CHARLIE
WILSON'S
WAR

18 March 05

For My Buddy Chips —
In honor of our great
friendship for many years —

Charlie Wilson

CHARLIE WILSON'S WAR

THE EXTRAORDINARY STORY OF
THE LARGEST COVERT OPERATION
IN HISTORY

GEORGE
CRILE

Atlantic Monthly Press
New York

Published simultaneously in Canada
Printed in the United States of America

Library of Congress Cataloging-in-Publication Data

Crile, George.
  Charlie Wilson's war : the extraordinary story of the largest covert operation in history / George Crile.
     p. cm.
   ISBN 0-87113-854-9
   1. Afghanistan—History—Soviet occupation, 1979–1989—Secret service—United States.   2. Wilson, Charlie, 1933–   3. United States. Central Intelligence Agency.   4. Military assistance, American—Afganistan.   I. Title.

DS371.2 .C75 2002
958.104'5—dc21   2002019074

Atlantic Monthly Press
841 Broadway
New York, NY 10003

03   04   05   06   07   10   9   8   7

To Barbara Lyne,
without whom this story would not have been told

"Four things greater than all things are,—
Women and Horses and Power and War."
—Rudyard Kipling, *The Ballad of the King's Jest*

CONTENTS

AUTHOR'S NOTE

In little over a decade, two events have transformed the world we live in: the collapse of our Cold War nuclear foe, the Soviet Union; and the discovery, after 9/11, that we face a new global enemy in the form of militant Islam. Both have profoundly affected the United States, and in each instance Americans were caught by surprise, unable to explain what had triggered these events.

9/11 was a watershed, as stunning in its boldness as it was frightening in its message. To this day, we know little about how it all worked or what was in the minds of the men who carried it out. Other than a shared religious identity, about the only obvious common denominator among the nineteen terrorists was having spent time in Afghanistan.

The fact that Afghanistan was the cradle of the attack should not have come as a surprise, for both the territory and the Islamic warriors who gather there are familiar to our government. Throughout the 1980s the Afghan mujahideen were, in effect, America's surrogate soldiers in the brutal guerrilla war that became the Soviet Union's Vietnam, a defeat that helped trigger the subsequent collapse of the Communist empire.

Afghanistan was a secret war that the CIA fought and won without debates in Congress or protests in the street. It was not just the CIA's biggest operation, it was the biggest secret war in history, but somehow it never registered on the American consciousness. When viewed through the prism of 9/11, the scale of that U.S. support for an army of Muslim fundamentalists seems almost incomprehensible. In the course of a decade, billions of rounds of ammunition and hundreds of thousands of weapons were smuggled across the border on the backs of camels, mules, and donkeys. At one point over three hundred thousand fundamentalist Afghan warriors carried weapons provided by the CIA; thousands were trained in the art of urban terror. Before it was over, some 28,000 Soviet soldiers were killed.

At the time, it was viewed as a noble cause, and when the last Soviet soldier walked out of Afghanistan on February 15, 1989, the leaders of the CIA celebrated what they hailed as the Agency's greatest victory. The cable from the CIA station in Islamabad that day read simply: "We won." But the billions spent arming and training the primitive tribesmen of Afghanistan turned out to have an unintended consequence. In a secret war, the funders take no credit—and no doubt that's why the mujahideen and their Muslim admirers around the world never viewed U.S. support as a decisive factor in their victory. As they saw it, that honor went to Allah, the only superpower they acknowledge. But for the few who know the extent of the CIA's involvement, it's impossible to ignore the central role that America played in this great modern jihad, one that continues to this day.

This book tells the story of the CIA's secret war in Afghanistan, of the men who dreamed it, and of the journey they took to see it through. If the campaign had different authors, men more associated with shaping foreign policy or waging wars, it might have surfaced earlier or been the subject of debate. But the unorthodox alliance—of a scandal-prone Texas congressman and an out-of-favor CIA operative—that gave birth to the Afghan jihad kept this history under the radar. It is the missing chapter in the politics of our time, a rousing good story that is also a cautionary tale.

Gust Avrakotos and Charlie Wilson

INTRODUCTION: A STRANGE AWARD AT LANGLEY

T he entrance to CIA headquarters is just off the George Washington Memorial Parkway, about a ten-minute drive up the Potomac from the White House. On a sunny, humid day in June 1993, an air-conditioned bus exited the parkway, onto Dolley Madison Boulevard and slowed down at the turnoff to the Langley headquarters. A bouquet of flowers had been left on the grassy island in the intersection. Each day now someone had taken to leaving a fresh floral arrangement here to mark the spot where three months earlier a young Pakistani with an AK-47 had calmly gunned down two Agency officials and made his escape.

It had never been easy for outsiders to get into the CIA's sprawling wooded compound, not even before the assassinations. The day the innocuous-looking bus pulled up to the security gate was some three years after the Berlin Wall had come down and a year and a half since the Soviet Union had ceased to exist. But although the Cold War was over, the CIA, that forty-six-year-old shrine to anti-Communism, was very much intact, and no one was talking about dismantling it. At the gate the uniformed guards immediately recognized the bus and the driver. It was a CIA vehicle with an Agency employee at the wheel, but the security men wanted to know who the others were.

"I'm Congressman Charlie Wilson, and they're fixing to give me an award in there," the tall figure in a dark blue suit announced as the guards mounted the bus. The congressman's voice is a bit startling at first—"booming" is the only way to describe it, a melodious, large Texas baritone that carries with it a sense of authority and importance. None of the other men or women in the bus looked terribly important. Generally speaking, no one ever looks impressive in a bus. But after listening to the congressman, the guard called the director's office and, without checking so much as a driver's license or searching any of the visitors' briefcases or handbags, waved the vehicle through the gate.

The woods of Langley were particularly lush that morning. It was June 9, 1993, a week after Charlie Wilson's sixtieth birthday, which he had celebrated with a party for three hundred at the Roof Terrace Restaurant of the Kennedy Center. *Casablanca* was the theme he had chosen for the event. It was his favorite movie, and he had appeared for the occasion in a white dinner jacket specially tailored to look like the one Humphrey Bogart wore when he played the role of Rick. A big band played dance music from the 1940s and '50s, and a characteristically bizarre collection of guests gathered to pay tribute to the rule-breaking congressman from the Bible Belt of East Texas. Six feet, four inches tall, square-jawed, Hollywood handsome, he had taken to the dance floor with one woman after another to relive the memories of his outlandish exploits.

No congressman or senator in anyone's memory had ever succeeded in flouting the rules so repeatedly for so many years and managed to survive. By this time, in the dull era of the 1990s, he had become the ultimate master of the Washington high-wire act, and that night his many strange and unusual friends had stood back and marveled as Charlie danced the night away, offering a toast to "Friends, to power, to passion, to black lace" before exiting with Ziva, a beautiful Israeli ballerina, on his arm.

A week later, riding in the CIA bus to his rendezvous with history, Wilson was preparing himself to rise to the occasion. He looked remarkably fit and useful. There was not a trace of gray in his full head of hair. On this day he actually had the look of a reliable, responsible, sober-minded man.

The others in the bus, mostly Wilson's staff, began gawking out the window the moment they passed the security checkpoint. They were all staring at the sprawling secret compound, trying to lock in a memory of this forbidden zone that their champion was making it possible for them to see and experience.

The well-kept jogging trails were still empty. They would be filling up in another two hours, once the lunch break began. None of this was any longer novel for the Texan, but he still marveled at this center of tranquillity where America plots so much of its espionage abroad. The CIA headquarters building is a somber cement structure that some still call modern even though it was opened just after the Bay of Pigs disaster. The bus slowed down at the entrance, then continued a hundred feet beyond to an oddly shaped, smaller building known to Agency insiders as "the Bubble."

Waiting in front was the new director of Central Intelligence, Jim Woolsey, and next to him, the Near East division chief, Frank Anderson. The congressman was late. He tried to apologize, but Anderson, a man of about fifty who bore a rather strong resemblance to Clark Kent, said, "No sweat."

With that they led Wilson into the Bubble, where close to a hundred people were already seated—men and women conservatively dressed in suits and dresses, uniformly white and middle class. Somehow, all at once, they sensed the arrival of Wilson with the director by his side. Without any apparent signal, these earnest men and women rose to their feet and a hush suddenly overcame the auditorium.

It was a strange sensation for the congressman, who had first come to the attention of this institution eleven years before as a virtual public outlaw—a seemingly corrupt, cocaine-snorting, scandal-prone womanizer who, the CIA was convinced, could only get the Agency into terrible trouble if it permitted him to become involved in any way in its operations. But now the director himself was leading this civilian into the Bubble and everyone was standing in silence, as if a holy man were passing.

The oddness of this moment is hard to exaggerate. America had just won the Cold War, a triumph every bit as significant as the victory over Nazi Germany, yet there had been no V-Day celebrations, no ticker-tape parades, no Douglas MacArthur to publicly celebrate. Life in the capital seemed to roll on as if there never had been a Cold War. At this moment, Charlie Wilson, of all people, was about to be honored as the architect of a great American triumph.

On a large screen on the auditorium's stage was a quotation—all that was necessary to explain why they were all there:

"Charlie Did It"
—President Zia ul-Haq of Pakistan, explaining the
defeat of the Russians in Afghanistan

The director quickly came to the point. "The defeat and breakup of the Soviet empire is one of the great events of world history. There were many heroes in this battle, but to Charlie Wilson must go a special recognition." Woolsey compared Wilson's role to that of Lech Walesa climbing over the fence at Gdansk to launch the Solidarity movement. He described how invincible the Soviets had appeared to be just thirteen years before and how Wilson had engineered one of the lethal body blows that had wrecked the Communist empire. Without him, Woolsey concluded, "History might have been hugely different and sadly different."

Sitting in the third row of the audience, a man in his fifties with thick glasses and a bushy mustache chewed gum manically, as if he were about to explode. Twenty-five years of clandestine service had accustomed him to looking beneath the surface of events. Wheels within wheels moved in his brain as he thought of the incredible irony of this ceremony. He hadn't been back to the Agency for three years, but one thing was certain: the men currently running the CIA weren't about to tip their hat to the role he had played with Wilson in turning a timid, uncertain operation into the biggest, meanest, and far and away most successful CIA campaign in history. The truth was, Gust Avrakotos was the only person in the room who understood how it had all happened, how he had broken the rules to make it happen, and how easy it would have been, if he had let the bureaucrats have their way, for things to have gone very, very differently. The gray man, so used to operating in the shadows, recognized that once again he would have to sit back and let Charlie take the honors for both of them.

The screen with the "Charlie Did It" slide on it was now being lowered into the stage floor as Frank Anderson took command of the proceedings. "To say that this is an unusual moment would be to underplay how unique it really is."

The Near East Division had been Anderson's home ever since he had been recruited out of the University of Illinois and joined the Agency's Clandestine Services. Now he was responsible for all American espionage activities from Morocco to Bangladesh. It was his great good fortune to have been in charge of the South Asia task force in the final years when his men, funneling billions of dollars' worth of weapons to the mujahideen, had chased the Red Army, tail between its legs, out of Afghanistan. Then, promoted to division chief, Anderson had watched the mystical process unfold as the entire Soviet bloc disintegrated, until an exhausted and helpless foe stood vanquished before America's secret warriors.

Anderson explained that he and the CIA were about to do something that had never been done for a civilian nonmember of the Agency. They were about to anoint Charlie Wilson as one of their own. "This moment is about elitism. Within the Clandestine Services we are a self-proclaimed elite unit called the Near East Division. It is an organization whose greatest weakness is hubris. One of the things about elites is that they only care about the approbation of the members of their own elites. So within the division we created an Honored Colleague award, something never before presented to anyone outside the service."

Perhaps no one but the handpicked officers of the Near East Division could fully understand how unusual it was to grant this recognition to an outsider, especially to a member of Congress. Any wariness and hostility that Congress seems to harbor for the CIA is more than reciprocated by the spies who suffer the politicians' scrutiny and endless criticism. But for some reason this man was different. "We really do feel that you are a member of our community," Anderson said with the look of a man who knew he was about to give out the most precious of all gifts. "So if you would, stand with me, Charlie, and be our Honored Colleague."

There were no television cameras present. No newspaper articles the following day would register the event. But curiously, even if the CIA had decided that day that it was appropriate to tell the real story of the CIA's Afghan war and how "Charlie did it," no one there would have been able to explain how it all began.

This book is the story of the biggest and most successful CIA campaign in history. It's the story of how the United States turned the tables on the Soviet Union and did to them in Afghanistan what they had done to the U.S. in Vietnam. The operation certainly contributed to the collapse of the Soviet Union; how critical a role it played is still being debated. But without doubt the Soviet invasion of Afghanistan and the Red Army's defeat at the hands of the CIA-backed Afghan rebels was a world-changing event. And what makes it all the more unusual is that at the heart of this drama is the story of two men, Charlie Wilson and Gust Avrakotos, and what they did in the shadows of the U.S. undergovernment.

This is the story inside the classified story. The version of events that Frank Anderson or the director of Central Intelligence would be capable of telling about the Afghan operation, were they so inclined, would only be a part of the real history. There is a peculiar phenomenon at the CIA that makes it almost impossible for anyone to have a complete picture of a covert operation that unfolds over a number of years.

To begin with, information is shared only on a need-to-know basis. That means that an officer in the European Division would have little, if any, idea what his CIA counterparts in Africa or Asia were doing. The men running the Contra war wouldn't have any way of knowing operational details of what was happening in Afghanistan. To further compromise any individual's field of knowledge, it is the institution's practice to freeze officers out of the information pool once they leave their assignment. That means the station chief who ran the Afghan war in 1981 will know next to nothing about what his successors did in 1984 and 1985.

Finally, there is the very human fact that the most interesting events are rarely put down on paper. Certainly that is the case with the conspiracy that Charlie Wilson and his CIA friend Gust Avrakotos engaged in during the mid-1980s to maneuver the United States into an all-out war against the Red Army in Afghanistan.

The word *conspiracy* is used with caution here. It means "an agreement to perform together an illegal, treacherous, or evil act." Neither Congressman Wilson nor the CIA's Avrakotos considered their efforts to be evil or treacherous. By their lights they were doing God's work as true patriots: moving a nation to fulfill its proper destiny. As to the illegal aspects, both acknowledge with pride that they joyfully broke the rules with abandon to achieve their daring goals.

The CIA's war in Afghanistan is, of course, a huge historical event featuring many players in prominent roles. But responsibility for transforming the American side of it into what became the biggest CIA operation ever belongs to these two highly flawed and perhaps heroic characters.

It can be said with absolute certainty that no one who knew or met these two men at the time the Soviets invaded and occupied Afghanistan could have imagined the circumstances that would cause anyone to give them responsibility for the most sensitive and highest risk of American covert policies. But no one ever gave them this commission. They seized it and this is the story of how they did it.

It needs to be underscored that this is a true story. It's purely by coincidence that, as in any good spy novel, we happen to come upon the leading man in the beginning of this account surrounded by beautiful women.

CHAPTER 1

Liz Wickersham and
Charlie Wilson

A HOT TUB IN LAS VEGAS

W hen Congressman Charlie Wilson set off for a weekend in Las Vegas on June 27, 1980, there was no confusion in his mind about why he had chosen to stay at Caesars Palace. He was a man in search of pure decadent pleasure, and the moment he walked into the hotel and saw the way the receptionists were dressed, he knew he had come to the right place. No doubt there were other members of the Ninety-sixth Congress who fantasized about orgies and altered states. But had any of them chosen to take the kind of plunge that Charlie Wilson had in mind, you can be sure they would have gone to some trouble to maintain a low profile, if not don a disguise.

Instead Charlie strode into the lobby of Caesars almost as if he were trying to imitate his childhood hero, Douglas MacArthur, majestically stalking ashore to take back the Philippines. He looked in no way ashamed or uncertain about what he was doing in this center of gambling and entertainment.

In truth, it wouldn't have been easy for Wilson to fade into any background. Six foot seven in his cowboy boots, he was handsome, with one of those classic outdoor faces that tobacco companies bet millions on. And he just didn't have the heart or the temperament to operate in the shadows; he felt like a soldier out of uniform when he wasn't wearing his trademark bright suspenders and boldly striped shirts with their custom-designed military epaulets.

Moreover, Wilson had never been able to shake the politician's impulse to take center stage. He covered ground rapidly, shoulders back, square jaw jutting forward. There were no volume controls on his voice as he boomed out greetings with astonishing clarity—and people in the Caesars lobby turned to see who was making such a stir. He looked like a millionaire, but the truth was, after eight years in the Texas legislature and almost as many in the House, he had nothing to show for his efforts but debt and a $70,000-a-year government salary that didn't come near to supporting his lifestyle.

Along the way, however, Wilson had discovered that he didn't need money of his own to lead a big, glamorous life. The rules governing Congress were far looser in those days, and he'd become a master at getting others to pick up the tab: junkets to exotic foreign lands at government expense, campaign chests that could be tapped to underwrite all manner of entertainments, and, of course, the boundless generosity of friendly lobbyists, quick to provide the best seats at his favorite Broadway musicals, dinners at the finest Parisian restaurants, and romantic late-night boat parties on the Potomac.

All of which explains how the tall, charismatic congressman with the blazing eyes and the ever-present smile had grown accustomed to moving about the world with a certain flair. And so as he arrived in Las Vegas, he was observing his hard-and-fast rule that whenever he traveled, he went first class and tipped lavishly. The bellhops and receptionists at Caesars loved this, of course, and Wilson, in turn, appreciated their outfits: little white goddess robes showing lots of cleavage for the girls, and Roman togas and sandals for the bellhops.

In all of Vegas, there was no place like Caesars Palace in 1980. It was the first of the great hotel emporiums to be inspired by the fall of a civilization. Its promoters had had the genius to recognize that the sins of Rome could seem far more enticing than any contemporary offering; and as the young Roman in the toga whipped out the gleaming, two-inch-thick golden key to the Fantasy Suite, he opened a door designed to lead even the most pious of visitors straight to hell.

Charles Nesbitt Wilson comes from a part of the country very familiar with Satan. The Second Congressional District lies in the heart of the Bible Belt, and it may well be that Wilson's Baptist and Pentecostal constituents spend more time worrying about sin and wrestling with the Devil than just about any other group of Americans. JESUS IS THE LORD OF LUFKIN reads the huge sign in the center of the district's biggest city where Wilson maintained a house, on Crooked Creek Road.

The congressman did at least have one dim justification for being in Las Vegas that weekend. He could say he was there to help a constituent: the striking twenty-three-year-old Liz Wickersham, former Miss Georgia, fourth runner-up in the Miss America contest, soon-to-be *Playboy* cover girl, and, later, host of a CNN talk show that an admirer, Ted Turner, would create specifically for her. The free-spirited Wickersham was the daughter of one of Wilson's main fund-raisers, Charlie Wickersham, who owned the Ford-Lincoln dealership in Orange, Texas, where Wilson always got special deals on his huge secondhand Lincolns. When Liz moved to Washington, her father asked Wilson to show her around, which he did with great enthusiasm. He even took her to the White House, where he introduced her to Jimmy Carter, proudly informing him that Liz Wickersham had won the Miss Georgia beauty contest the very year Carter had been elected president. There was never any question that Wilson would go all out to promote the career of his friend and fund-raiser's attractive young daughter. Now, in Vegas, he was doing just that—orchestrating an introduction to a producer who was casting for a soap opera.

A few months earlier, a young hustler named Paul Brown had approached him about helping to develop a *Dallas*-type TV series based on the real political goings-on in the nation's capital. It wasn't long before Brown had convinced Wilson to invest most of his savings—$29,000 and to sign on as the show's consultant. The reason for the Las Vegas weekend was to meet a big-time Hollywood producer who, Brown claimed, was eager to back the project.

It was a giddy moment for Wilson and Liz as they sat in the Fantasy Suite talking about a deal that was all but iced. Brown had already persuaded Caesars to comp the congressman's stay, and now he was making Charlie and Liz feel like they were the toasts of the town. He had brought up some pretty showgirls, and before long the whole party was acting as if they were part of a big-time Hollywood mogul's entourage, knocking back champagne as they congratulated one another on the deal that was about to be signed and the role that Liz was about to land.

Two years later, teams of investigators and federal prosecutors would spend weeks trying to reconstruct exactly what the congressman did that night after Paul Brown and the other hangers-on left the Fantasy Suite. It almost landed Wilson in jail. And given the very high wire he later had to walk to avoid indictment, it's quite astonishing to hear the way he cheerfully describes those moments in the hot tub that the investigators were never quite able to document. No matter how much hellish trouble it later caused him, the congressman leaves the unmistakable impression that he relished every single moment of his outrageous escapade.

"It was an enormous Jacuzzi," he recalled. "I was in a robe at first because, after all, I was a congressman. And then everyone disappeared except for two beautiful, long-legged showgirls with high heels. They were a bit drunk and flirtatious and they walked right into the water with their high heels on. . . . The girls had cocaine and the music was loud—Sinatra, 'My Kind of Town.' We all mellowed out, saying outrageous things to each other. It was total happiness. And both of them had ten long, red fingernails with an endless supply of beautiful white powder. It was just tremendous fun—better than anything you've ever seen in the movies."

As Wilson later framed the episode that almost brought him down, "the Feds spent a million bucks trying to figure out whether, when those fingernails passed under my nose, did I inhale or exhale—and I ain't telling."

Other middle-aged men have brought young women to the Fantasy Suite for activities not unlike Wilson's. But ordinarily there is something a bit desperate and tawdry about such aging pleasure seekers. It's unlikely that any of them would be able to talk about their debauchery in such a way that it would sound almost fresh and innocent. Charlie Wilson, however, had a genius for getting people to judge him not as a middle-aged scoundrel but instead as if he were a good-hearted adolescent, guilty of little more than youthful excess.

This survival skill permitted him to routinely do things that no one else in Congress could have gotten away with. One of the first to marvel at this unique capacity to openly flaunt the rules was the young Diane Sawyer, who met Wilson in 1980 when she was just beginning her career as a network correspondent. "He was just untamed," she recalled, "tall and gangly and wild—like a kid before they discovered Ritalin. He had this ungoverned enthusiasm, and it extended to women and the world."

The congressman was like no one Sawyer had met in Washington. He was simply outrageous. Sawyer recalled the experience of driving with

Charlie in his big old Continental on one of their few dinner dates: "Going down Connecticut Avenue with him, I felt as if we could have been driving into any *American Graffiti* hamburger place."

When Wilson was first elected to Congress, he'd persuaded a distinguished college professor, Charles Simpson, to leave academia and sign on as his administrative assistant. Simpson says Wilson was the brightest person he's ever worked with: "He had an uncanny ability to take a complex issue, break it down, get all the bullshit out, and deliver the heart of it. There's no question he could have been anything he wanted to be. His goal was to become secretary of defense. Certainly he intended to run for the Senate."

But Simpson gradually came to believe that his boss had a fatal flaw. That failing was perfectly summed up in a fitness report written by Wilson's commanding officer in the navy in the late 1950s: "Charlie Wilson is the best officer who ever served under me at sea and undoubtedly the worst in port."

There was little question in Simpson's mind in those days that his boss had a drinking problem. As with many alcoholics, it was not immediately noticeable; Wilson had an uncanny ability to consume enormous quantities of Scotch and seem unaffected. Also, he was a happy drunk who told wonderful stories and made everyone laugh. On the occasions when drinking would get to him, Simpson says, "Wilson would simply lie down on the floor for an hour, wake up, and act as if he had just had twelve hours of sleep. It was the most unreal thing I'd ever seen. He'd do this at his own parties—just sleep for an hour with everything going on around him, then get up and start again."

Most of the 435 members of Congress lead surprisingly anonymous lives in Washington. They are, of course, celebrities of sorts in their own districts, but the reality of life in the capital is that all but a few will leave Washington without much of anyone knowing they had been there. Wilson, in contrast, had begun to attract a great deal of media attention by the early 1980s, albeit the kind that any other politician would have considered the kiss of death. The gossip columnists called him "Good-Time Charlie," and they had a good time themselves describing the parade of beauty queens he escorted to White House receptions and fancy embassy parties. One Texas newspaper called him "the biggest playboy in Congress." The *Washington Post* featured a picture of Wilson and House

Majority Leader Jim Wright saddled up on white horses, riding down Pennsylvania Avenue to a nightclub Wilson had just invested in. The *Dallas Morning News* observed that there were more congressmen on the floor of Wilson's disco, Élan ("a club for the dashing" was its motto), than you were ever likely to find on the floors of Congress. When challenged about his lifestyle, Wilson replied good-naturedly, "Why should I go around looking like a constipated hound dog? I'm having the time of my life."

In truth, at age forty-seven, in his fourth term in office, Charlie Wilson was completely lost. Public officials are forever doing stupid things, but they don't step into hot tubs with naked women and cocaine unless they are driven to play Russian roulette with their careers. And it was hard not to conclude that this recently divorced congressman was a man in free fall, programmed for disaster.

Wilson himself would later say, "I was caught up in the longest midlife crisis in history. I wasn't hurting anybody, but I sure was aimless." If Charlie Wilson's midlife crisis had thrown him off course, it was nothing compared to the crisis America was going through. The night Wilson checked into Caesars Palace, Ted Koppel had opened his *Nightline* broadcast with a disturbing refrain: "Good evening. Tonight is the two hundred and thirty-seventh night of captivity for the hostages in Tehran." The United States, with its $200 billion annual defense budget, couldn't even force a taunting Third World nation to turn over fifty hostages. And then, when it finally screwed up its courage to mount a rescue mission, the whole world watched the humiliating spectacle of Desert One, as a U.S. helicopter pilot lost his vision in a blinding dust cloud and rammed into a parked plane, leaving eight soldiers dead and the rescue mission aborted.

Over and over again it was said that "Vietnam syndrome" had infected the spirit of America. And by the summer of 1980 a growing number of conservatives, led by Ronald Reagan, had begun to warn that the Soviet Union might have achieved nuclear superiority, that a "window of opportunity" had been opened in which the Soviets could launch and win a nuclear war. Other voices added to the unease, claiming that the KGB had infiltrated most Western intelligence services and that they were mounting devastatingly effective "disinformation" campaigns, which were blinding America to the danger it faced.

To the president at the time, Jimmy Carter, this kind of extreme worst-case thinking had created what he called "America's paranoid fear of Communism." A born-again Christian, a onetime peanut farmer and former governor of Georgia, Carter had almost no experience in foreign affairs when he ran for president, but he had won over an American public still traumatized by Vietnam and Watergate. The intelligence scandals in the late 1970s had only reinforced the widespread suspicion that the CIA was out of control—a virtual government within the government. Vowing "never to lie" to the American public and to introduce a new morality in Washington, Carter had all but promised an end to the CIA's dirty tricks.

Once in office, President Carter moved to discipline the Agency, coming close to suggesting that it was time to stop conducting covert operations altogether. His handpicked CIA chief, Admiral Stansfield Turner, went a step further and with great fanfare carried out a purge of the Agency's so-called rogue operatives. By the end of 1979, the new ground rules put down by the president and Congress had gone a long way toward altering the very culture of this embattled Agency. Even the CIA's most daring operatives had come to dread the prospect of having their careers destroyed for carrying out missions that Congress might later deem illegal. By Christmas 1979, the CIA's Directorate of Operations had voluntarily all but taken itself out of the dirty-tricks business.

What none of the CIA's leaders could have foreseen was that Jimmy Carter, the president who had gone to such lengths to tame them, was about to be reborn as a Cold War hawk. To say that Jimmy Carter was surprised by the Soviets' Christmas invasion of Afghanistan would be a gross understatement. It radicalized him. It made him suddenly believe that the Soviets might be truly evil and that the only way to deal with them was with force. "I don't know if fear is the right word to describe our reaction," recalls Carter's vice president, Walter Mondale. "But what unnerved everyone was the suspicion that [Soviet president] Brezhnev's inner circle might not be rational. They must have known the invasion would poison everything dealing with the West—from SALT to the deployment of nuclear weapons in western Europe."

Declaring Afghanistan "the greatest foreign policy crisis confronting the United States since World War II," Carter ordered a boycott of the Olympics scheduled for Moscow that summer. He embargoed grain sales to the

Soviets and called for a massive defense buildup, including the creation of a Rapid Deployment Force. Reflecting fears about further Russian aggression, he unveiled the Carter Doctrine, committing America to war in the event of any threat to the strategic oil fields of the Middle East. His most radical departure, however, came when he signed a series of secret legal documents, known as Presidential Findings, authorizing the Central Intelligence Agency to go into action against the Red Army.

The CIA's time-honored practice was never to introduce into a conflict weapons that could be traced back to the United States. And so the spy agency's first shipment to the scattered Afghan rebels—enough small arms and ammunition to equip a thousand men—consisted of weapons made by the Soviets themselves that had been stockpiled by the CIA for just such a moment. Within days of the invasion containers from a secretive San Antonio facility were flown to Islamabad, Pakistan, where they were turned over to President Mohammad Zia ul-Haq's intelligence service for distribution to the Afghan rebels. It hadn't been easy for Carter to get Zia to cooperate. Carter had targeted Zia—along with Anastasio "Tacho" Somoza of Nicaragua—in his high-profile human-rights campaign, and had cut off all U.S. aid to and military cooperation with Pakistan. Now, with the Red Army sweeping into Afghanistan, Carter had to do a 180-degree turn to win Zia's approval to use Pakistan as a base of his operations. Zia drove a hard bargain: the CIA could provide the weapons, but they would have to hand them over to his intelligence service for distribution. America's spies would have to operate exclusively through Zia's men.

Along with the first U.S. shipment, the Afghans soon began receiving arms and money from the Egyptians, the Chinese, the Saudis, and other Muslim nations. That response might have sounded impressive in a news dispatch, but the reality on the ground was that a bizarre mix of unsophisticated weapons was being handed over to tribesmen in sandals with no formal military training.

No one in the CIA during those early months had any illusions about the mujahideen's impotence in the face of the Soviet 40th Army. The full might of the Communist empire had descended on this remote, primitive Third World country. Giant Il-76 transport planes were landing in Kabul, the Afghan capital, one after the other, disgorging tens of thousands of combat troops. Columns of tanks were moving in the cities, while MiG fighter jets and helicopter gunships filled the skies. Very quickly the Agency's strategists accepted the invasion as an unfortunate, irreversible fact of life.

These CIA men were trained to be clinical when making geopolitical judgments. To them, there were more important things at stake than the fate of Afghanistan. There were many reasons for giving weapons to the Afghans, even if none of them had anything to do with liberating the country: it was a useful warning to the Soviets not to make any further moves toward the Persian Gulf or into Pakistan; it was a signal that the United States was ready to escalate a covert killing war aimed at Russian soldiers; and because it involved aid to Muslim fundamentalists, it was an extraordinary opportunity to make friends with the Islamic nations that had treated the United States as a virtual enemy because of its support of Israel and the Shah.

What was happening to the Afghan freedom fighters was tragic, of course, but if the truth were known, the CIA strategists saw a silver lining in the horrific accounts of the destruction of villages and the flood of refugees pouring across the border into Pakistan. As long as these "freedom fighters," as Jimmy Carter had begun calling them, continued to fight and the Soviets continued to murder and torture them, it was an unprecedented public relations bonanza for the United States. Never before had the CIA had such a powerful vehicle for blackening the image of the Soviet Union. The Agency began placing heartrending articles in foreign newspapers and magazines; academic studies and books were underwritten. To a certain extent this was unnecessary, however, since every account voluntarily played up the same theme: men of courage, armed only with their faith and their love of freedom, being slaughtered by the full evil might of a Communist superpower.

Curiously, the only ones who didn't see the Afghans as helpless victims were the Russians. One gets a sense of how terrified they were of these tribesmen and their methods of fighting from a story the Red Army used to tell each new group of combat recruits to discourage them from ever considering surrender. The story is said to be true, and although the details changed over the years, it goes something like this: At sunrise on the second day after the invasion a Soviet sentry spotted five bags on the edge of the tarmac at Bagram Air Base, close to the capital. The soldier was not initially concerned—until he pushed his rifle against the first of the burlap bags and noticed blood oozing onto the tarmac. Explosives experts were called in to check for booby traps. What they discovered was far more menacing. Within each bag was a young Soviet soldier wrapped inside out in his own skin. As best the medical examiner could determine, the men had died a particularly gruesome death: their skin had been sliced at the stomach while they were still alive and then pulled up and tied over their heads.

It was a message from the Afghans—an old, stylized warning, one that a famous Afghan chieftain had given to the commander of British troops in 1842. The warrior had been brought before the British general, who began to dictate terms to the tribal leader. Before he could finish, however, the Afghan started to laugh at him.

"Why are you laughing?" the general demanded.

"Because I can see how easy it was for you to get your troops in here. What I don't understand is how you plan to get them out."

One hundred and thirty-eight years later, across the length and breadth of Afghanistan in those first months of 1980, came the mullah's new call to jihad—to take up the holy war. It was not a campaign like the CIA's ongoing Contra war, in which the rich Nicaraguans fled to Miami and the peasants on the border were paid to take up arms. In Afghanistan, the whole nation of Islam responded to the call. In the capital, just a month after the invasion, the mullahs and rebel leaders decided to show the Russians that there was only one true superpower.

As dusk fell the first cry sounded from an elder in a turban: *"Allahu Akbar"*—God is Great. From the rooftops came the response, until the air was thundering with the sound of hundreds of thousands of Muslim faithful chanting the cry of the jihad: *"Allahu Akbar, Allahu Akbar."*

Across town in the Kabul Hotel, a Soviet reporter, Gennady Bocharov, was experiencing a terror like none he had ever known. In the streets and on rooftops around the hotel turbaned men and veiled women added to the basic chant: *"Marg, marg, marg bar Shurawi!"* Death to the Soviets—death, death, death! Bocharov had retreated into his room with a group of Soviet diplomats and the commandant of Kabul. He later wrote about his terror as they discovered that the phone lines had been cut and all they could hear was the swelling chant: "Each of us knew that the fanatics take their time about killing you. We knew that the first thing they do is pierce your forearms with knives. Then they hack off your ears, your fingers, your genitals, put out your eyes."

Bocharov's terror grew when they discovered they had only one grenade, which would not be enough to kill them all before the Afghans arrived with their knives. "I found myself shivering convulsively, uncontrollably," he reported. "We heard the nearby yells, breathed the smoke of nearby fires, and prayed to Fate to grant us instant death." Before the journalist and his friends had to face this specter, a company of Soviet paratroopers arrived to rescue them. By morning, a much-sobered Red Army was back in control, but the night of *"Allahu Akbar"* had been a rite of passage for the Afghans; they were now all in this together, to the death.

In the following months, the Afghan people would suffer the kind of brutality that would later horrify the world when the Serbs began their ethnic cleansing. Soviet tanks and jets would lay waste to villages thought to be supporting guerrillas. Before long, millions of Afghans—men, women, and children—would begin pouring out of the country, seeking refuge in Pakistan and Iran.

In those first months of the war Dan Rather made a dramatic trek across the border at a time when the world's attention had already shifted away from the sad story. Among other things, Rather was following up on reports that the CIA had already begun arming the mujahideen. Like most people, Rather assumed that if the CIA was now involved, they meant business. He disguised himself as a mujahid, and the curious sight of the familiar anchor dressed up as an Afghan in his *60 Minutes* report prompted the *Washington Post's* Tom Shales to dub him "Gunga Dan." The satirical account of his foray into this dangerous war zone diverted attention from Rather's unexpected and accurate conclusion: the CIA's support to the Afghans was almost meaningless. The mujahideen were facing Soviet tanks and flying gunships with World War I rifles and little ammunition.

Charlie Wilson was stunned by Rather's report. He admired his fellow Texan for having the courage to risk his life to expose what Wilson saw as a scandal. Once again, his president was failing to stand up to the test of history. Given the false hope of meaningful U.S. support, there seemed to be nothing in the future for these anti-Communist freedom fighters but defeat.

It was at this moment of despair for the mujahideen, in the early summer of 1980, that Wilson walked off the floor of the House into the

Speaker's Lobby, a rich, wood-paneled room that stretches along the full length of the House floor. A Teletype at one end spewed out stories from AP, UPI, and Reuters. Wilson was a news junkie, and he reached down and began reading a story datelined from Kabul.

The article described hundreds of thousands of refugees fleeing the country as Soviet helicopter gunships leveled villages, slaughtered livestock, and killed anyone who harbored the guerrillas. What caught Wilson's attention, however, was the reporter's conclusion that the Afghan warriors were refusing to quit. The article described how they were murdering Russians in the dead of night with knives and pistols, hitting them over the head with shovels and stones. Against all odds, there was a growing rebellion under way against the Red Army.

As he read the dispatch, Wilson found himself thinking of the Alamo and the letter Colonel Travis wrote to the people of Texas just before Santa Anna attacked: "The enemy has demanded surrender. I have answered the demand with a cannon shot. I shall never surrender or retreat."

The Texas congressman had first gone to the Alamo when he was six years old. He had been there many times since, and each time it had left him teary. Most Americans can't understand what the Alamo means to Texans. It's like Masada to the Israelis. It sums up what it means to be a man, what it means to be a patriot, what it means to be a Texan. Jim Bowie, Davy Crockett, and all who stayed with Travis that day paid the ultimate price, but they had bought time for Sam Houston to mobilize the Texas army to defeat Santa Anna. That is what brave men did: win time for others to do the right thing.

It would have been a sobering insight for the Communist rulers if they could have followed what happened in the few minutes after Wilson finished reading the Associated Press dispatch. The mysterious force in the U.S. government that was destined to hound the Red Army with a seemingly limitless flood of ever more lethal and sophisticated weapons was about to be activated.

No one, however, was paying attention, not even in the American government, when Charlie Wilson picked up a phone and called the Appropriations Committee staffer who dealt with "black appropriations," the CIA funds. The man's name was Jim Van Wagenen, a former college professor and onetime FBI agent. Wilson had just been named to the Defense

Appropriations subcommittee. He was now part of the band of twelve men in the House responsible for funding CIA operations.

The congressman knew enough about the eccentric workings of the subcommittee to know when a member can act alone to fund a program. "How much are we giving the Afghans?" he asked Van Wagenen.

"Five million," said the staffer.

There was a moment's silence. "Double it," said the Texan.

CHAPTER 2

Teddy and Charlie

DEFENDER OF TRINITY

S o far as anyone can tell, no congressman prior to Charlie Wilson had ever moved unsolicited to increase a CIA budget. From the beginning of the Cold War, Congress had granted that exclusive right to the president. But as dramatic as the doubling might sound, it had no visible impact on the war. It wasn't reported or debated, and it never even registered on the KGB's radar screen in Russia. At best, all it did was provide the mujahideen with a few thousand more Enfield rifles and perhaps some machine guns, so that they could go out and die for their faith in greater numbers.

Wilson's intervention had not cost the congressman much more than a telephone call to a key staffer and a few additional minutes when the subcommittee met to appropriate the nation's secret intelligence budget. The truth is, it was an impulsive action, a personal gesture to bolster a painfully inadequate U.S. program.

Wilson so easily crossed the line into this covert arena that no one stopped to question his right to be there or worry about the precedent he might be setting. It would be another two years before he would return to put this precedent to the test. But this is where, quite impulsively, he first demonstrated that there could be another power center in the American government, one that could act in a way that was totally unpredictable to drive a U.S. covert policy.

For a moment, a very different Charlie Wilson had surfaced—a master politician able to find tools that could be used in ways that others would not have considered. But it had all taken place behind closed doors, and just for a fleeting moment. Before anyone could notice, the congressman had resumed the inexplicable role he had chosen for himself as a hopelessly irresponsible public servant.

The truth is, there were always two Charlie Wilsons at work in Washington. But he was moving heaven and earth in those days to allow only one image to surface, and to promote that image so loudly that no one would go looking for the other. To begin with, he staffed his office almost exclusively with tall, startlingly beautiful women. They were famous on the Hill, known to all as "Charlie's Angels." And to his colleagues' amazement, whenever questioned about this practice, Wilson invariably responded with one of his favorite lines: "You can teach them how to type, but you can't teach them to grow tits." That was the way he tended to present himself in public, which was tame compared to the way he decorated his condo. It was almost a caricature of what Hugh Hefner might have designed as the ultimate bachelor's lair. Manly hedonism was the theme, down to the last detail: mirrored walls, an emperor's size bed outfitted with plush down pillows and a royal blue comforter, an entertainment center featuring a giant television and stereo, and a gleaming tanning bed to maintain his year-round tan. Finally, the congressman's most distinctive innovation: the Jacuzzi, not hidden away in the bathroom but so deliberately situated in the center of the bedroom that it forced the unsuspecting eye to draw all the worst possible conclusions about the man who slept in this room. Particularly when visitors came close and discovered silver handcuffs dangling elegantly from a hook within easy reach of the tub. The site of these instruments of hedonism invariably left his colleagues and distinguished guests speechless.

It would be an exaggeration to suggest that this was all a false front. Charlie Wilson, after all, is a bona fide hedonist. But he is also guilty of concealing his other identity. It's only when he's alone and everyone else is sleeping that the other Charlie Wilson surfaces. It's a nightly affair. Usually at about three or four A.M. he finds himself awake and turns to his library, with its thick volumes of military history. He's not like other insomniacs, who simply try to get back to sleep. He reads like a scholar steeped in his field but also like a man in search of something personal, poring through accounts of the struggles of the world and the men who counted—Roosevelt, Kennedy, and all the great generals.

But invariably, it is to the biographies and speeches and histories of Winston Churchill that Wilson always returns on these night journeys, to read again and again about the man who was cast into the political wilderness, written off as an alcoholic alarmist, and then, when all was lost, rose to the occasion to save his country and his civilization from the darkness of Hitler. It's no wonder that Charlie Wilson never shared his sense of personal destiny. It wouldn't have made much sense in his year of the hot tub had he even whispered of his inner conviction that he and Winston Churchill might have something—anything—in common.

Nor did he explain why the painting over his bed, his one steady nightly companion, was like a talisman to him. The painting—a lone pilot in the cockpit of a Spitfire, patrolling the night skies of London—had hung over his boyhood bed in tiny Trinity, Texas, at a time when the Nazis were sweeping across Europe. Night after night, on the second floor of the white frame house, in the corner room that Charlie shared with his uncle Jack, the boy would sit staring out the window, ever vigilant, searching the sky for signs of Japanese bombers and fighter planes, whose characteristics were burned upon the memory of this seven-year-old defender of Trinity. "They aren't coming, Charlie," his kindly uncle Jack would assure him. "But if they do, you'll be the first to see them."

There was nothing distant or unfamiliar about World War II for the citizens of this timber town along the railroad tracks in deep East Texas. Every night, not just Charlie and his family but everyone in Trinity gathered around their radios to find out how the war was going, knowing that everything rested on the outcome. When the Japanese struck at Pearl Harbor on December 7, 1941, Charlie Wilson, age eight, sat in the living room of the white frame house across from the Methodist church and listened to Franklin Roosevelt describe the "day of infamy." The young boy with the huge imagination had already become obsessed with the war and with the magical voices coming out of the RCA radio: Roosevelt with his fireside chats, Murrow from London under the Blitz, and particularly Winston Churchill. It was a voice from far away, heard on a radio in a tiny town in the back of beyond. But those ringing, defiant words of Churchill, mocking Hitler and infusing a nation with the will to fight on, no matter what the cost, never to be conquered, would leave Wilson forever struck by the power of one man's spirit to change history.

Young Charlie began reading everything he could find about war, saving his money to send away for a giant American flag from Sears Roebuck, which he draped from the front of the house each morning. He bought a Canadian Mountie's uniform and insisted on wearing it every day. He tried to stage mock battles with his friends, but no one would play the role of the Nazis or the Japs.

All of Trinity was transformed by the war. Everyone gathered scrap metal for the cause, even the aluminum foil that wrapped chewing gum. Charlie's mother prepared bandages, and he and his friends helped assemble medical kits, putting their names and addresses inside. It was a great event when a soldier wrote back to thank them and report that he had used their kit after being wounded.

Every soldier from Trinity had his picture in the window of the local drugstore. There were eighty or ninety of them, and whenever one would return, wounded or discharged, Charlie would sit at his feet at the soda fountain and listen to his stories.

Often he even saw the true face of the enemy close up. The War Department maintained a huge prisoner of war camp just seven miles from Trinity at a railroad depot called Riverside. Trains would unload German prisoners, who would then march three miles to the POW camp. As Wilson remembers, "It was a great treat in 1943 when the town doctor drove me to Riverside to watch the men of the Afrika Korps being unloaded—these were Rommel's troops. Those sons of bitches were goosestepping off of the train with great pride and arrogance in the very uniforms in which they were captured." The sight of goose-stepping Nazis burned deeply in the boy's consciousness. He had now seen the enemy. There they were—Hitler's men just ten miles from Trinity.

The young Wilson began going to the library each day to read up on weapons systems. He felt particularly menaced by the Messerschmitts, the German fighter-bombers that had savaged London. And he truly believed that Trinity might be next. "In the post office they had posters of all the Japanese and German airplanes, so we could spot 'em if they ever came over. Well, we had a little sawmill in Trinity, and all of us figured out it was probably a major target of the Japanese." Night after night, little Charlie Wilson would go to the window and scan the skies, Trinity's first line of defense, ready to spring at a moment's notice to alert the sheriff to a surprise attack.

The Japanese finally surrendered. While his mother played the piano at a service of thanksgiving at the Methodist church on V-J Day, the eleven-year-old boy was permitted to climb into the steeple to ring the bells in triumph.

Most boys his age did not follow the menacing transformation of America's World War II ally the Soviets. Wilson had been thrilled when Stalin's forces had turned back the Nazis at Stalingrad in late 1942. But with increasing alarm, he read and listened to the accounts of Stalin gobbling up Eastern Europe. When Churchill came to America in 1947 and warned of an "iron curtain" falling over Europe Charlie took his words to heart, and when the Communists tested the bomb Wilson was depressed for days, convinced that America had a new enemy every bit as dangerous as Hitler.

This was the early shaping of an American patriot and, for Wilson, just the beginning of a lifetime fascination with war, weapons, public service, and something else—a curious conviction that didn't come to him all at once but grew with greater and greater force and clarity as the war unfolded and the voices over the radio began to deliver a separate message to Charlie. As time went on, he would come to feel that one day, his would be the voice on the radio.

Wilson's father was an accountant for the timber company. They had little money but were better off than most people in town. They lived in a pleasant house and were pillars of their community. Charles Edwin Wilson had almost known despair when the mill closed down during the Depression and he was laid off. But the next day he had signed on with Franklin Roosevelt's New Deal jobs program, the Civilian Conservation Corps, where he worked as a roads supervisor, intensely proud of the fact that he had never missed a day's work.

Wilson's father had one fixed ambition for his son: to attend the U.S. Naval Academy. He insisted it would be a ticket to success. And so he lobbied his local congressman and, after two tries, got his son an appointment to Annapolis. Charlie flunked the first test because he was so scrawny. The second he passed only after wolfing down fifteen bananas, to bring his six-foot-four-inch body up to the academy's 140-pound minimum.

In September 1952 Wilson's proud parents drove their boy to Houston in the family's new Chevrolet and put him on a TWA flight for his trip across the country. Wilson remembers his first plane ride on the propeller-driven Constellation, which delivered him to the start of his military career. Wilson and his fellow midshipmen in the starting class of two thousand were warned that less than half of them would graduate; and over the years, it was always touch-and-go whether Charlie would make the

cut. He was a classic military screwup, constantly reprimanded for talking in formation, not having his shoes shined, leaving his light on after cur-
few. But somehow he made it through, in 1956 graduating eighth from the
bottom of his class and with the distinction of having more demerits than
any other graduate in anyone's memory.

Because of Annapolis, Wilson missed Korea. But at twenty-five, as a
gunnery officer on a destroyer sailing the world with the American fleet at
the height of the Cold War, he felt that he was at last coming into his own.
He was in command of the warship's weapons, and his gunnery teams almost always won the mock battles, in part because he had his men practice
more than anyone else. They always ran out of ammunition long before they
could get back to their home port to be resupplied. Wilson did this to sharpen
his men's skills, but also to empty the ammo boxes so that he could fill them
with cheap alcohol bought on shore leave in Gibraltar to smuggle back to
the States. Wilson's training style was unconventional, but he ended up with
the happiest men and the best shots in the fleet.

Wilson was now feeling the power of America, moving about sometimes with the entire U.S. Atlantic fleet and other times with NATO
naval units. "We were undisputedly the kings of the world, and everybody knew it. We were arrogant sons of bitches. But they loved us." He
sailed everywhere in those years—to Athens, Marseilles, Naples, Karachi,
Beirut—and everywhere he went he felt proud. America was rebuilding
Europe through the Marshall Plan, the dollar was powerful, and there
was more than a woman in every port for the smiling, open-faced, fun-
loving young officer in the starched white uniform.

There were also long stretches of downtime at sea that Wilson put
to good use, reading all of Churchill's wartime books, consuming each as
they came out and moving on to biographies of Roosevelt and George
Kennan's prescription for dealing with Communism.

From his destroyer on Christmas morning 1956, he wrote to his parents and kid sister, evoking the same spirit that had led the young boy to
keep vigil at his bedroom window in Trinity, scanning the sky for enemy
Messerschmitts.

Dear Mother, Daddy and Sharon:
    It's now 5:15 a.m. Christmas morning. I have the 4 to 8 watch so I am up
bright and early as always on Christmas. This will be my third duty day in a

row as I am standing by for some of the married fellows so they can be with their families.

This business of being away from home today is certainly not by choice, but neither is it something without reason. I can console myself and I hope you too, by simply realizing that we are doing a job here that must be done. It is only through constant vigilance on the part of the few that a secure, peaceful Christmas can be enjoyed by many.

These read like lines for a Jimmy Stewart character, but the sentiments were very much Wilson's own. In later life he would usually disguise such nakedly idealistic thoughts. That letter, however, without any hint of self-consciousness, is key to understanding Wilson's later compulsion to be the lone cowboy sounding the alert, mobilizing "the forces of freedom."

Patrolling the seas during those Cold War years, Wilson came personally to feel the menace and reach of Soviet power. His destroyer spent most of its time chasing the Soviet submarines that hounded the fleet. The destroyers purposefully badgered them with mock attacks, forcing them under for days on end. The great triumph would come when, after two or three days of pursuit, a sub would finally be forced to surface. The Americans would snap photos of the disgraced Russians and give them the finger, while the enemy would shake their fists in return. "I always kept my depth charges on total alert," Wilson recalls with bravado. On more than one occasion, the young gunnery officer appealed to the ship's captain to permit him to blast one of the subs. "I promised a clean kill," Wilson recalls. "Nobody would have ever known what happened to the fuckers, but they wouldn't let me do it."

After three years at sea chasing Russian submarines, Wilson was assigned to a top secret post at the Pentagon, where he was part of an intelligence unit that evaluated the Soviet Union's nuclear forces. Having chased Soviet submarines, he now found himself rehearsing for all-out nuclear war. Back then, the U.S. response time to an incoming Soviet nuclear attack was thirty-five minutes. There were frequent simulated attacks, and Charlie often stood in for the top generals, who had only seven minutes to dive into waiting helicopters to be flown to the "Rock," the secret underground bunker carved into a Maryland mountain. "I would be sitting there where the button is, and if you're twenty-seven, it makes you feel very cocky knowing that here's Moscow, and here's Kiev, and if they fuck with us I'll just hit all these buttons."

In spite of his bravado, the experience was sobering. Day after day he confronted the reality of an enemy he knew was rehearsing America's nuclear destruction, and he resented it. It became a lifelong obsession to bring down this evil power. And all of his idealism and patriotic passions, which had been building since childhood, suddenly found an inspirational outlet when John Kennedy launched his campaign for the presidency.

Kennedy appealed to every aspect of the young naval officer's imagination: a war hero, he was a dashing, handsome idealist rallying the country to greatness and making it all look like fun. After work each day, hours spent studying the Soviet intercontinental ballistic missile threat, Wilson would rush from the Pentagon to the Kennedy campaign headquarters, where he volunteered. Like so many others of his generation, Wilson became caught up in the aura of romance that Kennedy lent to public service.

It's not legal for active-duty servicemen to campaign for public office, but Wilson decided to disregard that detail. He took thirty days' leave from the navy and entered his name in the race for Texas state representative. Tall and skinny, always dressed in a suit, Wilson ran his campaign in East Texas the way the Kennedys had made famous in Massachusetts. His mother, his sister, and all their friends went door to door selling the idea of Charlie as a fresh, new idea in Texas politics. He won and managed to complete his Pentagon tour without anyone noticing his entry into the political arena. In 1961, at twenty-seven, he was sworn in to office in Austin, Texas, the same month his political role model became the thirty-fifth president of the United States.

For the next twelve years Wilson made his reputation in Texas as the "liberal from Lufkin," viewed with suspicion by business interests. He battled for the regulation of utilities and fought for Medicaid, tax exemptions for the elderly, the Equal Rights Amendment, and a minimum-wage bill.* Historically, the Second District congressional seat had been a hard

---

*He was often branded with the name "Timber Charlie" for the legislation he pushed through for the timber interests dominating his district; his political patron was the maverick lumber king Arthur Temple. Temple was not your usual southern robber baron; he was a model of progressive liberalism. His company, Temple Inland, never unionized because he always paid union wages. He personally integrated Diboll, his company town, in the early 1960s. He built the best library for any town its size in Texas. And at a time when federal programs to help the poor were considered anath-

place for a liberal Democrat to seek office. It was an ultra-right-wing political franchise, made famous by Martin Dies, a red-baiting inquisitor
who had unapologetically forced child actress Shirley Temple to testify
about her supposed knowledge of Communists in Hollywood. But fortune
knocked when Dies's successor, the incumbent congressman John Dowdy,
was caught taking a bribe. Wilson immediately threw himself into the special election, in spite of a recent arrest for drunk driving and its attendant
highly embarrassing mug shot. By that time he had become something of
a legend in Austin as a hell-raiser, and his opponent capitalized on this,
papering the district with blowups of the mug shot of the unmistakably
inebriated Wilson and the question "Do you want this man to represent
you in the U.S. Congress?"

In spite of this, Charlie won, demonstrating the intuitive understanding of and bond with his Bible Belt constituents that would allow him to
hold onto their support through the many scandals that lay ahead. Unlike
other politicians, Wilson never tried to hide his failings from his constituents. In fact, he seemed almost to turn his innocent sins to his advantage.
Time and again it seemed that the voters of the Second Congressional
District would forgive him almost anything if he was honest with them.
What they hated was hypocrisy, and whatever his shortcomings, Wilson
was no hypocrite. There was, perhaps, one other reason why the dour, supposedly puritanical voters chose to make Charlie Wilson their representative: the Second District can be a deadly boring place except when
Charlie was there. People couldn't help but like and forgive this boyish
politician who always made them feel good whenever he entered a room.

During the 1960s and '70s, as he built his political base in East Texas,
Wilson could never shake the feeling that he had cheated his country by
not giving the twenty years of military service expected of Annapolis men.
He had been too young to serve in World War II, he had been at the Naval
Academy during Korea, and when it came time for Vietnam he found him-
self as a freshman congressman reluctantly voting against the war. As he

---

ema, he did what local governments would not—he tapped federal aid to build housing projects, an airport, recreation centers, golf courses, and facilities for the elderly.
Arthur Temple helped bankroll Wilson's political career to perpetuate this tradition
as well as to help the timber industry.

saw it, America's South Vietnamese allies just weren't willing to fight, and for Charlie Wilson, that meant they weren't worth backing. In those days it was very much in the mainstream for a young liberal Democrat to vote against the war. But it always made him feel a bit like a traitor.

Wilson's first serious entry into the arena of U.S. foreign affairs came in his first year in office in 1973, when he discovered the cause of Israel. U.S. ambassadors and assistant secretaries of state, national security advisers, and CIA directors would invariably be puzzled by what prompted Wilson to take up the curious causes he chose to champion. Often they would suspect the basest motives—outright payoffs or some other ulterior temptation. The real explanation begins with his mother, Wilmuth.

Wilmuth Wilson was a woman of conviction. In Trinity, Texas, a conservative southern community, she was the town liberal and a force to be reckoned with. A mainstay of the Democratic Party and a pillar of her church, she stood out as a fearless defender of the rights of Trinity's black citizens. "I suspect ours was the only house in town where the word *nigger* wasn't used," Charlie remembers. She openly befriended blacks, and throughout the Depression, when hoboes and tramps would come to the back door to see if they could sharpen knives in exchange for a meal, Wilmuth would always send Charlie to talk with them, telling him that they were good people just down on their luck. "Always," she told her young son and his kid sister, Sharon (who would go on to become chairman of the board of Planned Parenthood), "always stand up for the underdog. If you're ever in doubt, back the underdog."

As corny as it may sound, the lesson took. It certainly helps to explain why, two years before he was elected to Congress, Charlie Wilson was the only person in Lufkin, Texas, who subscribed to the *Jerusalem Post*. He made this unusual move immediately after reading *Exodus*, Leon Uris's novel about the founding of the modern state of Israel. It was the ultimate story about worthy underdogs, the kind Wilmuth had taught him to honor.

Wilson had been in Congress only a few months and had just won a seat on the Foreign Affairs Committee when Egypt, Syria, Jordan, and the combined forces of the Arab League launched a surprise attack on Israel during the Jewish holiday of Yom Kippur. For a few days, as Wilson followed every news account, he thought the Arab forces might actually overrun the Jewish state. At one point he became so concerned that he put in a call to the Israeli embassy, asking the switchboard operator to connect him with someone who could brief him about the war.

In Washington during those days, the Israeli embassy was a center of remarkably effective intrigue. Its mission was to support the survival of Israel by ensuring the billions in economic and military assistance that the United States gives each year. Jewish congressmen and senators were natural allies and visited regularly. So, too, were elected officials with many Jewish constituents. What made the call from Charlie Wilson to the embassy's congressional liaison officer, Zvi Rafiah, so unusual was that Wilson is not Jewish and had virtually no Jews in his district.

Rafiah is a very short, very smart Israeli who Wilson always believed was a highly placed Mossad agent. He was used to dealing with all sorts of people, but he says he has never encountered anyone like Wilson. To begin with, Rafiah was not accustomed to having congressmen or senators come to him; they always summoned him, and he would appear at their offices armed with charts, maps, slides, military attachés, and ministers.

Wilson's arrival an hour after his call startled Rafiah. He was wearing cowboy boots and a Stetson and from the perspective of the five-foot-six Rafiah, the congressman looked like a giant. But what surprised the Israeli most was Wilson's impressive command of military history and his keen understanding of weapons and tactics. Rafiah quickly realized that Wilson had developed a powerful identification with the Israeli cause, and when the congressman said he wanted to go to Israel immediately, Rafiah was quick to accommodate.

Three days later Wilson was driving in a jeep in the Sinai with fellow representative Ed Koch. The Israeli army was taking them to the front of the Yom Kippur War, sweeping them past still burning Soviet tanks. He was ecstatic to be in the presence of these heroic warriors. It was the beginning of a ten-year love affair with everything to do with Israel. "I bought the whole thing—the beleaguered democracy surrounded by Soviet-armed barbarians—survivors of Nazi concentration camps—David versus Goliath."

Wilson would go on to become one of Israel's most important congressional champions: a non-Jew with no Jewish constituents. Years later Zvi Rafiah would muse on this curiosity: "I visited his district once, and I was very impressed with the oil pumps and the big fat cows lying in the shade. Every time I describe a rich country, I describe this scene in

Lufkin—the cows in the shade of the oil pumps. But believe me, there are no Jews in Lufkin."

There was perhaps another ingredient beyond his mother's exhortations that went into Wilson's embrace of Israel. His future co-conspirator in Afghanistan, the CIA's Gust Avrakotos, suggests that Charlie had a kind of James Bond syndrome: "As I saw it, the tie that bound us together was chasing pussy and killing Communists." Avrakotos' blunt language tends to turn people off, but the CIA man has a raw genius for understanding what makes Wilson tick. And his point is that, along with a worthy underdog to champion, two other ingredients were necessary to fully mobilize Charlie Wilson: a Communist bully to put down and a beautiful woman by his side.

In Israel it began with a raven-haired captain in the Israeli Defense Forces. She was the congressman's official guide to the war zone, and Wilson's infatuation began on that first trip into the desert to see the burning Russian tanks. Ed Koch still remembers his horror when the beautiful captain's commanding officer, offended by her growing fascination with the goy in the cowboy hat, ordered her not to return the next day. Koch saw Wilson as a potentially invaluable asset to Israel: a non-Jew on the Foreign Affairs Committee who was more passionate about Israel than any of its Jewish members. "He was unique," Koch recalls. "An oil man who was pro-Israel." Koch quickly took the commander aside. "Are you crazy?" he asked. "The woman is twenty-one. Let her take care of herself." Captain Lilatoff remained at her post.

Wilson admits that he was infatuated with the beautiful officer whose husband was off fighting in Egypt. But he says the relationship remained purely platonic, mainly because a few days later, in the lobby of his hotel, he was introduced to Israel's leading movie star, Gila Almagor. "I remember thinking, This is a hell of a place. You get Russian tanks burning on the desert, beautiful captains, and movie stars." To Wilson, Israel was filled with nothing but glorious underdogs who didn't want or need Americans to fight their wars for them. All they were asking for was U.S. military supplies and economic assistance, to counter the Arabs who wanted nothing less than to use their Soviet arsenals to annihilate Israel.

By the time he got back to Washington, Wilson had become, in his own words, "an Israeli commando" in the U.S. Congress. And quite to his surprise and delight, a remarkable thing happened: The Jews of Houston and Dallas discovered the congressman from Lufkin. Without any solicitation, contributions began rolling in from all over the country. "The AIPAC [American Israel Public Affairs Committee] people loved me because here I was, a cowboy from Texas, hysterical about their cause," remembers Wilson. The congressman soon found himself giving the major United Jewish Appeal speech of the year in Washington and addressing Young Jewish Leadership conferences all over the country.

This friendship with Israel grew so intimate that, years later, when Wilson determined that the CIA wasn't willing to provide Afghan rebels with an effective mule-portable anti-aircraft gun, he secretly asked the Israelis to design one. They came through, as they always did. And when Wilson was engulfed in a drug scandal that jeopardized his 1984 reelection campaign, Ed Koch mobilized supporters in New York and Jewish backers of Israel from all across the country to pony up $100,000 in campaign contributions and save the day. It was also the Jews in Congress who would rally to put Wilson on the all-powerful Appropriations Committee, where he could help make sure the annual $3 billion a year in aid continued to flow. Getting the Appropriations assignment as a junior congressman was an amazing political maneuver because his own Texas delegation opposed it; they backed a Texan with more seniority. The only other congressman to ever defy his own delegation and seek an Appropriations seat was Lyndon Johnson; but LBJ failed. It was Wilson's Jewish friends who made it possible.

From his new position on Appropriations, Wilson began to learn how Israel and other special interests use their power. He discovered that the authorizing committees, like Foreign Affairs, were little more than debating societies. He now served on a committee that doled out the nation's money: fifty men appropriating $500 billion a year. He watched and saw how one man, if he's on the right subcommittee and knows how to play the system, can move the entire nation to fund a program or cause of his choice.

By the late 1970s, Wilson was starting to feel his power. He had become part of a small tribe of Democrats alarmed by what they perceived to be a policy of appeasement by their own party. The Israelis had been whispering in Wilson's ear ever since Jimmy Carter came into office that the United States was getting soft, looking the other way as the Communists advanced everywhere unchecked. But Wilson's concerns were independent of the Israelis'. He genuinely believed that the Soviets were out to conquer the world. And he was unnerved when he saw the pictures of President Carter embracing Soviet premier Leonid Brezhnev and kissing him on both cheeks at the arms-control talks. To him it was an ominous replay of that critical moment before World War II when British prime minister Neville Chamberlain, pursuing his policy of appeasement, emerged from negotiations with Hitler to announce "peace in our time."

Timing is everything, and it was just at this moment, with these dark thoughts racing in Wilson's head, that Congressman Jack Murphy appeared in Charlie's office to make an appeal. Murphy was the kind of Democrat Wilson could relate to, a West Point graduate and decorated Korean War veteran. They were drinking friends, but Murphy had not come to socialize. The two considered themselves part of a lonely group of Democrats holding the line against the Soviets. And Murphy was preaching to the converted when he savaged the president for appeasing the Communists. Now, he said, Carter was about to betray America's oldest anti-Communist ally in Central America. It was unconscionable to stand by and let it happen, and Wilson was the only man in Congress with the power and the balls to stop it.

Anastasio "Tacho" Somoza was a particularly unattractive dictator, with thick black-rimmed glasses, weighty jowls, and a disturbing leer when he smiled. But over a bottle of Scotch in Wilson's private office, Murphy told a heartwarming story about how he had gotten to know Tacho as a schoolboy at LaSalle Military Academy in New York, and later as his roommate at West Point. Somoza had created a little U.S.A. in Nicaragua, Murphy explained; the U.S. Army had trained his entire army officer corps, and his son was a Harvard man.

More important, he reminded Wilson, the dictator had turned his country over to the CIA in 1954, when it had needed help to overthrow the Guatemalan government, and Tacho had played a critical role in the Bay of Pigs as well. His only crime, Murphy said, was that he always supported the United States, and now Jimmy Carter wanted to destroy him because the hand wringers at the State Department claimed he was violating human rights. At that very moment, Murphy announced to dramatize his point, the Cuban—and Soviet-armed—Sandinista guerrillas were attacking the cities of Nicaragua. If Wilson didn't use his leverage on the Appropriations Committee to try to protect Tacho, Carter would get away with cutting off all Somoza's military and economic aid, at a moment when it might just do him in.

The zeal with which Wilson took up the challenge caught everyone, particularly the Carter White House and the State Department, utterly by surprise. By the time Charlie intervened, saving Somoza seemed to be a lost cause. The Appropriations Subcommittee had already sent the bill that cut Somoza's funding to the House floor. The unwritten rules of the Appropriations Committee dictate that members don't challenge the overall subcommittee bills once they have been reported out. But in a stunning political maneuver, Wilson took the Nicaraguan-aid issue to the floor, where he threatened to scuttle the president's entire foreign-aid bill if Somoza's money was not restored. He told his colleagues that Somoza had done "an enormous amount of dirty work for the U.S., that he was virtually an arm of U.S. intelligence." It was hardly a popular cause. The columnist Jack Anderson had just labeled Somoza the greediest dictator in the world, to which Wilson responded, "No one is perfect, no one is pure." Miraculously, Wilson won the first round. To the disgust of liberals, the media, and the administration, Somoza's entire $3.1 million aid package was restored. A jubilant Representative Murphy insisted that Wilson accompany him to Managua over the July 4 recess to meet Tacho.

One of Wilson's more endearing features is an ability to understand how ridiculous he often looks to those witnessing his antics. Many years later he would recall with humor the lavish dinner party Somoza threw for him. "Everyone was looking at me with enormous respect," Wilson recalled, "as if I were Simón Bolívar. Tacho gave this great toast in which he credited me with being the only thing preserving freedom in the hemisphere. The entire oligarchy of Managua was there applauding. I will admit, it was kind of heady."

After the toasts, Somoza invited Wilson into his private underground office in the bunker. "It was kind of Hitlerian," Wilson recalls. Somoza would later spend his final days in Nicaragua in that bunker, vainly directing his army to bomb the cities of his country as the Sandinistas closed in on him. But that night Somoza, flushed with the victory in Congress, was brimming over with bravado.

The dictator was seated in front of a giant West Point flag. "I want you to know that dealing with Tacho Somoza is not a one-way street," he said, leering as he took a thick wad of greenbacks out of his desk drawer. He mumbled something about campaign contributions.

"I almost shit," Wilson remembers. "I said, 'Well, not now. I don't need any money now. Maybe in the future.'" The congressman says he was not about to take the money, but he couldn't quite get himself to turn it down completely. "It just looked so tempting," he says, remembering Somoza mentioning the figure of $50,000. "In those days that was a good bit of change, but I didn't take the fucking money."

Wilson says the rejection made for an awkward moment. In spite of this, the dictator managed to win him over. Wilson liked the West Point flag in the bunker, the dictator's easy American slang, his friendship with General Alexander Haig, and his bravado. Beyond that, they shared a common bond over Israel. Wilson's Israeli friends had spoken glowingly about Tacho's father, who had opened up Nicaragua for European Jews before World War II and voted for Israel's entry into the United Nations. "He was a soul brother to the Israelis," Wilson explains, someone they owed and supported to the very end. (There was even a shipload of Israeli weapons on its way when Somoza fell.) And Wilson was particularly swayed by the Israelis' insistence that Jimmy Carter's human-rights policy was shortsighted and that Tacho was by far less evil than anything that might follow.

Most of Wilson's Democratic colleagues, certainly most of the American press corps, and eventually most of the Nicaraguan people came to view Somoza as a corrupt dictator guilty of ruthless force against his own people. But Wilson saw him through his own peculiar lens as an abandoned and betrayed U.S. ally threatened by every Russian-backed leftist in the hemisphere. He was running a rearguard action from the Appropriations Committee to save Somoza, even threatening to torpedo the president's highest priority, the Panama Canal Treaty. But the tide in America had turned against such indiscriminate anti-Communism, and Wilson thought he had used up all his options to rescue Somoza. That is, until he found himself face-to-face with the renegade ex-CIA operative Ed Wilson.

The congressman's encounter with this outlaw came about by chance because of one of those peculiar problems that seem to beset Charlie Wilson. He had fallen hopelessly in lust with his confidential secretary, Tina Simons. Like many of the women in the office, Tina was curvaceous, upbeat, and available, but Wilson had imposed a most unfortunate discipline on himself when it came to romance: he would not woo any of the women on his staff. The smitten congressman decided there was only one thing to do: he asked a mutual friend to get her a job. As chance would have it, she ended up as the all-purpose office manager, decorator, and social secretary for Ed Wilson.

Memories fade, and the name Ed Wilson may no longer strike a chord, but in his day he came to represent something new and evil in the American experience. He was a former CIA agent who, like Kurtz in *Heart of Darkness,* had taken to serving the interests of dark forces. By the time the congressman met Ed Wilson, a *Washington Post* article had accused him of working for Muammar Qaddafi. But no formal charges had been brought, and the renegade managed to make many influential Washingtonians believe that he was, perhaps, operating under very deep cover on some convoluted mission.

The former CIA operative would later be indicted for selling sophisticated explosives to Qaddafi, or for recruiting hit squads to dispose of the Libyan leader's political enemies, but when Charlie Wilson met him, Ed Wilson presented himself as a multimillionaire with a sprawling horse farm in the hunt country of Virginia and a lavish town house in the capital where he held court with a daring collection of former and present CIA men and other mysterious characters.

Charlie had never met a full-fledged CIA operative before, and Ed Wilson appealed to his sense of what a CIA agent should look like. "He was taller than me, weighed about two fifty, just a very lethal-looking person, dark, ominous, but a good sense of humor and a good guy to drink with."

The congressman took to meeting his former secretary at this exotic town house, where, accompanied by much alcohol, Ed Wilson began telling Charlie how things really worked in the CIA. "Ed had convinced me that he personally killed Che Guevara and I thought, Shit, if he got Che, he can sure get that little turd Ortega," Wilson said, referring to the Sandinista guerrilla leader. This ex-CIA thug set off a lightbulb in Charlie Wilson's head; if Jimmy Carter wouldn't do what was necessary to save the United States, then, by God, he and Ed Wilson would come to the rescue of Tacho Somoza.

A meeting was arranged at the Palm Bay Club in Miami Beach, Somoza's favorite weekend retreat. The dictator brought along his hot-blooded mistress, Dinorah Sampson. Charlie Wilson brought Tina Simons and Ed Wilson. Somoza seemed more than intrigued when Ed Wilson described the one-thousand-man army of former CIA operatives he said he could mobilize to crush the Sandinistas. "We were all drinking, getting more excited, more excited, killing Ortega, killing everybody, and then Tacho asked Tina to dance."

Everything was going swimmingly when the dictator, now blind drunk with visions of a thousand CIA cutthroats doing in his enemies, began to fondle Tina. It all happened so fast that the two Wilsons could barely believe their eyes. Dinorah, a very fit weight lifter, began pulling apart the two dancers, screaming in Spanish at her lover, then ripped off Somoza's glasses and stomped them on the ground.

One can only imagine how a military dictator must feel when humiliated like this. It couldn't have been easy for Tacho to return to the table. Perhaps it was simply a need to reassert his manhood that changed his mind about Ed Wilson's proposal, which had so recently enchanted him. But more than likely it was the price tag. Somoza was a notorious tight-wad, and the congressman remembers to this day Somoza's look of horror when Ed Wilson said he could save the dictator for a mere $100 million— $100,000 per man. To the congressman's dismay, Somoza passed on the offer. He just said, "Out of the question." Wilson later observed that the whole exercise had been "very amateurish on my part." Putting the best possible face on this maiden effort to hijack a U.S. foreign policy, he explained, "I wanted to try to do something to hold the Ortegas of the world at bay, until Carter learned better or we got a new president."

Shortly afterward, Somoza lost the support even of his country's business community. On July 17, 1979, with the rebel forces closing in, the dictator fled Nicaragua. It had not been Wilson's finest hour, and the disasters were only beginning. Just over a year later, Charlie found himself looking at a picture of a screaming Dinorah Sampson on the front page of the *Washington Post*. She was running from the flaming wreckage of Tacho's white Mercedes-Benz in Asunción, Paraguay, the only country that had been willing to offer sanctuary to Somoza. The killers had pumped eighteen bullets into Tacho's body and face before finishing off the job with a rocket attack. Soon after, the man who had gotten Wilson into the affair,

Representative Jack Murphy, was caught taking a bribe in the FBI's ABSCAM sting operation and sent to jail. Meanwhile, Ed Wilson had become a hunted man after being indicted for his illegal dealings with Qaddafi. Captured in the Bahamas, he was tried and sentenced to fifty-two years in jail, where he languishes today.

From his maximum-security cell in White Deer, Pennsylvania, he insists that he had always been operating under the authority of what he calls the "inner CIA." The congressman's girlfriend, Tina Simons, suddenly found herself fearing for her life. After testifying against Ed Wilson, she permanently disappeared into the federal witness protection program. The Sandinistas, the Communist-backed guerrillas who Wilson had tried to stop, suddenly emerged as the preoccupation of Ronald Reagan in his not-so-secret Contra war.

Charlie Wilson escaped unscathed but unsettled. He had intervened, believing he was acting selflessly to counter a threat that the country had not yet recognized. His heart may have been in the right place, but his head certainly was not. And by the time it was over, he had managed to make himself look like a dangerous fool. It was in the aftermath of this debacle that Wilson slipped into his colorful midlife crisis—a despairing patriot, convinced that his country was headed toward disaster but no longer certain that he would have a role in its salvation. For a moment, when the courage of the Afghans temporarily inspired him, he shook off his stupor long enough to double the CIA's Afghan budget. But it was just for a moment, and then he disappeared back into what he called "the longest midlife crisis in history."

In retrospect, the Somoza fiasco was a turning point for Wilson, and only later would he realize its positive impact. He had discovered that, even with a wildly unpopular cause, he had the power to intimidate the most high-level bureaucrats. And most important for what he would later do in Afghanistan, he had crossed over a line and, in effect, experimented with running his own foreign operation with a renegade operative who wasn't afraid to break the rules.

CHAPTER 3

Gust Avrakotos

A ROGUE ELEPHANT IN THE AGENCY WOODS

G ust Avrakotos hadn't gone to Harvard. He didn't have important relatives or fancy summer vacations. He hadn't inherited tennis lessons, money, or classic good looks. He was the son of Greek immigrants from Aliquippa, Pennsylvania, and the CIA simply didn't go to places like that to recruit its elite case officers. Aliquippa was a steelworker's town, and for most of its early years, the Agency seemed to think its Clandestine Services should be filled with men of breeding.

That's how the British had always picked their spies, and the founders of the CIA had taken the British as their model. British spies belonged to clubs. They dressed like gentlemen. Their top officers had gone to boarding schools, then cemented their friendships as young men at Oxford and Cambridge. This was a class that had been at the spy game for centuries; they had learned that a man's family and schools stood for something.

That, at least, was the legend about the British. So it was natural, when Congress created the CIA in 1947, that the American leadership would look to the same class for its service. And to a remarkable extent, the CIA did manage to fill its ranks with sons of the establishment.

Take Theodore Roosevelt's grandson Archie. Brilliant at Groton and Harvard, a classical scholar with six languages and a robust appetite for healthy adventure, he was one of the first generation of Agency operatives. On the surface, he led a rather dull existence as a midlevel State Department officer. But "everyone" knew that Archie worked for the CIA, and there were few who didn't welcome an invitation to one of his elegant Georgetown evenings.

There was always a sense at the Roosevelts' of being at the center of things both past and present. As Archie's distant cousin the columnist Stewart Alsop used to joke at such gatherings, "A man should *have* furniture, he shouldn't have to buy it." In Archie's house there were ancestral portraits on the wall and that patrician glow that comes from the mix of old wood, Oriental rugs, gleaming silver, and the kindly faces of faithful retainers.

Archie presided effortlessly over these gatherings—actually thinking of them as "informal" because the dress called for dark suits instead of dinner jackets. There was little general conversation at the table. The ritual called for each man to speak first to the woman on his right and then, at an appropriate moment, to turn and converse with the dinner partner on his left. It was not until after the women left the men to their cigars and brandy that the talk would turn to matters of state.

Then Archie might talk about the latest rebellion of the Kurds or what his friend the Shah of Iran was up to. But even here it was all terribly discreet. The Agency would never have to worry about a Roosevelt being polygraphed—it was part of the noblesse oblige of the man to know intuitively how to keep a secret.

No matter how long he served or how far he rose in the CIA, Gust Avrakotos would always feel a bit like the poor street kid, nose against the glass, looking in at the party, knowing he would never be asked to attend such gatherings. And dinner at Archie's was hardly the only thing that made Avrakotos feel like an outsider. "Almost everyone was a fucking blue blood in the CIA in 1961 when I came in," he says. "They were just beginning to let Jews move up that year. But there still weren't any blacks, Hispanics, or females—just some token Greeks and Polacks."

Some of Avrakotos's friends actually schemed to wangle an invitation to Archie's. They felt it could help just to be seen with this patrician. But Avrakotos hadn't kowtowed to the plant manager's sons in Aliquippa, and he wasn't afraid to say what he thought about the Agency's blue bloods. As far as he was concerned, they operated in an "old boys' network" to keep his kind down and "the only reason half of them got anywhere is because they jerked off Henry Cabot Lodge's grandson at some prep school."

Avrakotos had a chip on his shoulder; there was no question about that. But he did make friends with some of the Agency's well-born officers, and he accepted the notion that some of the real aristocrats—originals like Roosevelt—were at least authentic. Nevertheless, as he rose through the ranks he came to loathe a certain type of blue blood with a rage that bordered on class hatred.

The CIA hadn't started opening its ranks to gifted "new" Americans like Avrakotos until 1960, and the move had had nothing to do with social justice. There were no quotas in those days. The fact was that these first-generation types, brought up on the streets of America and speaking the languages of the Old Country, had certain strengths that the CIA had come to feel it needed.

A kind of panic about the Communist threat had been sweeping over Washington. In every city in the 1950s air raid sirens were regularly set off. Tens of millions of children got used to scurrying into bomb shelters or crawling under their desks as part of drills to prepare for a Soviet nuclear assault. In every corner of the globe the dark hand of the Communists was seen to be at work.

The commission by which the CIA came to live during those years was spelled out in one telling paragraph from a blue-ribbon panel explaining to President Truman why it was essential for the United States to abandon its traditional sense of fair play in this all-out struggle for the world:

> It is now clear that we are facing an implacable enemy whose avowed objective is world domination . . . there are no rules in such a game. Hitherto acceptable norms of human conduct do not apply. If the United States is to survive, it must use more clever, more sophisticated and more effective means than those used against us.

It was almost as if Gust Avrakotos's early life in Aliquippa had been designed to turn him into the kind of back-alley spy that Harry Truman's advisers were urging the CIA to nurture and unleash on the Communists. The one thing no one needed to teach this man was how to "subvert and destroy" his enemies.

Aliquippa is one of those American company towns always described as a melting pot. Immigrants from all over the world poured in here for jobs in the huge steelworks that the Jones and Laughlin company built. But the hard people of this steel town never lost any of their ethnic pride, or their ethnic hatreds. You can still see the workingman's anger in Avrakotos when he drives up the hill to Plan Six, where the WASP managers used to live in their five- and six-bedroom stone houses. He calls them "cake eaters" and talks about them with the same contempt he uses for the Agency's blue bloods.

When Jones and Laughlin moved into Aliquippa on the rolling hills just north of Pittsburgh, it didn't specify where the workers should live. But every ethnic group insisted on living, marrying, partying, and going to church with its own. As recently as 1980, fourteen thousand steel workers earned their living there.

Today it's as if the bomb had struck. There's nothing but great hulking iron forms and rusting steel. About the only sign of life are a few teams of workers dismantling one of the abandoned steel plants to sell as scrap to the Japanese. But Avrakotos remembers Aliquippa the way it was when he was growing up and delegations of Japanese used to come in buses to study this marvel of industrial America. They brought movie cameras and notebooks to record everything about the workings of the largest integrated steel mill in the world. No one felt anything but pride as the plant operated at full tilt twenty-four hours a day, spewing out great clouds of pink and black smoke that would engulf the ethnic neighborhoods of Aliquippa.

"That's Plan Seven, where the Dagos lived," Avrakotos says, like a tour guide passing through the ruins of some past civilization. "Plan Twelve was all Irish. The Polacks lived in Plan Five. Plan Eleven is where the niggers were." For all his years at the CIA, Avrakotos has never stopped using the brutal street talk of his youth. He's as proud of it as he is of the scars that lace his body from teenage knife fights. "Each of the plans had a gang, and they fought like cats and dogs," he explains. "Each plan fought among itself, but when the niggers came we all banded together. You had to be very fucking practical. . . . The guys who made it out of Aliquippa had one thing in common: you can't fuck around all day trying to make up your mind. The niggers will overrun you."

This kind of talk is jarring, but it was the language of Aliquippa— and it shaped Avrakotos's brutal instinct for the jugular. There are legends in Aliquippa about the ones who escaped and made good: Henry Mancini, who got his start at the musical and political Italian clubs; Mike Ditka, Avrakotos's high school friend from Plan Seven, the former Chicago Bears linebacker whose name is synonymous with toughness; Tony Dorsett of the Cowboys. Becoming a sports hero was one way out.

The mafia was another. There were three thousand Sicilians in Aliquippa. Most of Avrakotos's friends were Sicilians, and he knew the Alamena family as "men of honor." Gust's father, Oscar Avrakotos, distributed Rolling Rock beer for them, and they always treated the Avrakotoses with respect. But the Sicilian mafia wasn't an option for a Greek-American. And anyway Oscar Avrakotos had high hopes for his son.

Like many other immigrants, Oscar's American experience had begun at Ellis Island, as an eight-year-old boy from the Greek Island of Lemnos. He had come over with his brother in 1894 and for three decades toiled in the sweatshops of New England and the "Iron House" of Aliquippa. But then Oscar broke away from the pack with a vision of making a fortune selling his own soda pop.

With his hard-earned savings he bought a bottling assembly line from the Smile and Cheer-up Company of St. Louis. He named his new company after the Greek sun god, Apollo. Apollo was his good-luck god, and he figured the name would win customers from the Greek Orthodox church, not to mention workers in the mills.

As the owner of the Apollo Soda Water Company, Oscar was a man of means, at least by the standards of Lemnos. He was close to fifty when he went back to the old country and took a bride, Zafira Konstantaras, twenty-one years younger and with a big dowry. Back in Aliquippa three years later, Gust Avrakotos was born into a household that would know nothing but unrelenting hard work. His earliest memories are of his father moving about in the kitchen at 4:30 A.M., eating his breakfast of pork chops and potatoes and polishing off several beers and a couple of shots, if it was cold, before walking downstairs to begin the day's labor.

By five A.M. he would have the bottling machine cranked up and moving. On one side was Louisa, a large black woman, who placed the dirty bottles on the beginning of the thirty-five-foot line. Miraculously, the chain apparatus would turn the bottles upside down as soap and water poured in and out, to prepare them for an infusion of Oscar's secret cherry and cola formulas. There were always incidents. The bottles would sometimes explode from the pressure like hand grenades, sending glass shrapnel all over the room. One such piece sliced into Gust's face and cost him a full day's work.

At first it was a thrill for the boy to be included. But by sixteen, he had accumulated forty quarters of Social Security and the novelty had worn off. This was the kind of punishing physical labor that quickly makes a man out of a boy.

It was at the Apollo Soda Water Company that Avrakotos developed his frightening convictions about revenge. His first mentor had been Wasil Rosinko, a Ukrainian who worked at the end of the bottle line, heaving cases into the trucks. Rosinko had found his wife in bed with another man and had murdered them both. After Rosinko spent fifteen years in prison, Oscar gave him his job back, and Wasil took it upon himself to help educate Oscar's boy. He warned young Gust never to trust a Ukrainian woman and taught him that revenge is sweet.

But Avrakotos's most powerful memory was of his mother at the kitchen table demanding to know what Oscar intended to do about an insult: "You're not going to let this pass, are you? You are going to get even, aren't you?"

In the Avrakotos household, revenge was a matter of family honor. As a boy of twelve, Gust would go with his father to the bars to collect unpaid bills. He learned not to show fear when Oscar would face down bartenders and begin hurling bottles, threatening to take the bar apart if the money due him was not paid immediately. The Avrakotos family did not tolerate freeloaders.

There was no TV in the house, and on Saturday nights Gust would be allowed to sit at the table in the kitchen to listen to his father and uncles talk politics and trade family stories. The men were particularly proud of the family name in spite of its ambiguous meaning in Greek: "without pants" or "those without pants." Whenever she became frustrated with Oscar, Zafira would suggest that some ancestor had been caught in a compromising sexual relationship.

The Avrakotos men insisted that the name referred back to men who functioned as a kind of praetorian guard in ancient times. These Avrakotoses were a fierce warrior class, so the family legend went, who would throw off all their clothes when going into battle and charge the enemy. The sight of screaming, naked warriors was enough to cause most opponents to break and run.

Whether or not the legend is true, these stories shaped the young boy's sense of his identity and destiny. And they help explain why his father made such extreme demands on his son. He forced Gust to take private lessons in Greek and Latin. "Each new language gives you a new set of eyes and ears, a new window on the world," he repeatedly told his complaining child. Even free time on Sunday was given over to torturous work at the Greek Orthodox Church, where, amid chanting priests and incense, Gust would spend four hours serving as an altar boy. But the main thing Oscar and Zafira did for their son was to fill him with the sense that he must get out of the steel town. And the path of liberation that Oscar chose gleamed like a vision directly across the street from their home.

Like Andrew Carnegie, the founders of Aliquippa had built a library. It was not a simple, utilitarian building but a shining citadel of limestone and bronze in the form of a Greek temple. On the cornices in great letters were carved the words HISTORY, SCIENCE, FICTION, PHILOSOPHY, BIOLOGY, and ASTRONOMY. Every evening after dinner, after hours of humping beer kegs and a full day at school, Gust Avrakotos would walk the two hundred feet across Franklin Avenue, pass through the great bronze doors of the Benjamin Franklin Jones Memorial Library, and take the seat at a mahogany desk reserved for him. There he would switch on the individual bronze reading lamp with its Tiffany-style glass shade and begin the serious work of the day. It was what his father expected and demanded.

The library was like a window into the world of the possible beyond the bars, the union halls, and a life of servitude in the Iron House. In the winter, it might be snowing when he entered the library, but the white accumulation would have already turned black with soot by the time he finished his evening studies. Inside the classics were all there; fine oil paintings hung on the wall; the beamed ceilings were high, the windows huge. At the doorway towered a bronze statue of the founder, Benjamin Franklin Jones, passing on his unspoken message to all who entered that here in this temple of learning was a way out for those willing to apply themselves.

Each night all the ethnic achievers of Aliquippa would be there—studying, wandering through the stacks, improving their minds. And none of the deserving working-class kids of Aliquippa worked so hard or did so well as Gust Lascaris Avrakotos, who graduated as valedictorian of Aliquippa High. Then followed two years working his way through Carnegie Tech in Pittsburgh, until disaster struck and Oscar had to close down his beloved Apollo Soda Water Company. Coca-Cola and Pepsi had moved into

Aliquippa, cutting prices. According to the family's Old World code, Gust had to leave school to pay off his father's debts.

For the first time, Gust went to work in the mill. Then he began traveling up and down the Allegheny Valley for the Greek-American Cigarette Vending Machine Company, selling cigarette machines to bars. He had never left Pennsylvania, but by the time he was twenty-one, he knew how people from numerous different countries talked and thought and drank and sang and argued. He knew the world the way few American boys his age do, because every one of those political clubs where he delivered beer and sold cigarettes was a virtual enclave of foreigners. There was the Syrian Club, the Cedars of Lebanon Club, the Pan-Slovak Club, the Russian-American Club, the Croatian Club, the Ukrainian Club—one for virtually every country of the Old World, and Avrakotos had discovered that he could increase his sales if he knew what each of these groups cared about.

"I started reading to find out what the fuck to say when I was trying to sell cigarettes in the different bars. To sell, you needed to talk to the Serbs and the Croatians and you needed to know what they cared about. And the one thing that was common was that not many of them were saying anything nice about the Communists. Not the Ukrainians, not the Serbians, not the Croatians, the Polacks, the Czechs, the Slovaks. . . . They all fucking hated the Russians. All of them were out of their countries because of the Russians. The Syrians of course hated the Jews. Maybe the only group not anti-Communist were the blacks. They were more practically biased. The others blamed the Russians for everything. For why we were working sixteen hours a day in the mill and paying taxes."

Avrakotos became a master at endearing himself to all of these prickly tribes. He can still say in perfect Slovak, "Take your balls and stuff them up your ass." This always pleased the Slovaks, who laughed appreciatively and offered the crazy Greek a boilermaker.

These forays into the ethnic enclaves of western Pennsylvania and the special skills required to maneuver there were not designed to serve any particular purpose beyond moving beer and cigarettes. Unbeknownst to Gust, they also constituted a remarkable introduction into the worlds he would later pass through for the CIA.

Curiously, it was not the Agency but IBM that first wanted to enlist Avrakotos. After paying off his father's debts in 1959, he had gone back to school at the University of Pittsburgh, graduating summa cum laude and Phi Beta Kappa, with a degree in mathematics. The IBM recruiter was so impressed that he offered Gust $15,500. "I was twenty-four years old and that was a lot of money in those days [roughly equivalent to $60,000 today]. All I had to do was get my master's and they'd pay my tuition." But then the recruiter started to tell him about IBM's corporate image and how they would expect him to adapt to some of their ways of doing things—a dress code, for one. And then there was the issue of his car.

It was a 1947 Dodge four-door, and it was the pride of Avrakotos's life. "We called it the fuckmobile," he recalls fondly today. "It had over three hundred thousand miles on it and was all souped up to look like a Lincoln Zephyr—like a gangster car. So I said, 'What's wrong with the car?'"

"It's old."

"It's an antique," Gust said.

"Around here we drive Pontiacs," the IBM man explained.

Avrakotos was on his way to his fourth interview with IBM when his favorite professor, Dr. Richard Cottam, suggested that he might like to speak to a man connected with American intelligence. Cottam, an expert on the Middle East whom Jimmy Carter would later tap for secret missions to Iran, was one of those men the CIA looked to in the country's universities to spot potential. Avrakotos still remembers the university room where he was told to report for the interview: 7 E21.

There was nothing physically interesting about the CIA man, but he knew how to talk Avrakotos's language. He registered pleasure that Gust had graduated summa cum laude. He said it was useful that Gust spoke Greek and that he was so good with figures. "But it was clear right away what really interested him," Gust recalls. "He recognized my real talent— that I was a fucking street guy."

"How do you feel about playing in dark alleys?" he asked.

"I love it," replied Avrakotos.

"You're just what I'm looking for."

When Avrakotos told him how much IBM was offering, the visitor said he was embarrassed and could offer only a third of that—$5,355 a year. "But I can give you one thing IBM can't," he said. "I can have you trained and overseas doing something for your country in one and a half years."

Avrakotos was hooked by the idea of becoming a spy for America. Instead, for the next three months the CIA spied on him. The office of security sent its sleuths to Aliquippa to ferret out any Communist influences in his family. They flew him to Washington (his first trip on an airplane) for a series of lie detector tests to see if he was homosexual or if he had anything to hide. Finally, the CIA told him they were going to induct him into their elite case officer–training program—not the office of security, not logistics or science and technology. They were going to take Oscar Avrakotos's son into their ultimate inner sanctum, into the Directorate of Operations, Archie Roosevelt's club.

When Avrakotos tried to read up on the CIA, he discovered there were no books or magazine articles explaining what the Agency did or what kind of people worked there. No one wrote about the CIA then; it was considered unpatriotic. The Agency was just moving into its $250 million headquarters hidden in the woods of Langley, Virginia, eight miles up the Potomac from the White House. Its design gave it the look of a modern campus or, perhaps, a corporate headquarters and some fifteen thousand employees worked there, but no sign acknowledged its existence from the road except a false one that read BUREAU OF PUBLIC WORKS. Any citizens who went looking for this nonexistent bureaucracy would find themselves facing a police barricade and a polite order to turn around.

It was into this mysterious world that Avrakotos descended on August 1, 1962. The majority of the fifty recruits in his class were from the Ivy Leagues—predominantly Harvard, Yale, and Brown. The others came from places like the Universities of Pittsburgh, Nebraska, or Kansas, or technological schools such as Carnegie Tech and Rensselaer Polytechnic Institute. The way Avrakotos computed it, "There were thirty-eight Ivy Leaguers and twelve of us." But he quickly developed a begrudging respect for all his classmates. He was impressed to find that the Agency had compiled a list of the country's valedictorians and had managed to enlist many of them. "When you grow up realizing the only way to get out of the shithole is by using your brain, you respect brains. And all these people were using their fucking brains, all of them."

Half had master's degrees; many spoke several languages. Avrakotos remembers one Harvard man who could recite Chaucer as if he were carrying on a simple conversation. For the next year and a half these fifty chosen ones stayed together, learning the tradecraft of the spy.

At Camp Peary, Virginia, the Agency's boot camp near Jamestown, Virginia, where the first Americans made their settlement, the new spies learned how to use firearms and detonate explosives. They went through a demanding survival course and parachuted out of planes. They traveled to different cities to practice shadowing and shaking surveillance. They learned how to sketch and diagram, how to make surreptitious entries, how to work with bugging experts and polygraph operators, how to pass messages secretly, how to infiltrate agents, how to compromise or recruit their adversaries.

There was a sense, in those days, of readying for war. The two superpowers were spending the bulk of their national budgets preparing to deliver an all-out nuclear attack within a matter of minutes. Over fifteen thousand nuclear warheads were aimed at each other's cities and military targets. On the border of Western Europe stood ninety Soviet divisions. The United States and its NATO allies conducted constant exercises in anticipation of an all-out conventional war. But no one doubted that it would inevitably go nuclear if so much as a division crossed the frontier. The superpowers had turned themselves into helpless giants, neither side willing to use its true might. With no other real outlet, the entire globe became the battleground of the spies. There was hardly a country where the KGB and CIA were not facing off in one way or another.

Avrakotos and his classmates assumed they'd be going into battle the moment they got their first assignment overseas. It was a time when places no one thought much about kept leaping onto the front pages as critical battlegrounds of the Cold War: the CIA's Cubans fighting the Soviets' Cubans; the American-backed Vietnamese against the Communist Vietnamese.

CIA agents came to view themselves as global cancer surgeons trying to identify and remove—or at least contain—even the most minor malignancies, lest they grow into full-scale threats that might later precipitate a nuclear confrontation. It was dirty business but deemed as necessary as the cut of a scalpel in the hand of a surgeon. A Castro in Cuba could spread his revolution not just to Central America but throughout Latin America. As the colonial powers began pulling out, all of Africa was up for grabs; a black Castro could infect the entire continent. There was no middle ground in this struggle. And everywhere the invisible generals in the only true battles allowed to be fought were the spies.

This was the world Gust Avrakotos moved into in 1963, when, after completing his training, he was given his first overseas post. It would be hard to underestimate the sense of destiny he felt when he learned he would be posted to the country of his parents' birth. Now he was going back, not just to defend Greece's freedom but, as President Kennedy put it, to be "a watchman on the walls of freedom."

Greece was not just the cradle of democracy; it was where the Cold War had begun. The Truman Doctrine had been created to counter the threat of armed Communist infiltration in Greece and Turkey. The Marshall Plan had poured in hundreds of millions to rescue the economy, and the CIA was determined to keep the Greeks, who were NATO allies, from voting for leftists.

By the time Avrakotos arrived, the Agency was intervening in every aspect of Greek life. It had created and funded the Greek Central Intelligence Service, whose operatives worked with it hand in glove. CIA men busied themselves planting stories, funding candidates, monitoring the Communists, neutralizing their champions, showering their own clients with gifts and services. It was a massive undertaking, but Avrakotos was surprised to discover that 142 agents were already in place. The station chief didn't even bother to introduce himself for two months.

This was a strange, insular world for a new CIA operative to get used to. There was a virtual taboo against befriending Americans in Greece, and most of the real diplomats at the embassy treated their spy colleagues as if they were untouchables. "They called us 'spooks,'" Avrakotos recalls. "It's different in a small embassy like in Dakar or Calcutta, where there may only be five people posted and you're the only Americans in town. But in the big embassies in Paris, Rome, Tokyo, London, spooks are separate. It's a real caste system. You can tell the way they spit it out when they ask for your opinion. 'Well, what do the spooks think?'"

The "spooks" themselves considered case officers green for their first two tours. Some of the veterans insist that you really can't be a true pro until you have twenty years of espionage behind you. But Avrakotos was an irrepressible self-starter. He spoke Greek like a native and knew how to build on opportunities. On April 21, 1967, he got one of those breaks that can make a career, when a military junta seized power in Athens and suspended democratic and constitutional government. Liberals in the United States and around the world were outraged, but overnight "the colonels' coup" turned Avrakotos into one of the CIA's indispensable, frontline players.

Well before this, he had made it his business to get to know the colonels. They had all started off life as peasants before joining the army, and they felt a kinship with this charismatic, working-class American whose parents had come from Lemnos. They could speak Greek with him. He drank and whored with them, and they knew from the heart that he shared their ferocious anti-Communism.

Avrakotos understood that the colonels had expected the United States to thank them, however discreetly, for preventing the anti-American candidate, Andreas Papandreou, from taking power. The polls had indicated that Papandreou would win the election, and the colonels suspected that the CIA itself was trying to sabotage Papandreou's campaign. But world reaction was so bitter and the move so brutally antidemocratic that the Johnson administration took to verbally attacking the junta and threatening to cut off U.S. assistance.

After the colonels arrested Papandreou, who had lived in the United States for years, the embassy sent Avrakotos to deliver a message to them. The United States had taken the unusual step of issuing the Greek leader an American passport, and the embassy wanted the junta to permit him to leave the country. "That's the official position. You should let him go," the young CIA man told the colonels. "But unofficially, as your friend, my advice is to shoot the motherfucker because he's going to come back to haunt you."

This was vintage Aliquippa wisdom and just the kind of statement made at just the right moment to cement a true conspirators' friendship. One can only imagine the trouble Avrakotos might have gotten into if the ambassador had learned about his private remarks—but he didn't, and now, at twenty-nine, Avrakotos had suddenly leapt to the front of the pack and transformed himself into the CIA's all-important agent at the very heart of the new power center of Greece.

For the next seven years, the colonels insisted on dealing with Avrakotos as their principal American contact. Ostensibly he worked for the Department of the Army as a civilian liaison to the Greek military. He moved freely in and out of their offices. He took them out on his boat at night and for picnics and outings on weekends. He was, for all practical purposes, an invisible member of the ruling junta.

Avrakotos tells of driving up to the Athens Hilton, where he lunched every day. The doorman saluted the CIA man and took his keys just as one of the colonels came up to meet him for lunch. "How come they let you park your car here?" the colonel demanded. "They won't even let me do that."

"Well, I don't know what you do, but I run the country," Avrakotos growled, and his buddy laughed with delight.

Accounts of Avrakotos at this high point evoke a Costa-Gavras character—a shadowy American in dark glasses, whispering to his fascist colonels. It was a time of coups and countercoups. Greece and Turkey came to the edge of war over Cyprus. Both countries were members of NATO, and Henry Kissinger and Assistant Secretary of State Joseph Sisco shuttled in and out, trying to keep the alliance from tearing apart. In spite of the significance of the diplomacy, the only American always welcome to the changing military strongmen was Gust Avrakotos. It's hard not to feel a certain unease about such a figure.

But those were days of Cold War, and the kinds of things he did were deemed crucial to the secret struggle. Just how dangerous a game Avrakotos was playing did not become fully evident until two days before Christmas 1975, when Richard Welch, the chief of the Athens station, was cut down on his front doorstep by three masked gunmen. Welch, one of those gentleman spies who spoke four languages and studied the classics, had supposedly been a mere first secretary at the embassy until that November, when an Athenian English-language magazine had identified him as CIA and published his name, photograph, and address.

It was a frightening moment for American operatives abroad. A CIA renegade, Philip Agee, had just set out to expose his former colleagues in a sensational book, *Inside the Company,* and radical newspapers were republishing the names of agents in their areas.

A Greek terrorist group, the 17 November, instantly claimed responsibility for the assassination. But Avrakotos and his CIA colleagues blamed Agee for deliberately exposing Welch. Six months later, Agee fingered Avrakotos as well. From that time on, Gust was vilified in the Greek radical press as the sinister force responsible for most of the country's many ills—preposterous stories that would have been amusing had they not carried with them the threat of death.

The articles described him as "the Head of the Dark Forces of Anomaly," the "Butcher of Cyprus," "the Fascist CIA Overlord of the Colonels," "the Brutal Killer of Cypriot Women and Children," even the "CIA collaborator with the Turks." The *Communist Morning Daily* was the most colorful. "Under every big rock, when lifted, live vermin, evil vipers and spiders. And under every questionable activity in our land is found the head CIA vermin and viper, Avrakotos."

Several of Avrakotos's friends from the junta were murdered, two with the same .45 that had killed Welch. Avrakotos became an even more intensely disciplined professional, systematically changing routes, cars, and meeting places, sometimes spending three hours of evasion getting to a five-minute contact. "Typically terrorists will have three targets," he says, "and they almost always pick the easiest to go after. I became a very hard target. That's how I stayed alive."

The terrorists and the ever pervasive KGB were not the only ones targeting Avrakotos and the CIA at that time. Back home, agents were being dragged before congressional committees to account for decades-old efforts to assassinate foreign leaders or overthrow governments. And for the first time, reporters were attempting to expose current CIA activities.

Every operative with an ordinary instinct for self-preservation was keeping a low profile. But for Gust Avrakotos there was unfinished business. His station chief, Dick Welch, had been murdered and, as he saw it, his job was to find and murder the murderers. It was the code of his family. It was the way of Aliquippa. "I wanted to go out and hit thirty-five or forty of the 17 November people," he recalls. "We had a list, and I didn't care if we hit some of the wrong ones. So what?" Furthermore, his friends in the Greek Central Intelligence Service (CIS) and the Athens police force would take care of the dirty work. All they needed was the signal.

"But I was ordered down," Avrakotos remembers philosophically years later. "'We don't do assassinations,' they said. I was just working at the wrong time." And so the tough steel-town kid backed off. But it was a different story when it came to Philip Agee. Like most of his colleagues, Avrakotos blamed Agee for having first exposed Welch, and he wanted to make the turncoat suffer.

In the U.S. media, however, Agee was receiving a surprising amount of sympathetic treatment. A number of journalists portrayed Agee as an American innocent, radicalized by the Vietnam War and the evil he had discovered. *Esquire* magazine published Agee's own apologia, in which he explained with righteous indignation why he considered it an act of conscience to try to destroy the organization in which he had served.

This was all much too much for Avrakotos, who began scheming with friendly intelligence services throughout Europe to label Agee a Cuban agent, thus getting him banned from their countries. It was at this moment, says Avrakotos, that the CIA's deputy director for operations flew to Athens to order him to cease and desist: "He said I couldn't use the same tactics that Agee was using against us and that my efforts were violating Agee's civil rights. He said I would go to jail if I continued."

The CIA's operations chief is like the commanding general of a secret army. His word is supposed to be law to case officers in the field. The man was clearly under tremendous pressure, but Avrakotos saw him as siding with a traitor. He flew into a rage. "'I understand you testified before the Pike Committee and used my name. Well, you just violated *my* civil rights, and if you come after me, then I'll come after you, you bastard!' I lectured him on what he should be doing. And you know what? That story went all over the world. Everyone was saying at all the stations: Do you know what Gust just did in Athens? He actually called the DDO a cocksucker."

Few case officers could have gotten away with that, but Avrakotos was one of those killer operatives that every spy agency comes to depend on. He had been indispensable in Greece, and he was saying things about Agee that virtually every CIA man agreed with. Beyond that, in spite of all his tough talk and his hatred of the blue bloods, no one who had worked with Avrakotos doubted that he loved and honored the CIA as if it were his own family. "I was never in a fraternity. The CIA is my fraternity," he said in retirement. "I still have people who know me in over three-quarters of the stations overseas, and even today if I call any of them and say I want something, it will be done, no questions asked."

The fact was that by 1977, Gust Avrakotos was head over heels in love with the Agency. When he returned to Aliquippa his father treated him as a man of honor: "You're the one who is educated, you've seen the world. Tell us, what's happening?" Oscar asked his son. "What are you doing about the Communists?"

"I told him that the Agency won't let us talk about our work and he said, 'Good, I'm proud.... Whatever you can do for your country, it's not enough.'"

There were moments in Athens, such as when a coup would hit and Henry Kissinger and the rest of the U.S. government would look to Avrakotos, that he would dream of climbing to the Agency's very top. Then Gust could visualize perfectly the moment when he, Gust Lascaris Avrakotos, from the long line of Greek defenders of the emperors, would be sworn in as director of Central Intelligence.

But those were Avrakotos's dreams before the intelligence scandals following Watergate rocked the CIA. Before Admiral Stansfield Turner took over the Agency for Jimmy Carter and sent out his cold form letters on October 31, 1977. That purge of the CIA's Operations Directorate, still known inside the Agency as the Halloween Day Massacre, changed forever the way Avrakotos felt about the CIA.

Until then Avrakotos had never complained about the death threats or the attacks by Congress or the press, because he and every other member of the Clandestine Services believed that "mother CIA would always take care of her own." It was similar to the confidence that U.S. fighter pilots feel when they are shot down in combat, knowing that everything possible will be done to rescue them, even to the point of risking more lives to save theirs.

That is why he was so stunned in 1978 when four of his agents opened envelopes from the new CIA director containing termination notices. The targets of the purge had all been first- or second-generation Americans, like him. They were the Greek speakers, the ones who didn't mind getting their hands dirty, the ones Avrakotos believed were the most valuable. When he checked elsewhere he discovered that other new Americans were also being let go: four Japanese from the Tokyo station, three Italians from the Rome station, three Chinese. The criteria seemed to be designed to terminate the men who knew the language and the culture and who had served the longest in one spot, agents just like him.

At first Avrakotos thought perhaps it was a mistake. He convinced two of the four to appeal. Langley's return cable to one of the men who had requested an explanation stung Gust like nothing he had experienced in his adult life. "We understand you have appealed," it read. "But you are a native Greek operating on native turf in a native language. You really are not an American."*

---

*The author has not seen the document, but this is the language and the message that came through as described to me by those who have read it.

"When they said that about him not being an American, I knew they could say that about me," recalls Avrakotos. "That's when I lost my loyalty to the bureaucrats. That's when I said, 'I don't give a fuck about my career or about trying to become the director. I'm going to fight these fuckers to change it and, if I can't, I'll leave.'"

The return cable that Avrakotos wrote, signing his friend's name, read: "I was born in the United States. I'm a second-generation American of Greek heritage. I served in World War II with honor. For you to call me anything else is a disgrace. I would like to send your comments to my senator in New York, Jacob Javits."

"Well, they shat in their pants. That's when they gave my friend his stay of execution. And do you know what he did when they reinstated him? He gave them thirty days' notice and resigned. Isn't that beautiful?"

Greece was now different for Avrakotos, murky and ambiguous. By 1978 he had been at this game for twelve years. He had been through eleven coups and four attempted coups; he had gone through the murder of his station chief and a thousand different dramas. He was bitter about the firing of his friends, and he had just broken up with his wife. He was burned out, and he didn't want to subject his son to any of these battles anymore. He put in for a transfer.

When he went to say good-bye to his counterpart, the chief of the Greek Central Intelligence Service, the man told him he was relieved Avrakotos was finally leaving: "You're good, but they would have gotten you if you'd stayed. It would only have been a matter of time."

And so the back-alley spy was finally brought home to America—to a post in Boston, where he was given command of a little-known operation to recruit foreign businessmen. He was good at this specialty.

For him it was like a sport. He would study his prey so that by the time he got to the liaison, he would know the man's family history, what he enjoyed eating and drinking, whether he liked boys or girls, what his material aims and psychological needs were. Years selling in the ethnic enclaves of western Pennsylvania had taught him how to hook a customer and close a deal. In the weeks before the hostage-rescue mission, he managed to convince two Iranians to go into Tehran to provide the Delta Force rescue team with real-time intelligence of any last-minute changes in security around the embassy.

His favorite deputy in Boston was John Terjelian, a physically menacing Armenian-American who "had one of those faces like Jack Palance's that scare the shit out of you." Avrakotos loved this man. There was something about him that was pure Aliquippa. His favorite story was about how the Turks had buried his four Armenian uncles alive up to their necks, poured honey on their faces, and watched as the insects ate their heads. "But you know they never talked," he told Avrakotos proudly. "And do you know what? I have the same attitude."

It was because of Terjelian that Avrakotos first began to consider the possibility that Afghanistan might be turned into Russia's Vietnam. On Christmas Day 1979, when the news came over the radio that the Russians were invading, Avrakotos went into the office to check the cable traffic. He opened the door to find Terjelian already there, eagerly reading the cables and laughing.

The huge Armenian was shouting out his favorite word: *muti,* which means something like "jerk" in old Armenian slang. "Those fucking *mutis.* The Russians are *mutis;* they're fucking *mutis.*"

"What the fuck are you talking about, John?"

Terjelian explained that he had spent three years in Kabul and that "no one fucks with the Afghans and gets away with it."

Avrakotos says, "John's the kind of guy who likes to do the things men do: skydiving, flying planes, ten whores at once, throwing spears, riding camels. He'd done all of that in Afghanistan. He'd even walked through remote parts of the country, and he was telling me that these were the only people who had ever frightened him."

This last admission made a large impression on Avrakotos because Terjelian was one of the only people who had ever made him feel physically menaced. Back in 1979 at this curious hidden CIA office in Boston, the idea of the Afghan tribesmen torturing and killing Russian soldiers gave these two lonely bachelors something to laugh about, and Avrakotos decided that Terjelian should write up a report for the DDO.

No one appears to have paid any attention at headquarters, but Terjelian's report had a huge impact on Avrakotos once he took over the Afghan war, particularly the warning he offered about these ferocious tribesmen: "Don't put white men in charge. Don't give [the Afghanis] a lot of money. Don't trust them. It would be like throwing money into a cesspool. All they need," he wrote, "is a little help and the Russians will be sorry they ever went into that country."

The idea that there was a nation of warriors waiting in the mountains to kill Russians took seed in Avrakotos's mind. But in 1979 he never imagined that he—or, for that matter, the CIA—would ever even consider the remote possibility of giving these people hundreds of thousands of weapons and billions of rounds of ammunition to take on the Red Army. Back then the CIA was rapidly pulling back from the world. It had gone a long way toward getting rid of the old street fighters like Avrakotos, and the talk was all about drawing down and avoiding the kind of high-risk covert operations that only created trouble for the Agency. A new and gentler CIA was being born, and it was not the kind of environment that seemed likely to permit such a rude figure as Gust Avrakotos to win a spot in the Agency's ruling elite.

After Avrakotos's three-year tour in Boston, the CIA brought him back to headquarters and started to use him for particularly difficult and sensitive missions. "My nickname was 'Dr. Dirty,'" he explains almost bitterly. He was still considered a valuable asset but too freewheeling to entrust with serious responsibility. So Avrakotos was thrilled when he learned that Alan Wolfe, head of the European Division, had handpicked him to become station chief in Helsinki. Wolfe was the legendary officer who had moved in advance of Henry Kissinger to set up the secretary of state's fabled opening to China. And the Helsinki assignment was one of the Agency's most important frontline posts targeted on the Soviets. For Avrakotos, it had an even greater significance. Until then he had been somewhat typecast as a back-alley operator, identified almost exclusively with Greek operations. The fact that Wolfe, whose judgment everyone respected, had picked him for a post that demanded worldly, diplomatic skills meant that, for the first time, Avrakotos would be moving out of his ethnic box and truly into the heart of the Clandestine Services. Once again, he could dream of rising to the highest levels.

Helsinki was a done deal and Avrakotos had already enrolled in Finnish-language school when Wolfe's tour as European Division chief ended and a new man, William Graver, took over. Graver happened to be another of the Agency's walking legends. At six feet seven inches he was an imposing figure who had been with the CIA ever since its founding. He held a rank equivalent to that of a four-star general and seemed to believe that the Clandestine Services should be staffed by the kind of gentleman spies that he had known when he'd served in the OSS, during World War II. On that score, Gust Avrakotos was all wrong, and rather quickly Graver decided he would not honor Alan Wolfe's appointment.

The morning after Labor Day 1981, Graver summoned Avrakotos to his large corner office on the fifth floor of headquarters. Avrakotos remembers a creepy feeling overwhelming him the moment he set foot in the room. Graver had spent much of his career in Germany, and as far as Avrakotos was concerned he might have walked into SS headquarters: "The most striking thing about Graver is that he was Teutonic. By Teutonic I don't mean the blond, handsome, Aryan type. By Teutonic, I mean stiff, wooden, no sense of humor." The only decorations Graver seemed to have were certificates and diplomas on the wall, mostly in German. Even Graver's aides looked like Teutons to Avrakotos, "the kind that carry briefcases and almost click their heels. It was like going in to see the führer."

Graver remained seated, leaving Avrakotos standing like an uncomfortable schoolboy. The division chief said that the coveted Helsinki station chief job was no longer his. The assignment was on the books, but Graver was taking it away. The conversation had barely begun when, contrary to all protocol, Avrakotos ended it. Not merely that, but he ended it by telling Graver to go fuck himself.

As Avrakotos turned and burst past the secretaries and case officers in Graver's outer office, he knew he'd transgressed in a world that is not generous to those who break the internal code of conduct. The CIA, and particularly its elite Clandestine Services, maintains a pretense of informality. Its officers dress in civilian clothes and call each other by their first names. But underneath, it is organized just like the military, and majors (Avrakotos's equivalent rank) don't get away with telling off four-star generals. Bill Graver was now in a position to effectively put an end to Gust's career.

Graver no doubt assumed that he had caught Avrakotos by surprise and that the poor fellow had simply lost control. But Graver had no idea who he was dealing with and what a dangerous enemy he had just made for himself. Whatever qualities as a gentleman Avrakotos may have lacked in Graver's eyes, when it came to espionage no one could outdo him. As was his practice, Avrakotos had cultivated a spy in the division who had tipped him off to Graver's plans weeks earlier. The source had even alerted

Gust that another officer had already been picked for a post Graver now had said he would consider giving to him. At that point Avrakotos concluded that Graver was not just taking away his promotion, he was out to destroy and humiliate him.

Perhaps if Graver had simply said he didn't want anything to do with Gust, it would have ended there. But a rage verging on violence had swept over Avrakotos when he was faced with Graver's calculated lie. The man didn't have the balls to say it straight; to the wounded Greek, it was simply the Halloween Day Massacre all over again. The Teutonic bastard seemed to think he could get away with this latest ethnic cleansing and expect Gust Avrakotos to just say "thank you very much" and disappear.

Something dark and dangerous detonated inside Avrakotos that previously he had unleashed only on America's enemies. He had an attitude about the blue bloods—the "cake eaters"—who ruled the CIA; there's no question about that. But the truth is, he revered the Agency and gave it and his country every ounce of his quite remarkable talents and energies. Graver had hurt him in ways that went beyond the crippling of Avrakotos's career. It was almost as if he had taken away all of Gust's previous accomplishments and declared him unfit to serve anywhere in his division. Now, after the outburst, this man who didn't even know him was in a position to make sure that Avrakotos would have no further prospects for advancement.

But life can sometimes be like a Dickens novel, with characters who meet early on destined to cross paths later, as if for a purpose. That was certainly the case with the friendship that Avrakotos had forged in Greece with Clair George, recently risen to become the second man in the Clandestine Services and heir apparent to take over the Directorate of Operations.

If there was any one person who owed Gust, it was Clair George, and Avrakotos fully expected that this old friend would come to his rescue. The two had forged their friendship over three years in Athens at the height of the 17 November terrorist campaign. George had volunteered to take over the Athens station just after Richard Welch was assassinated, and he had looked to Avrakotos to guide him through the treacherous landscape of Greece in the 1970s. For all practical purposes, he had shared with Avrakotos the responsibility for running the CIA's huge Athens station. Gust handled the underground side of the station—the network of safe houses, the security teams, and the liaisons with the military and the local police. In the wake of Welch's assassination, when everything important entailed dirty work, Gust was king, and Clair George depended on him. They spent their days and often their nights together, always the principal targets of 17 November and always plotting how to strike first. They drank together, they reveled together and, like a ferocious guardian angel, Avrakotos watched over George's safety, even passing on to him his long-time personal driver and bodyguard.

By curious coincidence, George and Avrakotos came from little towns just ten miles apart in Pennsylvania. George, a postman's son, found it easy and rewarding to adopt the manner, clothing, and attitude of the CIA's ruling elite. Gust would kid him mercilessly about being a Beaver Falls pussy, the kind of sissy Aliquippans used to love to beat up. But in truth, Avrakotos loved the man. He even approved of George's chameleon-like ability to assimilate and move onto the Agency's fast track. What Avrakotos valued most, however, was the way George had stood by him and the ethnic officers targeted during the Halloween Day Massacre. George hadn't signed his own name to any of the cables back then, but he had given his silent support, which was enough to make Gust feel confident that George would back him now. When Graver demanded that Avrakotos be punished, George had his old friend come up to the seventh floor for a heart-to-heart talk.

"Costa, Costa," George began, using Avrakotos's old Greek nickname. George didn't say anything explicit about what Gust must do. He was trying to be helpful—to make Gust recognize that he had a first-class problem that needed to be dealt with. He appealed to Gust not to offend Graver again. "He can hurt you badly."

"You know who I am," Avrakotos said. "I'm not going to kiss his ass; he didn't want me anywhere in his division."

"Yes, but you can't tell him to go fuck himself—he's very powerful."

When Graver's secretary called a few days later to schedule another meeting, Avrakotos assumed that George had smoothed things over. Nevertheless, he had his guard up as he walked back into the large fifth-floor office. The last time, Graver had asked him to close the door. He asked again this time, but Avrakotos decided to leave it open. "I didn't know what was going to happen, but I wanted witnesses," he explained. Once again, Graver remained seated.

"Well," Graver finally said, after a long pause.

"Well, what?"

"The ADDO [assistant deputy director for operations] said you were going to apologize."

It may be that Avrakotos had some kind of death wish. Perhaps he had allowed himself to expect good news from Graver. He may have been disappointed to find that Clair George had not delivered for him. But it didn't really matter, because he was now left with no good choices. Not all that much was being asked of him: a gesture, even some small effort to make peace. But it was suddenly too late for that. Once again Avrakotos was overcome with a feeling of class rage and anger that verged on violence. Once again he looked straight in Graver's eyes, and once again he crossed the line.

"You can go fuck yourself."

CHAPTER 4

Joanne Herring

A TEXAS BOMBSHELL

Years later, as he tried to explain how it all happened, how the CIA ended up with a billion dollars a year to kill Russian soldiers in Afghanistan, Avrakotos would offer a curious explanation. "It began with a Texas woman, one of Wilson's contributors. She's the one who got him interested."

Joanne Herring was a glamorous and exotic figure out of the oil-rich world of Texas in the 1970s and '80s. At the time nobody imagined that, in addition to her role as a social lioness and hostess to the powerful, she was simultaneously responsible for setting in motion a process that would profoundly impact the outcome of the Afghan war. When almost everyone had written off the Afghans as a lost cause, she saw potential for greatness in the most unlikely characters. In the pivotal first years of the jihad, she became both matchmaker and muse to Pakistan's Muslim fundamentalist military dictator, Zia ul-Haq, as well as to the scandal-prone Charlie Wilson.

Most of the women Charlie was seeing in those days—and there were many—were half Herring's age. But Joanne Herring was a woman of extraordinary resources who knew how to mesmerize a man on many levels—not the least of which was her ability to sweep this congressman from the Bible Belt into her dazzling world of black-tie dinners, movie stars, countesses, Saudi princes, and big-time Republican oil magnates. Invariably, when reporters wrote features about Joanne Herring, they invoked Scarlett O'Hara. The comparisons are found in clips from the

Washington Post, People magazine, and *Lifestyles of the Rich and Famous*. Few modern women can trigger such a comparison. But to appreciate her full impact, it helps to add Zsa Zsa Gabor, Dolly Parton, and even a bit of Arianna Huffington.

Something about Texas and its oil heritage seems to permit its citizens to reinvent their histories and to carry out their lives as if they were part of an ongoing theatrical experience. As Herring tells it, she was born on the Fourth of July, a direct descendant of George Washington's sister; her great-uncle had died at the Alamo; and there were suggestions of old family money and an ancestral home modeled after Mount Vernon. Hers was a family whose history embodied all the virtues of the American experience, Texan style. "You see, I'm descended from Washington, and all my life I've been told that by my family. It's kind of nice to know who you are down through the years, and I feel I know all my people who came before me."

But Joanne's story was nothing compared to that of so many other high-rolling Texans, like her best friend from high school, Sandra Hovas, who would become another link in Wilson's introduction to Afghanistan.

As a buxom teenager, Hovas was known affectionately as "Buckets." But as a young woman in the 1960s, she began to reinvent herself, and her friends soon went along with calling her Sandy, then Sandra, and then Saundra. When she met and fell under the influence of Baron Ricky di Portanova, a dashing young Italian who had moved to Houston to claim his share of the Cullen oil fortune, Saundra became Allisandra. When she married the baron, Buckets was reborn as Baroness di Portanova.

To the uninitiated, Joanne and the baroness appeared to be typical social butterflies, but they actually shared a conspiratorial past. As young debutantes, both had been inducted into the Minutewomen, an offshoot of the ultraright, paramilitary Minutemen. While other debutantes across the country were tittering and talking about boys, Joanne and Buckets were sitting at high tea listening to "patriotic women who cared about their country. They opened my eyes to the conspiracy that threatened our way of life," remembers Joanne. By the time the two girls were eighteen they had become part of a semisecret national organization of right-wing patriots so convinced of the possibility of a Communist takeover that they were organizing for guerrilla warfare. And like all good Texas girls, Joanne and Buckets had learned to ride and shoot from the earliest age.

"It is difficult talking about this now," says Herring. "You can easily be thought of as a nut or a nutty hawk." Nevertheless, she remains deeply proud of her involvement in the arch-conservative organization. That's where she acquired a "sense of obligation to act like a lady," which included a commitment to fight Communism. "I decided back then that I would dedicate my life to making the free-enterprise society survive for my children."

One would never have imagined such ambitions by reading about Joanne in the Houston society columns of the 1960s and '70s. Her Roman Toga party was so lavish and theatrical that *Life* magazine covered it, and everyone in Houston who counted was invited. Slave girls were auctioned off. Christians were burned to the accompaniment of fireworks. And to lend authenticity, ten-year-old black Boy Scouts, playing the role of Nubian slaves, moved about the gathering of Roman-clad socialites, filling their crystal goblets with wine.

By the 1970s, she was entertaining all of Houston daily with her own immensely popular television talk show. When she married a rich oilman, Bob Herring, who ran the largest natural gas company in the country, she began traveling with him through Arab lands. They met and befriended kings, sheikhs, and chiefs of intelligence. Arab oilmen have a special connection with Texas. Texans have drilled their oil and sold them machinery, and they have invariably visited Texas and watched cowboy movies. And when they met Joanne Herring, they all tended to turn to Jell-O.

Houston was a boomtown back then, and when kings and foreign leaders asked to visit, the State Department found it helpful to enlist the ever enthusiastic Herring to entertain. Her parties were always magnificently overdone. For the king of Sweden, there was a sheikh's-tent discotheque, complete with zebra rugs, stuffed tigers, and belly dancers. She so charmed Ferdinand and Imelda Marcos that when she and her husband visited the Philippines, the Marcoses reciprocated by meeting them with a brass band and an honor guard. Herring soon added Anwar Sadat, King Hussein, Princess Grace, the Shah of Iran, and Adnan Khashoggi to her list of intimate new friends, all of whom were extravagantly entertained at the Herrings' twenty-two-room River Oaks mansion.

In the midst of this heady swirl, Joanne departed for Paris to produce and narrate a "documentary" on the life of the Marquis de Lafayette, entitled *A Thirst for Glory, a Struggle for Freedom*. During 1976 she kept herself busy at Versailles directing thirty French aristocrats in the roles of eighteenth-century French nobles. She was a novelty, and the Parisian café society loved this Texas bombshell who talked of nothing but politics and the origins of freedom. There were even whispers of a romance between her and the elegant chief of the French intelligence service, the count de Marenches.

Until then, Herring had thought she was fully sensitized to the Communist threat. But the count opened her eyes to a new dimension when he took out maps and carefully described the "master plan" being carried out against the West: "'In every government and agency—even in the airports—there was infiltration,'" she recalls him saying. De Marenches explained that he had played a critical role in stopping the student riots in Paris in 1968. He was a center post in what Herring now describes as "a worldwide network of people ready to sacrifice everything: their lives, their fortunes, and their sacred honor, just like the Founding Fathers."

It can be said that Ms. Herring's future fixation on fighting the Russians in Afghanistan originated in Paris when de Marenches arranged for her and her husband to meet one of the key players in his network, the brilliant Pakistani ambassador to Washington and eventual foreign minister Sahabzada Yaqub Khan. At the end of the 1970s, Pakistan was a poor country and out of favor in Washington. Trying to build friendships, Yaqub Khan proposed that Bob Herring become Pakistan's honorary consul in Houston. Herring declined but suggested his wife instead. Thus began Joanne's love affair with Pakistan and certainly one of most bizarre diplomatic appointments ever made by a fundamentalist Muslim country.

Ordinarily, an honorary consul is not expected to do much more than get drunken sailors out of jail, ship dead citizens home, and generally show the flag. But Joanne Herring acted as if she had been made a full-fledged ambassador or minister of trade. She was suddenly organizing benefits, even one in which all of her designer friends—Pierre Cardin, Oscar de la Renta, Emilio Pucci—were shanghaied into coming up with designs for Pakistani craftsmen to use as patterns. She plunged into Pakistani villages on fact-finding missions, giving the poverty-stricken Muslims inspirational talks on capitalism and inspiring hope with her idea that each village could get rich selling beautifully made dresses and rugs designed by her famous friends.

There was no precedent for an American woman playing such a role on behalf of the Pakistani government, so Pakistan honored Herring with

the official status of "honorary man"; she was addressed as "sir." Back in
the United States, she managed to put the out-of-favor Pakistan diplomats
in the limelight, including them at elegant black-tie dinners with the likes
of Henry Kissinger and Nelson Rockefeller.

It was all going very well until the military seized power and hung
President Zulfikar Ali Bhutto, perhaps best known today as the father of
Benazir Bhutto. President Jimmy Carter led the charge in condemning the
new dictator, Mohammad Zia ul-Haq, accusing him of killing democracy
in Pakistan as well as of building an Islamic atomic bomb. Carter cut off
all military and economic assistance, declaring Pakistan unworthy of further U.S. aid.

When "Pakistan" became a dirty word in Washington, another honorary consul might have lost heart. Herring, however, reacted differently.
The count de Marenches had recently confided in her that there were only
seven men standing between the free world and Communism. Zia, he said,
was one of them. So that year she set off for Pakistan, prepared to find virtue in the maligned dictator Zia ul-Haq. In Islamabad, Zia quickly won
her heart. He invited her to dinner at his simple military headquarters,
explaining that he would never move into Bhutto's palace as long as his
people were starving. The unexpected surprise of this visit was the astonishing impact Herring had on Zia. He was a fundamentalist Muslim and
she a born-again Christian. Yet by all accounts, their bond grew so strong
that, for a time, she is said to have been Zia's most trusted American adviser, a development that Foreign Minister Yaqub Khan found alarming.
"She absolutely had his ear, it was terrible," he said.

It was all the more unusual given that Zia was in the process of
reimposing fundamentalist restrictions on women. But he was so spell-
bound by Herring, and took her so seriously, that to the utter dismay of
his entire foreign office, he made her Pakistan's roving ambassador to the
world and even awarded her his country's highest civilian honor, the title
of *Quaid-e-Azam,* or "Great Leader." Charlie Wilson says that Zia would
leave cabinet meetings just to take Joanne's calls. "There was no affair with
Zia," Wilson recalls, "but it's impossible to deal with Joanne and not deal
with her on a sexual basis. No matter who you are, you take those phone
calls."

When the Russians invaded Afghanistan in 1979, Zia's relationship
with the United States could not have been worse; nor could he have been

closer to his honorary consul, who took the novel position with the dictator that the invasion was a great blessing in disguise. "At last there were
Russians crossing the border," she told him. "Before, they were just using
nicknames like FMLN or FSMLN. But now they were Russians, and I
knew there was a possibility to do something."

That kind of bravado was typical of Joanne Herring, who, at age
forty-eight, was accustomed to seizing and holding center stage and refusing to let anything get her down. She had married two men, raised
two boys, and worked five days a week for twelve hours a day on her
television talk show. She was one of the social dragons of Houston and a
tireless promoter of Pakistan. But the year after the invasion, for the first
time in her life, she felt defeated. She found that no one seemed to want
to hear about Zia or Pakistan, much less about Afghanistan. It seemed
that life was passing her by, and she felt alone. After a long struggle, her
husband had died of cancer, and Joanne turned to her church in Houston, where she remembers sobbing at the altar, in a state of complete
despair. "I never thought I would laugh again," she says. "I thought my
life was over."

Joanne Herring remembers those dark days with a shudder, but
mainly she remembers how Charlie Wilson arrived to save her life. They
had met two years before at one of her River Oaks parties, after he had
passed an important piece of oil and gas legislation that her husband had
thought impossible. Joanne collected powerful men, and as she told him
about the virtues of Pakistan, she locked eyes with the handsome congressman. Wilson left with the distinct impression that Joanne Herring had been
flirting with him. So he was delighted when she called him one day out of
the blue, in the midst of her depression.

It is said that hypochondriacs make the best nurses, and if Charlie
Wilson was responsible for lifting Joanne Herring from her depression back
in 1981, then it was because he knew where she was coming from. Very
few were aware of the depths of Charlie Wilson's frequent depressions—
the insomnia, the alcoholism, the asthma, the trips to the doctor, the constant loneliness. He disguised it well. No matter what his inner mood,
whenever the public door opened, the darkness disappeared, replaced by
the bigger-than-life, can-do Texan.

For Joanne Herring, that overflowing energy was like a miracle cure.
"Charlie taught me to laugh again and made my life really wonderful," she

said. A curious romance began, with much talk of Christ, anti-Communism, and Zia ul-Haq. As the weeks passed, she found her spirits returning. "Everyone else's eyes would glaze over when I would talk about the Afghans, but Charlie was interested in these things."

As the romance bloomed, Herring found herself reborn as a ferocious champion of Zia and the Afghans, and she became convinced that Wilson was the one who could save the day. "I really gave Zia a story on Charlie," she recalls, "because I was scared someone could do an investigation of Charlie and write him off. I told Zia, 'This is the man who can really do it for you.' You see, they were very frightened of America." Joanne also began to use all of her wiles to pull Wilson into the Afghan war. "I knew that if he was serious about something, he went all out. I'd say to Charlie, 'You are powerful, you are wonderful, just think what you can do.' It had to be a sort of brainwashing," she explained. "But it was very easy, because Charlie thought in those terms too. You can raise that spirit in a Texan. It's there."

Wilson, now fully under Herring's sway, quickly accepted her invitation to River Oaks to meet the man who she said would explain it all. "You will adore this man," she told Wilson. "There have been eighteen books written about him. He has been decorated by every country in the world. To give you an idea, he was the first man in the Belgian Congo after the bloodbath, he married eleven Jewish girls to get them out of Nazi Germany and said he didn't have one honeymoon. Every time there has been a disaster in the world, Charles Fawcett was there. You will never meet anybody like him."

For those who don't know her, there are times when Joanne Herring sounds quite detached from reality. But the stories she told about Fawcett turn out to be largely true, including her account of how he had recently lured her into Afghanistan. She explained that six months earlier, she had been at home in River Oaks when a message from Afghanistan came in "via the underground." It was from her friend Charles Fawcett, a note scribbled with crayons on the back of a child's notebook: "Come immediately. Bring film equipment. The world doesn't know what's going on here."

It was hard for the congressman not to be impressed as he listened to Joanne describe how she had left immediately for Islamabad and then crossed into the war zone with Fawcett. "All this had to be very secretive," she whispered conspiratorially. "Zia sent his planes and helicopters with us to the border. He even sent troops to areas where they were not supposed to go. You see, the least little thing could have created a Russian invasion. Zia kept telling me that the Russians wanted nothing more than for his troops to cross over so that they could justify an invasion.

"They dressed me like a man. I had a bodyguard who was seven feet tall with a handlebar mustache and an Enfield rifle." At one point, Joanne told Wilson, this giant moved her about in a barrel to hide her. "It was so cold that all the men gave me their blankets. But it was like sleeping under a dead hippo. I was so cold, it was horrible, but it was the most exciting thing in my life."

As she told this story to Wilson, she played on themes she knew would move his Texas spirit. She described how these primitive tribesmen would bow to Mecca in prayer five times a day. She emphasized how few weapons they had and described how the Afghans treated their guns like library books—as soon as one warrior crossed the border, he would turn in his gun, handing it over to another man going off to face death. "It was so humbling," she went on. "Nothing ever affected me like seeing those twenty thousand men raising their guns and shouting to fight to the last drop of their blood."

When Joanne introduced Wilson to Fawcett, she was operating on the powerful conviction that they had two things in common: an impulse to stand up for the underdog, mixed with a thirst for glamour and adventure.

Charles Fernley Fawcett is an immensely likable man and, as Joanne had hoped, he immediately charmed Wilson with tales of nonstop swashbuckling, adventure, and good deeds. As Wilson learned, Fawcett had begun life as an orphan of sorts, watched over very loosely by an uncle from the well-heeled Fernley-Fawcett family of South Carolina. By fifteen, Fawcett says, he had commenced an affair with his best friend's mother; "a wonderful woman," he recalled warmly. "If that's child molestation, I would wish this curse on every young boy." But this mother of his dreams cut off the relationship, and at sixteen the handsome, powerful young man, already an all-state football player, escaped on a tramp steamer bound for the great fleshpots of the world.

The young Fawcett was one of those gifted all-purpose talents. He had a commanding voice; a strong, beautiful body, which he bared for sculptors; an artistic talent, which made him a gifted sketcher; and a musical ear, which allowed him to play the trumpet well enough to go backstage one night and get a few tips from Louis Armstrong: "What you do, my boy, is you pick up the trumpet thusly, and you put it to your lips thusly, and then you blow, boy, blow."

One day, after watching a professional wrestling match, he went backstage and asked the wrestler to show him some moves. For the next year he traveled through the back-alley theaters of Eastern Europe playing the role of the honest American boy heroically fighting underhanded opponents. "It got to the point that I didn't care that the villain always pinned me," Fawcett remembers, "because I was clean, and the others were dirty and the audience was always for me. So much so that they sometimes would storm the ring trying to get the other guy."

Fawcett still has scrapbooks, news clippings, and book entries that document an otherwise unbelievable life: an ambulance driver in France at the outbreak of World War II; an RAF pilot during the Battle of Britain, scrambling to his Hurricane to take on Messerschmitts over London; and even a tour as a member of the French Foreign Legion. At the end of the war, Fawcett came down with tuberculosis and was discharged from the legion. He was reduced to playing "Taps" at funerals and digging up graves to identify Nazi victims until an old friend rescued him with an offer of a bit part in a movie. Over the next two decades Fawcett reinvented himself as an actor, appearing in over a hundred B-grade movies, many of them in Italy. He was a star of sorts, but always cast in the role of the villain. He performed his own stunts, leaping out of buildings, brawling with Buster Crabbe, and riding horses off cliffs. He may have been a second-tier player during the day, but at night, in the words of the gossip columnists, he was "the king of Rome" and "the mayor of the Via Veneto." Warren Beatty remembers him as the centerpiece of the Dolce Vita of the city, loved and adored by everyone.

It was there that Fawcett met Baron Ricky di Portanova, who would later marry Joanne's childhood friend Buckets. At that time, di Portanova didn't advertise his title; he was penniless and relied on his deep voice to scratch out a living dubbing films into English. He and Fawcett shared a tiny apartment off the Via Veneto. Whoever had a woman for the night got the bed. The toilet was down the hall.

Had it not been for Joanne Herring, di Portanova might have remained an impoverished and forgotten member of the Cullen Oil clan. His mother was a Cullen, but she was mentally impaired and had virtually no contact with her family or its fortune. Joanne convinced him to stand up for his rights and to sue for his share of the family fortune. He did, and he won, and by the 1970s, had become a fixture in Houston's high society, the fabulously rich international jet-setter, Baron di Portanova. He was so rich that he once talked of buying the famous '21' Club restaurant in New York as a birthday present for Buckets.

Like many men who come into fortunes late in life, the baron romanticized his penniless days in Rome with his old friends. Twenty years later, alarmed to discover that Fawcett was in bad health and out of money, he insisted that his old roommate come to River Oaks to supervise the construction of his mansion's vast new swimming-pool wing. Fawcett accepted the plane ticket and the appointments with Houston's best doctors, and moved in with the baron and baroness, quickly becoming a prominent, much-loved extra man in Houston's roaring '70s society. But he didn't feel right about living in this lap of luxury. To begin with, all was not well in the baron's house.

The year before, di Portanova's loyal valet had been shot and killed while carrying a platter of cold partridges in to lunch. The baron insisted that he, not the valet, had been the real target. There were suggestions of rival kinsmen resorting to shady means in an effort to fight the baron's claim on the Cullen fortune. When the swimming-pool wing burned to the ground, the baron again suspected foul play. Fawcett was irrationally guilt stricken, convinced that he somehow could have prevented it. But beyond that, Fawcett was restless, without a cause, and feeling decadent. When the Soviets invaded Afghanistan, the sixty-year-old told Joanne Herring that he intended to leave Houston for the mountains of Afghanistan to pass on tactics he had learned in the Foreign Legion to the Afghan resistance.

No amount of cajoling from the baron and baroness could change Fawcett's mind, so they gave in and threw him an elegant going-away dinner in the wine cellar of Houston's finest restaurant. Joanne Herring saw him off at the airport the next morning, and six months later, after receiving his scribbled note, she was in Afghanistan with a camera crew to help Fawcett rally the conscience of the world.

Wilson was entranced by Fawcett, whom he considered a Renaissance romantic. "He loves beauty, he loves war, and he loves killing bad guys," Wilson remembered. As far as Wilson was concerned, Fawcett was a hero, an American who "had killed fascists in Spain, shot down

Messerschmitts over London, and had been in the Hindu Kush shooting Russians. How could I say no to a guy like that?"

But it was not so easy to be flattering about Fawcett's film. He had chosen Joanne to serve as his blond interviewer and persuaded Orson Welles, an old friend from the Via Veneto, to be the narrator. The baron threw himself into promoting the effort with a lavish black-tie dinner for the Houston premiere. The setting he chose was the newly reconstructed wing of his mansion, built around a giant Grecian swimming pool with oversized chandeliers.

As the lights went down, a lone mujahid warrior was seen on the back of a rearing stallion. An Afghan with a great white beard, bearing a startling resemblance to Fawcett, ran up to the mounted horseman and asked, "Commander, where are you going?" In the background, music straight out of an Errol Flynn adventure rose up. "I'm going to fight the Russians," the mujahid warrior growled. "But, Commander, how can you fight the infidel without weapons?" Onto the screen flashed the film's title: "Courage Is Our Weapon."

Joanne Herring watched with mixed reactions. "Fawcett just couldn't bear to cut any of it," she says. She acknowledges that the film is something less than sophisticated, particularly during her interviewing segments. "Here the Afghans were, telling me how the Russians had stuck a bayonet into a pregnant woman's stomach, and I'm trying to understand their language, and smiling, always smiling, because I'm trying to encourage them to speak English."

When the lights came on after the two-hour documentary, the baron tapped his champagne glass and stood to offer a toast. "Theeees," he said, gesturing to his lavish swimming-pool annex with the great chandeliers, "theees is not reality." Pointing theatrically to the projector, Fawcett, and Herring, he continued: "Theees movie, theees eeez reality."

Wilson was delighted to be included in the baron's social circle. "I'd never met any of those people before," recalls Wilson. "It's the kind of fantasy world that every Texan has always heard about and found exciting." But Wilson, the great anti-Communist, had to cope with the fact that Fawcett and Joanne had gone into the war zone. They had actually taken risks to do something about the Communists. He didn't quite know what to say when Joanne insisted that the CIA was playing a fake game in Afghanistan, that the U.S. consul she had met at the frontier was a kind of apologist for the Russians, and that brave men were dying because of congressional neglect. It didn't matter that he had made a telephone call to double the covert-aid budget for the mujahideen. A few million dollars more was a meaningless gesture, she said. Joanne Herring wanted Wilson to become the mujahideen's true champion. Wilson's manhood, she implied softly, was on the line.

CHAPTER 5

Charlie and his congressional office staff

THE SECRET LIFE
OF CHARLIE WILSON

No one questions the modern politician's reliance on spin doctors, press secretaries, and image makers. It's such a common practice that it can be stated as a virtual law of political physics that under normal circumstances, politicians will always emphasize the positive and never deliberately create a negative public image for themselves.

What always set Charlie Wilson apart was his impulse to do just the opposite: invariably, he promoted his vices and hid his virtues. As late as 1996 the *New York Times* would all but dismiss him in an editorial as "the biggest party animal in Congress." If Wilson made it hard for the *Times* to recognize the power and influence he wielded in 1996, it was nothing compared to the public face he projected during the early 1980s, when he seemed to be little more than a public joke. He almost never spoke on the House floor. He wasn't associated with any legislative initiatives. In this regard, his cover was nearly perfect.

But what every professional in the House of Representatives knew was that simultaneously another very different Charlie Wilson was at work. He was, in effect, running a tunnel right into the most powerful places in Washington. If there was such a thing as an underground ladder in Congress, then Wilson was climbing it speedily, so much so that *Washington Post* columnist Jack Anderson included the Texan in his list of the capital's ten most effective back-room operators. Wilson was a genius at the inside game of maneuvering in the Balkanized world where power is distributed in blocks and where deals are made when you have something to trade. And ironically, because Wilson was such a political pro, his outrageous lifestyle seemed to actually enhance his position. For one thing, from the very beginning, *everyone* in the House knew who Charlie Wilson was. He was impossible to miss: too tall, too handsome, too loud, with too many striking female staffers by his side.

He'd first broken from the pack and become a part of the legend of his party in 1976, when he'd defied his own Texas delegation and maneuvered his way onto the all-powerful Appropriations Committee. That move had made Wilson a player—one of fifty House members with a vote on how the government's $500 billion annual budget would be spent. The committee's power is so great that its twelve subcommittee chairmen are known collectively as the "College of Cardinals." The full committee holds the purse strings of the entire federal government, but it's such an immense job that responsibility for the various branches of government are broken down and delegated to individual subcommittees. In the end, that means that a lone appropriator who stays on a subcommittee long enough and knows what he wants can amass extraordinary individual power over agencies and the policies they pursue.

To most members, the payoff for winning an assignment to Appropriations comes from the fact that there is no better place in all of Congress to find pork. The man from Lufkin never shied from using his influence to get jobs for his constituents or contracts for local industry. He took enormous pride in reviving the fortunes of his poverty-stricken district. But just milking the system for all it was worth was not what had drawn Charlie Wilson to Congress. He had a grander vision. His passion, since boyhood, was foreign affairs, and from the moment he got on Appropriations he set out to position himself on the two subcommittees that dole out all money connected to national security.

His Jewish friends had helped get him onto the committee; once there, Charlie learned from these master politicians how to influence budgets and policies. When he won a seat on the Foreign Operations subcommittee, which allocates all U.S. military and economic assistance, he was suddenly positioned to champion Israel's annual $3 billion foreign-aid package. And since this subcommittee rules on the State Department's expenditures abroad, overnight he became one of twelve congressmen the State Department could no longer afford to alienate. In fact, these twelve legislators are treated as patrons who must be curried and pampered by ambassadors and even secretaries of state.

In 1980, just after being reelected for a fourth term and only a few weeks before his Las Vegas weekend, Wilson struck again, maneuvering himself onto the Defense Appropriations subcommittee. Now the Pentagon and the CIA were added to the list of federal bureaucracies that could no longer treat Charlie Wilson as a mere mortal.

The twin assignments were his tickets to play in the arena of world power. He was given the highest security clearance and an extra staffer and ushered into the soundproof hearing room under the Capitol dome, where he was shown his permanent seat—one of twelve large black leather chairs grouped around a horseshoe-shaped table. The room is closed off to the public as well as other members. Very little is ever written about what goes on when the twelve members meet in this chamber. But each year they preside over a kind of secret court, where huge deals are cut and important policies made or broken. Since hundreds of billions of dollars are at stake—and since only so many programs can be fully funded— enormous pressures and inducements are brought to bear upon these twelve men.

It's a big government, and everyone has a favorite weapons system or spy satellite, an embassy to be refurbished, a rescue mission to be funded, and assets to be traded. The White House, the defense contractors, the military services, fellow congressmen—all maneuver around and encircle the appropriators, seeking their support. Each year, in effect, the lobbyists create their own power list, a ranking indicated by the dollar amounts they dole out to congressmen in campaign contributions. Charlie Wilson was always at the very top of this list, usually occupying the second spot, right below his intimate friend John Murtha, chairman of the Defense Appropriations subcommittee.

"Anybody with any brain can figure out that if they can get on the Defense subcommittee, that's where they ought to be—because that's where the money is," Wilson laughs. "Once I got on Defense, I went from being the skunk to being the prettiest girl at the party." To the future Speaker, Jim Wright, Charlie Wilson was now critical for getting more contracts for the F-16s being built in Dallas–Fort Worth. For Texas Democrat Martin Frost it was the B-2 bomber. Wilson made it easy for his colleagues to come to him, always gracious, almost always helpful.

He was quickly accumulating powerful allies and IOUs. He was also playing a far more interesting and effective insider's game, in areas of the House that were not visible to outsiders. "You've got to look at the House like a college class where fraternities are everything," explains Denis Neill, a Washington lobbyist who is one of Wilson's oldest friends and allies. "If you're not in the right fraternities you're not in the game, and no one is in so many different important fraternities as Charlie Wilson."

At the time, Neill was one of the capital's greatest manipulators of Congress in the foreign-affairs arena. His firm, Neill and Company, represented clients like Egypt, Pakistan, Morocco, and Jordan. His job was to get them U.S. money, weapons systems, and good press; to do damage control; and provide influence in the corridors of power. One way he did it was by making campaign contributions and giving favors to congressmen on the committees that control foreign aid. He didn't waste his time or money on members who don't count, and in the foreign affairs world, he considered Wilson one of the two or three who were indispensable. When Neill starts ticking off Wilson's memberships, it quickly becomes apparent how his network of congressional fraternities later allowed him to speak for the entire House when he and Avrakotos set out to radically escalate the CIA's Afghan war.

"The way things normally work, if you're not Jewish you don't get into the Jewish caucus," Neill says. "But Charlie did. And if you're not black you don't get into the black caucus. But Charlie plays poker with the black caucus. They had a game, and he's the only white guy in it."

Part of the explanation here is that the House, like any other human institution, is moved by friendships, and no matter what people might think about Wilson's antics, they tend to like him and enjoy his company. His friendship with the insular black fraternity began with Barbara Jordan, the charismatic congresswoman who electrified the nation in 1973 with her stirring remarks during the Nixon impeachment proceedings. The two had served six years together in the Texas state senate before coming to Washington.

Former Speaker Jim Wright remembers how everyone initially came to know who Wilson was because he always sat next to Jordan on the House floor—this tall, good-looking cowboy and his constant companion, the dour, heavyset, scowling black woman. "I was her best friend for the whole six years she was here," Wilson recalls fondly. And for the mostly male black fraternity that played poker together—a group with a different set of priorities than Barbara Jordan—something about Wilson's lack of piety and his bad-boy aura appealed to them.

Wilson's archconservative friend Republican representative Henry Hyde identifies it as the Adam Clayton Powell factor. "Adam Clayton Powell's people loved him because he was always sticking it to the man, and Charlie is down there creating his own ground rules and in a weird way he's kind of a white man's Adam Clayton Powell. There is a kind of nonconformist relish about him. He leads the sort of life that many congressmen envy but wouldn't dare emulate." When Louis Stokes, the low-key black chairman of the Intelligence Committee, was arrested for drunk driving, Wilson turned it into a raucous act of friendship with one comment: "Mr. Chairman, I want you to know that I deplore the racist attack that the police of the District of Columbia just made on you with that totally fabricated charge."

Wilson even managed to sneak his way onto what could be considered the women's-rights fraternity. One might assume, given his well-earned reputation as a philandering chauvinist, this would have been impossible; however, he was one of the champions of the Equal Rights Amendment, having cosponsored and passed the ERA with Barbara Jordan back when they were in the Texas legislature.

And his credentials went beyond that. Even though his Bible Belt constituents were militantly pro-life, he always voted for a woman's right to choose. He took this politically risky position because of his kid sister, Sharon, who had risen in Planned Parenthood to become the chairperson of its national board. He would have loved to tell his ardently pro-life constituents that he would vote *their conscience* just as he always voted with them on opposing any kind of gun control. On that issue he always said that his constituents would permit him any failing, but the "one thing they would never tolerate was any vote to water down the right of an American citizen to bear arms."

Failing to rail against the murder of the unborn was almost as dangerous, but Sharon insisted that her big brother not embarrass her by doing the wrong thing. There was almost nothing Charlie Wilson wouldn't do for his little sister. And so at the Lions Club luncheons, at the Rotary and the church groups, he would simply say, "I know this is one of those things that we're just not going to agree on, but I'm voting for choice." Somehow his pro-life constituents let him get away with it, and in the House that translated into another base of support for the unconventional congressman.

By 1980 Wilson had established positions in a remarkably diverse network of congressional power centers: not just with Appropriations and his own Texas fraternity but also with the Jewish caucus, the black caucus, the hawks, and the women. Wilson was operating now completely outside the normal experience of American political life. Oddly, his pleasure seeking that year even served to propel him into perhaps the most powerful House fraternity—that of Speaker Thomas P. O'Neill. Only a true insider could have appreciated the significance of O'Neill's simultaneous appointments of Wilson that year to the House Ethics Committee and the board of the Kennedy Center for the Performing Arts. And certainly almost no one could understand what possessed Tip O'Neill to make such a strange choice for the ethics panel.

From today's perspective, the image of this philandering hedonist climbing out of his Las Vegas hot tub to render judgments on the conduct of his colleagues seems almost perverse. Even without knowing about the Fantasy Suite, a genuinely puzzled reporter had asked Wilson why he, of all people, had been selected for this sober assignment. Without missing a beat, Wilson had cheerfully replied, "It's because I'm the only one of the committee who likes women and whiskey, and we need to be represented."

It was an outrageous statement. The Ethics committee is supposed to serve as the conscience of the House and to rule on the conduct of its members. Any Speaker should have been furious at Wilson for this needless provocation, particularly at a time when the House was caught up in its worst scandal in years—the ABSCAM sting operation. An FBI undercover agent disguised as an Arab sheikh had managed to lure six congressmen and a senator into a Washington town house, where the bureau's hidden cameras captured them, one after another, taking $50,000 bribes.

"I have larceny in my blood," exclaimed one of the congressmen, as he thrust the bribe money into a brown paper bag. Another is seen stuffing the cash into his bulging pockets and asking the pretend Arab, "Does

it show?" When the tapes were aired, millions of Americans were left with
the impression that Congress, and the House in particular, had degener-
ated into little more than a den of thieves. It was a particularly bad moment for O'Neill, since nearly all of the ABSCAM bribe takers were
Democrats.

That fall, when the Republicans captured the Senate and Ronald
Reagan the White House, Tip O'Neill emerged as the unrivaled center of
Democratic power in the country. He recognized that the ABSCAM investigation was taking its toll, that something would have to be done to
restore public confidence. But the real crisis, as he saw it, was the immediate threat posed to those in his inner circle, who he relied on to help him
run the House.

A special prosecutor, Barry Prettyman, had just persuaded the
House to expel one of the ABSCAM defendants, a veteran lawmaker,
before he had even been convicted of anything. Never before had the
House expelled one of its own members. With the zealous prosecutor at
the helm, the committee was expanding its inquiry beyond the six members who had been indicted and was rumored to be offering deals in exchange for testimony that would take the scandal into the Speaker's office.
What finally caused O'Neill to draw a line in the sand was the
prosecutor's move against his intimate friend and key political lieutenant Representative John Murtha.

The Speaker immediately summoned Charlie Wilson into his office
to make an offer he knew Wilson would ultimately find impossible to
refuse. "I want you to go on the Ethics Committee," O'Neill said.

Wilson wasn't altogether sure if O'Neill was serious: "Tip, that's
crazy. I'm not on the side of the Ethics Committee and everyone knows it.
They'd laugh us off the floor if you put me on that committee."

The truth is the Speaker was operating in this instance much like a
spy chief. He didn't specifically tell Wilson that he wanted him to go rescue Murtha; he didn't need to. O'Neill knew that all he had to do was get
Wilson on the Ethics Committee, and the rest would take care of itself.

"Chally," the Massachusetts congressman continued with a twinkle
in his eye, "do you remember that appointment you've been asking about
for the Kennedy Center Board?"

There was nothing Wilson craved more than a seat on the board of
the Kennedy Center, and O'Neill knew it. To a married legislator, a life-

time appointment to the Kennedy Center for the Performing Arts might not mean much, but for a divorced congressman going through a midlife crisis, with so many beautiful women to romance and not enough money to properly entertain them, it meant just about everything. Wilson still has a childlike enthusiasm in his voice when he explains why he lusted for that appointment: "It's the best perk in town. It means that I get the box right next to the president's box for the ballet when I want it. I get to go to all the cast parties, meet all the movie stars, and I get an extra invitation to the White House every season."

Most important for Wilson, it meant that with no money down, he could dress up and play out his Good-Time Charlie role with a beautiful new girl on his arm as many as forty or fifty evenings a year if he liked, since he'd have free tickets to most of the shows. It was like a safety net for this broke romantic, knowing that on any given night he would always be able to give one of his girlfriends an evening of true glamour. For months Wilson had been pleading and lobbying the formidable House Speaker to grant him this appointment. But the tough old Irish pol hadn't come to rule the House by giving valuable perks away for free. And so Wilson's appeals had fallen on deaf ears—until now.

"Well, it's a package deal, Chally."

O'Neill understood that Wilson's identity as a noisy braggart was perfect cover for the covert operation he had in mind. "The word on Charlie was that he didn't talk," recalled O'Neill's former whip, Tony Coelho. "From time to time the Speaker needed to mount irregular operations, and Wilson was one of those irregulars Tip could count on."

Wilson accepted the Speaker's deal. Delighted at his lifetime appointment to the Kennedy Center board, he was a happy warrior as he raced to the rescue of his imperiled friend John Murtha.

He had his work cut out for him. Watching Representative Murtha on the ABSCAM tapes is not an experience designed to make a citizen feel better about Congress. A member of the Ethics Committee at the time, he did refuse the bribe, but he did not exactly close the door on a future negotiation: "You know, you made an offer. It might be that I might change my mind someday."

Others might have felt that Murtha had disgraced the institution and deserved to be prosecuted and thrown out of Congress, but Wilson genuinely did not. To begin with, he admired Murtha. The two were on Defense

Appropriations together; they were both fierce anti-Communists; and
Murtha was a decorated Korean War veteran who had volunteered for two
combat tours with the marines in Vietnam, which meant he started off as
a hero in Wilson's eyes. As Charlie framed the controversy, his friend had
actually done nothing wrong. He hadn't taken the bribe from the FBI's
"sheikh"; his only sin had been to say he'd think about it. And if the Ethics
Committee members were even thinking of lynching a patriot like Murtha
simply because he had lust in his heart, then it was time that the entire
committee be put to a very public morals test of its own.

Wilson arrived on the Ethics Committee just as O'Neill had hoped—
like a wrecker. He told a *Washington Post* reporter that the committee was
on a partisan witch-hunt and that what was really on trial was not John
Murtha but the integrity of the House of Representatives. He was clearly
spoiling for a fight, daring someone to take him on.

That was not the way things are supposed to work on the Ethics Committee. The members were supposed to sit around in a sober manner, quietly review the evidence, and make their rulings. It was a horrible thought
to have to go head-to-head with Charlie Wilson, a man who seemed to revel
in his reputation as a rule-breaking, skirt-chasing sinner. Ordinarily a special prosecutor in Prettyman's position could count on having enormous
leverage over members of the committee. All it took to damage a normal
representative's reputation was a leak to the press indicating that the member was trying to derail an investigation. But it was clear from his opening
statement that Wilson would have liked nothing more than to battle it out
in the press "on behalf of an innocent man who happens to be a war hero."

Prior to Wilson's intervention, the committee had given the special
prosecutor something of a free hand; but shortly after Charlie's arrival the
rules of the game changed completely and before Prettyman could fully
deploy his investigators to move on the Murtha case, he was informed that
the committee had concluded there was no justification for an investigation. "This matter is closed," proclaimed the newly appointed Ethics Committee chairman Louis Stokes, another of the Speaker's reliables.

Prettyman was stunned. But bound by an oath of secrecy, there was
nothing he could do other than resign in protest. Meanwhile, a teary
Murtha had confided to a colleague that Wilson's effort had saved his life.

The Murtha rescue operation was one of those small, unrecorded
incidents with far-reaching consequences. For O'Neill, the intervention

ended the threat to his hold on the House and unleashed him to become Ronald Reagan's liberal tormentor. Wilson would laugh off the incident as if it had been an entertainment: "It was the best deal I ever made. I only had to be on Ethics for a year, and I get to stay on the Kennedy Center for life." But he understood that something far deeper had taken place. Relationships had been cemented that would be crucial to Wilson's Afghan campaign.

Murtha would rise to become chairman of the awesomely powerful Defense Subcommittee that Wilson would turn to later when the CIA tried to resist his efforts to up the ante in Afghanistan. Whenever angry Agency officials tried to complain about this dangerous meddling, Murtha would always make it clear that when it came to Afghanistan, the subcommittee deferred to Charlie. "The thing about Murtha," says a respectful Wilson, "is that he always remembers." And looming over both of them would be the expansive Irishman with the big cigar, providing a special waiver for Peck's bad boy, "Chally," to cross over the line to work with the CIA. This was how things worked in Tip O'Neill's House.

Joanne Herring was one of the few outside Congress who truly understood Wilson's potential. As their romance blossomed, she looked deep into his eyes and got Wilson to spell out for her what he could do with his power. She was thrilled at what she heard and began putting her considerable wiles to work persuading him to take up the cause of the mujahideen.

Joanne was able to see things in Wilson that were invisible to others. She had cracked Charlie Wilson's code. She understood that underneath his devil-may-care lifestyle, Wilson was deeply ambitious, consumed with Churchillian visions for himself. She considered his womanizing of no particular consequence, the kind of thing that great men with large ambitions are prone to do. She was never disapproving. Instead she just whispered like a siren into his ear, telling him he could change history: "The mujahideen need you. You can do it, Charlie. You can do anything you put your mind to." That year, in spite of his many other flirtations, Wilson found himself beginning to fall under Joanne's sway, swept away by her charisma and stirred by her suggestion that he had a special destiny.

The war was not going at all well for the Afghans. While they were universally praised for their courage, their cause seemed utterly hopeless.

They didn't have any American champions of consequence, and those who did speak for them were a strange and offbeat group. A former Green Beret and Lithuanian-American put out a newsletter complaining about the antique weapons the CIA was giving to the mujahideen; reporters occasionally quoted him. A handful of enthusiastic, right-wing women in New York and Washington knocked on congressional doors, trying to appeal to the Reagan conservatives. And then there was Joanne's friend Charles Fernley Fawcett. The passions of this bighearted, white-haired American were so touchingly pure and his efforts to dramatize the plight of the Afghans so tireless that in 1981 General Zia had awarded him Pakistan's highest civilian decoration. Fawcett had then gone on the road in a quixotic effort to arouse the conscience of a world that didn't seem to care. He had taken his film, *Courage Is Our Weapon,* not only to Baron Ricky's living room but also to college campuses, salons in Palm Beach, and private clubs in Singapore—strange places where the rich gathered and invariably emoted generously but did nothing. The high point of Fawcett's efforts came when the well-bred sixty-one-year-old crusader managed to get Director William Casey to host a screening of his film at CIA headquarters.

In spite of this gesture from the director, Joanne continued to lecture Wilson about the CIA's appalling refusal to do anything of consequence to help the freedom fighters. Now, when Wilson came for weekends to her glamorous River Oaks mansion, she had him share a room with Fawcett in a separate wing of the house, to make sure the two got to know each other. Whether it was Joanne's wiles or those large candid eyes of Fawcett urging Wilson to do his part, the congressman finally threw in the towel that summer and told Joanne and Fawcett that he would go to Pakistan to meet Zia and their Afghans.

What he didn't tell her was that he intended to visit Pakistan at the tail end of a scheduled fall trip to Israel. In the political arena, Wilson was not a man to dilute his efforts. As he'd often explained to Joanne, the reason he was able to do so much was because he rarely went to the well, and then only when he knew he could win. His power in the House had come primarily as a result of his work with the Israeli lobby, and the cause that burned brighter than ever for him that year was still the survival of the Jewish state.

In the spring of 1982, many of Israel's strongest American supporters had been enraged when the Israeli army, led by General Ariel Sharon, had launched a blitzkrieg invasion of Lebanon under the guise of clearing out PLO strongholds. There was bitter controversy over the attack when Wilson flew into Lebanon, the first U.S. congressman to tour the battle-front. When he reemerged two days later in Jerusalem to hold a press conference, it was in the role of an unapologetic "Israeli commando," assuring the critics that Sharon had done the right thing.

The congressman began his remarks to the newsmen gathered at the King David Hotel by saying, "I come from a district with four hundred thousand white Baptists, one hundred thousand black Baptists, and no more than one hundred Jews." After establishing his supposedly neutral credentials, he went completely overboard in portraying the attacking Israelis as if they were the uncontested liberators of the people of Lebanon. "They have no complaints, except their houses have been blown up," he said. He talked about seeing an old Arab mopping the brow of a sick Israeli with a damp rag. "The biggest surprise I had was the enthusiasm, the universal enthusiasm, with which the Lebanese welcomed the Israeli army. In every instance their voices were of relief and appreciation of the Israelis. That's just the way it is. It ain't no other way."

The hard-line Israeli prime minister Menachem Begin was so impressed by this unsolicited endorsement that he sent a transcript to President Reagan and asked for a personal meeting with this marvelous congressman. They met in Jerusalem in Begin's apartment. The old Irgun commando thanked Wilson and asked if the congressman had any advice. "Well, you're not famous for taking advice," Wilson replied, "but if I were you I would let Sharon clean the PLO out while he has them by the throat before world pressure builds too much."

Begin was delighted at this suggestion, but in a matter of weeks Wilson would find himself back in Lebanon, traumatized by the sight of a massacre that caused him to regret any suggestion he might have made about egging on Ariel Sharon. Meanwhile Charlie's gushing endorsement of the invasion triggered his first registry on the Communist screen in Moscow. The Soviet daily *Izvestiya* ran a mocking column demanding to know how it had come to pass that this American congressman was touring the war zone with the Israeli army: "It is clear that he is a reliable man brought there by American Zionist organizations and the Israeli embassy in Washington."

Wilson found out about the *Izvestiya* complaint from the CIA, which monitored the Soviet press and sent him a copy of the article. All of this

delighted the congressman, who was reveling in his role as an indispensable protector of Israel. That year Wilson was also consumed by a grand
design that he and his old friend Zvi Rafiah had been working on for months
with the Israeli defense minister Moshe Arens. Arens had approached
Wilson personally with a request to see if he could win a waiver from the
U.S. government for foreign-aid money to be used by Israel to develop its
fledgling fighter-plane industry. The fighter jet was to be called the Lavi,
which means "young lion" in Hebrew.

For the Israelis, who depend totally on their air force as a first line of
defense, the Lavi was considered a matter of the highest national security.
It was going to cost a half billion dollars to develop, but according to federal guidelines, U.S. military-assistance grants could be used only to purchase American-made weapons. Arens and Rafiah were asking Charlie to
find a way to waive the rules.

Wilson was honored. Congress was filled with ardent supporters of
Israel, but with this commission Wilson felt himself advancing to the head
of the pack. He planned to return to Tel Aviv in October to finalize his
strategy for the Lavi. He had budgeted a few days for the Afghans, but only
after he finished with his real friends.

CHAPTER 6

Gust Avrakotos in Greece

THE CURSE OF ALIQUIPPA

I t had made absolutely no sense for Gust Avrakotos to have simply abandoned all discipline and, with the door to the European division chief's
office wide open, tell William Graver to go fuck himself for a second
time. Clair George, the powerful number two man in the Directorate of
Operations, had been incredulous. "Are you crazy?" he had demanded.

Suddenly, within the ranks of the Clandestine Services, Avrakotos
had become an untouchable. The CIA's Directorate of Operations is like
the mafia. You rise and fall with your friends and, with Clair George now
holding the number two job, it should have been Gust's moment to soar.
"I had taken care of Clair in Greece, and he owed me everything. I figured I was a pig in shit and about to go to the very top." Instead, Avrakotos
had not only created a dangerous enemy in William Graver but also completely alienated the ambitious Clair George, who wasn't about to have
his old friend's crude ways compromise his fast track. George didn't just
remove Gust's name from the Helsinki asignment; Avrakotos says he cabled
all the division chiefs to warn them about his old friend.

Gust's two verbal assaults on Graver had made no sense. But as he
later explained, "If you're looking for logic in the way things work, you're
not going to find it in me, the Middle East, or the Arab world, because that's
not the way things work." And no matter how counterproductive his dealing with Graver may have been, even years later, it's striking to hear the
pride in his voice when he explains why he faced down Graver.

"Greeks believe that we are truly God's chosen people. And even
when we go to Greek church and fourth-generation Greek-American
priests are talking to third-generation Greek-American kids, they're still

preaching that we are God's chosen people. And my mother led me to believe that among the chosen, I was one of the most chosen. That's very positive. So when you're thrown in with a group of brilliant Ivy Leaguers who know more about so many different things and who can humiliate you through what soup spoons to use, you just remember, 'Gust, you're the chosen among the chosen. You're a superman.' What an attitude that gives you to go through life—you're invincible. So you fuck up; so you make mistakes; but you do what you believe is right—what your gut feeling says you should be doing. You just remember that you're the chosen among the chosen. God will take care of you. God is on your side. It's sort of like the mujahideen going into battle: you cannot lose. If you survive and beat the enemy, you're the victor. If you die in battle, you go to Paradise. You can't lose."

But that September 1981 he was feeling very much alone and in need of help, and with the bitter memory of his interview with William Graver fixed in his mind, Avrakotos made a pilgrimage to the town of his birth. It was a six-hour drive to Aliquippa through the mountains on old Route 40. His destination was the home of an old and trusted friend of the Avrakotos family, a woman named Nitsa. She was in the midst of intense preparations when Gust arrived—an old crone dressed in black, cooking up a strange brew and preparing chants in Greek written a thousand years before. If Walt Disney had had to cast a woman to play a classic witch, he might have chosen Nitsa. She was, in fact, the town witch of Aliquippa, but ordinarily she only practiced her art benevolently—amulets for protection, cures for the sick, and talismans to ward off the evil eye.

Gust, however, was not only the son of her dear departed friend Zafira, he was the pride of Aliquippa, the young CIA warrior who had saved Greece from the Communists. If Gust was in need, all of her dark powers were available to him.

And so Nitsa began: "What does he look like?"

Gust had managed to extract a photograph of Graver from one of his security contacts in the CIA's badge office. "It was the only place I could get a picture. I explained I wanted it for my dartboard, and they loved that."

A puzzled look had come over Nitsa's face as she examined the photograph. According to Avrakotos she claims descent from an order of women in ancient Greece who were the intermediaries between the lords of the underworld and the gods of Olympus. This lineage was perhaps one of the reasons she approached her role that day with such an exacting manner. "He doesn't look evil," she told Gust after studying Graver's face. "Tell me, what he has done?"

"He's ruining my career, and all the cake eaters will pounce on me and rip me apart." She understood that, says Gust, "because her husband had been pulled apart by cake eaters."

She looked at the picture with new eyes, then nodded gravely. "You're right, he is evil."

Nitsa explained that her first move would be to strike where Graver already had weaknesses. Avrakotos then gave her a total physical description of Graver, first identifying his weak physical points, starting with his knees. "He looks like a tall scarecrow when he walks. And he has a bad back."

"Does he like women?" she asked, explaining that she would next move to take away those things he enjoyed the most. "I think she may have made him impotent," he later said matter-of-factly.

Every step of the way Nitsa insisted that Gust understand the consequences of the dark forces he was asking her to unleash. "Now, Gust, you have to want it," she warned. "You have to want evil to happen to him."

"Oh, I want it so bad, I can taste it."

"It will happen then. What are his favorite foods?"

"I know he likes potato salad and German food," Gust said, explaining that Graver had served many years in Germany. "The Nazis had killed Nitsa's mother and father and some of her relatives, and I told her he was a damn Nazi. You could see that her eyes just lit up."

It took her about twenty minutes to complete the curse. According to Avrakotos, her incantations, all in Greek, were taken from seldom-used biblical chants written by monks a millennium ago. "In the Greek Church," explains Avrakotos, "some of those monks were like Darth Vader, fallen angels."

All the while Nitsa kept rubbing Graver's picture. It was only a small photograph, but Nitsa belongs to that tradition of people who believe that a camera captures some part of a person's soul. "Can I keep it?" she asked.

"You can keep it. You can burn it. You can do whatever you want with it."

"Are you sure? You'll never see it again."

"Yes."

"How soon do you want the curse to take effect?"

"Immediately."

"I don't know how immediate is immediate. A professional curse will take effect before a health curse." But, she assured him, "both will take effect."

"Thank you," Gust said.

"Is there anything else you need?"

"No, that's it."

Certainly, had any of the teams of sleuths working out of the Offices of Security or Counterintelligence discovered what Gust Avrakotos had done with Nitsa, they would have immediately called him in for a psychiatric evaluation. And given his access to the most sensitive intelligence, they might well have considered him a serious security risk. But the session with Nitsa had been a private affair. And the act of drawing down curses and summoning forces from beyond had been miraculously therapeutic. By the time he approached the gates of the CIA, Avrakotos no longer considered William Graver a threat. Nitsa was seeing to that. Meanwhile, the whole experience had managed to revitalize his spirits and once again cause him to believe, as his mother had taught him, that he possessed some special destiny. He didn't know when or how his moment would come, just that he had to find a way to stay in place at the CIA until that time arrived.

On the face of it, his plan was quite simple. Instead of engaging Clair George in a head-on contest he could not possibly win, Avrakotos decided simply to vanish, to buy time until he could find a way to go back into action on his own terms.

The problem with that strategy is that it was not supposed to be possible. In the thinly disguised military environment of the Agency, no one is supposed to be able to exist even for a moment outside of a chain of command. Without orders, case officers can't do much of anything—they can't get paid, can't use the telephone, don't even have the ability to park their cars. The system had been painstakingly designed to guarantee that the Agency could never be compromised by its enemies.

Curiously, Avrakotos had been preparing for just this moment for years, ever since the Halloween Day Massacre firings in 1977. Back then in Athens, Clair George had stood with him when headquarters had tried to say that the firings were designed to purge the Agency of its rogue operatives. But Avrakotos knew better. To him it had been nothing short of bureaucratic ethnic cleansing and, ever since then he had believed that one day the blue bloods would come after him. So when it happened he was ready.

Gust had one piece of good fortune going for him. At that particular moment, he happened to be beyond the reach of the Clandestine Services—on administrative leave, supposedly completing his Finnish-language training. Avrakotos figured he had three, perhaps four more weeks before Finance caught up with him and cut off his salary ... and, unless he got new orders, all other privileges as well. But as only Avrakotos could see it, four weeks to build a route to survival was a gift from the gods.

By then he knew certain things that could help him in his odd quest. For example, he knew that the CIA forcibly places blinders on all of its employees. As the thousands of operatives and analysts and administrators cross one another in the halls, Avrakotos knew that precious few would have any idea what anyone else was doing. Even people in the same division or on the same floor understood that it was dangerous to look too curious and so Avrakotos, the master of deception, walked through the white halls of Langley with the knowledge that no one would be trying to figure out what he was up to. In fact, they would be doing just the opposite. And for the chance encounter with old colleagues, he knew exactly what kind of shrug to give, what kind of half lie to offer, what kind of air to affect. The whole exercise was remarkably simple—the idea being to make it seem as if he was engaged in something that others either should know about, if they were in the know, or shouldn't ask if they weren't.

The one thing Avrakotos could not afford was to physically run into Graver or Clair George. That would precipitate a formal review of his misconduct, and nothing good could come of that. The clock was ticking now and the challenge, as he moved through the white corridors of Langley, was to find someone in the Agency bold enough to give him a pay station before his administrative leave ended and the paychecks stopped coming in.

The first friend he went to—a man running a branch in the Latin American Division—didn't blink when Gust described the favor he needed, not even when Avrakotos explained that it might be illegal and, at the very least, there was the risk of Clair George's fury. Had his rank been one grade higher, George's office would have been automatically notified when Avrakotos took up his new post. As it was, Gust acquired this safe haven without registering on George's radar screen. Now, instead of having to formally seek a new assignment and trigger a reckoning, time was now on his side. "Without that pay station I couldn't have survived," he later recalled "That was my ante."

Avrakotos had bought himself time. But to survive the next series of challenges, he relied on a most unusual—and all but invisible—asset. Everyone knew that Avrakotos had a gift for making enemies within his own organization and this would always threaten to sabotage his capacity to rise to where his talents might have otherwise taken him. But even more distinctive was the unlikely network of allies he had acquired at the CIA over the years who were prepared to do the kinds of things to help him that almost no one could have imagined possible.

Avrakotos was hardly the first CIA case officer to recognize the value of lower-level members of an intelligence organization. Abroad, every CIA spy recognizes that perhaps the most promising targets for recruitment in an enemy intelligence service are low-level figures: the code clerks, the secretaries, the couriers. But it was rare indeed to find a case officer who made an effort to befriend such lowly figures within their own organization. In vivid contrast, Avrakotos had always found himself more at home with these fellow untouchables than with the well-born, high-ranking officers of the clandestine services, and from the time he first joined the CIA he had befriended them.

He made it a point to intervene when he could on their behalf. He became their champion whenever one of them would be unfairly treated. And he always shared the truth about the way he felt about the blue bloods.

The network's most distinctive feature was its racial composition: most of its members were African-American and no one could ever understand how they could be so devoted to a man who routinely called them "niggers" to their face. To Avrakotos it was simple. He identified with the Agency's African-American employees because they were just like him: "If you're from Aliquippa in the CIA, you may not be black but you're still a nigger." To Clair George's deputy, Norm Gardner, who witnessed the loyalty of this network: "It was just mystifying what Gust could get the blacks at the Agency to do for him," he recalls, "just mystifying!"

Throughout his seven-month disappearance into the Agency's underground, it was the CIA's African-American employees who, in small ways and large, protected Avrakotos by constantly passing intelligence on to him. "Don't go near the sixth floor today, Clair's going to be there; stay out of the cafeteria this afternoon." They even arranged for him to be able to park in one of the VIP lots. It may not sound like much but the only way to gauge the importance of anyone at the CIA is by the parking spot they are given. The agents who run the big programs are closest to headquarters and, most important for Gust, his VIP spot was next to a side door that let him avoid the main elevators. "They got the pass through security by saying I was a medical doctor on consultation," says Avrakotos. When asked if his black network had also monitored Clair George's and Bill Graver's traffic for him, Avrakotos replied: "I'll take the fifth on that one."

For seven months Avrakotos and his astonishingly loyal network managed to make a mockery of the Agency's entire system of security. With every extra day Clair George was pushed into an ever more complicated position. What could he say if Gust's bizarre operations were to surface publicly? What possible explanation could he offer for permitting a senior CIA officer to vanish without an assignment for months? It had been a stunning performance on Avrakotos's part—a somewhat unnerving demonstration of his skills as an operative. But in the end there was nothing to be gained from his victory if he could not get back into the field.

Fate has a curious habit in this history of stepping in at just the right moment. And it was during his time in limbo, just after Clair George had sabotaged Avrakotos's scheduled entry into the Contra Task Force, that Gust's black network tipped him off to an opening in the CIA's Near East Division, that would change everything for him. By chance, that posting, put him together with an old Agency friend, one of the few Ivy Leaguers

Avrakotos really liked. His name was John McGaffin, and he had known Avrakotos since his days as station chief in Cyprus. McGaffin was now running the Afghan program. In the CIA cafeteria, he was amazed when he heard the full story of Gust's recent adventures. "If it's really true that you have nothing to do," he said, "why not come upstairs. We're killing Russians."

CHAPTER 7

The Muj

HOW THE ISRAELIS BROKE
THE CONGRESSMAN'S HEART
AND HE FELL FOR THE MUJ

O f all the payoffs for being a member of the House of Representatives, Wilson would always say that none compared to the junkets: first-class, all-expenses-paid trips to exotic places, where
the American embassy and the host government treated him like visiting
royalty.

The junket that was destined to forever change Wilson's life and the
fate of the Afghans began on October 14, 1982, on a Pan American flight
from Houston. The first-class ticket and all other expenses were picked
up by the Appropriations Committee, for whom he was on a fact-finding
mission to review U.S. foreign-assistance programs. He was scheduled to
meet the Afghans but had tacked this on to the end of his itinerary only to
accommodate an insistent Joanne Herring.

En route to Israel, Wilson decided to stop off in Lebanon for another look at the Israeli intervention, which he had praised so effusively
in June. He lunched on C rations with the U.S. Marines, who had just
been sent to Beirut by Ronald Reagan on an ill-fated peacekeeping mission that would end in catastrophe and many deaths at the hands of a
suicide bomber. It was a sunny fall day, and Wilson enjoyed one of those
moments that make an old navy man feel good about being an American—in the company of lean U.S. boys in crisp uniforms keeping a troubled
peace.

His next stop was a visit to the Sabra and Shatilla refugee camps just outside Beirut, where thousands of Palestinians and Lebanese Shiites lived. Thomas Friedman of the *New York Times* had just reported that in September the Israelis, led by Wilson's hero, Ariel Sharon, had permitted Lebanese Christians to enter the camps and had stood by for two full days as their allies slaughtered hundreds of young men, women, and children. The Israelis claimed the operation had been aimed at PLO terrorists, and when Wilson approached the camps, no one had yet acknowledged that a massacre of innocents had taken place. "In my usual knee-jerk fashion I assumed there was a certain amount of sensationalism in the press and assumed Israel's culpability had been exaggerated, but I also felt it was my duty to see for myself."

Wilson, a student of military history, knew that war is never without horrors. He had met General Sharon with Ed Koch in the desert in 1973, when Sharon was the hero of the Yom Kippur War, and they had become friends. To him Sharon was an Israeli George Patton; he assumed that the general might have been heavy-handed but that he had done nothing more than what was broadly necessary. When Wilson walked into the camps, accompanied by his State Department control officer, he was still a true-believing defender of Israel. What he saw and heard shattered him.

"When we got into the camps," he recalls, "the grief and mourning was still going on. It had been maybe a week since the attack, and we walked down and ran into this woman who was an American Jew, obviously very liberal. She had been some sort of public-health nurse in an American humanitarian effort, and she was very impressive."

"She had on soiled clothing from tending the wounded, and she told me that her people had done something terrible. She walked us down to where the victims had been buried in a mass grave. And there were so many Palestinians weeping and bringing little pitiful flowers and I began to get a really terrible feeling in my stomach about it. And what was hanging over me was the Israeli guilt."

Wilson tried to believe the Israeli explanation that their soldiers hadn't known what was going on. "But then we walked about fifty feet and one of the American embassy people showed me where the Israeli command post was, and I looked at it and at that moment I lost it. My heroes were forever blemished because they would have had to be blindfolded not to have seen and heard what was happening. And then it was clear that they set up the whole thing and sat there and watched it."

Something dies in a man like Charlie Wilson when he loses his faith in the purity of a cause. Ever since he was a boy in Trinity listening on the radio to Winston Churchill defying the Nazis he had dreamed and prepared for the day when he would play his part in some worldwide struggle for decency. That's what he felt he had been doing by championing Israel. Each year he would feel the excitement mounting as he approached the King David Hotel, where he always stayed. But this time, with the terrible visions screaming in his head, the drive from Beirut to Jerusalem was an ordeal.

What kept his emotions in check as he crossed the border and headed down to the ancient capital was the realization that he would be having dinner with his friend Zvi Rafiah. Wilson personalizes everything, and when it came to the work he did on his various causes abroad, that was particularly true. In Afghanistan it was for Gust Avrakotos; in Israel, it had always been for Zvi, ever since he'd first met the smart, tough Israeli diplomat during the Yom Kippur War.

Over the next nine years, the two had worked together on a never-ending series of Appropriations efforts. Wilson had confided everything in Rafiah, and together they had tapped ever more funds for Israel from the subcommittee. Along the way Wilson had become close to Zvi's wife as well. When Rafiah had left Washington to join Israeli's largest defense company, Israeli Military Industries (IMI), Wilson had continued to help him. He'd gotten the Pentagon to buy a "bunker busting" bazooka from IMI, and almost every year after that Wilson had dreamed up some new congressional gift for Zvi's IMI and for Israel.

Congressmen usually have the American embassy set up meetings with government officials and organize their visits in foreign countries. But in Israel, Zvi always took care of Wilson's schedule. He understood the congressman's need to mix business with pleasure, and so along with the meetings with everyone who counted, there would be receptions and dinners with the country's leading musicians, scientists, artists, and writers.

Wilson could say things to Rafiah that he would tell no one else, and that night at dinner in Jerusalem, he shared his confusion and anger over the suffering he had just witnessed. Rafiah made it hard for him to blame the entire country; Wilson could feel his friend's personal distress at what had happened. Rafiah assured him that large numbers of thoughtful Israelis were just as horrified.

Wilson is a political pro, and professionals don't go running to the press or needlessly make enemies out of unforgiving friends like the Israelis. On the surface he conducted himself as if nothing had changed. He went through all the meetings at IMI and with the defense minister to discuss the Lavi, the Israeli fighter plane. But at the U.S. embassy he found himself in a shouting match with the ambassador, Sam Lewis, who tried to argue Sabra and Shatilla from an Israeli point of view. Wilson had liked Lewis's advocacy before, but now the fact that the U.S. ambassador was building himself a retirement home in Israel aggravated Wilson. He felt that Lewis had become little more than an Israeli agent.

The congressman felt marooned and betrayed by what he had witnessed. "I never recovered from that, but it wasn't something I wanted to make a big issue of. My history and everything with Israel was just too deep." In the following months and years Wilson managed to win funding for the Lavi. But back in October 1982, when he said good-bye to his friends in Tel Aviv, it was with the sense that he could never feel the same in Israel again. "I simply withdrew emotionally from my previous affection. It's a terrible thing to become disenchanted with your first love."

As Wilson progressed to the last leg of his trip, going to Pakistan to accommodate Joanne Herring, he was heading to one of the countries that the Israelis viewed with the greatest suspicion. For the Israelis, Pakistan's Zia ul-Haq was not quite a devil in the league of Saddam Hussein but he was close: his air force pilots flew interceptors for most of the Gulf States, a division of his army served as mercenaries for the Saudis, and, most alarming, the dictator was known to be building an "Islamic bomb."

The idea that Zia ul-Haq and the Afghans could replace the Israelis as the center of Wilson's world drama never occurred to the congressman. But as he took off for Pakistan, he was returning to a country that had charmed him two decades before when, as a young naval officer, his ship had sailed into the harbor at Karachi. He had expected to find a very backward people but in his letter home, he described the Pakistan navy men as better trained than their U.S. counterparts, their ships gleaming, their officers charming; and all pro-American. The only downside was the difficulty in getting the girls to consider a date, as he explained in his letter:

> I have seen a couple that really were knockouts but custom doesn't allow it. The girls themselves are really classic beauties, the essence of grace and femininity. Really captivating. Well enough I suppose for the lovely ladies of Pakistan. It seems that each part of the world excels in this realm. Or maybe I am just over susceptible to this particular attraction.

There was another reason why Wilson was inclined to smile on Pakistan: he had never liked India, and India and Pakistan are blood enemies. This prejudice is something visceral with the congressman. He doesn't like the way Indians talk or hold their heads. Furthermore, he considered them hypocrites, professing neutrality while firmly ensconced in the Soviet camp for decades.

These sentiments were music to the ears of the Pakistan military, which already had reason to view this congressman as a special friend. Back in 1971, just before Wilson was elected to Congress, India, with its Soviet-equipped army, had invaded and defeated Pakistan in the Bangladesh war. When Wilson was sworn in to office in 1973, the Indians were still holding 91,000 Pakistani prisoners in terrible conditions. Yaqub Khan, the elegant former general who was then Pakistan's ambassador to Washington, had desperately approached every congressman and senator on the Foreign Relations Committee, trying to find someone to help. Wilson alone had responded, immediately taking to the House floor to denounce the Indians and pressure the State Department to demand the prisoners' release. When the Indians finally disgorged the prisoners, Yaqub Khan gave much of the credit to Wilson, and a delegation of prisoners' wives were flown to Washington to present him with a citation of gratitude.

The Pakistan ambassador concluded that Wilson was a comer and decided to cultivate him. The future foreign minister was deliberately trying to assemble friends in America who might one day rally to support his country. The shrewd Yaqub Khan also picked Joanne Herring to be Pakistan's honorary consul in Houston, and it was at one of his black-tie dinners to honor Wilson that Joanne and the congressman met. These seeds that the general turned diplomat had planted back in the early 1970s were finally sprouting, almost a decade later, as Wilson's plane approached Karachi.

It was a murky landscape in Pakistan in late 1982 when the congressman landed to honor his commitment to Joanne Herring. The mujahideen had been fighting the Soviets for almost three years. Some 2.7 million Afghans had already made their agonizing trek over the mountains to seek refuge in this exotic Muslim nation. They were still pouring in at a rate of thousands a month, creating huge walled cities of mud huts. Close to one-fifth of the Afghan people were huddled in Pakistan's North-West Frontier province. Wilson didn't fully understand it at the time, but this zone of displaced Afghans had become the true front line of the Cold War.

The basic law of modern guerrilla warfare is that no insurgent movement can survive without a sanctuary for its fighters. The Vietcong depended on Cambodia and North Vietnam. The CIA's Nicaraguan Contras spent most of their time hovering in camps across the Honduran frontier. No guerrilla force could have survived in Afghanistan itself once the Red Army poured in over 100,000 combat troops backed by satellites and tanks, MiG bombers and helicopter gunships. Without Pakistan, there could not have been a sustained resistance. It was in Pakistan that the Afghans maintained their base camps, received their CIA weapons and training, and deployed for their guerrilla operations. The Soviets knew this and set out to intimidate Zia on two fronts: they built up the Indian army on Pakistan's eastern flank and began striking mujahideen bases over the border on its western flank.

Zia's chief of staff during those days, General Aref, says that the pressure got so intense that even Zia's own generals urged him to cut off the mujahideen. "The Soviets were saying that Pakistan, by arming the Afghans, was technically fighting the Soviet Union itself." The Soviets were shelling border towns, killing Pakistani civilians as well as Afghans and flying MiGs into Pakistani airspace. "A psychological image was created in Pakistan that we were earning this punishment because we were supporting the mujahideen against a superpower."

At Leonid Brezhnev's funeral in Moscow, Yuri Andropov, the new Soviet strongman, took Zia aside and threatened to destroy his government if he didn't cut off the Afghan "bandits." Zia, with his elegant Mao jacket and that famous gap-toothed smile, simply looked the Communist Party boss in the eye and replied that there were no Afghan guerrillas in his country. Zia's closest advisers all say the reason the general insisted on backing the Afghans so provocatively in the early years, well before he trusted the Americans to stand by him if the Red Army came into Pakistan, was because of his mystical religious convictions.

It's difficult for Westerners to understand the Islamic concept of jihad, but in Islam the word *jihad* is known and understood by all as a call to defend their faith in a "holy war." There has been only one pure holy war in modern times that rallied Muslims everywhere, and that was the jihad of the Afghan tribesmen.

Although he didn't know it, Wilson was about to enter a Muslim religious war in which Zia ul-Haq was the central player. Up close it was hard to think of Zia in a religious context. He was not the kind of Muslim that Americans were used to seeing on their television sets in those days. He wasn't anything like Khomeini, with his chanting Iranian Muslims flogging themselves with chains, and he bore no resemblance to Saddam Hussein and his radical anti-Western rhetoric.

No matter their differences, Muslims everywhere identified with the cause of the mujahideen. In the Muslim world it was incumbent on all to do what they could to challenge the Communist infidels. The Egyptians sent arms, and the Saudis gave fantastic sums of money; but only Pakistan was on the front line, for all practical purposes at war with the Soviets. "For Zia," General Aref explains, "it was a battle of right and wrong in which he felt it was ordained on us to support the right cause, irrespective of the risk."

Supporting the Afghans was never easy for Zia, and before all of his important missions abroad he would direct his pilots to stop in Saudi Arabia, where he would spend the night alone in prayer at the great mosque in Mecca. As powerful as his religious convictions might have been, Zia was also a political and military realist, constantly calculating how much he could get away with before his support for the mujahideen triggered a Soviet retaliation. For the Americans, convinced that they had to draw a new line of containment at the Pakistan border, Zia was the absolute arbiter. He assumed the stature of a benevolent despot who single-handedly, month by month, decided what, if anything, the CIA and the U.S. government would be allowed to do in his country.

Privately, the Agency, the State Department, and the Pentagon all gave him high-level assurances about the U.S. commitment to Pakistan. But Zia remembered how Jimmy Carter's administration had attacked him for hanging Bhutto, for being a dictator, and for trying to build a nuclear bomb, and how it had cut off military and economic assistance. Now, though allied with the Reagan administration because of Afghanistan, he was keenly aware of America's record of abandoning friends. It had been only a few years since South Vietnam, in spite of all the passionate promises, had been allowed to fall.

So Zia kept a wary eye on his Johnny-come-lately American friends and a particularly firm hand on the controls of anything to do with the Afghan mujahideen. To the Americans who came to see him during those times he would always say, "We must make the pot boil in Afghanistan, but I must make sure it doesn't boil over onto Pakistan."

The take-it-or-leave-it deal that Zia offered the Americans demanded the U.S. all but publicly renounce Jimmy Carter's attack on Pakistan. He insisted on an explicit understanding that the Reagan administration would not interfere in the "internal affairs of Pakistan." This meant no public complaints about his dictatorship and no attacks on his effort to build a nuclear bomb. The necessary assurances were made.

The next demand was equally tough. The CIA would have to accept radical limitations on its normal operating procedures. Zia fancied himself a distinguished professional soldier, not easily misled. He had read all about the Bay of Pigs, as well as Vietnam. Unimpressed by the CIA's paramilitary record, he refused outright to permit the Agency to operate directly with the mujahideen. The last thing he wanted was a horde of American agents stumbling about on his border, trying to tell Afghan fundamentalists what to do. Politely, the general insisted that the Americans run the entire operation through the "Afghan cell" of his Inter-Services Intelligence Directorate, the ISI. Under this agreement the Agency was permitted only to deliver weapons and ammunition by boat to the port at Karachi and by plane into the military airport at Islamabad. There the ISI's military officers took over, loading the Agency weapons onto trains and trucks for secret transport to the border.

By official U.S. policy, all weapons appeared Soviet-made. That way it was possible to maintain the fiction that they had been captured in battle. So well was the program executed that when the Afghans loaded their camels and mule caravans to set off over the mountains, they had no idea that they were carrying weapons paid for by the U.S. taxpayers. To them they were all gifts from Allah—weapons for the jihad that their Islamic brother Zia had provided.

By the fall of 1982, when Wilson arrived, this unusual CIA program had unquestionably kept the Afghan resistance from being crushed. In dollar terms (about $30 million) it was the largest Agency operation in more than a decade. But there were also serious troubles.

Joanne Herring had set the stage. She had called Zia from Houston on his private line and told him not to be put off by Wilson's flamboyant appearance and not to pay attention to any stories of decadence that his diplomats might relate. She was adamant that he win over this U.S. congressman from Texas: he could become Pakistan's most important American ally.

Wilson had met up with Joe Christie, his old drinking buddy from Texas, in Abu Dhabi, and the two men boarded the Gulf Air jet for the flight to Islamabad. They were seated in first class and served drinks. But shortly before take-off, they were forced to move to the back of the plane. The stewardess covered their first-class seats in plastic, and soon after, two rows of falcons were brought on board and placed in Charlie's and Joe's seats. When the plane landed in Islamabad, two cars sped onto the tarmac. The larger one pulled up to the plane, and before any of the passengers were permitted to leave, an official collected the sheikh's prized falcons. The little car was for the congressman, and his Texas pal took advantage of the contrast to rib his friend about the great status the Texas legislator had in that part of the world. In fact, Zia had taken Joanne's urgings to heart and had decided not just to make a giant effort with Wilson but to test him by asking for help with a very sensitive problem. Just after the plane landed, one of Zia's emissaries asked the congressman if he would be willing to meet with the general's army leadership for a private briefing that afternoon.

By the time Wilson emerged from his hotel room in Islamabad to meet the military escort he looked almost like a caricature of a western cowboy. The Stetson hat and the hand-tooled boots added at least six inches to his height, making him close to seven feet tall as he strode across the lobby and thrust out his hand to the officer. "Hello, I'm Charlie Wilson," he said in that huge voice of his. The Texan had that look on his face of an American who is just happy to be alive and delighted to be so much bigger and more optimistic than anyone in the Third World could ever dream of being.

The escort officer drove him fifteen miles from the dreary, recently built capital to Rawalpindi, an ancient city teeming with shops and street life that was the headquarters for Pakistan's sprawling military command. A delegation of air marshals and infantry generals was waiting for him. An orderly served tea from a gleaming silver pot as the Pakistanis launched into a highly classified briefing. They didn't immediately say what it was they were looking for. First they wanted the congressman to understand the risk Pakistan was taking by supporting the Afghans.

All Pakistan military men live with a primal fear of their blood enemy, India, and the briefing officer, with a large map and pointing stick, began with a description of the current disposition of Indian forces on the Pakistan border. They reminded him that India had exploded an atomic bomb in 1974 and now had greatly expanded its nuclear-strike capability. The Soviets, they said, were pouring money into the Indian army and the Indians were engaged in menacing maneuvers on their borders. In their understatedly British way, the Pakistani generals were doing their best to savage India without offending this American. Most Americans, they had found, were pro-Indian. It took them a while to understand that they were preaching to the converted. Finally Wilson simply explained that he despised Indians and that as far as he was concerned, they had been in the Russian camp ever since the days of Nehru.

With the meeting thus off on the right foot, Wilson listened eagerly as the generals turned to Afghanistan. They explained that the Soviet war was different from Vietnam. There was no media to record what the Red Army was doing, no antiwar movement in Moscow. Entire Soviet divisions were sweeping into highly populated valleys, killing everything they could find—people and livestock—and destroying irrigation systems and crops.

The best gauge of the campaign's ruthlessness was the refugees—almost three million in Pakistan, another two million in Iran. The congressman would be seeing them the next day. Each and every one carried stories of the brutality of the Soviet terror campaign. The camps were just forty-five minutes by air from the briefing room in Rawalpindi, the generals explained; at that very moment, Soviet MiGs and helicopter gunships were operating right on their border. And then the air marshal turned to the problem that Zia had decided to raise with Wilson. It had to do with F-16 fighter jets.

When the Reagan administration had fallen all over itself to restore relations with Pakistan, Zia had demanded that the Americans sell him high-performance F-16 fighter jets, the same kind Israel had used to bomb Saddam Hussein's nuclear facilities. In spite of predictable opposition from the Israelis, the sale had been authorized. Foreign-military-assistance money to buy the planes had been appropriated by Wilson's subcommittee. Pakistani pilots had already been sent to Texas to learn how to fly the planes. But the whole deal was now in jeopardy because the Pentagon was refusing to equip the interceptors with state-of-the-art "look down, shoot down" radar. As Zia saw it, Pakistan was putting its neck on the line to stop the Communists, and if the U.S. wouldn't equip his pilots with the same radar they'd given to the Israelis, he wouldn't accept the planes. And the air marshal warned it would also mean that Pakistan wouldn't help with the Afghan war. Could the congressman help?

That was like asking a fox if he wanted to take a private stroll through the henhouse. Charlie Wilson has always been an irrepressible arms salesman for America, and that was doubly the case when it came to F-16s. These jet fighters are made by General Dynamics in Fort Worth, Texas, then–House majority leader Jim Wright's district. The F-16 sale was not just good for the Pakistanis and bad for the Soviets; it was good for Wilson's powerful congressional friend, not to mention the defense contractors who poured $200,000 into his campaign chest every two years.

Wilson stretched out his long legs and smiled. He then began by explaining to the generals that Congress was a coequal branch of the United States government and that his Appropriations subcommittees controlled both Pakistan's foreign aid and the money for all U.S. government weapons purchases. In his heart of hearts, Wilson suspected that this problem would iron itself out even without his intervention. But ever the good politician, he told the appreciative generals that yes, he was confident that he could help. In fact, he would go personally to the Pentagon.

With that, Charlie Wilson put on his cowboy hat and he and Joe Christie went for a tour of Islamabad, ending up at the largest mosque in the world. It was a vivid reminder that in spite of the British demeanor of the generals, Pakistan was an intensely Muslim state. It was illegal to drink in Pakistan; to Muslims, alcohol is the Western equivalent of a narcotic and is forbidden by the Koran. Joe Christie, however, announced that he had found the only playboy in Pakistan and that he and Wilson were invited to a party in his secret disco. Wilson was thrilled, especially when he went down into the man's basement and found it equipped with blinking lights, mood music, and all the Chivas Regal anyone could possibly want. Once he realized that there would be no women, all the men, even his best friend, Christie, suddenly became quite unattractive to his eye and he proceeded to get wildly drunk. In his cups, he made a pact with himself never to return to this strange country without an American woman in tow.

Officially the congressman was on a fact-finding mission, and so, in spite of a horrible hangover, early the next morning they took off in the embassy's spy plane, for the short flight to the refugee camps. Just over the sharp mountains, one of the Cessna's twin engines failed, and the pilots began frantically leafing through their flight manuals. Their hangovers vanished as the terrified congressman and his friend watched the aircrew sweat as the tiny plane bounced back toward Islamabad.

Two hours later they set off again, this time on a commercial flight, which landed them safely in Peshawar, the capital of Pakistan's historic North-West Frontier. Peshawar is the last stop before Afghanistan on the famed Grand Trunk Highway, which originates in New Delhi. It's a historic smugglers crossroads, an intrigue-filled city that was home to the British colonial army, which maintained garrisons there and which Rudyard Kipling immortalized in his poems and novels. By 1982 it had also become the not very secret center of the Afghan resistance.

All the Americans who would later make this passage to Peshawar experienced the same giddy sensation of entering a time warp that Wilson and Christie felt that afternoon. There is a sound in the streets of this city that must be experienced to be understood. It's like being inside a beehive—a whirl of turbans, beards, ox-drawn wagons, brightly painted buses, motor scooters turned into rickshaws and driven by Pashtun tribesmen. Every face looks biblical, and everything is in motion on the streets: money changers, rug merchants, horse-drawn carts, men washing their feet and hands at the entrances of mosques, young boys scurrying about with trays of freshly baked Afghan bread and tea.

"It was all Kiplingesque," recalls Wilson about this first of fourteen trips to Peshawar. "I felt like I was about to see Kim sitting on the cannon. It was a very, very turn-of-the-century, British-garrison atmosphere. You would see all those elaborate gates to military bases with cannons in front of them and all those guys snapping heels and coming to attention."

Peshawar was only thirty miles from the Afghan border and minutes from the sprawling refugee camps. There were hidden storehouses, and Afghan commanders living behind walled compounds surrounded by armed bodyguards. This was home to the leaders of the seven mujahideen military parties that the CIA and Zia's ISI had created to organize the war effort. But no one offered to take Wilson to visit these secret warriors. He hadn't yet earned the right to pass freely into that world.

His schedule called for the traditional tour of the U.N.-supported refugee camps, a scene that appalled everyone who came to Peshawar: millions of proud Afghans living in mud huts without running water or the ability to feed themselves. That month twenty thousand more had poured in—young boys and girls dressed in bright tribal clothing; the women with their faces covered. They came from the mountains and valleys of a country where their ancestors had lived for centuries, a legendary warrior nation not easy to intimidate and uproot.

All brought horror stories with them of what had caused them to flee their country. In particular they talked of helicopter gunships that hovered over their villages—hounding them even as they fled. It began to dawn on Wilson that there were only Afghans in this part of Pakistan and that he was witnessing an entire nation in flight from the Communists. This spectacle of mass suffering roused him but he had been to refugee camps before and for him there was something almost impersonal about such a mass of humanity. What did catch his attention that day was the absence of men—no teenagers, not even forty or fifty year olds. He was told they were all fighting in the jihad.

It was at his next stop, the Red Cross hospital on the edge of Peshawar, that he lost his heart to the Afghans. Wilson's whole sense of himself rested on his self-image as a champion of the underdog. The victims of Sabra and Shatilla had shaken him, and he was not proud that he had chosen to remain silent in the face of such brutality. Perhaps this had something to do with his reaction in the hospital when he met his first Afghan warriors.

Scores of young men were laid out on hospital cots. The doctors sat with Wilson at the bed of a young boy and explained that his hand had been blown off by a Russian butterfly mine designed to look like a toy. This threw Wilson into a rage. A young Afghan who had stepped on a land mine explained he was proud of his sacrifice. "He told me his only regret was that he couldn't have his feet grown back so he could go kill Russians."

Wilson moved from bed to bed, undone by the carnage but increasingly aware why most of them were there. He spoke to a wounded commander as the effects of an anesthetic started to kick in. The man was waving his hand in a circle, speaking in Pashtun, describing the horror of the Russian gunship that had put him there. Not one of them complained about their lost limbs. But every one of them described their fury at the Russian gunships. And to a man, they asked for only one thing: a weapon to bring down this tool of Satan. Wilson wanted desperately to give something to these warriors and, before leaving, he donated a pint of his own blood.

His next stop was a meeting with a council of Afghan elders, hundreds of whom were waiting for him in a huge colorful tent, decorated with cotton fabrics that looked like floating Oriental rugs. As he walked in, Wilson was dazed by the sight of long white beards and turbans, and the men's fierce, unblinking eyes. The Pakistanis had told them that the congressman had come as a friend offering assistance, and as he entered they shouted, "*Allahu Akbar*"—God is Great.

To Wilson it was like a scene out of the Old Testament. When the elders invited the Texan to speak, he delivered what he thought would be just the right message. "I told them that they were the most courageous people in the world and I said, We're going to help you. None of your families will suffer from lack of shelter and food. I pledged that their soldiers would not be left to die in agony and that we would give them millions in humanitarian assistance."

An old man rose to respond. He told Wilson he could keep his bandages and rice. What they needed was a weapon to destroy the gunships. These old men were no different from the young warriors in the hospital. They were all fixated on the Russian Mi-24 Hind helicopter. If he wanted to help, he should get them a gun to knock this devil out of the sky. It was at this moment that Charlie Wilson realized he was in the presence of a people who didn't care about sympathy. They didn't want medicine or charity. They wanted revenge.

It's not uncommon for a single childhood experience—particularly if it is a traumatic one—to end up shaping an entire life. Sometimes it offers the only key to understanding what leads a person to make choices that would otherwise seem irrational. That certainly is the case with Charlie Wilson and his decision to embrace the lost cause of the Afghans.

As is true with many boys, Charlie's dog was his best friend, his constant companion. Everyone in Trinity knew that Teddy was Charlie's dog. Whenever the two would burst into Cochran's corner drugstore they would get equal billing: "Hello, Charlie. Hello, Teddy."

And that's where Teddy died—a hideous, agonizing end on the floor of Cochran's store with Charlie and a crowd of neighbors and friends watching in horror. Charlie's mother, Wilmuth, held the boy back, fearing the dog might have rabies. For ten minutes, he watched, completely helpless. He was thirteen.

Later, when the pharmacist discovered that Teddy had been fed finely ground glass, Charlie knew immediately who had done it. It was the work of his twisted neighbor, Charles Hazard, an old man who was forever threatening to do in any stray dog who soiled his well-manicured garden.

It was the spring of 1946, and that night Charlie poured gasoline over Hazard's precious plants and set his lawn on fire. But in the cold light of dawn, he realized that this wasn't sufficient revenge. That's when he had one of those brilliant flashes that never failed in later years to spring fully grown into his mind whenever he found himself in similar situations, facing bullies who needed to be reigned in. Hazard was a city official, and Charlie suddenly realized that an election was about to be held.

On this occasion, he found himself recalling his mother's fury at the way the liquor interests had managed to bribe Trinity's black citizens with beer and cash to accept a ride to the polls to vote down the referendum to outlaw alcohol. Looking out over Charles Hazard's blackened lawn, Charlie concluded that if he could only get a car, he could mobilize his own secret army of voters to defeat Hazard. In those days, farm boys could get special driving permits at thirteen. He got his permit and then persuaded his parents to let him use the family's new car, the first they'd ever had, a two-door Chevrolet.

When the polls opened, Charlie was waiting with his first carload of voters. He said only one thing before letting them out: "I don't want to influence your vote, but I'd like you to know that Charles Hazard poisoned my dog."

By the time Hazard arrived at the polling place that afternoon, his fate was sealed. About four hundred people had voted, and Charlie had bused in ninety-six of them. By a margin of sixteen votes, the reign of Charles Hazard had come to an abrupt and unexpected end.

That evening, thirteen-year-old Charlie Wilson strode down the street to Hazard's house and announced that he was pleased to report that his black constituents had just ended Hazard's career. "You shouldn't poison any more dogs," he said before leaving.

Thirty-six years later, something about the mujahideen's appeal to stop the Soviet gunships brought back memories of his dog. "I started to think to myself: Where are all the congressmen who are always talking about humanitarian aid, and the human-rights activists? Where are they now?" In the fall of 1982, the mujahideen had no congressional champions. In fact, they had no one in any position of power who believed that they had a chance for victory. Wilson had no logical reason to believe that he could help these tribesmen fight a ruthless superpower. But he felt the same rush of anger and clarity that had made it possible for a thirteen-year-old boy to bring down his dog's murderer. Surrounded by these determined men, Wilson saw a path to honor, if not victory. "It began to dawn on me right then and there that I didn't know what was going to happen, but with my rage and their courage I knew we were going to kill some Russians."

Standing by these biblical figures, he realized that Joanne Herring had been right. His whole life had been leading to this moment. This was the place where he could change history. "I saw how clearly it could be presented at home. I knew right then we would be able to overcome the liberals' objections to projecting American power. Because this was the Red fucking Army! This was simply an issue of good and evil."

Wilson had one final stop on his schedule, the most important of all—a meeting with Zia ul-Haq. When asked these days about his heroes, Charlie Wilson puts three at the front of the list: Winston Churchill, Abraham Lincoln, and General Zia ul-Haq. Zia's place on this list is, needless to say, unusual. In 1982 most of Wilson's congressional colleagues saw Zia as a smiling dictator who had hung his predecessor, killed democracy, and was building an Islamic nuclear bomb; and whose Muslim fundamentalism was robbing women of what little equality and dignity they possessed.

But none of this alarmed Wilson. He trusted Joanne Herring's instincts and he knew that if Zia could put up with her flamboyant ways, he was not an inflexible fundamentalist. Wilson was also shrewd enough to realize that Zia was the key to anything that might be done with the Afghans. When he returned from Peshawar and set off that night for dinner with the president, he was eager to meet this man and decide for himself whether they could join forces to up the ante in Afghanistan.

General Zia ul-Haq was a bugler's son, a child of the British army and, in his manner, British through and through. He had accumulated great power as Pakistan's military dictator, but he presented himself in a simple, even humble manner. He was waiting on the steps of the old colonial chief of staff's house when Wilson arrived. Up close, Zia did not seem remotely like the ruthless Islamist he was reported to be. He had a mesmerizing aura, and Wilson was immediately charmed by his warm greeting and the absence of any imperial trappings.

The congressman hated it when alcohol was not served, but he took the fresh fruit juice that was offered in good cheer. After the predictable exchanges about mutual friends, he found himself speaking with rage about what he had just witnessed. "Zia became very animated and talked about wanting to go fight the Russians himself," Wilson remembers as if it were yesterday. "He was all fire and passion, pounding the table, saying 'there is a way. We can win. We can beat them. We've got to all think about nothing but shooting down those helicopters.' I could feel the fire in his belly, and it excited me."

This was the first of many meetings to come where these two unlikely allies would sit alone, keeping the U.S. ambassador and other important dinner guests waiting while they plotted the demise of the Russian
empire. Wilson that night talked straight and tough with him about his
unconventional plans. "I told Zia that in spite of the opposition, as long as
he didn't detonate a bomb or execute any more Bhuttos, I could double or
triple the American commitment with a minimum of commotion. He looked
at me a long time and said, 'You know I've been promised many things by
Americans before.'"

Wilson was careful in responding: "'Mr. President, I'm a man of many
character flaws, but I can promise you one thing: I will never tell you I can
do something in Congress that I can't deliver.' Zia looked at me and said,
'That's very important. I believe that.'"

Before Wilson left Zia's residence that night, they embraced and
agreed to talk again the following month. Zia was scheduled to meet Ronald
Reagan in Washington, but first he would fly to Houston to attend an elaborate dinner that Joanne Herring was organizing in his honor.

In the scheme forming in Wilson's mind, he now had almost all the
elements in place to go back to Washington to work his Appropriations
magic. There was just one mystery to be cleared up: what was the CIA's
game? Why hadn't they been asking for more sophisticated guns and much
more money? The White House was behind the program. President Reagan
referred to the Afghans as "freedom fighters." No one in Congress had any
problems giving weapons to these men. So why wasn't the CIA giving them
what they needed?

Only one person in Pakistan could answer that question. And after
seeing Zia, he directed the U.S. embassy in the name of "the Honorable
Charles Wilson, member of the House Appropriations Subcommittee
on Defense" to request a meeting with Howard Hart, the CIA's man in
Pakistan.

CHAPTER 8

Howard Hart

THE STATION CHIEF

I t's a tribute to the CIA's cult of secrecy that by the time Charlie Wilson met Howard Hart, in November 1982, he had never, to his knowledge, talked to an active member of the CIA's Clandestine Services. He was on the subcommittee that appropriated the Agency's money, but he had no understanding of what the CIA really did or how its officers operated.

Howard Hart wasn't happy about briefing the congressman. The cable from headquarters had arrived in the crammed CIA station with this simple directive: "The Honorable Charles Wilson, Democratic representative from Texas, arriving Islamabad. As member of Defense Appropriations subcommittee he is entitled to full classified briefing on the Afghan war." The station chief figured there was almost nothing positive that could come from this meeting. But Wilson was on a committee the CIA couldn't afford to alienate, and Hart, ever the disciplined secret soldier, set out to do his duty.

Any successful case officer must have a capacity to charm and manipulate, and Howard Hart made sure to put on his most charming self when he greeted the congressman downstairs in the temporary U.S. embassy.

Ever since a mob of Muslim fanatics had burned down the new $22 million embassy to the ground three years earlier, life in the temporary mission had been a claustrophobic nightmare. Hart's team was unusually small, given the scope of its mission in Pakistan: only twenty-five people, including secretaries and technical workers, to keep the Afghan war going and to spy on the Pakistanis and their nuclear program. And all he could get for them was three windowless rooms on the fifth floor, so crowded that his agents had to take turns using the few desks and telephones.

The CIA, as a practice, locates its stations abroad in U.S. embassies. In Islamabad, Hart operated under the cover of being the first political secretary, the same job that Dick Welch, the Athens station chief, had held when he was gunned down outside his home several years before. Hart's operation was officially known as the Regional Affairs Office. He and his fellow officers were located on the fifth floor in what amounted to a vault with a combination lock on the door.

This was all very new to Wilson, who felt a bit like a kid when he realized he was about to enter his first CIA station. But he carefully took stock of Howard Hart. The congressman's only prior exposure to the CIA had been through the renegade operative Ed Wilson, now beginning his fifty-two-year sentence in a federal penitentiary. Ed Wilson had lectured him on how the Agency had been "deballed," as he put it, and taken over by careerists interested only in playing it safe. The congressman still had his suspicions about the Agency, but the one thing he did know for certain when he walked through the embassy with the handsome, blond forty-two-year-old American was that Howard Hart was the real McCoy. To Wilson, he seemed almost to be stepping out of a movie. The congressman thought he looked a bit like Nick Nolte, his voice eerily like William Holden's. Beyond that, Hart had the kind of command presence that an old navy man like Wilson always found deeply impressive.

For his part, the station chief was choreographing this experience for the congressman. He knew how the mumbo jumbo awed outsiders, and so he was playing his part to the hilt. He effortlessly punched the code into the combination lock and let the congressman into his secret room. Motioning for Wilson to sit down, Hart busied himself with a briefcase, which opened to disclose a row of dials. When he finished adjusting them, the sound of the 1812 Overture filled the room—a standard Agency technique to counter bugging. Not wanting to appear the amateur, Wilson did his best to look utterly accustomed to the ritual.

Hart pulled out satellite pictures and pointed to the map, prepared to give the congressman one of his tour de force performances. He had already heard from his sources that Wilson was carping about the level of CIA support. It was too bad he couldn't tell this blowhard with the pretty-boy hairdo and the cowboy boots how he had single-handedly escalated a set of village rebellions into an ongoing national war. But that would require confiding in a loose cannon about the way things work in the Directorate of Operations—and that was an inner sanctum that Howard Hart was not going to permit Charlie Wilson or any other congressman to enter.

The small, intense world from which Howard Hart came was Archie Roosevelt's old club, the same fraternity within a fraternity that had inducted Gust Avrakotos in 1962 and Hart four years later. Hart was so proud of his place within this elite that he would always say he had not joined the CIA but the Clandestine Services of the United States of America. Later in his career, when he was asked to talk to new recruits, that was always the message he would begin with: "You are not joining the CIA. You are joining America's Clandestine Services. There are fewer case officers operating abroad than there are meter maids in New York. You are America's spies. You were selected because you are the most gifted young men and women of your generation, but all we can promise you is that, after training, we'll send you to some terrible place. And when you finish your tour there, we'll send you to some other terrible place. And then the worst fate of all is that we'll make you come back to Washington for a year every once in a while, where you will have to live with the bureaucracy. And if you do anything good you can't tell anyone about it. Other than that, it is a wonderful life." The point Howard Hart was making to each class of new recruits was that they were joining a priesthood, and no one should apply or begin to serve if he didn't feel the sense of mission. It could not be for money or fame; it had to be for love of country.

Howard Phillips Hart had been a small boy when he first experienced the wonder of being an American. His father was a banker in the Philippines in 1941 when the Japanese occupied the country and put all foreigners in prisoner-of-war camps. There were about three hundred Americans, British, and Canadians living in the camp where Hart and his family were held captive. It wasn't such a bad life for a small boy who hadn't known anything different. There was just enough to eat and good fellowship, and the adults had time to spend with the children. But it got suddenly menacing when General MacArthur fulfilled his promise and began the liberation of the Philippines.

Around Christmastime in 1944, as the U.S. forces moved into Manila, word spread through the camp that all of the prisoners were to be murdered. Over the next two weeks, American forces captured 20,000 of the 400,000 Japanese occupying the Philippines; the rest fought to the bitter end or committed suicide. But the Americans had yet to free the camp prisoners. One bloodred morning in January 1945, on a day the Japanese were preparing to execute their charges, the young boy looked up and saw the sky filled with parachutes. As gunfire filled the camp, Hart's mother told her son that the American soldiers were coming to rescue them. Three hundred paratroopers began landing all around. Suddenly, the small boy was in the arms of a large American G.I. As shells exploded around them, everyone ran to the water's edge, where the U.S. Navy had sent a flotilla of amtracs to ferry the prisoners to safety across the lake. The four-year-old boy was impressed with the explosions, but the memory that would stay with him was of the G.I. carrying him to freedom.

After the war, Hart's father resumed his life as a banker in the Philippines. At night, when family friends would gather, they'd always end up talking about their wartime experiences organizing guerrilla forces to battle the Japanese. Hart stood in awe of these Americans who had risked their lives to fight for freedom. These late-night talks became a kind of ongoing seminar for the boy, who listened and stored away their wisdom on guerrilla tactics and strategy. When his turn came in Afghanistan, he would draw from those lessons and push that advice on the mujahideen: Never try to take and hold territory. Hit and run. Don't use radios to communicate; the enemy will intercept your messages and find you. Don't build base camps that need to be defended. Stay light and mobile.

Hart was like most Americans brought up abroad after World War II—he considered the United States to be the all-powerful beacon of freedom, and being an American in the Third World felt special. When he became old enough, his father sent him off for polishing to Kent, a boarding school in Connecticut for young men, and then on to college at Colgate. But midway through Hart's college career, his father went bankrupt, and he was forced to drop out. A friend told him that if he moved to Arizona, he could enroll at the University of Arizona for free. A surprising number of gifted academics were clustered at the University of Arizona, where Hart went on to receive a graduate degree in Oriental studies, specializing in South Asia and learning Urdu.

His decision to pursue a career in the service of his country came to him all at once on a cold January day in 1961, listening to John Kennedy's innaugural address: "Ask not what your country can do for you; ask what you can do for your country." Just as it did for Gust Avrakotos and Charlie Wilson, both of whom were listening at the very same time, the words had an explosive impact on the young man. With the memory of the huge G.I.

who had come out of the sky to carry him to freedom and the words of President Kennedy, Hart felt he had no choice but to serve his country, and he decided then and there that, if it would have him, he would join the CIA.

In June 1966, Hart was inducted into the Agency and spent the next two years at the Camp Peary spy school. After graduating, he was sent to India and Pakistan where he spent five years as a junior officer. But he got his first chance to play in the big leagues in 1978 when he was sent on a secret mission to Iran during the final days of the Shah's regime. The CIA case officers and staff at the huge Teheran station were all registered with the Shah's government, Hart's assignment was to operate deep under cover. Soon after revolution swept the Ayatollah and his virulent anti-American followers into power, the entire 125-man CIA station was evacuated.

Hart, still under cover, was left behind in enemy territory as the acting CIA station chief. At 35, a mere GS-13, he was now operating clandestinely as his country's eyes and ears in charge of a tiny collection of unregistered agents. For the next four months he lived with constant terror. Tehran was occupied by militant, gun-toting student radicals convinced that every American they saw was a spy. Rifles were always being pointed at his head. Crazed revolutionaries repeatedly hurled him to the ground, accusing him of being with the CIA and threatening to kill him.

Hart had made a pact with himself, back when he'd said good-bye to his wife and boys and had shaken hands with the departing station chief. A heavy smoker, he'd decided that he might well die one day from lung cancer, but he was not, by God, going to die at the hands of a Muslim fanatic. He realized that this challenge was what his whole life, and all his CIA training and experience, had been leading to.

Day after day Hart maneuvered through a terrifying landscape. He and his four agents had the keys to eighty cars and 250 apartments left behind by the departing Americans. They kept moving, maintaining their cover, and reporting back to Langley. When the student radicals stormed the embassy and took fifty-two Americans hostage, Hart transmitted his last dispatch, then made his way to the border and back to Washington.

It was one of those career-making events. The crisis had hit and Howard Phillips Hart had distinguished himself. He would receive the first of five coveted and rare intelligence medals—more, he was told, than any other CIA officer had ever been awarded.

Back in Washington, Hart was put in charge of the Pakistan-Afghanistan desk. He was there when the Russians invaded just after Christmas in 1979. When Jimmy Carter discovered old-time Cold War religion and asked the Agency to do something about Afghanistan, Hart helped write the first finding for the president to sign. And when the president ordered a rescue mission for the hostages being held in the Tehran embassy, Hart was tapped to head up the CIA's part of the operation. For the next six months he went underground, coordinating with Delta Force and the Pentagon's Special Operations Unit.

In Egypt, the night before launching the April 25 rescue operation, Hart met with the Delta Force team in a large hangar where the CIA had assembled a huge model of the U.S. embassy. Hart knew every nook and cranny of the place. Just the day before, one of the CIA's agents in Tehran had come up with the exact location where the Americans were being held, and Hart walked the secret warriors through every room they might have to enter. At the end of the briefing, as the Delta Force soldiers were filing out of the room, one young sergeant took Hart aside and asked, "Sir, where do I put the flag?"

"What do you mean?" Hart asked.

The soldier unbuttoned his camouflage suit and there, wrapped around his chest, was a large American flag.

"Oh shit, that's a good idea," Hart said. So the two went back to the model and Hart decided it should be nailed to the wall over the second-floor balcony of the ambassador's residence. "The revolutionary guards will take it down," he said, "but by then the TV crews will have filmed it. That's the place to put it."

Hart was on board the C-130 Hercules when the Delta Force team landed in the desert during the Operation Eagle Claw rescue attempt. He wore a flak jacket, carried an M-16, and was going in. But then the disaster hit. A helicopter collided with an airplane, and eight Americans died. The mission was aborted, and suddenly Howard Hart was at the door of his C-130 pulling one Delta Force soldier after another into the plane. When he reached out to pull the last man in, he saw tears smudging the dark camouflage paint under the soldier's eyes. It was the young Delta Force sergeant. "I'm sorry, sir," he said, "about the flag."

Back in Egypt, Hart wept. This could have been a chance for America to stand tall again. For Howard Hart, it could have been an opportunity to pay the country back for that moment in Manila thirty-five years earlier when he and his family had been rescued. But it was not America's day.

Back in Washington, when Hart received his second Intelligence Star for that mission, it was a bittersweet moment. But there wasn't time to look back. Ronald Reagan had been swept into office with a promise to restore America's standing abroad. His new CIA director, William Casey, was talking about going on the offensive. Casey wanted to bloody Russian noses in Afghanistan, and Hart was the logical choice to take on the Afghan operation.

Until then the CIA had been running a modest and uncertain effort out of Pakistan to back the mujahideen. When the Near East Division Chief, Chuck Cogan, tapped Hart to take over the program, he didn't presume to tell him what U.S. and CIA policies should be. The two men had gone through the Iranian hostage crisis together and now the rescue mission. They were soul mates, and Cogan was leaving it up to Hart to decide whether or not the Agency should move to expand its role in the war.

As the new chief of the station in Islamabad, command center of the CIA's Afghanistan operation, Hart quickly decided the time was right. As he settled into his command and presided over the steadily increasing arms flow to the mujahideen, Hart took on the air of a field marshal. Not since Vietnam had an American been responsible for putting so many men into battle, he would later note. Most compelling, he figured, was that he was the first officer ever to be given the mandate to kill America's true enemy, the troops of the Red Army. He was now the man of the hour, and it was inconceivable that the congressman he was briefing would ever have a significant part to play in the Afghan war. He had no idea that the two of them were headed on a collision course.

As far as Hart was concerned, this exercise was simply to give the congressman a memorable experience—to let him see the inside of a CIA station and hear a bit of secret talk before he was put on a plane back to Washington. Then Hart could get back to the business of killing Russians. Without any real sense of the man he was talking to, Hart launched into one of his boilerplate briefings, and for a time he had the congressman in the palm of his hand as he laid out the gruesome history of the Soviet invasion.

At the map, he explained to Wilson that over 100,000 Soviet soldiers were still in Afghanistan, garrisoned in all of the country's major cities, military bases, and airfields. In Kabul and the major cities, the KGB controlled the Afghan intelligence service, KHAD, and Soviet "advisers" were in all the ministries. The Kremlin, Hart said contemptuously, has the gall to say they only have a "limited contingent" of troops here. The official position in Moscow was: "there's no war being fought in Afghanistan."

Wilson's mind raced as he listened to Hart describe the mujahideen's indomitable fighting spirit. Hart explained that even as the two men spoke, this CIA-backed holy war was growing. The more Afghans the Russians killed, the more enlisted in the jihad. In the beginning, he said, they had acted as if they were still in the nineteenth century—sniping with Enfields, even mounting the kind of ambushes that T. E. Lawrence would have organized with his Arab units. Hordes of them would mass and run screaming at Soviet caravans led by tanks and armored personnel carriers and bristling with heavy machine guns, rockets, and tactical air support. Thousands upon thousands of Afghans died, but the mujahideen, fueled by their religious convictions and their legendary warriors' tradition, refused to accept defeat. Now, almost three years later, they were growing both in size and ability. What had once been a nuisance for the Soviets was becoming a bleeding wound.

The CIA man explained that he had watched them pouring over the border, heading for Peshawar. Some came from valleys where foreigners had never gone, where the language they spoke might be known to no one else in the world. Usually there had been no telephones or radios, not even postal delivery, but somehow they had all gotten word that Peshawar was the mecca of the jihad, the place to go for weapons. They came, not knowing what Afghans elsewhere were doing—all moving in the same direction, mystically organizing themselves into small bands that somehow, when it was all added up, turned into a strangely coherent guerrilla force. The mujahideen were moving on foot and on horseback across Afghanistan. They were bringing their families to Pakistan. The heads of the clans were arriving with their sons and nephews, their cousins and brothers, all looking for guns, to return as family and village military units.

Hart had no illusions about these people, most of whom were Pashtun tribesmen. He knew how stubborn they were, how primitive and impossible to reason with. How foreign the concept of unity was to them. How brutal they could be with their prisoners *if* they took prisoners. To Hart, ever the Cold War strategist, there was a simple equation: as long as the mujahideen were prepared to pay almost any price to kill Russians, it was a heaven-sent opportunity for America to help them against the common foe.

Charlie Wilson had paid careful attention to what Howard Hart said, and at the outset he had been impressed. "I felt better about Howard after listening to him," Wilson recalled years later. "I could see then that he had an enthusiasm for the fight. But it was a different fight than I had in mind. His idea was to be a burr under the saddle, an extreme nuisance, and he seemed very enthusiastic about this. But he never envisioned killing the beast."

The fact was, in Howard Hart, Charlie Wilson was confronting a CIA mind-set that had long before grown accustomed to fighting lost causes. There had been two Agency successes, always cited in the books—the government overthrows in Iran in 1953 and Guatemala in '54—but those were thunderbolt wonders pulled off with smoke and mirrors, *golpes* as they call them in Latin America.

The other interventions had invariably been grim affairs, designed to hold the line against Communism by launching spoiling actions all over the globe. Any officer who permitted his emotions to run loose in this cruel arena, where the "containment" game was being played, could have had his heart broken every year: all those sad campaigns to overthrow Sukarno; the colossal failure of the Cuban operations; the long and hopeless war in Indochina. It had almost become the trademark of the CIA's Operations Division to: fight and lose and finally be exposed and then mocked and vilified in the press, in Congress, and even at home by their children.

In late 1982, the suggestion that the CIA inflame the Afghans by giving them enough weapons to seek a victory over the Red Army would have sounded preposterous to Hart. No expert anywhere believed the mujahideen had a chance against the limitless reserves of men, armor, and air power of the country that had been willing to sacrifice over 10 million lives to destroy Hitler.

So when Wilson announced to Hart that money was no object and that he would personally see to it that Congress appropriated whatever amount Hart wanted for the mujahideen, the station chief was suddenly alarmed. "God protect us from our friends," he thought. At that very mo-

ment back in Washington, liberal Democrats in Congress were in an up-
roar over a *Newsweek* cover story about the CIA's latest "secret war" in
Nicaragua and here was this well-meaning fool, all puffed up and ready
to tell the world that the CIA needed millions more for a war against the
Red Army that fortunately no one seemed to even know was being fought.
Hart figured Wilson was the kind of politician who might just succeed in
compromising the entire operation, all in the name of rescuing it. "I looked
at him as a very dangerous man who could get me in serious shit if I wasn't
careful. I knew that Charlie was trying to draw me into some kind of statement that he could use. It was a trap I was not prepared for. I said, 'Wait a
minute. I have a risk of going outside my channels of reporting here.'"

It was hard also for Hart not to be offended by the congressman's
thinly veiled implication that he was not thinking big enough and that
the CIA was dragging its heels. This infuriated him because he believed,
with some justification, that he had almost single-handedly taken the CIA
into an involvement far deeper than anyone at the Agency had imagined
possible just a year before. Whatever this overeager congressman might
believe, there was a real war going on now in Afghanistan, and the reason why so many coffins were going back to the USSR had nothing to
do with Charlie Wilson. It was because of what Hart had pulled off the
previous year in Bangkok at the Agency's annual South Asia chiefs of
station meeting.

Like so much else to do with the CIA, that meeting had been one of
those invisible events no one ever hears about. But to Hart, Bangkok was
the watershed event of the Afghan war. That was when he had convinced
the Agency to take the risk of escalating. For Hart, Bangkok had been like
a class reunion. Near East Division Chief Chuck Cogan was the headmaster
who, along with his deputy, John McGaffin, presided over this annual gathering of spy chiefs from Turkey, Iran, Iraq, India, and all the other stations of South Asia.

The meeting was an exotic bazaar of spies with exotic stories to tell.
The station chiefs from Tehran and Baghdad were there with stories from
the Iran-Iraq War where over a million Muslims had already gone to their
graves. The man from Delhi had the latest on the increasing dangers of
nuclear war between India and Pakistan. Sri Lanka was descending into
absolute hell. The Kurds were stirring in northern Turkey. But early on,
Cogan and McGaffin split from the crowd to meet privately with Hart.

The three were part of that select world of the CIA's Directorate of Operations that Gust Avrakotos could never quite join, and as Hart sat down to brief them, it was with the ease that comes from belonging to the same family. Charlie Wilson and Avrakotos would later unite in hatred of Chuck Cogan, whom they came to see as the obstacle, preventing meaningful assistance to the mujahideen.

But Howard Hart adored Cogan and everything he stood for. Years later, looking back at that moment in Bangkok when he, Cogan, and McGaffin had sat weighing the fate of the Afghan resistance, he figured that they represented just about everything that was right about the United States and particularly everything that was right and honorable and important about the Agency's Clandestine Services. "We trusted each other," Hart said. "John and I were two of Cogan's bright young men. We were cut out of the same mold. We dress the same way. We had the same social confidence. For Christ's sake, McGaffin and I went to the same prep school together. And Chuck was so supportive. He always called me 'Howard of Afghanistan.' He was a GS-18, the equivalent of a three-star general, and a division chief. He was one of the barons of the Directorate of Operations, as we laughingly called ourselves."

Hart had come to Bangkok with a masterful presentation for his two friends, in support of a major CIA escalation. All three men knew there were two questions that had to be addressed. First, were the mujahideen for real? Could they sustain a resistance against the Soviets? Hart said they could—they were prepared to die in fantastic numbers, and he was convinced that, if supplied, they would fight hard for many years. Second, and even more important, would the jumpy Pakistan authorities, allow the war to expand? On this point Hart felt particularly proud to report that he had succeeded in forging a powerful relationship with Zia's intelligence chief, General Akhtar Abdul Rahman, who now supported the proposed initiative. Most important, Zia himself had signed off on it.

Cogan wanted to know what Hart had in mind. "I said we needed $12 million more or some figure like that," Cogan remembers. "I just picked the number from my head. It wasn't that much in raw dollars, but it was a very big deal because it marked a significant increase in the percentage of funding and it meant that Chuck would have to go back to the Agency's senior leadership and then to the White House and Congress for a new approval."

Hart didn't try to hide anything about the downside of this ferocious rabble. He knew what worried Cogan, so he anticipated the division chief's criticism by offering his clever observation about the nature of the Afghans. "'They're so crooked,'" he said, "'that when they die you don't bury them, you just screw them into the ground.' But then I explained that they probably would not rip us off any more than the American army would in a wartime situation. I said that the mujahideen might never be organized the way we would like, but there was a spirit and a commitment to a cause that lived in them now and might not be around in a little while if it did not get them more support."

"Carpe diem," Hart said after finishing his initial pitch. "Seize the day." It was the kind of flourish, perhaps, that only those who had gone to certain prep schools could get away with in such an encounter. The ball was now in Cogan's court, and Hart was sympathetic to his division chief's caution. It was risky business in 1982 for a CIA man to propose a large-scale covert operation. The Agency had basically been out of that business for years—ever since the accumulated impact of the congressional investigations, the press exposés, the Halloween Day Massacre, and Jimmy Carter.

Only two years earlier, when the Soviets invaded Afghanistan, Hart says, the Agency had nothing going against the Communists except perhaps a few insignificant undertakings like smuggling Korans over the Soviet border. He can recall vividly everyone's caution when the Agency was called upon to write the first Afghan finding for the president to sign. He was then the desk officer for Afghanistan, and no one could even remember what a finding was supposed to look like or what the language was supposed to be. So they had gone to the files and dug one up. Cogan and he had talked and reached the conclusion that they didn't dare call for anything radical right away; they proposed something like $700,000, much of it for communications equipment. But now Hart was asking the same division chief to sign off on millions to kill Soviet soldiers.

Hart says he was fully prepared to return empty-handed from Bangkok and had anyone else made the recommendation, Cogan might have held back. But the Clandestine Services are built on trust. "You're the guy on the ground," McGaffin had told Hart when he went to Pakistan. "This is your war out there. Just tell us what you need." In this same spirit, Cogan decided to run with his station chief. Together the three composed a cable to headquarters. "We spelled out what we wanted and why, and Chuck signed it. That was the beginning of the big time," he said.

If Howard Hart had explained any of this to Wilson, perhaps the congressman would have been more sympathetic. But Hart kept these stories within the family. It was hard to keep his mouth shut, however, when the congressman pressed to know what the United States was doing to stop the Red Army from sending its gunships to slaughter the freedom fighters. Hart found himself having to explain the basics—how, as a matter of long-standing Cold War policy, the CIA didn't use American weapons that would reveal the country's hand. It was critical to maintain the fiction that the Afghans had captured their weapons in battles with the Soviets. Hart wanted to help as much as Wilson, but surely the congressman would understand that it would be foolish to provoke the Soviets into a major retaliation against Pakistan.

These perfectly sensible arguments fell on deaf ears. Hart was a master at maintaining a poker face, but this congressman was driving him crazy. Of course it was easy for Wilson, in his dream world, to come in shooting his mouth off about pumping up the program to the bursting point with untold millions but Hart had to live in the real world.

It galled Hart to realize that Wilson didn't even understand that the U.S. embassy had been torched by a mob of Muslim radicals who hated America and had been quite ready to kill as many as they could find. That's why he was in this shithole of a station chief's office. Hart not only had to operate from cramped quarters but he had to be ready to destroy all his files in seven minutes—the time he figured he would have if the KGB ever decided to rouse the ever-ready Islamic mob. And at the heart of it all, something he could never explain to Wilson, lay his triumph in having won over General Akhtar, the stern and secretive intelligence chief.

Hart and Akhtar had met at least once or twice a week at the general's offices, the Inter-Services Intelligence Directorate headquarters in Islamabad. The general always dressed in uniform, and tea was served. By the time Wilson swooped in, Akhtar and Hart had all but fallen in love professionally. Part of the secret of Hart's success was the way on every public occasion he always deferred to the great General Akhtar, who took to affectionately calling him H2 because of the two H's in his name. Akhtar's affection for Hart was so enormous that when the next station chief took up his post, the general insisted on calling him H2, much to the CIA man's annoyance. The friendship was genuine, but it was also the product of a highly disciplined operational effort. As Hart saw it, his relationship with Akhtar was the best way the United States could effectively influence the one man who truly counted. "I would meet with Akhtar and talk strategy," he explained. "Then Akhtar would go to Zia, and Zia would approve every single item, every single incremental escalation."

Hart had gone to great trouble to establish his place in this process, so he found it aggravating to hear Wilson hinting that the Pakistanis were eager to fight a bigger war. What a laugh. Hart had sat in when the enthusiastic new CIA director, William Casey, had met with Zia in Rawalpindi, to offer more assistance, "What can we give you? How much do the Afghans need?"

Every time anyone asked that question, Zia always responded with the same speech. "Ah, Mr. Casey, we must make the pot boil for the Russians but not so much that it boils over onto Pakistan." Zia had given his little pot-boiling story so many times that Hart and Akhtar rolled their eyes at each other whenever he began.

But that was the crux of the matter: how far was Zia willing to go? "No one knew the answer," recalls Hart, "so one of my jobs was to figure this out. You must understand that, at the time, even Zia did not know the limits."

The station chief had no way of knowing that Wilson was then in the process of forging a direct relationship with Zia. Soon this link would end the convoluted process that Hart had so carefully erected to service his country's goals. Back then, however, Hart could not imagine the Pakistanis taking Wilson seriously. He saw only a dangerously energetic meddler.

The only overt tension that surfaced between the two men came when Wilson implied that Hart and the CIA were not doing enough to shoot down the Hind helicopters. Hart surprised Wilson when he argued that the weapons the CIA was already providing the Afghans—12.7mm DshK machine guns—were all that the mujahideen needed. Guns, including anti-aircraft guns, had been the congressman's specialty when he had been in the navy, and he thought that Hart's belief in the DshK was absurd: The Afghans didn't believe machine guns were the answer, and he knew that the Soviets had armor-plated their Hind helicopters specifically to resist a 12.7mm shell.

The congressman poured on the charm as he probed, trying to enlist the CIA man in his campaign. "Don't you need more weapons?" he asked again. What was Hart supposed to say to a question like that—particularly when it was being asked again and again in different ways? Finally he explained, "If what you are asking is 'Do I have as many weapons as there are Afghans who would like to be armed?' the answer is, 'No,' but we're doing very well."

The station chief had been very careful in making this final point, but Wilson heard something quite different than perhaps was intended. He heard Howard Hart sending a distress signal. He thought he could understand the code: Hart was asking for help.

The CIA man was now in that insecure position that bureaucrats so often find themselves when single-minded politicians burst into their lives. He could feel that Wilson was trying to grab the helm, but these were dangerous waters. The last thing Hart wanted was for this energetic amateur to screw things up by offering his noisy assistance. He and McGaffin and Cogan and Akhtar were doing just fine. In fact, they were doing brilliantly. What Wilson could do would be to go away and not come back. But as the two men said good-bye in Islamabad that day in November 1982, Howard Hart had the uneasy feeling that it was not the last time he would see this congressman from Texas.

COCAINE CHARLIE

W hen Wilson returned from Pakistan, Joanne Herring announced that everything was in place to give President Zia a reception he would never forget. At vast expense she had turned the main dining hall of the Houstonian Hotel into an exotic vision of a Pakistani palace. The heads of all the major oil companies had accepted, along with a surprising number of other CEOs from the Fortune 500. As she saw it, this was to be his coming-out party, designed to introduce America to the real Zia ul-Haq.

She had both Charlie Wilson and Charles Fawcett scurrying about from table to table, changing place cards up until the very last moment. In deference to the guest of honor's Muslim sensibilities, she even banned alcohol for the evening, but the congressman skirted the problem by occasionally excusing himself to meet Baron Ricky di Portanova at the hotel bar for fortification.

The event resembled one of those typical charity balls, which always seem to end with droning, laudatory speeches. But Joanne Herring had summoned her powerful friends for a purpose, and when she rose to introduce the Pakistani leader, she had a surprise for them: "I want you all to know that President Zia did not kill Bhutto."

Buckets, Baroness di Portanova, could not believe her ears. She knew how much Joanne liked the president, but she winced as her fellow Minutewoman proceeded to deliver an impassioned defense of Zia's role in the hanging of his predecessor, the former Pakistan president, Zulfikar Ali Bhutto.

"Bhutto had a trial," Joanne told the hushed gathering. "He was found guilty. President Zia did not commute the sentence, because the constitution of Pakistan is based on the Koran and the Koran believes in capital punishment. Zia did not murder Bhutto."

It was a curious maneuver, and if nothing else, Herring succeeded in stealing everyone's thunder: no longer could her guests harbor confidential thoughts about Zia's treachery. But, it was hard not to feel a little sorry for the dictator, forced to sit there with a genial smile as his honorary consul carried on.

American liberals and human-rights advocates would never change their view of Zia as a Third World thug, but his American visit was something of a triumph, and Joanne's dinner was part of the reason it succeeded. The Reagan administration was trying to encourage him to hold the line in Pakistan against the Soviets, and this state visit was part of that persuasion process. Zia had dangerous decisions to make in the coming months about the CIA's involvement in his inflamed North-West Frontier, and all of them centered on whether he could trust the United States.

Joanne's startling toast was strangely therapeutic for the much-maligned leader, who remembered how quickly Jimmy Carter had turned on him. In Houston that night, Joanne Herring saw to it that a host of powerful Americans actually honored him. And that same night, Charlie Wilson provided yet another dimension to Zia's growing partnership with the United States when he took the general into a side room for a private talk. The congressman had a novel proposition for the Muslim dictator. Would Zia be willing to deal with the Israelis?

This was not the sort of proposal just anyone could have made. But by now, the Pakistanis believed that Charlie Wilson had been decisive in getting them the disputed F-16 radar systems. As he saw it, Wilson had pulled off the impossible. Now the congressman, in his tuxedo, began to take Zia into the forbidden world where the Israelis were prepared to make deals no one need hear about.

He told Zia about his experience the previous year when the Israelis had shown him the vast stores of Soviet weapons they had captured from the PLO in Lebanon. The weapons were perfect for the mujahideen, he told Zia. If Wilson could convince the CIA to buy them, would Zia have any problems passing them on to the Afghans?

Zia, ever the pragmatist, smiled on the proposal, adding, "Just don't put any Stars of David on the boxes."

With that encouragement, Wilson pushed on. Just the previous month, he had learned that the Israelis were secretly upgrading the Chinese army's Russian-designed T-55 tanks. In Islamabad, he had been startled to see that the Chinese were supplying Pakistan with T-55s. The congressman now proposed that Zia enter into a similar secret arrangement with the Israelis. "I was trying to rig it for Israel to do the upgrade without the Chinese operating as the middlemen," Wilson explained.

It was no simple proposition. Three years earlier, a mere rumor that Israel had been involved in an attack on the Great Mosque in Mecca had so radicalized the Pakistani Muslim population that thousands had stormed the U.S. embassy in Pakistan and burned it to the ground. Zia was mindful of his people's hatred for both Israel and the United States, and he might have been expected to nip this in the bud. Instead, he encouraged Wilson to continue.

The congressman was acutely aware of the minefield he was walking through. Publicly, Pakistan and Israel would have to remain foes, he conceded. But as Zia well understood, Pakistan and Israel shared the same deadly foe in the Soviet Union. And the fact was that each could profit mightily by secretly cooperating with the other. If Zia would follow the lead of the Chinese, Wilson said, he could increase the striking power of his tanks, and there might be other areas of military and technological cooperation where both countries could mutually profit.

Pakistan did not have diplomatic relations with Israel, and Wilson certainly had no authority to serve as a quasi secretary of state. In fact, with this kind of talk, the congressman was walking dangerously close to violating the Logan Act, which prohibits anyone other than the president or his representatives from conducting foreign policy. But as the two rejoined Joanne's party, Zia left the congressman with an understanding that he was authorized to begin secret negotiations to open back channels between Islamabad and Jerusalem. Wilson would leave for Israel in March and travel on to Pakistan to brief Zia immediately afterward.

The entire evening had been a fantasy manufactured by Joanne to set the stage for Charlie to perform his magic with President Zia. It had worked beyond their expectations. As they compared notes at the after-dinner party that Baron di Portanova threw at his River Oaks mansion, this unusual Texas couple suddenly felt as if together they could conquer the world.

* * *

The CIA has a polite ruse for keeping senators and congressmen out of its hair. Whenever a member not on the House or Senate Intelligence Committee calls to request a briefing on a secret operation, the Agency always returns the call. The representative says they would be more than happy to accommodate the request, but—and this is a mere formality, of course—could the member please clear it with the chairman of the appropriate Intelligence Committee?

The catch, however, is that members of the Intelligence Committees are as human as anyone else. Information in the capital is power, and Intelligence Committee members don't like sharing it. Thus the CIA regularly manages to ignore the hundreds of individuals in the Senate and Congress who don't possess a key to the secret bureaucracy. The strategy is different, however, for members of the Foreign Affairs and Military Affairs Committees. The Agency talks to these committee members but doesn't feel obligated to offer much inside information.

Charlie Wilson's Defense Appropriations subcommittee is another matter. It controls the CIA's budget, even if historically its members haven't concerned themselves with the details of Agency operations. Yet here was Wilson enthusiastically seeking a meeting with someone in the CIA who had the authority to act on the Afghan problem. At first, the Agency merely dragged its heels but after he was put off repeatedly Wilson discovered, quite by accident, the magic words for summoning a high-level officer. "Don't worry," he innocently said to a deputy director at Langley who was explaining on the phone how busy they all were and how difficult it would be to come over to the Capitol. "I'll drive out there myself. I'll come this afternoon."

Bureaucrats at the Pentagon and the State Department consider it a boost to their ego and prestige when congressmen travel to their offices. But the CIA doesn't work that way. It is a forbidden place, so Wilson was not exactly surprised when his offer to pay a visit yielded a rather quick call back from Langley. The Agency's Near East division chief, Mr. Charles Cogan, would be in the congressman's office at five that afternoon.

The female members of Wilson's staff, the "Angels," were fascinated by the bustle of activity that preceded Cogan's arrival. The technicians came first, almost an hour before the appointment, looking like doctors with stethoscopes hanging from their necks. They probed the telephones, cleared the congressman's office, and moved about listening to his desk and walls. One of them explained that the KGB could place a beam on the windowpane from far away and pick up everything that was said inside.

By the time all of this curtain-raising activity had concluded and the two CIA technicians had tucked themselves away in an adjoining office to monitor any suspicious probes, the Angels were eager to see what this Mr. Cogan would look like. Right on cue at the stroke of five Charles Galligan Cogan, accompanied by two dark-suited aides, swept through the outer office and into Wilson's. But in that fleeting moment the Angels had glimpsed a figure out of another age. Cogan moved with the ease of the great natural athlete, exuding the air of a master spy. At fifty-five, the old Harvard man was still riding to the hounds and hammering the goals at polo.

Wilson was impressed, just as the CIA man had intended him to be. But for the congressman, everything that followed was devastatingly anti-climactic. "I had a thousand questions for him. I wanted to know about frost-bite, sleeping bags, boots, food, more Kalashnikovs, and, always, the problem of the anti-aircraft weapons. I needed to get a feel for what was going on, particularly to find out if they needed something." But Wilson soon realized that this mandarin of the Near East Division had come for no other reason than to patronize him. Cogan was pulling out all the stops with his noblesse oblige routine—exceedingly gracious, appreciative of the congressman's interest, full of impressive facts about the geopolitical situation. But in the end, he made it clear that it was rather premature to consider any new initiatives.

When a frustrated Wilson suggested that Cogan's man in Pakistan, Howard Hart, was dissatisfied with the weapons he was receiving, Cogan didn't blanch. This statement would later cause Hart no end of trouble, but Cogan let it pass with a smile: he would deal with Hart later. Yes, he admitted, the helicopters were a problem, but he elaborated on the CIA's argument that the DshK heavy machine guns were putting up a good show.

Wilson, the old gunnery officer, didn't buy it. He just wasn't able to figure out how Hart, Cogan, or anyone else could believe that the 12.7mm weapon was effective against those killing machines. Zia didn't think it was up to the job, and by that time, all sorts of Afghans had told Wilson the same thing. His office had become a visiting center for mujahideen coming to Washington. "All I heard twenty-four hours a day from these people was how the DshK bullets were bouncing off the Hind's bellies. So I said, 'Look, that's all well and good, but we ain't shootin' down the damn helicopters.'"

Chuck Cogan was not about to be deflected by such anecdotal evidence, and Wilson soon discovered that it is not easy to argue with a man who purports to be in possession of secrets that justify CIA policies. At that very moment, Cogan confided, his men were engaged in very sensitive and highly promising operations in Eastern Europe. They were on the verge of opening up a source of Soviet SA-7 shoulder-fired anti-aircraft missiles that would soon be making their way over the Hindu Kush mountains to the Afghans. Everyone was quite optimistic.

With that, Cogan rose charmingly, thanked Wilson for his interest, and insisted that they must keep in touch. It wasn't every day that the head of the Near East Division went to such lengths to accommodate an obscure congressman, and as he and his entourage swept out, he no doubt believed that this representative from East Texas would now leave the delicate work of espionage to the professionals.

The meeting left Wilson sobered about the problems he might face trying to rally his own government. "I was discouraged," he says. "I figured Cogan was formidable and shared none of my enthusiasm for the fight. I realized he was going to be one tough cookie to budge."

Just as Charlie was preparing to take on that battle, the lurid details of his hot tub weekend in Las Vegas surfaced on national television. Suddenly, it called into question Wilson's ability to stay in Congress, much less stay out of jail.

On the morning of January 21, 1983, NBC investigative reporter Brian Ross crouched behind a potted palm in Fort Worth's Mansion on Turtle Creek hotel. He and his camera crew were waiting for their prey. Ross had just received a tip that Congressman Charlie Wilson was the target of a federal drug probe. When Wilson walked out of his hotel room for breakfast that morning, he was confronted with an ugly question from Ross. Would the congressman comment on the charge that he had been snorting cocaine? So began Charlie Wilson's darkest hour.

It was all so unfair. Somehow, a congressional scandal the previous year centering on charges of congressmen engaging in homosexual relations with interns had escalated into a broader investigation by the Justice

Department into old and previously ignored allegations of recreational drug use by congressmen. Barry Goldwater Jr. and Ron Dellums were also targets. Wilson was included because of an accusation from his old friend Paul Brown, who had hosted the 1980 weekend in Las Vegas. Brown had later cheated Wilson out of a $29,000 investment and had gone to jail because of Charlie's testimony. The hustler had struck back in plea-bargaining sessions by offering to incriminate the congressman for drug use. Brown told the prosecutors that Wilson had taken cocaine as many as nine times in Las Vegas and that he had witnessed him snorting on Grand Cayman as well.

Until the story broke, Wilson's political star had been rising. He had been scheduled to be one of the Democratic Party's representatives to respond to President Reagan's State of the Union address. He was immediately replaced once newspapers across the country headlined the charges: "Lid Blown Off Big D.C. Drug Ring," "Drug Probe Targets Wilson." The congressman professed innocence to the reporter from the *Dallas Morning News:* "I don't think it's a Communist plot but I think it probably is a vendetta kind of thing." And to his constituents he promised, "I won't blame booze and I won't suddenly find Jesus." Under the circumstances he was doing as well as anyone possibly could, but nonetheless the nickname "Cocaine Charlie" began making the rounds.

Wilson was now a hunted man. Rudolph Giuliani, the then-famed prosecutor, was heading the Justice task force. G-men and DEA agents were working back through every nook and cranny of the congressman's past, locating his old girlfriends, playing tough with them, and taking depositions from all his employees, past and present.

Years later, Wilson would remember how easy it was to drown in suspicion: "You think your friends don't want to be seen with you. You're hesitant to say hello to your mother on the phone. You want to use the pay phone down the hall. You can't sleep. You want to talk all day to your lawyer until you realize that it costs $300 to talk, but you call anyway. And then you think of all the people in your life you've done things against who would like to bear witness against you."

Wilson's longtime administrative assistant, Charles Simpson, was genuinely worried about his boss. "There were four or five nights when I was almost afraid to leave him alone," he recalls. "He was that low, drinking straight vodka in the office. Just him and me."

At the center of this drama now stood a startled Liz Wickersham, the former *Playboy* cover girl who had accompanied Wilson on his Las Vegas weekend. Paul Brown told the FBI that Liz had been with Wilson in the Fantasy Suite when he'd snorted cocaine and in the Cayman Islands, where, Brown said, they had done it again. She had also been with him in the limousine coming back from Las Vegas, where, Brown claimed, Wilson had once again inhaled the white powder.

Wickersham was a potential time bomb, and Charlie's lawyer ordered him to cut off all contact with her. For the moment, any thought of Afghanistan was driven from his mind as he was forced to stand by, paranoid, and listen to the prosecutors' rumors about what Liz was telling them. "I just don't understand this, I can't believe she said that," he would tell Simpson in his cups late at night when he heard that Liz had confirmed that he had used cocaine in the Caymans. In fact, she told them she had taken a photograph of him "because he just looked silly and it was quite unusual . . . to see a congressman do that." She also reported that she thought she had seen him smoking marijuana in Washington.

Wilson took this news as a betrayal. He didn't yet understand that Liz was, in fact, his savior. At that critical moment in early 1983, this perky blond beauty queen found herself alone, holding the line against a federal posse threatening to make her swing if she didn't rat on the congressman. But all she would give the feds when she testified was information about Wilson's drug use outside the country, where U.S. law doesn't apply. Most important, she flatly denied any knowledge of cocaine use on the occasions Brown said he had witnessed it. She held the line in every area that could have brought Wilson down.

But back in February and March 1983, Wilson didn't yet understand that Liz was acting as his protector; he only knew that there were constant camera crews waiting for him to walk the gauntlet, three or four cameras following him everywhere. "They were like guns. I had an almost irresistible urge to grab them and pull them out of their hands." It was all getting to him and Wilson was beginning to act erratically, firing his lawyer one drunken afternoon, rehiring him the next morning. Meanwhile, the frustrated investigators were pulling out all the stops, sending out subpoenas to every major limousine driver in town, determined to find the driver who was said to have witnessed the congressman snorting cocaine in the limo.

In Wilson's mind it was as if a growing army of bounty hunters was moving about the capital, searching for any pretext to put him away. He might easily have left the Afghan playing field at this point for good, but his lawyers, upon learning of his scheduled trip to Israel and Pakistan, urged him to go. "Get out of the country. Keep to your routine," they advised.

This advice—just the thought of escaping from this nightmare—lifted the congressman's spirits. He realized that friends would be waiting for him everywhere he landed. Best of all, he already had a traveling companion who had agreed to come along for the ride. Two months earlier in Islamabad, while drunk in the secret basement disco, Wilson had vowed never to return to Pakistan without an American girl in tow. Incredibly, in a moment of drunken abandon, fate had led him to Carol Shannon.

Shannon was something of a local celebrity in the Dallas–Fort Worth area because of her skills as an exotic belly dancer. After watching her perform, and well into his cups, Charlie had asked her to dance and then impulsively had made the invitation.

"Now, darling," the congressman had said with mock gravity on the dance floor. "If you're really serious about this belly dancing, come with me to Cairo and I'll have you dance for the defense minister of Egypt." The invitation was made only half in earnest, but as time went on, Wilson began to think, Hell, that's not such a bad idea, bringing my own personal belly dancer. Now, in his lawyer's office, it was as if the clouds had lifted. Soon he would be far away from this city of cutthroats, traveling first class to countries where the leaders would treat him with respect. The light came back into his eyes as he prepared to rejoin the crusade.

CHAPTER 10

Carol Shannon

THE CONGRESSMAN TAKES HIS
BELLY DANCER TO THE JIHAD

At the age of six, in deep East Texas, Carol Shannon had felt the urge to dance. But her family's Baptist congregation viewed dancing as the work of the Devil. They preached a doctrine of the man as master of the house with the obligation to whip the evil spirit out of his children. At times the little girl didn't understand why her father shouted accusations and used his belt on her naked skin, causing it to break and bleed. Then one day, after he had caught her dancing and given her a particularly cruel thrashing, he struck her with his fist, again and again.

Afterward, alone in her bedroom, she was confused. And then mysteriously, she found herself turning on the radio and beginning to dance to the music, swaying before the mirror. As her body began to respond, she began laughing, then laughing louder, and finally laughing with joy.

Years later, when her husband, an archconservative Texas legislator, decided to run for the state senate, Charlie Wilson flew in from Washington to organize the opposition. Carol's husband told her that Wilson was a dangerous liberal who would ruin the United States and destroy big business. "He is the enemy," Carol remembers him telling her. But Wilson's candidate won, and Joe Shannon's political career was destroyed.

When Carol's marriage began to go sour, she signed up for belly-dancing courses to win back her husband's love. One night she asked him to turn the television off. She lit candles and performed for him. He said it was very interesting and then put out the candles and turned the TV back on.

But this Dallas housewife had an unmistakable genius for this unusual dance form. She was a beauty—once Miss Sea & Ski and Miss Humble Oil, she was now in her late thirties, with black hair and gleaming eyes. Men became infatuated when they saw her perform. Her dreams, however, went beyond such simple triumphs. She'd come to believe that in a previous life she had been Nefertiti, the ancient Egyptian queen of the Nile, and she found that when she danced, this bond with another identity released her spirit, freed her of her childhood terrors. Women started coming to her for lessons. She taught at the junior high school and danced wherever she could, at bachelor parties and retirement events. And then came the breakthrough.

In 1978, the Fort Worth Symphony invited her to dance solo in a performance of *Samson and Delilah.* The Devil's work or not, dancing had carried little Carol Shannon of East Texas onto center stage before Fort Worth's high society. A full symphony orchestra, the ultimate symbol of a city's culture, was validating her as a woman and an artist.

It was all too much for her husband, who left her a week later. But for the dangerously liberal congressman who had helped destroy Joe Shannon's career, the sight of this exotic housewife, appearing like a vision out of the *Arabian Nights,* was irresistible. He befriended her after one of her performances and soon found himself falling in lust, if not love. Later, when he was being hounded by the drug investigators, instead of turning to the elevated Joanne Herring, Wilson looked to the small-town girl from Kilgore, Texas.

Charlie found Carol Shannon to be a kindred spirit and when the drug charges mounted and he felt he had no choice but to hold a press conference she flew to Washington to be with him when he faced the newsmen.

That evening they sat together on the balcony of Wilson's condominium. From there they could see straight down the Potomac to the Lincoln Memorial, the Capitol, the White House, the Pentagon. Off to the right they could see the outlines of Arlington National Cemetery, but by far the most dramatic of the patriotic symbols, set just a hundred yards away, was the Iwo Jima memorial, where a marine honor guard was going through the evening ritual of taking down and folding the American flag. Wilson told her that he had chosen his apartment because of what the statue meant to him—and how badly he now felt for his people back home and for the grief he was causing them. "He said he had gone into politics because he wanted to make the country a better place for everyone and he really wanted to see peace in the world. There were tears in his eyes," she recalls. At the end of the weekend, Carol told the troubled man, "I love you to death. I'm only a plane ride away. If you ever need me, I'll always be there. I'm your friend."

Now, two months later, it was as if Carol Shannon was stepping into a fairy tale. She was in a first-class seat next to the smiling congressman, heading off to dance for the Egyptian defense minister. "You know that old television show *Queen for a Day*? Well, Charlie made me queen for three weeks."

When they landed in Israel, Zvi Rafiah was waiting at the airport. A U.S. diplomat was also there, by now so familiar with Wilson's routine that he didn't bother the congressman about his schedule. He just handed him a wad of cash—the per diem allotted to all traveling congressmen—and left Wilson to his Israeli friends.

Carol was thrilled to be in the land of the Bible. Wilson would disappear with Zvi every morning, sending her off in the embassy's chauffeur-driven Mercedes to see the holy sights. One afternoon, he came back "acting like a kid in a candy store," she said. She didn't completely understand what he was talking about, but she remembers that it had to do with T-55 tanks and secret deals with Pakistan. "I've never breathed a word about this before," she recalled. "And Charlie only gave me bits and pieces, but he was so excited because he thought he was going to be able to do something that no one else could. Charlie is a giver, and here he was saving the world."

What Wilson was doing during the day in Israel was scheming with Zvi's associates at IMI, the weapons conglomerate that produces the country's artillery, tank shells, and machine guns. It has the second biggest payroll in Israel and is inextricably entwined with the military and security apparatus of the Jewish state.

Wilson's scheming was conducted not merely out of Carol's sight but outside that of the U.S. embassy, which ordinarily monitors congressional activities abroad. One of the reasons for shadowing visiting members of Congress is to discourage them from engaging in negotiations that could place U.S. interests at risk. Wilson, however, never shied away from negotiating, in effect, on behalf of his government, and on this occasion he and his Israeli friends had a wide range of business to transact. The Lavi fighter plane was at the top of Israeli Aircraft Industry's agenda, but Wilson told them not to worry, everything was on track. They turned next to the T-55 upgrade proposal and to what their congressional friend could offer President Zia, on behalf of Israel, when he met with him in Pakistan at the end of the week. The Israelis were hoping this deal would serve as the beginning of a range of under-the-table understandings with Pakistan that the congressman would continue to quietly negotiate for them.

Wilson was in his element with these tough Israelis. He had already told Zvi of his frustrations with the CIA; now, in Tel Aviv, he was challenging IMI to invent a weapon that the Afghans could use to shoot down the murderous Hind helicopters. "You Jews are supposed to be so smart," he said, "so come up with something and I'll get the Pentagon to fund it."

Charlie Wilson was marching himself into a true forbidden zone. Congressmen are not allowed to commission a foreign power to design and construct a weapons system. Nor do they have the authority to commit the Pentagon to pay for such a weapon. But these were minor outrages compared to Wilson's potentially explosive attempt to bring the Israelis into the Muslim jihad that the CIA was funding against the Soviets in Afghanistan.

It's hard to conceive of anyone other than Charlie Wilson making such a proposition, much less being taken seriously. But such was the stature of this old congressional patron of Israel that the IMI chief immediately set his weapons experts to work. By the time Wilson was ready to leave, they'd presented him with an impressive-looking design, complete with detailed specifications. It was a mule-portable, multirocketed device named, to the congressman's delight, the Charlie Horse. Flushed with excitement, Wilson told Zvi and his boss that he would present it to the CIA with an ultimatum: either use it or come up with something better.

Somewhere in the deep recesses of his mind, the troubled congressman came up with an ingenious method to enlist the Israelis in the jihad. It helped put the memories of Sabra and Shatilla to the back of his mind.

The next morning, on March 31, 1983, five days into his trip, Wilson and Carol Shannon stepped into the world's most peculiar commercial aircraft. There were no markings on the plane, not even a tail number. This was the Jerusalem-to-Cairo shuttle mandated by the Camp David

Accords. It was the only flight linking Israel to any part of the Arab world in those days, and Charlie had managed to assemble a marvelously bizarre collection of traveling companions for the flight. Zvi Rafiah, the Israeli whom Wilson had always believed to be a Mossad agent, sat next to his wife, both of them visibly jumpy about this flight into enemy territory. Charlie's Israeli movie-star friend, Gila Almagor —no less jumpy—added a certain sparkle to the entourage.

The contrast among the passengers was almost comical: the Texas girl filled with innocent excitement at the prospect of seeing Cairo; the three Israelis quaking in their boots. They could barely believe they were on this plane. None of them had dared visit Egypt before, but the congressman wanted his Israeli friends to meet his great Egyptian friend, and he'd assured them safe passage. They would be under the protection of none other than the Egyptian defense minister, Field Marshal Mohammed Abu Ghazala. And the field marshal himself would be at the airport to greet them.

Wilson made it all sound so natural and easy. But by what strange coincidence had this Texas congressman come to be the Egyptian defense minister's intimate friend? The answer begins with Denis Neill, that resourceful Washington lobbyist who had gone to work for Egypt in 1980 after Camp David restored diplomatic relations between Cairo and Washington. Neill had sensed fantastic foreign-aid opportunities for his client and, knowing Wilson's power and his penchant for personalizing causes, he had urged Abu Ghazala to cultivate the congressman. It hadn't taken much of an effort. Abu Ghazala, it turns out, was just Wilson's kind of man: a hero of the 1973 war, a true hater of Communists, and, best of all, a Muslim who drank whiskey, loved women, and was possessed with an endless supply of ethnic jokes from every country in the world. Wilson saw him as just plain fun, and as Neill had shrewdly predicted, a friendship blossomed. As the connection grew, miraculously, Charlie Wilson, the old Israeli commando, added another identity to his portfolio: champion of Egypt's foreign aid as well as Israel's.

There was, of course, more to this story, and Denis Neill is quick to point out that he was merely piggybacking on the preexisting lobbying efforts of General Dynamics. "They're the ones who introduced Charlie to Egypt, because F-16s are the mainstay of Egyptian foreign aid and F-16s are made in Texas." But the essential ingredient that Neill added to the mix was the smiling face of Abu Ghazala. Once the issue of Egyptian aid became personalized in Wilson's mind, there was almost nothing he wouldn't do to get his friend Mohammed his fair share of the U.S. taxpayers' money. Now, whenever Abu Ghazala came to the congressman's office he was treated as Zvi Rafiah's equal, and that was saying a lot.

Rafiah had always acted as if he owned Wilson's office. One of the staffers kept a list of people he needed to lobby. He would use the phones, give projects to the staff, and call on Charlie to intervene whenever he needed him. Abu Ghazala's lobbying style was as industrious as Zvi's, and the office quickly learned to treat his causes as every bit as important. Wilson always delivered for his friend Mohammed.

When the congressman's plane approached the Cairo runway in March 1983, he had just shepherded through a foreign-assistance package for Egypt worth a billion dollars. Mohammed knew the importance of acknowledging such a gesture; and if it meant rolling out a red carpet for a collection of Israelis whom the congressman had brought along for the ride, so be it. When the door to the unmarked plane opened, a military band struck up "The Yellow Rose of Texas." Top brass were everywhere on the runway, cutting salutes to Wilson as if he too were a field marshal. For Carol, her fantasy about Nefertiti was being fulfilled on the spot. "I was received like a queen," she says. "A convoy swept us away."

At the hotel, the congressman signed Carol in as Mrs. Wilson, whispering that it was against the law to sleep in the same room if you weren't married. Carol had a moment of fright in the lobby when she overheard two Arabs from Saudi Arabia talking about a princess who had just been beheaded for sleeping with a man she wasn't married to. As a gesture to calm the worries of his Israeli guests, Mohammed placed armed guards outside the bedrooms of each of the congressman's friends. This only caused Gila to become convinced she had been taken prisoner. But nothing could diminish Carol's thrill when Abu Ghazala told her he was looking forward to her performance that evening.

One might think it would be like carrying coals to Newcastle for a U.S. congressman to bring his own belly dancer to entertain the second most powerful man in Egypt. But Carol Shannon had a surprise in store for him. In Egypt, in those years of renewed fundamentalism, it was dangerous for a belly dancer to perform moves deemed too suggestive by the Muslim hierarchy. To Carol's surprise, belly dancers were not permitted to show their bare arms or their bellies, which had to be covered with fishnet. No pelvic grinds were allowed, not even the floor routine that was the staple of her performance. That night in Cairo, with the nervous Israelis seated at the table and a beaming Charlie Wilson offering encouragement, Carol Shannon decided not to give in to the Muslim fundamentalists, any more than she had to her own Christian extremists back home. "I figured, just arrest me. I'm going to do it my way."

It's not possible to fully appreciate the impact of a belly dancer without being the person for whom the performance is given. In Carol Shannon's routine, the pasha—the great man for whom she performs—sits on a chair in the middle of the floor as the dancer, often with two or three other women writhing next to her, begins to circle.

"Don't breathe," she commanded as she pulled a sword out of a sheath and shimmied up to within inches of the defense minister's face. It was less than two years since the assassination of Egypt's President Sadat, and the minister's bodyguards lurched out of their seats; Wilson snapped at them to back off. Shannon, with her bare arms and undulating, naked belly, was now violating all of the taboos, surrounding the field marshal with her veils and exposing, for his eyes only, her heaving breasts and pelvic grinds.

Abu Ghazala had never before experienced this variation on his country's dance, and he was far too entranced to worry when she moved the sword from near his head and aimed it at his groin. This was the signature moment that this Dallas belly dancer had built into all of her performances. For her it had a special meaning. "It's the only time I have real power over a man," she explains.

But in Cairo that night it was all too much for the bodyguards when she pulled back her sword as if she were about to plunge it straight into the field marshal. They sprang to their feet, which only heightened the impact of her dance, as she laughed boldly and knowingly at the great and powerful man before her.

For a fleeting moment, she had threatened the field marshal's manhood, and now she was returning it with a laugh and a look that seemed to be an invitation. "He was foaming through his eyes," remembers Carol. "Charlie had to tell him, 'You can't touch her.' And he respected that, but he told me he wanted me to return to Egypt as his guest." That night Carol Shannon went to bed convinced that she was in the country of her ancestors.

There was also business to be transacted on this trip, so Charlie arranged for Carol, now accompanied by the Rafiahs, to ride camels into the desert and to visit the pyramids. Meanwhile, at the Defense Ministry he told Abu Ghazala that he needed to be able to do an end run around the timid CIA. Specifically, he wanted to know if Mohammed had any weapons in his arsenal that could make a difference for the Afghans.

Abu Ghazala smiled and declared that Charlie need look no further. Until Sadat changed sides in the late 1970s, Egypt had been a Soviet client state. Its warehouses were filled with Soviet weapons, and its factories were still tooled to manufacture Soviet-licensed material. Egypt was already providing some of the weapons in the CIA's Afghan pipeline, but Abu Ghazala explained that there was no end to the quantity and sophistication of what he could provide. And because of their friendship, he assured Wilson, there would be no problems whatsoever in getting Egypt to go along. No one else need be involved. No Foreign Office discussions would be necessary. If Charlie could get the money, Abu Ghazala would supply everything else to bring down the gunships.

The Texan was now in full throttle, violating diplomatic taboos at every stop: bringing Israeli spies and movie stars to Cairo, commissioning the Israelis to design an anti-aircraft gun for the CIA, and negotiating secret weapons deals with the Egyptian defense minister. He had also made Carol Shannon's life complete. She could go home now knowing that she had danced in Cairo and won the heart of a modern pharaoh.

"Ladies and gentlemen, we will be arriving in Karachi, *Inshallah*, God willing, in four hours. This is the prayer that the prophet, Muhammad, peace be upon him, always recited at the start of any travel . . ."

When Wilson's Pakistan International Airways jet glided to a halt in Karachi, the U.S. embassy's control officer was waiting on the runway. The ambassador had been cabling frenetically, "Please advise re identity of Congressman Wilson's traveling companion." Wilson had been careful not to reveal Carol's identity to the American press corps, which had hounded him in both Texas and Washington. They would have had a field day if they had discovered that the scandal-ridden congressman was headed off on a junket with a belly dancer. (In fact, Carol was so sensitive to Wilson's precarious political position that she never even developed her photographs from the trip.)

In Jerusalem, the congressman had felt so safe in the hands of old friends that he'd told them everything about Carol. In Cairo, he had artfully dealt with the prohibitions against cohabitation by saying Shannon was his wife. But by the time he reached Zia's rigorously Islamic nation, Wilson realized it was not safe to flout local custom. Here it wasn't uncommon to see women dressed in burkas, and Wilson decided not to take any risks. He sternly told Carol to wear lots of clothes, show no skin, and avoid seeming too friendly. The congressman had come to Pakistan on a mission that not even his own government knew about, and he was doing his best to be discreet. He now introduced his belly dancer to everyone as a member of his staff. It was his one gesture to propriety, and amazingly, he thought people would believe him, even though Carol insisted on wearing the skin-tight jumpsuits she had bought specially for the trip.

Wilson's first objective was to visit the victims of the so called "toy bombs," tiny antipersonnel mines that the Soviets were reported to be spreading all over the Afghan countryside—maiming children who unsuspectingly picked them up. And so, for the second time, he flew to Peshawar and visited the International Rescue Committee Hospital, where he once again gave blood for the jihad. He wouldn't allow Carol to come along; he said it was "too sad."

For Charlie Wilson, however, it was always strangely energizing to visit these warriors whose conviction was so great that they never complained. Going to the front did not seem all that dangerous to this self-destructive congressman. On the contrary, losing himself in the presence of these fearless victims, knowing that the Red Army was just over the border, always liberated him from the terrors of his personal life. He was engaging in what psychiatrists call counterphobic behavior—finding one horror to force out the memory of another.

At home he was his own worst enemy. In Pakistan, there was a real enemy just across the mountain range. Throughout the entire Afghan campaign, twice a year or more, Wilson would always visit this hospital. He would do it to renew his fury at the Soviets, almost like Zia's repeated visits to Mecca for inspiration. Wilson's entire imagination and value system as a boy had been shaped by the wonder of the outgunned British fighting on against the Nazis to defend everyone's freedom when there seemed to be no hope. Here in the hospital, the words of his boyhood inspiration, Winston Churchill, would swirl in his consciousness as he moved about the wounded Afghans: "We shall fight on the beaches, we shall fight on the landing grounds, we shall fight in the fields and in the streets, we shall fight in the hills; we shall never surrender."

At such moments, Wilson always experienced an adrenaline rush. To him, the Afghans were not victims. They were almost mythological characters out of a legend, with their long beards, their burning eyes, their refusal to admit pain or fear or doubt. To him, they symbolized the raw essence of freedom and self-determination. His inner voices would tell him that it was his destiny to be the only congressman to come here, to be the only one who could see what these warriors could do to wreak havoc on the Soviets, if they were only given the tools.

In a curious way, Howard Hart came the closest of anyone in a position of power in the U.S. government to sharing Wilson's passion for the Afghan cause. By this time, however, Hart had come to loathe Charlie Wilson, and he was horrified to learn that the congressman was back in his territory.

Hart was careful not to criticize Wilson openly. But with winks and inflections he went to some trouble to make sure his counterpart, Pakistan's chief of intelligence, General Akhtar, knew that Wilson was bad news and that it would be best not to deal with him. Even a decade later, Hart would still be under the impression that Akhtar and Zia shared his dislike and mistrust of the congressman.

Hart's reading of the Pakistanis' reaction to Charlie Wilson may well have been his single greatest intelligence misjudgment. Still, it is hard not to be sympathetic with Howard Hart. By the rules of the Cold War, the only way an American station chief could operate effectively was if he could play with a hidden deck of cards. Otherwise, the CIA might as well have turned its account over to the State Department.

According to this logic, Hart needed to be the source of all secret U.S. information to his Pakistani counterparts. Yet Wilson was running about stripping the bedcovers off his delicate operation, not only suggesting that Hart and the CIA were timid but claiming that he could force them to play a bigger and bolder game. He was, quite simply, wrecking the special advantage that a CIA official like Hart has in dealing with a country like Pakistan.

Hart did not realize all of this at first, but he intuitively understood that there was an alien force moving about in his carefully seeded garden. His disadvantage was that Wilson had a far larger field of vision than he did, larger even than that of the CIA director or the White House, because the bottom line in all government programs is money from Congress. And unlike almost everyone else, Wilson always had a sense of what was possible and what was not in his world of Appropriations.

He was certain of one thing: it would be easy to get more money for this CIA program. In fact, he suspected that he could get his committee to appropriate more money whether Langley wanted it or not. In reality, what he was already plotting with the Pakistanis was far more radical than anything Hart could have imagined.

For example, years later, when Hart was asked if he knew about Wilson's efforts to bring the Israelis into the Afghan war, he dismissed this story out of hand, insisting that the Pakistanis would never have permitted it. "I would have burst into hysterical laughter and locked myself in the bathroom before proposing such a thing," he said. "It was bad enough for Zia to be dealing with the Americans, even secretly. But the Israelis were so beyond the pale that it would have been impossible. You have to understand that the Pakistanis were counting on maintaining the image of holding the high moral ground—of a religious brother helping a religious brother. . . . It's beyond comprehension to have tried to bring the Israelis into it."

Yet right under Hart's nose, Wilson had proposed just such an arrangement, and Zia and his high command had signed on to implement it. Seven years later, Hart still knew nothing about it. He had seen only the grotesque vision of a drunken congressman, stained by a drug scandal and blundering about the Islamic world with a belly dancer in tow. "He was just a terribly egregious fellow," he says. "I found Charlie to be repugnant." As far as Hart was concerned, this was a man no true Muslim could tolerate.

He might have asked why this congressman, so offensive to the Pakistanis, was permitted to take his "secretary" to the Khyber Pass when just a week before Hart himself had been denied permission to go there. In fact, President Zia had exercised his martial-law authority to grant Charlie the right to show his girlfriend the legendary gateway to Afghanistan. For Carol Shannon, sitting queenlike in the convoy's lead vehicle as it made its way up the forbidden mountainous road that spring day, it was yet another fantasy come true.

Five miles out of Peshawar, she was told they were crossing into the tribal zone, where no nation's law prevails. Pakistani law would protect them as long as they remained on this narrow road, but once they were off it, for hundreds of miles the tribes ruled. The convoy took them past giant walled compounds where the Afghan drug lords lived and then into Landi Kotal, the last town before the pass, where the Afridi tribesmen openly pursued their ancient and honorable trade in opium and hashish.

When Rudyard Kipling wrote about the goings-on in these lands, he described the endless war of espionage that the British and Russians waged against each other here during the nineteenth and early twentieth centuries as "the Great Game." Neither imperial power had been willing to permit the other to gain control of this keystone of central Asia, yet neither was willing to resort to all-out war; for most of the time, they had chosen to fight through surrogates.

The Soviets had rewritten the rules of the Great Game on December 27, 1979, when they'd sent their 40th Army in to occupy Afghanistan. At the Khyber Pass that spring day three years later, Carol Shannon watched with wide eyes as her hero made his own move to enter the Great Game. At the barracks of the Khyber Rifles, a Pakistani colonel pointed down to the legendary pass where invading armies since Alexander had entered and exited Afghanistan. Carol could actually hear artillery fire and see puffs of smoke where the Red Army was punishing the resistance. "It was not like a movie. It was real. You could just feel how powerful Russia was."

While Carol was getting her first look at war from the Khyber lookout point, off to the side Wilson was meeting with a group of Zia's generals, urging them to let Israeli technology multiply their tanks' killing power. He told them they would need it if the Red Army ever followed through on its threats and stormed the frontier, or if the Indian army continued its massive buildup. He explained that he wasn't asking them to like the Israelis or to acknowledge any dealings with them. He was simply saying it was good for Pakistan, good for the Afghans, and it could be kept a secret.

For these generals, talking to Charlie Wilson was an altogether new and seductive experience. For once a powerful U.S. official was not harping on what *couldn't* be done or what *shouldn't* be done or suggesting anything other than triumphant outcomes. He was, in an eerie way, the very messenger for whom they'd been longing.

Yaqub Khan, that towering intellectual figure who had served as Zia's commanding officer before becoming his foreign minister, has a theory about why Charlie Wilson had such a large impact on the Pakistan military. He explains, "Armies exist to win on the battlefield, and once defeated they cannot rest until defeat has been avenged." By this logic, the Pakistani army had developed a deep psychological need for victory by the time of the Afghan war. In each of its three wars with India, Pakistan had been overwhelmed by the far larger and more powerful Indian army. Even though its commanders believed that in all respects—from general to rifleman—the Pakistanis were superior soldiers, they had been vastly outgunned. On top of that, the Indians had the bomb. This was one of the reasons the Pakistanis were racing to build a bomb of their own, and it helps explain why they had been so quick to intervene so deeply in the Afghan war. By the time Wilson visited the Khyber Pass, Pakistani officers and special-forces enlisted men had begun slipping into Afghanistan dressed as mujahideen. The Pakistanis were now playing a very dangerous game. But as Yaqub Khan suggests, it was potent therapy for Zia and his military. By becoming the indispensable link between the mujahideen and the West, the Pakistanis were able to lash out at India's superpower patron, the Soviets. Afghanistan's conflict had become the Pakistan army's war of redemption, but not even the generals understood this at the time, says Yaqub Khan.

Khan's theory helps explain why Wilson had such a huge impact on the Pakistani military establishment. They were entranced by his conviction that the mujahideen could win this war. Even more seductive was Wilson's message that they could play this greatest of all games on their terms. As he presented it, they didn't need to be guided by the CIA's caution. If they simply did what they yearned to do anyway and backed the Afghans to the hilt, they could count on the U.S. Congress giving them hundreds of millions to reconstruct their army. Wilson said he could personally guarantee that.

None of this reflected the current thinking of the U.S. government. But most Pakistani military officers had grown up on Hollywood films, and dealing with a larger-than-life Texan like Wilson was a far more fa miliar experience to them than the gray figures from the CIA and the State Department, who always behaved so properly. The Pakistanis tended to suspect that bold characters like the ones they had gotten to know in the movies were the real powers in America.

The only thing that troubled President Zia ul-Haq stemmed from the rumors about the congressman's peculiar lifestyle and his needlessly provocative traveling companion, the woman he lamely called his "secretary." Realizing that he needed a reality check before going any further with this congressman, Zia put in a call to the American he relied on for advice.

There is a thirteen-hour time difference between Pakistan and River Oaks, and the courteous dictator was careful to wait until his honorary consul, Joanne Herring, was awake. "Why has the congressman brought a belly dancer with him to Pakistan?" he asked. Basically, the dictator needed someone to tell him that he was not dealing with a crazy man.

"Well," she recalled, "I said, 'I just don't know what to say about the belly dancer. I haven't met her, but you can depend on Charlie.'" That was enough for Zia. Joanne had saved the day. Shortly thereafter, the president's private secretary called Wilson to set up a dinner at Government House in Rawalpindi. At the president's request, the congressman would come alone at 7:30 P.M. It was to be an all-male affair in Mr. Wilson's honor. Dinner would begin at eight, but President Zia would like to have a few words with the congressman before the others arrived.

The conversation in the president's study that evening dealt with a range of military and political issues. It would have astonished Howard Hart that the military dictator would even discuss such matters with any American official. A very different Charlie Wilson surfaced—sober, impressive, with a bold strategy that caught Zia's attention and enthusiasm.

The congressman began by showing Zia the design for the Charlie Horse and describing the Israelis' T-55 proposal. After establishing what Zia wanted him to convey back to the Israelis, Wilson came right to the point: they both wanted the same thing—to expand the Afghan war—and Charlie had a plan to make it possible. Then, just as he had with Zvi Rafiah and Abu Ghazala, Wilson set about giving Zia the keys to understanding what he could do for Pakistan by explaining how things really worked in the U.S. government.

Zia's problem was that he did not dare permit a radical escalation unless he could be guaranteed huge amounts of U.S. aid, both to build up his army and to demonstrate to the Soviets that the Americans stood ready to protect Pakistan. That could be done, Wilson said, but not by relying on the State Department and the CIA to deliver. The key to opening the foreign-aid spigots and keeping the money flowing, Wilson explained, was one man—someone Zia had never heard of.

"His name is Doc Long," Wilson told the president. "Forget the big-name senators or even the secretary of state; this is the man you have to win over. He's a very strange, if not bizarre, character, but he's the chairman of the Appropriations subcommittee that doles out foreign aid. He's so powerful that he can sabotage any program he doesn't like, or he can be a Daddy Warbucks."

Wilson said he was prepared to bring Doc Long to Islamabad during the next congressional recess. "He's hostile to military dictators, but he's an unpredictable man and he can be won over if the case is made correctly." He explained that Joanne had already agreed to come along to help make the case, but he would not even approach Long unless Zia was prepared to roll out the reddest of carpets.

When Wilson missed his scheduled flight out of Islamabad the next day, Zia arranged to have his presidential plane take the congressman and his companion to Karachi to catch the Pan Am flight home. As would become his custom for all of Charlie's subsequent guests, he included a gift for Carol—a green onyx jewelry case with his personal card inside.

On the plane ride home, Wilson proceeded to get himself very drunk. For Carol Shannon, it was nearing midnight in this fairy tale. The next day she would be back in Fort Worth to resume her difficult life as an exotic belly dancer in a city that doesn't pay a living wage to practitioners of the art. For her Prince Charming, the adjustment was going to be even harder. The congressman might be received as a hero in Jerusalem, Cairo, and Islamabad, but when Wilson landed in the capital, there would be no brass band waiting for him, only a federal posse closing in to destroy him.

CHAPTER 11

THE REBIRTH OF
GUST AVRAKOTOS

Gust Avrakotos had taken to the Afghan program like a duck to water. There was nothing like killing Communists to give him a sense of well-being. He had begun helping his old friend John McGaffin on the Afghan task force the same month in late 1982 that Charlie Wilson first discovered the mujahideen in Peshawar. Just like Wilson, Avrakotos had felt something stir inside himself the moment he met the Afghans. They were killers, and he understood these people. They wanted revenge. Avrakotos wanted revenge. And he liked their food. Lamb. That's what Greeks eat. He even liked the Pakistani military men who were running the mujahideen for the CIA.

It didn't take Avrakotos long to throw himself into this operation that was actually drawing Soviet blood, and he soon made himself indispensable to McGaffin. By the middle of 1983, when he learned that his friend was about to be promoted to another job, Avrakotos, who had made something of a cult out of pretending he didn't care about anything, realized that he desperately wanted McGaffin's job.

By this time, however, he had made a mess of things, and somewhere deep down he knew that at least part of the reason was because he just wouldn't compromise. There was nothing to gain from telling a powerful division chief to go fuck himself—twice. And there was everything to gain from being a bit more diplomatic in the way he dealt with his colleagues. But Avrakotos had no stomach for this game and, in a curious way, felt he shouldn't have to play it.

He had been recruited to be a street fighter for America, and he was proud to offer his brilliant mind and his ruthless skills to the country that his father had taught him to honor above all else. As he saw it, he was providing something through his work at the CIA that America desperately needed. One night, in a moment of introspection, Avrakotos came up with a historical analogy to explain the role he has played over the years in defense of America. "Have you ever heard of the Janissaries?" he began. "The Turks, when they conquered the Greeks and ruled much of the known world, had an elite group known as the Janissaries. Most were Christians, taken from the best families and made into fanatic Muslims. They were the sultan's SS. They were his CIA. Every totalitarian regime, every government, every democracy has its equivalent of the Janissaries, people used for missions that no one else wants to touch."

This was definitely not the sort of analogy a Yalie at the CIA would have offered to explain why he had joined the CIA, but it was typical of Avrakotos to put forth such a grim analogy. It may not be pretty, but to his way of thinking there could be nothing more honorable or important than to serve as an elite guardian of American democracy.

Even before the run-in with Graver, Avrakotos had come to wonder if the CIA had lost its way, and if there was still a place for a modern Janissary. But when he went to the border in Pakistan that first time and saw the Afghans loading camels and mules with Agency munitions, everything leapt back into focus. This was the CIA he had joined back in 1962. The Afghan operation was still small, but as he realized what was already under way and what these tribesmen were prepared to do if given more support, Avrakotos lusted to take over the program.

The CIA is a surprisingly large organization. Although the number of people who work there is classified, it can be said with some authority that there are over twenty thousand employees. When it comes time to fill a major operational post like McGaffin's, however, the CIA suddenly becomes a very small and unforgiving place. The only real contenders come from the Agency's true inner circle, the Clandestine Services, that tiny tribe of handpicked, hard-trained, general case officers to which Avrakotos had been admitted in 1962 in spite of his shabby social credentials. These men and precious few women are the ones who organized the overthrows of governments in Iran and Guatemala for Eisenhower; who tried to assassinate Lumumba and Castro during the Kennedy years; who ran the secret wars in Laos for Johnson; who helped overthrow Allende in Chile for Nixon; and who created the Contra army for Ronald Reagan. They were the ones who even Jimmy Carter had turned to when he'd decided he had to do something about the Soviets in Afghanistan.

The number of these elite case officers at any given time is about 2,500, but even this gives a grossly inflated impression. As one veteran explains, "Out of that twenty-five hundred a certain number are simply burned out or their wives have cancer or they are the walking dead. Maybe five percent are super, twenty percent good, and five percent should be shot. By the time you get to choosing an officer for a major post there may only be two or three serious candidates available."

Technically, Gust Avrakotos was in the running. He now had more experience with the Afghan program than anyone at headquarters. But this crude and defiantly uncompromising spirit was simply not a contender and not only because he had made so many enemies. He just wasn't presentable in the way that Chuck Cogan or Howard Hart or John McGaffin were. And the CIA had powerful reason to be extremely cautious when it came to filling its most visible posts.

In the interest of national security, the CIA is given a responsibility that calls for routinely violating the law in the countries where it operates. In any democracy there is a natural, built-in tension over the mere existence of any such organization; it's one of the reasons the American spy service conceals itself and acts as if it doesn't really exist. No government likes to acknowledge what its spies are doing—particularly when it's dirty business. For that reason, there is an understandable impulse to hire men for this line of work who, when seen in public, present a sober, upright image.

The idea of Gust Avrakotos, the beer salesman from Aliquippa, interacting with a Saudi prince or even a British MI6 chief was scary enough. But even more frightening was the prospect of such a loose cannon representing the Agency in meetings with other branches of the U.S. government—particularly now that the CIA was once again under bitter attack from Congress for its secret war in Nicaragua.

The man chosen instead of Avrakotos to take over John McGaffin's post was Alan Fiers, the politically astute chief of station in Saudi Arabia who years later would burst into the limelight when indicted by the independent counsel for his Iran-Contra dealings. He would become infamous in the CIA as the first Judas to turn in another officer in order to save his own skin.

But back in the early 1980s, he had caught the eye of Ronald Reagan's exuberant CIA director, William Casey, as one of the Agency's leading covert operators. Fiers was known as an outspoken, anti-Communist zealot, a former marine and college football player under Woody Hayes at Ohio State. Casey was looking for bold, risk-taking officers, and Fiers not only passed the enthusiasm test but he had long since adapted perfectly to the Agency's culture. He had a Brooks Brothers appearance and was diplomatic in any setting. All in all, he seemed to be the perfect man for the job.

Since Fiers's Saudi tour was not scheduled to end for several months, an acting chief had to be found, and no one on the Agency's fast track wanted this lame duck slot. The comers all knew that headquarters wouldn't even want a temporary chief to set up liaison relationships with foreign services for fear it would compromise the efforts of the permanent director soon to take over.

John McGaffin, either out of respect for Avrakotos or perhaps in a less than helpful gesture to Alan Fiers, his bureaucratic competitor, urged Gust to take the post. "Who knows, you're good enough that you may be able to keep the job," he said. With that Avrakotos began plotting to push Fiers aside, keenly aware of the unwritten rule in the Directorate of Operations: if you hold a major post for three months as acting chief, it's yours.

Avrakotos's job title was acting chief of the South Asia Operations Group. It was a big job with responsibility for, in addition to Afghanistan, India, Pakistan, Iran, and Sri Lanka. Though he was little more than a caretaker, Avrakotos marched in with none of the caution of a lame duck. He figured that however many months he had in this job, he was going to use it to make a difference in the mujahideen's war.

No one was asking for heroics from the temporary chief. McGaffin had told Avrakotos that the Agency's job was not to think about winning but to make the Soviets bleed. "It wasn't a defeatist attitude," says Avrakotos. "It was positive—making the enemy hemorrhage. But I don't play ball that way. It's either black or white, win or lose. I don't go for a tie."

In Islamabad, Howard Hart viewed Avrakotos's promotion with almost as much disgust as he had Charlie Wilson's entry into the war. "I had known Gust for years and never liked him. He's just a horrible man. . . . Had I stayed on much longer I would have gone to Chuck Cogan and said, It's either him or me."

Talking to Hart about Avrakotos is like hearing an old Yale alumnus bewail the entry of women into the hallowed halls. "Most of us were fourth-generation Dartmouth types," he explained. Hart did, however, acknowledge one area where Avrakotos excelled: whether it was the black market or negotiating with a corrupt Communist official, no one could cut a better deal. And from day one, without asking for a penny more from Congress, he began to dramatically increase the purchasing power of the Agency's weapons budget—just by introducing a bit of competitive shopping.

This is something of a euphemism given the way Avrakotos operates when he goes to buy almost anything. Years later, when he joined Wilson on a congressional fact-finding mission to Baghdad, he hovered all afternoon in the main bazaar, haggling over a prayer rug. Wilson, whose personal style calls for big tipping and a generous manner, was always appalled by his friend's ferocity over the cost of trinkets. On this afternoon in Saddam Hussein's capital, Avrakotos waited until the bazaar had emptied out and then, with an evil stare, presented the merchant with a virtual threat. "This is a fair offer. You either take it or you won't have a single sale tomorrow."

The merchant succumbed, and Avrakotos gloatingly explained to the unhappy congressman that Muslim merchants are superstitious and feel it critical to begin and end the day with a successful sale: "If you know when to move, you can make them feel it's not only bad luck for their business but bad luck for their family as well."

When Avrakotos had started working with McGaffin in 1983, this compulsive bargainer had made the rounds of seven CIA stations, explicitly looking for ways to make an end run around the Agency's procurement specialists. From his point of view, the 450-man Covert Action Procurement and Logistics Division always found the least risky and therefore the most expensive way of buying weapons on the black market. There was an art to getting a good deal with these merchants of death, and it did not include paying whatever price they attached to a weapon or a supply of ammunition.

By the time Avrakotos came into the picture, the procurement operatives were buying just about any Lee-Enfield .303 ammunition available on the world market. The Agency had already slipped more than 100,000 of these World War I–vintage rifles to the Afghans. It takes an enormous amount of ammunition to feed that many rifles, and the procurement people weren't able to get as much as the mujahideen needed.

The bigger problem was the cost. Once the arms merchants caught on to the Agency's appetite for this obsolescent ammunition, the price soared. And to Avrakotos's disgust, his procurement colleagues simply paid it. He looked into the records and found that the Agency's first buys were for three cents a round. "But then it doubled to six, and when they discovered we were coming back every three months it went to twelve cents. When it hit eighteen cents I said, We're being taken."

Through one of his old Greek military buddies, Avrakotos learned of forty million rounds stored in a Yugoslav mushroom cave, which represented almost half of what Howard Hart needed to fill his annual budget for the mujahideen that year. It was a perfect setup. The Yugoslav army wanted money and didn't like Russians; the farmers wanted their caves back so they could grow mushrooms; and all the Agency had to do was provide phony end-user certificates so that it would look as if the ammo was going to someone other than the Americans. Instead of eighteen cents a round, Gust was able to buy the stash for seven cents a round. It was a mini coup.

"The Office of Logistics didn't like this deal because it was embarrassing," remembers Avrakotos, "but I never cut them off completely, because they have ways of getting back at you. So I'd throw a little their way and say, 'Okay, we're getting .303 rounds for seven cents, let's see what you can do.'"

Avrakotos now began asking his friends at stations around the world to work their military sources to find out what else was available. "It's not what spies usually do, but I figured we have the contacts and who is better at finding what's available."

It was during this time that he supervised a nerve-racking operation centered on a Polish general ready to sell Soviet SA-7 surface-to-air missiles to the Americans. This called for lifting these tightly guarded weapons from right under the nose of the Red Army, which was then more or less occupying Poland. "My hair turned white on this operation because of the risks we were taking," remembers Avrakotos.

If the guerrillas could acquire Soviet SA-7s, they could achieve a breakthrough in their war; the weapon might enable them to bring down the murderous Hind helicopter. The fear at Langley, however, was that the general might be part of a KGB sting. That was the year that Ronald Reagan branded the Soviet Union "the Evil Empire." It was the height of the Cold War, and high-ranking Polish, East German, and Czech military men were all assumed to be either loyal Communists or under the control of those who were. And beyond that, the general's demands were strange.

He had signed off on a particularly high-risk operation. He would remove the missiles from their containers, put stones in their place, and sneak the SA-7s out of the country under false labels. In return, he wanted money, but more important, he told his CIA contact, he wanted to know if the Agency would put up a tombstone in Quebec in honor of his grandfather.

The general's explanation was that the old man had gone to Canada in the 1930s when he couldn't find work in Poland. He had sent money home to take care of his family, and when he returned years later he had filled his grandson, the future general, with a sense of the wonder of Canada and a hatred for what the Communists had done to enslave Poland.

To many this might sound a bit like those Cold War stories that used to appear in the *Reader's Digest*, so corny that it's suspect. But to Avrakotos, that was the way things worked in the real world. His own father had gone to America to find a job and had sent money to support his family back in Greece, just like the general's grandfather. The story had a plausible ring to it, particularly after Gust had the Canadian service do a check confirming that the grandfather had once lived in Quebec.

There were also other things that made Avrakotos buy the general's story. He could remember, as if it were yesterday, those "captive nation" rallies he had attended as a boy and all those drunken nights at the political clubs in Aliquippa listening to the Polacks swear to liberate their motherland. It made perfect sense to Avrakotos that there could be a general in Warsaw who wanted nothing more than to stick it to the Red Army and to honor his grandfather.

In his typical compulsion to reduce human truths to a sexual analogy, Avrakotos explains, "You just have to find out what a person has a hard-on for and give it to them." So often money was not the determining factor. What Avrakotos knew from so many experiences was that you can never underestimate the cravings of the human spirit.

In the small Canadian town in the Lake Superior region, it never occurred to the local stonemason that there was anything unusual about the request from the innocent American to chisel a tombstone for his Polish grandfather. A plot in a pretty cemetery was chosen, and once the tomb-stone was erected, the bereaved American snapped two rolls of film with his thirty-five-millimeter Nikon. By the time Gust's special courier had rushed them to Warsaw, the deal was done. Soon the Soviet SA-7s were in the CIA's pipeline on their way to Afghanistan.

But Avrakotos was not content to limit his role to haggling over the cost of war material. As he saw it, now that he was acting chief, his task was to find ever more ingenious ways to kill and maim Soviets. And he knew just whom to turn to for help.

Kutsher's Country Club sits in the heart of the Catskill Mountains two and a half hours from New York City, in what Charlie Wilson affectionately calls "the Hebrew Himalayas." Kutsher's is a high-priced family hotel, and every Yom Kippur holiday throughout the nine years of the Afghan war, Art Alper made it a point to spend time there with his aging father.

The conversation at the dinner table at Kutsher's in the fall of 1983 was hardly scintillating. Two old ladies who had taken a shine to the CIA man's father always seemed to find seats at the Alpers' table. The women didn't pay much attention to the fifty-eight-year-old "youngster" with the yarmulke and the potbelly and the ample jowls. And anyone looking at this table would have assumed that the younger Alper was about as bor-ing a dinner companion as could be imagined.

But Art Alper was a man who made his living surprising people, and his head was alive that fall with the deadly assignments he was beginning to work on for Avrakotos. For thirty years he had specialized in the crea-tion of nasty and often lethal devices. His division, with its joyless bureau-cratic title, the Office of Technical Services, had given Alper the best window in the business on the full range of covert operations the Agency had pursued over the years.

When the Agency wanted a chemical to make Castro's beard fall out or a poison pen to assassinate him, Alper's colleagues in the Office of Technical Services got the call. Almost any time the CIA undertook a daring or dangerous operation, it invariably required some devilish input from the OTS.

Despite Alper's nondescript, grandfatherly appearance, he was an ad-venturer, a man with an eye for the ladies, a lust for travel, and a love for his work. In the 1960s, this eminently forgettable-looking man had been given the assignment to direct the covert action division of the CIA's Office of Technical Services. He spent a year in Laos helping run the secret war and three years in Vietnam with thirteen devilish tinkerers serving under him at the old Saigon embassy. There he was given carte blanche to play dirty with the Vietcong. One of his favorite tactics was to secrete both a homing device and Semtex plastique into typewriters offered for sale at shops the Vietcong were known to frequent. Alper was then able to follow the typewriter by its signal and identify the enemy nest. When ready, this American with the kindly face would detonate the Semtex charge with an electronic signal, striking a blow for the war effort.

Alper loved this work. But then the war ended and the Church Committee investigations all but wiped out his beloved specialty. By the time the Soviets invaded Afghanistan, the CIA no longer had a stable of deadly tinkerers to call on. Not only had many of the old covert operators been fired, but the storehouse of ingenious gadgets to support special operations was simply not there anymore.

The task to rebuild the inventory was given to Alper, who began roaming the world in search of deadly hardware, dividing his fieldwork between Central America and Afghanistan. At that point the Reagan administration was focusing its energies and hopes on the Contra war, where it believed victory was possible; Afghanistan was deemed a lost cause. So in 1983, Art Alper found himself on the Nicaraguan-Honduran border at the vast CIA Contra base camp known as Las Vegas, directing a most unusual operation.

Alper felt it was critical to do more than just support the CIA's Contra army. Out to win the hearts and minds of the Nicaraguan people, he sold the Agency on a plan that called for floating huge propaganda-stuffed helium balloons into Nicaragua. For years the Agency had tried to convert the Communist Chinese by bombarding Red China with such propaganda balloons launched from Taiwan. For the Nicaraguan operation, Alper added his own grandfatherly touch by including little packets of candy, soap, toilet paper, toys, and toothbrushes in the aerial bombardments.

Every Sunday, Alper would fly from Washington to Tegucigalpa. At four A.M. Monday morning, he would be at the border with his helium pump, ready to float his propaganda offensive into the morning air currents. Alper took particular pride in this effort. It filled him with a sense of

American virtue, knowing that his little creations would soon be delivering their message of hope into the hands of honest peasants eager for a non-Communist alternative.

But then the CIA got caught mining the harbors of Nicaragua, and when John McMahon, the Agency's cautious deputy director, reviewed the Nicaraguan operations, he grounded Alper's balloons. Congress had just passed the Boland Amendment, making it illegal for the CIA to do anything that might be aimed at overthrowing the Sandinista government. McMahon concluded that the balloon offensive might be construed as a violation.

For Alper, the game was up in Central America. The only place left for the kind of vigorous anti-Communist guerrilla warfare he loved was Afghanistan, especially now that Avrakotos was taking over the program.

Art Alper was prey to an occupational hazard common among many of the CIA's specialists: he believed that only his specialty offered the key to success. The Agency's mine expert, for example, had the same conceit, and by all accounts was virtually psychotic in pushing his belief that mines alone could inflict maximum pain to the occupying army. To Alper, sabotage via small, portable devices that disable, surprise, and kill was the answer.

When he first reviewed the mujahideen's tactics he spotted all kinds of ways to make a difference. Ambushing was the meat and potatoes of the Afghan's strategy, but their antique approach reminded Alper of old cowboy movies he had seen as a child: an Afghan standing up in the hills with a plunger connected to an explosive. The guerrilla in his turban or Chitrali hat would wait for the tank to get to what he hoped was just the right spot before making the connection to drop and blow it up.*

The OTS technicians proposed as an alternative a small, black device about the size of a Walkman and not much heavier. Alper still has a

---

*In those days it was a very rare event when the rebels could stop a tank. So rare that Alper says a picture of a downed Soviet tank was received at Langley in 1983 with almost as much excitement as the later pictures of helicopters brought down by Stingers. The interview was conducted the day after the San Francisco earthquake, and Alper said the tank looked just like one of the cars stranded on the Bay Bridge. The main difference was the context, in which the mujahideen posed triumphantly with gleeful grins for the camera, which revealed a Russian dangling from the turret with his genitals removed. "It looked like a beached whale," Alper says, "and the poor bastards had to get out of the tanks once they were trapped."

few of these "blasting boxes" on a shelf in his consulting-firm office just outside Washington. Their most attractive feature, he explains, is that they are very light and user-friendly. Whereas a mujahid would have to struggle to carry a bulky wood box and plunger up and down the mountains, these six-ounce devices could be hung from a belt and used ten times or more before requiring a change of batteries.

Alper had discovered this blasting device for sale in Europe for $113. After taking it apart, he'd decided that he could have it made in the United States for about $90. It would look exactly like the European model, which was important in those days when American involvement had to be concealed. Even better from Alper's perspective, since he is a fierce "buy American" man, it would put some Americans to work. "Remember," he explained with genuine conviction years later, "we were just coming out of the Carter years and there was great unemployment."

Commissioning a U.S. company to arm the mujahideen called for breaking the prohibition on American-made weapons. But in Avrakotos Alper found a risk-taking, rule-breaking boss who figured that even if the Soviets did capture some of these little black boxes, they would never be able to point the finger at the CIA. "And what was the KGB going to do even if they found out—sue us?"

Avrakotos says Alper was something of a bureaucratic misfit, somewhat adrift in the Agency, until he put the technical expert to work. "He's fat, and people passed him over. He was only a GS-14. Some of his ideas were off the wall, and we'd have knock-down, drag-out fights. But two out of ten of Art's ideas were great." Gust also maintains that some of the work Alper ended up doing on the Afghan program advanced the tenets of modern conventional warfare.

Bear in mind that Avrakotos was talking here about Alper's effort to design ever more lethal ways of killing Russians. "He'd sit down with the Egyptians and design some new plastic device that the Soviet mine detectors couldn't detect. When the Russians made plastic-mine detectors, we made screaming meemies. We'd put steel rods on the side of a hill and make the limpet mines look like stones covered with mud. It was all point-counterpoint, and Art always knew the counter to the counter and had started to build it. Here was this fifty-eight-year-old guy calling me at eleven o'clock on a Sunday night saying, 'Hey, I've got a great idea. Can I come over?' You can't get that enthusiasm out of a fourteen-year-old."

Like most of the CIA veterans who got caught up in this secret war, Alper loved doing to the Soviets in Afghanistan what they had done to the Americans in Vietnam. One of his most satisfying moments came right at the beginning of his work with Avrakotos. When the mujahideen captured a collection of Soviet 122mm rockets, the fuses wouldn't work and no one knew what to do with them. But Alper knew this terror weapon well from his Vietnam days. One of the Soviet 122s that the Vietcong fired from the jungle had hit next to Alper's office, and the concussion had been so great that it had hurled the desks and safes all over his room. He loved the idea of turning some of those Soviet rockets back where they came from.

After a bit of tinkering, Alper declared that he could make them work just so long as he was allowed to use American fuses, which he would attach with his own specially tooled thread adapters. Again that meant breaking the prohibition on *any* American-made items, even components. "Art's the type of nice little Jewish boy who always checks with his mother, and since he didn't have his mother he always checked with me," recalls Avrakotos, who immediately signed off without consulting the lawyers. "If I asked them they would have jerked off for three months trying to figure out why we couldn't do it."

There weren't all that many 122s, but the mujahideen reacted with childlike delight when they fired these magnificent noisemakers into Kabul. It was a morale booster for the freedom fighters to be terrorizing the infidel in his own lair.

Avrakotos was now working to toughen the Agency's tactics, but by later standards the war he was presiding over in 1983 was remarkably tame. Congress had appropriated only $15 million for the Afghans that year, concealed in an air force appropriation. The Saudis, convinced that the Soviets would come after them next if they were not stopped in Afghanistan, had agreed to match the U.S. commitment to the mujahideen dollar for dollar and to permit the CIA to direct the program.

This still meant only $30 million to run a guerrilla war twelve thousand miles away, against a superpower then able to intimidate every nation in the world. Thirty million dollars is what two F-15 fighter jets cost, or six Black Hawk helicopters.

It was not just insufficient funding, however, that Avrakotos saw as the central problem. It was bureaucratic cowardice. He talks about a

"Nuremberg syndrome" loose in the upper echelons of the bureaucracy, where officers like Chuck Cogan lived in terror of another congressional investigation or of being hauled up by a special prosecutor. "By the time the lawyers were finished talking to the 'Chucks' of the Agency," he says, "we couldn't do anything but play with our dicks because the lawyers worried that our weapons would be perceived as terrorist devices, or worse, as assassination devices."*

Later, when Avrakotos took over the Afghan program, he dealt with this problem by introducing an Orwellian change in the language he directed his staff to adopt whenever describing weapons or operations in the Afghan program. "These aren't terrorist devices or assassination techniques," he would inform his staff. "Henceforth these are *individual defensive devices.*" Sniper rifles were finally shipped out to the mujahideen, but only after Gust renamed them: "long-range, night-vision devices with scopes." Once, when the Islamabad station sent a cable describing a lethal tactic being introduced, Avrakotos shot back a return communiqué saying that the cable had been garbled and adding, "Please do not send anything more on this subject ever again."

Avrakotos talks about the lawyers during these days almost as if they were predators patrolling the halls of Langley: "Even *Saturday Night Live* couldn't do justice to the way the lawyers made us deal with Afghanistan." It got so bad, he says, that when he planned to begin planting anti-Soviet stories in the European press, an assistant secretary of state objected, claiming that the propaganda might bounce back and mislead Americans, in which case the Agency would be in violation of congressional laws that prohibit the CIA from operating inside the United States. Soon groups of State Department lawyers and CIA lawyers were caught up in endless

---

*What this meant in a practical sense is that the lawyers ruled that the Agency couldn't provide the Afghans with sniper rifles or, for that matter, with satellite target studies if they focused on an individual. As extreme as it might sound, they argued that it might constitute a violation of the 1977 congressional ban on any assassination plotting. It didn't matter that the Agency was dispensing hundreds of thousand of assault rifles, machine guns, mines, rockets, mortars, and RPGs for the Afghans to use in their killing war with the Soviets—in all, some ten thousand tons of weapons and ordinance in 1983 alone, according to the Pakistan intelligence officer directing the combat activities of the mujahideen. The lawyers dug in their heels and held to their strict interpretation of the law.

meetings debating whether the possibilities of this blowback were strong enough to deny the operation.

Avrakotos's solution to this internal sabotage was to enlist an old CIA friend—"a New York Jew, a lawyer who had balls"—to join the Afghan task force as "my consigliere." Larry Penn was another of those nondescript, slightly overweight middle-aged men you would never notice in an airport. Technically he was the task force operations officer. But Avrakotos says he deployed Penn regularly to design methods of countering the Agency's other lawyers.

Penn would constantly warn Avrakotos that he was going to end up in the slammer. But the balding, bug-eyed consigliere happily carried out the tasks Avrakotos gave him. When sensitive initiatives were being proposed and lawyers were expected at an Agency meeting, Avrakotos would send Penn to represent him. The consigliere's instructions were to employ euphemisms and to drone on with boring double-talk so long that he would make the entire operation seem tedious.

As Avrakotos saw it, he almost had to run a covert operation inside the Agency to get things going out in the field. But he wasn't quite as radical as he might appear.* The main reason for his boldness with the lawyers was that he interpreted the Presidential Findings differently than they did.

When Avrakotos talks today about the findings Jimmy Carter signed shortly after the Russians invaded, he makes them sound almost as if they were sacred documents. He says they are far and away the most comprehensive lethal findings ever commissioned, the equivalent of a presidential declaration of war. What makes them doubly unusual is that they were authored by that ultimate liberal and supposed critic of CIA covert operations, Jimmy Carter. Avrakotos, however, also insists that Carter had no idea he was signing such a blank check. And this would appear to be a reasonable conclusion, given the fact that ultimately the findings authorized operations that helped kill as many as 25,000 Soviet soldiers.†

---

*The problem was that the Agency was operating on a small budget in the beginning and the procurement office could make buys only when they had funds, thus playing into the hands of the suppliers, who sensed the growing appetite and a limited supply.

†For years Russia put the Afghan death toll at 13,000. The most recent official tally, based on previously classified files, puts the number at over 28,000.

Ironically, Avrakotos says his predecessor, who authored those find-ings for Carter to sign, also had no intention of having them used for an all-out killing war. "They were," he says, "quite literally written to pro-vide the Agency with an insurance policy. My predecessor wrote it that way because he didn't want to be left there with his dick hanging out if Carter forced him and the CIA to do stupid, counterproductive, dirty tricks in Af-ghanistan and Congress decided to investigate. He did it to cover his ass and his troops from Watergate-type, Nuremberg-type, Church-type attacks, and this guy is smart and he had the balls to do it."

Avrakotos was at the helm when most of the weapons that did the killing were funneled to the Afghans, and he says he always kept those Carter findings in his desk. "And I told everyone with me to make sure they were always there and to take copies whenever we left. They are the orders of the president of the United States until rescinded. I told our law-yers [meaning Larry Penn] never to ask for a clarification, never to ask if the findings authorized what they authorized. When the war winds down, I thought, maybe we would have need for them again. I'd hide them and keep them, but then I'm a dinosaur. To get those four findings again would take a miracle."

It's easy to identify with Avrakotos's frustration. For the first time in the Cold War, the CIA was operating with Presidential Findings that au-thorized the CIA to mount operations to kill Soviet soldiers in Afghani-stan. Given that fact, it made little sense to claim that it was somehow legitimate to provide guerrillas with hundreds of thousands of AK-47s, tens of thousands of heavy machine guns, land mines by the thousands, not to mention millions of rounds of ammunition, all given with the explicit hope that they would be used to kill Russian soldiers—and then at the same time to claim that providing the Afghans with sniper rifles would somehow violate presidential bans on assassination plotting.

But then, the lawyers had a different agenda than Avrakotos. They were trying to protect the Central Intelligence Agency, and they had a vivid memory of what happens in Washington when the political winds start shifting. Their job was to identify the most unfair interpretation anyone could possibly put on a covert operation. And if it could be somehow con-strued as prosecutable, no matter how absurd, they took the position that the Agency should back off.

Throughout his Afghan tour, Avrakotos did things on a regular basis that could have gotten him fired had anyone chosen to barge into his arena with an eye toward prosecuting him. But then Avrakotos was not just lucky. He was brutally worldly wise, keenly aware of the internal risks he was taking. And so he always made it difficult for anyone to get him, should they try.

He left no paper trail. He always surrounded himself with like-minded outcasts who understood and approved of his code of conduct. Above all, he became a master manipulator of the system, capable, by sheer bureaucratic skill, to take the Agency into areas others would not have thought possible.

As Avrakotos is the first to acknowledge, however, none of the astonishing things that he was able to do later to transform the Afghan war would have been possible had it not been for Charlie Wilson. But back in the summer of 1983, Wilson didn't look like anyone's champion. In fact he looked like a sorry old drunk who was about to be knocked off by his own government.

CHAPTER 12

Ronald Reagan and Charlie Wilson

THE UNITED STATES
V. CHARLES WILSON

Wilson's drug lawyer, Stuart Pierson, is a good-looking, virile man with enormous self-confidence. As he approached Charlie Wilson's office in early 1983, about the last thing on his mind was the war in Afghanistan. He was a specialist in white-collar crime, and he was on a mission to rescue yet another endangered politician.

Such lawyers are accustomed to feeling powerful as they move through the wreckage of great men's lives. But when Pierson walked into the congressman's office, past the gorgeous receptionists, and shook hands with the charismatic Texan, he was keenly aware of the physical differ-ence between himself and his new client.

Pierson is a short man, and he actually experienced a curious shrink-ing sensation as he dropped several inches into the cushions of the huge hand-tooled and leather-upholstered chairs that Wilson kept in front of his desk. It was ridiculous, but it quickly seemed apparent that Wilson was trying to put him in his place. The congressman remained on his feet, strut-ting about the room, all six foot, four inches of him, talking cheerily in that booming Texas voice, as if Pierson had dropped by for nothing more than a social visit.

Pierson, however, sensed danger in the congressman's aggressive state of denial and decided he had better introduce an element of reality. When Wilson finally offered him an opening by asking, "What's the worst that can happen to me?" Pierson devastated him with his answer: "It's not just your political career you can lose, Charlie. You could go to jail over this."

Pierson went on matter-of-factly to explain that the FBI agents were not stupid, and that they would assume that Wilson was deeply involved in a distribution network on the Hill: "A congressman who is allegedly using cocaine has to get it from someone safe. So the natural assumption of any prosecutor is that there has to be a sophisticated network."

In a practical sense, said Pierson, what that meant is that every employee, friend, and drinking buddy of Wilson's would be visited by federal agents. Anyone could turn on him, for real or imagined crimes. "This is not just about Liz Wickersham's testimony," he said. "There are other people in your office who could hurt you." Pierson's physical stature was suddenly enhanced as the shaken Wilson realized that his fate might well rest in this man's hands.

The first thing any criminal-defense attorney does upon taking a case is to impose a damage-control mechanism to prevent the clients from getting into more trouble. But even before this meeting, Pierson had felt a particular urgency. He had been studying Wilson as a psychoanalyst might his patient, and he figured that the congressman's performance to date had been just about as bad as it could be. When Brian Ross of NBC had cornered him with his camera crew, Wilson had made the mistake of looking like a burglar caught in the beam of a cop's flashlight, turning on his heels and fleeing back into his hotel room.

What had alarmed Pierson even more was how Wilson had compounded the disaster by subsequently inviting Ross into his room for an off-the-record talk, in some kind of crazed belief that he could charm his way out of his predicament. Pierson couldn't quite understand why, after four terms in Congress and after weaving his way through so many scandals, Charlie had not simply beamed confidently at the reporter, like Ronald Reagan always did, and kept moving. Ross's story might not even have made the evening news had Wilson handled himself like a pro.

As far as Pierson was concerned, this client was a walking time bomb. If he was to have any chance, Wilson would have to be fenced in, and Pierson proceeded to read him the riot act. Absolutely no talking to the press. Perhaps even more important, he stressed the danger of talking to Liz Wickersham. Everything depended on her. The feds were pressuring her to testify that the congressman had been snorting cocaine. He could end up with an obstruction-of-justice charge for almost anything he said to her. The congressman was all ears now, and Pierson was not about to miss

the opportunity to drive home just how grave the situation was. He warned
Charlie that it was highly likely that Justice would bug his phones.

This was particularly terrifying news to Wilson, who suddenly remembered Chuck Cogan's visit to his office just a few weeks earlier. Security
officials had told him how easy it would be for the KGB to listen in on everything Wilson was saying merely by casting a beam onto his window.

Soon after Pierson's warning, window washers suddenly appeared
outside the congressman's window. The staff informed him that furniture
cleaners had arrived uninvited. The whole office was reduced to near paranoia as Wilson's intake of Scotch began assuming alarming proportions. It
was at this point that the depression kicked in, so badly that some of the
people around Wilson began to worry that he might kill himself. Wilson
says he never even considered taking such an action. But his lawyer, Stuart
Pierson, fearing that he had perhaps gone too far in arousing his client's
fears, began a massive effort to reassure Charlie. "I almost destroyed my
liver on that case," he remembered years later. "It was hard not to drink
with Charlie because I quickly developed a lot of affection for him, and in
any of these investigations, you have to provide comfort as well as legal
advice." The lawyer remembers those drinking and therapy sessions today
almost with disbelief. Once, in the congressman's office, he'd watched with
amazement as Wilson filled a four-inch tumbler with ice and Scotch. Over
the course of an hour and a half, Wilson downed a total of four of these
sledgehammers.

At first Pierson thought the alcohol was necessary—a tranquilizer
for his unstable client. But then he began to worry that Wilson was in such
a dangerous state of mind that he needed round-the-clock watching. That's
when Pierson discovered the loyalty of Charlie's friends, who in the end
saved the day.

The first to impress Pierson were the Angels, who quietly took over
the office, shielding Charlie from the media, doing his work for him, com-
forting him, and—best of all, from Pierson's point of view—keeping their
mouths shut. So did all of Charlie's friends, starting with the most vulnerable of all, Liz Wickersham, who spoiled everything for the prosecutors
by holding the line.

Another friend with more guilty knowledge than perhaps anyone,
the famous Texas author Larry King, also found himself being grilled about
Charlie's habits. King had been a wild, two-fisted drinker who had spent

many years getting into all sorts of trouble carousing with Charlie, particularly during the time Justice was interested in. King had almost joined Wilson as an investor in Paul Brown's plan to produce a soap opera with Liz Wickersham as its star.

On the occasion of his seventh year in AA, and his seventh year of being sober, King stopped to recall his answer to the authorities who wanted to know about Charlie. "I'd like to help you," he had told the investigators, "but just after the period in question I went into rehabilitation, and everything from that time frame is a blank."

It had to have been grotesquely frustrating for the feds, who ran into one stone wall after another as they deposed the congressman's conveniently forgetful staff and friends. But then that summer they got lucky. The dragnet that had been thrown out to find the limousine driver who had taken Charlie and Liz and Paul Brown back from the airport after the Las Vegas weekend came up with its man.

One can only imagine the excitement in the halls of the Justice Department as the investigators prepared to interrogate the driver, twenty-year-old Bill Cheshire. The young man told them he remembered the congressman well and said he would be happy to give them a deposition. Now all Justice had to do to put Wilson into a concrete cell was to get Cheshire to confirm what Brown had already told them—that the Texas congressman had snorted cocaine in the back seat of the limousine.

While the authorities were busy laying their traps for Wilson, the congressman was busy projecting himself publicly as a man without a care in the world. For his fiftieth birthday that June he threw a party for himself on a huge boat that motored up the Potomac. When police helicopters buzzed the party ship repeatedly, flashing blinding spotlights on the deck, the startled guests assumed that the feds were checking Charlie's party for illicit activity. No, *Texas Monthly* magazine reported, the police in the copters were not looking for drugs; they just wanted to "check out the female duo performing Motown songs."

Wilson followed this up the next month with a Fourth of July extravaganza in honor of the woman he now claimed was his one true love. The invitation read, "Charlie Wilson invites you to a birthday party for Uncle Sam and his Yankee Doodle Sweetheart, Joanne Herring." Everyone had a grand, drunken evening watching the fireworks from his condominium terrace, unquestionably the best seat in the capital.

All of this merrymaking, however, was a smoke screen concealing a desperate man. Wilson's office was being held together those days only by the extraordinary efforts of the highly competent and protective Angels and his paternal administrative assistant, Charles Simpson. They made it possible for Wilson to maintain the appearance of normality. But his depressions were deepening. And as the feds closed in on him that summer, Pierson came to believe that the main drug that soothed Wilson's nerves and kept him whole was Afghanistan. It was the only thing that allowed him to function as a man of honor on the Hill, the only thing, perhaps, that made him continue to believe that he had some self-worth. "If he hadn't had Afghanistan, I think he probably would have jumped," Pierson says.

To Pierson, Wilson had seemed almost a different man after returning from Pakistan. He had immediately called a press conference to denounce the Russian's use of "toy bombs." At that time the press hadn't been paying particular attention to the Soviets' brutality, but they gave Charlie a lot of play. In spite of his drug troubles, he had managed to seize the high ground, and for a moment, at least, he was the public prosecutor, indicting the Soviets for their crimes.

This aggressive posture carried over into Wilson's dealings with the CIA as well, where, no matter what Chuck Cogan and the others at Langley might have thought about the endangered congressman, they always went to his office when summoned to fill him in on the latest war developments and listen stoically to his demands that they do more.

It was actually somewhat of a miracle that Wilson was able to maneuver so effectively during this time. To the mujahideen, who flocked to his office whenever they came to Washington, Wilson was never anything but a buoyant presence, always leaving them with a sense that more help was on the way and that he personally guaranteed it.

When General Ajaz Azim, the new Pakistani ambassador to Washington, came to call, Wilson assumed the role of his political counselor, furnishing him with explicit strategies for their common campaign to generate new funds for the Afghan struggle. The foreign minister, Yaqub Kahn, was another regular who came to seek Wilson's help. And there were ongoing communications with Zia himself, as well as with the Israelis over the back channel and the tank-upgrade proposals.

That was all part of what held Wilson together that summer of 1983—his plan to force the CIA and the Reagan administration to radically escalate the war in Afghanistan. As he had told Zia in April, the one obstacle that had to be overcome was Doc Long. He had to be converted, or at least neutralized.

As chairman of the House Appropriations subcommittee on government operations, Clarence D. Long presided over the twelve men who doled out the State Department's entire budget as well as *all* foreign military and economic assistance. Few outside the U.S. government had ever heard of him, but Chairman Long was one of the barons of the feudal world that is the U.S. Congress, and he made sure that everyone who came before his Appropriations subcommittee understood the power he held over them. He even had what he called his "golden rule" inscribed on a plaque and hung in the hearing room, to make sure there was no confusion over who was in control. It read, "Them that has the gold makes the rules."

As chairman, Long was so powerful that no secretary of state or U.S. official, no matter how high the post, could afford to alienate him. He was called Doc Long because he had a doctoral degree in economics from Princeton and had once been a college professor. He was also easily one of the strangest and most cantankerous members of Congress—so crazy in appearance that Charlie Wilson describes him as being a dead ringer for the bug-eyed crazed scientist and time traveler in the movie *Back to the Future.*

As the chairman's longtime aide Jeff Nelson explained, "It was always an ordeal for anyone to approach the chairman for anything: Doc had this horrible habit of spitting in the halls. He'd spit as we were walking, often hitting the baseboards on the wall. I remember the capital police looking the other way and just rolling their eyes." Nelson told of one meeting when Doc summoned the secretary of defense, Caspar Weinberger, and much of his high command to his office, where he slowly and sloppily munched on a tuna-fish sandwich while they briefed him. It was an ugly way of making a point, but Doc liked to remind the higher-ups who wrote out their checks.

He was strange in the extreme, but highly intelligent and dangerous to anyone who crossed him. Once staffers had to pry apart Doc and David Obey, the subcommittee's second ranking member, who were literally attempting to strangle each other.

On the face of it, Wilson had no real reason to think he could win over Doc Long. To begin with, Doc was an ardent supporter of Israel and an equally ardent foe of human-rights violators. For that reason, he didn't like anything about Zia. Jeff Nelson remembers Long regularly referring to the Pakistan dictator as "that greaseball." He considered Zia's Islamic program to be a basic violation of human rights, and he was enraged at the idea of Zia building an Islamic bomb; he saw it as a threat to Israel, and on that subject he was uncompromising. Nelson recalled his astonishment at a hearing when Long warned, "We must be wary about the reproductive rate of Muslims. It's much faster than Jews."

Wilson, however, was not one to be intimidated by Doc's theatrics. For one thing, he knew that the chairman liked him. They were both staunch supporters of Israel as well as old-fashioned anti-Communists. Beyond that, Charlie knew that Doc had a weakness that could be exploited: he happened to be extraordinarily responsive to flattery. Charlie had watched how easily the Israelis had seduced him, so effectively that Long's aide had concluded that the main reason Doc had become so passionate about Israel was simply because the Israelis were so wildly attentive to him.

In the summer of 1983, Wilson first had to find a way to get his foot in the door with Doc Long. That's where Wilson's peculiar genius as a master of unconventional strategy kicked in. Doc had a problem: he liked junkets. More importantly, the chairman had developed a taste for grandiose junketing. In particular, he liked to travel to Europe, and he liked to go better than first class on specially detailed air force jets. Long's problem that summer was that he couldn't convince enough congressmen from his committee to go with him to justify the cost of the government plane. The members didn't say so openly, but Charlie knew the reason: no matter how grand the trip, they couldn't bear the thought of having to spend any time at all with this rather disgusting and hopelessly eccentric tyrant.

In one of those negotiations that Wilson is a master at putting together, the congressman cut an explicit deal with his chairman. He would convince enough of his colleagues to go if Doc would include a trip to Pakistan to give General Zia and the Afghans a hearing.

It was an offer Doc could not refuse, and Charlie negotiated it so skillfully that Long didn't feel in the least offended. He even listened to Charlie's argument that Zia was not only a nice man when you got to know him but an invaluable ally, absolutely critical to the mujahideen's war.

After agreeing to put Pakistan on the itinerary, the chairman directed his staff to have the CIA send someone to brief him on Afghanistan and

Zia's importance to the war effort. Wilson welcomed this initiative, until he looked up to find his least favorite CIA man, Chuck Cogan, sweeping into the hearing room with his retinue. True to form, Cogan sat down in the witness seat in an imperial manner. It was to be a classified briefing—no press, no public—but to Wilson's growing alarm, the CIA's Near East division chief proceeded to stonewall the chairman. He actually refused to tell him anything whatsoever about the Afghan operation or about Pakistan's role in supporting it, answering quite reasonable queries with "I can't share that information."

In fairness to Cogan, it can be said that he was playing the game according to the rules. In his mind, Doc Long was just another congressman sticking his nose where it didn't belong. Long wasn't on any of the committees cleared for CIA briefings. It didn't occur to this mandarin of the CIA that it would be prudent to at least accord the chairman the same respect that was second nature to secretaries of state and defense when they approached Doc's throne. Nor did it occur to Cogan to think that this peculiar old man, who did not control the CIA's budget, could hurt him or his Agency.

Long's reaction to Cogan startled even Wilson, who had witnessed a number of the chairman's more excited tirades before. The former economics professor began shrieking, "Poppycock, this is poppycock. I'm not going to sit here and have the Congress of the United States insulted by some two-bit little bureaucrat." Wilson says the chairman then began hurling chairs about the room, knocking inkwells off his desk, sputtering, and ordering Cogan to leave, vowing that he would never be permitted back into his committee as long as Clarence D. Long was in Congress.

Wilson was now convinced that all was lost. Long considered Cogan's performance to have been an attack on a coequal branch of the U.S. government. It was an offense that had to be avenged. And, according to Wilson, Long decided to retaliate against the CIA by cutting off all U.S. foreign aid to Pakistan.

Wilson was so alarmed that he immediately forced his way through on the phone to alert the CIA's number two man, John McMahon. Wilson explained that it was highly likely that Long was about to strike out against the Agency by making massive cuts in the administration's proposed $600 million foreign-aid budget for Pakistan. Charlie did not have to explain to McMahon the consequences of suddenly cutting Pakistan's military and economic assistance. It would be a slap in the face to Zia, the man whose cooperation the CIA relied on to mount its Afghan operation. The $600 million in aid was part of a quid pro quo, and if it was lost, there was no question that the CIA would immediately suffer the consequences.

The next day a highly solicitous John McMahon appeared before Doc Long, utterly responsive to all of the chairman's questions. He was there to repair the damage, to kowtow to the chairman. As Wilson saw it, the CIA deputy director's virtuoso performance was the only thing that kept Doc Long from sabotaging the entire Afghan program.

As the society columnist for the *Washington Post*, Maxine Cheshire had often written about Charlie Wilson before leaving journalism to marry one of Wilson's Texas friends. Charlie was happy to hear from her when she called from Houston that summer, but he had no idea what she was talking about when she said, "I sure am glad Willie has been able to help." It was another of those bizarre coincidences: the limo driver that the Justice investigators had finally tracked down turned out to have been Maxine's son.

Bill Cheshire had told Justice that he keenly remembered the time he drove the congressman home from the Baltimore airport. But, no doubt to the dismay of the federal sleuths, he'd declared that no drugs were present. And he'd explained that he certainly would have remembered such a thing, since he had recently left his rock band out of disgust for the drug habits of his musical colleagues.

Justice had now lost out on its most promising lead, but Wilson's political antenna told him that some bigger force was, perhaps, moving to help convince the department that it needn't pursue its investigation any further. As Charlie saw it, it was a stroke of good fortune that his fellow target was none other than the only son of that icon of Republican conservatives Barry Goldwater. Whatever the actual reasons, in late July the federal prosecutors announced, "We have insufficient admissible, credible evidence to support criminal charges." As to the specific Wilson investigation, Justice included a statement that there had been a jurisdictional problem (a clear reference to Liz's testimony that Wilson's cocaine use had been confined to the Caymans, where U.S. law does not apply).

At his desk in the Rayburn House Office Building, Wilson, staring out the window to the capital lawn, told a group of assembled reporters, "I feel relieved." He then asked a staffer, "Would you bring me a glass of wine, to calm my nerves a little bit?"

There was still the House ethics investigation to cope with, but Wilson, instead of adopting a saintly and repentant demeanor, immediately went out and celebrated. The *Austin American-Statesman* soon reported to its Texas readers how "Good-Time Charlie's" friends had thrown him a "Beat the Rap Party."

It seems almost inconceivable now, but sometime during this year of women and alcohol and constant scandal, Joanne Herring, the socialite who appeared regularly in the society pages as the "Queen of Texas," had found herself falling hopelessly in love with Charlie. It had happened in late May at the Paris air show. Wilson had invited Joanne to come along to see his world of defense contractors and military men at this biennial extravaganza. She was going to reciprocate by introducing him to her world of European royalty. They had an early celebration for Charlie's fiftieth birthday at Maxim's, and during the six-day trip Joanne walked with him through the acres of weapons displays as he doggedly searched for a mule-portable anti-aircraft gun to give to the mujahideen.

She went with him as he launched into animated discussions with the Bofors arms salesmen from Sweden and the Oerlikon reps from Switzerland. No one else in the U.S. government was hunting for mule-portable anti-aircraft guns. To begin with, the CIA hadn't asked for them. But here was Wilson, with Joanne by his side, openly discussing whether the Bofors RBS-70, a three-man portable anti-aircraft gun, made sense for the Afghans.

There is an innocent feel to these air shows. They're organized almost as social events, disguising the rather obvious fact that the defense contractors and weapons merchants are there to court buyers. It's nothing short of a massive arms bazaar, not unlike a car or boat show, only the buyers tend to be governments or, sometimes, people trying to overthrow governments. It was the greatest of all places for Charlie to impress Joanne because here Charlie Wilson was not just another congressman. As an outspoken hawk on the Defense Appropriations subcommittee during the Reagan arms buildup, he was treated as one of the greatest arms patrons in history.

Much of what Charlie was doing in Paris was unclear to Joanne. So many different people representing so many strange interests seemed to have business with him. Bertie van Storer, the aristocratic representative

from Oerlikon, the Swiss gun manufacturer, took them to Maxim's for
dinner and insisted that, unlike the Swedes, Oerlikon not only had the right
weapon for the Afghans but would have no trouble selling it to the CIA.
The Washington lobbyist Denis Neill was omnipresent, as was his client
the Egyptian defense minister, Mohammed Abu Ghazala, whose country
was now receiving $900 million in U.S. aid. The field marshal, who was at
the show as Egypt's all-powerful arms merchant, was gallant with Joanne,
and said nothing about Charlie's belly dancer. He, too, insisted that he had
the perfect gun for the Afghans and that Charlie must bring Joanne and
return to Egypt to see for himself.

Strangest of all to Joanne was the couple from Israel. True to form,
Wilson explained that this was the same raven-haired Israeli captain who
had so entranced him in the Sinai on his first trip to Israel with Ed Koch.
Wilson suggested that she and her husband were true Israeli war heroes
and were engaged in clandestine business. "Charlie had told me he was
working with the Jews," Joanne says, "but I didn't see how he did it—arms
for Israel and arms for Egypt." In this case, Wilson did not tell Joanne that
he was pursuing his secret negotiations to put together the Israel-Pakistan
back channel.

The world Joanne introduced to Charlie at night in Paris was as
bewildering to Wilson as his arms bazaar was to her. She took him to elegant black-tie dinners where many of the guests seemed to be pretenders
to the ancient thrones of Europe. At one point Wilson found himself seated
next to an elderly lady whom Joanne had introduced as royalty, and he
braced himself for an evening of dutiful conversation.

"Do you know Imelda Marcos?" the woman asked the congressman
in a rather affected voice.

"No, I'm afraid I don't," he said, taking a sip of his soup.

"I do," he remembers the matronly lady saying. "You haven't missed
much. She's such a greedy cunt."

Wilson says he had a hard time keeping himself from spitting the soup
out on the table. When he recovered, he said in his most courtly manner,
"Baroness, I think you and I are going to have a lovely evening."

Joanne was not like any other woman Wilson had known. Old-
fashioned about their courting, she stayed with her Parisian friends instead of at the Le Meridien hotel, where Charlie was camped out in U.S.
government–financed splendor. But they partied and stayed up well into

the night, whereupon he would leave Joanne to walk home along the Avenue Foch and engage in playful conversation with the ladies of the night.

Paris was a marvelous interlude from the horrors of Washington. Pampered and flattered by defense contractors during the day, amused and impressed by aristocrats at night, Wilson found himself being swept off his feet by this woman who had managed to turn him into her champion to rescue the mujahideen.

After their fourth dinner at Maxim's and while dancing at a disco, Wilson stopped and told Joanne that he loved her. Before the night was out, they were talking about marriage and beginning to make plans. "He started asking me if I thought I could lead his kind of life," Joanne recalls. "And it was a very good question and I really wasn't sure. I remember I didn't answer, but then I decided that I loved him."

Back in Washington, Charlie discovered just what it meant to sign on with Joanne as she began throwing her enormous energies into her future life with Charlie. First of all, her mother had the congressman's family "checked out." She told Joanne that he came from "people of modest means, but fine people."

Years later, trying to explain why she had agreed to marry Wilson in the midst of the cocaine scandal, Joanne said, "I never gave a thought to the drug business." While others might have seen him as a hopeless sinner, Joanne saw a flawed but heroic figure fighting the Communist devil, doing God's work, and she meant to be a part of it. She says that she had been reborn with Charlie and that "part of this came from thinking I had to do something with my life that was worthwhile. And what better way than to serve your country and to serve your Lord."

Meanwhile, Joanne was moving into Wilson's office. Agnes Bundy, who handled Charlie's Appropriations work, remembers Joanne sweeping in "like Scarlett O'Hara in her canary-yellow dress and a black cape to organize all of us. We wondered who this woman was."

She was Charlie's girl, and the congressman now had her picture on his desk and was talking to her six or seven times a day. The two of them started to go out looking at apartments together, and Joanne summoned Charles Fawcett to Washington. Her idea was to create a salon that would change the course of history. Fawcett was to be a lobbyist for the Afghans as well as others enslaved by the Russians. In her mind the salon would be the meeting place for the greatest minds of the age. She saw it as a revolutionary cell that would spread the conservative gospel to the rest of the country and the world.

But before rescuing the world, the Afghans had to be saved. According to Charlie, that meant they had to win over Doc Long. With that objective in mind, Wilson had invited Joanne to come along on the chairman's upcoming junket, not however, as Wilson's official companion but in her curious diplomatic position with General Zia's government.

Officially, Joanne was only Zia's honorary consul in Houston, but she had such astonishing sway over the Muslim dictator that in a moment of abject weakness that had horrified the entire Pakistan Foreign Office, he had committed to making this blond American woman his roving ambassador at large, and had further agreed to provide her with a turbaned Pashtun tribesman to serve as her footman in Washington.

At last, everything seemed to be falling in place for the embattled congressman. He had beaten the rap, he had won the heart of the "Queen of Texas," and now he had three weeks to give to the jihad.

From his office on the Hill, he called Joanne in Houston. They exchanged little endearments of unending love and agreed to meet the next day in Paris, where they would begin their mission to convert Doc Long.

CHAPTER 13

Joanne Herring and Zia ul-Haq

THE SEDUCTION
OF DOC LONG

When Wilson had bought his secondhand Lincoln Continental from Liz Wickersham's father in Orange, he'd joked that its hood was as vast as the flight deck of an aircraft carrier. He had named it "the Nimitz," after the greatest of Texas admirals, Chester W. Nimitz, who had fought his fleet across the Pacific to bring down the Japanese empire.

Wilson's always delighted in the feeling that came over him whenever he took its wheel. On August 11, 1983, the night before his long journey to the front, he was feeling particularly heroic as he swung onto the Key Bridge and began to accelerate. He had just finished a romantic dinner with Trish Wilson, a warmhearted and good-looking blonde he had dated off and on for years. He was scheduled to meet Joanne the following day in Paris. But Paris was an ocean away and it had always been hard for the congressman to deny himself such simple pleasures as an evening with an old friend. They had gone to the Trieste Restaurant, and Charlie had gotten himself a little drunk. He could never resist Manhattans on such occasions—the glasses were so elegant—and with Trish staring admiringly into his eyes, he'd outlined the dangerous mission upon which he was about to embark. It had made him feel like a heroic character in a movie, perhaps an RAF pilot in a London bar the night before a big raid. By the fifth round, Trish had agreed to spend the night with him, and after his eighth Manhattan, he had set off in the Nimitz while Trish drove back to her apartment for a change of clothes. They were to meet at his place in half an hour.

It was raining as the congressman roared across Key Bridge. And then—bang! A twenty-two-year-old motorist who had just moved to Washington from Minnesota found his brand-new Mazda hurtling sixty feet before slamming into a guardrail that saved him from plunging into the Potomac.

Mr. and Mrs. Steven Standiford, who later provided eyewitness accounts of the rear-end bashing, said they had been concerned when they'd noticed the big blue car weaving from lane to lane in front of them. They'd watched horrified, as the Lincoln smashed the little Mazda, then lurched back from the wreckage. The hood of the Nimitz was crunched straight into the air, and its driver seemed to be craning his neck anxiously out the window to take in the scene. With a sweeping maneuver, the Lincoln then sped away into Virginia, but not before Mr. and Mrs. Standiford had noted the car's unusual license plate: Texas 2.

Behind the wheel of the Nimitz, Wilson was now thinking clearly. It was dangerous to drive any further; the mangled hood blocked his vision. The only way for him to see the road was to stick his head out the window. But it was just two more minutes to the Iwo Jima statue and his apartment building. And once in the Wesley's underground garage, he would be safe. He was moving quickly now, scurrying from the car, hitting the elevator's ninth-floor button, then flinging his front door open and, just as quickly, locking it from inside.

Years later, he reconstructed this moment: "I was drunker than shit. I had hit this car and knocked it forever. I knew that if the cops came I was dead meat. So, after determining that the driver was not hurt, I just drove home and locked myself in my apartment. The police must have the world's fastest computer in northern Virginia, because they found my car and were banging on my door in thirty minutes."

On the other side of that door, Charlie Wilson cowered in silence. The hammering and the loud, demanding voices wouldn't stop. Finally he crept to the phone to whisper instructions to Trish not to come: "The police are after me. They're in the building."

Wilson's administrative assistant, Charles Simpson, was jolted awake by the phone call: "Simpson, I've really screwed up this time. Here's what you've got to do." By this time Wilson had already called his lawyer, who'd advised him that the police might well attempt an arrest, but that he would be safe as long as he drove directly to Congress. Federal law prohibits local authorities from arresting a national legislator on his way to or from Congress. But Wilson didn't want to go to Congress. He had to get to Doc Long's plane, which was waiting for him at Andrews Air Force Base. There was every reason to believe that the frustrated Virginia police might attempt an arrest once he left the Wesley. But again Wilson's good luck held.

The Key Bridge, it turned out, falls under the jurisdiction of the District of Columbia, not Virginia, so the Arlington police banging at the door had been outside their authority. Simpson would always say that his boss's finest moments were when he was backed into a corner. With the authorities closing in, Wilson proceeded to make his own luck. His main threat now was from the D.C. police, yet until recently he had been chairman of the Appropriations subcommittee that funds the District of Columbia.* He had always been very generous with the federal city, particularly with the police force, whose budget he had always protected. And just before the sun came up he put in a call to one of the friends he had made in the police department.

Wilson explained his problem: an air force jet was scheduled to take him out of the country on government business in a matter of hours. "I may have told him that it was a mission that had to do with saving the world from Communist aggression in Afghanistan," Wilson recalled with some humor years later, "and that there might well be substantial raises in store for the District police." The bottom line was this: could he leave the country? "No problem, Mr. Chairman. Just check in with us on your return."

Wilson still had to cope with the likelihood that the Virginia police might attempt an arrest. But the Pentagon solved that problem for him. As is its custom when providing flights for members of Congress, they dispatched an escort officer and car to pick Wilson up at his apartment to make sure he arrived safely at the plane. The congressman tried to look calm as the officer opened the door to the car, but he hadn't slept and he was agitated. He couldn't help but glance around nervously as they glided through Arlington, past the scene of the crime, back into the District, and finally to the safety of Andrews.

*The District of Columbia, a federal city, is governed by the U.S. Congress, and all its funds are governed by the Appropriations Committee. This gives enormous influence to those subcommittee chairmen able to slash or augment budgets without much trouble.

On board Wilson asked for a bullshot, as his hangover was fierce. For a moment, looking down on the capital, it all seemed peaceful. Then the cables started coming into the cockpit.

Back in the office, the Angels were frantically trying to reach Charlie to warn him that cameras and questions were likely to be waiting at Orly. With each news bulletin detailing the congressional hit-and-run, a new cable from Washington arrived and was sent back to the unhappy congressman.

The plane was filled with Wilson's Appropriations colleagues and their wives, and soon Charlie had confided the whole sorry story to Doc Long. Another, more conventional chairman might have thought Wilson was compromising the delegation or perhaps besmirching the reputation of the entire U.S. House of Representatives. "Doc kind of looked at me as if I was Peck's bad boy," Wilson says, referring to the old Jackie Coogan silent film. "He was very tolerant. I've gotten by on that many a time in my life."

But Wilson's loyal administrative assistant, Charlie Simpson, felt that he couldn't put up with it anymore. The only reason Simpson had quit his job as a tenured professor of history at Sam Houston University was because he'd believed that Charlie was one of those politicians who come along only once in a decade. When they had flown into Washington together in 1972, Simpson remembers, Wilson had asked the taxi driver to pull over at the Lincoln Memorial. "I have to learn how to be a congressman and you need to learn how to be an AA [administrative assistant]," Wilson had told Simpson. "And this is the first thing we have to do." The cab waited as the two men climbed to the top of the white marble steps. "Charlie read every word written on the walls," Simpson recalls. "And as we were leaving, there were almost tears in his eyes." The experience left the AA believing that perhaps the two of them shared a special destiny.

Over the years, Simpson had learned to cope with Charlie's women, his drinking, his dictators, his outlaw friends, his short attention span, his overall irresponsibility—and even the drug business. But when Wilson had called that morning to say he had just rammed a motorist and run away, something in Simpson had snapped.

"There's a young man with a Mazda RX-7," Wilson had told Simpson. "If he calls you, get his car repaired." Simpson remembers his rueful response: "Okay, I'll take care of it. You go along." Somehow he managed to put out the fires that Wilson had left raging behind, explaining with a straight face to the press why the congressman had left the scene of the accident: "He thought he'd hit a bridge railing and came on home."

Simpson then contacted the aggrieved motorist and offered to have his car fixed. It had been a nasty accident. The repair bill was $3,800, but Simpson handled the victim so well that he never even discussed litigation. "The kid was new in town, been here two months. He just didn't know when he had us by the balls."

It all worked out fine, but for the first time Simpson felt dirty. "From that day on, I didn't give a shit what Wilson wanted," Simpson said. He would never look at Wilson with the same blinders that had served them both so well over the last decade. Now he saw only an irresponsible, overgrown boy. A year later, when the senior senator from Texas, Lloyd Bentsen, offered to make Simpson his administrative assistant, he sought Wilson's blessing and, upon receiving it, accepted.

On board the air force plane the morning after the wreck, Wilson felt about as low as a snake's belly. For the first time, he too wondered if he had any legitimacy left. The Afghan cause had sustained his self-respect throughout the worst of the drug days, but now he didn't know if he could even go through with this campaign to win over Doc Long.

Luckily, Joanne Herring was waiting for him in Paris—ready to breathe pure inspiration back into the deflated and badly hungover congressman. Right away he told her that his career might be over, that the hit-and-run on top of the dope charges might well be the last straw. He was offering to let her off the hook.

But nothing that Charlie did that year seemed to shake her—not the drugs, not the stories of Liz and the hot tub, not even the belly dancer in Pakistan pretending to be the congressman's secretary. The hit-and-run on the Key Bridge she treated as little more than a speeding violation. Perhaps the best explanation as to why she was so forgiving is that Joanne Herring, that summer, was very much in the throes of her born-again revelations.

Just the year before she had found Christ. And like all born-agains, the Tempter was a very familiar figure to her. As she saw it, the Devil was throwing roadblocks in her man's way—trying to derail him because Charlie was headed into a mighty battle with the forces of evil. Herring was a product of Texas oil and the John Birch Society and, most recently, a disciple of the Count de Marenches's vision of a global Communist conspiracy in which even well-known capitalists were agents. All of this somehow coalesced for her into a clear vision once she was born again. She now saw an apocalyptic struggle in which she and Charlie had become instruments of Jesus.

She told the self-flagellating Wilson that there was no time for moping, that he was wonderful, and that they had God's battle to fight. It was to begin that very night at the home of the Viscomtesse de Grèves, "the most beautiful woman in Paris." It had been no small matter persuading this French patrician to host a dinner for a group of unknown American politicians, and Charlie had to play his part.

Joanne had long since evolved a theory about the way she, as a Texas socialite, could influence the course of world events. It had to do with grand dinners and glitz and fun and how you bring people together. For her, a dinner party was not entertainment alone but deadly serious business. It all came down to the mixture: business with pleasure, high society with the people who actually make the world work, moving them around from course to course, matching them with partners they would never otherwise encounter, always maneuvering to bring together the ones who could change the world according to her designs.

Doc Long was hardly the sort of person you'd expect to be the guest of honor at an aristocratic gathering in Paris, but the viscomtess had been sympathetic to Joanne's seduction plan and had summoned "le tout Paris." As Joanne articulates it today, the strategy was very simple: "What we wanted to do is make Doc Long have so much fun that when he got to Zia, the ground would be prepared, just like it had been for Charlie when he first went to Pakistan."

She saw the evening as a perfect first step and was fast on her way to becoming each of the congressmen's new best friends. The pictures from this interlude in Paris show Joanne dressed in fanciful pink Little Miss Muffet outfits, sexy affairs with a parasol and a very short skirt. In each of these photos she is the center of a sea of smiles: Doc Long is grinning from ear to ear, and Mrs. Long is smiling too. "It's always a big mistake to ignore the wives," Joanne explains, and on this trip she concentrated much of her attention on making sure all of them were on board.

The delegation next stopped off briefly in Syria, then went on to Israel, where the chairman was treated with great respect. Nobody needed to tell the Israelis to make an effort with this man who, along with his planeload of appropriators, sent large amounts of U.S. aid each year for every man, woman, and child in the country.

Charlie, meanwhile, went off on his own to visit his old Israeli friend Zvi Rafiah, and Rafiah's boss, Michael Shore, the chairman of IMI. As always, the Russian gunships were foremost on Wilson's mind, and he was eager to find out where things stood with the Charlie Horse, the antiaircraft gun IMI had agreed to design for the Afghans.*

After briefing Wilson, the two Israelis brought up a personal matter: they were worried that their friend might lose the upcoming election because of the scandals surrounding him. They wanted him to know that Israel needed Wilson in Congress and that since they couldn't contribute to his campaign directly, they would make sure their friends in America did. They then gave him a captured PLO Kalashnikov, which Charlie proudly carried onto the air force plane with utter disregard for the rigid rules prohibiting such illegal arms shipments. "Doc got a kick out of me having it on the plane," Wilson recalls. "He also liked the fact that the Israelis liked me so much."

The Israelis had gone out of their way for Joanne as well after Charlie had alerted them to her religious passions. "He knew that the first thing in my life is Jesus Christ and he arranged for the Israelis to take me everywhere Jesus had gone," Joanne recounted with appreciation years later. Her experience visiting the Stations of the Cross managed to make her even more convinced of the sacred nature of the mission she had embarked on with Charlie. It seems hard to imagine, but on this trip she says that she succeeded repeatedly in getting the congressman to join her in intense prayer sessions. "We prayed that the dinners would go well, that Zia would be well received," she says. "We prayed for Charlie and for him to have the strength to get through it all, and for the Lord to guide us with Doc Long."*

---

*Rafiah and Shore said they were convinced that the Charlie Horse could work for the mujahideen, but the 2.75-inch ammunition it used would be expensive unless it turned out, as they believed, that there were enormous stockpiles of the ammunition left over from Vietnam. Wilson decided to put in a special appropriation to commission an inventory to find out how much ammunition could be raided from the leftover Vietnam arsenal.

*Wilson later claimed that he was not praying on his knees but was just a passive participant, holding hands with Joanne.

As they left Jerusalem for Pakistan, Joanne really set to work. She moved from seat to seat, telling not just the members but their wives all her stories about bringing capitalism to little Pakistani villages, and about how the wonderful General Zia was sacrificing everything to help the Afghans. She knew that Zia had a horrible reputation, and her way of dealing with it was to confront head-on the "false accusations" that Zia had in effect murdered his predecessor, Bhutto. From seat to seat she carried her curious and impassioned message: "I want to make it really clear to you that Zia did not kill Bhutto," she said, until on her third stop she encountered a blank stare from one of the congressmen. "He said to me, 'Who's Bhutto?' and I thought, These guys are going out here to visit this country and they don't know doodle-de-twat about it." Undeterred, Herring smiled charmingly, filled him in on the real history, and, like a pro, moved her pitch on to the next seat.

Doc Long, that magical dispenser of U.S. foreign-aid dollars, had grown accustomed to being made much of by governments. But General Zia, at the prodding of his honorary consul, made sure that the chairman got a reception he would never forget—literally, a red-carpet affair with a brass band, braided generals in full-dress uniform, lines of soldiers at attention, and small children with arms full of flowers running up to honor the suspicious old man.

Wilson and Joanne now had Doc trapped in their choreographed sequence of events. Pakistan might have been in bad odor with the chairman because it was a military dictatorship, but that also meant that when Zia ordered the military to put on a good show, the whole country performed. The golfers in the delegation were taken to the local country club and served tea at the ninth hole with linen and silver. The merchant at the antique shop in Rawalpindi offered such incredible bargains that the wives were convinced that General Zia had ordered discounts.

The centerpiece of the trip, however, was a helicopter trek to the front. It began in Peshawar at the refugee camps, with two and a half million destitute Afghans in their mud-walled compounds. Then on to the Red Cross hospital, where the delegation saw Afghan boys and young men without arms, legs, some without eyes, none complaining. Doc Long was the only member of Congress with a son who had been wounded in Vietnam, and it was impossible for him not to be impressed with the quiet courage of these men.

As always, Charlie gave a pint of his own blood for the mujahideen—the kind of act that humbles those who don't participate. Then the delegation, wives and all, left to meet the Afghan elders, who had assembled in a tent to greet the old American chief they had been told could help them.

Long's aide Bill Shursh remembers being awed by the sight and smell of the Afghans as he walked with Doc into the tent. One after another, the leaders stood up to address Long, in every instance telling him about the Russian gunships that were slaughtering their people and were invulnerable to the bullets from their rifles and machine guns. Shursh himself remembers thinking that these were real freedom fighters. "They made the Contras and the Cambodians look like urban cowboys," he says.

Like every other visitor from the United States who came here in those days, Doc Long could not help but respond when the entire assembly of Afghans began roaring in unison the cry of jihad, *Allahu Akbar,* God is Great. Suddenly, he too could feel the presence of the Red Army just across the mountains. He was with men his own age who were bearing arms—men with gray beards and fierce eyes telling him about the murderous helicopters. They wanted someone from the delegation to speak to them, and Wilson shrewdly declined, offering the stage instead to his chairman.

Doc began by making a reasonably supportive but not excessive statement about the horror of the Soviet atrocities. From the tent came another great cry of *Allahu Akbar.* Wilson watched with amazement and some amusement as the seventy-two-year-old former professor of economics seemed to have an adrenaline rush. Suddenly, the old man was roaring to these Muslim warriors that he was going to get them what they needed to knock the helicopters out of the sky. *"Allahu Akbar, Allahu Akbar,"* they cried. Every time Doc said anything at all, the Afghans would clap, throw up their hands, and thunder back their battle cry.

It was like the most heated revival meeting in East Texas. By the time Doc Long left the tent, Wilson realized that he had just witnessed the conversion of this enemy of the CIA into an honorary mujahid. That night, back in Islamabad, Zia administered the coup de grâce.

Ordinarily, he shunned his predecessor's luxurious palace, but Joanne and Charlie had told Zia how responsive Doc was when much was made of him. And so Zia had turned Bhutto's palace into a vision out of the *Arabian Nights,* and Joanne even got him to relax his Islamic restrictions for this one event. She understood that he could not include women at the dinner, but she insisted that he gather everyone together at the end of the evening or else the wives would feel insulted.

As usual, Zia listened to his honorary consul and after the final course, before inviting the women in, Zia asked Doc for a word alone. Like most Americans, about the only thing Doc Long knew about Zia was bad: he was a military dictator who presided over a fundamentalist state. But Zia had a way with Americans that always caught such suspicious visitors utterly by surprise.

Twenty years before this dinner, as a young Pakistani captain, Zia had been assigned to a year of military training at Fort Knox, Kentucky. One Friday evening, shortly after arriving, the Muslim officer was sitting alone in his austere quarters feeling homesick. There was a knock at the door. A man and his wife from Louisville introduced themselves and said they were interested in making friends with foreign officers. Would he like to go to dinner with them?

Captain Zia ul-Haq had never forgotten that generosity of spirit, nor that of the many other Americans he had come to know. In later years, whenever he received Americans in Pakistan, President Zia always returned the hospitality he had found in Kentucky with a warmth that was clearly genuine. Like everyone else, Doc Long found himself entranced by this man of charm, intelligence, and seeming sincerity.

Wilson was not present at the encounter, but he quickly recognized that a communion of sorts had been established that night. The United States might have lost its nerve, but Chairman Clarence D. Long, an elder of the College of Cardinals, had personally committed himself, the entire Appropriations Committee, and the government of the United States to pouring hundreds of millions of dollars in aid to Pakistan and, specifically, to providing those marvelous Afghan warriors with the weapons they needed.

That night in the ornate Islamabad Holiday Inn, Wilson was alone in his bedroom. For all his womanizing, he was not prone to pressing himself on his paramours. The door opened, and his true love entered with just a towel wrapped around her. For Wilson, all the nightmares were over. It was a return to the fairy tale.

At the airport the next morning there was an amazing farewell: bands, flowers, carpets, gifts from Zia for everyone. As the plane headed west from Pakistan, Doc sat next to Charlie and told him, "Now my honor is at stake.

I made a promise to those old men and I gave my word to the president of Pakistan that I would get them the guns."

The plane was locked into its final flight path back to Washington when Doc, after an intimate conversation with Joanne, suddenly ordered the pilots to land in Venice for an emergency refueling. By now entranced with Joanne, he had responded to her damsel-in-distress appeal when she'd explained that an important "Save Venice" film festival was under way and that she was already a day late.

As they said their farewells on the runway, Charlie and Joanne embraced each and every member of the delegation. They had accomplished their mission with Doc Long and now had Joanne's business to attend to. They were to be guests of the Machiavelli family, admitted into all the elegant dinner parties and homes in Venice. There are pictures of Joanne with Charlton Heston and Roger Moore, the second James Bond, who impressed Wilson with his tales of the lovely ladies who wanted to meet 007 offscreen.

As the two of them sat drinking by the Grand Canal one night, Joanne found herself overwhelmed with the realization that, as she says, "We were just so good together." They conducted a postmortem, reviewing their triumphs. With Doc on board, Charlie told her, more money for Pakistan and the mujahideen was a sure thing. The next step was to ensure that the money was used to get them the right guns. But for the moment, it was time to bask in their glory. "We thought we were invincible," Joanne recalls.

Then, to put the icing on the cake, paparazzi came by and began taking pictures of the glamorous couple. Soon a crowd gathered, asking for autographs. Joanne signed hers Ava Gardner and Charlie, Gary Cooper.

CHAPTER 14

Gust

GUST'S SECRET

In retirement in Rome in 1992, just after the collapse of the Soviet's puppet government in Kabul, Gust Avrakotos strolled across town to the Spanish steps to buy the daily newspapers. Life was good but tame these days. It was the curse of all operations officers to be put out to pasture at fifty, after almost thirty intense years of scheming on behalf of their country. Avrakotos was working on several moneymaking ventures, but nothing had come through yet and there really wasn't much to do but see the sights and remember.

A column in that day's *Wall Street Journal* immediately caught his eye. Entitled "The Afghan Who Won the Cold War," it was about an old friend of sorts, the legendary Afghan commander Ahmad Shah Massoud, and the writer claimed that "as much as Lech Walesa, Pope John Paul II, and Ronald Reagan, Mr. Massoud broke the back of Soviet imperialism."

Avrakotos knew something about the columnist, Robert Kaplan. He was one of the more gifted writers on Afghanistan. A few months before he had somehow gotten Gust's name and number and tried to get him to talk. But Avrakotos hates the press and hadn't even made an effort to be nice when he said no.

Now, as he read Kaplan's article, he found himself enthusiastically agreeing with the writer's assertion that the Afghan war had played a decisive role in bringing on the collapse of the entire Communist empire. Not enough people understood just how devastating the CIA war had been to the Soviets. But the author was not praising the Agency. In fact, he seemed to believe that most of the credit for defeating the Red Army was due to this one guerrilla leader, so great that he belonged in the historical company of Tito, Ho Chi Minh, Mao Tse-tung, and Che Guevara. After conferring this recognition, Kaplan ended with a swipe at the CIA for having failed to recognize and adequately support this one true, independent Afghan commander.

Avrakotos smiled. He always smiled when he read these attacks. It was like receiving a medal. All the reporters had taken up this line about the CIA giving short shrift to the Lion of the Panjshir. Now that the war was over, they were all complaining about how the Agency had backed the wrong horses, giving the weapons and support to Khomeini-style Muslims instead of the noble Massoud.*

What prompted Avrakotos to smile so broadly that day was his little secret. Massoud hadn't just come out of nowhere. It was he, Gust Lascaris Avrakotos of Aliquippa, and the Central Intelligence Agency, who had made it possible for Ahmad Shah Massoud to realize his greatness. And what made it all such a perfect spy's delight was that nobody knew.

The story of Avrakotos's machinations on behalf of the great commander begins with his trip to London with John McGaffin in 1983 to meet the "cousins" at MI6. It had been a generous invitation, and Avrakotos had been grateful when McGaffin invited him to come along to meet their British counterparts. Though Gust was expected to be acting chief for only a few months, McGaffin introduced him as his replacement, which immediately conferred status upon him and gave him a license to operate independently with the British service.

MI6 members always did their best to be good hosts when their Agency friends came over on these official visits. McGaffin and Cogan loved the routine: the dinners at the venerable men's clubs, the personal introductions to the best tailors on Savile Row, and the gushing but understated reception from the staff of the Basil Street Hotel, MI6's choice for its favored guests. The hotel reeked of Old World charm.

But none of this worked for Avrakotos. It made him feel claustrophobic. He didn't like the quaint wooden toilet seats in the hotel's tiny bathrooms. McGaffin good-naturedly asked him, "Well, what do you shit on in Aliquippa, Gust?"

---

*In fact, this was a legitimate criticism. Even Avrakotos acknowledges that Pakistan all but forced the CIA to back its favorites, who were of the hard-line variety.

What Avrakotos says he found particularly distasteful about the British spies were "the fucking teas. Can you believe it, they interrupted meetings every day at three-thirty or four for tea and cookies."*

Gust's escort officer was only trying to make this unpolished American feel at home. "Now that you'll be coming here frequently," the distinguished Englishman in the dark suit offered, "perhaps we could suggest a few things you'd like to shop for." He mentioned a visit to his tailor, or perhaps his shoemaker. "I was patient with him until he exhausted my patience," Gust says. "Look, fuckhead, I didn't come here to buy shoes," he had growled.

Part of the reason for his explosion was a certain sensitivity to his class. Long ago Avrakotos had realized that he could never look like an Ivy Leaguer, much less a British aristocrat, so he had taken to defiantly dressing in marked contrast. Since he had decided not to play the clothes game at Langley, he wasn't about to get seduced into trying to look like one of Smiley's people in London. "Look, if you're trying to make me look like a Brit and it takes going to your tailor to get into your club for dinner, it's not going to happen," he snapped. "Besides that, I prefer pub grub!"

At this point the unflappable Englishman won Avrakotos over. "Without missing a beat he looked at me and said: 'Pub grub, yes. Well, pub grub it shall be.'" Later, McGaffin told Gust how unfortunate it was that he couldn't have experienced the club. Avrakotos didn't have the heart to explain.

The MI6 spies were impressive as they moved about their old imperial capital. But Avrakotos's eye is keenly trained to spot what's known in the trade as "recruitable weaknesses." Like everyone else, he had heard about MI6's financial problems, but at their headquarters he was nevertheless struck by the extreme shabbiness of their operation. Before long he realized that this once proud service, in whose image the CIA had been formed, was virtually bankrupt. It was Avrakotos's cunning that allowed him to sense, in

---

*After he became acting chief, Avrakotos actually interrupted one of these afternoon teas to declare that he did not come to London to drink tea and eat little cookies and if they wanted to do business with him, there would be no more interruptions. The ever-accommodating MI6, eager to win more CIA money for their Afghan programs, discontinued their afternoon custom.

this financial despair, a unique opportunity to bypass the Agency's lawyers and play tough through a surrogate.

What initially caught the CIA man's interest in the British was how knowledgeable they were about the war. It made sense: they'd been operating in Afghanistan and Pakistan since the nineteenth century, and some of their agents were sons or grandsons of operatives who had worked for the British Raj. "They have guys who have lived there for twenty years as journalists or authors or tobacco growers," explains Avrakotos.

When the Soviets invaded, MI6 activated these old networks. In spite of their lack of resources, both the British government and MI6 wanted to continue to play a role on the world stage. From their days of empire, Afghanistan was a very familiar arena. They knew the players and the terrain, and figured they could make a mark even with very little money by focusing their efforts on Massoud, the Afghan leader who controlled the one critical area of the country. It was because of MI6's intimate connections to Massoud that Avrakotos had come to London. The commander had stopped fighting, and the CIA wanted to know why.

By the Agency's reckoning, there were about three hundred reasonably serious commanders in action against the Soviets at that time. But the critical factor of terrain made Massoud indispensable. His Panjshir Valley lies close to the Afghan capital and airfields where most of the Soviet's 40th Army was based. Even more significant, the Soviets depended on the narrow Salang Pass and Highway that snaked through Massoud's mountains from their border. With over 100,000 troops totally dependent on everything from spare parts and ammunition to medicine, vodka, and Russian food, the supplies moving down the Salang had become the lifeblood of the 40th Army. It simply couldn't survive without keeping this line open. "Geographically, it was the key," says Avrakotos.

Throughout the early years of the war the Red Army repeatedly invaded the Panjshir in division strength. These engagements were like scenes out of *Apocalypse Now,* with artillery barrages, helicopter assaults, and carpet bombing, followed by great sweeps with overwhelming numbers of men. Each time, the Lion of the Panjshir had followed the age-old guerrilla tactic, ordering his people to fall back to the mountains and passes beyond, to bide their time sniping and ambushing until the Russians moved out.

As Avrakotos saw it, the Soviets were being sucker-punched almost every time they tried to march into Massoud's narrow valley: "It was like every cowboy movie where the wagon train comes in and then the Indians attack on either side."

The French doctors from Médecins sans Frontières who had gone into the Panjshir early in the war had come out with film and stories that promoted Massoud as the ultimate freedom fighter. Ken Follett would later make him the demigod of his best-seller *Lie Down with Lions*. He was the only Afghan to capture the imagination of the world beyond the Hindu Kush.

But in 1983, when Massoud stopped fighting, Agency intelligence came to the disturbing conclusion that he had cut a deal with the Soviets. What made this particularly worrisome was that it was not the first time. In 1981 and again in 1982 the Afghan commander had also stopped fighting, in exchange for Soviet offers of food and guarantees that the Red Army would leave his villages alone.

Avrakotos, ever the prepared student, had read everything he could find in the Agency's files about Massoud and the tribes who made up the CIA's army of freedom fighters. What he learned made him think that perhaps Massoud was not being handled correctly.

The CIA had deeded to the Pakistan intelligence service, the ISI, the right to decide which mujahideen leaders would receive the Agency's weapons, and without question, Massoud was being shortchanged. The overwhelming bulk of CIA weaponry was being funneled to the renowned Pashtun tribesmen who had long dominated Afghan politics. No one could question the ISI's backing of the Pashtuns, fierce warriors renowned for having repeatedly humiliated the British in the nineteenth century. They were fighting heroically against the Soviets, dying in staggering numbers, and refusing to give up. Zia's intelligence chief, General Akhtar, himself part Pashtun, harbored the deepest suspicions about Massoud. He resented the gushing publicity about this Afghan who wouldn't fight. He knew that MI6 agents masquerading as journalists were part of the Massoud propaganda machine. As for the French, he told Howard Hart that the only reason they were enraptured was that the so-called Lion of Panjshir was "poking the French nurses." It was all Hart could do, drawing on his close relationship with Akhtar, to convince the ISI chief not to reduce the meager supplies set aside for Massoud.

Hart himself, however, was deeply suspicious, even angered by Massoud's refusal to move on the Salang Highway. He passed on his doubts to Langley, along with the ISI's crude joke about the unmanly nature of

Massoud's Tajiks: "When a Pashtun wants to make love to a woman, his first choice is always a Tajik man."

Avrakotos came to see things differently once he discovered that there was a venerable blood feud running between the Pashtuns and Massoud's Tajik tribe. The campaign against Massoud became even more suspect once he realized that many of the Pakistani ISI officers were themselves Pashtuns and that they maintained a formal relationship with these Afghan resistance leaders that had begun years before the Soviets invaded Afghanistan. Avrakotos figured that whatever the cause for Massoud's sit-down strike, the ISI wasn't helping matters by withholding the CIA's weapons. As far as he was concerned, it would be a disaster to write Massoud off. Somehow, a way had to be found to get the commander back in action, and Gust knew that it was useless to look to the ISI.

The Agency, under McGaffin's direction, had already been using the British for information about Massoud. Unlike the CIA and the U.S. government, which operated with a strict taboo against any Americans crossing into Afghanistan, British SAS commandos had been going in and out of the Panjshir since the beginning of the war. They even had a way of moving supplies to Massoud independent of the Pakistanis. In London, Avrakotos asked for a personal meeting with MI6's Massoud expert.

He turned out to be a young, blond SAS guerrilla-warfare expert with the peculiar nickname of Awk, a name said to vaguely resemble the grunting noise he would make on maneuvers. Awk had just returned from three months inside the war zone. It was about a two-week journey in those days, walking north from the Pakistan border through Nuristan and the Hindu Kush to reach Massoud's valley. Awk had gone in with two other SAS commandos. Their report had astonished Avrakotos.

"There was one passage in there that really got me," remembers Avrakotos. "This guy was sleeping with a couple of his buddies and he said he awoke one night and heard horrible groans. He didn't get up but was able to put on his night-vision goggles and saw a group of Massoud's guys literally cornholing a Russian prisoner."

The Afghan presiding over the rape was one of Massoud's lieutenants. Awk described in his report how uncomfortable he and his two friends had felt, particularly because they were good-looking blond boys and Massoud's man seemed to have developed a crush on one of them. For the last two weeks of their stay in the Panjshir, he said, they went to sleep with their weapons by their sides, always ready to fight it out if their Afghan friends approached in the dark. Then one day the three Englishmen and their Afghan escorts were lured into a Soviet ambush. The British were dressed as mujahideen, and Awk said that they absolutely would have been killed but for the lieutenant who had so terrorized their nights. Suddenly he bolted from them, running into the open field to draw the helicopter's Gatling guns away from the men he sought to protect.

At MI6 headquarters Awk told Avrakotos that watching that man die had made him finally understand the Afghans' ancient code: "Honor, hospitality, and revenge." Raping an infidel invader was not the atrocity it would be in the West; it was simply revenge. Above all, Awk had come away convinced that these were men of honor. When it came to picking an ally to fight the Soviets, he told Avrakotos, there was no shortage of Tajik courage. They were every bit as good as the Pashtuns.

Now the only question for Avrakotos was how to get Massoud back in the field. Awk and his MI6 superiors took the position that Massoud would return to the fight as soon as he was adequately supplied. They made it clear that they were able to secretly funnel weapons to Massoud without the ISI's knowledge. It was almost embarrassing, however, for the British division chief to have to explain how little they were able to provide.

It's often a small detail that says it all, and when the MI6 division chief told Avrakotos why they were having difficulty finding Afghans willing to drive supplies up to Massoud, Avrakotos realized they were hopelessly broke. "They keep getting maimed," the officer explained, "because the route is mined and we don't have any mine detectors to give them."

"How many could you use?" Avrakotos asked.

"Would ten be too much?" the MI6 man inquired nervously.

Gust insisted that they accept twenty-five, and even a decade later he remembers this exchange with amazement: "Do you know what mine detectors go for? Three hundred bucks! Can you believe it? They were losing drivers and loaders because they couldn't afford twenty-five mine detectors."

Technically, Avrakotos was in London to consult with a coequal intelligence service, but during this visit he realized he had something that these able and ambitious British spies desperately needed. With his American money he could put them back in the game. They had something equally valuable to offer Avrakotos in return—no lawyers to contend with and, as Gust enviously put it, "a prime minister to the right of Attila the Hun."*

Almost immediately, on that first visit to MI6, Avrakotos began sketching in his mind a grand design for putting the British to work. Later he would reflect that they had given him options that were simply denied to the CIA. "They had a willingness to do jobs I couldn't touch. They basically took care of the 'How to Kill People Department.'"

Gust knew he would be skating perilously close to the edge. But with MI6 he was in the presence of old pros, and he figured that as long as he never *specifically* discussed what they would be doing with the money he planned to provide them, he would, technically, not be breaking any U.S. laws. So at the end of their talks Gust committed to a major increase in the CIA's subsidy to the Brits with just one condition: they must not tell him or any other Agency official about any lethal operations. "If I'm ever brought up before a committee," he explained, "I'll have to say what I know. Please, don't tell me for your own good and mine."

Later, when Charlie's money began to roll in, Avrakotos says, "The Brits were eventually able to buy things that we couldn't because it infringed on murder, assassination, and indiscriminate bombings. They could issue guns with silencers. We couldn't do that because a silencer immediately implied assassination—and heaven forbid car bombs! No way I could even suggest it, but I could say to the Brits, 'Fadlallah in Beirut was really effective last week. They had a car bomb that killed three hundred people.' I gave MI6 stuff in good faith. What they did with it was always their business."

But Avrakotos wasn't about to pay the British to completely take over such an invaluable asset as Ahmad Shah Massoud. Immediately after expanding the MI6 account, he set about to create an independent U.S. channel to Massoud as well. Not that he didn't appreciate MI6's efforts; it's just that interests inevitably diverge, and he wanted America to have its own piece of Massoud's war.

---

*As always, the experiences of the CIA in Central America stood in marked contrast. While Avrakotos was in London his counterparts on the Central American task force were about to be strung up for commissioning a so-called assassination manual. Not only the Agency's lawyers but Congress, the press, and hordes of concerned Americans moving about Nicaragua and Central America were attempting to stop the CIA's war.

During this time Gust showed up in Peshawar in disguise—a fake limp, different hair color, elaborate security—to meet Massoud's brother. Avrakotos was now beginning to assert his independence, even from the ISI, which until then had enjoyed total control over the Agency's Afghan efforts.

In their secret meeting in Peshawar behind Dean's Hotel, Avrakotos made one of those offers to the Lion's brother that cannot be refused. By late 1984, Agency money would immediately begin to flow into Massoud's Swiss bank account, and with Art Alper's input, all kinds of exotic hardware for killing Russians started to move on the backs of camels and mules toward the Panjshir. It would prove to be important aid during this moment of intense Soviet escalation in 1984 and 1985. All Gust asked for in return that day was that Massoud keep killing Soviets and remember who his friends were.

Avrakotos is quite matter-of-fact about the reason for sidestepping his British pals: "You can't allow even a friend to have a monopoly on the most effective fighter. The ante to get into the game was money, and by giving it directly we had a voice at the table." One of the main reasons for fixing an independent American channel was to make sure the Agency was in the game if, for example, Massoud captured a KGB communications van. The last thing he wanted was for the Brits to walk away with such a prize.

It didn't take Avrakotos long, once he started funding such programs, to discover that there wasn't nearly enough money to do the things he knew would be effective. He began stretching the rules to the breaking point. Years before, an Agency finance officer had taught him a trick for surviving when an operational budget runs dry. By law any money not spent by the end of a fiscal year is automatically returned to the U.S. Treasury and lost to the Agency. It's one of the ways Congress keeps Central Intelligence accountable—by preventing the buildup of a discretionary war chest. A neat way to undercut this safeguard is to get other division chiefs to divert their extra moneys to your project. "We all know the routine. What you do is get someone in, say, the Tokyo station to pick up the tab. This is where a good finance officer is invaluable," explains the master at walking the bureaucratic tightrope. "On the q. t. they can find out who has surpluses. No one likes to have surpluses. It looks like you can't spend it, right? So I would go to a guy with a surplus and say, 'Will you help? When I'm fat one day I'll help you.' John, my predecessor, lived off the fat of others with promises, and when I got in and got some money I paid them all back."

Avrakotos acknowledges that what he had in mind went far beyond anything the division chief, Chuck Cogan, would have tolerated. But then Cogan hadn't grown up in Aliquippa.

CHAPTER 15

The Oerlikon

THE OPENING SALVO

W hen Doc Long returned from his junket, he moved quickly to fulfill his promise to President Zia and the freedom fighters. This time when the mercurial chairman asked the CIA to send someone to see him, the Deputy Director, John McMahon, was determined to avoid triggering the kind of explosion that had followed Chuck Cogan's encounter with Long the previous spring. This time, when he tapped Norm Gardner for the job, McMahon spelled out the mission: at all costs the case officer must pacify Long.

Gardner is one of those CIA men who've actually participated in secret warfare. A former Green Beret, he had signed on with the Agency in the 1960s for its campaigns in Vietnam and Laos. But he was also smart and later would run operations in Africa and eventually become the right hand of Clair George, the Agency's director of dirty tricks. It was on the way to this most sensitive of jobs in the Clandestine Service that Gardner was handed the Long assignment.

That year, 1983, the CIA was already in serious trouble with Congress. It had been caught building a Contra army to overthrow the Sandinistas, and the Democratic majority in the House was in full revolt. That's when headquarters selected Gardner to serve as its liaison officer to this troublesome body.

At five foot four, Gardner tends to give off a little-boy appearance when he puts on his blue suit and Brooks Brothers wing tips. He's incapable of looking mean or dangerous or in any way out of the ordinary. But Gardner is easily underestimated.

The first thing he did after receiving his assignment was to take his lunch, in a brown paper bag, and sit outside the Capitol. He treated the House of Representatives as if it were an intelligence target and he wanted to know how it worked. For three days he prowled the halls—watching, talking, reading—and quickly reached the conclusion that precious few of the 435 representatives mattered.

He figured there were only two committees to worry about: the Intelligence Committee, which was supposed to serve as the Agency's watchdog, and the Defense Appropriations subcommittee, which meted out its money. Probably no more than forty representatives and staffers were cleared for Agency briefings, and Clarence D. Long was not one of them. But when Long summoned Gardner to his office in September, the CIA's diminutive liaison officer promptly appeared, and did his best not to look surprised at the spectacle that began unfolding in front of his eyes.

The chairman was expectorating into his spittoon and shouting for his shoes. A nervous aide explained apologetically that the chairman had just sent them off to be repaired.

"Oh, all right, goddamn it. What's the name of that missile?"

No one could remember.

"Well, goddamn it, then bring me my briefcase."

With that the aide scurried off, only to return a minute later to report that the chairman had left the briefcase in his car and the car was also at the repair shop. As Doc Long proceeded to curse his staff, the poker-faced CIA man waited patiently, wondering where this was all heading.

Finally a breathless aide arrived with the briefcase and Gardner watched with much amazement as Long began pulling out glossy brochures and shouting that this was what he wanted the CIA to buy for the mujahideen. They were pictures of British Blowpipe and Javelin anti-aircraft missiles, and the excited old representative seemed to assume that Gardner would immediately take the brochures out to Langley and put the missiles into the pipeline for the mujahideen.

Gardner was careful to be respectful in discussing the missiles' merits, and before leaving, he assured the chairman that immediate consideration would be given to his most helpful suggestions. He had read about the eccentricities of Congress, but a trip to Doc Long's office was disorienting, like visiting a loony bin.

Wilson, however, was thrilled by the chairman's zeal. "Doc was now more ferocious than I was," he says. "It was no longer a question of me going to him for his help. He was telling me to do whatever I had to do to get the guns."

Even with Doc Long's support, what Charlie wanted to do should have been technically impossible. To begin with, funding for a covert program had always been the exclusive preserve of the president, and neither he nor the CIA had requested the weapons. In addition, the critical first phase of the legislative session had ended. And while the Appropriations Committee is the ultimate arbiter of funding, it cannot dole out money for any program without a legislative committee having first authorized it.

But "Them that has the gold makes the rules" said the sign over Doc Long's desk. And since Long was one of the barons of the committee, and Wilson a veteran insider with chits aplenty, they decided to reverse the process and back-end the money through.

Wilson had worked his magic with his own subcommittee, and everything seemed on track for him to make his legislative strike when Doc Long stumbled across an article recounting the plight of a young, blind, orphaned Pakistani girl who had been raped. To the chairman's disgust, the article explained that by Islamic law, rape can be proved only if there are four witnesses. Since here there was only one, and since the girl admitted that intercourse had taken place, the Pakistani authorities promptly tried her and threw her in jail for fornication.

All bets were now off. Hair swirling, eyes bugging out in fury, the chairman was suddenly calling his newfound friend General Zia a barbaric dictator. "Zia is not going to get a dollar of foreign military aid. Period," screeched Long. "I want him to know that I control the bucks." Long dispatched his aide Jeff Nelson to inform the Pakistani ambassador that if the girl was not immediately pardoned, put in a home, and cared for, Pakistan would be cut off.

For a moment, the plight of this unfortunate teenage girl became the most sensitive issue in U.S.-Pakistan relations. In Wilson's view, Long was just powerful and crazy enough to sabotage the entire Afghan war effort if Zia did not yield.

The next day Zia's ambassador General Ajaz Azim appeared in the chairman's office and announced, "His Excellency the president has asked me to communicate to you that the matter about which you communicated with him has been resolved in the exact terms which you requested."

Doc stared at the ambassador, shouting back at his aide, "What the hell does that mean?"

Very quickly, General Azim assured Long that the girl would be taken care of in a private home for life. The president, he said, wanted the chairman to know that he personally guaranteed this. "As far as I'm concerned," says Nelson, "the blind girl was the key to everything."

With Doc back in the fold, Wilson felt dramatically bolder. But before choosing the dollar amount to put into his Appropriations request, he summoned Chuck Cogan for a final review of the situation. The Near East division chief, still smarting from his encounter with Doc Long, was not about to talk to another congressman without a witness. Unfortunately, the man he wanted to accompany him was off at language school, so he was forced to tap the acting chief of the Afghan task force, Gust Avrakotos.

There may have been another reason why Gust was chosen to go along with Cogan. John McMahon had not liked having to repair the damage from Cogan's last briefing of a congressman. "So the mission from McMahon," says Avrakotos, "was to prove to Wilson that we weren't sissies, that we were tough guys."

Before setting off for the fifteen-minute drive down to the Hill, Avrakotos was familiarized with the sins of Congressman Wilson: a boodling, boozing, indiscriminate skirt chaser who was giving the Agency no end of trouble. Unlike Cogan, however, Avrakotos was interested in having a look at this Hunter Thompson of the Hill. And unlike his division chief, who numbered kings among his personal friends, Avrakotos prided himself on being tough to intimidate.

Avrakotos knew he was going to enjoy himself the moment he passed the threshold of the congressman's office and took note of Charlie's Angels. He liked the Truman and FDR pictures on the walls, the statue of Churchill, the giant painting of George Washington at Valley Forge, the blowups of the mujahideen, the map of the world covering an entire wall. But the congressman struck gold with Avrakotos the moment he began talking to Cogan. "Rays were coming out of him," Gust recalls, "and I could sense that he had an immediate dislike of Chuck. He was the only congressman I ever met who used the word 'fuck' in the first forty-five seconds."

Wilson began by asking Cogan what the Agency had done to come up with a weapon to shoot down the Hind. It was one of those questions designed to put the CIA official on the defensive. The only realistic answer was "Nothing effective," but to Avrakotos's annoyance it took Cogan some time to concede this simple point.

"All right, then what about the Charlie Horse?" Wilson demanded impatiently. Cogan explained that the mujahideen would never accept an Israeli weapon, and it would jeopardize relations with the Saudis, who were putting up half the money. "Well, if that's your only problem, I can have my Israeli friends put swastikas on the guns," Wilson said.

"Cogan looked as if I had farted," Wilson remembers. "He always acted as if people farted right next to him whenever you challenged him." Part of the problem no doubt is that Wilson insisted on calling Cogan "Mr. Coburn," despite at least one correction. Avrakotos loved watching his division chief squirm.

Now Wilson was on a roll, hurling questions at the now-defensive "Mr. Coburn," who didn't know how to respond to the congressman's accusations that the CIA was sitting on its hands. The congressman said that he and Doc Long were not going to wait any longer. In fact, he was thinking of a special appropriation to buy Oerlikons. What did the Agency think about these mule-portable Swiss anti-aircraft guns?

Wilson directed this question to Avrakotos, who had been introduced as Cogan's expert on anti-aircraft weapons. "I don't know what the fuck an Oerlikon is," Avrakotos responded. Wilson was not impressed. "I thought they had hauled him in to be a big dumb target, to take my abuse," Charlie says. "I didn't take him seriously at all." There was also the question of Avrakotos's appearance. "He had a peasant's physique and those fucking tinted glasses that looked like they came off a shelf at Woolworth's. And very thick shoes. He was a real low-rent-looking guy."

Across the desk, Avrakotos was anything but disapproving of Wilson. He was delighted by the way the Texan was sticking it to Cogan with a shower of references to his intimate friendships with Zia and Akhtar; his Texas benefactress who had Zia's ear; his high-level Pentagon contacts who were advising him about how the CIA should be running the war; even informing Cogan that he had convinced his great friend the Egyptian defense minister to sell 894 SA-7 anti-aircraft missiles for use in the war. Reading between the lines, Wilson was saying that since the Agency wasn't doing anything to counter the Hind, he damn well would. And what was Chuck Cogan going to do about that?

Cogan managed to push Wilson to the breaking point when he offered a long-winded explanation about why the Agency could not possibly introduce the Oerlikon into Afghanistan. It had to do with concealing the American hand, "plausible deniability," the CIA's time-honored rule permitting only weapons of Russian origin in a secret war with the Soviets.

"Why?" Wilson asked defiantly, pointing out that President Reagan was publicly acknowledging U.S. assistance to the Afghans.

As the exchange started to break down, Avrakotos felt a certain institutional loyalty and jumped in to save the day. "We'll be happy to look into your suggestion," he said with uncharacteristic diplomacy. "Mr. Cogan is absolutely correct that it is not what we have been doing, but I'll have my experts look into it."

The ride back to Langley was exquisite for Avrakotos. As he says, "I mean, what boss wants to get reamed in front of his subordinates?" Cogan didn't talk much except to say he really didn't want to see that man again. Avrakotos, on the other hand, figured he had spotted a kindred spirit, a congressman with power who talked dirty and who wasn't afraid to say he wanted to kill Russians and get even for Vietnam.

On the Hill, Wilson was now in the middle of the annual Appropriations feeding frenzy. Secretaries and undersecretaries of the navy, army, and air force and the long chain of defense contractors from General Dynamics, McDonnell Douglas, GE, Lockheed, and LTV all lined up, waiting their turn to plead their cases with the always receptive big spender on defense. Denis Neill and the main foreign-aid recipients were also putting in appearances: Zvi Rafiah from Israel and Mohammed Abu Ghazala from Egypt.

Wilson would take care of them all, but his mind and energies were now focused on getting more help for Pakistan and the mujahideen. By his side was Joanne Herring, a full-fledged conspirator in their secret campaign. They began using code language on the phone, talking about "eagles" and how many hawks had landed that week. Wilson also had her sit in on one of his CIA briefings and encouraged her to explain why they needed to do more. One can only imagine what the officials reported back to their bosses at Langley.

The two Texans went to visit Wilson's old adviser on Israeli strategic concerns, Edward Luttwak, described on the dust jackets of his many books as "the most brilliant and controversial defense analyst and military historian writing today." Luttwak would later burst into the national consciousness during the Gulf War with his numerous network appearances warning that the U.S. Army would take horrendous casualties if General Norman Schwarzkopf launched a ground war against Saddam Hussein. He was dramatically wrong but, as always, impressive and full of authority.

When Joanne and Charlie descended on him in 1983, he had just completed an assignment for the Pentagon to design the mix of weapons that a light infantry division could use to battle the Soviets in mountainous terrain. Because of this he had become unquestionably the most knowledgeable figure in Washington about light, portable anti-aircraft weapons.

Luttwak had some bad news. The Afghan war could never become Russia's Vietnam, he said. It was a lost cause. The best mujahideen fighters were being wiped out and the CIA was right not to provide American weapons to the tribesmen.* It would be foolish to provoke the Russians into an attack on Pakistan.

But Charlie and Joanne were not there to be told they were chasing a lost cause; they wanted to find out which gun to buy. Luttwak said there were only three non-American versions available on the world market. He was partial to the Swiss Oerlikon. He had actually visited the Swiss mountain forces and was confidant that although the primitive Afghans were not up to using most sophisticated weapons, the Oerlikon could work for them. It wasn't complicated, and it was light enough that the barrel could be carried on a line of mules.

Now the amorphous drive to help the mujahideen had a specific focus. Wilson was envisioning Oerlikons on every mountaintop in Afghanistan. He told Joanne that his first challenge was not likely to take place in the House. He owned the Appropriations subcommittee. But the Senate would have to sign off on it, and there the most important man would be the Alaska

---

*Luttwak shared the CIA position, championed by John McMahon, that plausible deniability was critical, that it was in effect an unstated bargain with the Soviets. The Soviets would not invade Pakistan if the United States concealed its hand. And the American public did not want to take responsibility for defending Pakistan.

Republican Ted Stevens, chairman of the Senate Defense Appropriations subcommittee.

This was Joanne's territory—the Republican establishment—and she quickly applied her formula for making things happen by organizing a dinner for the senator with Lord Robert Cranborne as the guest of honor. This was vintage Joanne. Cranborne had one of those titles that inevitably impress Americans. A friend of Charlie Fawcett's, Cranborne had been actively involved in the Afghan war from the beginning. He flew over on the Concorde for the dinner with the specific mission of lobbying the senator.

That night the English lord talked eloquently about how the U.S. media had no compunction about reporting every negative thing it could find about Vietnam, but in Afghanistan, the press seemed willing to give the Red Army a free ride as it pursued a policy of near genocide. It was hard not to be impressed with Cranborne, who was then running Afghan Aid, a foundation that provided assistance to Ahmad Shah Massoud in the Panjshir, helping Massoud keep his men in the field.

It was an effective evening, a creative exercise on Joanne's part, carefully designed to cast Charlie in a new light with the powerful senator who chaired the Defense Appropriations subcommittee. For the Oerlikon bill to sneak through, Wilson was going to need Stevens's support.

Joanne was systematically putting Charlie together with other powerful Republican friends as well. Wilson had met Caspar Weinberger, the secretary of defense, and CIA director Bill Casey when they'd testified before his committees, but that had been bloodless and very different from being known as the honored friend of the fascinating, well-connected, archconservative Joanne Herring.

"I'd give them all the pitch about Charlie," remembers Joanne. "I'd say he isn't just a boll weevil, he's better. He's your most significant instrument, because he's a real Democrat but he believes what you believe."

"All of this was done," Joanne acknowledged years later, "so that when d'Artagnan came charging with his light brigade, he wouldn't meet an irresistible force."

One of the peculiarities of the CIA's Afghan campaign was that none of the Agency officers knew or dealt with the Afghans they were supporting. This was one of Zia's conditions that the CIA had agreed to in order to win the right to operate out of Pakistan. But Charlie Wilson was not bound by any such restrictions. And so in the fall of 1983, when an Afghan doctor who lived in Orlando, Florida, called to say that his brother, the interim chief of the CIA's mujahideen alliance, was in town, Wilson quickly agreed to a meeting.

Professor Sigbhatullah Mojadeddi is a small man with glasses and a gray beard, and the story he told that day moved and enraged Wilson. Mojadeddi, a Muslim intellectual who speaks six languages, comes from a family said to be descended from the third caliph. By the time he shook hands with Wilson, more than a hundred members of his immediate family had been assassinated, killed, or simply lost somewhere in the mountains of Afghanistan. He himself had been jailed and tortured in 1978 after protesting in Kabul. What caught Wilson's imagination as he listened to the Afghan leader was his insistence that the Soviets could not win: "They are not a superpower. There is only one superpower: Allah."

Interspersed with this inspirational talk of faith was a challenge: "Why can't the United States do something to stop the gunships? We can't hold off the world's largest power with our bare hands. The DshK bullets only bounce off the armor." What could they do with no modern weapons and so little ammunition? The slaughter was intolerable.

Wilson invited Mojadeddi to join him and Joanne for lunch at the Democratic Club. Almost immediately Joanne began to sing the praises of an Afghan leader she had gotten to know when making her documentary with Charles Fawcett. Gulbuddin Hekmatyar was his name, and she had found him marvelous beyond words. The meek-looking professor became instantly agitated and began, in a most remarkable fashion, to denounce Gulbuddin as a true monster and an enemy of Afghanistan. He accused Gulbuddin of being a dangerous fundamentalist, busy assassinating moderate Afghans, a man no self-respecting nation should support.

If nothing else, Joanne Herring has the courage of her convictions. Zia himself and the Pakistani leaders had told her that Gulbuddin was the Afghan they respected most. She held her ground. It was an explosive argument, with neither side yielding but with Mojadeddi saying some very disturbing things about Gulbuddin's alleged bloodthirstiness and his Islamic radicalism. America would be sorry one day if it didn't stop favoring him, he warned.

In the aftermath of 9/11, the CIA would find itself agreeing with Mojadeddi. In March 2002, it launched a satellite-guided missile in an attempt to assassinate Gulbuddin Hekmatyar, the Afghan leader who had been the largest recipient of CIA weapons during the jihad. But back then, Wilson figured that he had just stumbled into some ancient tribal rivalry and that it made no sense to try to figure out who was right and who was wrong. The only relevant question, in the face of the great Soviet evil, was whether they both were trying to kill Russians. Of that he had no doubt, so he temporarily put out of his mind an issue that would later cast a shadow over the CIA's great victory in Afghanistan.

Wilson decided that Mojadeddi could be a powerful advocate for the Afghan cause and set about trying to arrange an audience with CIA Director Bill Casey. Wilson knew all about Casey's dream of finding a country where the United States could begin to roll back the Communists. Casey believed it would happen in Nicaragua, but Wilson thought that if the old OSS spymaster could just meet the Afghans, he would buy into the plan to fund a radical escalation of the war.

Only after some bullying did Casey agreed to receive Wilson, Mojadeddi, and his brother in the corner office he maintained in the Old Executive Office Building, next to the White House. The great patron of anti-Communist freedom fighters listened as Professor Mojadeddi described the experience of having a Hind helicopter sweep in on an Afghan village. Mojadeddi was still recounting the horror stories to Casey fifteen minutes later when he and his brother asked if they could excuse themselves to pray.

Wilson describes Mojadeddi as a born performer and says he suspected that the Mojadeddi brothers orchestrated the call to prayer for effect. But at the time, even Wilson was moved as they took their prayer rugs to the far corner of the suite, turned to Mecca, and began to pray loudly.

While this unusual scene was unfolding in the CIA director's office, Wilson saw a moment to drive home his point and whispered, "Bill, we're just allowing these brave men to sell their lives too cheaply."

"Charlie, there is no silver bullet," Casey replied sincerely.

"Well, there's got to be some way to knock those Hinds down, or at least make them think they're going to be knocked down," Wilson answered. The Mojadeddi brothers rejoined the conversation just as Wilson started to talk to Casey about his wish to put Oerlikons into the war.

"I'd like to have a heavier cannon too, but it's just too expensive," Casey said.

"Mr. Director, you don't understand that money is not the issue here. We'll fund anything you want. You ask for it and I'll pay for it."

Wilson remembers Casey looking at him as if he had come from a different planet. Congress was trying to close down the Contra war completely, and he did not seem to believe that Wilson was for real when he declared, with the Mojadeddis listening in amazement, "Mr. Director, I'm going to drown you in money."

What Charlie Wilson did next has no precedent. Throughout the Cold War, the CIA and the White House had always acted alone in deciding how much money would be spent on covert programs. Congress's only role was to rubber-stamp the requests or try to stop them. Never before had a congressman presumed the right to throw money at the Agency to escalate a secret war. More unthinkable, however, was Wilson's chutzpah in dictating what kind of weapon the CIA should introduce into a covert operation.

Radical as his plan might have been, Wilson had no real doubts about his ability to win the votes of his eleven colleagues on the Defense Appropriations subcommittee. Each year they gathered behind closed doors, like justices of the Supreme Court, deciding how to spend hundreds of billions of dollars for the nation's defense. They wrestled, of course, with the awesome responsibility of spending enough to protect the country while maintaining fiscal responsibility. But there was also the very human question of pork. Each of the eleven men had to stay in office, and there was no better way to do this than to bring home the bacon—the jobs, the schools, the highways, the bridges—and as everyone in Congress knew, there was no more effective pork than a piece of the giant defense pie.

Wilson occupied a special place on this committee because he asked for little and almost always supported everyone else's pork-barrel proposals. Murtha had his research grants for Penn State, and Norm Dicks was always trying to relocate much of the defense establishment to his district in Washington. Charlie was always gracious in his support, and since he had absolutely no defense contractors in his district, it was never a question of a quid pro quo. And now, in the case of the Oerlikon bill, Wilson was not asking his colleagues for billions. All he wanted was $40 million for a cause (shooting down Soviet gunships) that not even a liberal Democrat could find fault with. He was like Fred Astaire sweeping across the ballroom when he floated from the subcommittee with approval for the full $40 million— $17 million of it earmarked for an anti-aircraft cannon to bring down the Hind.

This first step had been almost anticlimactic in its ease, but next, he had to persuade the defense appropriators from the Senate to go along with his unprecedented maneuver to escalate the CIA's war. Here anything could happen, so when the House and Senate defense appropriators met, Wilson adopted a simple strategy of building up chits. "I voted for everything anyone proposed no matter what," he recounts. "I kissed every ass in the room." Wilson voted for hundreds of millions of dollars' worth of weapons—systems that more often than not were to be built in districts where the men he sat with came from.

He waited until his friend Senator Ted Stevens asked if there was anything else to be considered from the House side. "Yes," Wilson said, rising to his feet. "I'd appreciate $40 million for the Afghan freedom fighters with $17 million of that specifically earmarked for getting them a better anti-aircraft gun than they presently have." He used a phrase that Doc Long had first coined and that would later become his trademark in such deliberations: "This is the only place in the world where the forces of freedom are actually fighting and killing Russians."

The House appropriators, of course, stood as one with Wilson. To his surprise, no one on the Senate side objected. "I looked around the table and was flabbergasted. No one blinked. No one said no." Wilson says that moment was a revelation: it was as if he had pushed on a door and discovered that there was no lock and no one to complain if he charged in.

CHAPTER 16

Howard Hart

HOWARD OF
AFGHANISTAN

The press had no pictures of Howard Hart. They didn't éven know his name. The few congressmen on the Intelligence Committees who had met him had received only the most general briefings. Not even the State Department was aware of how he ran his operation. No one in the Islamabad embassy, where the station was housed, dreamed of asking him what he was doing. Strangest of all, only a very small group of people in the CIA knew the details of Hart's campaign. Although Hart and the CIA worked with many branches of the government and drew heavily on the Pentagon's support, no one attempted to dictate to the station chief what tactical decisions he should be making in the most sensitive of covert wars against the Red Army—no one but Charlie Wilson.

That was why Hart reacted so badly when news of Wilson's $40 million legislative gift reached him at the station in Islamabad. Charlie had innocently assumed that the CIA would appreciate what he had just done. After all, Tip O'Neill and his House Democrats were virtually at war with the Agency. They had just cut off all funding for the Contras, and the last thing any of the Agency's leaders expected from that same Congress was a $40 million appropriation earmarked for secret warfare in Afghanistan. It was an enormous sum for those days—$10 million more than the entire U.S. contribution to the mujahideen the year before—but to Wilson's dismay, no one at the Agency seemed to appreciate the gesture, least of all Howard Hart.

Case officers are different from most people. They're trained to be paranoid. Their job is to identify and evaluate threats, and the one thing

Hart could spot from a mile away was a first-class challenge to his command. To him, Wilson's Oerlikon maneuver was nothing short of a direct slap in the face. Yet that was precisely what Wilson had just done with the bill that he had somehow gotten through Congress. Taken literally, the legislation virtually ordered the CIA to deploy an anti-aircraft cannon in Afghanistan, and Hart quickly determined that the only weapon that fit the congressman's specifications and that made sense for the CIA to buy was the Swiss Oerlikon. It was definitely not a Soviet weapon, and if Wilson was going to force Hart to put this big, Western gun into the war zone, he might just as well write "CIA" in neon letters all over it. In fact, in one fell swoop, this extraordinarily meddlesome congressman was threatening to upend the inflexible Cold War rule that the American hand never be displayed in a proxy war.

In retrospect, the CIA's efforts to conceal its role in those early years of the Afghan war seem extreme. Only Soviet weapons that the Afghans themselves could have captured or acquired were allowed into the Agency's pipeline. U.S. Air Force planes would then fly the CIA's war goods to Saudi Arabia, where they would be unloaded, repackaged, and flown to Pakistan on Saudi cargo planes. Additional weapons and ammunition came by ship. Pakistani intelligence agents, not Americans, passed the weapons on to the mujahideen. Even the satellite targeting studies drawn up in Washington for the freedom fighters were translated into primitive hand-drawn pictures so that they looked as if they were the work of an Afghan scout.

Hart had another reason, beyond knee-jerk dogma, for worrying about the consequences of introducing Wilson's Oerlikons into the war zone. Over the long years of the Cold War, a kind of unwritten understanding had emerged between the superpowers about rules of engagement in proxy wars. The implicit understanding in Afghanistan was that the United States would not taunt the Soviets with an overt demonstration of involvement. That, at least, was the way Hart and his CIA colleagues saw it. Of course, it was an open secret that the CIA was arming the mujahideen, but no one admitted it and the voluntary discipline of concealment engendered a certain restraint. As long as the United States observed this self-restraint, Hart and the CIA high command assumed, the Soviets would also refrain from upping the ante.

Hart's very specific fear about the Oerlikons was that the expensive Swiss automatic cannons would startle and anger the Kremlin and cause it to reevaluate its entire war strategy. If the Red Army were to move with a million troops—or even only a half million—instead of its current force level of 120,000, it could break the resistance, Hart believed. And then the Soviets would surely move on Pakistan.

Under this scenario the Red Army wouldn't even need to invade. With tens of thousands of troops on the frontier there would be endless ways to make life hellish for Zia—cross-border raids, sabotage of CIA arms depots, stirring up of trouble among the three million Afghan refugees. Bombings and assassinations were already plaguing the refugee world in the North-West Frontier, and Hart could see how easily things could rage out of control if the Soviets ever decided to go for broke. Would the United States be prepared to send American boys to defend Zia ul-Haq, the man who'd murdered Benazir Bhutto's father, the dictator building a Islamic bomb?

All these thoughts and more were running through his head as he sat down with his paramilitary expert and composed a return cable to headquarters attempting to explain why it would be lunacy for the CIA to buy the Swiss gun. For starters, the weapon was incredibly heavy, requiring at least three mules to transport it. On top of that, each round cost upwards of $50, and firing at a rate of several hundred rounds a minute, the Oerlikon could eat up its sixty-round magazine in a matter of seconds. How could the Agency move all that ammunition through the mountains to keep such a gun in action? And how could the Oerlikon be used except in one fixed location? Guerrillas were supposed to be mobile. Hart suggested that even his counterpart in Pakistan intelligence, General Akhtar, shared his reasoning.

When the cable reached Langley, Cogan and Deputy Director John McMahon embraced its conclusions. But what moved them to join Hart in resisting the Oerlikon had less to do with the gun's limitations than it did with the underlying principle to which Hart needed only allude. The station chief's coded red alert had come through loud and clear. This was a test case that went beyond the immediate danger of testing the Soviets with the Oerlikon: Wilson's bill was challenging the CIA's historic right to run its own operations.

The Agency's professionals had long since become accustomed to congressional efforts to close down operations or to investigate supposed excesses. But this move of Wilson's to force the Agency to be more provocatively aggressive blindsided everyone. Hart and Cogan had assumed they could wait out Wilson and he would eventually go away. Instead, he had simply bullied his way into their poker game and now, with his $40 million appropriation on the books, was directing them to do something that they claimed was madness. They had little choice but to try to reason with him.

The problem Hart and the other CIA officials had in talking to Wilson in those days was that they had such radically different notions about what would constitute a victory in Afghanistan. Hart never had trouble explaining the logic behind his Afghan strategy to professionals like Louis Stokes, chairman of the House Intelligence Committee, or Daniel Patrick Moynihan, vice chair of the Senate committee, when they came through Pakistan wondering where the growing CIA campaign was going.

He would always begin by explaining that even if they didn't quite see how it would all end, there were compelling reasons why the best scenario for the United States was simply more of the same. For starters, the CIA's analysts now believed that every dollar that the United States slipped into the insurrection cost the Soviets at least ten to counter. That was the beauty of being on the right side of the guerrilla war; it's expensive to fight men who are not afraid to die. They just go around blasting hardware and soldiers without warning—bleeding the occupiers at will.

There was another factor. The Soviets were not using their old weapons in Afghanistan; they were deploying frontline troops along with their most sophisticated Hind helicopters, MiG fighters, and T-72 tanks—men and machinery that otherwise would be committed to the European battlefield, where as many as fifty divisions of U.S. and Soviet troops sat eyeball to eyeball. Every ruble they spent and every soldier they committed to Afghanistan was one less available for the European front.

Beyond that, the Pentagon was ecstatic with the war booty the CIA was capturing. Whatever the Soviets were using in Afghanistan was thought to offer a window into how the Red Army would fight when the big one broke out on the NATO frontier. The Agency, on behalf of its military cousins, began offering the mujahideen huge rewards for the capture of a Hind, and even more for a KGB communications van. A million dollars was said to be the reward for one of these treasures, but the bounty was extravagant for all sorts of items. The Pentagon's Soviet analysts seemed to have an indiscriminate appetite for everything the 40th Army used—tanks, mines, recoilless rifles, flak jackets, medical kits.

No one in the press, and certainly no one in the U.S. government, was talking about a victory in Afghanistan. In fact, all of the media accounts continued to portray the Afghans as heroic victims, doomed to be destroyed. But Howard Hart saw things differently. Now well into his third year as the CIA's field marshal, he felt that he was on the verge of pulling off a historic covert triumph. By that he didn't mean a conventional victory over the Red Army. The resistance was not only intact, contrary to almost all of the experts' predictions; it was now a genuine problem for the Soviets. Hart calculated that perhaps 400,000 Afghans had been armed in some fashion or other with CIA weapons. He would be the first to acknowledge that the mujahideen were hardly an army. They were more like a rabble-in-arms— but what a rabble. The veteran of the Khomeini humiliation sometimes had to pinch himself at the thought of having hundreds of thousands of Muslim fanatics moving about Pakistan and the Hindu Kush, all living for the moment when they could aim their CIA weapons at a Soviet infidel.

"It was the first time the Soviets had to pay," recalls Hart with passion. "We had watched Hungary; we had watched Czechoslovakia; we watched East Germany; each day we watched the Wall. This repulsive, repugnant machine was out there, and we finally found a place where we could get at them."

By the time Wilson intervened with his Oerlikon legislation, Hart figured he was riding the most ferocious beast ever to confront Communism. Hart thought of himself as facing off against the commander of the Soviet 40th Army in Kabul, and he was so confident of his long-term strategy that he would later boast, "I had him by the balls. I was killing his men and there was nothing he could do about it." As Hart saw it, every day that the Soviets stayed in Afghanistan with their existing force levels, the United States won.

His one consuming fear was that the Soviets would wake up and realize just how much pain the CIA and Zia were exacting and either withdraw or, more likely, escalate. As Hart saw it, he now had the war on a footing where there was simply no downside to the American involvement. The only thing looming on the horizon that could spoil it all was Wilson. The congressman was on his way back to Pakistan, and Hart decided he had no choice but to go out of channels and somehow try to reason with him.

When Wilson arrived in Pakistan in January 1984, Hart was not even on his list of people to see. The congressman was so frustrated with the CIA that he was deliberately making an end run around it. Much to Hart's annoyance, Wilson immediately began a round of private meetings with Akhtar and Zia, who expressed amazement and gratitude for what he and Doc Long had achieved—not just for the $40 million Afghan appropriation but for saving the entire Pakistan aid program from drastic cuts. "Mr. Wilson, you always surprise me," declared a pleased Zia.

Wilson's main reason for coming, however, was to personally bring news to the Afghan rebels of the Hind-killing Oerlikons. Professor Mojadeddi had genuinely alarmed him in Washington with his grim accounts of the gunship slaughter. Wilson intended to play the role of cheerleader, talking up the miraculous new weapon in the pipeline to keep Mojadeddi and the other Afghan leaders from losing hope in the months before the Oerlikon and the other weapons could be delivered.

It was a mission with noble intentions, but Charlie could never deny himself a bit of pleasure from even the most sensitive of his national security efforts. He had chosen for his traveling companion on this trip a five-foot-nine, Nordic blonde named Cynthia Gale Watson, whom he introduced to everyone as "Snowflake."

Wilson's practice of always bringing a beautiful woman along on his foreign adventures was far more complicated than just making sure he had a romantic partner in the deserts of Islam. He thirsted for glory and respect, but his lifestyle had left him with a reputation for little more than scandal and excess. All of his remarkable feats of derring-do abroad took place in the shadows. No one at home, none of his constituents, not even anyone on his staff fully understood what a key player he was in the countries where he was now operating. Even his sister, Sharon, perhaps the most important person in the world to Charlie, had no idea what he was about. It was only on the junkets, when the brass bands came out to greet him and he was received as a statesman—in Israel, Egypt, and Pakistan—that the role he was playing in these flash points of history became public.

But what good was it all without a witness—without someone to tell him how very wonderful he was? Charlie needed a witness to validate the experience, and this time it was Snowflake. Like most of Charlie's loves, she was a beauty queen, the former Miss Northern Hemisphere, a farm girl from Minnesota who could plow a field, break a horse, make her own clothes, and run faster than any woman in the state, and who now, at twenty-eight, dreamed of becoming a movie star. Most important, she was a good American girl, filled with enthusiasm and a sense of wonder at this man who was performing miracles, not only for her but for his country.

Snowflake fell into her part effortlessly, weeping over the wounded mujahideen at the Red Cross hospital, watching her hero give blood for the freedom fighters, walking arm in arm with Charlie through a sea of refugees as little children sang him their song of the jihad. All of this was just boilerplate for Wilson, who had come to Peshawar to meet "with the seven tribes," as he explained to Snowflake. "There are seven ruling leaders. They all banded together to fight this war, and they're coming to meet with me to see if they can get some arms."

Snowflake was thrilled when Charlie told her she could sit in on the war meetings. Not wanting to offend the fundamentalist warriors, she went to great lengths to dress conservatively—in a pink nylon jumpsuit with a zipper straight down the front. She even braided her hair and wore combat boots, feeling that a "semimilitary" outfit would put the visitors more at ease.

The first of the mujahideen leaders to arrive in Charlie's room, the engineer Gulbuddin Hekmatyar, was biblical in appearance, with his long, black beard and turban. He was then only thirty-eight, but there was a timeless air to him, an almost feline quality and a gentleness to his manner and speech. Even at that early moment in the war he awed his fellow mujahideen as the most ruthless and uncompromising of them all.

Gulbuddin was the darling of Zia and the Pakistan intelligence service. Like other mujahideen leaders, he had been working with the ISI since the early 1970s, when Pakistan had begun secretly backing fundamentalist students at the University of Kabul who were rebelling against Soviet influence in the Afghan government. Back then Gulbuddin was very much a part of the emerging global wave of Islamic radicalism, opposed to any attempts at altering fundamental tenants of the faith. By all accounts, he was responsible for the practice of throwing acid in the faces of Afghan women who failed to cover themselves properly.

The Red Army had a legend of its own about Gulbuddin. To the Soviets he was the bogeyman behind the most unspeakable torture of their captured soldiers. Invariably his name was invoked with new arrivals to keep them from wandering off base unaccompanied, lest they fall into the hands of this depraved fanatic whose specialty, they claimed, was skinning infidels alive.

Gulbuddin's reputation would grow to such sinister proportions by the latter part of the war that many U.S. newsmen would almost agree with the Soviets in comparing him to Khomeini and would accuse the CIA of backing the wrong horse. He ran his Hezb-i-Islami organization like the Communist Party, with utter ruthlessness. Nevertheless, Gulbuddin was the "freedom fighter" whom Charlie Fawcett and then Joanne Herring had come to know and love when they had made the movie *Courage Is Our Weapon*. And Charlie Wilson was fascinated with him because he had heard that Gulbuddin could kill Soviets like no other. Furthermore, Wilson had a specific question for the engineer that he wanted to put to him without the CIA's knowledge.

That New Year in Peshawar, into the lobby of the Pearl Intercontinental Hotel swept Gulbuddin and his entourage—a tall figure in white with five bodyguards carrying AK-47s. Up to Wilson's suite he strode, the ascetic fundamentalist holy warrior finally coming face-to-face with his American patron. As if on cue Cynthia Gale emerged from the congressman's adjoining room in her pink jumpsuit, her hand thrust out in greeting: "Pleased to meet you."

What could the engineer possibly have been thinking? By his Muslim standards, Snowflake was half naked. Whatever his reaction, Gulbuddin's face remained neutral, almost benign, as he and the congressman began to talk.

"It was just very, very exciting to be in that room with those men with their huge white teeth," remembers Snowflake. "It was very clandestine. There was this secretive feel to it." To her Gulbuddin, as well as all the other Afghans who visited the suite that night, looked on Charlie as "the great god that was going to save their lives."

This last observation would doubtless have come as a particular surprise to Gulbuddin, that disciplined worshipper of Allah, the one and only true god. Seven years later he would reveal just how much he appreciated all that Charlie and the United States had done for the jihad by siding with Saddam Hussein in the Gulf War. But that evening in Peshawar, sitting with the Texas congressman and his blasphemous traveling companion, Gulbuddin was all smiles.

Wilson began by telling the commander about the Oerlikons and the flood of more and better weapons soon to come. Then he put his question to the engineer: the congressman had certain important contacts with the

Israelis, but the CIA was giving him no end of trouble on his proposal to take advantage of a significant opportunity. If Wilson could get the Americans to buy Soviet weapons that the Israelis had captured from the PLO, would Hekmatyar have any trouble accepting them?

"We take Russian weapons from dead Russians to use against them—I don't see why we can't take them from the Israelis," replied the engineer wryly. In fact, Gulbuddin seemed to have no problem with the origin of any weapons for the jihad. "Allah has many mysterious ways of providing for his faithful," he said.

Wilson was delighted. He resolved right then to disregard the CIA's objections and ratchet up his efforts to pressure the Agency to buy the PLO weapons and fund the Charlie Horse.

The next Afghan to find himself face-to-face with Snowflake that night was Professor Mojadeddi, the mujahideen leader Charlie had taken to meet Bill Casey at the White House. The small professor was surrounded by an even more menacing band of bodyguards than Gulbuddin had brought with him. "Do they really have to worry that much about the Soviets trying to kill them?" Wilson asked a Pakistan ISI man later. "It's not the Soviets they're worried about," the man said matter-of-factly. "It's each other. They're all trying to keep from being killed by their rivals."

Howard Hart would have choked had he witnessed the comic opera of Wilson and Snowflake that evening—singing the praises of the Oerlikons, suggesting to the fundamentalists that they link up with Israel, and then asking that hopelessly naive question about the bodyguards. It would only have confirmed Hart's conviction that Wilson didn't have a clue as to whom he was dealing with.

Hart understood that, like most Americans who'd discovered the Afghan war, Wilson was in the initial stages of unconditional adulation. Typically that meant seeing the mujahideen as pure of heart, brave, intensely religious, and worthy of total support. Like all newcomers, Wilson appeared even to have embraced the fantasy that these tribesmen could weld themselves into a single unified resistance.

Hart had gone down this path himself, but that had been long ago. "Akhtar and I used to sit around talking about how nice it would be if they could create the equivalent of the Free French and find themselves an Akbar de Gaulle," remembers Hart. "But the Afghans are hardly a people, much less a nation. They are a nation of tribes constantly at war with each other. They are very heterogeneous, with an extreme ethnocentricity which makes them not only hate or suspect foreigners but Afghans living two valleys away."

Hart had made his peace with this profound flaw in the Afghans and had even come to believe that a large part of their potency as a guerrilla force came from the fact that they were disunited. It made it hard for them to coordinate their military activities, but it also meant that there was no single leader whose head could be cut off to destroy the insurgency. In fact, there was no centralized anything except a distribution system for weapons and support that, in utter frustration, the Pakistanis had finally created to impart some measure of organization and control.

The ISI, with the consent of the CIA, had chosen seven leaders from a mob of heroic chieftains. To a certain extent, the power of the seven and their respective political parties was a creation of Pakistan intelligence. The desperate mujahideen were told that in order to get weapons, food, medical supplies, training, or assistance for their families, they had to join one of these authorized groups. So began the only form of unity that would exist in this war. It was just an illusion, however, and the only thing that kept the Afghans from one another's throats was their common hatred of the Soviet infidel and hence the need to restrain their tribal fighting in order to retain access to the weapons and money that the CIA was making available to them.

This would become frighteningly clear in 1989, just weeks after the Red Army's withdrawal, when Gulbuddin's commanders in the Helmand Valley would trick a delegation of Massoud's warriors into negotiating. They guaranteed them safe passage, even swearing on a Koran that they would honor this commitment. But once the trusting Tajiks came into the Pashtuns' territory, they were set upon, tortured, and killed. What Hart knew well, even back in 1984, was that there was a cruel and disturbing side to the Afghans.

Which is not to say that Howard Hart did not feel deeply about his clients and their cause. Like everyone else, he had been swept up by it. But he put limits on his emotional attachments. Professional detachment was necessary to play "the Great Game" effectively. All seasoned commanders are faced with the need in war to sacrifice one flank in a feint, or to lose an entire unit, if necessary, for the good of the whole. To Hart and the CIA, the mujahideen had become a division, albeit a strange and unpredictable division, in a much larger struggle against the advancing Soviet empire. The station chief's task in Afghanistan was to keep the mujahideen in the field, to give them enough so that they could hope for victory but not enough to endanger the larger goals of the United States.

Above all else, the head of the Islamabad station prided himself on being a realist, and there were profound limits to what was possible in Afghanistan. For him and his Agency, the central reality was that the Red Army did not lose wars. Not since 1921, when the Treaty of Riga had ended the Russo-Polish War and ceded Russian land to Poland, had the Soviets been forced from territory they had paid for in blood. Afghanistan would not be another Vietnam. The Soviets didn't operate with the same restraints as the Americans. There was no horde of journalists and politicians questioning every military action. Just across the border from the mujahideen camps and the great refugee centers in Pakistan, the Soviets were busy carpet bombing villages, poisoning wells, killing livestock, causing over half the Afghan population to flee their homes. Perhaps it wasn't yet genocide, but the Red Army was capable of almost anything.

What was so grating about having to deal with Wilson was that he just didn't understand the game. He seemed to think that the interests of the Afghans and the CIA should be identical. Hart, however, underestimated the twists and turns of Wilson's thinking both about the mujahideen and about what he was hoping to accomplish in Afghanistan.

On one level the station chief was right: Wilson did romanticize these mountain warriors. It was the old business of his dying dog Teddy. Only a Dr. Freud could have fully explained what compelled Wilson throughout his adult life to champion the cause of underdogs. But there was never any question that his mind always raced back to that moment with his mutt writhing on the drugstore floor, dying from the ground glass that the selectman had poisoned him with.

Forty years later, Wilson didn't just want to help the Afghans; he needed to help them. They too had been poisoned, their children maimed with toy bombs. Old men were being thrown down wells by the Communist thugs. Gunships were swaggering through the skies, looking for caravans of mules or camels to mow down. They were wiping out villages friendly to the rebels. They were even murdering columns of refugees just for sport as the women and children tried to walk out of the country. In the landscape of Wilson's mind, the Hind had become the murderous selectman. But the mujahideen weren't giving up, and Wilson wanted revenge for them.

As a boy, he had been inspired by the struggle of World War II, where the United States had demonstrated that it had the power to work its will when it had the courage to fight. The lines he had read on the marble walls of the Lincoln Memorial the day he had arrived in Washington to take office had never left him—the lines about the soldiers who had died at Gettysburg. "We here highly resolve that these dead shall not have died in vain—that this nation, under God, shall have a new birth of freedom." To Wilson, Afghanistan was every bit as important a battlefield for democracy as Gettysburg, but the United States was asking the mujahideen to give their lives too cheaply.

Charlie Wilson wanted to make the Red Army suffer. He was after revenge, and he would prove tireless and maniacal in his drive to arm the mujahideen. But he was also in ways an unlikely champion of these stoic, bloodthirsty warriors.

On a personal level, Charlie was a near pacifist. He had hunted only once in his life, as a twelve-year-old. He had shot a squirrel in a tree, and when the furry creature had fallen to the ground yelping, Wilson had been horrified at the agony he had caused. The shaken boy had been horrified to have to put the animal out of its misery. Never again would Charlie Wilson raise a gun against a living creature.

You would never know this looking at the gun case in his house on Crooked Creek in Lufkin. It is filled with weapons from around the world—Uzis from Israel, M-16s, Russian assault rifles, Enfields, shooting canes, shotguns, .30-06s, and pistols large and small. But never would this congressman fire one to take a life.

Outside his home, along the creek, he's installed forty bird feeders and countless varieties flock to take advantage of the New Deal breakfast he provides year-round for the cardinals and sparrows and blue jays. There are also specially designed feeders with corncobs and a sitting perch, where the squirrels can eat with the knowledge that no one will be coming after them in this game preserve.

But when it came to the Afghan war, this softhearted bird lover was out for blood. What Howard Hart did not understand was that Wilson was not just swept away by the romance of the freedom fighters; there was a more pragmatic side to his embrace of them, something akin to the friendship that Winston Churchill developed for Joseph Stalin during World War II. "I like that man," Churchill had told Anthony Eden in an impulsive moment.

Churchill, however, had not been naive about Stalin. More than anyone in the West, he knew that the Soviet leader was responsible for the murder of millions. But context is everything, and in the 1940s, during the struggle for the world, the prime minister found it nothing short of exhilarating to have the guns of this thug and his Red Army targeted on Hitler. Before the war was over the Soviets would pay the price of twenty million lives to put down the Nazis. Having an ally like that was no small thing.

What Hart could not quite comprehend was that, in the end, what the congressman liked most about the Afghans was their terrifying passion to kill the common enemy, their refusal to bow under in spite of the odds. He even admired their revenge taking, when they would put their prisoners to gruesome deaths.

Although Hart didn't yet know it, any ability that he might have had to modify Wilson's designs was all but lost late that night in Peshawar at the Pearl Intercontinental. Well after the last Afghan leader had left and Charlie and Snowflake went to bed, there was a knock on the congressman's door. Snowflake was frightened, at first, to hear the whispering voices of the mujahideen. Professor Mojadeddi, accompanied by his bodyguards, entered the room carrying something in a pillowcase. Snowflake said she backed off as Mojadeddi pulled a captured Russian AK-47 out of the pillowcase.

"It was very hushed, and this private, quiet ceremony unfolded," she remembers from her cramped quarters in Beverly Hills, where she is still trying to get established. The professor presented the AK with great solemnity—it was the sincerest thanks he could offer for the Oerlikons. This was the kind of gesture that moved a Texan like Charlie Wilson. He'd be with them now to the end; and the only end was victory.

Wilson would illegally ship that captured Russian assault rifle home and place it on the wall of his living room in Lufkin. Whenever he was in trouble politically, he would turn to it almost as if it were a talisman. It would become the centerpiece in a political ad that moved his constituents and became famous among his congressional colleagues for its brazen appeal to John Wayne–style patriotism.

"This is a Russian Kalashnikov assault rifle," Wilson intoned in the ad. "It's the instrument of Communist terrorism worldwide—in Rome, in

London, in Lebanon, and in Afghanistan. Everywhere except here, because we're big and we're strong. With continued adequate military strength and eternal vigilance and God's help, we'll never see a Kalashnikov on the banks of the Neches."

In slow motion, with a weird, frightening sound in the background, the congressman from the Second Congressional District hurls Mojadeddi's captured AK into the river. Perhaps only in Texas could such an ad have found a sympathetic audience. But it was not created for cynical political reasons. This was the way Wilson saw himself, and this heroic self-image made him see Howard Hart not as a daring spy but as a timid bureaucrat unwilling to take a risk for freedom.

The station chief was not authorized to seek out visiting congressmen to discuss classified matters, particularly not legislation. It was taboo, and under normal circumstances, he would never have considered it. But now, with the threat of the Oerlikon looming, he deliberately crossed the line, sought out Wilson, and asked for the opportunity to brief him.

The two men acted as if they were pleased to see each other when they met in the old Agency for International Development building, which was still serving as the temporary embassy. On the fifth floor Hart ushered Wilson into the cramped suite that functioned as the CIA's Islamabad station, and in the secure room known as "the tank," Hart once again put on the 1812 Overture. His paramilitary expert was already there, and the two men began their carefully prepared presentation. It was designed to explain how much more effective it would be to the war effort if Wilson would let the Agency use the Oerlikon money to buy 12.7mm DshKs and 14.5mm machine guns.

Charlie had, of course, already heard Hart's spiel about the DshK's effectiveness. But this time Hart felt he was making a far more compelling argument. The paramilitary expert had prepared plastic overlays to place over the station's war maps. The first one showed a handful of blue dots representing the Oerlikons that could be deployed with the millions of dollars Wilson had laid aside for them. Afghanistan is about the size of Texas and Hart, pointing to the handful of dots, made it clear how little damage they could do.

He then superimposed another overlay, with hundreds of red dots indicating the number of heavy machine guns that he could deploy with that same amount of money. "I can kill more Russians with these than with the Oerlikons. And the Oerlikons will just piss the Russians off and might provoke them to attack a base camp they might otherwise ignore."

Perhaps it was the music in the background that imparted a sense of history and drama. The station chief felt the power of his own argument and simply could not imagine how the congressman could fail to see its logic.

Wilson was polite. They had made a fine case, a persuasive case, but he had studied this problem and the Oerlikon was just what the mujahideen needed. At this point Hart got a creepy feeling that to Wilson the Oerlikon had become "sort of a messianic cause of his, the magic weapon."

But Wilson was not talking about an either-or situation. "Howard, you can have more 12.7s, too," he said. The idea of just throwing more money at a CIA campaign was simply outside of Hart's experience—and, for that matter, outside the experience of the CIA. He paid no attention to it. Instead, he reminded the congressman of the danger to Pakistan if the Oerlikon were introduced, and he said that General Akhtar agreed with him.

Wilson had the station chief outflanked here as well. He had just finished talking to Akhtar and, indeed, to Zia himself. "Howard, the Pakistanis ain't stepping back," he said. "They're steppin' up."

The two men might just as well have been speaking different languages. Hart was ostensibly addressing the narrow subject of the Oerlikon but was really making one last stab at keeping the program in the hands of the professionals. And Wilson was confusing the issue by trying to be accommodating, doing his best to make Hart understand that money was no longer an issue. He was offering a bigger pie—for that matter, many more pies if that's what the warriors wanted.

"Howard, you don't seem to understand," he said in frustration. "We're going to buy you every fucking Oerlikon, every fucking Blowpipe, every fucking SA-7 we can get in Eastern Europe. And Howard, you just tell me how many DshKs you want and you can have them too. Just tell me how many."

It was all very sad, this confrontation. Hart was thinking about managing perpetual conflict, using the Afghan war to help slowly erode the strength of the enemy in a global campaign that might go on for decades. Wilson was running with the logic of the old Barry Goldwater line "Why not victory?"

It was particularly offensive for Hart to be treated as if he were some kind of timid bureaucrat. It had been no easy task convincing the Pakistanis to permit the war to escalate. Hart had built the relationship with a nervous and suspicious ISI. He had become a personal face that General Akhtar could look to and trust. Good old H2. Akhtar knew that with Hart in place it was safe to move forward together on this most dangerous of tiger hunts.

By 1984 Akhtar's special-forces operatives were moving in and out of Afghanistan dressed as mujahideen, leading special operations and ambushes and killing Russians. That was truly provocative, and Hart was proud that he had helped bring about an escalation of the CIA's efforts far larger than anyone had thought possible when he'd taken over. When Akhtar complained to Hart about his discovery that the English were trying to sneak ordnance and support to Massoud in Panjshir, Hart could draw on their friendship and say, "Oh, General, leave them alone. You know the British are only a Third World army, and you have the fifth largest in the world. They won't hurt anything."

That was Howard Hart the pro. His Afghan program may have been modest by comparison to what was to come once "Charlie's money" started pumping billions into the war, but everything that was done later with the mujahideen was built on the back of the relationship Hart had forged with Akhtar. Perhaps it was in part pride of ownership that caused Hart to refuse to play with Wilson now. Perhaps it had something to do with their unpleasant last meeting. Whatever it was, Hart could not cope with Wilson's pompous offer of unlimited weapons. Good God, the man talked as if he wanted to declare war on the Soviet Union. What good was it to have the CIA run a covert operation if a P. T. Barnum was allowed to hop into the ring and start barking out circus lines?

Five months later, Howard Hart would pack his bags, take his wife and two teenage sons, and leave Pakistan and the Afghan war for good. He longed to stay on, but perhaps it was fortunate that his three-year tour was up.

On his last night, the station chief and his three-man Afghan team had a farewell dinner with General Akhtar. At the end of the evening, the ISI chief took Hart aside and hugged him. The Pakistani would never shake the habit of calling the next station chief by Hart's affectionate nickname, H2.

Back at Langley, Director Casey honored him with the Agency's highest decoration. But as is the custom of the Clandestine Services, at the end of his Afghan tour, Hart saluted, closed the door, and never looked back. He wouldn't really ever find out what Avrakotos and Wilson did next to transform the war. He had left the encounter with Wilson knowing that he had done everything possible to stop a disaster in the works. Now it was up to Chuck Cogan; he would have to hold the line back at Langley. There would be many new arenas for Hart to go into—many other challenges the CIA would have in store for him. But in the end, he would always look back on Afghanistan as his proudest hour.

CHAPTER 17

Joanne, Charlie, and friends

COGAN'S LAST STAND

Chuck Cogan had come of age in the CIA in the 1960s—long before Congress demanded or even claimed the right to serve as its watchdog. By the time Cogan had climbed to the top of the Agency, he had not found it easy to adapt to the idea of politicians intruding into this private world. But he was a good soldier, and ever since the law establishing intelligence oversight committees was enacted in 1980, he had done his part to brief members and staff on the House and Senate side.

Cogan had drawn the line, however, when Wilson had moved to insinuate himself into the operational details of the Agency's business. In his quasi-military world, Cogan enjoyed the status of a three-star general. He didn't just oversee the Afghan operation; he had to deal with the hostage nightmare, with Khomeini, with Saddam Hussein, with the spread of nuclear weapons, and on and on. This was no playground for amateurs. He had been quite up front in telling Wilson that the Agency would not go along with his request to fund the Charlie Horse. The whole idea of an Israeli anti-aircraft gun for a Muslim jihad was absurd. Nor was he going to permit any non-Soviet weapons into Afghanistan. Wilson's response had been crude, almost threatening, but the CIA veteran had assumed that this was just congressional bluster. The fact was that Wilson had been trespassing in areas where he did not belong, and Cogan had politely shown him the door.

No doubt Cogan would have been happy never to see Charlie Wilson. Unlike his colleagues and predecessors, however, Wilson did not accept Cogan's implied premise that the CIA had an exclusive right to decide the nature of this war. Things may have worked that way before, but Wilson had decided to change all that. It was really quite simple, as he saw it.

Congress not only represented a coequal branch of the U.S. government, it had the power of the purse. The bill he had muscled through called on the CIA to spend $17 million for a Swiss anti-aircraft cannon (as well as another $23 million to be left to the CIA's discretion) to be deployed in a campaign that everyone knew the president enthusiastically endorsed. Just to be sure the CIA got the message, Wilson had included language obligating it to inform him in advance of how it intended to spend the balance of the $40 million appropriation he had sponsored. And so, when the congressman requested a meeting, the Agency found itself with no real choice but to send Chuck Cogan back to try to sort things out.

The way Wilson saw it, "The CIA basically woke up one morning to discover they had an extra $40 million they hadn't asked for. It was kind of a good news–bad news deal. Good because they like money; bad because it specified that the money should be used for an anti-aircraft cannon they didn't want. But then a lot more money for the things they did want—boots, morphine, and saws to cut off legs and arms. They had to come and clear it first."

Left with the unpleasant task of returning to Wilson's office to try to reason with the congressman, Cogan again tapped Avrakotos. As the two men moved through the cavernous white marble halls of the Rayburn office building, Cogan, with the slightly thuggish-looking Avrakotos by his side, was still convinced that he would be able to put this meddling congressman back in his cage; but best, he thought, to wear the man down with good arguments.

Wilson received Cogan and Avrakotos at his desk, next to the giant map of the world that covered an entire wall of his office. He was all business, interested only in hearing when the guns would be deployed. Unfortunately, the division chief had some bad news: "preliminary studies" indicated that the Oerlikon was simply too heavy for the Afghans to carry up to the heights where it could be useful. An even bigger problem, he explained, were the shells. So many would be needed that scores of mules would have to be provided. The Agency would end up having to go into the mule business. Wilson recalls Cogan suggesting that as many as two hundred of these pack animals might be needed just to take care of one Oerlikon over the course of a year.

Cogan stressed the top-secret nature of the briefing. Another congressman might have been intimidated, but Wilson had been studying the

Jane's series of weapons reference books, as well as conferring with his own arms expert, Ed Luttwak. He knew that the Agency was already giving the mujahideen Soviet 14.5mm machine guns, which weighed more than the Oerlikon. So what was the big deal about his guns?

Cogan shifted gears: end-user certificates were a big problem. The Swiss, with their fetish for neutrality, would be compromised if the Soviets cornered them and demanded to know who had paid for the guns. The U.S. cover would be blown. It could have nightmarish ramifications, he confided. It would require finding a government willing to lie for the CIA and assume responsibility for the Oerlikons.

Wilson found this argument empty. With twenty thousand employees, the CIA should be able to take care of a simple concealment problem. Cogan was clearly feeding him a lot of sludge, and he didn't like it. He was demanding a specific answer, and Cogan didn't want to tell him outright that he wasn't going to buy the guns.

"Well, how about the $4 million we put in for boots?" Wilson asked with contempt. "There hasn't been one damn boot delivered. And I understand there were eighty-two cases of frostbite last week. Do you need end-user certificates to send boots, Mr. Coburn?"

Avrakotos, meanwhile, sat quietly, fascinated by the spectacle of this congressman viciously reaming his boss, whom everyone else treated with such reverence. Over the course of the next few months, while Cogan stonewalled him, Charlie would come to hold him personally responsible for the slaughter that continued in the mountains. "The only thing I care about, Coburn," he had said at the end of that meeting, "is shooting down those helicopters, and I don't care if it hurts your feelings or not. There is nothing I won't do, absolutely nothing."

While Wilson was doing battle with Cogan, Joanne Herring was in a state. All of her grand plans were suddenly in jeopardy. She had organized a party that was designed to put her and her political salon on the map, but to her horror, most of the important people she had been counting on were turning her down. The party was billed as a "Welcome to Washington" dinner for Prince Bandar, the dashing young American-trained fighter pilot serving as Saudi ambassador to the United States. Joanne had known Bandar ever since his flight training in Texas, when he'd attended

her extravaganzas in River Oaks. Since then, the prince had married King
Fahd's daughter and become, for all intents and purposes, a surrogate
son of the Saudi monarch.

"I just assumed that because of his history everyone would accept,"
recalls Joanne. That assumption would have been sound had she given the
party a couple of years later, after Bandar emerged as the most powerful
and influential ambassador since World War II. In those days, however,
Bandar's most impressive accomplishments stemmed from his work in the
shadows.

Just a few months after Joanne's invitation, Ronald Reagan's national
security adviser, Robert C. McFarlane, would visit Bandar at his palatial
house overlooking the Potomac to ask the Saudi prince to secretly fund
the Contras. Bandar would quickly win approval from the throne to pay a
million dollars a month to keep the CIA's Contras in the field. Soon enough,
Bandar's many discreet favors for the American government would raise
his profile with Washington's power elite. George Bush would take the
prince and his family on fishing vacations; Colin Powell would come over
to his house to play handball. Indeed, during the Gulf War, Bandar would
become a de facto member of the National Security Council.

But back in early 1984, his name was not working for Joanne. It was
all doubly embarrassing because she had taken Charlie to lunch at the
prince's house, where she had gone over the guest list and promised a party
to end all parties. As always, she was mixing pleasure with business. By this
time, thoughts of marriage to Charlie had passed, but Joanne was as deeply
committed to their common crusade for Zia and the Afghans as ever, and
she knew that few men in Washington could be as helpful to Charlie as
the young ambassador.

It was a tightly held secret, but Wilson knew from classified briefings that the Saudis were secret partners of the CIA in the Afghan war,
and he was eager to meet Bandar. The Soviet invasion of Afghanistan
had had an even more dramatic impact on the desert kingdom than it
had on America. The Saudis sit on at least one-third of the world's known
oil reserves—perhaps the greatest treasure trove any nation has ever possessed. But the 870,000-square-mile kingdom with a population not much
greater than that of Los Angeles County has no real army to protect its
wealth. The royal family was convinced that once the Red Army invaded
Afghanistan and took up positions a few hundred miles from the king-

dom, the Kremlin's grand design would call for moving on their oil fields next.

In Washington shortly after the invasion, Jimmy Carter had announced the creation of a Rapid Deployment Force and committed the United States to protecting Saudi Arabia and other Persian Gulf oil states from any aggression. For their part, the Saudis had moved to turn their country, in effect, into a forward base for American military forces. They'd commenced building vast underground facilities where weapons and ammunition could be prepositioned for an American-led intervention. They'd built airfields with hardened hangars able to withstand two-thousand-pound bombs, erecting hundreds more than were needed for their own air force, making it possible for the United States to fly in naked and be instantly ready for war. Fuel and bombs and bullets and food had all been placed in storage for the day when they might be needed for an American rescue mission.

When the Gulf War erupted a decade later, all those immense secretive preparations made the colossal American and allied operations possible. The underground command centers, where U.S. and Saudi generals worked side by side, rivaled anything in the Pentagon. Suddenly it became clear that the United States and Saudi Arabia enjoyed a very special relationship indeed.

But back in the early 1980s, the billions of dollars' worth of high-performance jets and AWACS radar planes that Saudi Arabia was seeking to purchase from the United States were the source of deep and bitter political battles in Washington. And Prince Bandar, then in his early thirties, was at the center of the campaign to convince Congress to grant the Saudis' requests. It was a knock-down, drag-out fight, and the Israelis, who had mobilized all their forces to block the sales, were horrified when Wilson, one of their most trusted champions, broke ranks.

So intense was the 1982 AWACS battle that scores of the congressman's most important Jewish backers, who had scheduled a major fund-raiser for Charlie, canceled the event the day after Wilson voted to sell the AWACS. Despite this, Wilson held the line, actually lecturing his Jewish friends on how Israel's very survival depended on reaching out to moderate Arabs.

Bandar was well aware of the significance of Wilson's AWACS support, but that was history. What clicked when Joanne put them together at lunch was their mutual fascination with Afghanistan. Bandar had been the king's point man three years earlier, when the new CIA director, Bill Casey, had approached the prince about helping fund an escalation in the Afghan war. Bandar had flown to Jidda with Casey to serve as the Director's translator for the meeting with the king.*

"What can you do to help us?" Casey had asked King Fahd. But Fahd, no stranger to the workings of American politics, had countered by introducing a note of reality into the discussion: "That's not a fair question. What I tell you I'll do, I'll do. But you have your Congress to deal with. So you do what you can—and I'll match it." Knowing the king's vast resources, Casey had sprung to his feet, arms extended, saying, "You've got a deal."

By the time Bandar hosted Joanne and Charlie for lunch, the arrangement had been in place more than two years. Wilson was eager to find out if the Saudi commitment would extend to his $40 million special Oerlikon appropriation. Beyond that, he wanted to know how the Saudis would react to the far larger increases in the CIA's Afghan budget he had in mind.

As it turned out, Wilson could not have found a more willing accomplice. Bandar not only supported the Afghan war; secret dealings with the United States were now in his blood. Wilson could see that just by looking at the huge photograph in the gold frame displayed on a pedestal in the prince's living room. It showed one of Charlie's early political heroes, Franklin Roosevelt, talking to Bandar's grandfather, King Abdul Aziz, the founder of modern Saudi Arabia. The picture captured the two men in the middle of World War II scheming to undermine British influence in the Middle East.

From grandfather to grandson, little had changed in the way these tribal patriarchs conducted their affairs. Abdul Aziz had grown up before oil transformed his desert kingdom, and he'd passed on to Bandar's generation the highly personalized Bedouin tradition of diplomacy. That day in 1984, Bandar did not need to consult his country's legislature to tell Wilson that the Saudis would embrace a gun that could shoot down the

---

*The royal family was concerned not only about oil; they also had to please their own intensely fundamentalist religious establishment. The Saudi mullahs had been among the first to begin sending financial support to the Afghan jihad, and the king, as protector of the two holiest shrines of Islam, Mecca and Medina, could not afford to be indifferent toward this most passionate of Islamic causes.

Hind. He knew that the king would smile on any increases Wilson might make in the CIA's support for the jihad.

Charlie did not look or talk that day as if he were anything but an equal of Bandar. But sitting at the prince's table with Joanne was an exotic experience for the man from the tiny town of Trinity. Dining with kings and princes, moving in the world of characters who shape history was what he had dreamed about in that dusty Depression town. Wilson had always managed to fill his life with characters who looked and acted as if they had escaped from a novel, but Bandar was in a class of his own: a U.S.-trained fighter pilot with a house in Aspen so large that it would create a town crisis over the right of millionaires to build such oversized structures.

Everything he said that day pleased Wilson. It wasn't a contract, but Bandar left the clear impression that the Saudis would match any future appropriations Wilson might make. To Charlie, that meant anytime he struck on behalf of the mujahideen, it would double the blow against the Soviets.

Many years later, after the Red Army had withdrawn from Afghanistan, Bandar would arrange a hero's welcome for Wilson in Saudi Arabia. But even back in 1984 one can imagine how pleasing it must have been for the prince to meet such a refreshingly different U.S. representative. Bandar was used to Democrats dependent on Jewish contributions, who always seemed to vote against Saudi arms sales even as they privately told him how much they respected the kingdom's moderate positions. He was keenly aware that most Democratic congressmen didn't want anything to do with the CIA unless it was to reign the Agency in. Joanne had brought him a congressional powerhouse who not only sided with Saudi Arabia in its historic confrontation with the Israel lobby but could single-handedly force massive increases in U.S. funding for a Muslim jihad.

Within a year of the lunch, Gust Avrakotos would take advantage of this budding relationship between the prince and the congressman. As the Afghan budget doubled, and then doubled again into the hundreds of millions, the king would inevitably be late with his matching funds. Casey and Avrakotos would fly to Riyadh or Jidda to personally collect, but more often than not there was no time for this flattering diplomacy. Bills would come due and the program's relationship with its suppliers would be placed in jeopardy. Avrakotos, not wanting to alienate the king by being too pushy, would turn to Wilson.

"Allah will not be pleased if the king abandons his freedom fighters," Charlie would tell Bandar in a voice that seemed at once playful and serious. "If you don't do this soon, I'm going to tell Joanne." Bandar would laughingly feign alarm at this bogus threat: "Oh no, don't do that! Allah will soon be smiling, Charlie. You will see."

Much of the business in Washington is transacted in this manner. That's why in 1984 Joanne felt so menaced by the many regrets to her dinner invitations. Bombing out on a high-profile party like this one could be terminal, politically as well as socially.

"I spent three weeks on the telephone, personally calling everyone. We had to get them back," she recalled of her efforts. "I got Charlie to call his friends on the Armed Services Committee and at the Pentagon." Wilson was already going the extra mile for Joanne, even assigning some of his secretaries to help her with logistics, just as he had done the year before for her Zia party. It was clearly stretching the rules to deploy congressional staff for such work, but an argument could always be made that Joanne's parties were critical to some aspect of U.S. diplomacy.

Meanwhile, Joanne's other friends were also rallying. A financially strapped Charles Fawcett took the train from Los Angeles to Washington. Joanne had sent him a plane ticket, but out of pride he had sent it back. On the train he was robbed, and he arrived without suitable clothes to wear to the party. But the ever-resourceful ex-RAF ace, king of B-grade movies and defender of the Afghans, penciled a vividly accurate sketch of the robber, and his black tie was returned by the police just in time for the party.

By this time, Joanne had taken a romantic interest in another Texan, Jimmy Lyons, who flew into town in his private jet. Lyons was the son of the woman who had first introduced Joanne to the John Birch Society and the Minutewomen. Lyons proudly describes himself an "ultraconservative" who believes that the Trilateral Commission and the Council on Foreign Relations were, in some sinister fashion, the real forces behind the Communist Party.

Joanne's romance with Charlie was always centered on Afghanistan. When Jimmy Lyons came into the picture, she adopted another romantic crusade: Angola and Jonas Savimbi's anti-Communist freedom fighters. The way Lyons saw it, big business was in bed with the Communists, and nowhere was that more apparent than in Angola, where Gulf Oil and other

U.S. corporations were shamelessly doing business with the Marxist government. When Congress prohibited the CIA from helping Savimbi, Lyons personally intervened. He not only flew the guerrilla chief about in his private plane, he urged Savimbi to blow up Gulf Oil's facilities. Joanne was entranced by Lyons's zeal and by his willingness to throw his own resources against the dark forces. "Whatever I needed," gushed Joanne, "Jimmy would provide. And he had this wonderful plane."*

The night of her party, Lyons, Fawcett, and Wilson attentively served as Joanne's uncomplaining lieutenants while she made last-minute changes to the place cards and settings in the grand ballroom of the Hay-Adams hotel. Perhaps only Herring could have designed an event with such strange bedfellows and such grand visions.

By the time the first guests arrived, Zia's honorary consul had once again created a vision of a Pakistani palace. The room was ablaze with hand-embroidered, sequined tablecloths and brass candlesticks. Joanne had been magically transformed into the most frivolous devil-may-care southern belle. No one would have guessed the heroics that had gone into making this potential disaster a triumph. It was part of Joanne's grace under pressure, and in the end, the party was a smashing success.

Henry Kissinger, who often stayed with Baron di Portanova in Acapulco and who was part of Joanne's circle, flew in to toast Bandar. The smiling prince was seated on Joanne's right and her childhood friend White House Chief of Staff James Baker was on her left. A glittering collection of Texas oil money, military chiefs, senators, astronauts, and diplomats filled the room.

Wilson was hardly the center of attention that night, but Joanne had given him a seat of honor, placing him between Buckets and Barbara Walters. Di Portanova regaled Wilson with stories of the dangers that would befall the United States if San Marino, the tiny Manhattan-sized republic for which he served as honorary consul, were to return to Communism. For Charlie, the party was another exhilarating triumph of networking chez Joanne. It did not hurt to have a special channel to the richest Muslim power on earth, or to the conservative elite like Baker

---

*One of the most distinctive moments of the Reagan anti-Communist era came at a 1986 gathering in Washington of conservatives who rose to their feet chanting, "Get out, Gulf, get out, Gulf" as Savimbi marched down the aisle to address them.

and Caspar Weinberger. And it was reassuring to know that even if marriage was no longer in the cards, he and Joanne would still continue crusading side by side.

The first indication of just how committed the CIA was to blocking Wilson's Oerlikon initiative came from the Pentagon. While Wilson was still in Pakistan, General Richard S. Stillwell, in charge of all the Pentagon's black activities, had stormed into the congressman's office demanding to speak to the administrative assistant. When Charles Simpson appeared, the very first words out of Stillwell's mouth were "Who the hell is Charlie Wilson and what the hell does he think he's doing with the Afghan program?"

The retired general was not even trying to be diplomatic as he laid down the law to Simpson. No one had asked Wilson for the appropriation, and even if the Agency had additional funds, it wouldn't be able to use them effectively. Finally, he barked, Wilson should know the $40 million was scheduled to come out of existing Pentagon funds, and he was in a position to block that. His parting wisdom was that the congressman had no business sticking his nose into operational details of a covert program.

Wilson was not overly distressed when Simpson reported the encounter. A mere general could never frustrate one of the key defense appropriators. But a far more effective coalition was mobilizing, and it took Wilson a while to figure out who the real enemy was. He would have been well served to follow what had been happening at the other end of the Capitol, where an able and well-liked U.S. senator was also running into trouble when he sought to expand support for the mujahideen.

There was only one other serious champion of the mujahideen during this time, a liberal Democratic senator named Paul Tsongas, who managed, in spite of ferocious opposition from the Reagan White House, to win passage of a congressional resolution calling for increased support for the mujahideen. It remains something of a puzzle why Tsongas and Wilson, two ingrained liberals, emerged as the only early champions of the Afghan rebels. No one in those days would have dreamed of calling the Reagan administration soft on Communism, but Charlie Wilson couldn't find anyone in the administration who seemed to want anything more than a safe bleeding campaign.

For him, Afghanistan had become a political mystery. Why was it that Ronald Reagan could invade Grenada, commission Star Wars, bypass

Congress to keep his secret Contra war alive, and frighten everyone by branding the Soviets the Evil Empire, yet when Wilson made his move to up the ante and counter the most egregious Soviet aggression, he met only resistance?

Stillwell had at least been up front; no one else was. According to Wilson, the CIA initially blamed the State Department for the resistance; the Pentagon said it was the fault of the Office of Management and Budget, which was refusing to release the $40 million. But the OMB people Wilson spoke to said the Pentagon had refused to take the money out of existing naval funds, as the bill had specified. The reason for the delay was "congressional confusion."

At first, Wilson thought he might be up against a turf battle led by the Senate Intelligence Committee, whose staffers were up in arms about the way he had usurped their role. Ordinarily, a CIA program can be funded only if it is first authorized by the two Intelligence Committees. Having bypassed that step, Wilson now found himself having to make the process legitimate. Because the money had to be taken from existing Pentagon funds—"reprogrammed"—he had pursued the chairman and ranking members of the House and Senate Arms Services Committee, as well as Intelligence, to sign off on the bill.

The House was no problem. Mel Price, the chairman of the Armed Services Committee, was so senile that Charlie got a staffer to sign for him. Lee Hamilton, the highly respected House Intelligence Committee chairman, appeared ready to block the bill until Wilson warned his old ally Speaker Tip O'Neill that he was prepared to take to the floor and accuse the Democrats of selling freedom down the river. It was Wilson's way of cashing in an IOU, and O'Neill put in a call to Hamilton, who dropped his opposition.

That left the Senate—a distasteful place for any congressman to have to go hat in hand. Nevertheless, the Texan booked an appointment with Senator Sam Nunn, who surprised Wilson by quickly signing off. Nunn would turn out to be a quiet and forceful backer of this and all future Afghan programs. Wilson's next stop was Senator Moynihan, the ranking Democrat on Intelligence, whom he lured out of a hearing; Charlie soon won his approval. The last remaining obstacle was the chairman of the Intelligence Committee, Barry Goldwater. Here Wilson figured he had a certain in if he dared to use it. The senator's son, Barry Junior, had been a target of the same federal drug-prosecution effort that had hounded him, and Charlie had always suspected that the senior Goldwater had been helpful in getting the case dismissed. So he took a gamble on a joke: "Both Barry and I were subjected to police brutality by Rudolph Giuliani and the Justice Department," he said with that infectious, rumbling laugh of his, and Goldwater told him to come into the office.

"I know this was turf trespassing on my part," Wilson began, "but what we want to do is shoot down the Russian helicopters." Goldwater was an old air force pilot and a legendary anti-Communist, and Charlie told him it was unacceptable for the greatest power on earth not to give the mujahideen an effective anti-aircraft weapon. Wilson was at his patriotic best, and he struck a responsive chord.

In the 1960s, Goldwater's best-selling political manifesto *The Conscience of a Conservative* had set the conservative revolution in motion with its warning of dire consequences should the United States fail to act boldly and counter the Soviet menace. "Well, fuck the turf," the silver-haired senator said after listening to Charlie's appeal.

Wilson realized that this congressional rebellion had been much ado about nothing and that his real problems were not at State, the Pentagon, OMB, or on the Hill. They were coming from Langley. Wilson had thought that the CIA's main stumbling block must be money, and on this point he was sympathetic. His Democratic colleagues in the House had been so antagonistic to the CIA for so long that it was no wonder the Agency didn't believe Wilson when he said money was no object. He had assumed that his $40 million gift would have established his bona fides with the CIA's leaders and encouraged some bolder thinking.

Even after the war was over, Wilson would always remain convinced that Director Casey supported everything he was trying to do for the mujahideen. The director was the last of the adventuring World War II heroes, a man who had been responsible for dropping spies behind the lines in Germany and who talked Wilson's Churchillian language of standing up to tyranny. And Charlie had witnessed Casey's emotional response to Mojadeddi that day in the White House when the Afghan leader had turned to Mecca in prayer.

As the months wore on and the Agency surfaced as the problem, Wilson chose to believe that it was the bureaucrats who were poisoning Casey's thoughts. In Wilson's mind there was no question who was responsible for this cynical policy of leaving the Afghans helpless in the field. It had to be Charles Galligan Cogan, a man no one had elected, who thought he should decide what the United States would and would not do for the Afghans.

In later years, while affiliated with Harvard's John F. Kennedy School of Government, Cogan would acknowledge that the CIA had overestimated the Soviet Union and that, in retrospect, the rigid concerns about concealing the American hand to prevent Soviet retaliation had been exaggerated. But back in 1984 he believed that the way to run a U.S. proxy war was the way the CIA had always done it.

If these two men had met when Cogan was starting off at the Agency, Wilson might have found much to admire. Certainly back in the early 1960s he wouldn't have branded the handsome young case officer a wimp. At twenty-eight, Cogan was the deputy station chief in the Congo; there he ran South African mercenaries, sent Bay of Pigs veteran pilots on interdiction missions against Soviet-backed troops, and rescued nuns from savagery. During this time, headquarters was even bold enough to send assassins down to murder Patrice Lumumba. In the Congo, Chuck Cogan was no pantywaist, nor had he been while serving in the Sudan. But gradually, it is said, he developed airs. Perhaps it began in India, where he learned to ride horses and play polo, or perhaps when he won the patronage of Archie Roosevelt and, later, the friendship of Morocco's King Hassan and Jordan's King Hussein. After thirty years in the Agency, Cogan was the perfect choice for royals but the wrong man for Charlie Wilson.

"So, how many reasons have you come up with this week not to do anything, Mr. Coburn?" Wilson asked Cogan. A week after their unpleasant last encounter, Wilson did not yet understand that the Agency's leadership was united in its opposition to the Oerlikon. He proceeded to heap abuse on Cogan: "You just don't give a shit about the mujahideen, do you? The Vietcong shot down two thousand of our helicopters in Vietnam. How many have you shot down?"

Cogan had initiated this meeting. The Agency was obligated to spell out how it wanted to spend the non-Oerlikon portion of the appropriation, and Cogan wanted to know how much flexibility it had.

Wilson says, "He came in to talk to me about the boots and blankets and shit. And I said, 'Fuck this, Coburn! What about the fucking guns?'"

Cogan said they were initiating several steps. "Yes," Wilson yelled back, "and the fucking helicopters are killing people right this second while you are studying. As best as I can tell, you ain't got but two things to study because that language says 'a cannon.'" Wilson then spelled out the choices to him: "Either buy the Oerlikon or the ZSU twenty-three-millimeter Soviet gun." (It was the only other applicable cannon.)

Only at one point did Avrakotos intervene, suggesting that the Oerlikon would force the Afghans to defend fixed positions instead of relying on more effective hit-and-run guerrilla tactics. "We'd just end up losing the Oerlikons, which cost a hundred thousand dollars each, or the Afghans would all die trying to defend them."

Wilson was completely unimpressed with Avrakotos and his argument. "I don't care if you lose them all, just so long as one Soviet helicopter is shot down. If it takes ten million dollars' worth of Oerlikons to shoot down one ten-million-dollar Hind, that's a good investment. And if you shoot down two, you're way ahead," he said.

Gust found himself agreeing with the argument. In fact, he found himself secretly agreeing with almost everything Wilson was saying. At one point, Cogan slipped and told Wilson that the Oerlikon just cost too much and he wanted to use the money for other things. "You either buy these cannons or you take that money and stick it up your ass," Wilson said. But Cogan wouldn't back off.

It became clear to Wilson that he was up against something far bigger than Chuck Cogan. In any other year he would have gone to the mats immediately, but an old politician's instinct told him that Cogan, the Agency, Stillwell, and all the others were just waiting him out. They read the papers, and the headlines about his upcoming primary said it all: "Good-Time Charlie in Trouble," "Wilson's Lifestyle Tests Supporters," "Shenanigans Could Cost Representative Wilson."

For the first time since he had come to Congress in 1973 he was in trouble at home. His all-forgiving constituents were reconsidering the blind support they had always offered their playboy congressman. A collection of Democratic challengers smelled blood, and so, Wilson suspected, did the CIA.

Charlie Wilson—The Texas Congressman was obsessed with finding a weapon to bring down the lethal Soviet Hind helicopter.

Left, Joanne Herring, the woman who inspired Charlie to champion the Afghans. *Above,* Charles Fawcett in *Afghanistan*—the man who enlisted Joanne to the jihad. *Below,* Joanne using her wiles to convert powerful congressman Clarence "Doc" Long to the cause.

"Them that has the gold, makes the rules."—Doc Long

Gust and Charlie in Egypt, buying weapons for the jihad

"What brought us together was chasing pussy and killing Communists."—Gust Avrakotos, explaining his relationship with Charlie

Left, Field Marshal Mohammed Abu Ghazala, Egypt's minister of defense, admiring Charlie's belly dancer, Carol Shannon
Above, Gust with Charlie and his belly dancers

Milt Bearden, the CIA station chief who presided over the final victory

Left, Mike Vickers, the CIA's brilliant young strategist, and Art Alper, the grandfatherly demolitions expert
Right, thousands of Tennessee mules carried the CIA's weapons to the jihad.

Clockwise from top left, Liz Wickersham, Charlie's companion on his Las Vegas hot tub weekend. Annelise "Sweetums" Ilschenko, former Miss World contestant at the heart of the DIA plane scandal. Charlie and Cynthia Gale Watson, a.k.a. Snowflake, in front of the notorious DIA plane. Bush, Reagan, and O'Neill. Charlie, Liz, and President Carter. Barbara and George Bush joking with fellow Texans Charlie Wilson and former governor Ann Richards.

"The greatest foreign policy crisis since World War II."—Jimmy Carter on the Soviet invasion of Afghanistan

"I used to tell him: 'I don't want to know what you are doing [with the CIA]; you just go ahead.'"—Speaker Tip O'Neill

Above, Charlie's money transformed a rabble of shepherds and tribsmen into an army of techno holy warriors.

Above, Charlie with Jalaluddin Haqani. Once the CIA's favorite commander, after 9/11 he became a prime target of U.S. military forces who believed that he was harboring Osama bin Laden. *Below,* Charlie greeting Gulbuddin Hekmatyar, the Pakistanis' favorite commander who received the greatest amount of U.S. support. Branded as a terrorist after 9/11, he was the target of a failed assassination attempt from a CIA-launched Hellfire missile.

Carol Shannon,
Charlie's personal belly dancer

Gust Avrakotos, the CIA's blue-collar James Bond. It was Charlie Wilson's war but it never would have happened without Gust Avrakotos.

Charlie Wilson, patron of the greatest modern jihad and
architect of the CIA's victory in the last campaign of the Cold War

CHAPTER 18

Gust and Charlie

THE BIRTH OF A CONSPIRACY

There are thirty-three churches in Trinity, Texas, population 2,648. The Second Congressional District, which Charlie Wilson represented in 1984, lies in the very heart of the Bible Belt, as attested to by the JESUS IS THE LORD OF LUFKIN billboard. Just down the road are the huge Pentecostal summer revival camps. A kind of fundamentalism flourishes in the religious practices of its citizens, not all that dissimilar from the intensity of feeling the Afghans have for their god. Religion is a way of life in East Texas, and at the heart of that experience is a belief in the presence of Satan.

Almost everyone in Wilson's district is an authority on sin. In a curious way, the God-fearing people of East Texas are far more familiar with sin than people in more sophisticated parts of the country, even those without religion. The ministers here rail constantly against the Devil's handiwork. They talk about the temptations, always present, that every man and woman succumb to at some point in their lives. The ministers look out over a flock of sinners and preach the need, indeed the responsibility, for all to come to the altar and cast Satan out. Many find Jesus again and again.

It is in this rhythm of sin and redemption that the key to Charlie Wilson's political survival can be found. Charlie was in a curious way the Second Congressional District's designated sinner, a highly visible presence whom they could live through vicariously. And because he was forever getting caught and forever coming home and owning up to his backsliding, entreating forgiveness, the generous-hearted faithful regularly took him back into their hearts.

Beyond this, Wilson had also been a remarkably effective and accessible congressman. That spring, as the primary campaign got under way, he was on the road every day, zigzagging about his New Jersey–sized district in an elaborate mobile office, complete with three workstations to receive constitutents seeking help in dealing with the government. Since 1980, this ingenious motorized command post had doubled Charlie's effectiveness, permitting him to increase his constituent services while chalking up an enormous amount of campaigning at government expense.

Ordinarily a congressman will buy or rent a branch office in addition to his or her main office in the district's largest city. Instead, Charlie had used his government allowance to buy this $70,000 custom-made van, which served to project his presence everywhere at once. Throughout the year, notices would go out announcing the arrival the following week of Congressman Charles Wilson. Charlie himself would rarely appear, but the van, filled with competent staffers and volunteers, would zoom up to the designated neighborhood and help constituents with Social Security, Medicare, veterans issues, or any other problems they had getting the federal government to work for them.

The people Wilson did the most for, the very poor, rarely voted. But ever since his father had avoided the stigma of unemployment through FDR's Civilian Conservation Corps, Charlie had been a true believer in the positive role of government. The district boasted a vast civic center and a veterans' hospital, solely due to him. And everywhere, from the shipyards in Orange to Lufkin Industries, constituents were working thanks to Charlie's way with defense contractors.

A surprising number of people in the Second Congressional District adored him, particularly its senior citizens. Every fall Charlie hosted a dominoes tournament in the Lufkin Civic Center that set his campaign back $25,000, because every player got a set of dominoes with VOTE FOR CHARLES WILSON engraved on the back. More than a thousand gray-haired people showed up each year, and Charlie was there to bestow on the lucky winner a trip to Washington for the Cherry Blossom Festival.

Lufkin's black citizens voted for him almost en masse. Reverend Nordstron, their spiritual leader, would explain that Charlie was a courageous champion of their interests but that he and other black leaders would never allow him to stick his neck out too far. In this district, where pockets still held that the Klan was king, the black vote belonged to Charlie. Despite this goodwill, as the 1984 primary unfolded, it became clear that there was only one thing that could save Charlie Wilson: money—enormous quantities of campaign contributions.

The four candidates who had filed against him were convinced that Wilson had finally crossed the line. The business about the hot tub was bad enough. But even those who forgave the drug investigation had a hard time explaining the hit-and-run incident; it just made Wilson look like a bad person.

It is said that even if a yellow dog ran for Congress in East Texas, as long as the dog was a Democrat he could win. The only race that counted was the primary, and Wilson knew that the only antidote to his scandal-stained image was television and radio. He had to overwhelm his rivals with carefully packaged campaign ads, a strategy that doesn't come cheap.

In moments of need, politicians turn to those who owe them favors, and no group was more beholden to him than the defense contractors. Wilson had a reputation for never having met a weapons system he didn't like, and they anted up $100,000 for their benefactor. They were not alone. All the special interests beholden to Wilson came through that year, and he ended up taking in the second largest amount of PAC money in Congress. But it was the friends of Israel who rallied most impressively. Ed Koch organized a fund-raiser in New York and made an emotional pitch for generosity: "This is a man who has less than ten Jewish constituents, but he helps Israel because he believes in it." By Election Day, Wilson's Jewish friends had come up with another $100,000 for his campaign.

Unquestionably the greatest individual stalwart turned out to be the ever loyal Joanne Herring, who set about corralling all of her rich, archconservative friends and business contacts. Her efforts were typically spiced with glamorous enticements, including a weekend retreat at a friend's exotic wild-game ranch. She would reflect afterward, "It was the most difficult thing I've ever done. I told my friends that the things they had heard about Charlie weren't true, that he was so bright and that he was doing something that would change the world. And then he arrived for dinner and fell asleep right at the table. It was terrible," she recalled with an all-forgiving laugh. "The heads of everything were there and Charlie couldn't even answer questions. But some of them gave money anyway. They did it for me."

After this incident, Joanne and Charlie Fawcett decided they had to rescue Charlie from the bottle. Together they composed an anonymous note "from a true admirer who only wants to see you realize your destiny." "Alcohol is going to ruin you," it warned. "For your own good and for the country, you must stop." Together they took this anonymous communiqué and slipped it into Charlie's mailbox—a touching gesture that didn't seem to have any impact at all.

In spite of her concerns, Joanne stood by her man and single-handedly raised close to $50,000. In all, the congressman pulled in an amazing $600,000—an astounding sum for a primary campaign in a depressed rural district where the local contributions totaled a mere $20,000.

His war chest notwithstanding, Wilson was running scared. His chief opponent, Jerry Johnson, was precisely the kind of candidate one would expect the voters of the Bible Belt to support. A fifty-year-old rancher and family man, he was a deacon and Sunday school teacher at a Baptist church. "Unlike the incumbent," his political ads promised, "I won't go into the Washington real estate and nightclub business and forget where I come from and who I'm working for. He's forgotten that we didn't elect him to sightsee the Khyber Pass and sit with Moslem refugees."

The other opponents, like Lloyd Dickens, echoed the same theme of ridding the district of an embarrassment: "Charlie Wilson has shown that he is against the concept of the American family, from his Playboy lifestyle to his pro-abortion stand."

As Election Day approached, the polls weren't improving, but somehow Wilson seemed to pull himself together. Something seemed to be energizing him. It was a dream—a recurring dream that began coming to him almost nightly. It always began the same way, in an Afghan village where four or five Hind gunships are sweeping in low. A young Afghan boy and a couple of men in baggy pants are firing frantically with their rifles and pistols, but their bullets bounce off the armored bellies. And then, as in a movie close-up, the pilot's Slavic face comes menacingly into focus, leering as he opens fire with his guns, mowing down the villagers.

It was a nightmare, but to Charlie Wilson it always seemed real—as if he were there in that village night after night, watching those brave men being murdered in cold blood. Instead of feeling haunted, somehow he almost welcomed its nightly arrival. It seemed to cleanse him and leave him feeling that there was a reason why he should win this election.

The slaughter in Afghanistan was at its peak that spring. With the knowledge that his own government was not willing to give the Afghans a weapon that could protect or at least avenge them, Wilson would wake from the dream energized, thinking, "What am I going to do to those fuckers tomorrow?" And by "those fuckers," he didn't mean the Soviet pilots. He meant the polished bureaucrats in Washington.

He began calling Langley from his mobile campaign office the day after the dream first came to him in Texas. "You just don't give a fuck about the Afghans, do you?" he found himself shouting in frustration at Chuck Cogan. When the CIA's number two man, John McMahon, tried to argue once again that an escalation would be dangerous to Pakistan, Wilson cut him off: "As long as Zia's not afraid, that's not your concern, John."

When Wilson demanded a timetable for the Oerlikons, McMahon would only say, "Keep your britches on, we're working on it." When Wilson got through to Casey, the director would fob him off with sympathetic words: "I hear you, I hear you. Get back to me in a few days if nothing happens."

Once when Wilson was particularly incensed, he reached a surly General Stillwell at the Pentagon, who told him that the Oerlikons were the wrong weapon and that the CIA shouldn't even be running the war if it was going to get that big. Wilson's response caught the powerful general by surprise. "If I remember correctly," Stillwell recalled years later, "the congressman said something like he was going to put my pelt on his wall if I kept up my opposition."

The reason the CIA and their allies in the Pentagon and elsewhere were prepared to risk Wilson's fury was because they were counting on the voters of the Second Congressional District to rid them of this meddlesome politician. Given the accumulated scandals, it seemed inconceivable that his constituents would return such a persistent sinner to office.

But in the final days of the Wilson campaign, something noticeable began to happen. It had to do with an atmosphere around him. Anyone who studies television knows that it is less important what a person says on TV than how he projects himself. Afghanistan wasn't an issue in the campaign, but something about the way Charlie felt about the cause of Afghanistan and his mission there burned so brightly inside him that it made him look as if he had been "born again." He may not have found God, but Charlie Wilson's constituents could see that his needle was once again pointing north.

On primary night everyone who counted in Charlie's life gathered at his house on Crooked Creek—his mother and sister, staffers and friends.

Charles Fawcett and Joanne added a touch of glamour by driving in from River Oaks in an exotic recreational vehicle that had been a gift to Fawcett from the king of Morocco. The house was full of friends, but there was, among them all, a sense that this might be Charlie's Waterloo, particularly when disastrous early returns from Nacogdoches came in: Jerry Johnson, the Sunday school teacher, had swept the county.

A concerned Charlie Fawcett took Wilson aside to try to cheer him up: "That doesn't mean a thing, Charlie—you can be far more effective for the mujahideen out of Congress than in." Wilson was horrified by this well-meaning pep talk. The fact was that he would be utterly useless to the mujahideen if he lost. In fact, he didn't really know what value he could be to anyone.

Arthur Temple, the timber baron who had been Charlie's political patron since he'd first gone into politics, sat Buddha-like and disapproving as he watched the election reports. Temple was a kind of surrogate father to Charlie, an influential businessman and progressive reformer who had once believed that Charlie could go all the way to the top. Even Charlie's mother looked concerned. She had been by his side ever since he first ran for office, campaigning at teas and going door-to-door like the Kennedy women. What was there to say to her now except that he had brought this ruin down upon himself? Finding it too trying to put on a brave face, Charlie asked Joanne to come with him into the bedroom. "He told me things didn't look good," she remembered. "I just told him he was wonderful. He was a real hero to me."

When all seemed lost, the tide began slowly to turn. By the end of the night, the tally stood at 55 percent for Wilson, 45 percent divided between the four others. Miraculously, at his lowest moment, Charlie had found his moorings. He hadn't told his born-again constituents that he wanted their vote so that he could save the Afghans or even because he wanted to do in the Evil Empire. He hadn't had to. Whatever it was about him, they liked what they saw. He was there to stay, with all his seniority and unsettling allies. And when he returned to the capital two days later, all his pent-up energy was turned on Langley.

At this very moment, Gust Avrakotos's fortunes were also shifting. He had managed to win himself a powerful new patron. Ed Juchniewicz (pronounced Gin-oh-witz) was Clair George's number two man, the associate deputy director for Operations. Like Gust, Juchniewicz was not part of the Agency's old-boy elite. He was a second-generation American whose father had been born in Poland. A former marine, he had spent most of his first twenty years at the CIA in the Soviet division. Juchniewicz was a dyed-in-the-wool Communist hater, and by 1984 he was the second most important man in the Clandestine Services. Day in, day out, his primary responsibility was selecting officers for the division's key assignments, but when Clair George was out of town he served as deputy director for Operations. He could be a powerful friend, and his thinking ran very differently from that of Chuck Cogan and the rest of the seventh floor.

Juchniewicz didn't like the idea of a wasting action in Afghanistan. No doubt because of his own family history, he responded personally to the plight of people enslaved by Communism. He had been to the mujahideen training camps near the Afghan border, had sat with the elders, and watched shoeless young boys preparing to go fight the Red Army. His response was understandably moralistic, from a man whose father's homeland was behind the Iron Curtain: "How in Christ's name could you send these guys into battle and say, You don't have much of a chance, but do your best. That is despicable."

Juchniewicz had watched Avrakotos take command of the Afghan account with growing admiration and then cheerleading. Gust was only the acting chief, but he was playing as if he were there for the long haul.

While Wilson had appeared to be going down and out in East Texas, the Soviets had gone on the attack. There were scenes that spring in Afghanistan of military striking power not witnessed in the world since Vietnam. Great clouds of dust rose as the 40th Army marched twenty thousand troops into the Panjshir Valley to finish off Massoud once and for all.

Unlike earlier campaigns, these Soviet troops were highly trained and motivated. They rode into battle in tanks and armored personnel carriers, with MiGs and helicopter gunships overhead providing close air support. Any previous distinction that the Soviet command might have made between the mujahideen and the civilian population that provided assistance of any kind suddenly disappeared as silver-bodied Tu-16s operating from bases in the Soviet Union began carpet bombing even primitive mud-walled villages where the mujahideen might have received support.

At Langley, Avrakotos was not surprised. He had been waiting for the escalation, knowing that the Agency had been egging it on. As he saw it, the Soviets had no choice. Given their mentality, they couldn't let a bunch of ragheads openly defy them. The 40th Army was now moving to crush the resistance, and Avrakotos took the position they might just succeed if the Agency didn't start playing tough.

It was precisely because of Avrakotos's killer approach to the job that Juchniewicz became his advocate. He had become angry at the way the war was being run. "The Paks were in charge of everything, running the whole show, and I said, 'That's bullshit. We want to help plan battles, want to look at the kind of training they're getting.'" So Juchniewicz went to the director and said that Afghanistan was going nowhere and that the Agency had to get tougher. According to him the director said, "Go ahead, make your call, you're in charge."

That simple statement of Casey's is the kind of murky opening that men like Juchniewicz and Avrakotos are wont to take advantage of. One day when Clair George was out of the country and Juchniewicz was the acting chief, Avrakotos burst into the ADDO's office with a challenge: "It's been almost a year that I've been helping McGaffin as acting chief, and the rule is that if you have the job for three months and you want it, you get it. I want it. Unless you want another fucker in here who just follows orders."

Juchniewicz was not the kind of man who was ruffled by such a presentation. "You're right," he responded. "I'm going to do it. I shouldn't, but Clair's gone." Chuck Cogan was reportedly appalled and tried to challenge the appointment. According to Avrakotos, Juchniewicz silenced Cogan with a communiqué of unusual clarity: "Higher authority wants a mean fucker in the job."

Juchniewicz had the technical authority to make this appointment, but given Avrakotos's intensely complicated history with Clair George, it had required some guts. Now, unless George was prepared to overrule his deputy, it was a fait accompli. Recalling that moment, Juchniewicz observed that his boss was furious but somehow compromised in his ability to challenge the appointment. "Clair had a secret admiration for Gust from their time together in Athens. People didn't understand the depth of their relationship. But it was one of those love-hate relationships." He says the two had had a falling out over something that no one fully understood. "In my own heart I always felt Gust had something on Clair, something he knew about Clair himself or about the family. Clair didn't like that. Gust would never betray a trust or confidence, but Clair couldn't stand it."

According to one account, George spent the better part of fifteen minutes shouting at Juchniewicz until the deputy said that he had already spoken to Casey and McMahon about Gust and they thought his appointment was a good idea. Perhaps George should check with them, he said, knowing that was about the last thing George would want to do.

In the end, the DDO chose not to overturn the decision and instead congratulated Gust, saying that he was happy to have been able to do it for him. Avrakotos, who knew exactly what George had been doing, played along. Why not? He now had the job.

Part of the pleasure of that circumstance involved watching his rival, Alan Fiers, slowly self-destructing. Denied Afghanistan, Fiers would end up in charge of the Contra war, which would soon be outlawed by Congress. He would play a role on the fringes of the Iran-Contra arms-for-hostages scheme. Finally, it would be his fate to become the Clandestine Service's first Judas. Faced with near-certain imprisonment for lying to Congress about the Iran-Contra affair, Fiers would take the special prosecutor's offer of immunity if he told all. In a courtroom filled with former brothers of the Clandestine Service, a weeping Alan Fiers would give the testimony that would doom his old chief, Clair George.

Juchniewicz would later look back on his act of bureaucratic daring and say that pushing Fiers aside and gambling on Avrakotos might well have been his most prescient decision in a long CIA career.

By the time Avrakotos had maneuvered himself into his new post, Charlie Wilson and the CIA were in a virtual state of war. What would soon become clear to Avrakotos is that Wilson had the will and the ability to win. That first came into focus at Langley when Wilson drew on his real strength, the power to punish. He called Jim Van Wagenen, the Defense Appropriations staffer responsible for black programs and asked, "What are the CIA's crown jewels?" Recognizing the veiled threat in the question, Van Wagenen sprang into action, informing John McMahon that Wilson was going to go after the Agency's pet programs if they didn't back off. The staffer made it clear that Wilson enjoyed the support of the full subcommittee on this one and that the Agency was now on the verge of alienating those very legislators on whom they relied for money.

Wilson even managed to make the CIA believe he would go after crown jewel number one, the Contra war in Nicaragua. "I'm sure I implied that I might go over to the other side on the Contras," admits Wilson somewhat sheepishly, because it would have been a bold defection from the anti-Communist camp. "But at that point I was willing to do anything I could to embarrass them. I probably threatened them well beyond what I could have done, but I always try to make people think I'm a little crazy."

This, of course, is the madman theory of how power is best exercised, the notion that a reputation for unpredictability and excessive use of force makes threats more effective. It's worth noting that Wilson was making these rumblings at a time when the Democratic majority in the House had already mobilized against the CIA because of Nicaragua. Had the hawkish Wilson taken his conservative following and made common cause with the opposition, it might well have been a rout for the Agency.

In retrospect, Wilson acknowledges that this debate over the Oerlikon, a weapon that ultimately proved to be of marginal value, was really not about the weapon itself. It was about his personal march, under the aegis of the U.S. Congress, onto the seventh floor of Langley to force the Agency into a bigger war than it wanted to fight. As he sees it now, this bureaucratic battle in 1984 was the defining moment of the Afghan war. Every other tactical decision to escalate, including the introduction of the American Stingers two years later, followed from it.

"They were offended to the point of despair and they weren't going to let it happen," remembers Wilson. "But I knew there was no point to this war if you couldn't shoot down the helicopters. They wanted to fight to the last Afghan and not expose the United States to any risk at all. But I didn't have any interest in killing a million Afghans to cause the Russians some mild embarrassment, and it still absolutely enrages me to think of it."

Wilson and the Agency's seventh floor were now locked in a dangerous confrontation that Avrakotos likened to a bureaucratic "Showdown at the O.K. Corral." And he knew that the first thing to suffer would be his

Afghan budget. Director Casey was also beginning to sense danger—so much so that he asked Avrakotos to explain what Cogan had been saying to Wilson and what might be done to defuse the situation.

Avrakotos was typically blunt: "If you didn't know better you'd say Cogan was working for the Soviets," he told the director. This was mutually understood hyperbole, and he then explained that he couldn't understand why the Agency wanted to pick a fight with Wilson. "Buy the Oerlikon, see if the gun works," he urged Casey. "We're pissing all over our friends. "

The director was famous for the way he would often mumble in such moments, so that it was hard to know what he was saying. Avrakotos interpreted the mutter as a go-ahead to take independent action. "In that game on the seventh floor, if the director hints at something, that's a green light," he explained. "No one was going to question me."

Avrakotos was never one to wait for written instructions. He was a patriot, but he drew his operational inspiration from the Janissaries, the elite warriors of the old Ottoman emperors. "You're a Janissary when you play your own game—when no one knows what the rules are," he explains. "And once you get a band of adventurers working for you, it's a bit much to expect they won't have some adventures of their own." So with that mumble from Casey the modern Janissary moved into action.

As a boy in Aliquippa, Gust's favorite game was playing chicken in the dead of night on the long empty roadways next to the steel mills. All the high school girls and their boyfriends would come out and stand by the side of the road to watch these feats of daring. Two cars would face each other in the same lane a quarter of a mile apart, then accelerate from a dead start to maximum speed. The first to blink, to veer off into the other lane, would be the chicken.

Early on, Gust developed a reputation for never blinking. He would throw his souped-up four-door Dodge into first, and by the time it was ready for second he would have the look of the early Avrakotoses, the ones who would rip off their clothes before battle and charge the enemy screaming. What manner of man would want to fight such a foe? In that car in the dark of night, with pretty girls on the sidelines, the Greek would barrel for glory, and the lesser gladiators of Aliquippa would yield. "Never blink" was the rule that Avrakotos had drawn from these early nights of combat.

Thirty years later he took an Agency car and left the driver out in front of the Rayburn building. He should have called Norm Gardner, the congressional liaison, to accompany him. A CIA nanny was always supposed to be present for meetings with politicians. But Gust was on an operation, and it had to be done one-on-one. By the time he reached Charlie's office he had gained a momentum not visible in the speed of his walk. He was cordial with the Angels, perfectly controlled, but once inside the office he strode directly to Wilson's desk.

The congressman was caught completely by surprise. Until then, he had dismissed Avrakotos as "a bumpkin from the coal fields" and "Chuck's pacifier," another of those timid souls from the CIA. But the frightening-looking Greek standing just inches from him was saying quite disturbing things. "It seemed to me that he made some aggressive, physical move," remembers Wilson. "He said, 'Let's get it straight right now. You don't want to kill those fuckers any more than I do. So let's just figure out a way to do it together.'"

It took a moment for Wilson to compose himself and to realize that this finally was the CIA he had read about in the novels. Whoever Gust Avrakotos was, he was not to be trifled with: "It stunned me. He took my bluster away," admits Charlie.

At the heart of every CIA case officer's existence is the business of recruitment. It's a dirty game—buying people for one's country. To excel at it, the case officer must be empathetic and supple. He must have the capacity to charm and to make friends. But in the last analysis he has to be a con man. What he's looking for are "recruitable weaknesses." And once he spots them he has to know how to put in the hook and land the fish.

Avrakotos had spent three years as Station Chief in Boston doing nothing but recruiting agents—nuclear scientists, American businessmen, Iranians to take part in the rescue mission. Each was a major accomplishment and Avrakotos' office was credited with fifteen, a remarkable record indicating an almost disturbing ability to use the tools of idealism, sex, money, and blackmail for America.

There was no question in Avrakotos' mind about what he was doing in Charlie Wilson's office that April of 1984: he was there to recruit the congressman. But it was by no means an official CIA operation. No one at the Agency even knew that Gust had gone to Wilson's office. The

Agency's leadership never would discover the plots that these two men later hatched.

But almost immediately, the seventh floor at Langley understood that something had transformed Wilson from a highly dangerous adversary to a peculiarly supportive advocate. Everyone knew that Avrakotos had performed this small miracle and Gust played it for all it was worth—letting it be known that he had tamed the congressman's fury over the Oerlikon issue with a ruse. "There are a lot of ways to kill a program," he explained. "One is to fight it to the bitter end but we realized we couldn't do that with Charlie. So we came up with an internal 'pilot program' to buy a limited number of Oerlikons to test and evaluate. We knew we could create delays for at least a year and then see what happened."

This maneuver elevated Avrakotos in the eyes of McMahon and Casey. They now viewed him as a kind of political lion tamer, able to contain the Agency's most dangerous and persistent congressional critic. Up until this point Avrakotos could argue that he had not exceeded his authority since he was quite prepared to claim a clear go-ahead based on his interpretation of the director's mumbles. But two weeks later, when he returned to the congressman's office, he was guilty of such a flagrant violation of the CIA's rigid rules that no excuse could have protected him if exposed.

This time he didn't set out to physically intimidate Wilson. Instead, he opened by making it clear the enormous personal risk he was about to take. No one knew what he was doing and if Wilson accepted his proposition he must never let on where the idea came from. Then he dropped his bombshell. He wanted another $50 million.

It was an outrageous request. Agency officers are not permitted to lobby congress for money. They're not even permitted to talk to members of congress without an authorization and then only when accompanied by a minder.

In this case, Gust Avrakotos was not only asking for money that no one on the seventh floor knew anything about; it was money that no one at Langley was remotely interested in asking congress to give them. Indeed, some were still balking at the $40 million Wilson had just rammed down the Agency's throat. The congressman was seen as a wild man to be restrained rather than egged on. More important, any request for new funding in the middle of a congressional session could only be introduced if the director was willing to take his case to the president. The $50 million that Avrakotos was now asking Wilson to push through was more than the CIA's entire Afghan budget that year.

No matter how you look at it, this series of moves amounted to a direct recruitment effort. No CIA recruitment comes without an element of danger. In extreme instances abroad a case officer might get shot or beaten or jailed when a recruitment effort goes bad. There is always the risk of being exposed to hostile authorities—in Avrakotos's case the hostile authorities would have been the CIA itself. But as if the ice was not thin enough already, Avrakotos made it sound as if Wilson's manhood was at stake if he didn't deliver. "You do a lot of talking about killing Russians. Now for someone as tough as you, you ought to be able to get $50 million bucks, and I'd rather not have to wait until Christmas for it."

CHAPTER 19

Charlie and Gust

THE RECRUITMENT

O stensibly Gust Avrakotos was the moving force in this recruitment drama. And certainly had he not made the first move nothing further would have happened. But the fact was, he had just walked into a trap that Charlie Wilson had set long before. Wilson, too, was relying on his political instincts. He knew that somewhere in the CIA there had to be people who thought as he did. He had tried to woo the Agency with offers of money. When that failed he had stood on the outside and threatened to lay siege to their fortress if they didn't accept his offer. Avrakotos was the one who took the bait. The result was a mutual recruitment and the birth of a secret partnership that would soon transform the Afghan war.

The way Charlie recalls that first encounter, Avrakotos actually asked for only $40 million whereupon Wilson responded by upping the amount to $50 million. "That day, we recognized that we could be good for each other," says Avrakotos. "I think Charlie realized that I'm loyal and brutally honest and I knew I could call on him. He would protect me."

Initially Avrakotos took the lead as he began to introduce Wilson to the intricacies of political life inside the CIA. They both understood that the first battle they must fight would be against the CIA's cautious leaders. Together they worked out a ritual dance that they would refine and put to use with great effect time and again in the coming months. Following Gust's instructions, Wilson telephoned Casey and said he was prepared to give the Agency $50 million more for Afghanistan. Could the director use it? Charlie added that he had already taken it upon himself to put this question to Avrakotos.

That left Casey with little choice but to check with the actual orchestrator of this charade, Gust Avrakotos—who confirmed that Wilson had called him and that, in response to the congressman's demanding questions, he had admitted that the program could use more cash. The director had little choice but to sign off on the offer. With that in place, Wilson set out to work his magic on the Appropriations Committee.

"By this time I had everyone in Congress convinced that the mujahideen were a cause only slightly below Christianity," Wilson remembers. "Everyone on the subcommittee was enthusiastic. I gave them the sense they could lead the way on a just cause. I told the conservatives it was time we fucked the Russians. Told the liberals it would prove that they were against Communism even if they didn't support the Contras."

The CIA was in very bad odor in the House that summer. There was some grumbling from the liberals who had just defeated the administration's $19 million request for the Contras. Wilson realized he couldn't just rely on political clout. He would have to sell this one. "So I defended the $50 million in front of the whole committee. We ordered the staff to leave. It was the only time I ever had to do this."

Above all, Wilson is a masterful storyteller, and he began by describing the events of Christmas Day, 1979, when the great unconquerable Red Army began airlifting troops into Afghanistan. "But the Russians picked on the wrong guys," he told his colleagues. "Even as we speak, illiterate shepherds and tribesmen are confounding the Soviets. They are making them pay and pay and pay. The money we're talking about represents one-tenth of one percent of our appropriations bill, and this one-tenth of one percent is the part that could change history. And even if it doesn't," he concluded, looking about the room with unquestioned sincerity, "it is our sacred duty to make valuable the lives that these people are laying down."

Wilson directed a final point to the instinctive mistrust of his liberal colleagues for CIA interventions. "The U.S. had nothing whatsoever to do with these people's decision to fight. The Afghans made this decision on Christmas and they're going to fight to the last, even if they have to fight with stones. But we'll be damned by history if we let them fight with stones."

Whatever opposition had existed before vanished by the time of the full committee vote. "I don't remember one nay," says Wilson, who would use variations on this speech at other critical junctures over the coming years when the outcome of a vote was uncertain.

When Charlie called Avrakotos the next day, it was to announce that he would soon have the entire $50 million. "We were just gleeful," remembers Wilson. "That $50 million was a direct Avrakotos-Wilson conspiracy. We had made our first move together." The figure grew to $100 million when the Saudis' matching funds came through a few months later, a fact made all the more astonishing because Congress was simultaneously moving to completely close down the Contra war.

Bill Casey had no choice now but to take notice. He had just been raked over the coals by Barry Goldwater, the Senate Intelligence Committee chairman, who was furious about the CIA's operation to mine the Nicaraguan harbors. The House, meanwhile, under Tip O'Neill's leadership, had succeeded in banning all military assistance to the Nicaraguan rebels. Casey was perceived by many congressional Democrats to be running an outlaw Agency, and when it came to the Contra war he was prepared to do almost anything to keep it going.

Alan Fiers, who took over the Central American task force after losing out to Avrakotos for the Afghan job, recalled to the *Wall Street Journal* the enormous significance Casey attached to the Contra war. Casey told him, "Alan, you know the Soviet Union is tremendously overextended and they're vulnerable. If America challenges the Soviets at every turn and ultimately defeats them in one place, that will shatter the mythology . . . and it will all start to unravel. Nicaragua," Casey said, "is that place."*

The CIA director and Oliver North at the White House were just then starting to plot alternative routes to fund the Contras and bypass congressional restrictions. One can only imagine the director's confusion at Wilson's ability to tap huge sums for the Afghans while neither his nor President Reagan's direct appeal for Contra support had yielded anything.

By most accounts Casey was repelled by Wilson's carnal lifestyle. Ed Juchniewicz, who shares an intense Catholic background with the director, explained that "Casey was a prude when it came to lifestyle issues. He was educated by Jesuits and nuns, and the stories about Wilson—the belly dancers, the drugs, the drinking, the constant womanizing—offended him."

---

*Fiers offered this account to David Rogers of the *Wall Street Journal*. It was Rogers who first broke the story of the $50 million supplemental.

Avrakotos also noted the director's initial disapproval of Wilson's overt hedonism: "This whole thing about cocaine really bothered him. The perception about perverted sex, about drug use, and about being Mr. Five Percent. Casey just didn't want that black cloud to land on the Agency's image."

But the director's pet, the Contra war, was now in jeopardy, and Casey was the ultimate pragmatist. In spite of his concerns about Wilson, he decided to try to enlist the congressman to help with the Contras. By that time, Casey had discovered Wilson's role as the great defender of Tacho Somoza and had deduced that Charlie would want to do his part to punish Somoza's enemies, the Soviet-backed Sandinistas. Adding to the argument was the fact that much of the leadership of the CIA's Contra army came directly from Somoza's U.S.-trained National Guard.

Wilson felt almost triumphant returning to Casey's office, assuming that he would be recognized as the mighty CIA patron he had become. The director, whom he so revered, congratulated him on his extraordinary ability to put through so much money for the Afghans. "You know the entire administration is going through unmitigated hell trying to get a few million for the Contras—who are next door to us—and you've just increased the Afghan program by $90 million. I don't understand this."

Wilson was elated by the director's praise until he realized the real reason Casey had summoned him: Could Wilson see a way of sharing just 10 percent of the Afghan appropriation with the Contras? The director insisted it would make all the difference. "We could win the war in six months."

It was no small request. The president desperately wanted to keep the Nicaraguan "resistance" alive, and the director was asking the patriotic Texas congressman to do his part. "I'd like nothing more than to do that, but Tip wouldn't like it," Wilson told the director, referring to Speaker Tip O'Neill. He added that he would only destroy his ability to work for the Afghans if he set out to champion the Contras.

When Casey asked if he wouldn't at least try, Wilson quite bluntly explained that the Contra war was a lost cause. Clearly the director didn't understand what Nicaragua had come to mean to liberals in America. Influential leaders in every city in the country were agitated about the Agency's operations. Hundreds of Americans were actually working for the Sandinista government. Every Friday afternoon, they would gather in front of the U.S. embassy to protest the war, often joined by many more Americans visiting Nicaragua. O'Neill's niece was in Managua, and housewives and ministers from Witness for Peace were going up to the border to symbolically interpose themselves between the Contra army and the Sandinistas. Reporters were flying in and out of the country filing dispatches about the Agency's hopelessly public covert operation.

All that was tame, Wilson told Casey, compared to the white passion that he was seeing close up from his Democratic colleagues. Even his close friend level-headed majority leader Jim Wright acted as if getting the CIA out of Nicaragua was his life's crusade. The most powerful and intractable foe, however, was still the Speaker, and nothing anyone said was going to change his mind.

What Wilson didn't tell the director that day, because it would have enraged Casey, was that he had already cut a deal with O'Neill—an implicit quid pro quo arrangement in which he'd agreed, in effect, to sell out the Contras in exchange for leading the House when it came to funding the Afghan war.

"I can tell you that we would not have been involved in Afghanistan had it not been for Charlie," says Tony Coelho, the Democratic whip at the House. "Most members didn't know where Afghanistan was, and the majority didn't care." Coelho, one of the true scholars of power in the House, explained why the arrangement was necessary.* "Nicaragua was a bitter, bitter, vicious fight with State, CIA, the military, and the White House against us. If Charlie had gotten caught up in any of those battles he wouldn't have gotten anywhere."

It was not the first time Wilson cut a private deal with the Speaker. O'Neill had tapped him during the Abscam scandals on behalf of his great friend Representative John Murtha. "He would do things like this for O'Neill," explains Coelho, "and the leadership learned that it could count on him."

---

*Coelho further explained, "During the eighties we had a divided government. The Republicans controlled the Senate, and the only institution controlled by Democrats was the House. We were not just the opposition party, we were the opposition government. It was a heady time for us. After the 1982 elections a political stalemate occurred and that stalemate gave Tip power and we were aggressively willing to take on Reaganism."

George Crile

Wilson's conservative anti-Communist colleagues had repeatedly tried to get him to join their Contra crusade. But he'd always stayed out. O'Neill didn't expect him to vote with the Democratic majority, but the understanding was that he would not use his influence or energies to work against them.* Deep into the Scotch one night, Wilson recalled the bargain with genuine remorse: "Even though I knew they were a lost cause, I'll always have to live with the fact that I sold out the Contras." But for the Afghans, the rewards that came from this Contra betrayal were extraordinary.

In retirement, the former Speaker was surprisingly candid in describing his machinations with Wilson: "I knew that Charlie was doing undercover work with the Defense Department and the CIA and everyone else, but we blinked while he was doing it. I figured Charlie was on the right side and I knew that no American soldiers were going to be involved. I used to tell him: 'I don't want to know this Charlie; you just go ahead.'"†

The one place where O'Neill drew the line was over Wilson's fierce efforts to win an assignment on the Intelligence Committee. As Coelho explains, "That committee was supposed to be controlling the CIA. If we had let Charlie on, it would have been like giving up one of the spots to them." But that was just about the only thing the Speaker denied Wilson when it came to Afghanistan.

Ever since Reprentative Leo J. Ryan had been murdered in Guyana during the Jim Jones Kool-Aid mass suicide, congressmen had been prohibited from traveling alone on congressional business; but Tip waived the rule for Wilson. Congressmen aren't supposed to become embroiled in the

---

*Once, however, in a particularly close and important vote on Contra aid, Wilson was confronted with an awkward choice. He had just voted with the administration when he was approached by Eddie Boland, the distinguished chairman of the Intelligence Committee, whose amendments were responsible for curtailing and then cutting off the CIA's war. Boland was not only deeply respected in the House, he was Tip's Washington roommate. "Charlie," he said, "haven't we always given you what you wanted on Afghanistan?" Wilson says he only thought for a second. He withdrew his card and voted with Boland and the Speaker.

†"The president used to say I got my ideas of what policy should be from the priests and the Maryknoll nuns," he said. "Which was true, of course. But I say I'd rather listen to them than to these people the president called freedom fighters. I was convinced that the only thing that kept us from invading Nicaragua is what we were doing in the House to stop the president."

mechanics and decision making of a covert killing war; rather, they are expected to act as a watchdog over such things. Again, Tip chose to give Wilson license to operate as a virtual member of the CIA. "We had our differences," recalled the Speaker warmly, "but I always admired and respected Charlie for what he did down there in Afghanistan. I've never known a congressman to take a role like that before. If you asked, 'Did Charlie do it with my approval?' No. But he did it with my consent."

Coelho adds one other intriguing observation about Wilson's success in bringing about radical increases in the CIA's Afghan funding. "The only reason the political institutional atmosphere would permit something like this to develop was because of the cover of Nicaragua. We were so concentrated on Nicaragua that Afghanistan was not on the radarscope. No one paid any attention to it, and they would have had it not been for Nicaragua."

There was another thing Wilson did that would have enraged the director. He never missed an opportunity to tell his liberal friends that they were safe voting against the Contras only if they covered their tracks by voting with him on Afghanistan. That way they couldn't be accused of being soft on Communism in the midst of the Reagan revolution.

Bill Casey had no idea that this was the game Wilson and the Democratic leadership were playing, and he emerged from his Contra fundraising effort empty-handed. He had asked Avrakotos to join him in the effort to recruit Wilson for Nicaragua, but Gust had diplomatically bowed out of the meeting.* He didn't want anything to compromise his plans to escalate the war in Afghanistan. Flush with Charlie's money, he was able to operate effectively in the international arms bazaar for the first time. Under his direction, the Agency commissioned the Egyptian Defense Ministry to set up a production line for ammunition to feed all those Enfield rifles. He was sick of being shaken down by black marketeers, and with this government-to-government contract he could count on a guaranteed supply at a fixed price.

---

*Casey's efforts to find a legal route to funding the Contras were fast disappearing. Soon, he would begin scheming with Oliver North and a weird collection of characters inside and out of government to raise money from private citizens—from the Saudis, even the sultan of Brunei. Ultimately it would lead to the disastrous arms-for-hostages sales to Khomeini, where the profits were diverted to the Contras.

Nothing is ever simple in the clandestine world, and Gust was soon beset with complaints from the Pakistanis that they should have been given the contract. No doubt some general wanted to skim profits, but Avrakotos didn't care who stuck his hand in the till just so long as the price the Agency paid was less than he could get anywhere else. It was important to keep the Pakistanis happy, so he gave them a contract as well.

All of this was insignificant, however, compared to what happened when Avrakotos moved to play the China card. Like the Egyptians, the Chinese army had once been equipped and trained by the Soviet Union, and the military alliance between these two powers had terrified the West. But by the time of the Afghan invasion they had become bitter foes. Thirty Soviet divisions were massed on the Chinese border, and China had good reason to believe that an attack (perhaps nuclear) might be launched at any time. They never missed a chance to urge Western countries to take a hard line toward the mounting Soviet threat.

Still, no one thought the Chinese government would risk Soviet wrath by becoming the major arms merchant for the Afghan rebels. This came about through the efforts of a brilliant young station chief in Beijing, Joe DiTrani. Fluent in Mandarin and married to a Chinese woman, he presented headquarters with the novel suggestion that the Chinese might be willing to manufacture Soviet-designed weapons for the jihad. DiTrani reminded Avrakotos of a young Frank Sinatra; "Broadway Joe," Gust called him. "The thing we had to do in China," explains Gust, "was to convince the Chinese that we not only wanted to fuck the Russians . . . [but] we were going to win. Joe did that."

DiTrani had asked his Chinese counterparts, "Do you think we'd have people in Kabul and Pakistan who are not like me? Look at me. I speak your language. I married one of your people. We have people like me everywhere. We can't lose."

"He did a marvelous con job," says Avrakotos admiringly. The Chinese connection was one of the most tightly held secrets of its day. Only two or three of Avrakotos's colleagues from the task force knew about it. Perhaps no more than ten people in the whole Agency were read in. The Chinese still do not acknowledge that they provided such arms.

To Avrakotos it was delicious revenge: "Just the thought of using Chinese Communist guns to kill Russians—just the irony of it. Getting two guys on the same side fucking each other makes it easier for you to fuck both of them, and aside from just the general idea of fucking each other, their equipment was good—top-notch—and it was cheap."

The first order was for millions of dollars' worth of basic weapons: AK-47 assault rifles, Dashika 12.7mm machine guns, antitank RPGs, and lots of ammunition. To explain the significance of this new source of high-quality, low-price weaponry for the mujahideen, Avrakotos offered another sexual analogy: "Operating in the black market is like trying to get laid in a city you don't know. In a strange city, if you have enough money, you're bound to find something, but there might be a disease contracted, you might get rolled or arrested, and there's no telling how much it will cost. With your wife, it's predictable and in a steady quantity."

By mid-1984 Avrakotos was using Charlie's money to take the CIA out of the world's black-market whorehouses and into contractual relationships with governments that could provide the Agency with sound, reliable killing devices at a fixed price. He was amazed at how eager the Chinese were to get into this game. To his delight, he discovered that they were prepared to sell at close to cost. That increased his purchasing power dramatically.

"It was like the old days, when the Italians would produce shoes for forty dollars and the Chinese would come in at two dollars for the same thing," says Avrakotos. "For example, AK-47s on the black market were going for $299. Once I got the Egyptians to start up a production line, the price went down to $139. With the Chinese in it, I was able to get them for less than $100." Mines offered an even more dramatic savings. "On the black market some were going for as much as $500 apiece. With the Egyptians it dropped to $275. But with the Chinese in the game, it went down to $75, and then the Egyptians had to match it."

Of Wilson's $50 million, $38 million went to the Chinese. The pipeline to the mujahideen suddenly filled up with a quantity of goods unimaginable just a year before. By late fall 1984, cargo ships filled with Soviet-designed weapons began moving from Shanghai, disguised as junks for the 5,200-nautical-mile run to Karachi.

At about this time Avrakotos received a small gift from the gods. As well as things were going, the Agency was still deeply reluctant to undertake the kind of sustained escalation he had in mind. The concern was not just fear of Soviet moves on Pakistan but the trickier charge that the Agency was pursuing a cynical policy of fighting to the last Afghan.

A compelling answer to this accusation came right out of the sky, from the National Security Agency, whose job it is to eavesdrop on enemies and friends abroad. No one knows exactly how many intercepts the NSA's sensitive ears picked up listening to the Soviet's 40th Army in Afghanistan. Day after day, week after week, teams of aging Russian émigrés sat about secret Agency facilities, translating every sort of Soviet communication. By chance one of these was a tape of a Soviet operation in the spring of 1985 against a 12.7mm Dashika heavy-machine-gun warrior.

This was the gun that Howard Hart so admired and upon which he had rested the entire anti-aircraft capability of the mujahideen. The Dashika had profound shortcomings, most notably its inability to break through the armor of the helicopter. But when fired down on a helicopter from a mountaintop it could be lethal, and on this occasion the radio intercepts revealed an amazing drama.

The tape began as one helicopter went down—$10 million worth of Soviet hardware felled by a lone man in a mountain perch with a single 12.7mm burst. Enraged, another chopper came in to finish the mujahid off, and it went down too. The pilot had wired through to Kabul for reinforcements, so in came a Spetsnaz platoon—the Soviet's Green Berets—in a troop transport helicopter. The gunner shot this down too, killing some twenty more soldiers.

This was Audie Murphy in the mountains of Afghanistan, and the radio intercepts vividly captured the Soviets sense of utter impotence as they talked back and forth about the terrible losses this Afghan warrior was inflicting on their troops. It is not clear whether the Soviets ever did finish off the mujahid. It's possible that he was assisted by another Afghan handling the ammunition, but what emerged with great clarity was that one man with one $6,000 machine gun had managed to wipe out dozens of the Soviet' most elite soldiers and perhaps $20 million worth of equipment. The story of this one man's heroics energized everyone on Gust's team. If one mujahid could pull off such a stunt, imagine what might happen to the Soviets over the course of several years.

This tape of "Mohammed the Conqueror" became a powerful piece of mood music. Avrakotos gave a copy of it to Casey, who ended up playing it in his limousine coming from and going to Congress. There were few stories of mujahideen triumphs, and this one bought Avrakotos some much needed running room with Wilson, who was fanatically pushing Gust to buy the Oerlikons.

The two were now meeting at least once a week in Wilson's office. Avrakotos played his role to the hilt, leaving a slight question mark in the congressman's mind as he jokingly threatened to rub Wilson out if he ever blew Gust's cover, and delighting Charlie with demeaning stories about Chuck Cogan. These two bureaucratic outlaws seemed to have found a common bond in ridiculing the polo-playing Harvard elitist. The jokes would also extend to Cogan's deputy, the milquetoast Tom Twetten, who, both decided, bore a striking resemblance to the children's television host Mr. Rogers. A few years later, to Gust's intense dismay, that "wimp" would replace Clair George as the director of Operations. But back then Avrakotos and Wilson saw themselves as mounting a rear-guard action to revitalize a CIA that had become paralyzed by cowardice. They were determined once and for all to move their country to stand up for freedom and to punish tyranny. On that score, they might as well have had as their mantra an old Barry Goldwater slogan: "Moderation in the pursuit of liberty is no virtue; extremism in the pursuit of justice is no vice." Since the conspiratorial part of their partnership was hidden, none of the Agency's leaders on the seventh floor was ever prepared for the precision attacks that Wilson was now able to deliver in order to open the doors for Avrakotos to put his own bureaucratic black arts to work. What this meant was that for the next two years, while Chuck Cogan was, happily, out of Wilson's line of fire in Paris and Tom Twetten was skillfully avoiding any confrontation with the excitable congressman, Charlie and Gust opened the secret-war throttle to levels never before deemed possible.

CHAPTER 20

Gust and the Eldorado

NO WASPS NEED APPLY

A vrakotos was not a morning person. By the time he left his row house in McLean, Virginia, and placed his plastic coffee cup on the special holder next to the driver's seat, most of the Agency's senior officers were already at their desks. It was just a four- or five-minute drive to Langley, and everyone would immediately recognize the Greek by his car. It was a 1976 emerald Coupe de Ville, the last of the truly big Cadillacs, with tufted green damask upholstery and a CB radio antenna jutting up from the back. Avrakotos had bought it in Philadelphia from "a Mafia teamster guy in a bar." It was a strange sight, this would-be wrecker of the Soviet empire maneuvering into the line of spaces reserved for Chuck Cogan and the other understated senior officers running operations around the world.

Bill Casey would arrive in a chauffeur-driven car. Most of the other cars in the line where Avrakotos was authorized to park were BMWs, Mercedes-Benzes, or Saabs. There were a Jaguar and a few Porsches, even a Ferrari. As far as Avrakotos could make out, there wasn't an American car in the whole row.

The Greek took a perverse delight in pulling into his parking spot and greeting his fellow officers with excessive good cheer. The preposterous hubcaps on the Cadillac were priced at $200 each. He knew it embarrassed his well-bred colleagues to see a fellow officer in the kind of car, as he says, "that only gangsters and niggers drive."

After work, Avrakotos would sometimes stop in front of the building to offer his secretaries a ride home. Susan, the beautiful black woman who always passed on information to him and who'd had a shouting incident with Alan Fiers, used to complain each time she got into the gaudy machine. "I hate it. Everybody's looking at me. They think I'm some kind of whore. Why can't you buy a white man's BMW or something?" she'd ask him.

But the Cadillac was his badge of honor as well as a kind of shield. His mother had taught him about the evil eye, that ancient belief that certain people have the power to do all kinds of harm just by wishing ill on an enemy with a stare. Gust had more than his share of enemies, and the Cadillac was a kind of amulet, a message to all those who might have bad intentions that they shouldn't screw with this street fighter.

He was now forty-seven. His entire adult life had been spent in the CIA; it was home. But once he left the car, Avrakotos only occasionally entered through the Agency's front door, where lines of nameless stars—each commemorating an officer killed in the line of service—are chiseled into the white marble walls. He figured he had known almost half of the case officers on the wall—eight alone lost in the bombing of the Beirut embassy more than a year earlier, in April 1983. Gust had particularly mourned Deputy Station Chief Ken Haas, one of those brilliant, exuberant tough guys who'd reminded Avrakotos why he loved the CIA. The two had gotten drunk together in Frankfurt. Gust had known he could count on Haas if there ever was a crisis, but some Iranian scum had wasted him.

Avrakotos was not the type to stop and stare, but the symbolism, designed to inculcate a sense of mission and sacrifice in the minds of the agents of the Clandestine Services, was not lost on him. The reason he chose not to pass this way was because of a new scanning device that tended to reject his plastic ID card. Throughout the day he treated his card like a string of worry beads, picking away at its edges, bending it back and forth and thus altering the electronic signature. It was embarrassing to be turned back from the front door, so he usually took the side entrance, where an old scanner never denied him entry.

His office was on the sixth floor, but it didn't really matter what floor you were assigned to at headquarters. All of them looked the same. Occasionally, Gust would think how weird it was to be back in this white-walled sterile atmosphere where everyone wore coats and ties and pretended to fit into a mold. He knew it was a lie.

He understood the thinking behind the minimalist architectural style. Its Spartan design was supposed to promote discipline and purpose, but it was a fraud: overseas, a case officer was an individual, swimming in the inky sea of the culture he was part of. He led a life without any real rules. "You can do almost anything except screw naked little girls. But then you're supposed to come back to Langley and be Mr. Goody Two-Shoes. No one likes it."

At times Avrakotos would wander the halls, just to see the way everyone lived and worked. It wasn't really done in this compartmentalized world, but Gust knew he would find a certain amount of jazz once he opened one of the white office doors lining the corridors of Langley. Acording to Avrakotos, the Agency at that time allowed its officers to paint the inside of their doors whatever color they wanted. So there were blues, yellows, and greens. It was a way of establishing one's independence. Farther inside there were the trophies from days abroad: menacing masks from Indonesia, shrunken heads, Buddhas, icons, and always posters from the exotic places where these case officers had once roamed. Avrakotos understood that this was what kept everyone sane, kept them from feeling humiliated by the sterile bureaucratic sameness that made it seem as if they were all lab technicians, instead of espionage agents for the greatest country in the world.

The South Asia Operations Group, the formal name given to the agents assigned to the cluster of countries through which Gust exercised so much clandestine power, was located on the sixth floor, one down from the director's floor in what is called the "vaulted area." These case officers were responsible not only for the Afghan war but for India and Iran as well. The entire suite that made up the South Asia Operations Group was nothing less than a giant strong room with a heavy metal door and combination lock. They didn't even have to put their classified documents into safes when they went home at night: the office was the safe.

It was easy to know which suite belonged to the Iran branch. Persian rugs covered the floor, maps and Iranian flags hung on the wall, along with a huge picture of the young Shah, entitled "The Hope of Democracy of Iran." His father, Reza Shah Pahlavi, had been installed by the CIA in 1953. Now, five years into Khomeini's virulently anti-American regime, Gust's Iranian agents had pulled off what they considered a master technical strike. They had blocked the TV signals on all Iranian channels and broadcast a speech from the young Shah. There had been a caviar-and-Russian-vodka party in the Iran section that day to celebrate this stunt.

There was little the Agency could do directly against Khomeini. But indirectly it was doing tremendous damage by providing covert assistance to Saddam Hussein and the Iraqis for their bloody war with Iran. As explained by Ed Juchniewicz—Avrakotos's patron and the number two man in the Operations Division at that time—they were just leveling the playing field: "We didn't want either side to have the advantage. We just wanted them to kick the shit out of each other."

Gust's Iranian officers would look at satellite photographs that showed "the human waves" surging into battle. Hundreds of thousands of Iranian teenagers—all carrying plastic keys that the Ayatollah insisted would grant them entry into Paradise if they died in battle—had already perished in this mindless Muslim war. Gust, too, looked at the satellite images and felt no remorse.

Bleeding the Ayatollah was what the Iran branch was all about. In Gust's mind, there was nothing wrong with a bit of realpolitik; he approved of it wholeheartedly and knew he had good men in place in the Iranian section. There was little more that could be done, and he only spent perhaps 15 percent of his time supervising them. His real passions lay in the neighboring suite of offices.

The Pakistan-Afghanistan branch was located in the vault, in an area totally lacking in character: government-gray walls partitioned to create semiprivate work spaces. Although every desk had a telephone and typewriter, there were few computers. It could have been mistaken for an old-fashioned newsroom, save for the huge map of Afghanistan and the romantic, poster-size pictures of mujahideen on horseback. A doctored photograph showed a Russian tank with the hammer-and-sickle insignia looming in front of the Houses of Parliament. The inscription read, "This year Afghanistan, next year London." Gust's propaganda team had the same tank in front of the Arc de Triomphe—"This year Kabul, next year Paris"—as well as ones for Germany, Holland, and Italy.

On the surface, officers working in the Pakistan-Afghanistan branch looked like everyone else in the operations directorate. They were respectably dressed and well turned out. But there was a difference. For all practical purposes, Gust might as well have placed a sign on the outer door that read, "No Wasps Need Apply."

The entire staff of the Afghan branch numbered only fourteen men and women—rounding off, Gust referred to them as "the Dirty Dozen." It would remain an article of pride with Gust that the core group stayed small, even as the program grew to almost $1 billion a year. The numbers were deceptive because the fourteen were able to draw upon hundreds of Agency people, both at headquarters and around the world. "If we wanted a pamphlet in German, one guy could go get sixty people to work on getting those pamphlets out. Each person could network and draw on anyone he wanted."

Nevertheless, when it came to the core group, this was as large as Gust would permit it to grow. After all, it was good cover: how could so few people be directing something so big? Avrakotos took particular pride in comparing his lean staff to the Central America task force, with its ninety agents bumping into one another as they micromanaged the disastrous Contra war.

"I took people no one wanted," he says. "I took the outcasts. It was my way of demonstrating that you don't have to go to Amherst to succeed. Hardly any of us were Ivy Leaguers. I had the worst band of derelicts ever assembled: "There was Dwayne, the intelligence analyst, all twisted up from childhood bouts with polio. He could barely walk. It would take him ten minutes to go take a piss. But he had a passionate, underdog streak. He was my walking encyclopedia about the Russians and everything to do with the mujahideen. And I would use him to grind out bureaucratic memos defending the program from its attackers."

Avrakotos was convinced that the CIA's Intelligence Directorate, where the analysts came from, was professionally invested in the mujahideen's defeat; that's what they had been predicting all along and were still predicting in their papers. He tapped Dwayne to counter them. "I could tell him. 'Okay, we need three memos this morning: one to answer the Pentagon, one to answer some stupid article in the press, and one to counter our own analysts.'"

Soon Gust had Dwayne publishing a weekly Afghan update that he distributed as a top-secret document to forty of the main policy makers at the State Department, White House, Pentagon, and inside the CIA. It showed that the mujahideen were hurting the Russians and that they were unwilling to quit. Gust knew that if he gave these reports a high enough classification, they'd be sure to leak—which was his intention.

Then there was Larry Penn, "the New York Jew." A Latin America specialist, he spoke Spanish and Portuguese. He and Gust had gone through the Agency's Camp Peary boot camp together. And they had both seen themselves as outsiders. "Larry was the only Jew ever sent to Saudi Arabia from the Afghan program," Gust recalled. "He has the map of Tel Aviv on his face, but on his visa he put down 'Unitarian' on the line that asks about religion." Under Avrakotos, the balding, bug-eyed Penn was in direct charge of the Afghan war effort. He was also a lawyer, and that turned out to be immensely valuable to Gust, who was convinced that if he listened to the Agency's in-house lawyers, nothing would be possible. Gust insisted that Penn double as his "consigliere."

Time and again Penn who would warn Avrakotos, "You'll go to the slammer for this." But then he would set about finding ways to bypass the lawyers' most recent prohibitions. "These aren't terrorist devices or assassination techniques," he would conclude. And this lovely euphemism would become the official description of a particularly lethal weapon for the mujahideen.

Penn's legal rulings were of enormous importance, since he interpreted how Avrakotos could delegate the dollar-for-dollar matching grants that the Saudis had contributed to the secret war. According to Penn, those funds were not subject to the same restrictions that guided congressional appropriations. So Gust committed $44 million of those liberated CIA-controlled funds to acquire $44 million worth of British Blowpipe anti-aircraft missiles, non-Soviet weapons that otherwise would have required special authorization for the CIA to pass on to the Afghans.

Moving money into the black market and through all of the secret channels of the world of espionage was the special preserve of a man whom everyone called "Hilly Billy." Avrakotos describes him proudly as a man with a "huge chip on his shoulder." Gust knew well how easy it was to get stymied moving millions of dollars of unacknowledged funds. "Have you ever tried to open an unnumbered Swiss bank account for the U.S. government? It takes six months because of all the red tape. The Agency can do it in four to six weeks because they're good. But this guy, Hilly Billy, could do it in twelve hours." By late 1985, Hilly Billy would be moving $1 billion a year through those secret channels. A sign over his desk read, "War Is Not Cheap."

The man tapped to run psychological warfare was Paul Broadbent, a second-generation American who had grown up in a Russian neighborhood of Cleveland. "He was the 'hearts and minds' expert," Gust says, "the kind of guy who pulls the wings off of flies, dangerous if you don't channel him properly. I told him, 'The first time I see you treating any of my people mean, I'll fire you. Take it out on the Russian cocksuckers.' Paul knew the Russian mind. He kept trying to get me to give him twenty portable radio stations that he could program with demoralizing psychological broadcasts. He finally got two portable man packs to beam stuff into the Russian troops. The problem is that none of the mujahideen wanted to do it. They didn't think it was manly. Who would want to carry a radio transmitter when you can fire a missile?"

The team met at 9:30 A.M. each Monday, with Avrakotos presiding over his fourteen specialists. "There was one basic question: what do we need to win the war? Each guy would come in with his dream sheet. Some guys came up with real wild dream sheets. No one had any streak of mercy in him when it came to hurting the Russians."

Art Alper, the grandfatherly demolitions expert, was one of the team's more idea-filled members. Along with developing demolition kits, special fuses, and new techniques to smuggle weapons and ordnance into enemy territory, he helped develop portable amplifiers and devices to spread Broadbent's psychological war. The inspiration for this effort came from North Korean radio broadcasts to U.S. troops: "Hey G.I., we're fucking your sister." The CIA's idea was to place powerful amplifiers on hills across from Soviet garrisons. When the mujahideen turned them on, a Russian voice would boom out: "While your wives and mothers and sisters are sleeping with political commissars and you are dying on the battlefield, we mujahideen laugh at you" or "We Dushman [the Russian name for the mujahideen], we herders of goats and sheep, challenge you women to come up to this hill and fight."

"I thought the portable broadcasts were ridiculous, but it hit my funny bone," says Avrakotos. "And it did promote fear. If you get some fucking Dushman without shoes challenging you to fight and you go up there and get bushwhacked or sniped, you realize this guy is clever. You start fearing him."

Alper's amplifiers would broadcast at irregular intervals, even after the mujahideen had left their positions. When the Soviets discovered that the equipment was on automatic pilot, it spooked them further; the mujahideen were a more sophisticated foe than they had previously thought.

Some of the other psychological-war efforts weren't quite as successful. The sinister messages that Broadbent had dreamed up for leaflets rarely made their way to the Red Army troops. Each pamphlet had a different pitch. One said, "If your commanding officer is a real Communist who wants you to fight many battles, frag him. Otherwise, eventually we're going to get you." But the mujahideen, who didn't understand the concept of propaganda, tended not to be very helpful. Avrakotos says they found it far too temping to treat Broadbent's leaflets as if they were exotic CIA-issued toilet paper.

Alper was a particularly offbeat presence in the office, with his grandfatherly face, his violent schemes, and his burgundy plaid pants. "All the secretaries saw him as a dirty old man," says Gust. "But he was a genius with mines and at demolition. I'm sure it was the first time in his life he really felt wanted." Gust was trying to promote just such a sense of belonging, in essence creating his own CIA tribe within the tribe.

The heart of everything the CIA was trying to do in Afghanistan, though, was arm the mujahideen. Here the man Avrakotos most strongly relied on to acquire and move staggering quantities of ordnance was longtime veteran Tim Burton. Never in the Agency's history had there been such a challenge for the Office of Logistics. It would be up to Burton to move millions of ammunition rounds, thousands of AK-47s, night-vision goggles, medical kits, and herds of mules, all through hidden channels, from a dozen countries into one of the most inaccessible lands in the world.

"If you know who Radar is in *M*A*S*H*," Gust says, "that was Tim. In the social pecking order of the CIA, the case officer is at the top of the totem pole and the logistics people are near the very bottom. Case officers don't usually associate with the logistics men; they're known as 'logs pukes.' People call them when the toilet breaks down. But if you really want to have a good ship, you make sure you include all your people." Avrakotos made it a point to elevate Burton to a position of status, and when he finally left his post he passed on a piece of advice to his successor: "If you get rid of this guy, you're losing your right tit."

Avrakotos still stands in wonder of Burton's mastery. "We had fifty major sources feeding information to us on a daily basis about weapons and material that we were purchasing for the mujahideen," he said. "Tim had positioned people all over the world—in Cairo, Frankfurt, Switzerland. He could place an order, get a contract obligated, and get the weapons there in three months. It was fantastic. He could get seven C-141 planes in forty-eight hours—something that would ordinarily take a CIA task force four weeks."

Once things got rolling, so many people started coming in to the task force with so many wild proposals for screwing up the Red Army that Avrakotos had to assign two women case officers just to screen the ideas; they put together target studies and provided the mujahideen with maps and operational intelligence for striking purposes.

Providing the mujahideen with real-time satellite intelligence had the potential to transform the Afghan soldier's combat power. In time, Avrakotos won over another ethnic soul brother, Colonel Walter Jajko, who worked out of General Stillwell's Pentagon office and who took it upon himself to task eighty of his people with producing target studies for the program. Jajko would make sure that satellites made extra runs over Afghanistan, and his technicians would translate the photographs into simple sketches to make them appear to have been drawn by the Afghans themselves.

Close to half of the officers in the Afghan branch, including Avrakotos, were divorced. "Everyone worked six and a half days a week, twelve to fourteen hours a day. After work we only went out with Agency people. We drank with them, slept with them, and if you were lucky you'd get laid three times a week, always with an Agency person. And one Sunday a month I'd head for Deale, Maryland, and eat crabs and smell salt water."

Avrakotos has an intense love for most traditional American pastimes. He is, for example, an ardent sports fan who gambles on professional football. Under the surface, however, few Americans were as tied to the superstitions of the Old World as he was. One only had to look at his office walls to appreciate that this chief of the CIA's South Asia Group was guided by his parents' Greek Island mentality.

The most distinctive object in his office was a *phylacto*, an intricate dark weaving laced with silver and gold threads, that hung on his wall to protect him from evil spirits. Avrakotos's mother, Zafira, had stitched it for Gust when, at age five, he was sick with jaundice and the doctors had given him up for dead. In desperation, his father, Oscar, brought in an herbalist from the islands. She moved into the house, fed the small boy terrible-tasting mixtures of herbs, and rubbed a hideous black paste onto his gums. The old healer cured the boy, and when Gust came to say good-bye before going overseas with the Agency on his first assignment, his mother took the *phylacto* off the wall and admonished him to always keep it with him. "You are going to all these foreign lands. I know how it feels," she said. "Take this with you. It helped me. It will help you."

Throughout his travels, Avrakotos brought it along. He didn't talk about it to his colleagues, but he was every bit as superstitious as his mother. He remembered how feuds in Aliquippa would begin when someone approached a woman with a baby, saying, "May your child have a long and happy life." The mother, fearing that the speaker was pronouncing a curse in code, would be convinced that the person meant the opposite. Gust also remembered the interminable Greek Orthodox church services of his youth, when elders would walk the aisles slapping any young boy foolish enough to cross his legs; crossing one's legs was considered bad luck. Drinking water out of a faucet also brought bad luck, according to Gust's mother. No matter where he was, Gust drank bottled water, just as he always closed his bedroom windows and shades at night, much to the annoyance of his wives. These were the ways of Lemnos, the island where Zafira had been born and raised.

Next to the *phylacto* on Gust's office wall was a giant photograph of a Greek fishing boat, the *Trident*. The innocent-looking vessel was actually a high-speed armored ship used by the CIA in the 1950s to infiltrate agents into Albania. Gust had spent many a drunken evening aboard the *Trident* entertaining Greek military officers and their lady friends, and the *Trident* had also cemented the bond between him and his son Gregory during their frequent weekend boat outings together.

One of those trips had been particularly momentous. In early 1976, five weeks after CIA station chief Richard Welch had been assassinated and the 17 November terrorist group had marked all senior Athens station agents, Gust decided to take his wife and Gregory, then ten, out on the *Trident* to escape the tension. They went to a remote beach far from the capital. "It was a gorgeous morning," he remembers. "You could see for miles. It was one of the few moments I could relax and not carry a gun. All of a sudden this gypsy woman was walking down the beach toward us. It was just weird. She was wearing twelve layers of clothes—a lot of white and purple and some red."

"The gypsy walked up to me and asked for a cigarette. She had a tiny, shriveled, weather-beaten face and a deep, resonant voice. 'Ah, American cigarettes. Obviously you are American,' she said, not waiting for an answer. 'You have a blond wife and a little boy with a bathing suit. Only Americans buy bathing suits. Also, you are Greek, but there are many Greeks who don't like you. There is a group that wants to kill you. They have already killed one of your coworkers. You have much to be afraid of.'"

It was impossible for Gust to turn this woman away. Greeks have a great mistrust for gypsies but inevitably seek them out for protection when someone has put the evil eye out on them. "Your name is Costa," she said. This statement surprised and frightened him—Costa was his Greek nickname. "Tell me more, old lady," he said.

"I have to look at your hand, and I have to touch you. It's going to cost you lots of money—one thousand drachmas," she told him. When Avrakotos began to protest, she brushed off her request. "The money isn't important. I like you." Then she proceeded to tell him about his family history. "Your father died at a very old age. He died a good death. Your mother died shortly after of a horrible death."

That unnerved Avrakotos because it was true. His father had recently died at eighty-nine of a heart attack; his mother had been killed in a gas explosion three weeks later. "This was something no one in Greece knew. I tried to find out how she did it," he said, "but she said she didn't know, that a flash came over her and she could see it. If she was a flimflam artist, she was damn good." As the morning drew out, Gust shared his wine-and-cheese picnic lunch with the old woman, who offered to make him a *phylacto*. 'I know you believe, even if your wife doesn't. As long as you carry this, you won't have to worry that someone will hurt you or take your money. But as to health, only God can protect you."

Gust agreed: "Two out of three isn't so bad," he said, whereupon she brought out grotesque things from under her clothes, including dried animal parts and bits of bats. When he asked what they were for, she replied, "You don't want to know." She put together the *phylacto*, then wrapped it carefully in waxed paper and said, "Put it in a safe pouch. Don't ever throw it away because you'll be throwing luck away." To this day Avrakotos never moves without this black, shiny, composite of bat wing, unknown animal parts, and whatever other ingredients gypsies employ to protect their charges.

All of these superstitions help explain what led Gust to embrace Charlie Wilson in the summer of 1984, when everyone else at the CIA was trying to stiff-arm him. Avrakotos could see that something was protecting this congressman from the fate of mere mortals. Every charge in the book had been leveled against him, and yet he had shed them all and given what amounts to the evil eye to General Stillwell, Chuck Cogan, the State Department, and the entire seventh floor of Langley.

But more than his apparent power to ward off enemies, what pulled Avrakotos to Wilson was the thing that all Greeks are looking for: Wilson was the man with good luck. Greeks are gamblers at heart—they look for signs; they bet with winners. And to Gust, Charlie Wilson was the quintessential man with whom to place a bet. He was the ultimate amulet, the good-luck charm.

This, then, was the man in overall command of the largest CIA operation in history—Gust Lascaris Avrakotos, age forty-seven, a CIA "super grade" making $59,000 a year, with twenty-two years invested in his pension plan, a *phylacto* on the wall, another in his pocket, and an outlaw congressman he counted on for the ride to victory.

The only ones more irrationally optimistic than Wilson, Avrakotos, and his Dirty Dozen were the mujahideen, who were being slaughtered that year in record numbers. To them it was all so obvious: there was only one superpower, and since He was with them, they could not lose. Allah would choose the instruments of their salvation.

In the end, however, it would not be some piece of hocus-pocus or anything mystical that would give Gust and Charlie and the United States the capacity to ride the mujahideen's guerrilla war to victory. The true transformational element arrived at Langley that fall in the form of an unassuming young man who had only been in the CIA a year and a half.

He was without superstition, entirely rational, and no one looking at him could ever have imagined that within a matter of weeks, he would completely redesign and transform the nature of the CIA's Afghan program. Looking back at it years later, Avrakotos would see the arrival of Mike Vickers into the ranks of the task force as part of the peculiar destiny that seemed to be guiding this drama.

CHAPTER 21

Mike Vickers

MAN OF DESTINY

W hen Mike Vickers arrived at the door of the South Asia Operations Group for his first interview, he was a GS-11, the civil service equivalent of a captain in the army. At thirty-one, with just a year and a half in the Agency, he was so low in the pecking order that had he joined the ninety-man Contra task force, he would have been one of its most junior officers.

It wasn't exactly easy to find Avrakotos on the sixth floor. Every other office in the Near East Division, the mother hen of the South Asian enterprise, had a sign next to its door: N.E. SUPPORT, N.E. FINANCE. Vickers had only a number to go by, 6C18, so he searched for a white door in a white hallway with no markings—just numbers in very small print next to the entrance.

The idea behind this studied anonymity was to discourage those without a need to know from dropping by. Anyone could enter, however, and once inside, the unsuspecting visitor was confronted by a huge Soviet soldier in the combat uniform of a chemical-warfare specialist. The uniform was the real thing, stripped off a Red Army trooper killed in Afghanistan. There was a bullet hole in the chest alongside the hammer-and-sickle insignia, and with its rubber gloves and gas mask, the looming figure had a Darth Vader quality about it.

Such was the Dirty Dozen's innovative approach to security. They didn't like the rigmarole of locking and unlocking the door each time they came and went, so they deployed this Soviet scarecrow as their first line of defense. The threat was not some Soviet mole but the Office of Security, which was sure to send an agent incognito one day to try to penetrate the vault to prove the branch wasn't protecting its secrets. Gust had prepared for such an incursion by installing a secretary next to the Russian soldier with instructions to deny entry to suspected security sleuths.

The secretary was expecting Vickers, however, and escorted him past the burn bags into Avrakotos's suite. It, too, was part of the vaulted area, but the Office of Security had insisted on sealing it off with special doors equipped with cipher locks and peepholes.

Avrakotos hadn't protested. One of his ironclad rules was never to cross the security people. He got around them by just keeping the doors open. Other officers loved to wrap their daily routine in the spookery of "need to know." The ritual of closing their doors made everyone believe that important clandestine business was being transacted.

But Avrakotos hated that game. Anyone who made the mistake of closing the door to his office would find themselves staring at what was probably the only pitch-black door in the Agency. Avrakotos had a thing about black. He always wore it when he went on challenging operations, particularly when he wanted to intimidate someone. That was the idea behind the door, and he took a perverse enjoyment out of watching the reactions. To those few who dared ask, he would explain that he hated to be closed in and wanted people who did that to him to know that there better be a good cause. But Vickers was not the sort to needlessly close a door; nor was he intimidated by anyone.

The face of the CIA is often disappointingly bland, and with his glasses and quiet demeanor, Vickers was a particularly bland-looking fellow. He had the manner of an eager but young stockbroker who had perhaps attended a good college. He just didn't look like a candidate to take over the design of the largest CIA operation in history.

Avrakotos, however, had never gone about staffing his units conventionally. For starters, he didn't trust the Agency to pick candidates for him. He began his recruiting drives by tapping into his informal network: the secretaries of the Clandestine Services. As far as he was concerned, they were the only ones who could be counted on to tell him who was good and who was a loser. "They overhear their bosses' conversations," explains Avrakotos. "They know about jealousies. They know if a guy gets thirty-five calls a day from his wife." More than anyone in the Agency, the secretaries in Operations were the ones privy to the real dirt.

Over his twenty years roaming the world and checking in at the Agency's stations wherever he went, Avrakotos had built up a virtual network of these women. By 1984, he figured, he knew 90 percent of the secretaries in the Operations Directorate, certainly all of the twenty-five or thirty in Near East. He cultivated them almost as an agent network, treating them as equals and taking them to lunch even after he'd ascended to McGaffin's job.

He knew how hard it was for them to come back to headquarters, trying to live on $18,000 or $19,000 a year. Overseas, in Dacca or Tegucigalpa, they had housing allowances, and when the dollar was strong they could live lavishly. At Langley, they were so poor they had to cluster together in tiny houses or apartments to make ends meet. Gust always made sure they got as much overtime and as many cash bonuses as he could justify, and more than once he proved that he was willing to fight for them.

One time, when his personal secretary was slated for an overseas assignment, the area chief responsible for the country where she was to be posted blackballed her, declaring that she was a "jezebel." Her crime was having been caught in an affair with a married case officer—who, of course, suffered no consequences.

Avrakotos immediately rallied to the defense of his humiliated secretary, a pretty blond divorcee. When Gust confronted the branch chief, demanding an explanation, the man made the mistake of telling him that his secretary was a "fornicator" who might disrupt the station if he gave her the assignment.

"Well, if that's the case, then you're going to have to fire your own secretary and one of your agents as well."

"Why?"

"Because I fucked them both. They're both fornicators."

Back in his office, Gust summoned his secretary and the case officer with whom she was consorting. "It's all cleared up—you can have the job if you want it," he said. "But if I were you, I'd probably tell them to go to hell." He added, "I'm sorry, but you're going to have to call off the affair."

Such stories make the rounds, and the secretaries knew they had a friend in Gust Avrakotos. Had it not been for them, Gust wouldn't even have considered hiring the man who would quickly become indispensable to him. The secretaries said he was special—the best writer in the branch, a near genius, and the target of jealousy in the paramilitary branch, which hadn't even passed his name on as a candidate for the job.

The CIA's paramilitary unit, officially known as the Special Operations Group, was still in the process of rebuilding after years of firings and retrenchment. It had once been a major component of the CIA, a full division with land, air, and sea branches. When the Agency took on Castro, at the Bay of Pigs, it was two cowboy PM officers who had led the Cubans ashore and fired the first shots. PM officers had been at the heart of the successful overthrow of the Arbenz government in Guatemala in 1954. Close to a hundred of them had run a massive air-support operation in Laos in the late 1960s. They had always been a critical component of every major covert operation involving force because the general case officers rarely had such expertise.*

Avrakotos instinctively liked these men, most of whom had begun their government service in the military. "Most of them never would have survived in the regular military," he explains with admiration. "They're the kind who like to tell generals to go fuck themselves. They don't like to shine their shoes. Some were pilots for Air America and were crazy, but that's what you want on your side. They talk straight and tell you what they believe. They hate bureaucracy. They get in trouble, drink too much—probably beat up a lieutenant colonel in a bar—so then they decide to get out of the army and go to where the action is, and that's the CIA."

These men and Gust were kindred spirits. But there was a reason these PM specialists were known inside the Agency as "knuckle draggers"—so many of them had limited vision. Now that he was in charge of the Afghan program, Avrakotos felt that he needed a different kind of paramilitary specialist, and left to its own devices, he didn't think the PM branch would find him the right man.

The Afghan operation was unique, not just because of its size but because the Pakistani intelligence service, General Akhtar's ISI men

*The paramilitary branch had been radically reduced during the Carter years. Under Bill Casey it had once again expanded to staff the Agency's burgeoning paramilitary campaigns in Nicaragua, Angola, Cambodia, Libya, Chad, and Afghanistan.

were responsible for the hands-on supervision of the mujahideen. In time, Avrakotos would send teams of American PM officers on temporary training missions to the Pakistani camps. But for his personal military adviser he didn't need a knuckle dragger to perform heroics behind enemy lines. He needed a weapons expert who was above all a strategic thinker.

As Avrakotos had sat in his office paging through the résumés of the ten PM officers he was considering for the job, Vickers's file had stood out: ten years a Green Beret, the first five on the NATO frontline studying the Soviets and preparing for guerrilla warfare behind enemy lines. A series of internal citations: Special Forces Soldier of the Year. Fluent in Czech and Spanish. Officers Candidate School, second in class. Training in demolition, light and heavy weapons, raids and ambushes, high-altitude free-fall parachuting, advanced mountain climbing. Three years running counterterrorism missions out of Southern Command, Panama. Then a career change: at thirty he entered the CIA's elite career-training program. What caught Avrakotos's eye were two entries indicating missions to Grenada and Beirut in the midst of what should have been a routine desk job. For one of them, Vickers had gotten a citation for bravery under fire. That was enough to make one want to pursue this man's background more thoroughly.

Gust had begun by wandering through the PM branch to eyeball Vickers. He wasn't impressed. "He was the only nerdy-looking guy in the whole group; most of those guys are Neanderthals, and he looked like a bookworm." Avrakotos decided that he needed to know what this man was all about. What tipped the balance was a piece of intelligence from one of the secretaries in his network: as far as the women were concerned, Vickers was no nerd, and he was dating the prettiest girl in the case officer program.

To Gust's great annoyance, Rudy Enders, the Special Operations chief, declared that Vickers was too junior and couldn't interview for the position. This wasn't Avrakotos's first run-in with the PM branch, and he wasn't about to roll over. Earlier that year he had locked horns with the previous PM chief over another officer he had wanted to borrow. A vicious turf battle had broken out over the phone. "You better apologize," Avrakotos had shouted, "because if you don't I'm going to come down and shove the telephone up your ass." By time he had stormed down to the PM branch, to the knuckle draggers' lair, the chief had vanished. Later

Avrakotos discovered that the officer had left only because he had a history of brawling and it would have jeopardized his career had he stayed to slug it out.

That man was William Buckley, who shortly afterward was sent to Beirut as chief of station. By the time Gust was scheming to enlist Vickers, Buckley had already been taken captive by Iranian-backed terrorists, who'd proceeded to torture him. They had sent a videotape of their captive's agony, leering into the camera as they broke every bone in his body. As best the Agency specialists could judge, his ordeal had lasted many days.

Avrakotos never had any doubts about what he would have done to the Iranians had he been in charge. He would have ordered the bombing of their most holy shrine at Qom or taken his anger out on Khomeini's family. As he saw it, the tape was a classic sucker punch, designed to make the Agency strike out impotently. He told Casey that unless they were prepared to do something truly awful, it was better to do nothing at all. But he argued that the tape should be released to at least inform the world who these people were.

Buckley may have been his foe internally, but once the enemy had him, the case officer became very much a part of Gust's family. He would later give him the ultimate accolade: "Whoever kidnapped him got the wrong guy. He would have given them no satisfaction. He was a stubborn goat."

Buckley's replacement in the paramilitary division was no less prickly a personality. Rudy Enders wasn't about to let Avrakotos fill one of the Agency's plum PM jobs with the most junior case officer in his branch. But Gust was painfully aware of his own inadequacy in the area of weapons and strategy. With Charlie's money pouring in and so many critical decisions to be made, he was ready to do whatever was necessary to get Vickers.

The last officer PM had sent him, Dwight Weber, a full marine colonel, had driven him crazy. "He was a by-the-book, straight-missionary-position kind of guy with absolutely no initiative," says Avrakotos. The colonel didn't think beyond the next fiscal year. "If the funding level were to double he would have been inclined just to double the existing order, keeping the same ratio of weapons to ammunition that Howard Hart had long ago established. There was no thought of changing the kind of weapons—just more of the same year after year."

To make matters worse, Colonel Weber had crossed a line by asking Larry Penn, Gust's consigliere, whether the entire program made sense. He seemed concerned about the mounting casualties, given the tremendous odds against a successful resolution of the war. A livid Avrakotos dressed him down. "What kind of military man are you?"

Everyone else in the program was there to kick ass, and Avrakotos considered this kind of self-doubt unforgivable. The grandfatherly Art Alper wasn't rent with doubts when he designed his lethal sabotage tactics; he felt virtuous about it. "Here's a guy who could go to the synagogue, pray, and have a good night's sleep. That's the kind of killer I wanted on my team. We had right and God on our side."

Weber had actually driven Avrakotos to the breaking point once before, when he and another PM officer had accompanied him to Switzerland to explore the purchase of the controversial Oerlikons. They were told they were there to examine the guns, but the real reason Gust had brought them was to protect his backside. "I didn't want anyone to suspect that I had made a private deal with Charlie or to suggest that he was somehow getting a commission."

Avrakotos took special precautions because he knew quite a bit about the company he was dealing with. "We were negotiating with two savvy Swiss, Herbert and Johan. Oerlikon is the company that sold weapons to both sides in World War II. They had collaborated with the Nazis. They were selling guns to Iraq and Iran and to Israel and the Saudis the same time we were talking to them. These are international scumballs, and I guess I couldn't conceal my feelings because one of them said to me in the midst of dinner: 'Gust, I sense you don't like me.'"

Herbert and Johan were like any other salesmen. They stood to make a lot of money off the CIA, and they were going out of their way to be accommodating. They asked where the Americans would like to have dinner. Weber volunteered that he had always wanted to go to a restaurant where they yodeled. Avrakotos was appalled. "For the Swiss, that's as low class as you can get. Herbert knew I was embarrassed, but they were trying to please us, so they took us to a yodeling place. I ordered a vodka. Weber ordered a Diet Coke. And then Tom, my other weapons expert, asked, 'Do you think they have chocolate milk?'"

Herbert responded graciously, "No, but they probably have milk."

"Don't they have chocolate they could put in the milk?" Tom asked with a forlorn look.

Avrakotos couldn't believe it. "Here I was, trying to buy arms to beat the fucking Russians, and one of my tough guys orders Diet Coke and the other chocolate milk. These are my fucking tough guys. Meanwhile Herbert's ordering cognac and saying, 'Ah yes, that chocolate milk is a good American drink.'"

The two Swiss knew that the Agency had been given $40 million in Wilson's appropriation, and they were doing their best to persuade Gust to spend it all on Oerlikons, instead of the 50 percent that he had in mind. The rewards to the arms manufacturer would come not just from the initial sales but from the ammunition. Each Oerlikon round cost $50, and the gun fired hundreds of rounds a minute. That could quickly add up to a lot of money if the gun were ever put to use in a big way.

In Zurich, Avrakotos says, the Oerlikon officials used every conceivable argument and incentive to encourage a large sale. At the close of their visit one of the company executives, a cultivated aristocrat, hosted a fancy dinner for Gust. The suggestion was reportedly made that a three-year contract for $600,000 might be available to Gust once he left the Agency, with $500,000 of that up front.

"Shove it up your ass," Avrakotos shot back. "I'll pretend I didn't hear what you just said, because the last thing you want is for me to tell Congress you were trying to bribe me." The worldly Swiss executive did not seem insulted or in any way put off, instead he responded with a question more to Gust's liking.

"Do you like blondes?"

"Well, that's different," Gust replied.

Avrakotos says he reported the incident to his superiors. Whether or not he ended up with a blonde that night, it can be said with confidence that Oscar Lascaris Avrakotos's son had not gone into the CIA to profit at the expense of his country. Beyond that, he was keenly aware that when it came to Oerlikons he was living in a glass house. It took nerves of steel and good judgment to walk the tightrope he was now on, and it was not helpful having marines by your side who were totally lacking in imagination and good sense.

This became doubly clear back in Washington, when it was time to testify before Congress about the Oerlikons. Gust was fully prepared to buy a small number of these weapons, knowing that this was the unspo-ken quid pro quo with Charlie—giving him something for his money to shoot down the Hind, even if it wasn't effective. After explaining this to Weber, Avrakotos told him to testify that the Agency didn't really need the Oerlikons but could certainly use them.

"No," Weber replied, "the honest answer is that the Oerlikon is su-perfluous."

"You're not going to testify," declared Avrakotos.

"Yes, I have to," Weber protested.

"No, you're not, you're sick. Go home. That's an order. Are you dis-obeying orders?"

The story, of course, made the rounds inside the PM branch, as did Gust's next move, to hire Vickers. The paramilitary chief, Rudy Enders, refused to let Vickers go until Avrakotos threateded to have the director personally intervene. As he had predicted, Enders caved in.

Vickers was unaware of the bureaucratic maneuvers that Avrakotos had gone through to get him. He was told only that he was being consid-ered for the Afghan paramilitary slot. His interview took thirty minutes, and while it would be an exaggeration to say that Avrakotos fell in love at first sight, it was close.

To begin with, Gust discovered that Vickers was an ethnic. He didn't look or dress or talk like a new American, but his grandparents had all taken the Ellis Island route—two from Italy, two from Slovakia. The Slovak grandfather had worked in the steel mills in Chicago, had been thrilled by the money he was earning, overjoyed to be in the land of opportunity. The flag flew in front of both grandparents' homes. Gust could spot a kindred spirit from a mile away. Like him, he had made it in life all on his own by using his brains. And he could not help but respect the fact that this non-descript-looking nerd could probably kick his ass.

It's initially disorienting to listen to Vickers talk about guerrilla war. He makes it sound as if it were a business school course. Avrakotos him-self was taken aback by the young man's bloodlessly precise responses to questions about weapons and strategy. It was as if he were quoting from a textbook, but there is no such textbook.

Avrakotos, a math star himself, was mesmerized. This man seemed to have studied guerrilla warfare the way others study medicine. He seemed to know exactly what to prescribe and in what dose, when to be alarmed by developments, and when to stand back and let time take its course. Some deep organizing principle was at work; and Gust could sense an exuberance behind the calm exterior, particularly when this utterly self-confident young man announced that he saw no reason why the mujahideen could not win. Avrakotos hired him on the spot and turned him loose to review the entire program.

Vickers is a grind, and once he began poring through the Agency's files and the history of the war, he didn't look up until he had assimilated everything. What he saw both pleased and dismayed him. The good news was that the resistance was intact and growing in the face of unbelievable casualties. (Special Forces doctrine held that if a guerrilla insurgency survives and grows, then it is by definition winning.)*

The rest of what he saw appalled him. By his way of thinking, whoever had been responsible for choosing the weapons and the broad strategy for backing the freedom fighters had verged on criminal negligence. Vickers had already been alerted that the Afghans had no meaningful anti-aircraft capacity. But he was amazed to find that they had no modern communications; no battlefield radios to coordinate attacks; few mortars; few antitank weapons; no light machine guns to speak of; no proper medical kits; no boots, which resulted in a number of cases of preventable frostbite; not enough food to keep their families from starving unless they returned from the front regularly; no mine-clearing devices; no sniper rifles; and far, far too few modern assault rifles. For some reason, the basic weapon the CIA had given the mujahideen was the bolt-action World War I Lee Enfield.

That might have worked in the early years of the century, when armies faced off against each other from fixed positions in trenches, but now? Clearly the thinking behind Howard Hart's decision to flood the Afghans with Enfields was to give a sense of empowerment, however ill-equipped they might actually be. The Enfields were cheaper than the modern AKs, and given the small early budgets, it must have seemed

---

*Vickers was particularly struck to find that after throwing the best they had at Massoud, the Soviets had not been able to crush him. From the ledgers he could see that Massoud was only one of some three hundred significant commanders. That was a very telling indication of the fighting spirit of the mujahideen.

the way to go. Standard guerrilla doctrine, however, called for giving the mujahideen the same rifles that their enemy used. It was the only way they could use captured ammunition. Needless to say, the Soviets didn't use Enfields. Nevertheless, the Agency had robotically supplied the mujahideen with hundreds of thousands of these antiquated weapons—and nowhere near enough ammunition.

It became instantly clear to Vickers that there was no way for the Afghans to wage sustained combat. All of this leapt out of the CIA's secret ledgers to offend Vickers's sense of professionalism. By Agency protocol, Vickers was far too junior to go shooting off his mouth about his conclusions. In fact, he was so low on the totem pole that had it not been for Avrakotos, he would have had no right to take any initiative.

What makes Vickers's story so remarkable is that the organization and support of a giant covert military campaign is a highly esoteric specialty. The U.S. government doesn't train anyone with this particular discipline in mind. But as chance would have it, Mike Vickers had spent his entire adult life preparing for just such a commission.

Underneath his controlled exterior, Vickers is a romantic. It's unlikely that this side of him would have surfaced had his father not left Chicago, where he ran a funeral home, to move the family to California. Vickers was still in elementary school when his father reinvented himself in Hollywood as a master carpenter, helping to build fanciful movie sets on the lots of Twentieth Century–Fox.

The senior Vickers had been a genuine war hero who had always stirred patriotic ambitions in his son. He had won the Silver Star in a bloody bomber raid over Germany, and as a boy, Vickers would look with awe and pride at his father's citations. Later, as a teenager, he had a sense that he was born to do something big in life, but for years he thought it would be on the sports field. He couldn't have been a more lackluster student, rarely cracking open a book and graduating from high school with a C+ average. But he would pump iron religiously in the garage, and he performed well enough as a varsity quarterback and pitcher that he hoped he would make it as a football or baseball star.

The unlikely ambition to join the CIA came to him by accident in his senior year, when he found himself in a class taught by a teacher who talked tough and straight. This professor was able to break through to him, and spoke to him about the basic realities of power and how things really work in the world of international relations. It was the height of the Vietnam protests, and the teacher gave Vickers an article to read about the CIA's secret war in Laos. It didn't praise the CIA; quite the contrary. But Vickers was riveted by what he read. Already intrigued with spying because of the James Bond movies, he could see himself playing such a role one day—the heroic loner, empowered by sophisticated technology, taking on fantastic odds for his country. The article on the war in Laos clinched it: one day he would join the CIA and run a secret war of his own.

At a community college the next year, still preoccupied by football, he met with disappointment: Mark Harmon, later to become the star of *St. Elsewhere* and *People* magazine's "most handsome man in the world," beat him out for starting quarterback. Stuck on the bench, a young man looking for action and adventure, he decided to enlist in the Green Berets. It wasn't an impulsive move; like everything else in his life, the decision to try out for the Special Forces was highly calculated. Vickers knew that the Green Berets train men to run irregular armies, and he figured that this was the best way to acquire the preparation he needed to join the CIA. He took a military I.Q. test and for the first time learned that he was endowed with remarkable potential. He got a 160, the highest score possible.

It's said that 85 percent of those who enlist in the Green Berets don't make it to graduation. Vickers not only won his beret but was soon honored as the Special Forces Soldier of the Year. At twenty-one, he began his apprenticeship under true military heroes. In the 10th Special Forces Group, the other men in his unit were ten- or fifteen-year veterans of almost every irregular military adventure the United States had to offer. Most had volunteered for repeated tours in Laos and Vietnam. They were an unconventional elite who had learned the hard way what a guerrilla army filled with committed men can do to destroy the will of a much larger force.

The bulk of the U.S. Army in those years was preparing for an all-out war in Europe. But Vickers's Green Beret unit had a special mission: training year-round to fight a guerrilla war deep behind Red Army lines—exactly what the mujahideen would be doing in real life ten years later.

Vickers threw himself into intensive study of Soviet weapons and tactics: how the Soviets organized themselves, what their counterinsurgency methods were, how to set up networks to exfiltrate downed U.S. aircrews. The target was always the Red Army and the tactics those that the Afghans would have to perfect: raids, ambushes, sniping, mines, booby traps, sabotage, even some relatively large-scale conventional operations. Vickers became an expert at using every type of Soviet weapon, from pistols to mortars to heavy machine guns to surface-to-air missiles. But he also trained with weapons from all over the world so that he could be dropped in anywhere to advise an insurgent movement on how best to use whatever armaments they happened to possess.

During his early years with the Green Berets, Vickers was driven to prove his warrior's worth. He became an expert in the martial arts, so good that he was sent to West Point as an instructor in hand-to-hand combat. He trained with the navy SEALs in infiltration techniques and long-distance swimming. He went to England for counterterrorist training with the crack British SAS regiment, learning how to storm a room and pick out every terrorist for the kill without imperiling the hostages. He even volunteered for the ultimate assignment: in the event of an all-out war with the Soviets, Vickers was to parachute into enemy territory with a small tactical nuclear weapon strapped to his leg. His mission was to place the device in a mountain pass or some similar terrain to halt the advance of the Red Army. Theoretically, there would be time to escape the blast, but everyone knew this was a one-way mission.

When the Soviet's 40th Army and KGB liquidation squads descended on Kabul in 1979, Vickers was driving across the country toward the Special Forces school at Fort Bragg, North Carolina, where additional training led to a job as part of a secret twenty-man unit tasked with assessing the vulnerability of U.S. embassies and responding to terrorist incidents. He moved about Central America, picking locations for snipers, gathering intelligence from embassies and other locations that might someday have to be infiltrated to rescue American diplomats. His ultimate job was to be first on the scene in the event of a terrorist incident—to pave the way for the Delta Force shooters and to serve as the ambassador's military adviser in the event of a hostage incident, a job he performed with distinction twice in the 1980s.

By 1983 Vickers figured he had learned what he needed from the Green Berets. An enormous buildup was underway at the CIA and he judged it time to make his move. Typically he researched the career paths in the Agency exhaustively before choosing a specialty. His Special Forces experience would have allowed him to jump right into one of the paramilitary slots but he had larger visions of becoming Deputy Director for Operations one day and the only route to that post was to become a general case officer. This would require going through the same fifteen-month training course at Camp Peary that had prepared Hart and Avrakotos for their CIA careers.

The paramilitary course had little to teach Vickers. He was already an expert skydiver, trained to leap out of planes from high altitudes. He was even able, by steering his chute with his feet, to maneuver laterally thirty miles and to land, alongside a team of black-suited warriors, within yards of a preassigned target.

Camp Peary wasn't all drudgery for Vickers, mainly because he shared the boot camp experience with a pretty young case officer. They parachuted together, rappelled out of helicopters, trained with all sorts of rifles and set off plastique: a touch of James Bond glamour in what might otherwise have been drudgery for this overly qualified military specialist.

It is said that all the determinants of success, luck is the most important. And as luck would have it, Vickers turned out to be the right man in the right place at the right time. But that's not the way it looked to Vickers when he learned of his first on the job training assignment with the Caribbean Task Force. He was desolate: the Caribbean was where people went on vacation, not where great foreign policy issues were played out. But shortly after his posting, the tiny Caribbean nation of Grenada became the focus of the world's attention. For months the Reagan Administration had been complaining about the large number of Cuban advisers on the island and a suspiciously long airstrip being built with Soviet funds. When the already leftist government of this island nation was overthrown, the U.S. suddenly made the decision to invade.

The Caribbean branch chief was directed to accompany the invasion force and was told he could take one aide. As he saw it, he was going to be driving a stagecoach through the badlands and he needed a man by his side who knew how to ride shotgun. It turned out to have been a wise decision. They arrived in Grenada the day after the first troops landed and were promptly ambushed while inspecting a captured ammunition cache. Vickers comported himself with distinction in the firefight

that ensued and for the next ten days impressed everyone with his organizational skills.

Back at Langley, Vickers was given a citation and another urgent assignment: to the Lebanon task force, in Beirut, to identify the bombers of
the American embassy and the marine barracks. In the embassy bombing
in April, the Agency's national intelligence officer for the Near East, Bob
Ames, and six other Agency men had died. The barracks attack, coming
on top of the embassy bombing and all the other humiliations at the hands
of the Iranians, had pushed the White House to the point of wanting revenge. Vickers's mission was to figure out whom to target and how to get
to them.

Vickers and his team quickly made their way through a list of suspects in Hezbollah and the region's many other terrorist groups. Unhesi-
tatingly, his team recommended that no action be taken. There was no
reliable identification, no appropriate targets, and no reason to strike out
blindly. It may not have been what the White House wanted to hear, but
it was obviously honest.

Shortly after Vickers completed his training at Camp Peary, Avrakotos
interviewed him for the military-adviser and program officer position. In
Vickers's mind, there was no question what needed to be done in Afghanistan, and drawing on his years of preparation, he quickly came up with a
grand design for the war. The obvious problem, however, was that no one
was about to listen to a GS-11 proclaiming that everything the Agency
had undertaken was misdirected; the only person who could initiate the
kind of radical change Vickers envisioned was his boss. So he gathered together his disconcerting set of proposals, and thus began the education of
Gust Avrakotos.

Coordinated firepower is the key to effective combat, but rather than talk
in jargon, Vickers began by offering his new boss a metaphor. The key
to success, he said, rested with the mix of weapons, and having the proper
"clothing" for the job. Vickers explained that the mujahideen's needs were
not all that different from those of a Green Beret team, which relies on
a wide variety of weapons and skills to be effective. The guerrillas also
needed to be cross-trained in communications, map reading, first aid,
demolition, and small arms. But all of this was secondary to giving them

the right combination of weapons—guns to kill a Russian soldier, to disable a tank, to shoot down an aircraft, to lay siege from far away.

Everything needed to be rethought with the weapons mix in mind, Vickers explained. He wanted to immediately stop all purchases of those obsolescent Enfield rifles and switch to AKs. They should think of the basic mujahideen unit as a one-hundred-man force, he said. Each one of these units needed three Dashikas but no more, and Vickers figured there were already more than enough of these heavy machine guns to satisfy that ratio. Stop the purchase of them, he suggested; instead, buy the longer-range 14.5mm heavy machine guns with rounds that can break through the skin of a Hind. He wanted long-range mortars that could hit targets from a distance and not bring down instant reprisal.

His projections for ammunition, however, forced Avrakotos to recognize the inadequacy of the existing budget. If you have one gun, explained Vickers, the key question is how much ammunition will be necessary to feed it over the course of a year. Take an AK-47 assault rifle, which could easily consume 200 rounds in a firefight. Ten firefights in a month, say, would eat up 2,000 rounds. And given an annual fighting season of three or four months, one mujahid would require about 7,000 rounds a year. At a cost of fifteen cents per round that comes out to approximately $1,050 per man per year simply to keep a $165 AK-47 in ammunition. Howart Hart had already distributed more than 400,000 rifles—Enfields and AKs—to the mujahideen. It would break the budget to fully supply all of these existing weapons with ammunition, Vickers explained. Just to keep 100,000 holy warriors' AK-47s in ammunition for a year would cost over $100 million.

The Agency had already decided to use the added funds to buy more rifles, but these, Vickers asserted, would only leave more men with little ammunition and without the kind of weapons that could really make a difference. Everything needed to redesigned with a new weapons mix in mind.

By the time he finished describing the range of weapons and amount of ammunition that should be supplied, he was proposing heretofore unthinkable quantities and costs of ordnance. And that was only the beginning. Once the decision was made to escalate, it would trigger huge parallel investments up and down the line to make the logistics workable: cargo planes and ships, trains and trucks, camels and mules. New warehouses would be needed, quality-control inspectors, and, always, the specialists to disguise the American hand.

In his unassuming way, Vickers was walking Avrakotos into a completely new dimension as he talked about what the resistance should look like two, three, four years down the road. This was not about bleeding the Soviets. Vickers, a trained killer, was presenting a systematic plan for putting the Red Army through its own Vietnam.

As Vickers sat in Avrakotos's office, his highly specific blueprint in hand, Gust found himself almost unnerved. He had sent the junior case officer to his task feeling cocky about how much money there was to spend. What he and Wilson had done with funding was nothing short of a political miracle, and he had expected Vickers to recognize this. Instead, Vickers announced that to make a difference they should be prepared to ratchet up to a budget as high as $1.2 billion a year.

This kid was talking about more money than the CIA was spending on all of its other covert operations put together. This was more than even Gust had bargained for. He quickly convened his team to challenge the numbers. The logistics man in particular was skeptical. But in the end the senior officers could fault little. "We ended up going with nine out of ten things he proposed," says Avrakotos.

Meanwhile, the paramilitary branch had gotten hold of Vickers's paperwork and was calling the whole plan into question. At a showdown with twenty veteran warriors, Vickers reiterated that existing policy was little different from giving the mujahideen clubs instead of rifles. If they had to live with existing funding, better to stop buying any new weapons and throw the entire budget into ammunition. That way, at least the Afghans could have something to fire at the Red Army, even if they didn't have the right weapons.

As it now stood, the mujahideen could not fight year-round, and they couldn't really engage the Soviets in intense combat. To infuse them with the kind of resources he was calling for, he argued, would quickly turn them into year-round warriors. All they needed was enough ammunition, food for their families, medical kits, and a supply line to keep them in the field. With his remarkably low-key presentation, this warrior-strategist was quietly seizing control of the program by sheer force of logic.

Avrakotos knew that Chuck Cogan, with his extreme caution, would have nixed this plan before it had a chance to be considered by higher authority. But the stars were moving all the right figures into place that year; as luck would have it, Cogan's successor was the rugged veteran case officer Bert Dunn.

Dunn was an old military man who had served in both Afghanistan and Pakistan. He knew the terrain and the players, and he was bowled over by Vickers's strategic plan. Equally important, he trusted Avrakotos and chose to stand back and let him run the show. That would prove to be of enormous consequence in the coming years.

After Dunn signed off on the plan, the two men went upstairs to present it to Clair George. Once again fate played its hand. Dunn had been George's deputy in the Africa Division and enjoyed his complete confidence. "Clair doesn't like a lot of details or number crunching," explains Avrakotos. "He just said, 'Bert, if you endorse it, it's okay with me.'" But the Agency's top spy then suggested that the entire discussion was somewhat irrelevant because Congress would never give them the kind of money the plan called for.

As deputy director for Operations, George was always overwhelmed with a world of problems. He had to choose where to throw his energies and where he could afford to delegate responsibility. With his old deputy Bert Dunn riding herd over Avrakotos, he didn't feel he had much to worry about or reason to involve himself in the details of the Afghan program. Avrakotos made it easier by being uncharacteristically diplomatic with George, saying only that there was nothing to be lost by giving the plan a try; surely they would get at least some of the money. He didn't for a moment flirt with telling Clair his little secret—about how he and Wilson were thick as thieves, plotting together to up the funding.

Avrakotos did have one simmering problem with Wilson that he knew he had to sort out quickly. When it came to spending for the CIA's war effort, Charlie was virtually a Johnny-one-note, insisting that the money go first toward weapons to shoot down the Hind. The nightmare was still waking Wilson up in the middle of the night, and he was constantly on the phone to Gust, wanting to know whether any Hinds had been shot down and where things stood with the Oerlikons and the other weapons he was pushing the Agency to buy.

By the fall of 1984, when Vickers entered the picture, Wilson had been way out in front of everyone at the CIA for almost two years in trying to solve the anti-aircraft problem. He still had the Israelis working on the Charlie Horse, though Gust had told him he wouldn't fund that program. The Muslim world considered itself at war with Israel, and he wasn't going to risk everything by letting the Jews into the jihad.

Now both Wilson and the Agency were urging Avrakotos to buy the British Blowpipe, a shoulder-fired missile said to have been effective in the Falklands War. Gust had looked over the weapon at a recent air show and had already spoken to the Shorts Brothers, the manufacturers. But that, too, was a sensitive matter requiring the highest-level clearances from the British government. Avrakotos was increasingly aware of how dangerous it was to stonewall on this issue, particularly since he had basically tricked Wilson with the Oerlikons. Wilson had come to think of the Swiss guns as a kind of magic weapon; he kept a little model of one on his desk and would show it to visiting Afghans, telling them that this was the weapon that would deliver them. Gust knew it would be at least a year, however, before the first Oerlikons got into the field, and then there would be so few that they would only be of marginal importance.

It was embarrassingly clear that the Agency had not figured out how to combat Soviet control of the air. It had no plans in the works, and Gust knew it was only a matter of time before Charlie turned his guns on him.

As with everything else, Vickers did not miss a beat when Avrakotos asked him what they should do. He said that Wilson was thinking about the solution to the problem the wrong way. Rarely, in war, is the battle won by a single weapon. It wasn't necessary to find the *perfect* weapon. Once again, the answer lay in the broad concept of the weapons mix.

After hearing Vickers out, Avrakotos decided to break protocol and bring Vickers into Wilson's office. It's unheard of for a new case officer, a mere GS-11, to go to a congressman's office, much less to make a sensitive and controversial presentation. But Avrakotos was desperate. "This is going to be the most important briefing of your life," he told Vickers. "Go practice in front of the mirror."

Even years after the Soviets pulled out, Wilson would not have any idea of the role Vickers had played in the war. He never did learn—or at least could not long remember—the names of any of the briefers that the CIA sent to him through the years. To him they were all anonymous, generic figures who worked for Gust and later for Jack Devine or Frank

Anderson. Everything that started to go right in the war during those early
years he would always credit to the handiwork and daring of his secret partner, Gust.

On this occasion, Wilson assumed that the young man with glasses
who talked with so little charisma was a brilliant technician, but certainly
not the author of a plan to give the mujahideen a chance to win. Vickers
had been his normal impressive self, talking about how a new weapons
mix would radically change things for the mujahideen on the ground.
But it was the part about the helicopters that finally broke through for
Wilson.

Vickers explained that it was not necessary to look for a single new
weapon to serve as a "silver bullet." The way to defeat Soviet air power
was by introducing a symphony of different weapons that, when put together, would change the balance in favor of the mujahideen. He then
painted a verbal portrait of the mélange of weapons he was urging Gust to
deploy to bring down the Hind.

Avrakotos watched silently from the sidelines as Vickers worked his
spell on Wilson. Instead of just the 12.7mm machine gun—the Dashika—
with its one-thousand-meter range, the Afghans needed far more 14.5mm
heavy machine guns, with twice the range and greater penetrating power.
And while Oerlikons were expensive and static, their shells, which explode
on impact, could fell an aircraft from thousands of meters away. The final
element in this mix, Vickers suggested, should be an increase in the number of surface-to-air missiles purchased by the Agency, by twenty to thirty
fold, in order to take the air war to the Soviets. The heat-seeking Soviet-
designed SA-7 was able to fly five thousand meters up into the tail of a
MiG while the British Blowpipe was operator-controlled and could not
be thwarted by flares.

It was like having his own intellectual hit man, and Gust could feel
Charlie's excitement as Vickers concluded by conceding that none of
these weapons individually would be that effective, but the whole would
be greater than the sum of the parts. It was their collective impact that
must be considered, because all they needed to do was convince the
Soviet pilots that this mix of diverse anti-aircraft weaponry existed and
was in the hands of the guerrillas. Every Soviet pilot would then know
that there was no one diversionary tactic they could rely on. As it stood,

the Hind could stay well out of range of the Dashikas and blast the mujahideen with impunity. And by dropping a few flares they could throw off any heat-seeking SA-7. But once the weapons mix was in place, they simply wouldn't know what the mujahideen might have coming up at them. "The idea is to make their assholes pucker up," Avrakotos threw in.

More important, Vickers concluded, once this mix of anti-air was employed, it would force the pilots to fly higher; and once they did, they'd be far less effective and wouldn't be able to terrorize the mujahideen on the ground.

The day after Vickers's virtuoso performance, Avrakotos returned to Wilson's office and the two men talked money. With Wilson's help, the Afghan program was now being funded at $500 million, half of which was from Congress and half from Saudi matching funds. Avrakotos informed Wilson that they might need more money.

Avrakotos was now moving deeper into his embrace with this potentially dangerous congressman. The Agency still suspected that Wilson might have some financial interest in the Oerlikons, and while these suspicions were still running strong, Charlie announced that his great friend Mohammed Abu Ghazala, the defense minister of Egypt, would be willing to sell the CIA the weapons the Afghans needed to bring down the Soviet helicopter.

Avrakotos, of course, knew that the Soviets had previously equipped the Egyptian army. The Agency was already doing some business with the Egyptians, but it was never easy to organize anything with them. Abu Ghazala's message was that he had eight hundred SA-7s and a mule-portable Soviet anti-aircraft gun called the ZSU-23 that he was willing to sell. He had already invited Wilson to inspect them, and Charlie wanted Gust to go to Cairo with him to check them out.

For Gust, this was a truly nerve-racking proposition, both tempting and menacing. Mohammed Abu Ghazala was widely considered to be the second most powerful man in Egypt as well as a friend of the United States. But the Justice Department was reportedly investigating a shipping company that Abu Gazalla and a former Agency case officer had set up to transport goods provided by U.S. foreign assistance to Egypt. There were allegations of corruption.

It was doubly awkward because the ex-CIA man, Tom Clines, was an old friend and shady business partner of that greatest of all outlaw ex-CIA men, Ed Wilson. As chance would have it, it was Clines who had drafted the multimillion dollar plan for Ed Wilson that Charlie had presented to Somoza so many years before. This complicated tangle was hardly worth unraveling except for the stark question that sprang out in Avrakotos's mind: was he going to get to Egypt only to discover that Charlie Wilson, the congressman he had now entered into a noble conspiracy with, was corrupt?

CHAPTER 22

The Arms Demonstration in Egypt

MOHAMMED'S ARMS BAZAAR

In the fall of 1984, Charlie Wilson defeated his Republican opponent in the general election easily. Back in official Washington, and particularly on the seventh floor of Langley, Wilson was now perceived as a permanent fact of life in the capital—an unpredictable, rule-breaking maverick who was dangerous to cross.

His most important House ally in the Afghan struggle hadn't been so lucky. Doc Long was defeated that year in spite of a $600,000 war chest—a major setback for Israel, which lost its most well-positioned and fanatically supportive congressional patron. For Wilson, it meant he would have to champion Zia's aid package on the Foreign Operations subcommittee all by himself.

It was a time of many transitions for Charlie. Joanne Herring had accepted a marriage proposal from a Houston millionaire, Lloyd Davis, a particularly suspicious Texan who didn't approve of Wilson and insisted that his fiancée stop seeing him. Charlie wasn't invited to the wedding Joanne organized in Lyford Cay, in the Bahamas. It was typically grand. She had everyone dress in white, and then she and her new husband left on safari for their honeymoon.

All of a sudden, Charlie's muse was gone. But by then he was already swept up by the momentous forces that she had set into motion. She had pulled him out of his midlife crisis, taught him once again to believe in the special destiny that awaited him, inspired him, and then selected roles for him and Zia ul-Haq to play as champions of her freedom fighters. It wasn't easy for her to turn away from this shared crusade to rid the world of Communist tyranny. Wilson, however, faced a new set of challenges for the game, which now had to be played against the Red Army. For that battle, his newfound friend from the CIA was a far more suitable companion.

The two men had agreed to meet in Cairo the week before Thanksgiving to buy, or at least consider buying, anti-aircraft weapons that Field Marshal Mohammed Abu Ghazala had told Wilson would be perfect against the Russian gunships. The entire American entourage was to be received as the official guests of the defense minister, who'd promised to let them review the Egyptian military's entire arsenal.

True to his vow never to move in a Muslim land again without a good Christian girl by his side, Wilson had invited along Trish Wilson, the pretty blond congressional secretary he'd had dinner with the night of his hit-and-run accident. The coincidence of their shared last names would be helpful when booking rooms in the stricter Muslim states. As usual, Charlie's traveling companion was not brought along for romance alone. Her principal role was to serve as the wide-eyed innocent witnessing and appreciating the astonishing status Wilson enjoyed in the worlds he was about to take her through.

Traveling out of the United States for the first time in her life, Trish was in awe as they flew first-class, then checked into a lavish suite at the Marriott—a colonial extravaganza built for Empress Eugénie in 1869, when she came to open the Suez Canal. The hotel was close to the pyramids and, as the days unfolded, Charlie's girl played her role perfectly—she saved every napkin, menu, bar of soap, and postcard, and even took photographs of their seats on the plane.

Gust's trip was a bit more mundane. Unlike Charlie, he flew tourist class and checked in at the decidedly more pedestrian Ramses Hilton across town. Accompanying him were three tough and deeply skeptical paramilitary experts: Art Alper, the demolition and sabotage man from Technical Services; Nick Pratt, a marine major on temporary duty with the PM branch; and his new military adviser, Mike Vickers. All three had warned Gust on the flight across the ocean that the gun Abu Ghazala was hawking, the ZSU-23, was even less suitable than the Oerlikon. But Gust had explained that part of their mission was diplomatic. They had to give the weapon a chance, and if it didn't work he needed them to back him up with explanations.

The three military pros were all a bit tense since they knew full well that it was highly unusual to have a congressman pushing specific weapons for a covert program. The general assumption among them was that Wilson had a piece of the action. The marine, Nick Pratt, who had just come back from test-firing the Oerlikons in Switzerland, was a particularly straitlaced fellow who viewed Wilson with such distaste that he used an alias when introducing himself to the congressman, steadfastly refusing to reveal his real name. Avrakotos, meanwhile, was simply hoping against hope that Charlie would not fail the ethics tests that lay ahead. But for now the congressman, because of his relationship with the defense minister, was calling the shots. So Gust checked in with the station and set off across town to find Charlie.

Avrakotos is an extreme type-A personality. He can't bear to be trapped in traffic and actually drives on sidewalks to circumvent traffic jams. But that's not possible in Cairo, a city so overcrowded that an estimated two million people sleep in cemeteries. Stopped in hopeless gridlock, he cursed Wilson and the fates for causing him to be stuck in a seamy hotel all the way across town.

By the time he arrived at Charlie's door he was sweaty and stressed, which made Wilson's appearance even more startling. The congressman acted as if he were on the second week of a Riviera holiday. Gust reacalls, "Charlie was in an open white shirt. Next to him was Trish in a white jumpsuit and I said to myself, 'Motherfucker, look at this piece of ass.' Some women can wear panties that show through their clothes in a way that drives you crazy. This one brought out the Greek in me and Charlie, of course, knew it."

A more unsettling sight for Avrakotos was Denis Neill, a lobbyist for the Egyptian Defense Ministry, standing behind Trish. It was more than Gust could believe. Neill might have been Wilson's good friend, but it was hard not to conclude that he was walking into a corrupt bit of wheeling and dealing. How was he going to explain the presence of this particular American lobbyist, who seemed to be traveling with Wilson, to his three already suspicious colleagues?

Gust tried to be diplomatic, explaining that there were rules he had to follow and he could not talk business with Neill in the room. When Charlie asked if Trish could stay, Gust responded, "I don't mind. I'll stare at her all night. But I won't be able to talk very much." So Neill was dismissed and Trish sent into the adjoining bedroom, where she immediately put her ear to the door.

Once they were alone, Charlie told Gust that he had dined with the field marshal the night before and that everything was set up for the CIA's purchases. At that dinner, Mohammed and Charlie had placed rival fifths of Cutty Sark in front of each other and begun swapping jokes and matching drinks. It was a particularly exquisite exchange because the two had delightful business to transact. There was money to be made for Egypt but, more important, a noble crusade to save the Afghans. To every weapon Charlie reported the Agency was seeking, Mohammed responded, "No problem. We have exactly what you want." As Wilson recalls the dinner, "After the first fifth of Scotch I started telling Mohammed what we were going to do for him: we were going to save the Egyptian economy, modernize their ammunition factories, and together destroy the godless Communists."

Charlie Wilson's amazingly intimate relationship with Abu Ghazala was another remarkable coincidence that seemed to shape the buildup of the Afghan war. As defense minister, Abu Ghazala was one of America's most important partisans in the Middle East, decidedly pro–United States, and, above all, not fundamentalist. In an economy and society so overloaded with corruption and bureaucracy that nothing worked, he had managed to create a separate world for the military—their own schools and housing, even their own farms. In its own way, Abu Ghazala's army, with its opportunity for advancement based on merit, was far more democratic than any other institution in Egyptian life. And from the standpoint of U.S. interests, it was his military alone that made it possible for Egypt to remain stubbornly pro–United States, in marked contrast to most other Arab countries, which tended to side with the Soviets.* Mohammed was easily one of the most important men in Egypt, but no one in the U.S. government other than Charlie Wilson had such a raucous, intensely personal relationship with him. "We were soul brothers in every way," explains Wilson. "Pussy, whiskey, and conversation."

They had met in Washington during the Camp David negotiations when Abu Ghazala, now a two-star general, was a military attaché. Wil-

---

*Just the year before Wilson's visit, he had been the linchpin in a secret effort with the United States to trick Libya's Muammar Qaddafi into provoking an Egyptian retaliatory invasion. At the last minute the plan to cut the Libyan leader down to size had been scuttled, but the effort had demonstrated Abu Ghazala's paramount significance to the United States.

son had been moved by Egypt's willingness to establish relations with Israel, and Mohammed was the man through whom he personalized it all. Beyond that, Abu Ghazala was a big drinker with a robust personality. Charlie invited the dashing young general to all his Washington parties. "He liked my women and wanted to know their friends," Charlies says.

After Mohammed returned from Washington, Anwar Sadat gave him his third star and appointed him defense minister. Abu Ghazala had been on the parade-reviewing stand when the Muslim Brotherhood gunned down Sadat in 1981. Mohammed was hit in the ear, and the television clips from the event show him taking charge of the counterattack, ordering the bodyguards into action against the assassins. By that time, Wilson had become a passionate congressional champion of Egyptian military and economic assistance, so important to Egypt that he had been invited as a guest of honor to that very parade—indeed, to sit between Sadat and Abu Ghazala. Only a last-minute cancellation had spared Charlie this brush with death.

Since then Wilson had become perhaps Egypt's most valuable congressional champion. Denis Neill had skillfully lobbied his old friend, but as always, it was the personal connection that energized the congressman. "I liked Egypt, I liked Sadat, and I love Mohammed," he explains. "Helping my friends, what the fuck?"

With Trish exiled to the bedroom, Charlie had fleshed in all of this history, culminating with the unusual commitment that his friend the defense minister had made: the field marshal was prepared to waive all rules and regulations in selling Egyptian equipment to the CIA. No paperwork would be necessary, no governmental approvals. Not even President Mubarak need be consulted. It could all be done with a handshake because of Abu Ghazala's confidence in Wilson.

Abu Ghazala arranged for a demonstration the following morning of the weapon he insisted would be perfect for the Afghans, the mule-portable ZSU-23. The field marshal didn't attend; it was below his dignity. He left the fieldwork to his generals, who were all waiting anxiously as the Americans gathered in the desert. Gust noted with dismay that Denis Neill was once again with Charlie, all dressed up in his "Alan Ladd desert suit.'" Avrakotos was still offended at the idea of a lobbyist for the Egyptian defense minister glomming onto a CIA mission, so he perversely enjoyed watching Denis "sweating his balls off in his suit."

A surreal sight awaited the odd delegation of Americans as they drove through the desert to the spot the Egyptians had chosen for the demonstration. Abu Ghazala's generals had not only brought the ZSU-23s into the desert but also a collection of round white tables with umbrellas and red-and-white-checked tablecloths, so that the honored guests could sit in comfort. Each table sported a lunch box filled with Kentucky Fried Chicken.

The conditions couldn't have been less pleasant, however. Wanting to simulate the mountainous terrain of Afghanistan, the Egyptians had chosen the sloping incline of a landfill over a sprawling desert garbage dump. Furthermore, no parasol could tame the desert heat that day. It was at least 110 degrees in the shade, everyone was soaking, and the hot wind made Avrakotos feel like he was in a sauna with a fan running. There were pitchers of Pepsi-Cola, which the Americans drank incessantly, but no one could think much about eating the fried chicken.

Then things began to take on a comedic dimension, so much so that it was hard for Alper, Pratt, and Vickers not to smirk at one another. The Egyptian gunners were standing at attention as a three-star general who talked as if he had been educated at Oxford gave a rousing description of the ZSU-23's attributes. The key point he made—at the urging of his advisers, Gust had insisted on this demonstration—was that after his men fired at a target across the desert, the Americans would see how easily the gun could be broken down and moved by mule up the incline.

Even the doubting weapons experts were suitably impressed with the first part of the exercise. They could see through their binoculars how smoothly and accurately the guns fired. The Egyptians then began to strip the gun down to move it up the hill. The object, after all, was to have a gun that the mujahideen could actually transport among the mountains of Afghanistan.

Charlie was still sitting tall in his seat, not at all bothered by Vickers's tactful effort to explain why this gun simply would not work. By this time, the Egyptians had put the six-hundred-pound base of the gun on wheels, and several mules had been harnessed to haul the dead weight up the long, steep incline.

"Commence the exercise," shouted the general, whereupon a squad of soldiers pulled the blocks out from behind the ZSU's wheels and began urging the mules forward. Gust is charitable in his memory of this moment: "Egyptians win my heart because no matter how bad they fuck up, they always smile. Those fucking mules started going backward. They were in danger of going ass over head backward, whereupon twenty Egyptians appeared from nowhere trying to hold the mules and push them back. They almost lost all the Egyptians as well."

Vickers watched with astonishment as the soldiers desperately jammed rocks behind the wheels to keep the gun cart from racing backward down the landfill. Once it was stabilized, they would bravely began again, each time with even more desperate efforts to stop the inevitable movement in the wrong direction. "If there had been a way to will it up the mountain, they would have," recalled Avrakotos. Finally, after repeated Egyptian tries and failures, Wilson himself ordered an end to the exercise. In an effort to spare the Egyptians further embarrassment, Gust said with enthusiasm, "This chicken is great. Thanks for the demonstration."

Avrakotos then turned to Wilson and said, "Charlie, I can't buy it." Without missing a beat Wilson responded, "You're right." In Gust's mind, Charlie had just passed the first ethics test. He wasn't trying to pressure the Agency into buying a weapon that wouldn't work for the Afghans. There would soon be a second test for Charlie.

The entourage was then ferried back across the desert to eyeball Mohammed's next offering: a warehouse filled with eight hundred Soviet SA-7s left over from the Yom Kippur War. These were the same type of shoulder-fired anti-aircraft weapons the Agency had gotten so excited about when they were able to buy a small supply of them from the Polish general who'd wanted a tombstone in honor of his grandfather erected in Quebec. But the station had tipped off Gust that the Egyptians tended not to maintain their old weapons well. Avrakotos, still worried that Wilson might try to put the fix in, had said, "Charlie, if the SAMs are operational, I'll buy them. But if they're not, I don't want to hear another fucking word about them."

Abu Ghazala had assured Charlie that every SAM was in mint condition. But when they walked into the warehouse, all three of Gust's experts rolled their eyes. SA-7s, like all sophisticated electronic weapons, are supposed to be stored in temperature-controlled, sanitary conditions. This desert warehouse was filled with dust, and the SA-7s were actually sitting on dirt floors. Art Alper whispered to Gust, "They aren't worth the metal put into them." The wires were burned out, and the connections were no good.

Gust explained to Wilson that Vickers and Alper, the two men he trusted, said the SAMs were useless, but another expert from the station had suggested that Gust take samples back to headquarters for testing. What did Wilson want to do? Gust asked. "Forget the SAMs," Charlie said. "We can't give something to the Afghans that won't work."

Before leaving for Egypt, the CIA's deputy director, John McMahon, had called Avrakotos into his office and issued a warning: "I want you to know that you are dealing with dynamite with Wilson. If he ever does anything that looks to you as if he is using the Agency to personally profit, you let me know immediately." Wilson had now passed Avrakotos's final ethics test. "It proved to me that he wasn't out for the commissions," Gust says. It made me one hundred percent certain he was not Mr. Five Percent. And having watched him now for all these years, I can honestly say, in my opinion, there is no question that Charlie never made a dime on any of this. His motive was just to get even with the Russians. If his friends made money he didn't give a shit, just so long as the weapons killed Russians."*

After the disastrous day in the desert, Gust was not very hopeful about doing much business with Mohammed. Charlie, in his typically charming manner, called the field marshal to tell him the bad news. "Mohammed, I'm afraid some of your mules fainted this morning," he said, adding that the defense minister would be furious to discover that his officers had not properly stored the SA-7s and that the CIA couldn't consider buying them either.

---

*Wilson, unaware of Gust's and the Agency's suspicions, had attempted to put the best spin on the weapons disasters by suggesting that his friend Mohammed had been deceived by his generals. In retrospect, he acknowledges, "Abu Ghazala was probably also trying to dump his old shit from his warehouses." What Wilson came to realize was that his friend was eager to help the CIA but also deeply interested in getting as many dollars as possible for his huge obsolescent inventories of Soviet weaponry.

On a later trip, Avrakotos would be amazed to see just how ambitious a merchant of death Charlie's friend had become. He remembers talking to Mohammed's aide General Yahia al Gamal, whom everyone referred to as "General Ya-Ya." Yahia kept running in and out of a perfumed room next door to his suite of offices. There was a heavy aroma of incense, and Gust finally asked, "Who the fuck do you have in there?" Yahia answered, "The Iraqis are in one room, the Iranians in another." Avrakotos instantly put it all together: "Mohammed was selling weapons to us to kill Russians in Afghanistan, selling weapons to Iraq to kill Iranians, and selling weapons to Iranians to kill Iraqis."

"Someone is going to die," Abu Ghazala told Charlie, who says, "I'm sure a few heads rolled that day."

Although a bit embarrassed, Mohammed did not seem overly concerned. He quickly assured Wilson that he had many other weapons to offer and that the following day he would even arrange for a visit to Egypt's most sensitive new-weapons development center. That night, he insisted, the entire delegation must join him for dinner and an evening at the leading belly-dancing casbah of Cairo, where Fifi Abdul was performing.

The scene in the casbah was right out of *Casablanca*—swarthy Egyptians drinking and watching the middle-aged belly dancers, Mohammed at the best table surrounded by equal numbers of Egyptian generals and Agency operatives, and Charlie and Gust as the guests of honor. As always, flanking the table were Mohammed's bodyguards, understandable in a country where religious zealots had recently gunned down the president.

As head of the purchasing commission, Gust was seated next to the defense minister. The Agency's analytic division had prepared him for this encounter by providing a psychological profile of Ghazala, which Avrakotos had studied on the way over. It reported that Mohammed smoked, drank, had a roving eye, and, most fascinating of all to Gust, loved ethnic jokes. Wanting to build a bridge to this powerful potential ally, Avrakotos decided to ingratiate himself by telling Mohammed a politically incorrect joke that made fun of a certain Greek stereotype. "Did you hear the one about the little Greek boy?" he asked. "He went with the Greek girl for three months until he finally got into her little brother."

"It's not that funny when you get down to it," acknowledges Avrakotos, "but Mohammed fucking loved it. He said, 'You're Greek, aren't you?'" The delighted defense minister then proceeded to spin out a series of Greek, Armenian, and Israeli jokes and ended up by saying, "Well, I have to give equal treatment to the Arabs. I can't let you think I'm anti-Semitic." With that, Mohammed let loose several hilarious jokes mocking his own countrymen.

As Gust and Mohammed began to bond, Gust discovered how valuable a relationship with Abu Ghazala could be. The quality of the weapons and ammunition the Egyptians had been producing for the Afghan operation was so mixed that the Cairo station had been requesting the right to inspect the factory, but after four months they had been unable to get anyone to even give them an answer. At dinner, Abu Ghazala just waved his hand and told Gust that everything was possible for Charlie's friends; they could visit the factory in the morning.

The rest of the trip was a dizzying roller coaster. The previously inaccessible .303 factories sprang open just as promised. The CIA contingent found it hard to believe their eyes as they watched the Egyptian men loitering about, smoking next to the explosive stores of gunpowder, while women, their hands moving like machines, filled cartridges with thimbles full of the black substance. To Gust it was like stepping back in time. The factories looked just like the descriptions he had once read of conditions in nineteenth-century New England textile mills.

"Mind you, we were in a Muslim nation where women are not supposed to participate but all the quality control stations were run by women," he says. When Avrakotos queried General Yahia about all the women supervisors, he replied, "Apparently you've never been married to an Egyptian woman—they're real sons of bitches."

"Okay," Gust responded, "I'm going to keep buying from the Egyptians."

Most of the Egyptians' initial efforts to sell weapons to the Agency resembled a Keystone Kops movie. The most preposterous moment came during a test firing of Mohammed's new briefcase-size tank destroyer. Once more a general delivered a rousing briefing and a stalwart Egyptian fired at the target, but this time the round, acting like a boomerang, turned back on the watchers. "Oh shit!" Charlie yelled as they all hurled themselves flat. "We decided not to buy any of those," Wilson remembers.

There had been much wringing of Egyptian hands before the demonstration, ostensibly over the disclosure of such valuable state secrets to such known friends of Israel. Art Alper had gone to some lengths to conceal his religious affiliations. After scrambling up from the ground, Gust had quipped to the embarrassed General Yahia, "I don't think the Jews have to worry about this one."

As compensation for these little setbacks and to the confusion and dismay of his security officials, Mohammed offered to let the Agency delegation go into the army's most sensitive research-and-development facility, where his weapons people were finishing production of a shoulder-fired anti-aircraft missile that he said was not only more effective than a SA-7 but would prove superior to the American Stinger.

No one at this plant was ever prepared for visitors, but unlike everything else the Americans had seen in Egypt, this facility was operated like a sophisticated high-tech laboratory in the United States. "It was the cleanest place in Cairo," remembers Avrakotos. "The men and women wore white coats like doctors and seemed to have been educated at technical schools in the U.S. like Carnegie Mellon."

At first Charlie figured he had led the CIA to the silver bullet that would at last bring down the Hind, and once inside, Gust could not restrain his impulse to snoop. On a later trip with Paul, the psychological-warfare expert whom Gust complimentarily describes as "a sneaky son of a bitch," the visitors dispersed to explore as much of the facility as possible. The Egyptians always looked quite terrified when the American spies, taking advantage of Mohammed's license, entered areas ordinarily forbidden.

In one sealed-off room Paul and Gust came across three scientists who didn't look Egyptian and Gust said, "*As Salaam Alaikum*," Arabic for "hello." Two of them responded with *"Bonjour."* Gust now knew that French were working with the Egyptians. It was not long ago that Egypt and Israel had been at war, and the fear was that the Americans would run off and warn Jerusalem. But once again Gust, with Charlie as a guarantor, gave his word that all of the Agency's dealings with Mohammed would remain a secret. In keeping with all of Mohammed's other antiaircraft solutions, this weapon never lived up to the field marshal's promises and wasn't even ready to be tested when the CIA was prepared to buy it.

After all those disastrous mishaps at Mohammed's arms bazaar, the CIA contingent finally stumbled across a number of things they very much wanted. Thanks again to Charlie, Mohammed had offered to let the CIA men exchange information with his unconventional-warfare experts. The Egyptians had something to talk about here because they had gone through a brutal guerrilla war in Yemen just a few years before. Fighting with tribesmen in mountainous terrain similar to Afghanistan, they had learned what works and what doesn't. They might have bombed out in the big-ticket items that Wilson had wanted the Agency to buy, but at the Egyptian Special Warfare School, the counterinsurgency experts began showing Alper, Vickers, and Pratt items that would clearly be devastating in the hands of the mujahideen.

What got Alper and then Avrakotos particularly excited was the cornucopia of city-warfare devices that the Egyptians had stored in this facility. "It was incredible stuff that most American minds are not devious enough to think up," remembers Avrakotos. "But if you've been around five thousand years like the Egyptians and survived, you come up with some great ways of killing your enemies." He was referring to such things as bicycle bombs. "They had hundreds of ways to conceal bombs or, if you will, terrorist devices. But they had worked out bombs that were concealed in wooden carts that carry manure, or special wheelbarrows."

The only question, as Avrakotos saw it, was whether this deadly cornucopia could be effective against the Soviets in Kabul and the other cities of Afghanistan. Alper insisted it would be very useful. "Then the decision was left to me," Gust recalled. "Do I want to order bicycle bombs to park in front of an officer's headquarters? Yes. That's what spreads fear."

Another senior CIA officer in Avrakotos's shoes might well have chosen to pass on the offering of urban terrorist devices. That's the kind of thing the CIA was not supposed to be doing. But Avrakotos decided they would be quite effective. Beyond that, Gust calculated that the congressman who had opened the door for him to make these purchases happened to be on one of the committees that serves as a watchdog for the Agency. Gust could hardly be accused of trying to pull a fast one on Congress.

Thanks to Mohammed's tour, the CIA's military team soon discovered a whole range of low-level weapons they wanted for the jihad, like Egyptian limpet mines that Alper later modified so they could be attached magnetically to Soviet trucks heading down the Salang Highway. The Egyptians taught Alper how to delay the fuses beyond the time period he thought possible. "It was very useful for going after tunnels. We managed to block the Salang for days. The Yemenis had done it to the Egyptians, the Egyptians showed our guys how to do it, and our guys showed the mujahideen how to do it." The Egyptians' list also included screaming meemies, plastic mines, mines that popped out of the ground, trip mines, and wire mines.

Gust was now sensing genuine opportunity, enchanted with his status as Charlie's running mate as they drove in air-conditioned cars through the desert to be given red-carpet treatment at whatever facility they might choose to descend on. It was on one such visit that he stumbled across a weapon that thrilled him like no other.

The Agency had been looking for a rocket with a range of over ten kilometers that could not be traceable to the United States or NATO, and they found it in one of Mohammed's warehouses—the Katyusha. During World War II, at the siege of Stalingrad, this 122mm rocket had made the difference. A huge, screaming artillery round, it chilled the Wehrmacht with its terrible noise and striking power and had been immortalized in such Soviet patriotic songs as the "Stalin Organ." "We didn't think we could ever find the fucking thing," says Gust. But after spotting fifty-four of them in a warehouse, he had the Egyptians test-fire one, and he still remembers his terror. "If you've ever heard one of these come at you, there's no way you wouldn't crap in your pants. I was three miles away from where it hit and I was scared. It was a frightening experience, like being in a minor earthquake. You just can't imagine what it would be like to be within fifty feet of one of those things."

Gust bought every one of Mohammed's Katyushas at tens of thousands each, and soon the mujahideen were blasting away at the airport near Kabul, creating holes the size of football fields as far away as the city's outskirts. The French ambassador reported that although the rocket had landed seventeen blocks away, it had cracked the foundations of his Kabul embassy. The Russians were mortified. Ultimately, terrorizing the Soviets and making them leave was the name of Avrakotos's game. The discovery of the Katyusha at that point in the war was just what the doctor ordered. Gust didn't care that the rocket wasn't accurate. He wanted to frighten and demoralize the 40th Army, the KGB, and all those Communist Party bastards ruling the roost in Kabul. The Agency had already started trying to "turn the lights out" in the occupied capital by having the mujahideen blow up electricity pylons. The night always belonged to the mujahideen, but particularly when there was no light. And if a screaming Katyusha could be added to the mix, well, that was just the perfect twist of the psychological dagger.

Avrakotos first saw the rocket fired at the end of 1984. By February 1985, he had commissioned the Egyptians to open up a production line of Katyushas, ordering seven hundred of them by year's end. They also became a part of the weapons mix against the previously invincible Soviet air force. By firing these rockets at the airfields, the Afghans could at least spread fear in the pilots' minds and occasionally take out a target. "We had the mujahideen firing the Katyushas from ten kilometers away twice a day," says Gust. "They sound like thirty freight trains coming in all at once."*

Things were falling into place on this trip, with Gust acquiring odd, diverse instruments for Mike Vickers's symphony of armaments. "You could imagine what the Russians were starting to discover once we started pouring in all of these new weapons," he says. "When they went into a village in 1983 or 1984 they would find a few .303 rifles. But a year later they'd have a much bigger fight on their hands, and at the end they'd find twenty-five AK-47s and all sorts of ordnance. They could sense the enormity of the volume."

At one point near the end of this Egyptian shopping spree, it occurred to Avrakotos that no other CIA officer had been able to play such a hand as he was in the campaign against America's great enemy, and all because of this Texas congressman. As far as he was concerned, Charlie Wilson was a partner he could go the course with. Wilson had not only passed Gust's ethics tests, he had demonstrated that he could be more valuable to the Agency in dealing with Egypt than anyone else in the U.S. government. "What we did in one month with Charlie would have taken us nine years to accomplish."

Gust would learn to operate in Egypt without Wilson's presence. With Charlie's blessing, Avrakotos would deal with low-level problems by telling whatever Egyptian blocker might be in his way that Congressman Wilson had already spoken to the defense minister about the matter and perhaps the officer would like to call Abu Ghazala if he insisted on overriding the field marshal's wishes. This was Gust's old game of bureaucratic chicken, and as long as he was moving under the mantle of the magical congressman, the keys to the Egyptian kingdom were his.

But frequently in those early months, Avrakotos had to call on Wilson to intervene directly. Thanks to Charlie, Gust was able to build his own storage facilities at Port Suez and then send Egyptians to the United States for training as production inspectors. Once, Wilson decided that a major crisis over quality control was too big to be dealt with by phone, so he

---

*There is some disagreement here among experts as to the date and identity of the weapon that Avrakotos is describing in this passage. This account was used because it reflected the memory of both Avrakotos and Wilson.

invited Mohammed for a weekend at the Hawkeye Lodge, a "good old boy" establishment in the pine woods of East Texas where legendary Texans like John Connally, Nelson Bunker Hunt, and Ross Perot go for rest and recreation. It's a place where a man can ride, shoot skeet, hunt, fish, and hang out and drink with the boys. It's expensive, but Charlie arranged to have some of the defense contractors who sell their wares to the Egyptian military pick up the tab. And for icing on the cake, he thoughtfully summoned Carol Shannon, his personal belly dancer, whom Mohammed so adored, to come for the weekend with her entire troop of liberated Fort Worth belly-dancing housewives.

There is a tradition at retreats like Hawkeye that no one talks about the recreation pursued on these visits, so before the festivities began, Gust took Mohammed aside and said there would be no wiretaps, no photographs. His word of honor. This was to be a weekend of pure, free play. The two men instinctively understood each other. Mohammed, coming from a land of intrigue and omnipresent dangers, did Gust the singular compliment of taking him unreservedly at his word. So, with secret servicemen and local police patrolling the wooded perimeter, Carol danced, Charlie drank, Mohammed entertained everyone with his endless store of ethnic jokes, and Gust resolved his problems. As always, it was wonderful fun doing business Charlie's way.

Before his tour of duty was over, Gust would place orders for tens of millions of dollars' worth of weapons. The consignments grew so large that he bought a special ship to move them in containers to Karachi. For the next two years he was treated like a visiting monarch whenever he went to Egypt. And because of his expanding business with the Chinese, he was in the catbird seat when it came to organizing competitive bidding. Avrakotos was able to drive prices down to half the going black-market rate. On one occasion, Mohammed's trusted General Yahia whined, "We're only making a half cent a round. I'd like to make more."

"Well, I'd like to fuck Marilyn Monroe, but she's dead," Avrakotos responded. "Take the money and be happy." After brooding for three weeks, the Egyptians folded.

By the end of this first trip to Egypt, Gust had come to feel that he was poised to provide a steady stream of weaponry at a predictable price without fear of any sudden cutoffs. This was critical to everything that Mike Vickers was teaching Gust about the weapons policy the CIA must pursue.

There was one lurking concern that Gust could never quite shake: the threat posed by Islamic extremists. Once, while being driven through Cairo by an Egyptian officer, he came upon an entire block that had recently been burned to the ground. Demanding that the car stop, he got out and learned that the Egyptian security forces had wiped out the entire neighborhood because it was thought to harbor radicals. Cairo's politics were clearly unpredictable, which meant that Abu Ghazala's hold might not last forever. But for the time being, Gust figured Mohammed was firmly in control of the armed forces, and that meant things couldn't be better for the CIA.

For Wilson, the Egyptian trip was a small right of passage. He had now been inducted into the CIA's Clandestine Services. Beyond that, he had gone through a dramatic learning experience. "Up until that time I thought we just needed to buy the guns and get them into Afghanistan," he says. But in Egypt he had been sobered, witnessing how one weapon after another that he had wanted Gust to buy sight unseen proved to be worthless. Furthermore, Charlie had learned that it didn't help to put guns in the field if you didn't have a proper supply of ammunition to feed them and a pipeline to get that ammunition to the fighters.

One thing that had not changed was Wilson's spirit, still completely untamable when it came to conniving for his freedom fighters. Gust had told Wilson that the CIA was running a Muslim jihad and he would not buy weapons from the Israelis. But Jerusalem was Charlie's next stop on his trip with Trish, and once in the Israeli capital, he and Zvi went back to work scheming to get the Charlie Horse into the Afghan war.

By the time Wilson arrived, the Israelis had come up with an ingenious argument as to why their anti-aircraft gun would be more effective and cheaper than anything else the Agency could acquire. It was to be fed by 2.75-inch rockets, and Zvi's people at Israeli Military Industries were convinced that the U.S. Army had vast stocks of such ammunition left over from the Vietnam War. If Wilson could tap into this treasure trove and acquire the ammunition for free as surplus, the Israeli gun would cost the CIA precious little to operate, and IMI, for its part, could disguise it as a Soviet weapon, or anything else for that matter.

As always, Wilson was scheming on many fronts but looking like nothing more than the ultimate boondoggling congressman. From Israel he took Trish to Marrakech, where they checked into the Churchill Suite at La Mamounia hotel. Charlie, of course, dropped in on the highest military command to justify the U.S. government picking up the tab. With the CIA on board and the Egyptian arsenal now open, Charlie could feel the tide turning.

For Gust Avrakotos, Cairo was hopeful right up until the very last hours when, without Wilson by his side, he ran into the horror of dealing with the Egyptians as a mere mortal. A single parent, he was rushing to catch the last plane back to Washington that would get him home for Thanksgiving dinner with his son Gregory. But there was the usual bottleneck at customs.

Almost a decade later a CIA friend would tell Gregory the story of what he saw in the airport that day. The Greek-American with the bushy mustache, wearing blue jeans and a dark blue jacket, leapt into the baggage area and started hurling suitcases about until he found his, then bolted toward the gate. Grabbed by security guards, he brandished his diplomatic passport, roaring at them to call Abu Ghazala.

It was one of those borderline situations where a security official might go either way—either be intimidated or believe that he had just apprehended a true terrorist. Choosing the bureaucrat's route, the Egyptians put in the call and watched with amazement as Avrakotos dressed down Mohammed's aide, growling that the aide had exactly four minutes to get him moving toward the plane. Otherwise the field marshal should be informed that the CIA was not buying anything more from Egypt.

When last seen, Gust was not only on the plane jetting back for his turkey dinner, but had been elevated to first class, compliments of the Egyptian Ministry of Defense.

CHAPTER 23

Senator Gordon Humphrey

THE SENATOR AND HIS EVEN CRAZIER RIGHT-WING FRIENDS

By the time Charlie Wilson returned from Cairo he had, for all practical purposes, become an integral part of Avrakotos's Afghan operation. This recruitment (or voluntary enlistment, if you will) of an agent at the very heart of the congressional establishment came just in the nick of time, because three weeks later, on December 26, 1984, the Far Right unleashed a devastating public attack on the CIA.

It came from New Hampshire Senator Gordon Humphrey, one of those pure conservatives from the state that has the slogan "Live Free or Die" on its license plates. Humphrey was for prayer in the schools, against abortion, against big government, and always against Communism in all of its manifestations.

What made his assault so noteworthy was that everyone in Washington knew that Gordon Humphrey was a close ideological and political ally of the president. So when he rose before a crowd of reporters at the National Press Club with two bearded mujahideen commanders by his side, it was hard to ignore his charge that the Agency was playing a role so wimpish in its support of the Afghans that it verged on betrayal of the freedom fighters. The senator added many embellishments to his attack: mismanagement, incompetence, lack of will, failure to honor the president's commitment. The bottom line, however, was a declaration of war against the CIA from one of the leading spokesmen of the Reagan Right.

What Gordon Humphrey didn't know that day was what the CIA had just done, thanks to Avrakotos and Wilson, to transform the Afghan operation. Drawing on "Charlie's money" and following Vickers's grand design, Avrakotos now had unbelievable amounts of ordnance moving in the pipeline toward the Afghan border. But the CIA was in no position to defend itself against Humphrey's charge of betrayal. Covert operations are considered state secrets at Langley, not to be commented on, even in the face of ignorant or damaging claims. This attack, however, had the smell of danger to it because the senator made it clear he was not about to drop the issue.

Humphrey, who kept to his promise to serve only two terms in Washington, has all but disappeared from public view outside of New Hampshire. During the Reagan years, however, he was a ferocious and vocal promoter of conservative causes. He didn't sit on any of the committees that oversee the CIA, but out of fear of his access to the president and because of his penchant to fight to the death for his causes, the Agency chose to deal with him as if he were a full member of the Intelligence Committee.

The senator tended to operate in those years out of a secret hideaway carved out of the curve of the Capitol dome. The intelligence officials who met him there invariably left feeling that he was a truly eccentric and somewhat disturbing figure. Avrakotos recalls a particularly creepy feeling on first encountering him there: "When I went into his inner sanctum I kept looking for pictures of little boys half mutilated on the walls. He reminded me of Himmler with those chicken-farmer eyes. I didn't like going to see him."

The senator reportedly spent long hours alone in this room, communicating with his staff via computer. Avrakotos had been told that Humphrey was a former Eastern Airlines copilot and, upon being admitted to the windowless room, Avrakotos had been struck by its resemblance to the cockpit of a plane. The senator, in front of his word processor, seemed as if he were busy at the controls.

"Is he going to fly us out of here?" Avrakotos whispered to Norm Gardner, the Agency's congressional liaison man who had come along to keep Gust on his best behavior. "Shut up, we don't want to piss him off," Gardner whispered back. Wilson had already told Avrakotos to be careful with Humphrey because "he may not be all there." Avrakotos's Pentagon friend Walter Jajko had been blunter: "The fucker's crazy." Gust had repeated all this to Gardner on the way over, but the tough little CIA man had responded pragmatically, "Yeah, but Clair tells me he's a personal friend of the president's."

Just how zany and out of touch with modern times the senator was is conveyed by his hard-and-fast rule that none of his staff were permitted to speak to Communists, no matter what the circumstances. Any infractions were cause for immediate dismissal. This created a considerable dilemma for Humphrey when he discovered that the aide he had come to rely on most, Mike Pillsbury, was an old China hand who had spoken to untold numbers of Reds for years. Pillsbury had the unfortunate task of having to explain the confusing news to the senator that the Communist Chinese were key allies of the CIA in backing the anti-Communist mujahideen in their war against the Soviet Union.

This came as something of a shock; Pillsbury reports that it took the senator some time to assimilate the information. But that December 26 at his press conference, Humphrey was anything but muddle-headed; he was the picture of clarity and passion as he laced into the CIA. For the next six years, Afghanistan would become his all-consuming passion. Within weeks of his debut he would create a congressional "Afghan task force" and, anointing himself chairman, would then preside over unofficial hearings on the state of the CIA's war. Almost immediately he would become better known than Charlie Wilson as the American champion of the Afghan cause. His method of support, however, would be so exceedingly bizarre that the Pakistan ambassador, Jamsheed Marker, would observe privately that Gordon Humphrey "was a most embarrassing friend."

The senator became so obsessed with the cause that he went so far as to commit over 60 percent of the efforts of his Senate staff to Afghanistan. Most of those efforts consisted of harassing the bureaucracies involved in the war effort. His aides were expected to grind out a constant flow of accusatory letters to the CIA, State, AID, the Pentagon, and the White House, demanding more action and immediate explanations for failures to properly support the mujahideen. His letters resembled interrogatories sent to a hostile side in litigation.

The sudden appearance of this vocal negative force was no small problem for Avrakotos and the CIA. To begin with, it forced Gust's officers to spend hours or even days a week just answering the senator's questions. Unlike Wilson, Humphrey's approach was not to work with the CIA from the inside but to push them through bureaucratic terror tactics. The threat most worrisome to Langley came from the senator's ability to create a forum where all sorts of critics of the CIA, including some very zany ones, could have their voices heard.

As with so many of the public assaults on the Agency's Afghan program in those early years, Humphrey's could be traced back to a maniacally energetic Lithuanian-American, Andrew Eiva, the same former Green Beret who had convinced Senator Paul Tsongas to push through his congressional resolution calling for total support of the mujahideen. While Charlie and Gust were in Egypt, Eiva had managed to insinuate himself into Humphrey's mind. The senator, who acknowledges that he hadn't thought much about Afghanistan before launching his CIA attack, had been searching about for a good conservative cause to champion, when Eiva came into his life.

The night of the press conference the team divided its labors: Eiva to *Nightline* to accuse the CIA of selling out the freedom fighters, Humphrey to *MacNeil/Lehrer* for a twenty-minute tirade. The papers, notably the *Los Angeles Times* and *Washington Times,* as well as a number of newspapers overseas, gave his accusations front-page billing.

The reason reporters were drawn to the right-wing senator and his Green Beret adviser had little to do with a shared conviction that the CIA should be involved in Afghanistan. They paid attention only because a senator was bad-mouthing the Agency on the record. (He and Eiva were specifically accusing the CIA of double-dealing by providing the freedom fighters with antique and joke weaponry and permitting the Pakistanis to steal them blind.) Perhaps it was hard for the press to avoid giving full attention to these kinds of harsh accusations, but it is remarkable that Eiva was able to get his campaign off the ground.

Eiva was a very shabby-looking fellow, with disheveled hair and a long scraggly beard. Quite overweight, he always had a haunted look, like a character out of a Russian novel from the days of Rasputin. In what seemed to be his only suit, he resembled almost anything but a former clean-cut American Green Beret.

The CIA came to loathe Andrew Eiva, and it appears that officers suggested more than once to congressmen and staffers that Eiva might be a Bulgarian or East German agent. But it seems more likely that he was just another of those passionate believers, like Charles Fawcett and, to a certain extent, Charlie Wilson, who got caught up in this cause. The idea that he was a Communist spy would become quite ludicrous years later, in 1990, when he was found behind the barricades in front of the Lithuanian Parliament, where he had joined his countrymen for the final assault on Communism.

The penniless Eiva had been working out of a phone booth in 1984 when a particularly extreme, right-wing Mormon operation, Free the Eagle, decided to put him on their payroll as an Afghan lobbyist. The group's leader, Neil Blair, believed that Eiva could rally conservatives who felt that the CIA, like the Council on Foreign Relations and the Trilateral Commission, was dominated by people of suspect patriotism.

With Free the Eagle's Xeroxing and mailing resources, Eiva began bombarding reporters and congressmen with the Agency's long record of betrayals and its current failures in Afghanistan. Many of his points were hard to deny, and a breakthrough for the crusader came when he convinced Leslie Gelb of the *New York Times* that the CIA's effort was insignificant when compared to the estimated $700 million a year's worth of weapons that the Soviets had furnished the North Vietnamese and Vietcong. A favorable *Times* profile gave Eiva all the legitimacy he needed.

It might seem that Gust Avrakotos would have found Eiva's public criticisms useful. The two were, after all, saying much the same thing, and certainly they were pursuing the same objective. But Avrakotos had many reasons for fearing the public attacks once Gordon Humphrey got into the mix. For one thing, the civilian Pentagon officials involved in security affairs were starting to maneuver to take over the Afghan operation, claiming that the CIA did not know how to run a military campaign. Furthermore, Humphrey and Eiva were enlisting other conservative senators, and the idea of Congress gearing up for a sustained public attack threatened to erode confidence in the program just when Gust and Charlie had finally managed to get the resources the Agency needed to show what could be done.

Here Wilson orchestrated another cunningly effective campaign to soften these challenges to Avrakotos's Afghan program. Early on he decided that most of the activists involved in lobbying for the Afghans were highly peculiar and excessive in their criticism, not only of the CIA and the U.S. government but of the other groups that were involved in the same cause. Indeed, he would soon come to view them as very much like their Afghan clients—ostensibly sharing the same broad cause but caught up in internecine warfare.

Many were even more extreme in their zealousness than Eiva and Free the Eagle. There was the Washington-based Committee for a Free Afghanistan, originally led by an intimidating former army officer, Karen McKay, who had once undergone limited jump-school training and would sometimes appear at conservative gatherings in uniform, wearing a green beret. Two other equally formidable women worked out of a respected New York foundation, Freedom House: Rosanne Klass and Ludmilla Thorne. Wilson's political antenna told him right away that it would be highly dangerous to cross any of these zealots. For one thing, they all seemed to hate each other. The Committee for a Free Afghanistan, for example, refused to let Eiva into any of its meetings, and Eiva reciprocated by accusing the committee of being a CIA front.

Wilson made it a point to see them all whenever they called, to offer encouragement but diplomatically avoid signing on publicly with any of them. He played his role masterfully here. By now he was for all practical purposes a critical player in the very center of the CIA's Afghan operation, though he managed to make the entire range of ardent critics believe he was with them in their bitter attacks on the Agency. In the councils of his Appropriations subcommittees and in conferences with the Senate, however, he had already assumed the role of Langley's advocate, able to make the case for the way the Afghan operation was being run. It may be that Wilson was better informed at that time than anyone in the Agency except a few members of Avrakotos's inner circle.

He could tell his colleagues that he had been to Cairo, had seen the weapons being bought, had been to Pakistan and the mujahideen camps, and could state from firsthand experience how effective the program was becoming. He was already playing the part that the CIA's number two man, John McMahon, would later call that of the Agency's "case officer on the Hill."

There was an element of duplicity in Wilson's dealings here. In truth, it suited him just fine to have these crazies moving menacingly around the fringes hurling virtual bombs and attacking bureaucrats. For example, Charlie would always defend John McMahon in public, but he recognized that the deputy director was in fact a conservative force at the Agency and that other CIA officials were even more dubious about escalating. It didn't hurt to have the bureaucrats feel the pressure. On occasion, when he sensed resistance at State or the Agency, he would deliberately stir Eiva up.

Perhaps Wilson's most masterful maneuver on behalf of the CIA effort came in his dealings with Senator Humphrey. Here Charlie chose to have his role inside the Agency remain invisible and to allow Humphrey to assume the public spotlight as the Afghans' key congressional champion. Humphrey was so extreme when it came to Afghanistan that he would camp outside a fellow senator's office, if necessary, to corner him for a commitment on a vote. He didn't sit on Appropriations or Intelligence. He couldn't initiate funding increases the way Wilson could. But as an enforcer of senatorial discipline on behalf of the mujahideen, he managed to make his fellow senators feel that they would have a political enemy for life if they stood in his way, and few cared enough about the issue to choose to alienate such a man.

All of this made it possible for Wilson to play the role of the good cop, able to assure the Agency capos that he would always cover for them. At the same time, he made it clear that they should recognize that within the range of strident criticisms were some points that ought not to be ignored.

Meanwhile, Avrakotos had to deal with the fact that Gordon Humphrey, with all of his conservative credentials, was preparing to try the Agency in public. As he saw it, the CIA's credibility and right to continue its escalating operation was in jeopardy. Early in 1985, Gust decided it was time to co-opt the senator. Mike Vickers was put in charge of organizing a dog and pony show at the Agency's Camp Peary training ground.

Humphrey tried to bring Eiva, but Avrakotos pointed out that Humphrey, who did not sit on the Intelligence Committee, wasn't even cleared for what he was going to be shown. Bert Dunn, the Near East division chief, came along, and he and Gust sat back as Vickers did the briefing. Gust had samples of most of the weapons the mujahideen were using flown in from all over the country. The contrast between Humphrey's public accusation about the CIA's failure to adequately arm the mujahideen and the range of sophisticated weaponry from the arsenal displayed before his eyes was so stark that no one mentioned it directly. As Humphrey was shown the impressive arsenal that he had claimed did not exist, three battle-hardened Agency paramilitaries told of their experiences training the mujahideen and then helped the senator fire the weapons.

This carefully choreographed performance was designed to persuade Humphrey that the Agency was not wimpish, and after exploding a particularly lethal mine for the senator, Gust said with studied forethought, "You think we're putting chicken-shit mines in? Did you see this fucking round? It went through the son of a bitch better than Joe Louis penetrating a white woman."

"He didn't like that comment," Gust remarked years later, but that was the reason why Avrakotos had chosen such an ugly and crude analogy. He was out to intimidate Humphrey into silence. At one point the senator asked if Avrakotos could account for all the money and weapons being given to the Pakistanis and the Afghans. "We can't. Can you account for all the money going into New Hampshire from the federal government?" Avrakotos asked in return. "We use satellites as best we can. We put beacons on some packages and various crates, and overhead we study what happens to the shipments. And we do a pretty good job of it."

The entire Camp Peary exercise had one simple objective—intimidation—and Avrakotos saved his most effective ploy for the end, when he explained in front of his fellow operatives that the Agency wasn't able to refute the senator's charges publicly because it didn't want the Soviets to know what the mujahideen were getting. "You're undermining what we're trying to do. You're a fifth column. . . . Now that you've seen everything we're giving to the muj, you certainly should know that Andy Eiva is incorrect, and I assume you are satisfied."

Unlike Wilson, Humphrey never did become a partner of the CIA and no one connected to the Afghan program seems to have anything but unflattering things to say about him. But Avrakotos maintains that by the end of that day at Camp Peary, Gordon Humphrey had been largely neutralized.

For Avrakotos, 1985 was a year of right-wing craziness. About the same time Humphrey surfaced as a menace, he was confronted with a far weirder and more threatening problem from inside the government. A band of well-placed anti-Communist enthusiasts in the administration had come up with a plan they believed would bring down the Red Army, if the CIA would only be willing to implement it.

The leading advocates of this plan included Richard Perle at the Pentagon, so intense in his Cold War convictions that he was nicknamed "the Prince of Darkness." Oliver North also checked in briefly, but the man who set Avrakotos's teeth on edge most was Walt Raymond, another NSC staffer who had spent twenty years with the CIA as a propagandist.

Their idea was to encourage Soviet officers and soldiers to defect to the mujahideen. As Avrakotos derisively describes it, "The muj were supposed to set up loudspeakers in the mountains announcing such things as 'Lay down your arms, there is a passage to the West and to freedom.'" Once news of this program made its way through the Red Army, it was argued, there would be a flood of defectors.

This vision was based on Vlasov's army, a German-backed effort during World War II to persuade Communist soldiers to join an anti-Stalinist front. It had met with some success before collapsing, enough at least to excite the passionate efforts of its latter-day advocates. Andrew Eiva, not surprisingly, was deeply involved in this effort. He had gone to Pakistan in the early 1980s trying to find Russian prisoners to demonstrate how effective such a policy could be, but he had learned that the mujahideen did not have much interest in keeping prisoners alive. At a White House meeting, North and Perle told Avrakotos they wanted the Agency to spend millions on this program, expressing the belief that as many as ten thousand defectors could be expected to pour across the lines.

Avrakotos thought North and Perle were "cuckoos of the Far Right," and he soon felt quite certain that Raymond, the man who seemed to be the intellectual ringleader, was truly detached from reality. "What Russian in his right mind would defect to those fuckers all armed to the teeth?" Avrakotos said in frustration. "To begin with, anyone defecting to the Dushman would have to be a crook, a thief, or someone who wanted to get cornholed every day, because nine out of ten prisoners were dead within twenty-four hours and they were always turned into concubines by the mujahideen. I felt so sorry for them I wanted to have them all shot."

The meeting went very badly indeed. Gust accused North and Perle of being idiots. Larry Penn, Gust's consigliere, actually giggled in their faces. Avrakotos said to Walt Raymond, "You know, Walt, you're just a fucking asshole, you're irrelevant."

Avrakotos thought that would be the end of the Vlasov idea, but he greatly underestimated the political power and determination of this group, who went directly to Bill Casey to angrily protest Avrakotos's insulting manner. The director complained to Clair George, who responded by forbidding Avrakotos to attend any more interagency meetings without a CIA nanny present. George gave the job to his executive assistant, Norm Gardner, who worked out a system so that whenever Gust started to feel the anger coming from his toes he would tap Gardner and let the more diplomatic officer do the talking. But Gardner, who shared Avrakotos's frustrations with the Vlasov business, would often sit back and let his charge have at least a preliminary run at Raymond and the others.

At one point Avrakotos arrived for one of these White House sessions armed with five huge photographic blowups. Before unveiling them he explained that they would provide a useful understanding of the kind of experience a Soviet soldier could expect to have should he surrender to the mujahideen. One of them showed two Russian sergeants being used as concubines. Another had a Russian hanging from the turret of a tank with a vital part of his anatomy removed. Another showed a mujahid approaching a Soviet with a dagger in his hands. "If you were a sane fucking Russian, would you defect to these people?" he had demanded of Perle.

In spite of the angry complaints, Claire George and everyone else on the seventh floor agreed with Avrakotos's position. He says that Director Casey even privately told him, "I think your point is quite valid. What asshole would want to defect to those animals?"

But the issue wouldn't go away. Perle, Raymond, and the others continued to insist that the Agency find and send back to the United States the many Russian defectors they seemed to believe, despite Avrakotos's denials, the mujahideen were harboring. They had visions of a great publicity campaign once these men reached America. As soon as their stories were known, others would defect. They refused to believe Avrakotos's claim that there were no defectors.

Avrakotos describes what happened next with the kind of pleasure he feels only upon achieving revenge. It had been almost impossible to locate two prisoners, much less two defectors. The CIA found itself in the preposterous position of having to pony up $50,000 to bribe the Afghans to deliver two live ones. "These two guys were basket cases," says Avrakotos. "One had been fucked so many times he didn't know what was going on. The other was an alcoholic. We brought them back to the United States and I said to Walt Raymond, 'Do you want me to give them your telephone number? They're yours now.'"

Finally, Avrakotos turned the Soviets over to Ludmilla Thorne at Freedom House. "One guy had hallucinations of the KGB murdering him.

The other started fucking with boys." At that point, Avrakotos says, he went to Perle to announce the good news that the Agency had twelve more willing to come over. "I turned the tables on them and demanded they take them all. And they didn't want to. That was the new Vlasov's army. In all I think we brought three or four more over. One guy ended up robbing a 7-Eleven in Vienna, Virginia."

By 1985 the CIA had become a dangerous place in which to hold a position of power. Avrakotos and Wilson had led the Agency into completely uncharted territory. No longer bound by the historic Cold War doctrine of containment, it was, for the first time—unapologetically, almost openly—in the business of killing thousands of Russian soldiers by funding a Muslim jihad.

But nothing that year, or in fact in the Agency's history, compared to the unprecedented public attack launched from the Right on the CIA's number two man, John McMahon. The moving force was Andy Eiva, who explains now that he was "looking around for a rock to throw" when McMahon's name came onto the screen. Eiva says he discovered this presumed "enemy" of the Afghans on May 20, 1985, a date he remembers vividly. He had been making his usual rounds of congressional and press offices pushing for better weapons, including the American Stinger, for the mujahideen when a staffer from Senator Humphrey's office arranged for him to meet an NSC staffer at the White House named Vince Cannistraro.

Eiva was awed just to be admitted to the Old Executive Office Building and to find that the president's man in charge of overseeing intelligence operations seemed to take him seriously. Cannistraro, an old Agency man himself, was immediately sympathetic to Eiva's critique of the CIA but told him that he was missing the point. "The real enemy of the freedom fighters," Eiva remembers him saying, "is John McMahon." It was like a biblical revelation for Eiva, as if Cannistraro was deputizing him to put a stop to John McMahon's treachery.

Vince Cannistraro was not exactly a neutral source on the deputy director of the CIA. Until recently he had been the operations chief of the Contra war, but he had been reprimanded and moved out of Central America affairs because of the scandal over CIA-produced assassination manuals, which had enraged Congress. John McMahon had been largely responsible for his demotion and subsequent exile to the White House staff. Eiva didn't know any of this and probably wouldn't have cared, because he also learned that McMahon was the Agency official who had urged the Senate not to pass the Tsongas resolution. And so—on the same day that Humphrey launched his public attack on the CIA—Eiva appeared on *Nightline* and specifically accused McMahon of misleading Congress when he'd testified that the Afghans were being adequately armed. It was just the first of a vicious series of public attacks that Eiva would make against the CIA's deputy director, all of them suggesting that McMahon's record verged on treason.

Given what was already being done, it was a perverse twisting of reality. That fall, the mujahideen in the Pakistani training camps were not only receiving a flood of lethal weapons, they were also being trained to wage a war of urban terror, with instruction in car bombings, bicycle bombings, camel bombings, and assassination.

Just how vicious a campaign the CIA was sponsoring is suggested by the Pakistan brigadier Mohammed Yousaf, who directed the training with and distribution of CIA weapons at that time. In a matter-of-fact passage in his memoirs, he describes the range of assassination tactics and targets he was preparing the mujahideen to take on in Kabul. They ranged from your everyday "knife between the shoulder blades of a Soviet soldier shopping in the bazaar" to "the placing of a briefcase bomb in a senior official's office." Educational institutions were considered fair game, he explains, since they were staffed by "Communists indoctrinating their students with Marxist dogma."

What made Cannistraro's whispering campaign charging cowardice and timidity in the Afghan arena so perverse was that it came at a time when Avrakotos was responsible for over a half billion dollars' worth of weapons and training going into the funding of an exceedingly dirty war. Yet somehow Eiva, backed by conservative senators who followed his lead, insisted that the CIA was guilty of cowardice.*

According to Avrakotos, Casey came to loathe Cannistraro, calling him that "fucking dago." Clair George was also up in arms, according to

---

*Needless to say, the kind of tactics the CIA was at least indirectly responsible for promoting would have resulted in mass firings and Watergate-size scandals had any of them been implemented in Central America. Cannistraro, for example, was reprimanded and transferred for mere words in a manual urging assassination as a tactic.

Gust, and came to him to explain how Cannistraro could be neutralized. This was the kind of special assignment that had won Gust his old Agency nickname, Dr. Dirty, and he accepted it with relish. Gust knew that the politically ambitious Cannistraro would want to try to recruit the most powerful congressman on Afghanistan as an ally, so he arranged to have Vince meet him in Wilson's office. "I wanted to put him totally out of place," remembers Avrakotos. "He had no business doing what he was doing, and I figured that if he and the NSC were going to slap me around, I wanted to show him he'd have to deal with Charlie."

Cannistraro, who later appeared regularly as an intelligence expert on ABC News and such TV shows as *60 Minutes*, remembers feeling quite out of place that day—not being able to get a word in edgewise and amazed at the intense camaraderie he and Charlie shared. "They loved each other," Gust says. "I sat back and watched them talking about big tits and guns."

Gust's next move was pure Greek melodrama. He arrived at the airport for a trip with Vince to Pakistan dressed all in black. Before boarding the plane, he says he cornered Cannistraro and read him his rights: "You know you went to Central America and gave the Agency heartburn and you're not going to get away with it on this one."

But it was an incident on the flight from Pakistan that gave Cannistraro a real look at the side of Avrakotos no one would want to have to deal with. They were traveling on diplomatic passports and Gust managed to upgrade them to first class, where they met the interior minister from one of the Gulf States. The Arab, who was drinking heavily, ended up insulting Gust. Gust belted him and followed this up by pulling out his knife and loudly threatening to cut the man's balls off. Cannistraro watched with horror as Gust proceeded to hurl insults at the bug-eyed minister, accusing him of sinning in the eyes of Allah by drinking.

Cannistraro remembers being quite unnerved by this excessive aggression. "I was afraid to be sitting next to him. I thought the man was going to come back at us with a knife. Gust is not a gentle person." After describing this incident, the soft-spoken Cannistraro added that there was another moment in Pakistan that was every bit as bad: "He almost throttled the head of the motor pool at the embassy because the man didn't give him the car he wanted."

Gust was making a point with Vince. He made only one direct threat at the very beginning of the trip; afterward he was very courteous with his traveling companion, only demonstrating in his inimitable way how he dealt with minor aggravations. No doubt Cannistraro must have wondered what Avrakotos might be prepared to do if he determined someone was a true enemy. This was Dr. Dirty operating in his prime, but as far as Avrakotos is concerned the crowning blow came at dinner in Peshawar, when Gust followed the explicit prescription of his division chief, Bert Dunn, "to make sure to take him to a fucking restaurant where you can get him sick."

Over the years, Avrakotos had built up a stomach immune to foreign microbes. He says, "I even ate everything in Bujumbura, Burundi, where every white man got sick. I have a cast-iron stomach." He took Vince to a native restaurant in Peshawar, full of character, singing the praises of the food—calling it "very clean." Gust ate everything with relish, knowing full well that the next day Vince Cannistraro would be out of the picture. "Bert was absolutely delighted," Avrakotos recalls. "Bert just loved that Vince was sick for two days and couldn't do shit. He was like a little country boy who just shot his first squirrel when I told him about it."

By the time the two returned, Gust felt he needed to say nothing more. He had made his point, and he says that Cannistraro's report evaluating the CIA program had nothing damaging in it. "It started off by saying the Agency had a well-run program, and it was so wishy-washy that it was meaningless—chicken-shit criticism about procurement and storage of perishables. Nothing about important stuff."

Although most of this test of wills had been about personality conflicts, the Agency leadership had felt that a principle had been at stake. Never before had any outside agency attempted to investigate and critique the operation side of the CIA's work, and Gust's effort to back down Cannistraro was received as an important victory to prevent a dangerous precedent from being established. But that was just round one, and Avrakotos knew that Cannistraro would be back. "Vince could be greatly underestimated by his opponents, including Casey. He has certain qualities that I admire—revenge being one of them."

Avrakotos found himself in the midst of this unprecedented covert escalation, repeatedly threatened by bizarre challenges from totally unexpected quarters. It was all so strange that he actually came to see himself as a voice of reason facing down perfectly deranged figures, who happened to have the potential to do great damage. The archconservative senators, who had always been so blindly supportive of the Agency in the past, now became the kind of friends who make it unnecessary to have enemies. In the name of trying to help, they seemed quite prepared to bring the whole program down.

Ironically, the only real impact of all of these hard-right assaults may have been to give the program the cover it absolutely needed. The scope and the disquieting details of the Muslim jihad that the CIA was then sponsoring surely warranted Congress's attention. The Agency was not just flooding Afghanistan with weapons of every of nature; it was now unapologetically moving to equip and train cadres of high-tech holy warriors in the art of waging a war of urban terror against a modern superpower. But reporters did not choose to examine these themes in any depth. And before any congressional skeptics could investigate or seriously question whether the program might be growing too large, Humphrey, Eiva, and Free the Eagle shouted to anyone would listen (and many who didn't want to) that the CIA was denying the Afghans the weapons the president wanted them to have.

Meanwhile, Democratic liberals and reporters, who might ordinarily have questioned the wisdom of these programs, simply couldn't figure out how to overcome the impression left by right-wing critics that the CIA's crime in this case was not doing too much but too little—that McMahon and the Agency were subverting the president's clear mandate. While the CIA threw itself into arming, training, and funding the largest Muslim jihad in modern history, the only ones to register their outrage and demand change were those who seemed to believe that the CIA's support was so meaningless as to constitute a betrayal of the Afghans.

CHAPTER 24

The Freedom Fighters

TECHNO HOLY WARRIORS

One morning in early 1985, Gust Avrakotos noticed a strange phenomenon: a number of junior officers were addressing him as
"sir." Even more peculiar was an encounter with the deputy director for finance, a stuffy functionary who Gust says "always acted like he
was Saint Peter at the gate deciding whether you went to heaven or hell."
The man had never even asked Avrakotos to sit down before, but now he
got up from his desk to shake Gust's hand and offer him coffee and a dough-
nut. And then, one day when Gust arrived for a task force meeting where a
group of officers from different departments had been invited to offer advice, a hush came over the room. Most of these officers outranked Avrakotos,
but he remembers vividly that "they were quiet and smiling when I came
in, and moved aside for me." Afterward Larry Penn, Avrakotos's old friend
and "consigliere," couldn't help commenting that they had acted as if he—
Gust Avrakotos, of all people—was "Moses parting the waters."

What soon became clear to Avrakotos was that he suddenly had enormous power, by virtue of the fact that by 1985 his Afghan program was
getting over 50 percent of the CIA's entire Operations budget. Within a
year it would explode again, becoming almost 70 percent. His bosses, Bert
Dunn, the Near East division chief, and Clair George, deputy director for
Operations, had, of course, far higher rank and responsibility. But he was
the one with the authority to dispense hundreds of millions of dollars for
killing Russians. That was power.

On the floor below, where the Central American task force operated,
Gust's counterpart Alan Fiers had literally no money for his Contras.
Congress had cut the Agency off completely and forbidden them to con-

tinue any military support whatsoever. Yet Gust had a half billion to spend, and his "freedom fighters" seemed to be loved by everyone on the Hill. No one spoke ill of them, not even the press. As Gust recalled, "We were the only game in town where you could have excitement, a war, a chance to make a name for yourself. But also it was the holy cause—the one program everyone could be very proud of and identify with."

What finally convinced Avrakotos that he had arrived was when the grand old man of the Near East Division, Alan Wolfe—who had played such a critical role in setting up Kissinger's fabled entry to China and who was then serving as chief of station in Rome—asked Gust for dinner and an afternoon of antiquing in London. That meant something huge to Avrakotos, who says, "Wolfe is the kind of guy who only speaks to Cabots, Lodges, and God." Wolfe was the division chief who had picked Gust to be chief of station in Helsinki—until Bill Graver had come on board and taken back the assignment. For Gust, it was like being invited to Archie Roosevelt's. That afternoon, the incredibly short and impressive veteran officer talked Afghanistan with Avrakotos. Wolfe spoke seven languages, including Chinese. He had served in Kabul, knew the terrain, knew the culture, and he had just wanted to tell Gust that he was on the right track and "to keep at it."

After twenty years of being an outsider, it was as if this former renegade was finally part of the establishment of the Directorate of Operations, even flying off alone with the director to the desert kingdom. Once again, the Saudis were late on their payments. It was like pulling teeth to get them to cough up their matching grant, and this time, with the CIA putting up $250 million, Avrakotos was no longer sure they could be counted on. He had urged the director to go personally to collect, and Casey had invited Gust along for the ten-thousand-mile flight in his huge C-141 Starlifter, a kind of flying hotel with a planetary-range communications center.

The Saudis treated Casey as if he were a head of state. In Riyadh, Avrakotos was given his own villa. Casey's had eleven rooms with thirty exotic bowls, each one filled with a different kind of cashew, the director's favorite snack. Gust had given his chief a paper with talking points, which Vickers had prepared for the meeting. "I told Casey," he recalls, "that he should talk to the king about 'your Muslim brothers,' about using the money for food for the families, for clothing, weapons, for repairing the mosques. You should talk to him about being the 'keeper of the faith.'"

"Jesus, fuck, I like that—keeper of the faith," Casey said. "Oh fuck, I like that—keeper of the faith."

Avrakotos found the director's handling of King Fahd masterful. "Casey admired the Saudis. He didn't look at them as strange fuckers, scratching their balls and wearing funny headdresses. He told them that the mujahideen were getting stronger day by day, and that his men were inspired and motivated by them."

When the director finished his briefing, the king said, without asking for anything in return, "We will fulfill our promise." It was a desert agreement. No papers were signed.*

The amazing feature of the Saudi grant is that the king did not dictate terms. He was content to let the CIA use the money as it saw fit. Gust realized that because of King Fahd's commitment, the CIA's Afghans would now have twice the bite.

By the time Avrakotos returned to Langley, he knew he had won more than a massive increase of the Afghan war budget. He now possessed the mystique of having traveled alone on a secret mission with the director. As Avrakotos saw it, half the game in a dicey operation like Afghanistan was getting enough room to operate, and he knew that his superiors would now assume that something had happened on that long flight. The director loved risk-taking operatives. He was a notorious rule breaker himself, famous for bypassing the chain of command to deal directly with the men running his covert operations.

The seventh floor now had to adjust to the likelihood that Avrakotos and Casey had a private understanding. The director's mumbles could be interpreted to mean almost anything, and Avrakotos, confident that no one

---

*The Saudis received Casey regally, and the director took to the role. Avrakotos was impressed with how effective his briefing was. The king signed off on the money transfers without asking any questions. The director had other business as well. As a favor to President Reagan, the Saudis were, at the time, secretly providing the Contras with a million dollars a month. Prince Bandar had flown in as translator, and when Casey began to talk about what the Saudis might do to help out in other arenas, Avrakotos quickly excused himself. Gust already knew that things were being done for the Contras and in Iran that he wanted no part of. He could almost picture himself under the bright lights of a congressional hearing having to answer questions about what he and the director had been doing with the Saudis on this visit. He was content to confine his rule-stretching to his arena alone.

would dare go to the old man to see if he really agreed to what Gust might claim, was fully prepared to exploit the situation to the hilt. "If I had a problem I'd say, 'Casey called me; that's not what he wants.'"

Meanwhile, Gust's task force was a beehive of secret activity. The Dirty Dozen were now striking secret deals on a daily basis with intelligence services in China, Egypt, Pakistan, Saudi Arabia, Britain, Canada, France, and Singapore. They were spending tens of millions in a shot as they began moving unbelievable shipments of weapons and ammunition to the Afghans—millions of AK-47 rounds, divisions' worth of rifles, mortars, RPGs for hitting tanks, rockets for terrorizing Kabul, 14.5mm heavy machine guns with tracers to fend off the gunships, Dashikas, 120mm mortars—thousands of tons of deadly material.

With hindsight it can be argued that this was the critical year of the war, not just the year of the great U.S. buildup but also the year when it appeared to many at Langley and in the U.S. government that perhaps the CIA had moved with too little, too late and that it might be on the verge of creating an all-time covert disaster.

With hindsight, this was the year the Soviets might actually have succeeded in breaking the resistance. Had it not been for the huge CIA escalation, but specifically the new mix of weapons that Vickers introduced that year, the Soviet offensive might have worked.

The moment of panic—when it seemed as if the Wilson-Avrakotos escalation might backfire—came early in 1985. Ironically, the problem came not from the conventional hard-liners in the Kremlin but from the man usually thought of as the voice of reason and the architect of glasnost, Mikhail Gorbachev.

The first to get a look at the dark side of Gorbachev were the Pakistanis. Zia and his foreign minister, Yaqub Khan, were in Moscow in 1985 for Konstantin Chernenko's funeral, when the newly elevated Gorbachev took them aside at the Kremlin and all but threatened to destroy their country if they did not halt support for the mujahideen. He was reportedly brutal in his delivery, declaring that Pakistan was in effect waging war on the Soviet Union and that he was not going to stand for it. Summoning all of his courage, Zia looked Gorbachev straight in the eye and insisted that his country was not involved. With that, the CIA's key ally left Moscow for Mecca, where he prayed to Allah for courage to continue the jihad.

The CIA didn't wake up to what Gorbachev had in mind for them until later, when the Kremlin put General Mikhail M. Zaitzev in charge of the Afghan campaign. Zaitzev was the legendary officer who had executed the brutal invasion of Czechoslovakia in 1968, and his appointment was viewed as virtual proof that the Soviets were now committed to prevailing no matter what the cost. Almost immediately upon Zaitzev's arrival, the 40th Army took to the offensive everywhere.

The battlefield reports coming in that spring were deeply disturbing. Whereas the Soviet forces had previously operated only with huge shows of force, easy to detect and hide from, they were now moving in all kinds of ways and on all fronts. For the first time, the Red Army itself was howling at the doors of Pakistan, its fighter-bombers striking border towns, Soviet battalions and regiments sweeping in to cut off supply lines. There was more of everything—more bombing, more shelling, more gunships prowling the countryside looking for mule and camel caravans to blast. But most unnerving was the introduction of thousands of elite Spetsnaz troops into the fighting.

The Spetsnaz are the Russian equivalent of America's Green Berets. The most highly trained elite soldiers in the Soviet Union, they had previously been used only for the most technically demanding and sophisticated operations. But in Afghanistan Zaitzev and his commanders were now bringing in these skilled killers by helicopter at night, inserting them behind mujahideen lines to organize ambushes and sabotage raids. For a time they seemed to be an invincible and omnipresent force, spreading terror among the usually stoic mujahideen.

Gorbachev, alarmed at the price the Soviet Union was paying for its Afghan campaign, had given Zaitzev a year to break the back of the resistance. And by the summer and fall of 1985 many Western analysts seemed to think the Soviets were on the verge of pulling it off. The escalation had taken its toll on the mujahideen, who, in spite of their warrior discipline and their astonishing faith in Allah, had become a bit war weary. At the funerals of their fathers and sons and brothers and cousins they rarely wept. They claimed to believe that they were happy for their loved ones who were now in Paradise, but it was hard not to detect a certain exhaustion setting in. They were, after all, just people. The war had been going on for five years, and instead of things getting better they were now facing an enemy that was increasing his ability to punish in ways they had never had to worry about before.

For the first time that year, Avrakotos had to consider the possibility that for once he was playing chicken with an adversary who might not blink. He says, "This was the escalation that scared us because here we were pouring in stuff that would soon double and triple their casualties and that's what caused them to escalate in the first place—the casualties. We had to ask ourselves, What would be left for them to do after that other than to invade Pakistan or to use tactical nukes?"

The well-publicized appointment of Zaitzev had created a kind of panic among the Afghan hands in Washington, but it turns out he was not the real commander. Instead, a far more lethal and politically important figure had been placed in charge.

It seems almost incredible that a general as significant as Valentin Varennikov could have served so long in Kabul and been so little known to his American adversaries. Zaitzev was the subject of constant conversation; Varennikov none. It was as if the Kremlin had never focused in on the role that General Westmoreland had played in Vietnam.

Certainly in his own world, Varennikov was anything but invisible. To begin with he was an authentic war hero, possessor of the Golden Star of the Hero of the Soviet Union, a man whose history embodied the legend and mystique of the invincibility of the Red Army. It was Varennikov who was given the honor as a young captain at the end of World War II of presenting a captured Nazi flag to Stalin.

From that moment on, the Red Army had been his life, and he had never known anything but victory as he'd risen through the ranks to become one of the three most significant officers of the Soviet General Staff. By Christmas 1979, when the Soviets marched into Afghanistan, he was the Soviet General Staff's man in charge of drawing up the master plan for all-out war against the United States and the West. As Varennikov matter-of-factly puts it, it was his job to design the strategy for the Red Army to fight the entire world at once and win, and he had no doubt that his side would prevail.

In 1985, when the grand old strategist of Soviet power took command in Kabul, he was alarmed by developments in Eastern Europe, what he saw as a subversive anti-Communist alliance between the Reagan administration and the Polish pope of Rome. He concluded that the Soviets would have to choose a place to halt the momentum. As he set off to draw the line in Afghanistan, he was prepared to use Soviet power without compromise. During the 1980s, while Wilson and Avrakotos were still maneuvering to get into positions of power, Varennikov was in charge of Soviet military affairs in the Third World—Cuba, Nicaragua, Angola, Ethiopia, Yemen, El Salvador, and South Africa. In all those areas where the United States felt threatened, the anonymous hand of Valentin Varennikov was at work stirring the pot. In 1993, surrounded by rich Oriental rugs in the Moscow apartment building where former generals are still given gracious housing, the general agreed to speak about Afghanistan as he awaited trial for his part in the failed coup against Gorbachev.

He quickly made his American visitor understand how significant Afghanistan had been to him and to the Kremlin leadership when he laid out his dark vision of U.S. intentions during the Cold War. "It was America that started the arms race as a way of bankrupting the Soviet economy," he explains. "America loved blackmailing the world with its nuclear might."

The general found himself even more alarmed when he learned that Reagan had launched a missile attack against the Soviet's Libyan ally Muammar Qaddafi. The White House and the Pentagon openly rubbed salt in this wound to Soviet pride by releasing a videotape from a tiny camera that had been placed in the nose cone of the American rocket so that the whole world could see and feel, via television, the experience of riding a U.S. Air Force bomb right into Qaddafi's tent. "What was I to think? I knew Qaddafi very well. We were friends. I had just visited him in that tent the month before. How could we ignore these things?"

From the standpoint of the Kremlin, the early returns on Varennikov's series of offensives must have looked very promising indeed. By the summer of 1985, new floods of Afghans were pouring over the border seeking refuge in Pakistan, telling horror stories of saturation bombing, a new scorched-earth policy, and the dreaded night-fighting Spetsnaz troops.

What Gorbachev and Varennikov had no way of knowing that spring, however, is that they were moving with too little, too late. Back in Langley, Avrakotos had his own personal General Varennikov in place, thirty-two-year-old Mike Vickers, and Vickers was going to turn out to be the better general.

On one level it was preposterous for Vickers to be playing such a role. He was so junior in grade that he couldn't even sign his own cables. But he was now speaking and acting in Avrakotos's name, with a half-billion-dollar war chest to use to wreck General Varennikov's campaign. And never for a moment did Vickers have any doubts about exactly what needed to be done.

What Vickers, operating even more invisibly than Varennikov, came up with was a radical departure from Hart's concept of a massive mountain army. The brash young officer conceded that Howard Hart had accomplished much by arming a baseline force of more than 400,000. But because of the way the Afghans were armed and because of their lack of training and sophistication, he was convinced that the law of diminishing returns had long ago set in. In fact, he concluded that even if the Agency were to arm an extra 300,000 mujahideen, it would not improve their capacity to fight one bit.

Vickers's first bold act was to cut off hundreds of thousands of mujahideen from the Agency's main support program. Instead of giving the same arms and ammunition to 400,000 or more conventional guerrillas, Vickers decided to create an elite force of 150,000. Basically, he was betting everything on this new army within an army. The "holy warriors" who didn't make the cut would continue to be supported but would be treated essentially as a militia.

To an outsider, it might have appeared to be a scaling back, but 150,000 was still a huge number. The Contra army in Nicaragua, for example, was said to be no more than 20,000. More important than the size, however, was what Vickers had in mind for this core group of Muslim warriors. He intended to give them the most sophisticated weaponry and turn them into a force of late-twentieth-century "technoguerrillas."

Drawing on Gust's authority, Vickers was already channeling a torrent of new and varied weapons to the mujahideen, but that was only half the battle. He had been appalled when he'd discovered that the Agency was offering the mujahideen only four or five training courses in weapons and tactics, none any longer than a week. Now, under the supervision of marine Colonel Nick Pratt, the straitlaced officer who had been so repelled by Charlie Wilson on the Egyptian trip, the Agency began giving twenty different courses covering a range of irregular warfare disciplines, some lasting a month or more.

It seemed to Gust that the mujahideen had some genetic gift for learning how to use weapons and instruments of destruction. His PM operatives, dressed in *shalwar kameezes* with beards and Chitrali hats, set out to train the Afghans in their Pakistani border camps. They were taught not only how to fire their new weapons but how to work together in combat and how to mount a range of different kinds of operations, from urban sabotage to huge, combined-arms ambushes.

By the end of the year, the Agency began sending in frequency-hopping radios and burst transmitters. Now, instead of waiting days for messengers on horseback, a commander like Ismail Khan in Herat, near the Iranian border, could communicate with the ISI in Pakistan instantly. With basic combat walkie-talkies, these biblical warriors were finally able to talk to one another in combat and coordinate attacks.

That year Art Alper's Technical Services people even came up with a small device that the mujahideen could carry with them to give an early alert when a gunship was approaching. It would be many long months before Vickers could introduce his "symphony of weapons" to combat the Hind, but this exotic noise sensor, not much bigger than a quarter, was a godsend. It didn't just predict the approach of a helicopter but identified the direction it was coming from, thus giving the Afghans time at least to hide. On every front, the CIA was turning its guerrillas into a far smarter and more lethal fighting force.

Throughout the entire buildup, only a handful of people understood the role Vickers, hiding behind his lowly GS-11 rating, was playing. He would be in England negotiating to buy Blowpipes one day and back the next; in Pakistan for four and back for two; in China for seventy-two hours, placing orders for hundreds of millions of dollars' worth of weapons, and back to the sixth floor, operating as if he had never been away. As Avrakotos explained, "He was our brain. I couldn't afford to have him away for more than four days at a time."

When things went badly and the reports made it sound as if all was lost, Vickers would be there to reassure Gust. It was only logical, he explained, that the Soviets would finally make their move. As for the Spetsnaz, Vickers suggested that there might be something hopeful about their introduction.

No rational army, he explained in his role as Gust's tutor, uses its most valuable soldiers for semiconventional battle. Spetsnaz soldiers are the army's equivalent of jet fighter pilots. You don't treat such thoroughbreds as if they were ordinary grunts. "You wouldn't send me to lead a raid on the Kabul garrison," he went on. "It's a waste. There's something desperate about it."

It was always reassuring for Avrakotos to talk to this cool strategist. Vickers, with his white shirt and tie, looking out calmly through his owl glasses, invariably responded to such crises as if he were being asked to solve a simple arithmetic problem. Avrakotos had been genuinely alarmed about the Spetsnaz and told him they needed a counterstrategy fast.

Vickers was soon presiding over a meeting of three knuckle draggers from the Ground Branch of the P.M. division and two of the Pentagon's leading irregular-warfare experts. Within days, three Agency types turned up in Pakistan, armed with a very specific set of countertactics to pass on to the freedom fighters. One tactic, for example, called for the mujahideen to lure the Spetsnaz into restricted areas, which would have been mined in advance and would be covered by machine-gun fire. Soon the Afghans were actually hunting the Spetsnaz: never easily or without a price but now at least able to hold their own. Before the year was out, the cost to the Soviet special forces would be enormous.

Gust's war room during this time was electric, infused with patriotic purpose. The PM types would always stop by to see him before going off on their missions. As Avrakotos saw it, "Sending one of these people to Afghanistan was sort of like giving Itzhak Perlman a Stradivarius. Give him an AK-47 and he's home. He suddenly lurches from being an asshole at Tyson's Corner into being an honorable killer." Gust would always leave these warriors with a few words of encouragement. "I told them to just teach the mujahideen how to kill: pipe bombs, car bombs. But don't ever tell me how you're doing it in writing. Just do it."

One of the secretaries remembers the sense then in the war room of being "surrounded by heroes." The case officers were all framed by huge blown-up pictures of mujahideen warriors. After hours they would tell the wide-eyed young women about the nobility of the Afghans. "I got the feeling that the Russians had come in and taken their land, their homes," recalls one of the secretaries. "People were being massacred, children were dying, and the mujahideen were fighting impossible odds. When you found out what was happening you couldn't be involved and not care."

For this woman, watching Vickers grow a beard before leaving on a trip or listening to Gust say good-bye to the paramilitaries as they set off for Pakistan was like watching a World War II movie with RAF pilots heading off to fight the Luftwaffe. In reality, however, these PM officers did not actually go into combat. Throughout the war, the CIA was rigidly prohibited from having any American agents operating inside Afghanistan.* In fact, for most of the war, they were only permitted to train the Pakistanis, who in turn trained the Afghans.

Some of the hard-right enthusiasts complained about this, arguing that Americans would be more effective, but Avrakotos and Vickers knew that direct involvement would be a prescription for disaster. Besides, they saw General Akhtar's ISI as first-rate military men, many of them highly experienced and well trained (some out of the American Special Forces schools at Fort Bragg).

Beyond that, they knew it would be absurd for non-Muslim Americans to accompany the Afghan holy warriors in combat. The Pakistanis, many of whom were of Pashtun origins, spoke the same language, shared the same geography and religion. They were now constantly going with the mujahideen as advisers on combat runs into Afghanistan, a fact that Gust knew could cause him no end of trouble because of the explicit prohibition on any direct CIA involvement. "I got around that by asking if the Pakistani advisers had any Pathan blood," explains Avrakotos. "'Yes,' was the response. 'Okay then, they are not Pakistani. They are Pathans or Uzbeks.'"

To the CIA men who had operated on the ground in Pakistan, it was clear that American spies would have made a mess of things trying to deal directly with these Afghans from another time and place. "Akhtar's troops did something for us we couldn't," explains Avrakotos. "It would have cost us millions to try to do what they did—all the movement of weapons, the training of the mujahideen, the coordination of everything."

There was another plus. Because most of the ISI trainers were virtual blood brothers to the Afghans, they were more than eager to do things that would have been political suicide for Americans. For example, they had no hesitation when it came to training for sabotage and assassination.

---

*That did not apply to agents operating under technical cover from the U.S. embassy in Kabul. The station chief during this time was a short, feisty man who rode his bicycle around Kabul as a means of gauging the morale of the Soviet soldiers. Avrakotos eventually had to replace him when he appeared to be acting erratically under the strain.

And unlike their American counterparts, they could even offer bounties to hit the targets deemed most valuable.

Without so much as a second thought, the ISI officers promoted the value of selective killing. This was war, and as they saw it the idea was to convince the mujahideen that some of the enemy were more important to kill than others. They went to some lengths to teach their Afghan charges how to identify a Soviet general or commanding officer by describing where he would normally stand in a group of soldiers and what position he would take when walking about a base. An Afghan soldier could more easily decide whom to shoot first once he not only knew who the general was but also understood that the higher the rank of the Soviet soldier killed, the bigger the bounty he could collect back in Peshawar.*

Avrakotos was careful never to associate the Agency with such activities—that would be a political time bomb. Killing Russians, however, was what this operation was about, and he was determined to put every kill to his advantage. He agreed to the idea of using Soviet soldiers' belt buckles as a way of measuring the body count. And he loved the rewards the Pakistanis offered for these trophies: cash, more guns, sometimes even alcohol—whatever a given commander or warrior most wanted. Avrakotos made sure every one of these kills was tabulated and the totals distributed in highly classified reports to the policy makers he needed on board.

In many respects, the war on the actual battlefront was the least of Gust Avrakotos's concerns in 1985. He left the operational decisions to Vickers. His combat took place in very different and varied arenas. That year he had a particularly ticklish problem to cope with from the all-important Pakistan intelligence service, through which the CIA had to conduct all of its operations.

The ISI brigadier responsible for arming the Afghans with the CIA's weapons was Mohammad Yousaf, a big, bug-eyed, former infantry officer who maintained a very complicated relationship with the Americans. After the war he wrote a book in which he complained sharply about the CIA's

---

*These explicit goals of the CIA campaign were never discussed in any official capacity. The Agency's lawyers, not to mention high-ranking officials like John McMahon, were adamant about not becoming involved in anything remotely resembling assassination.

inefficiency and its timidity in introducing the kinds of weapons, like the Stinger, that the mujahideen needed.

But if you listen to Avrakotos and the other CIA Afghan hands, it was Yousaf who wouldn't let them escalate. A fundamentalist Muslim, Yousaf bore considerable suspicion and even bitter resentment against the American spy agency, which he believed was forever machinating behind the scenes to manipulate the Pakistan government and to undermine his religion.

President Zia was the ultimate authority in Pakistan; he always told his American friends that he was the one who decided how much to let the pot boil in Afghanistan. He assured Charlie Wilson and others several times that he had given his okay to the escalation that year. But Yousaf felt it was his obligation to decide how much to permit the Americans to force down Pakistan's throat, and he emerged in those months as a genuine block to the massive increases Vickers had in mind. His official explanation was that he did not want to do anything that would precipitate a Soviet invasion of his country.

Part of the problem, however, was no doubt personal. On a CIA-sponsored trip to Washington that year, the proud ISI brigadier was deeply insulted when he was led, virtually blindfolded, to the Agency's "sabotage school" in North Carolina. Vickers escorted the burly Pakistan general in a plane whose windows were blacked, then in a car with its shades drawn. Yousaf, who suffers the chip on the shoulder of many proud Third World types, was deeply offended at this slight. He reasoned that if he was trusted enough to be permitted to run the CIA's operation in Pakistan, why was the Agency treating him as if he were about to reveal the location of the sabotage school?

At dinner back in Washington, things deteriorated even further when Vickers and Avrakotos took Yousaf and one of his colleagues out for a fancy dinner at the Four Seasons Hotel. Yousaf, perhaps because he still felt the sting of the sabotage-school humiliation, complained when Avrakotos ordered a second bourbon and water. Being a pure Muslim, the Pakistan general reacted to this rather natural Western custom almost the way an American might respond if Yousaf had taken out a syringe and begun shooting up with heroin just as the appetizers were arriving.

Avrakotos lost his cool. It was one thing to suffer this kind of repression in Pakistan, but Yousaf was playing on Avrakotos's home turf. Beyond that, Avrakotos was paying for the guns and the ammunition and making it possible for the Pakistanis to organize this jihad. He was even paying for dinner, and he didn't like this chain-smoking, tight-assed Muslim trying to tell him what not to drink in his own hometown. "I'll stop drinking," Avrakotos barked, "when you stop smoking. My doctor says it's like suicide to smoke, and Allah does not permit suicide."

The Agency was not doing a good job on this trip of winning the heart of the man they needed on board to make the Afghan program work. There was also another slight, one that seems almost incredible, given the effort the Agency was making to strengthen its relationship with Yousaf.

For reasons that were quite inexplicable to Vickers, the CIA protocol team in charge of organizing the brigadier's schedule had decided that Yousaf would enjoy going to the theater. Brigadier Mohammad Yousaf is a fundamentalist Muslim who turns to Mecca five times a day in prayer and who has made the pilgrimage to Mecca; by nature he is suspicious of Christians. The play the CIA selected for him to attend with Vickers and Avrakotos at Ford's Theater was *Godspell.*

It was, needless to say, a very grim-faced Pakistan general who sat between Vickers and Avrakotos that evening. His arms folded over his barrel chest, he scowled at the musical, whose author clearly had not understood that Muhammad was the greatest of all the prophets.

All was not lost, however. The Agency's relationship was saved in part by Yousaf's enormous respect for Avrakotos's boss, Bert Dunn, the Near East Division chief. Dunn had served in Afghanistan and had been responsible during the Kennedy years for helping Pakistan establish its own special forces unit. He spoke Dari and Pashto and was much loved by the Pakistan military, which had known and trusted him for years.

Yousaf was pleased to receive Dunn's praise for all he was doing for the jihad. But things broke down with Yousaf again over the most basic question of how to arm an insurgent movement. Yousaf didn't want to let the CIA ship the huge amount of ammunition that Vickers felt was absolutely necessary to keep the fighters in steady combat. When Yousaf cited insufficient infrastructure to transport the ammunition, Vickers countered by getting Gust to offer to build warehouses, upgrade train tracks, buy thousands of new trucks, even ship in mules and camels.

More complicated was Yousaf's adamant insistence that the CIA equip all of the mujahideen with AK-47s. Vickers had been the biggest critic of the bolt-action Enfield in favor of the AK, but his objective now was to create a lean, tough, well-armed guerrilla army. The last thing he wanted was to buy hundreds of thousands of AKs and then not be able to give anyone enough ammunition for sustained combat.

The Agency was not about to make this point directly, and Vickers, the rough equivalent of an army captain in Brigadier Yousaf's eyes, was not inclined even to suggest such a thing. So something of an impasse was reached in which Vickers could not say either that he was worried about corruption or that he felt Yousaf was an imbecile when it came to military strategy and tactics. The net result was a logjam, which appeared to be unmovable until Avrakotos intervened with a bit of baksheesh distributed skillfully at just the right moment.

At one of those dreary official receptions in Islamabad where the Muslim government serves only fruit juice, Avrakotos ran into Brigadier Raza, the Pakistan ISI general who had held Yousaf's job during Howard Hart's tour. Unlike Yousaf, Raza was no fundamentalist. He liked Americans and they liked him, and Raza was not offended when Avrakotos showed him the flask he had concealed in his suit and offered to spike the general's fruit juice.

After accepting his fourth ration of Russian vodka, Raza volunteered a suggestion. Perhaps the CIA would have more luck with the ISI if Avrakotos would consider giving a contract for ammunition to a certain Pakistani arms manufacturer.

Avrakotos had a half billion dollars to spend on arms that year, so he quickly gave $8 million of that to the Pakistanis to make .303 ammunition for the mujahideen. "It was chicken feed," he said. "We paid a penny or two more per round, but we didn't have to pay for transportation. I had Charlie come out and go through the factories with me, and we complimented the Pakistanis on their quality control." In such a manner, apparently, was the barrier to the historic CIA escalation removed. Avrakotos does not assert any direct quid pro quo or claim that Yousaf's troublesome positions were anything but the product of his wrong-minded professional judgment. But for whatever reasons, the Agency officials most knowledgeable about these negotiations do say that after the placement of this relatively small arms contract, the Pakistani resistance disappeared.

For Avrakotos, dealing with crises became routine, but at one point in 1985 he found himself having to cope with a screaming problem that seemed to belong to another century: mules. The challenge of secretly moving tons of weapons into position for the Afghans was always a logistical nightmare. The CIA had literally hundreds of millions of rounds of ammunition constantly traveling by sea and air to Pakistan. Once in Pakistan, the lethal goods were transported by train and truck to the border. At that point, however, everything had to move the old-fashioned way: if not on a man's back, then by mule or camel.

The Russians therefore placed the highest priority on hunting down and slaughtering the mujahideen's long mule caravans. So many of these beasts were wiped out by gunships that in 1985, an urgent call suddenly came into the task force headquarters warning of a crisis that had placed everything at risk. "Where the fuck do you go to buy donkeys?" Avrakotos remembers asking Vickers. Later an incredulous CIA director called Avrakotos: "You've got to be kidding me. You're buying mules?"

In fact, Avrakotos soon had agents all over the world looking for the best deal on mules. When the Egyptians landed one of the first major contracts, the Pakistanis got insanely jealous and began complaining about health hazards because a number of mules had died shortly after arrival. They insisted on health certificates for the next batch, presuming this would force the Agency to buy locally.

But Mohammed Abu Ghazala's resourceful arms salesman General Yahia al Gamal wanted the next contract for 2,500 mules at $1,300 each, cash on delivery, so he engineered a great Egyptian put-down. "You have to realize that donkeys and mules are the lowest form of life in Egypt," explains Avrakotos. "Even a camel has greater status. But the Egyptians provided each donkey and mule with an ID card and vaccination certificate." As if that wasn't enough to make fun of the Pakistanis, General Yahia outfitted every donkey with a piece of plastic sporting an Arabic name. "Yahia thought it was hysterical. He even gave them passports."

According to Avrakotos, the Pakistanis only reluctantly accepted this zanily credentialed herd, but they were sufficiently insulted that they refused to permit any more Egyptian mules into Pakistan. The experiences of the CIA buying and shipping mules to Afghanistan over the next few years became the subject of legendary stories in the halls of Langley. At one point, the Pakistanis became so ornery that they wouldn't permit the CIA's transporter to leave the mule manure in Pakistan. They made the planes carry the smelly droppings back to Europe.

It would take months to establish the mule-supply lines. One early shipment of sorry creatures purchased in Brazil arrived in Pakistan with all the animals dead. Eventually the mujahideen were moving their supplies on the backs of Tennessee mules, and the halls of Langley were soon filled with rumors (later confirmed by the Agency's spies) that the freedom fighters were copulating with these animals.

In an attempt to paint a bright face on this curious practice, Avrakotos explained that in Greece and other Near Eastern cultures there is no scorn placed on buggery as long as the person in question assumes the right position. "The key question is whether you are the fucker or the fuckee," he said. The mujahideen were taking the dominant male role here; thus, by their code of honor, Gust explained, there was no cause for shame. The Office of Logistics, however, was not as understanding as Avrakotos. They were quite appalled by the stories, particularly when they learned that the mujahideen had also eaten a number of their prized Tennessee mules.

No sooner had Avrakotos's operatives dealt with the mule crisis than he was faced with a new and truly threatening challenge. The White House had taken Andy Eiva and Gordon Humphrey's accusations of corruption in the CIA pipeline to heart and had demanded a major policy review. Now that hundreds of millions of dollars were at play with an uncertain outcome on the battlefield, Avrakotos understood that it would be devastating if the conclusion were drawn that the Pakistanis were stealing the CIA blind.

It isn't easy to control graft in a massive covert arms operation like the Afghan war, and certainly some level of corruption is part of doing business in the Third World. Gust found it perfectly acceptable to dole out an $8 million contract now and then if it bought him cooperation. At the same time, he understood that crude corruption could bring them all down.

For that reason, the task force had adopted all kinds of extraordinary measures to keep their allies honest. Here Art Alper's boys made all the difference by placing tiny sensors in random shipments of weapons, which were then followed by satellite, to see where they ultimately went. Spies were recruited among the mujahideen themselves, as well as from the ranks of the Pakistani military. Finally, the Agency also ran a network of fifteen "third-country agents," neither Pakistani nor Afghans but Europeans operating inside the war zone under the cover of being foreign journalists, doctors, or documentary filmmakers. They reported how the mujahideen were doing militarily, as well as whether the money, food, and arms shipments were getting through. Beyond that, satellites were now regularly being used to verify Afghan claims of downed planes and tanks.

The task of responding to the White House fell on Vickers's shoulders, and instead of looking at it as a defensive exercise aimed simply at keeping the bureaucrats from closing the operation down, he saw it as an opportunity to win their support. He quickly spelled out the full range of measures that had already been put in place to prevent the kind of corruption that Eiva and Humphrey alleged. He had no doubt that his detailed explanation would lay the corruption matter to rest. One of the questions from the White House asked for an explanation of the program's overall objective; clearly the volume of weapons and support flowing into Pakistan now dwarfed the intent of the original Presidential Findings, so Vickers went on the offensive.

Rather than pretend that Afghanistan was still a bleeding campaign, Vickers urged Avrakotos and Bert Dunn, the division chief, to come clean and to acknowledge that the Agency now believed that the policy should unapologetically be to win the war. Avrakotos and Dunn signed off, and Vickers reduced the answer to a simple and momentous line for the president to endorse, which he did in National Security Decision Directive (NSDD) 166. The object of the CIA's campaign, he wrote, was now to drive the Soviets out of Afghanistan "by all means available."

"THE NOBLEST SMUGGLING OPERATION IN HISTORY"

I n the first week of 1985 Wilson hired a new administrative assistant, a fifty-five-year-old Texan named Charlie Schnabel. Technically, Schnabel was supposed to spend his days in the small office next to the congressman, watching over the staff and making sure legislation was being tended to and constituents' problems were being solved. Strictly speaking, Schnabel, who had never been out of the country except for a brief visit to Mexico and who had never given a serious thought to the workings of U.S. foreign policy, was expected to stay in the capital and certainly not to have anything to do with a CIA war in Afghanistan. But years later, Wilson's former assistant, Charles Simpson, would remark that the twin impact of his departure and Schnabel's arrival removed the one restraining influence that had previously kept Wilson somewhat straight. It may be hard to believe that anyone could outdo Charlie Wilson when it came to the art of rule breaking, but Charlie Schnabel turned out to be every bit his boss's equal and then some.

Schnabel is a slow-moving man who wears cowboy boots, speaks with a southern drawl, and subscribes to *Soldier of Fortune* magazine. You see his type often on the dusty back roads of East Texas: driving a pickup truck, a rifle hanging on a rack in the back window, a hound by his side, heading off into the woods for a weekend of hunting. But he's also reminiscent of that breed of cunning southern lawyers who open trials by saying, "I'm just a country boy."

Schnabel was nobody's fool. For twenty-two years he had been secretary of state of the Texas Senate, responsible for running the institution that Wilson's famous drinking friend Larry King immortalized in *The Best Little Whorehouse in Texas*. This experience taught him just about everything there was to know about the way things work in American politics. Over the years he had broken in or done serious business with just about every major Democratic political figure ever to come out of Texas.

He had watched over all the newcomers in their turn. On more than one occasion, the ever understanding secretary of state had carried Wilson home drunk in his arms. He'd gotten Wilson out of the jail and had sometimes even managed to get his DWI charges dropped or modified. So prepared was Schnabel for the inevitable foibles of his many wild Texas charges in those days that he had the wife of the county prosecutor and the wife of the county clerk on his payroll.

All of which is to say that Schnabel had not kept his post in the Texas senate because he was a timid or cautious bureaucrat. As his wife, Nadine, commented one day when a visitor to their capital apartment noted how curious it was that her husband had a Soviet RPG grenade launcher, an AK-47 with a large supply of live ammunition, and other captured weapons from the Afghan war, "Oh, Charlie's rule in life is: 'Don't pay attention to the rules.'"

Schnabel was in fact something of a Texas legend—and in spite of his penchant for stretching the rules, the senators who had known him over the years never felt he had ever done anything bad. They figured that the Schnabels of the world are the ones who make the system work in spite of itself. There had been one embarrassing incident, a prosecution centering on a political favor he had done for a college sports program. He was indicted but plea-bargained his way out with a misdemeanor conviction. His old senatorial friends stood by him, and in a Wilsonesque statement, Schnabel remarked to the press, "I always like to do what I can for American sports."

Wilson was not one to be put off by the accusations of some mean-spirited prosecutor, and in late 1984 he called Schnabel and asked him to take over Simpson's job as his administrative assistant. "The answer was no. Schnabel had had many other offers to go to Washington over the years, but he liked his life in Texas. He liked his 120-year-old farmhouse near Austin, he loved his hunting and fishing, and he was a part of the life of the state—a man with so many debts owed him that he could almost live out the rest of his life just calling in the chits.

"Don't say no," Wilson implored, and thus began a full-court press. "Don't worry about the hunting," the congressman said on the phone. "I'm on the Defense Appropriations subcommittee, and anywhere in the world where we have a defense facility you can fly there and hunt. They'll take care of you."

This curious offer caught Schnabel's attention, so when Wilson sent him a plane ticket and spending money to come up to the capital to look it over, he accepted the invitation. He wasn't planning to be swept away, but the romance of Washington started to work on him, and Nadine, who had joined him on the trip, turned out to have relatives who lived nearby. She wanted to stay.

The next day Schnabel went out and bought a house—an act that he purposefully concealed from Wilson when he went in for a final chat. "I told him I was still worried about the hunting," remembers the cunning negotiator. Wilson then iced the deal with a hard-and-fast repetition of his commitment: "Don't worry about the hunting."

In Schnabel's scrapbooks from these Washington years, gory documentation of Wilson having made good on his promise is revealed on page after page. The pictures show the congressman's AA in camouflage uniform near a military base with bow and arrow by his side, holding up a gentle-faced Bambi by its antlers. In another location Schnabel, with Texas Speaker of the House Gib Lewis, is grinning into the camera. The two good old boys are in northern Pakistan, on the Silk Route from China, in search of the nearly extinct Marco Polo sheep. The animal is very much on the endangered species list, but Schnabel explains proudly that President Zia himself waived this prohibition and provided the congressman's esteemed assistant with an official guide and a Mercedes to hunt the beast. In another picture we see Schnabel beaming as he presents Zia with a ten-gallon hat, custom-made in Texas for the Muslim dictator.

One particularly gruesome set of photos reveals a pickup truck piled high with deer from the grounds of the Indian Head, Maryland, navy base. Schnabel explains that this deadly harvest of deer came from the night he led a SEAL team on a hunting spree, everyone wearing night-vision goggles and shouting *"Allahu Akbar"* before unloading their high-powered weapons into the unsuspecting prey. The resulting venison, properly blessed before slaughter, was then given to a collection of visiting Afghan fundamentalists.

In a sense, Washington never knew what hit it when Charlie Schnabel came to town. To a certain extent, Charlie Wilson didn't either. Until Schnabel's arrival, Wilson had worked the Afghan account in Congress all alone. His defense staffer rarely knew what the congressman was up to. But Schnabel is a self-starter with a gift, if not a genius, for getting along with people, and he began making friends with the mujahideen who visited the congressman's office.

In the beginning, Schnabel admits, it was not so much the purity of the Afghans' cause that got to him as much as the romance of it all and the fact that "it was just exciting, just so much goddamn much fun. I'd talk to these muj when they'd come into the office and ask them, 'What can I hunt in Afghanistan? I want to kill something.' And they'd say 'Come to the Panjshir, it's the greatest hunting in the world—the Panjshir Valley.'" So while other adventuresome Americans who became fixated on Afghanistan always wanted to go to the Panjshir to meet Ahmad Shah Massoud, the great mujahideen commander, Schnabel was drawn to Massoud's valley for very different reasons. He was desperate to go because the Panjshir is where you find the Marco Polo sheep and the ibex.

When it came to all things to do with Afghanistan, Wilson's relationship to his administrative assistant was eccentric in the extreme. The two never really coordinated their efforts, and Wilson rarely chose to include Schnabel in his CIA dealings. But he always encouraged his AA's Afghan interests, and before long the two men had worked out an implicit understanding of the rules of engagement they would follow.

It went something like this: Schnabel had Wilson's blessings to intimidate bureaucrats in his name: he could smuggle contraband to the mujahideen; he could also carry stationery from the office, write letters requesting unusual assistance from, say, the Pakistan intelligence service, and sign them "Charles Wilson." All of this Schnabel was empowered to do, and as his passion for the Afghan cause grew, he came to operate with such frequency and effectiveness in Wilson's name that Abdul Haq, one of the legendary Afghan commanders and a favorite of American reporters, remarked, "We used to think of the two Charlies as one." And President Zia, after receiving a ten-gallon hat, took to affectionately calling Schnabel "The Other Charlie."

In effect, during those years, Charlie Schnabel came to operate as a virtual second Charlie Wilson. The result was to substantially enhance

Wilson's ability to influence events. During this period the real Charlie Wilson would take the high road as the patron and defender of the CIA's Afghan program. Schnabel, meanwhile, as the congressman's representative, moved about as the undercover bomb thrower, organizing the Andy Eiva–Gordon Humphrey–style crazies who saw the Agency as the enemy. Schnabel himself had come to see the Agency as the problem and his boss as an apologist of sorts. But he forgave Wilson this sin because the two of them were playing a kind of good cop, bad cop routine.

Without any direct commission, Schnabel was soon operating along the fringes, helping to menace bureaucrats, including some at the CIA, and stirring the pot for the muj in ways that Wilson felt he could not afford to do openly. In a sense he became the dark side of Charlie Wilson, free to operate but with the implicit understanding that if he got in trouble he was on his own.

The way he got to the front was by wrangling seats on the Pentagon's humanitarian-aid flights to Pakistan. Inevitably, in those early years before the prohibitions on the CIA's support program were lifted, Schnabel could be counted on to be overloaded with contraband for the mujahideen. On one of his first flights it was long-range sights for sniper rifles. John McMahon wouldn't let the Agency give them to the mujahideen out of fear that Congress might accuse the CIA of supporting assassination efforts. Schnabel had gotten his rich Texas friends to put up the money for the telescopic sights, and as was his custom, he told Wilson about his smuggling exploits only after the fact.

The old Texas politician always greased his way with charming stories and gifts for everyone on every end: captured Soviet war trinkets for the American officials who manned the humanitarian-aid flights, and American military items or congressional pens and seals for the Pakistani ISI agents waiting at the airfield. They looked the other way because he was such a charmer, because he was speaking in Congressman Wilson's name, and because Schnabel would do such things as get their children scholarships to Texas universities, or visas or medical care through the burgeoning programs that would be opened up in the coming years.

As Schnabel got deeper and deeper into the war, he began crossing lines further and further into no-man's-land. There would be live ammunition strewn about his small office; Makarov pistols, AK-47s, and an RPG grenade launcher under his bed at home; and down in the congressional storeroom, so many rugs and fur coats from Pakistan that it resembled a small market.

But it was his love of the Afghan people that burned deepest in Schnabel's sensibilities. In the scrapbooks he keeps are scores of photographic portraits of different mujahideen. All those faces of old men and young boys, faces of noble warriors wearing turbans and Chitrali hats. "You don't see much ferocity in the eyes of a mujahideen," he explains paging through the books. "Rather it's the steady, calm, 'I'm going to get you' look. They would tell me, 'We won't stop till the blood is flowing in the streets of Moscow.' They'd say it as a matter of fact 'because God is on our side and Allah will prevail, but we are willing to fight to the last man' and it was no bullshit. They all grew up that way. They grew up as hunters."

Soon after falling in love with the mujahideen, Schnabel dressed himself up in their clothes and went off with them on operations, in violation of the strict embassy ban on any U.S. officials crossing the border. Inside Afghanistan he would discover the wonder of *naswar,* the opiated snuff that the Afghans put under their tongues for inspiration. They would come to call him "Naswar Charlie," and back in Washington, one emotional night, he would even go so far as to convert to Islam, taking the name Abdullah.

All of this Schnabel did very much on his own, but in the eyes of everyone he dealt with, he was always operating in Charlie Wilson's name. And what made it possible for him to operate so effectively in what was supposed to be the CIA's arena had nothing to do with the U.S. spy agency. It was, rather, his relationship to a seemingly innocent, humanitarian-aid program run by the Agency for International Development (AID). In large measure because of the two Charlies, this seemingly innocent program would be transformed into an indispensable second front in the CIA's Afghan war.

The State Department official initially responsible for setting up this effort, known as the Cross Border Humanitarian Aid Program, was Assistant Secretary of State Gerald Helman. As he tells the story, by early 1985 Afghanistan had suddenly become a hot program in the National Security bureaucracies. The conservative revolution was in full swing. Ronald Reagan had just won reelection by a landslide, and the State Department did not want to look as if it were failing to support the Reagan Doctrine, which called for U.S. support of anti-Communist guerrillas.

State first sensed an opportunity when the tough old veteran U.S. ambassador to Pakistan at this time, Dean Hinton, met with Helman and began to urge action to counter a crisis that he saw developing on the Afghan border. Hinton was one of the handful of career diplomats who during the Cold War always seemed to be posted in spots where the CIA was active.* In 1984, before going out to Pakistan, Hinton had talked to all the experts and found no one who thought there was any chance whatsoever of pushing the Red Army out of Afghanistan.

But as the CIA funding mushroomed that fall, so did Hinton's enthusiasm for the operation. "For the first time we were playing offense instead of defense," he explains. He was unnerved, however, by a series of intelligence reports that concluded that the Soviets were laying waste to a huge strip of land between the Pakistani border and their major garrisons and cities in Afghanistan. Villages were being bombed, irrigation canals destroyed, livestock slaughtered, crops burned, and civilians murdered, tortured, and forced to flee the country. If this were permitted to continue, it was argued, the war would be lost before the new military assistance could have an impact. Guerrillas simply couldn't wander on foot across vast uninhabitable areas. Famine and disease were said to be moving at a terrifying pace. As important as anything else was the total absence of any medical care. If this continued, the entire military program would be in jeopardy. Hinton warned Helman that something had to be done to stop the flow of refugees and keep the Afghans in their villages as sources of support for the warriors. He used the term *genocide* to describe the war policy the Red Army was pursuing over the border.

Helman was not exactly a daring official. Diplomats are good at sensing which way the political winds are blowing, and the leadership of the department had already taken note of the fact that Congress was not just smiling on the CIA's Afghan program; it was hurling money at the problem and browbeating the administration to do more. Specifically, the State Department's leaders noted that Congress, through Charlie Wilson's Oerlikon bill, had earmarked money to provide humanitarian aid to the

---

*Hinton had just come off a tour in El Salvador, and the Reagan administration was constantly under attack in Congress and by the press for its support of the Salvadoran military, which was engaged in bloody death-squad murders.

mujahideen. After listening to Hinton's warnings, Helman decided to endorse the veteran diplomat's proposal that the State Department contribute to the war effort by starting a humanitarian-aid program under its banner.

Thus was born the Cross Border Humanitarian Aid Program. It was initially conceived as a modest program to smuggle food and some medical care across the border—a total of $6 million for 1985. The State Department considered the program to be highly provocative, since it would be the first U.S. effort to openly provide aid to the mujahideen in the war zone.

In truth, very little could be done with $6 million. To complicate matters, the Agency for International Development, which was assigned the task, had little interest in running a program that sounded a lot like a CIA operation. During Vietnam, AID had gotten burned rather badly for providing cover to CIA operatives and for running programs that were very much part of the CIA's efforts. As Helman explains the dilemma, "We were violating a lot of ground rules that said you shouldn't interfere in the private affairs of another country and certainly should not be operating covertly against another country's will." As a result, the AID leadership would have preferred to have nothing to do with this program. They initially planned only to provide the Pakistanis with humanitarian goods and let them distribute the material to the Afghans. And had it not been for Charlie Wilson, the program almost certainly would have remained small, cautious, and not particularly worthy of comment.

But the Cross Border program happened to come on-line just as Wilson had decided to use his appropriations muscle to fund an effort devised by a California doctor—a friend of Charles Fawcett's—to train and send cadres of combat medics into Afghanistan. This zealous figure, Dr. Bob Simon, had already enlisted one hundred American volunteers, doctors and nurses, a third of them from Texas. They were to teach the Afghans themselves how to care for their wounded and ill. His ambitions went beyond simple battlefield medicine; he wanted to use this American volunteer effort to focus world attention on the atrocities being committed by the Red Army. As far as Wilson was concerned, this was precisely what the Cross Border program should support.

The idea of encouraging, much less openly funding, Americans to enter the CIA's proxy war was just about the last thing State and AID wanted to permit. The task of explaining to Wilson why it was not going to be possible to fund his doctor was given to Assistant Secretary Gerald Helman. And for Charlie Schnabel, who had just joined Wilson's office, the experience of witnessing what happened to the veteran diplomat was an eye-opening introduction into the kind of leverage he would later put to use as Wilson's surrogate.

Helman was solicitous with Wilson. He said the State Department was indebted to the congressman for his role in helping launch the program. Then he explained that, as Wilson could well understand, there were national security concerns that demanded certain restraints in the kinds of support that the United States could provide. Chief among those was an absolute prohibition on any Americans crossing the border. "It's too risky to expose Americans to danger and perhaps cause them to be taken hostage," he said.

To this day Helman is amazed at Wilson's response: "Hell, that's exactly what I'm aiming for. I want to use American doctors as bait so they'll be captured and force our chickenshit government to give the muj an anti-aircraft cannon that will take care of the Hind Mi-24 helicopter." Wilson remembers a somewhat tamer response, but acknowledges that he made it clear that if American doctors wanted to go into the war zone, that was their privilege. Whatever his actual words, they were enough to startle the diplomat.

"I had to pinch myself," remembers Helman. "I couldn't figure out if he was pulling my leg. No one in his right mind would want that, but he said this in a room full of people."

When Helman dug in his heels and refused to budge, Wilson finally summoned Under Secretary of State Michael Armacost to his office for a showdown. Under secretaries are particularly solicitous of the few senior members of the Foreign Operations subcommittee. There can be terrible problems if one of these representatives decides to seek vengeance, and the way Wilson put his question to Armacost left the official in a precarious place. "Look, Mike," he said, "if it's State's position that the president's policy is wrong, then say so directly. Clearly, the president intended for wounded mujahideen to have medical care, and if you don't want to do it then you better tell me."

Wilson remembers this confrontation as "one of my better performances. I was still drinking and at my absolute meanest. I told him that in my twelve years in Washington I had never seen any single bureaucrat so able to frustrate the will both of the president and Congress as Gerry Helman."

Soon after, Helman was relieved of his responsibilities for the Cross Border Program, and Simon, over Helman's dead bureaucratic body, was given a $600,000 grant to set up operations in Peshawar close to the border. Schnabel marveled at Wilson's ability to take down an assistant secretary. The congressman would soon offer an equally vivid illustration of his power to reward as well as to punish.

The congressman had assumed the very worst when Larry Crandall, the man AID had picked to head up the Cross Border program, asked to see him. The pink-faced bureaucrat with the somewhat self-satisfied air had reminded Wilson of Helman, and he had been harsh with him, saying, "Until you prove to me that you have vials of morphine and medical care going into the mujahideen, I don't want to see you in here."

What Wilson had no way of knowing at the time was that Larry Crandall was a bureaucratic gunslinger—another of those self-appointed crusaders who somehow found themselves being pulled into Charlie Wilson's orbit. Crandall had reached that time in his life when he wanted to make his mark, and it was as if all of his professional years had been spent preparing him for this assignment. As a young AID officer in Vietnam, he had worked intimately with the CIA, supervising an interrogation center. Just before the Soviet invasion, he had served two years in Kabul. He knew the people and the terrain. Equally as important, Crandall was respected at AID and something of a genius at knowing how to push his timid agency to the absolute breaking point.

His first move, once he arrived in Peshawar on September 2, 1985, instantly put him into a league of his own. He had $6 million to spend by September 30, the end of the fiscal year. It was money the president had taken out of a Syrian AID program, and if he didn't spend it by the deadline, it would be lost to the Treasury. Another AID man might have taken the safe course and thrown the money into the bottomless pit of refugee assistance.

But Crandall had visited the same border clinics that had radicalized Wilson. "I saw what kind of damage was being done and I started to think, These no good S.O.B.s can't get away with this." Crandall wasn't interested in playing it safe with the Agency for International Development's money. He was already into the war and sensed that anything he might want to do required a relationship with the mujahideen leaders. With what appeared to be reckless abandon, he issued orders to buy hundreds of brand-new Isuzu and Toyota four-wheel-drives and trucks, which he promptly presented to the leading Afghan commanders. The only condition was that the vehicles be used in the fighting and absolutely not for commerce inside Pakistan.

"I wanted to make a big impression on them quickly," Crandall explains. "I wanted to hit them fast with something big so they would take us seriously. It got us into a lot of trouble with AID, because AID likes to think when it buys vehicles for the government they are in a parking lot at night so that they can be counted. In this case most of the trucks disappeared, never to be seen again, and AID couldn't understand this. But it established our bona fides with the mujahideen. All of a sudden those bastards loved us. And all of a sudden it gave me access that no one else had."

That was typical of Crandall—a bold move early on to get the attention of the men he would need later. To his surprise, he had discovered that neither the CIA nor the U.S. embassy had any overt contact with the mujahideen. In fairness to the embassy, that was because Zia had outlawed it. So when Crandall asked to meet some of the resistance leaders, the consulate couldn't help him. By chance, while walking down the streets of Peshawar, he ran headlong into one of the locals who used to work for him at the U.S. embassy in Kabul. "I told him my problem— that I had to get in touch with the resistance but the embassy didn't know how to do it. That was at six P.M., and by two A.M. my hotel room was filled with mujahideen."

For the first time, a U.S. government official was talking and negotiating with the warriors the CIA had been arming for five years. The CIA was still not permitted to meet these people, but Crandall reasoned that since he was running an overt program, supposedly dealing only in humanitarian aid, the prohibition did not apply to him.

No one had told him to do this and certainly none of his bosses would have liked the idea, but Crandall was now beginning to operate his AID program the way the CIA would ordinarily have moved in any other country where it was supporting a rebel force. The specific objective and the exact nature of all of Crandall's plans would remain essentially concealed for many years, even though the program was technically overt and would grow to over $100 million a year.

Avrakotos tends to dismiss Crandall's efforts as inept and clogged with unnecessary bureaucracy, but the truth is that this program fast became a critical second front in the CIA's war, in more ways than one. Certainly Crandall had the kind of mind and experience that could rival that of most chiefs of station, and everything he did in designing and running this rapidly expanding and supposedly open humanitarian-aid program was designed to make a difference in the mujahideen's fighting power.

Crandall was actually no stranger to the CIA. His first big AID job had been in a Vietnam province, working side by side with the Agency's Phoenix program operatives. They were selectively killing suspected Vietcong while he was trying to win the loyalty of the local Vietnamese. He had walked away with a keen sense of how easy it was for a determined guerrilla force to wreak havoc with a superpower.

During Crandall's two years in Kabul he had not been particularly charmed by Afghanistan. But he'd left with profound respect for the Afghans' orneriness and had paid little attention to the pessimists who'd seemed to dominate the policy circles around the Afghan question. He was stunned by how down the embassy officials were about the Afghans' prospects when he arrived to survey the situation. "Everyone was constantly talking about Russian stick-to-itiveness as opposed to U.S. jumpiness."

His own very different conclusion, after meeting the Afghans, was almost identical to that of Mike Vickers: there weren't enough Soviet troops to pacify that country. The key was to keep the Afghans in the battle; as long as they didn't become demoralized, they could do the same thing as the Vietcong and the North Vietnamese. He set out to use AID's money to win the hearts and minds of the Afghans.

The vision of America buying Third World hearts and minds in Vietnam had become discredited. But as Crandall saw its Afghan application, it simply meant doing more than just giving out guns. The Cross Border program had been started to counter the Soviets' scorched-earth policy—to stop the flow of refugees out of Afghanistan. That meant, first of all, getting out food and medicine and a reason for people to stay in their villages. As Crandall saw it, that could only be done if the commanders became true leaders able to care for their own families and to offer things of material value to their people.

But how do you offset the horrors of a war zone? To begin with, it meant he had to take AID into the smuggling business in a big way—with trucks and mules and camels and donkeys to slip in food and medicine. Later he organized training for teachers and supplied kits for them to pack in over the mountains to establish underground schools in devastated villages. Within a year he would be doling out tens of millions of dollars to the private volunteer organizations that began to flock into the Muslim stronghold of Peshawar, so that American nurses, doctors, and health workers could set up shop, not only providing care in Pakistan but constantly training new cadres of Afghan men and women to provide health care inside the war zone.

As Crandall saw it, the significance of the effort in those first few months was that it showed the American flag for the first time and filled the Afghans with hope that the superpower was standing tall alongside them. "We created a mentality," he explains. "When we would go to big rallies at refugee camps they would talk about how the Americans are coming, the Americans are coming. Even at mosque prayers we heard it."

Wilson, who had first seen only "a horrid little shit" of a bureaucrat standing before him, would soon come to love this man. Schnabel would arrange for Crandall's daughter to intern in Wilson's office. The congressman would throw fancy parties for him on his return visits, and above all, Charlie would conspire with Crandall against his bosses at AID.

Soon after their first meeting, Crandall returned to Wilson's office. He closed the door and, just as Avrakotos had done a year and a half earlier, said in a very different voice than Wilson had heard before, "Now, this conversation never happened. And if you ever say I came here, I'll deny it. But we could use twice as much money next year, and this is what we can do with it to change the war."

One reason for this conspiracy was that Crandall's bosses were determined to kill this program. In a meeting of fifty AID officers, one of the assistant directors had said that the Cross Border program was less important than the program operating in East Timor. And there was no AID program in East Timor.

When the same official accompanied Crandall to tell Wilson that he was offering far too much money for the Cross Border program and that AID did not feel it could assimilate it, Wilson cut him off. "You're here to listen, not to talk," Wilson said. When the official made another appeal to reason, Charlie cruelly laid down the bottom line: "Every time you talk, I'm going to take $15 million from a place where you want to be spending it, and I'll add that $15 million to the Afghan program."

By this time Wilson was coordinating his efforts with Senator Gordon Humphrey, who was even more adamant about upping the ante. And so the program, begun at $6 million in 1985, leapt to $15 million in 1986; to $30 million in 1987; to $45 million in 1988; and finally topped out at $90 million in 1989. By then Crandall would be deep into war logistics, building highways and bridges in Afghanistan so that ordnance could be moved in days rather than months to supply Massoud in the Panjshir Valley. He was sending in huge amounts of wheat, much more than needed, knowing that the Afghans would sell it to generate operating funds. And by then he would have taken over the business of supplying vital Tennessee mules, officially to carry humanitarian cargo only. But no one bothered to tell the mujahideen at the border that they might be violating AID rules by adding a mortar or box of AK ammo to the load. All of this was coming at the same time as the massive weapons program, and in many respects, Crandall's operation initially had a larger impact. The reason the Afghans had succeeded in holding out against the Soviets was not because they were winning battles. Basically, they lost every direct contest they engaged in. Nor was it because they inflicted such tremendous casualties or costs on the Red Army. It was more because they simply kept in the game in spite of fearful losses both to their warriors and to the vast majority of the population that stood with them. It's estimated that by 1985, one of every three Afghans had been forced out of the country by the Red Army. Hundreds of thousands had died as a direct result of the invasion and occupation, and that year it appeared to many, even to Mike Vickers, that a certain war weariness was setting in.

The flood of new weapons and the training programs made an enormous difference. But in a curious way, Crandall's Cross Border program may have provided the greatest lift to the spirits of the warriors because, for the first time, the Afghans could say and believe that the United States was moving in behind them. Until this point, they did not really know where the CIA guns were coming from. The weapons were all of Soviet origin and were handed out by the Pakistanis. But now Crandall was handing out brand-new Toyota pickups, and the word was getting out about the giant cargo planes that landed in the night and disgorged incredible amounts of U.S. goods for the mujahideen. Crandall and his team were holding regular meetings with the mujahideen leaders, filling them in on the programs they were going to start and have the Afghans run.

It was a stunning concept. Crandall was going to provide them with the wherewithal to roll back the scorched-earth policy. For five miserable years, the Afghans had retreated from their country, watching as their villages were destroyed and their families forced into exile. Now the pink-cheeked bureaucrat was talking about setting up clinics, training medics and doctors, creating schools, and teaching Afghans to read. Crandall wanted them to begin preparing for the time when they would be returning to Afghanistan to rebuild their country.

It wasn't long before Crandall was operating a kind of shadow CIA program. Wilson sometimes thought that Crandall might actually be a CIA man. His program supported the same fighters and shared the same ISI infrastructure for moving goods. In Islamabad and Peshawar, he became a pasha, no doubt the greatest smuggling lord that that ancient caravan route had ever known. He took gracefully to the role, surrounding himself in his embassy office and home with fine Afghan and Persian rugs, and mahogany furniture hand-tooled by Peshawar craftsmen in the old style.

At first, Crandall says, he tried to shield his officers from the shadowy role that his programs were playing in the CIA's campaign. But soon they came to revel in their role, describing themselves boisterously as "the other Agency." And when Schnabel would arrive everyone would receive him as if he were the patron himself. AID occupied a suite on the embassy's second floor, sealed off by a combination lock, just like the CIA station on the floor above. Crandall soon gave Schnabel the combination; cars and drivers were put at his disposal. The AID director would not assist the other Charlie's smuggling efforts, but he would smile broadly and look the other way when the sniper sights and other contraband passed through the AID-maintained International Medical Corps (IMC) clinics.

The most telling indicator of the Cross Border program's relevance was the station chief's invitation for Crandall to sit in on the CIA's war sessions. Since Crandall's men were the only Americans dealing directly with the mujahideen, they had become an invaluable new and reliable source of information. Crandall was now able to offer better tactical advice on how long it would take to get supplies to a given commander, or what tribes were likely to hijack a caravan, or who would take bribes from the Red Army, or which mujahideen were doing the most fighting.

There was another factor, impossible to quantify but nevertheless critical. In the fall of 1985 and into the next year, the Kremlin had to wrestle with a difficult choice: whether to take the war to Pakistan or to get out altogether, as the United States had with Vietnam. Central to the Politburo's thinking was the need to evaluate just how far the United States was prepared to go in Afghanistan.

Clearly the discovery of the exotic and public non-CIA programs Wilson was funding must have made for a sickening moment in Moscow. Until late 1985, in accordance with the Presidential Findings, the U.S. had moved in stealth: no American components were even allowed to go into any of the mujahideen's weapons. Indeed, few Afghans even knew where the weapons came from.

Before this, the courageous French doctors from Médecins sans Frontières had been virtually the only ones to go into the war zone. But now into Peshawar burst a flood of American doctors, nurses, and health-care workers. All shapes and varieties of private American volunteer organizations were setting up shop in Peshawar, and all of them seemed to be settling in for the long haul.

It was a community of free spirits that Crandall began to fund. He gave two former hippies a grant to operate a clinic on the actual border, under the name of Freedom Medicine, and sent his daughters out for weekend experiences in freedom fighting. Behind one walled compound in Peshawar he installed professors from the University of Nebraska, working under a Cross Border grant to develop plans for creating the new government of Afghanistan. Thanks to a program sponsored by Gordon Humphrey, at the edge of the city, behind a rather nondescript building, a school was being formed to teach mujahideen how to shoot war footage with small video cameras.

A pretty young pediatrician from Manhattan came to Crandall for a grant to organize a harrowing trek into Nuristan to inoculate Afghan children against the great killers of the war—measles, mumps, and chicken pox. And at night, all these adventurers were gathering noisily at the newly formed American Club in Peshawar, drinking and acting as if they were operating in the days of the Berlin airlift. "Three years in a row, Charlie doubled my budget," remembers Crandall. "He would always say, 'What do you need? There are no limits.'"

What happened in the months and years that followed, to the great displeasure of and opposition from AID's leaders, was the explosion of this seemingly innocent little program into what Wilson provocatively called "the noblest smuggling operation in history." But it also served as a Trojan horse of sorts for the CIA. Operating with its innocent cover, this AID program would soon merge directly into the CIA's ongoing operation by providing the first direct American link to the Afghans themselves.

Up until the Cross Border program Zia, Akhtar, and the Pakistan ISI had steadfastly forbidden the CIA from any direct contact with the mujahideen. But now Crandall's people were everywhere on the Afghan frontier. They were operating with the mujahideen, smuggling contraband into the war zone. The whole policy of trying to conceal the American hand was suddenly moot. Inadvertently, the Cross Border program was clearing the way for the introduction of the ultimate Hind killer, the thirty-five-pound General Dynamics surface-to-air missile known as the Stinger.

CHAPTER 26

Charlie and Sweetums

DR. DOOM DECLARES
CHARLIE DEAD

Control of U.S. foreign policy is supposed to rest with the president. As a practical matter, highly popular presidents, like Ronald Reagan, are almost always able to mount foreign initiatives without serious challenge. But in 1985 Tip O'Neill and his House Democrats seized control of two of the president's most passionate causes. Everyone who read the papers that year knew about the first challenge—the House-led attack on the CIA's Contra war in Nicaragua. In spite of Reagan's appeal to a joint session of Congress, the Democrats cut off all funding for this CIA operation.

Opposition to CIA secret warfare was seen as a core principle that the Democratic Party wanted to be identified with. That identity was so strong that the second Democratic-led initiative went all but unnoticed. At a time when the Contras could not get a dime from Congress, Charlie Wilson had managed to turn the CIA's cautious bleeding campaign in Afghanistan into a half-billion-dollars-a-year operation that dwarfed any prior Agency effort. For all practical purposes Wilson had hijacked a U.S. foreign policy and was busy transforming it into the first direct winner-take-all contest with the Soviet Union. And the only reason he was able to take on this role was because of the license to operate given to him by Tip O'Neill.

With Tip's eyes voluntarily averted and with the Democratic majority's acquiescence, Wilson was operating behind the lines like a ban-

dit. He was now engaged in the kind of sensitive diplomacy that is technically illegal for anyone other than the White House to conduct: cutting
arms deals with the defense minister of Egypt; commissioning Israel to
design weapons for the CIA; negotiating all manner of extraordinarily
controversial matters with the all-important U.S. ally General Zia. There
was even a moment when Wilson would find himself outside of a hotel in
London introducing two delegations of the highest-level representatives
of Israel and Pakistan. It was Charlie's very own peace initiative that would
result in the creation of a back channel between the two ostensibly enemy
nations. "I figured that that may have been one that no one else could have
put together," he reflected in later years.

None of these initiatives was ever cleared with State or the White
House, and had Wilson chosen to seek prior approval it is almost certain
he would have been told in no uncertain terms to back off. As a matter of
policy, touring members of Congress always have an embassy representative present when they meet with high-level officials of the host government. To the great aggravation of the tough U.S. ambassador to Pakistan,
Dean Hinton, Zia always insisted on meeting privately with Wilson on
every one of Charlie's numerous visits to Islamabad. At these sessions the
two men would talk as partners, often as virtual co-conspirators. To Zia a
personal commitment of continued U.S. financial support to the Pakistan
army made by Charles Wilson of Defense Appropriations was as good as
gold and far more reliable than anything anyone else in the U.S. government might promise. The two men horse-traded and schemed, and only
after they had completed their sensitive matters would Wilson invite the
ambassador to sit in on the latter half of the discussion.

At the heart of everything Wilson was able to do, however, was the
conspiratorial partnership he had entered into with Avrakotos. Gust was
now coming by his office every week, sometimes visiting two or three times
a week, and they would talk on the phone incessantly. Wilson, in his huge
office in the Rayburn building with the twenty-five-foot ceilings and the
great map of the world on his wall, would never look or sound awestruck
when Gust arrived. But this was indeed Charlie's greatest adventure, and
he lived for those meetings with his CIA friend.

Gust, who would arrive alone, was now filling his patron in with the
kind of operational details that even senators and congressmen on the Intelligence Committees are not permitted to know. In fact, because of the

Agency's rigid code of compartmentalization, not even division chiefs in other areas of the Agency knew what Charlie did. "There were times in those early years when I felt as if I were some character in a great spy novel," recalls Wilson.

Indeed, by early 1985 Wilson was moving invisibly in so many areas at once that it would have been next to impossible for anyone to assess his overall impact. In a front-page story in the *Washington Post* Bob Woodward surfaced one of Wilson's key roles as "the catalyst" responsible for funding the biggest covert operation since Vietnam.

Now, just as Gust was shaking his outcast identity and experiencing a rush of recognition from his CIA colleagues, Wilson began to notice a shift in the way Washington insiders were treating him. For the first time, he could sense genuine respect from the people he cared most about—the admirals from his Annapolis class, senior Pentagon officials, the inner Reagan crowd, and, most vividly, from his congressional colleagues, some of whom started to call Afghanistan "Charlie's war."

The mujahideen, who had always visited Wilson's office when they came to Washington, were now arriving with a special fervor, acting more like they were attending a *majlis* with a Saudi prince. They would listen in amazement as this ebullient Texas cowboy pointed to the tiny model of an Oerlikon on his desk and boasted how hundreds of these million-dollars-a-unit anti-aircraft weapons would soon be inside Afghanistan shooting down the Hinds.

Had the CIA's analytic division been asked to turn out a psychological portrait of the congressman at that time, as it did of Zia and other world leaders, it surely would have revealed a perplexing pattern of behavior: whenever things start to go well for Wilson, some Freudian impulse seems to prompt him to create havoc. And since everything was going so close to perfection in early 1985, Charlie went to work to spoil it all.

As usual, the incident was connected to a woman. One of the high points in Wilson's social calendar each year was the black-tie White House reception for Kennedy Center board members. As always, Charlie went to extraordinary lengths to make a dashing appearance. And according to his well-established ritual, that meant he needed a beauty queen on his arm. This year he chose a former Miss U.S.A., Judi Anderson. But no sooner had he introduced his date to the president and first lady than he found himself thunderstruck by a striking young woman on the arm of a colleague from the Ethics Committee, Don Bailey. This was the woman Charlie would soon be introducing to Zia, Gust, and CIA station chiefs all over the world as "Sweetums."

"Hi, I'm Judi Anderson," Charlie heard his date say.

"That rings a bell," said the woman who was destined to become Charlie's constant companion on all his Afghan travels for the next four years.

"It should," replied Wilson's date. "I was Miss U.S.A."

"Well, isn't that a coincidence," replied Sweetums in one of those thinly disguised notes of triumph, "I was in the Miss World pageant."

Following the unwritten rules of the House calling for honor among thieves, the next day Wilson approached his Ethics Committee friend to ask if the beauty from the White House reception, Annelise Ilschenko, was spoken for. Bailey good-naturedly gave his blessing, but then Charlie discovered that Annelise was ill disposed to be seen in public with him.

"He had a sleazy reputation," recalls Ilschenko. "He was known as a womanizer, and I didn't want it. The rumor was that when he went on the floor Charlie would look up at the boxes for pretty blondes and then have the pages go up and say, Charlie Wilson wants to meet you."

Ilschenko recalls him falling down the stairs drunk at the River Club one night and lushing about "with his belly dancer" on another. "He was just not to be taken seriously," she says. But in spite of this she was drawn to him, and she did accept occasional dinner and dancing invitations, finally agreeing to accompany him for a weekend he promised she would never forget. The U.S. Navy had agreed to host the senior member of Defense Appropriations and his personal delegation aboard the 4,300-man aircraft carrier the U.S.S. *Saratoga*. Charlie, who had also invited three of his Texas drinking pals, thoughtfully brought along his twenty-seven-year-old defense aide, Molly Hamilton, "so that Annelise would not feel so isolated being the only lady on board."

Of all the Angels, Hamilton was the one who turned Gust's knees to jelly. She didn't know anything about defense, but Charlie didn't rely on staffers to do his thinking for him and he loved to watch the reaction on his guests' faces when he would ask his defense aide to sit in on conferences. As he saw it, a big part of the job was entertaining the defense lobbyists who contributed mightily to his campaigns. Hamilton, however, was not exactly a good-time girl, and she was frankly appalled on this weekend junket by what she perceived to be a clear abuse of congressional power.

Charlie's entourage was jetted onto the carrier's deck, where the great hooks brought the U.S. Navy jets to a screeching halt. That night, the captain, in dress uniform, had a marvelous dinner on the deck with the sounds and sights of the U.S. empire playing in the background. To Hamilton's discomfort—she was well aware of the strict prohibition against alcohol aboard a U.S. Navy vessel—Charlie had somehow managed to bring a healthy supply of liquor along. He hadn't served as a gunnery officer sneaking whiskey aboard in empty shell casings for nothing. Hamilton's unhappy memories of the evening are of a frightening sea of seventeen-foot waves, people drinking, and everyone going to excessive lengths to accommodate the congressman and his date.

It was meant to be one of those "old boy" weekends where a bit of good, clean fun can be carried out without anyone tattling. But nothing Charlie does ever remains a secret for long, and to Annelise's horror, Jack Anderson's column, carried in the *Washington Post* and some four hundred newspapers across the country, spelled out in humiliating detail how the congressman had taken a beauty queen for a weekend boondoggle at the taxpayers' expense.

The story, which made page one of the *Cleveland Plain Dealer,* didn't sit well with Ilschenko's parents. Charlie personally apologized to them, then magnanimously offered to pay the navy $650 for Annelise's expenses. In response to reporters, he explained that he had only brought Ilschenko along so that Hamilton, his staffer, wouldn't feel so "isolated being the only lady on board." Finally, after tending to this damage control, he begged Annelise for another chance, promising that next time he would take her on the trip of her life and he would pay the bill.

The experience Charlie offered his new true love was the product of much thought and a kind of boldness about junketing that only a compulsive risk taker like Wilson could propose. The trip began in Marrakech, where he had the Pentagon reserve the Churchill Suite at the exotic La Mamounia hotel. Since Charlie was officially on a "fact-finding trip" for Defense Appropriations, the Pentagon sent along a liaison officer to take care of logistics.

There had to be a technical reason for being in Morocco, so Charlie paid a visit to his friends in the Royal Moroccan Army to watch them blast guns in the desert. "You see, I was evaluating anti-Communist activities because I was getting my way paid. But then, of course, I had to find time to lie out in the swimming pool with Sweetums and take her to the ba-zaar." It was even better for Sweetums in Venice, where Charlie had arranged a magical dinner and gondola ride on the Grand Canal. This leg of the journey was more difficult for Wilson to justify, but he managed to. "Fortunately," he explains, "the air force base in Naples felt a great urgency to give me a briefing in Venice and sent two generals, as I recall."

And then the pièce de résistance: the overnight trip to Paris on the fabled Orient Express. Wilson had the good sense not to bill the U.S. government for this exotic leg of the trip. But the Pentagon added a pleasant flourish by sending along an escort officer to make sure everything was perfect during their travels. It was June 1, 1985, Charlie's birthday, and the the young officer came dressed in formal uniform for the champagne dinner, with Charlie in black tie and Sweetums in the stunning dress he had bought her for the occasion.

This spectacular Morocco-to-Paris junket for Sweetums was clearly stretching the rules of reasonable conduct, even for a senior member of Defense Appropriations. But in fairness to the congressman, he was only doing what he had been taught to believe was standard operating practice. As with most things, one's first experience is seminal, and few newcomers have been offered such a blinding insight into the way things work in Congress as when Charlie Wilson first joined the Foreign Affairs Committee in 1974 and was invited by the chairman, Olin "Tiger" Teague, to attend the Paris air show. "Well, Tiger, I don't have the money," explained the embarrassed freshman. Teague laughed, and Wilson remembers his astonishment at discovering that the U.S. government pays for first-class plane tickets and first-class hotels, provides funds for meals, and supplies limousines, foreign service officers as guides, and, of course, the best seats at the air show. All of this is free, with the objective of providing the legislators with a fact-finding experience that will make them wiser when they come back after the break to design legislation.

What left the deepest impression on the novice congressman, however, was the way the senior foreign service officers at the embassy threw themselves into helping the committee members' wives find the best shopping deals in Paris. After Charlie had spent two weeks living better than he had ever imagined possible, the air force plane landed at Andrews Air Force Base to reveal a demonstration of respect for the power and prestige of the House that would linger with Wilson for the rest of his days in

Congress. Two lines of station wagons were lined up on the tarmac, each one with the name of a member of the delegation prominently displayed on the windshield. No sooner had the plane pulled to a stop than a collection of uniformed men quickly moved into the cargo hold and placed the fruits of the junket–shopping spree in the cars. Without so much as a thought about customs, the uniformed officers swept the chairman and his booty—two station wagons filled with antiques—off the air force base and into the District.

That was when Charlie discovered how much fun being in Congress could be if you're on the right committee and if you know what to ask for. Over the years, Charlie became one of the all-time master craftsmen at bending the business of his Appropriations subcommittees to the fancies of his private life. That was critically important for Charlie because he had absolutely no money to spend. In fact, in the spring of 1985, the local Texas papers revealed that he had the distinction of being the poorest member of the Texas delegation, with a negative net worth estimated as high as a million dollars of debt. For Charlie, the joy of being a congressman was that on a junket money was not necessary. And as the Paris-bound Orient Express made its elegant way through the night on Charlie's fifty-second birthday, the magic was working its spell on Sweetums. She was fast forgetting the humiliation of the U.S.S. *Saratoga* and finding it quite pleasing to be with this charming, handsome man who could make her feel like she was once again walking onstage at the Miss World pageant.

For Wilson, however, this junket was fast turning into an agonizing and increasingly frightening experience. By the time he toasted Sweetums at his birthday dinner, he had begun to think he might be in serious physical trouble. There had been an incident in Morocco when he couldn't swim across the La Mamounia pool. He had assumed the chest pains were caused by dysentery, probably from the local cucumbers he had eaten with the Royal Moroccan Army. On the train in his tuxedo, in between laughing and telling charming stories, he convinced himself that the lingering hollow feeling and the cold sweat was just the tail end of the intestinal problem.

In Paris, Charlie was just one of a slew of senators and congressmen who make the annual pilgrimage to the air show. But since he was a senior member of Defense Appropriations, he knew that Sweetums would be pampered and spoiled by every defense contractor worth his salt. And sure enough, the lobbyists had messages piled up at the hotel—invitations to dinners, cocktail parties, the theater.

Paris was supposed to be the high point of the trip, but it was Sweetums's fate to have nothing but disasters accompany her on all of her travels with Charlie. Coming back from dinner that first night, Wilson took three steps out of the restaurant and couldn't continue. "I took him up to the room," she remembers. "He couldn't breathe and he couldn't lie down. Later we found out he was literally drowning with blood in his lungs."

A lifetime of drink had finally caught up with Charlie Wilson. His heart was literally soaked in alcohol and barely functioning, a condition not uncommon to alcoholics. When he got to the American hospital where Rock Hudson had just died, his blood pressure was so low that it took the nurses thirty-two tries to get an IV into his veins. In critical condition he was evacuated to the U.S. military hospital at Rhine Main, Germany, for preliminary treatment.

The doctors there put him on blood thinners and drugs to force his devastated heart to continue beating. In his fog, after discovering that the hospital had been built by Hermann Göring for the Luftwaffe pilots, his imagination offered him an explanation as to why he was there: "I imagined myself as a wounded pilot from the other side who had just made it back with my Messerschmitt shot to shreds."

Ten days into this fog, as if he were in fact a great war hero, he woke up to find the general in charge of the military hospital at his bedside saying there was a call from the White House. The president needed him in Washington. Would he fly home immediately to cast a vote for Ronald Reagan to save the Contras?

For an anti-Communist from East Texas, this was a command performance. A giant air force plane was flown into Rhine Main with a medical team on board to carry the congressman across the Atlantic to rescue the Nicaraguan "freedom fighters." "It made me feel like a big shot of immense proportions," he remembers.

It was a critical moment for the Contra war, a congressional face-off where two or three votes would make the difference. When two of Wilson's liberal colleagues, Tom Downey and Bob Mrazek, spotted him being wheeled onto the floor of the House in his navy pajamas and sustained by an IV, they ran over and threatened to unplug his life-support system if he didn't vote right.

Charlie felt heroic enough to bark them down with his typical banter. "They had to fly my skinny ass all the way from Germany to keep you pinkos from wiping out freedom in Central America," he said. It was hard for anyone to be upset with Charlie no matter what he did. Not even Tip O'Neill would ask this famous war hawk to turn down a direct appeal from the president.

There was little joy back in the hospital, where the naval doctor whom Charlie would come to call "Dr. Doom" presented him with what amounted to a death notice. The tests had indicated that the congressman's alcohol-soaked heart was functioning at only 16 percent. That was the amount of blood that comes out when the heart beats (a normal person has a 50 percent rate). The doctor told Wilson, his sister, and Charlie Schnabel that he didn't think Wilson was going to get any better. The best he could hope for, Dr. Doom suggested, was eighteen months.

"I wanted him to tell me I would have to give up corn on the cob or I'd have to take an extra pill," recalls Charlie, who was reacting like a typical alcoholic. He simply couldn't accept some doctor telling him that he could never have another drink and that he was going to die in eighteen months, whether he had a drink or not. Restlessly, Wilson insisted on a second opinion—and then many other second opinions—but every new specialist only confirmed Dr. Doom's terrible diagnosis.

With some sixth sense that destiny had not yet called his number, Wilson, living on oxygen and unable to walk up even a few steps, announced to his physician, "Dr. Doom, you don't know what you're talking about." He booked a flight to Houston to consult an eminent cardiologist, Dick Cashion. As he saw it, he was appealing Doom's unjust verdict. If all else failed, Charlie thought, at least Cashion might arrange for a transplant. That way he'd be able to maintain his boozing lifestyle.

Just being in Cashion's hospital made him feel better. He recalls his pleasure the first night when a waiter arrived in a black tuxedo to offer him a choice of six entrées. The waiter also said he could arrange for wine and cocktails for the congressman's guests. This was the kind of healing atmosphere that Wilson could identify with.

The next day Cashion told him they would be taking a piece of his heart out with a procedure that would start in his jugular. For the first time, Charlie began to realize there might not be any good news at the end of this story, and he began to put in calls to all of his closest women friends—

Sweetums, Snowflake, the Israeli dancer Ziva, and Trish. Guardedly he asked one after another, "Will things be okay? Can they be like they always were if I'm not drinking anymore?" Curiously, he thought that without alcohol, he wouldn't be good company.

Charlie Schnabel, who witnessed this performance, remembered Wilson's relief after discovering that his girlfriends wouldn't desert him if he had to go on the wagon.

A cable from the station in Paris had alerted Gust to the problem: "Wish to inform headquarters that Congressman Wilson appears to have suffered a heart attack." Avrakotos had been in the cafeteria when Deputy Director John McMahon paged him to come up to the seventh floor to read the cable. He recalls, "When I walked in, McMahon said, 'It may be serious. In fact, he may not make it. Did you know he was an Annapolis graduate?' And then McMahon added, 'It sure would be a bad day for us if we lost him.'"

Over the next few days, as Wilson made his way back across the Atlantic and into the military hospital in Bethesda, Avrakotos suddenly came to feel almost alone and exposed. To a certain extent he had thought of himself as the architect of the conspiracy with Wilson, but now he was forced to recognize that without Charlie, he might still be the pariah of the Directorate of Operations, roaming the halls without purpose.

The program was the first thing Gust thought about. The Agency was now committed to pushing the Soviets out "by all means available." Everything depended on sustaining congressional funding. As he articulated it years later, it was a frightening bottom-line concern: "How the fuck do you get more money for the program if Charlie's gone? But the other bottom line I discovered was that I didn't want to lose this friend."

That was the discovery that caught the tough Aliquippan by surprise. The man who tried to pretend nothing could hurt him discovered that he actually loved Charlie Wilson. "He risked an awful lot for us. He was unique. He ran with the CIA instead of hitting us from the outside. How many fucking congressmen in the last forty years have gone to bat publicly to get the CIA more money? That made him unique. Even in the heyday of Eisenhower and John Foster Dulles, when the Cold War was one big fucking goatfuck, no one was publicly calling for more money for the CIA to use in Guatemala or Cuba or anywhere."

Avrakotos now recognized what Wilson had done for and meant to him. Mainly he realized that Charlie had given him legitimacy. For twenty-three years he had served in the shadows, never recognized outside of his bureaucracy and even there shunned as a kind of thug and outsider. But now, in large measure because of Wilson's patronage, Gust had been inducted into the CIA's most celebrated inner circle—the career executive service, one of perhaps forty officers from the Clandestine Services to be so recognized.

It had been a long trek for this roughneck from Pennsylvania. Gust Avrakotos, a Greek beer distributor's son, could eat in the executive dining room with the Ivy Leaguers and Mr. Casey. Charlie had not just given his career a gigantic boost, he had made him feel like he belonged. The glamorous congressman with all the girls and all the power had also reached out and touched him as a friend, and it meant everything to Gust. "I was honorable in Charlie's eyes. Charlie really liked me, and I can't say that about many people."

From his hospital bed, Wilson made the first move with a call to Gust's secret number and a question that immediately made Avrakotos feel much better. "Gus," Charlie asked (he still hadn't learned that there was a *t* at the end of the agent's first name), "how many planes have you shot down today?"

"I'll be right over," Avrakotos responded, not minding in the least the mauling of his name. As always, Avrakotos wasn't authorized to visit a member of Congress without prior approval and then only with a CIA nanny present; the trek to Bethesda Naval Hospital was yet another trip off the reservation.

Instinctively he understood that Wilson would not want conventional sympathy. And so he appeared at Charlie's bedside with a giant bottle of Scotch, a package of condoms, and, most important, a stunning secret satellite photograph. "You didn't see this, Charlie," he began.

Wilson was genuinely lifted by the satellite photograph, which revealed what had just happened at the Shindand air base in Afghanistan. Fifteen Soviet MiGs destroyed on the runway, the damage visible in explicit and stunning detail. Best of all was the story Gust told Charlie about what had happened. It might as well have been a scene out of the movie

Rambo, as Gust explained it. The Afghans, armed with satchel charges, had slipped onto the base, fixed the charges, and destroyed fifteen fighter jets on the ground. The photograph was so clear that it showed wings and twisted metal on the runway, and Gust boasted that this little act of mujahideen daring had cost the Kremlin at least $150 million. "We got our money back on that one hit alone," he told Wilson.

Later John McMahon arrived at the hospital room proudly bearing the same strictly classified picture to cheer Charlie up. McMahon, however, had Office of Security agents clear the room first. To Avrakotos's enormous relief, Wilson did not blow his cover by admitting that he had already seen the photo.

Charlie's hospital room was witness to any number of strange visitors that June, not just CIA friends but Pakistani and Egyptian ambassadors bringing personal greetings from Dictator Zia and Defense Minister Abu Ghazala. Charlie's sister, Sharon, was in the room one day when Sweetums, Trish, and Ziva all appeared at the same time. "I thought he was going to have a heart attack," recalled Sharon. "It was a bit awkward," Charlie remembers, "but it raised my prestige on the floor considerably."

But mostly, for this bigger-than-life character suddenly laid low and struggling to breathe, it was a time of desperation. Curiously, Wilson turned his concerns away from his own condition and instead found himself preoccupied by the fate of the Afghans. "I'd lay in the bed and think about those helicopters and I worried that maybe Dr. Doom was right," he says. "I worried that without me, Gust would lose his edge at Langley, that the money would dry up, that Cogan would be made director of the CIA, that Helman would become secretary of state." Wilson had always romanticized the Afghans, but with his own fate so much in jeopardy, he came to see the mujahideen's war as almost a holy cause. "To me they were just these mythical heroes who were totally good and who somehow might change the world. And I just felt that if I died they would die as well."

Then came the miracle. In Houston, Dr. Cashion, the eighth specialist Wilson had sought out, announced that there was hope. "He said if I stopped drinking, I had a thirty-three and a third chance of getting well, the same chance of staying like I was, and a thirty-three and a third chance of deteriorating." To a man who had been living with what amounted to a death sentence, this was not just a stay of execution. As he walked out of the hospital he felt overwhelmed with a sense that he had been given a reprieve for a purpose. "It was a beautiful day at the end of June and I re-member thinking, You'll never have another drink. I always figured I had nine lives, but this time I realized I'd better really go after what I wanted. I thought, Well, let's just put all our energy and thought into our little project in the Hindu Kush."

Something deep was now stirring in Charlie Wilson. "You always have religious thoughts when you come face-to-face with your mortality," he says. "I felt at peace with what I'd done with my life because, even in my darkest days of alcohol abuse, I'd never neglected my constituents, never for a minute. But that day I left the hospital, I really felt I had been given a new lease on life and all my energies would be channeled into really draining the last drop of Russian blood out of Afghanistan. I was still think-ing there had to be a way to shoot down those fucking helicopters, and I was going to find it." It was an altogether new Charlie Wilson who arrived back at his office to pick up where he had left off.

CHAPTER 27

Charlie Schnabel and Friends

CHARLIE'S IRREGULARS

For Avrakotos, there was something slightly unnerving about Wilson's miraculous recovery. It would be another eighteen months before Charlie took a drink, and for the first time in his adult life he was soberly focused. Schnabel had ordered all alcohol removed from the congressman's house in Texas, from the condo in Arlington, and from the offices on the Hill. But for once it wasn't necessary. Wilson was observing his own ban, and it was transforming his mood.

Each morning he would take the members' underground subway from his Rayburn office to the Capitol, striding past the security guards into the sealed room under the dome where the CIA provides a copy of the national intelligence daily brief for members with the highest security clearances. Charlie was usually the only congressman present as he poured through the Agency's most up-to-date intelligence on battles and Soviet casualties.

There were times when Gust found it almost intimidating to brief his revived patron. Wilson was acting like a man with little time left, particularly frustrated that his Oerlikons were still not in action, and always asking the question Avrakotos hated to answer: "How many Hinds have you shot down this week?"

"It takes time Charlie," Gust would begin before launching into Vickers's standard refrain. "It's the mix that's important. And you've got to teach the mujahideen how to use these weapons." But Wilson wasn't willing to let it go at that. He had full confidence in Avrakotos, but Afghanistan had been a journey of discovery for him. By the fall of 1985 he had come to know that the CIA was not the only force he could call on. He had learned that his influence on Appropriations gave him the ability to run his own operations should he sense an opportunity. That's where Charlie Schnabel came into the picture.

By that time Schanbel had become Wilson's envoy to an assortment of odd characters who made up the American Afghan lobby. The tendency is to call them right-wingers, but they really defied labeling, with views even more extreme than Gordon Humphrey's. Wilson thought they were all a bit crazy but potentially useful, as long as he didn't have to deal with them personally. Schnabel made that possible since all of them seemed to feel a kindred spirit for the "other" Charlie. Just weeks after Wilson got out of the hospital, Schnabel urged the congressman to meet with one of these people.

Vaughn Forest was an obscure and somewhat abrasive aide to a little-known congressman. He was not the sort of man who instills trust in most politicians, but Wilson was intrigued when Schnabel explained that this former Florida cop and Vietnam Special Forces medic had just returned from a monthlong trek into the Afghan war zone. As an aide to Florida congressman Bill McCollum, he'd been well aware that the U.S. government absolutely prohibited any of its employees from crossing into the war zone with the mujahideen. But that kind of rule-breaking zeal appealed to Wilson, and he graciously agreed to a meeting.

Forest's route to Afghanistan, like that of so many of the Americans who would become infatuated with the mujahideen's cause, was a curious one. It had grown out of a passionate Catholicism that had caused him to spend his vacations providing humanitarian assistance to war refugees in Central America.

To his enormous surprise, in 1984 this work came to the attention of a group of Catholics, who invited him to join the ancient order of the Knights of Malta. At a ceremony in Washington, the famed trial lawyer Edward Bennett Williams performed the ritual induction, forever altering Forest's life. According to legend, the original knights had been crusaders from noble families. To Forest, it was as if he had been ordained by some mystical power to fulfill the obligations of this exalted order, which called on its knights to devote their lives to rescuing those in distress.

It was this new commission that caused him to fly to Pakistan on his vacation to contact the mujahideen, and then to walk over the mountains with one of their bands for a month of fighting. Vickers's new flood of weapons had not yet made it through the pipeline, and Forest, who knew nothing of the program under way, was appalled by the way the Afghans were being armed and supported.

Drawing on his Vietnam experience, he began preparing his own detailed plans for revamping everything. On the way home he stopped in Rome to visit the headquarters of the Knights of Malta. The headquarters, which is located on two acres of sovereign territory near the Spanish steps in Rome, is actually a country, the smallest in the world and the only one with a front door. Forest had been a bit disappointed by the building's fading architectural features, but he emerged from his meeting there with the name of a fellow knight whom he was told might be of use to him. Back in Washington, from his desk in the overcrowded Longworth Building congressional office, he called the number he had been given. "Hello, this is Vaughn Forest," he said. "I believe the grand mufti of Rome wrote to Director Casey about me. Is he in?"

Forest heard a muffled voice saying, "Tell him to come out." He was an anonymous aide to a congressman who served on no committee dealing with intelligence or foreign affairs. He had no realistic way of gaining access to William Casey, America's spy chief, but suddenly and effortlessly Vaughn Forest found himself seated in the director's office talking knight-to-knight.

This kind of experience can do strange things to an enthusiast like Vaughn Forest. Casey flattered him and applauded the young man's interest and then passed him on to another good Catholic, Ed Juchniewicz, the associate deputy director for Operations. Juchniewicz says he liked Forest, took him seriously. "Let's face it, he was an extreme right-winger," Juchniewicz recalls. "But here was a kid with all of the best intentions. He wanted to help and he had all the right credentials as far as Casey was concerned. So I spent some time with him and found he had a lot of neat ideas."

The truth was, Vaughn Forest managed to rub just about everyone else in the Agency the wrong way. Avrakotos, who was asked to see him, recalls, "He was a real odd bird, plus what he had to say was really off-the-wall." But now, thanks to Charlie Schnabel's recommendation, this persistent knight was sitting in Charlie Wilson's office, and the congressman liked what he was hearing.

Forest explained that after returning from Afghanistan he had scoured the bureaucracy to find out if anyone in the U.S. government was trying to make high-tech, user-friendly weapons for anti-Communist guerrillas. No one was, not at the CIA or in the military. But Forest said he had discovered a group of weapons tinkerers in the Pentagon's Tactical Land Warfare Division who were filled with notions of how to develop offbeat, mule-portable devices to help the mujahideen kill Russians. They would like nothing more than to be given the opportunity.

Vaughn Forest was so low on the Washington totem pole that he hadn't even been able to get anyone at the Pentagon to listen to him, much less think about how to get Congress to fund a program to design and produce lightweight exotic killing devices. Under the best of circumstances—with a conventional-weapons plan that no one opposes—moving a program through Congress would take at least a year. But not for Charlie Wilson, once he turned to his fellow appropriators to shortcut the system and turn Forest's vision into a reality. Within a few weeks of hearing Forest's implausible proposition, Charlie emerged from a House-Senate Appropriations conference with a commitment to fund the most unconventional weapons program of the decade.

Its official name was the Weapons Upgrade Program, but it might just as well have been called "Charlie Wilson's personal Afghan war chest." One of the more unusual features of the program was a clause that exempted it from having to follow the rules and regulations that guide all of the Pentagon's other weapons procurement and development programs. It was such a radical departure that Wilson knew it would have no chance of ultimately being implemented unless it first won the endorsement of the secretary of defense, Caspar Weinberger.

Thanks to Joanne and her carefully orchestrated dinner parties, Charlie had come to know Weinberger socially. Beyond that, for almost four years, in spite of being a liberal Democrat, he had been a critical ally on the Defense Appropriations subcommittee, voting for each and every item in Reagan's massive arms buildup. At one hearing, he'd even told Weinberger, "Mr. Secretary, there are a lot of things I don't understand and some with which I don't agree. But because you say they are important, I'm going to vote for them all." As Charlie saw it, the bottom line was that he had done a lot for Weinberger, and it was time to cash in his chips.

At breakfast with the defense secretary, Wilson began by saying, "All I want is $10 million"—but then came the catch. For starters, he wanted the Pentagon to give the program a complete waiver on all red tape—no specs, no feasibility studies, no minority contracts, not even competitive bidding. There wasn't time, he argued. The mujahideen were fighting and dying for America. They were fighting America's war against America's principal enemy and no one in the government was trying to create weapons and devices that could give these primitive freedom fighters a chance. Money was not the issue, said Wilson. This was war, and he wanted Weinberger to unleash the Pentagon's most devilish inventors and tinkerers to think big and small and to begin delivering the goods within weeks. He added one final request: he wanted to be granted some measure of personal control over the program. As Wilson recalls this moment, Weinberger initially expressed concern about the legality of such a program, but only for a moment. Yes, he said; Charlie could count on his support.

The rest—getting the trusty staffers on the subcommittee to conceal the appropriation in a line item that no one would ever find—was hardly a challenge. Charlie Wilson was now presiding over another congressional first: his very own invisible $10-million-a-year exotic-weapons program. There were days in his office when he felt as if he were playing the role of M in a James Bond novel, summoning the government's most ingenious inventors to decide what weapons and devices to commission for his freedom fighters.

Wilson had originally intended to fund this program through the CIA so that Gust could run it, but Avrakotos wanted no part of it. It was a year and a half since Charlie had come up with the money to buy the Swiss Oerlikons, and not so much as one had been given to the mujahideen. In frustration Wilson had begun lobbying the Agency to give the Israelis a contract for the Charlie Horse, the weapon Charlie had commissioned Zvi's engineers to design for the mujahideen.

But bringing the Israelis into the CIA's Muslim jihad was not what Avrakatos considered a reasonable option. There were many reasons why he was adamantly opposed to dealing with Israel. To begin with, it would risk alienating the Saudis, who were putting up half the money for the program. Beyond that, why risk alienating the legions of Muslim hotheads around the world who would draw the most extreme conclusions if it became known that the CIA was sneaking Jewish weapons into the jihad?

Avrakotos had an even greater concern, which he wasn't at liberty to share with Wilson. It centered on his suspicions about the role Israel was playing with Oliver North and the White House in their ill-fated arms-for-hostages negotiations with Iran. From the time he'd first learned about North's operation he had smelled a disaster in the making. The more he learned, the more he came to believe that the Israelis were walking a naive and inexperienced Oliver North and, with him, the United States into a trap. Repeatedly he would try to keep the Agency from being sucked into what was to become known as the Iran-Contra scandal. As it turned out, he didn't have the power to do that, but he was determined not to permit the Israelis to become identified with any direct CIA commission connected to Afghanistan.

So instead of the CIA taking on the Weapons Upgrade Program, it went to the Pentagon. But, in fact, Charlie Wilson himself ended up overseeing much of this eccentric program out of his own congressional office, and it turned out to be a wild and remarkable success story. "There were all these little scientists in the Pentagon—bureaucratic misfits who just needed to be freed," Wilson recalled years later. "We gave them a little money and made them immune to procurement laws. They're mad-scientist types. They love to tinker with things that blow up but hate to fill out forms. Hate to follow the chain of command. Hate to wait."

Typical of the characters who gravitated to this program were Chuck Barnard and his brother. They had grown up working in their father's auto garage, and as far as they were concerned the Pentagon didn't just buy $600 toilet seats; it made $20 million tanks that couldn't survive in a face-off with one of their $1 million stripped-down Volkswagens armed with a range of their favorite high-tech weaponry. In their view, almost everything the Pentagon did to develop and buy weapons was wasteful, ineffective, and designed to fight some previous war.

For the first time, thanks to Wilson, these tinkerers were free to innovate at will and more or less without restraint. Within weeks, they began developing an astonishing collection of weapons. The Spanish mortar, for example, was designed to make it possible for the mujahideen to communicate directly with American navigation satellites to deliver repeated rounds within inches of their designated targets. Global-positioning technology is well known today, but back in 1985 it struck Wilson as the most astonishing capability. Just the thought of Afghan tribesmen who had never seen a flush toilet signaling an American satellite to fire precision rounds at a Red Army stronghold was almost too much to believe. The weapon's name was purposefully misleading, chosen to conceal the fact that major portions of this "Spanish mortar" were being built by the Israelis.

Milt Bearden, the station chief who would dominate the war's later years, actually came to rely on the steady stream of crazy new weapons that kept coming on-line from this offbeat program. His strategy called for introducing a new weapon into the battle every three months or so, in order to bluff the Red Army into thinking their enemy was better armed and supported than it was. The Spanish mortar, for example, with its satellite-guided charge, was rarely deployed and may only have succeeded because the Pakistani ISI advisers were along to direct the fire. But the Soviets didn't know that. When the weapon was first used it wiped out an entire Spetsnaz outpost with a volley of perfect strikes. And as soon as Bearden learned from the CIA's intercepts that the commander of the 40th Army had heli-coptered to the scene, he knew that from that day on, the Soviets would have to factor in the possibility that the mujahideen had acquired some deadly targeting capability. For that reason alone, the weapon was a suc-cess even if never fired again.

Bearden became so intoxicated with this kind of psychological war-fare that he later developed plans to have a group of mujahideen shoot dead Russian soldiers with crossbows. To him, the vision of men who might kill you with a bow and arrow one day or with a satellite-guided mortar the next would be unnerving to any army.

Neither Vaughn Forest nor Charlie Schnabel were officially part of the program, just as Wilson's name never appeared on any organizational chart. But both men became so intimately involved with the tinkerers and the decisions about which weapons to develop that they began to hold their own informal meetings, which Wilson often attended and which Schnabel nicknamed "the Sewing Circle." Wilson reveled in the decidedly unbureau-cratic spirit among these happy warriors as they talked about the next killing machine they planned to smuggle to the mujahideen: "I'd like to see the look on Ivan's face when he gets this one up his ass," they would say, laughing.

While Charlie and the tinkerers were starting to tap into the outer realms of twentieth-century technology, their freedom fighters were often stuck in another age. In a meeting with the elderly fundamentalist mujahideen leader Yunis Khalis, Wilson managed to remain respectful when the Muslim commander said he had just seen a movie with soldiers wearing thick Spanish armor. The red-bearded Afghan explained that the Russians had placed millions of mines throughout his country and his men were taking fearful losses. Could the congressman arrange to send several thousands suits of armor so his men could navigate safely through the minefields?

No, Wilson explained, because he had even better devices in the works. Sometimes Charlie could hardly believe what the tinkerers were coming up with for these medieval warriors. He could picture a bearded mujahideen on a mountaintop looking like a child flying a large toy airplane. But the tinkerers had built this model airplane with a video camera mounted on its wing so that an Afghan could guide this flying bomb right through the window of a Soviet compound from miles away. The concept was incredibly simple. It drew on the marvel of fiber optics, which allows signals to be passed in two directions simultaneously. In this case it meant that an Afghan operating the drone could see the camera's images in a monitor and use a joystick to direct the explosive load wherever he might want to send it. In deference to Wilson's commanding influence, the tinkerers would call this weapon, powered by a chain-saw motor, "the Texas Chainsaw."

The Weapons Upgrade Program, dominated by its band of free thinkers, was dramatic in more ways than one. The tinkerers turned out to be wildly productive, in large part because they weren't restrained by any of the normal bureaucratic controls. But the downside of this freedom became painfully evident early on when a freelance tinkerer on his way to Charlie's office to demonstrate a weapon he had designed blew up a Texaco gas station not far from the Capitol.

For a moment it looked as though the incident might bring down the entire operation. The man responsible was one of Vaughn Forest's protégés, Colonel Bill Dilger, a retired air force pilot with two hundred missions over Vietnam. Dilger had flown an A-10 air-to-ground-support plane after Vietnam, and he had come up with an ingenious scheme to turn the plane's GAU-8 Gatling gun (with its depleted uranium ammunition) into a portable single-shot, long-range tank destroyer that the mujahideen could carry with them on the ground. He was just one of the slew of enthusiasts who were offering ideas for doing in the Russians, and thanks to a call from Wilson, Dilger had been given a small development grant from the upgrade program.

As chance would have it, Dilger had met Charlie Schnabel and Vaughn Forest for lunch to rehearse the presentation he planned to give Wilson later that day. After several drinks the exuberant inventor had insisted on showing off his wondrous device, which was in the back of his Dodge pickup. He boasted about its lethal characteristics: its ability to fire from a mile away and penetrate a four-foot-thick concrete Russian fort or burst right through the armor of a tank. For some reason he had loaded the huge gun with live ammunition, and it appears that it inadvertently fell when he left it propped up on a pedestal in the back of his truck at a gas station.

Schnabel happened to be walking by that afternoon with a load of laundry when he heard the detonation. Dilger's demonstration had begun prematurely. The live shell had discharged and gone straight through a truck, two gas pumps, and into another car before the entire station went up in flames. Dilger, panicking, leapt into his pickup and fled the scene. The weapons manual, however, which he had just had translated into Pashtun, spilled from the back of the Dodge as he pulled away. Within minutes the local news channels were reporting frightening alerts: terrorists had just blown up a gas station at the edge of the nation's capital and terrorist literature had been found in the wreckage.

By the time Dilger came to his senses and returned to the gas station, the authorities were quite convinced that he was, in fact, a terrorist. That evening Wilson and Schnabel would watch this Weapons Upgrade grantee on the local news programs shielding his face as he left the Arlington courthouse.

A sensitive and complicated set of negotiations followed. Dilger was forced to sell his house to cover his legal bills. Although he had been utterly irresponsible, the government had no choice but to assume responsibility for the damage, since Weapons Upgrade money had gone into developing the gun. The Pentagon paid off the two wounded bystanders. Schnabel's car was shrapneled, but he claimed nothing. Needless to say, the CIA chose not to buy the weapon; miraculously, Wilson and the program managed to escape the scandal. Such minor setbacks aside, the program's return on the dollar was so high that it continues to this day, a testimony to how effective government can be without government rules and regulations.*

*In honor of the congressman's role as the founding patron, he was taken to the program's secret facility fifty miles from Washington shortly after the U.S. victory in the Gulf. He was surprised to find the facility to be little more than a huge garage, where the tinkerers were still operating, and he was deeply moved when he was ceremoniously told that he was visiting the Charles Wilson Building.

Some of the program's weapons, like the Texas Chainsaw, were never used in Afghanistan. Prototypes were put through preliminary testing in Pakistan, and there were serious plans to kamikaze one into a Soviet Il-76, the world's largest plane, when it landed at Bagram Air Base loaded with Scud missiles near the end of the Soviet occupation. But ultimately the seventh floor at Langley worried that if such a weapon was deployed, terrorists worldwide would discover how easy it is to build such delivery systems and turn them against the West.

Much later, a version of the Chainsaw did make an appearance in the Gulf War. And in that same campaign the Charlie Horse 2, a multibarrel rocket that hurls so much ordnance of such diverse and devastating nature that it can literally wipe out everything moving along a huge perimeter, was also deployed. "My little babies were at play all over the Gulf," Charlie would say, beaming with paternal pride, when he discovered how effective his tiny $10-million-a-year research-and-development program had become.

Back in the fall of 1985, Wilson listened to another of Vaughn Forest's grandiose schemes, and like a genie granting wishes, he turned to the Appropriations well to make this one come true as well. The knight of Malta explained that on his visits to the refugee camps and on treks inside the war zone he had seen that the mujahideen and their families were in desperate need of almost everything—boots, tents, sleeping blankets, medicine, canteens, winter coats, cooking utensils. You name it, they needed it, and the irony was that the U.S. military had vast stores of these very goods that they had long ago designated surplus and that were wasting away in warehouses.

Forest had looked into the law and discovered that the Pentagon could give away as much of this surplus as it liked just so long as the gift was for "humanitarian assistance." The next challenge was finding a way to transport the goods to Afghanistan, and that's where Forest came up with a truly innovative proposition. Each month, he told Wilson, U.S. Air Force reserve pilots spent hours flying huge, empty C-5A transports in continental-length circles to maintain their flight proficiency. Why not have them fill the C-5s with surplus and task the reserve pilots and navigators to put in their time flying "humanitarian-aid shipments" to Pakistan? It wouldn't cost the U.S. government much of anything.

This time Wilson called on his Foreign Operations subcommittee to insert an extra $10 million into the State Department's open budget to fund the program. Forest had appealed to Charlie to name the flights after his then little-known boss, Congressman Bill McCollum. (Such gestures are the way passionate aides like Vaughn Forest manage to win a free hand to operate in their congressman's name.)

Officially, the McCollum flights were part of an open U.S. humanitarian mission. But there was nothing remotely open about the way they operated. In fact, the Pakistanis originally balked at letting the flights in at all. Wilson used his influence with Zia and won clearance, but only with very severe restrictions. The C-5s were required to land in the middle of the night and be gone before sunrise.

For the uninitiated, the stealthlike arrival of a McCollum flight was an eerie and impressive experience, from the moment a giant C-5A cargo plane started circling the military airfield in Islamabad, waiting for darkness to fall. Landing without lights, the plane became a growing shadow as it approached the group of Pakistanis and Americans clustered by the runway. Then light suddenly poured out as the back of the plane began to open, revealing a hold half the length of a football field able to transport over a quarter million pounds of supplies. It was a scene out of *Close Encounters of the Third Kind*. The behemoth's hydraulic lifts began to hiss, and miraculously the beast knelt down, as a colossal ramp was lowered to the runway, where young American airmen supervised the unloading of what appeared to be a city's worth of sleeping bags, boots, field hospitals, medicines, uniforms, binoculars, and body bags. The entire show, from touchdown to takeoff, was run by the ISI.

It was never easy for the U.S. embassy to figure out exactly which of these American night visitors fell into the McCollum category and which might be carrying a load of SA-7s for the CIA. On more than one occasion the wrong U.S. agency would be on hand to greet and unload the plane.

By the war's end, the quantity and variety of surplus goods flown into Pakistan was breathtaking—literally tens of thousands of tons. But almost as distinctive was the way Schnabel managed to commandeer the McCollum flights as his private airline. He went to Pakistan twelve times, perhaps more than any other Washington official. Without it, he never would have become a force in his own right. A McCollum flight took two full days, with a stop in Turkey or Saudi Arabia. And each time this other Charlie took the trip, his stature with the CIA station, the ISI, the U.S. embassy, and the Afghan commanders grew.

Schnabel not only used the McCollum program to smuggle sniper sights and walkie-talkies to Pakistan; coming back he would bring Afghan rugs and fur coats for the Angels, and a constant flow of captured Red Army memorabilia for the boss and his friends. He remembers one flight when he smuggled three Kalashnikovs, two thousand rounds of ammunition, three rifle grenades, and a Tokarev pistol, all rolled up in two carpets.

Schnabel never mounted a McCollum flight without packing a surprise. One C-5 carried thousands of fruit trees, which were then moved down the Grand Trunk Highway in trucks to the North-West Frontier, to be smuggled over the border to start reforesting the scorched earth of the war zone. On another trip he brought along two of the weapons upgraders—demolition experts who trained navy SEALs in their dark arts. To a certain kind of American, there was nothing so romantic and exciting as this war against the Evil Empire, and these two were so eager to get their hands dirty helping the mujahideen kill Russians that they spent their two-week vacation with Schnabel teaching his friends how to make the most deadly pipe bombs and booby traps.

Schnabel managed to turn all of this crusading into enormous fun. The flights would take him to the Karakoram Highway, the old Silk Route he'd traveled when hunting for the great curve-horned, nearly extinct Marco Polo sheep. He also arranged to have one of his Texas patrons donate sixty black buck to replenish the dwindling herd of the same breed that the war was wiping out; somehow Schnabel managed to convince the McCollum flight authorities that such cargo fit into the broad category of humanitarian assistance.

By this time he had taken over Wilson's liaison chores with the Afghan lobby in Washington, in particular with the Committee for a Free Afghanistan and its much-loved director, Mary Spencer, who was constantly asking Wilson to help raise money to finance surgery for badly wounded Afghan fighters. Schnabel ended up spending an inordinate amount of time fund-raising to buy tickets to fly the fighters to the United States for treatment. Soaring homeward on a McCollum flight late one night, the resourceful politico was struck by how empty the huge C-5A was. It came to him all at once: if he could put the wounded mujahideen on these cavernous planes, he wouldn't have to raise any more money. Wilson was so intrigued with the idea that when he next visited Pakistan he told a group of war-weary commanders that he would soon bring a planeload of wounded freedom fighters back to the States for specialized treatment.

This was the beginning of a sometimes touching, sometimes ludicrous chapter in the war, in which Charlie Wilson caused America to open its arms to these exotic freedom fighters. At first, it all seemed quite wonderful. Joanne Herring came out of political retirement to join Charlie in welcoming the first load of wounded heroes to arrive in Houston. It was a dramatic event: wounded mujahideen in wheelchairs with their freedom hats, local Afghans cheering and noisily stamping on a Soviet flag as cameras recorded it all for the six o'clock news. And everywhere these Afghan martyrs were sent for medical care in those days, sympathetic stories about their cause would follow.

But then the problems began. For one thing, these puritanical mountain men with their fundamentalist Islamic ways, which required that proper Afghan women cover themselves from head to foot, weren't prepared for the virtual nudity of the American nurses. The mujahideen were, however, just men, so one can imagine their reaction upon seeing young blond women with much of their legs and arms and even portions of their necks and upper chests stark naked—the Devil's own temptresses reaching down to touch them. This nightmarish diplomatic problem fell upon its author, Schnabel, to deal with. In most instances he was able to smooth things over with the agitated nurses by explaining the cultural divide. But he had no idea what to say to the hospital boards once tribal war broke out in the hospital ward.

The problem began with the arrival of a rather fanatical fundamentalist from Yunis Khalis's faction, the same leader who had asked Wilson for the suits of Spanish armor. The Afghan was a large man by the name of Afridi who had a sensitive medical problem. His wife couldn't have children, and since he was a major commander and something of a mullah in his own right, he'd managed to get a McCollum flight for the two of them, to revitalize her reproductive system.

After a bit of investigation Schnabel discovered that the real problem was not with Afridi's wife. According to Schnabel, "Afridi didn't have any bullets in his gun, and he went through terrible psychological anguish." Apparently he compensated by becoming aggressive toward rival tribesmen, at one point precipitating a fight that terrified the nurses. The Afghans, being Afghans, had broken up into fundamentalist and nonfundamentalist camps, as well as dividing along tribal lines, and Schnabel received a frantic call in Washington warning of an impending slaughter.

By the time he arrived, on the day's last flight into Dallas, they were all brandishing knives. "I hear you want to kill each other," he said. "I want you to know that you're all going back on the next plane if you don't straighten out. Now give me your knives." No one moved. The veteran political fixer then tried appealing to the common cause. "Allah loves you both," he urged, getting between them. "Allah loves you, just like Allah loves you. That ought to make you feel good. He loves all of you."

It was a heartfelt effort on Schnabel's behalf, but the Afghans only glared more menacingly at one another. "They argued, got mad, thrust their forefingers out at each other," recalls Schnabel, "but after this the arguments suddenly stopped and they hugged. We all hugged. You know, right side, left side, and right side again. We hugged so much that my face got scratched up by all those beards."

Schnabel returned to Washington feeling a bit like a hero, quite convinced that he had pulled off a masterly reconciliation. But a few days later came another frantic late-night call from the hospital. They were at it again, and this time it was really serious.

It just wouldn't do to have Charlie's boys cutting one another's throats in a distinguished Texas hospital. Clearly Wilson's reputation was on the line. In fact, the whole program for the Afghan wounded was on the line. And, to a certain extent, Schnabel felt the entire war effort could be placed in jeopardy. A lesser spirit might have given up on these incorrigible tribalists, but Schnabel hadn't served as secretary of state of the Best Little Whorehouse in Texas for nothing, and as he flew west he came up with a plan.

The fundamentalists among the Afghans had been unhappy about their food. They couldn't eat the hospital fare because their religion demanded that animals be sanctified before slaughter. Schnabel seized on this as an opportunity to flatter and co-opt the leading troublemaker, Afridi, by turning him into the party's mullah. And so now Wilson's ever-resourceful aide found himself and the burly fundamentalist looking over a sea of chickens in the local processing plant. Afridi, with appropriate solemnity, was uttering the "*Allahu Akbar*" chant. That night, the mullah seemed at peace with himself over the chicken dinner.

But Afridi's troubles were deep-seated, and in no time he was back stirring the pot, telling the mujahideen that they were all entitled to two calls home per week and that his personal enemy in the next ward, Rashid, was being allowed to make calls when they were not. With that the knives came out again. Schnabel, in desperation, called Afghan's military commander in Peshawar, who warned Afridi that he was compromising the jihad. But nothing could calm this agitated Muslim, and when the McCollum flight returned him to his tribe, according to Schnabel, "they hung him by his neck with a rope and took him out of his misery."

The wounded program nevertheless proved to be stunningly effective at building goodwill in America. There were other mishaps, but the more typical experience for the hospitals and communities that took in the Afghans was the discovery of an incredibly brave and impressive people. Up until that time the press had not paid much attention to the Afghan war, but now local news stories about the noble Afghans were appearing all over the country wherever mujahideen were being placed for treatment.

The wounded program was transforming Wilson's entire office as well. Charlie had previously kept his Afghan work all to himself, not even sharing basic details. With Schnabel enlisting everyone in the effort, however, it was as if Charlie's district lines had suddenly expanded to take in a large slice of South Asia as well. Wilson's press secretary, Elaine Lang, was planting stories about the wounded program everywhere. His aides—arguably the most effective on the Hill, with a record of getting more satisfaction from the federal government on behalf of Charlie's constituents than any other congressional office—were widening their focus to taking care of Afghanistan's wounded, as well.

All of the programs that Wilson was expanding or helping launch were soon taking on lives of their own. More important, they were beginning to fit into one another as if by design, even though there had been no grand architect, other than the now sober and single-minded congressman. His office, meanwhile, was coming to resemble a zany Hollywood stage set as an unlikely procession of exotic figures began appearing with greater and greater frequency: bearded mujahideen commanders, Pakistani generals, Mossad agents from Israel, Saudi princes, Egyptian arms merchants and field marshals, CIA station chiefs, division chiefs, intelligence analysts, Russian experts, demolition experts, Pentagon weapons designers. The talk was always about war—about killing Russians in a campaign thousands of miles away, a conflict that few in America seem to know or care about. And yet had any of this congressman's liberal colleagues known what kind of plots and vicious killing devices were being dreamed up and ordered into production during these astonishing sessions, they surely would have been horrified.

The incongruity of it all struck each and every one of the visitors as they moved past the bank of tall and dramatic young Texan women in the reception area and were greeted by the beaming cowboy congressman, who acted as if he alone spoke for America when it came to Afghanistan. Down the hall and throughout the capital, his Democratic colleagues were noisily at war with the CIA—launching investigations, trying to shut down its secret wars in Central America. But in Room 2265 of the Rayburn Building, Wilson made it seem as if America and the Democratic House and just about everyone was completely behind this effort to take on the Russians, and he calmly commited Congress to producing sums of money that no president or CIA director would ever have imagined requesting.

Needless to say, it was unusual to find a Capitol Hill office dedicated almost exclusively to a CIA campaign to kill Russians in Afghanistan. And curiously, as the war unfolded, the congressman's growing role became more and more obvious, as huge heroic photographs of mujahideen commanders began going up on the wall. Soon there would be a giant picture of the congressman himself inside Afghanistan, sitting astride a white horse surrounded by fierce-looking freedom fighters and appearing as striking as a Hollywood movie star. The strange part about the goings-on here was that almost no one ever took these clues to his real role seriously. Almost everyone assumed that this Texas congressman was just playing out some little boy's fantasy. As Avrakotos would always marvel, it was just about as good a cover as he had ever seen.

CHAPTER 28

Muj on the Move

THE SILVER BULLET

From the Los Angeles airport, you get to the Stinger factory by heading east on the Santa Monica Freeway. It's about an hour's ride east
toward the mountains before you're into the other southern California, a small-town world of Taco Bells, car washes, and Sizzlers. And then
just beyond the Humane Society shelter in Rancho Cucamonga, the General Dynamics plant suddenly springs out of nowhere.

Building 600 is about as anonymous a structure as can be found anywhere in America. But in the fall of 1985, the ladies of Rancho Cucamonga
were busy inside it, assembling the silver bullet that would soon wreak
havoc on the Red Army in Afghanistan. Had any of the holy warriors seen
this facility in 1985, they would have been deeply confused, for Building
600 is truly an infidel's factory.

To begin with, almost all of the workers were women—and California women at that. Most were in their twenties or thirties, many were blond,
and more than a few favored tight jeans. They tended to be young mothers from two-income families or single mothers raising kids of their own.

Their work—connecting miniature wires, looking through micro-
scopes and large magnifiers to solder circuits—required a careful hand and
patience. Starting pay was $4.80 an hour and went as high as $11 for those
with seniority. The ladies normally pulled eight-hour shifts, but in 1985
the Stinger was considered so vital to the defense of the United States that
work in Building 600 continued around the clock.

Some areas of the plant were sealed off and temperature-controlled. It was like a hospital operating room; the women and few men dressed in white gowns and plastic caps. They worked with tiny gyroscopes and miniature motors; some of the coils they handled had only one five-thousandth of an inch clearance between parts. The whole exercise was exceedingly delicate, but miraculously what emerged at the end was a thirty-five-pound dark green tube that could be dropped on the ground, frozen, thrown in a lake, or kept around for ten years.

Even after all that abuse, the electrical engineers and rocket scientists from Building 600 insisted, their Stingers would be ready for action. They were designed for American soldiers to use, but as it turns out, they were sufficiently user-friendly to make it possible for a simple man with no technical knowledge to put the dull tube on his shoulder, get a MiG or helicopter in his sights, pull the trigger, and bring down a $20 million jet fighter or gunship.

The U.S. Army thought so highly of the Stinger in those Cold War years that it stockpiled them in Europe as fast as the ladies of Building 600 could make them. The Joint Chiefs, citing the need for as many as possible to prepare for all-out war with the Red Army in Europe, claimed that none could be spared for a CIA sideshow, and they asked Deputy Director John McMahon to block any efforts to deploy them in Afghanistan.

On the wall of the warehouse where these thirty-five-pound shoulder-launched anti-aircraft missiles were warehoused was the motto "If it flies it dies." But for the Afghans in the fall of 1985, the Stinger was still not an option the U.S. government was prepared to consider.

For Charlie Wilson, the quest for something to shoot down the Hind gunship had become a total obsession. When the CIA director, Bill Casey, told Wilson that there was no silver bullet to deal with the Hind, he was alluding to the ancient belief that certain enemies of mankind surface now and then with such power and evil that they are virtually invincible and can be stopped only by a magical weapon—a silver bullet. The Lone Ranger, the hero in the cowboy stories that Wilson and Avrakotos listened to on the radio as boys, always carried with him such magic bullets to guide into the hearts of the evil ones he was pitted against.

For all practical purposes, the Mi-24 Hind flying gunship was the superweapon of the Afghan war. In 1985, it remained the Soviets' one invincible, bloodcurdling instrument that threatened to finally rob the mujahideen of hope. Perhaps never had any soldiers enjoyed such total superior force as the men who flew the gunships against the Afghans. Descending out of the clouds they would hover just out of range of the mujahideen's machine guns. The pilots would look down on tribesmen as if they were ants. Their only question was, Which to shoot first and with what weapon? After firing a burst from a Gatling gun at a thousand rounds per minute, or laying down napalm bombs, or launching one of their 128 rockets, they knew it was just a short flight back to their comfortable barracks at Bagram, where vodka and a hearty meal awaited them. For these dark gods of the sky, flying the gunships was a routine mission of death—so far removed from the ground that they would never hear the sounds of men screaming or feel the sweat and terror and agony they were inflicting.

To be caught by a Hind was the nightmare of the Afghan freedom fighters, and it was literally Charlie Wilson's nightmare as well. The gunships were still flying into his dreams—the same leering Slav mowing down the helpless fighters. From the moment Wilson had sat by the bedside of a mujahid who had been mauled and tortured by this beast, he had become determined to find a silver bullet to bring it down.

But the Texan was not looking for supernatural intervention. He was an old gunnery officer with an almost religious faith in America's ability to come up with technological fixes that verged on magic. The issue was deciding to do it. It had taken the United States only four years to build the A-bomb once Hitler and Tojo looked as if they might win. Kennedy had been able to put a man on the moon in a decade when the Soviets seemed to be pulling ahead. So why, Wilson kept asking, couldn't the mighty United States figure out how to shoot down a helicopter?

The Stinger was no secret to Charlie or Gust. They knew it was the best mule-portable plane killer in the world. But in the fall of 1985 the CIA was adamant about not introducing an American weapon. Putting in the Stinger would have been like advertising the CIA's involvement in the war in Red Square. What possible reason did the Agency have to be running this war if not to maintain cover for U.S. involvement? And if the Agency were to hand out these instruments to the fundamentalist holy warriors, who would control them? The idea of a Khomeini loyalist shooting down a TWA flight with a General Dynamics Stinger was too much.

For Charlie Wilson, denied the weapon, the restless quest continued. He was relentless and single-minded in his conviction that there had to be a weapon to challenge the Hind. If not the Swiss Oerlikon, then the Israeli Charlie Horse. If not the Charlie Horse, then perhaps the Swedish RBS 70, which he had forced the upgraders to buy and try out. If not the Swedish weapon, then perhaps his plan to place a phosphorus charge in the 12.7mm machine-gun ammunition. Once lodged in the Hind's armor, he argued, the bullets would act as incendiary devices. He became fixated on this, and by that fall, Mohammed's Egyptians, as well as the Communist Chinese and the tinkerers, were all trying to develop this version of the silver bullet.

Even Gust Avrakotos, who had long since abandoned the idea of finding a single weapon to deal with the Hind, was so infected with Wilson's mania that one day he too went over the edge. A twisted old Agency veteran named Sam, whose son had died in the Vietnam War, told him he could build a Stinger from scratch using cannibalized parts. What Sam described was an amalgam of all the anti-aircraft missiles then in operation—the SA-7's great motor, the "beautiful fins" from the Blowpipe, the wonderful aerodynamic casings from the Redeye, and the Stinger's great warhead. The only problem, acknowledged Sam, was with the patents. "Fuck the patents. This is a covert war," Gust told him. "Let them sue us."

Mike Vickers, meanwhile, was coolly insisting that they already were assembling the equivalent of the silver bullet. No one weapon, not even the Stinger, could do it all, he argued. The secret was in the mix, in the combination of weapons that were just then being introduced into the field. As usual, he was taking the long view, explaining how their efforts were just beginning to come together and how it would be another six months or more before the weapons and training could all be introduced and begin paying off.

It was not an easy argument to make at that point, because the mujahideen seemed to be in big trouble. That fall, General Varennikov, in a bid to break the resistance, sent twenty thousand troops up to the Pakistan border to overrun the mujahideen stronghold at Khost. A *Time* magazine article reporting the loss quoted a dramatic message from the Afghan commander, Jalaluddin Haqani: "We have been without sleep for forty-eight hours. It is the biggest battle of the war. We have lost many men but we will not lose the war."

To many, it looked like a full-scale disaster, but Vickers told Gust that Khost was nothing to be alarmed about. It was like all the big battles in Vietnam. What good had it done the army to win the battle of Hamburger Hill? After tremendous casualties, the U.S. soldiers had discovered that they were king of a desolate hillside in the middle of nowhere. They had won a great victory, but then they simply left Hamburger Hill and the Vietcong moved back in.

Vickers was now seeing in Afghanistan the mirror image of what had happened to the United States in Vietnam. The Soviets were supposed to be providing support to the independent Afghan government. It was, in fact, their puppet government. The Red Army was supposedly just serving as advisers and suppliers of the Afghan army, which had been close to 100,000 strong at the beginning of the war. Now, after the tremendous infusion of Soviet arms and money, it was down to 30,000, and units were defecting en masse to the mujahideen. Once the Soviets had determined that the Afghans wouldn't fight, they'd found themselves with no choice but to take over the fighting. It had been the same for the United States. And just as in Vietnam, the Soviet infantry hadn't been organized to cope with a dedicated, cunning, and increasingly well-armed guerrilla force. To compensate, the Soviets, like the Americans before them, had grown increasingly dependent on air power.

The main reason why Vickers did not overreact to the Khost defeat, however, was because of the intelligence reports he was studying from a very different mujahideen experience with the Red Army. The ex–Green Beret didn't show emotion easily, but he was clearly ecstatic as he brought out the most recent satellite photographs to show Avrakotos how the mujahideen had just wasted an enormous armored convoy along a fifty-mile stretch of highway running from Kabul to Gardez. The incredibly sharp pictures revealed the carcasses of seventy-five smoking Soviet vehicles.

What excited this young strategist most about the ambush was that the CIA had played no role in planning it. They had not even known it was about to happen. To Vickers, that was the ultimate confirmation of the effectiveness of his new mix of weapons and training. In just a matter of months these mountain warriors had suddenly leapt into the late twentieth century—operating burst transmitters and frequency-hopping radios, coordinating different units, and using timing devices and a wide range of weapons in a carefully sequenced pattern. Looking at the satellite photographs of the wreckage, the Special Forces veteran wasn't all that sure that his old outfit could have done any better.

It wasn't the first time the mujahideen had mounted successful ambushes. The resistance had often hit convoys during Howard Hart's tour. But the Soviets assumed that anytime they moved with armor on the ground and Hinds flying shotgun, their convoys would be essentially invulnerable. Now, Vickers told Gust, it was a completely new ball game. If the muj could mount this kind of ambush regularly, it would throw the Soviets' entire Afghan strategy into a cocked hat.

It didn't take much for Gust to grasp the significance. The 40th Army's strategy called for controlling the major cities as well as maintaining invincible garrisons across the country. Early on, the Soviets had conceded the countryside to the mujahideen. But they'd assumed that from their strongholds they would always be able to move in strength with near impunity to wipe out villages and create free-fire zones and thus slowly grind down the resistance.

What Vickers saw in the Gardez-to-Kabul ambush demonstrated that the Soviets' entire Afghan strategy was vulnerable; this, he argued, was the moment to reinforce success. The Soviets were doing their best to trumpet Khost into a major public relations victory, but Vickers believed that the battle was nothing more than a predictable setback for a guerrilla force. He said the Red Army would now have little choice but to pack up and leave Khost, because if they stayed they would just become a fat target for the mass of guerrillas right across the border in Pakistan. And sure enough, the Soviets and their Afghan allies soon pulled out and the mujahideen moved back in. The supply lines from Pakistan were reestablished, and the war went on.*

The simple truth, as Vickers saw it, was that in this lone encounter the mujahideen had proved that they could become the army of technoguerrillas that he had set out to create. They were the true magical weapons in this war, and he could suddenly see with blinding clarity that they could win.

---

*No insurgency had ever enjoyed such a range of support: a country (Pakistan) completely dedicated to providing it with sanctuary, training, and arms, even sending its own soldiers along as advisers on military operations; a banker (Saudi Arabia) that provided hundreds of millions in funds with no strings attached; governments (Egypt and China) that served as arms suppliers; and the full backing of a superpower (the United States through the CIA). All of that plus various kinds of support from different Muslim movements and governments, as well as the intelligence services of England, France, Canada, Germany, Singapore, and other countries.

That fall Vickers and Avrakotos put in requisition orders for hundreds of millions of rounds of rifle and machine-gun ammunition—and that was just for one year. The only real question in Vickers's mind now was whether, for the foreseeable future, the CIA would be able and willing to continue to serve as the arsenal of the holy warriors' increasingly expensive jihad. Around the same time, Charlie Wilson appeared, almost as if on cue, with an almost ludicrous question: "Could you use another $300 million?"

"Try me," Gust said jauntily, fully realizing how strange this question would have seemed coming from anyone other than Wilson. The congressman was operating out of his subcommittee like a political alchemist, looking about for ways to magically expand Gust's budget. On this occasion he had just discovered a $300 million warfare program that the Pentagon had decided to abandon. If the money wasn't spent by the end of the fiscal year, just eight days away, the full $300 million would revert to the Treasury. Charlie told Gust he figured he could persuade the Pentagon to give it up for Afghanistan if the CIA could be convinced to ask for it.

"Reprogramming" Pentagon funds was the way Wilson had paid for all of his special gifts to Gust. But the odds against pulling off such an immense diversion of moneys into a covert program in eight days were immense—by normal standards, quite impossible. Even if anyone at the CIA could be convinced to initiate such a proposal, Gust figured, it would take a minimum of nine months just to move the idea through the Agency's bureaucracy. Everyone would be terrified about asking for such a gargantuan sum. There would have to be elaborate studies commissioned, reports written to justify the money. The White House would have to get into it. The Intelligence Committees would hold hearings. The director would have to testify before both the House and Senate watchdog committees, and then he would have to do it again before the Appropriations subcommittees.

But Charlie Wilson wasn't talking about business as usual in the covert-funding department. He was telling Gust they could push through $300 million (really $600 million with a Saudi matching grant) in eight days if Gust was willing to stop everything and make a run for it. Varennikov had launched his attack on Khost that same September, but in terms of the ultimate fate of the Afghans, the significant contest was unfolding back in Washington as Gust, Charlie, Mike, and the task force threw themselves into an almost impossible race against the clock.

The first obstacle came from an unexpected quarter. "The Pentagon started to bitch about not wanting to give up the money," recalls Wilson, "so I told the comptroller, 'If you don't like giving us the $300 million, how would you like it if we just cut $3 billion from your budget next year?' And I meant it. I told them they didn't just have to get out of the way, they had to get out of the way fast."

Once the Pentagon rolled over, the battle shifted to Congress, where eight separate committees had to be convinced that there was a compelling reason to divert such a huge sum to Langley. The entire exercise would have been impossible if Vickers, in his normal fashion, had not already worked up a budget explaining precisely how he could use this money. The supremely confident GS-11 was now saying that the optimum annual budget for this supposedly secret war was $1.2 billion.

This was an insanely large sum for a covert operation, particularly given the intense anti-CIA passion then running in Congress. The only reason Vickers and Avrakotos were even able to propose such radical budgets inside the CIA was because of Gust's boss, Near East Division Chief Bert Dunn. In the Agency, Dunn was known as Mr. Afghanistan. He had not only served in Kabul, he spoke the languages, and he was a weapons expert with a great deal of experience working with the military. All of that counted for a lot when an officer like Dunn assumed a post with the equivalent rank of a four-star general with command of an entire division of the world.

Dunn had been Clair George's deputy in the African Division. Clair George, of course, knew Avrakotos intimately and respected his talents. But he also knew how extreme and unpredictable Avrakotos could be, and their relationship was strained. In marked contrast, Dunn was the steady, honest broker, the pro. There was only so much any operations director could cope with; he had to delegate. He had to trust someone. And if Bert said it made sense to add $600 million to the Afghan budget, that was enough for Clair George and probably for John McMahon as well. In this case, even Bill Casey was actively lobbying for the money.

While the Agency stood united, Wilson was operating on the Hill as if he were Gust's mole and the CIA's one-man lobby. The tall Texan was using every opportunity—riding the elevators with other members, walking onto the floor for votes to smoke out what questions might be asked in the different committees, calling Gust to pass on suggested answers.

By this time, Wilson had become the great educator of Congress on all matters pertaining to Afghanistan. In the Defense Appropriations subcommittee, in conference with the Senate, with Tip O'Neill and the Democratic leadership, with Republican friends like Henry Hyde and archliberal allies like Dave Obey, Wilson was constantly entertaining everyone with riveting stories about what was going on in this secret James Bond world. Gust kept him informed, in part to serve as the Agency's spokesman, and Charlie made it all come alive for everyone.

He would describe the wonder of the CIA's exotic alliances—with Saudi kings and princes serving as bankers, with earnest Communist Chinese offering their weapons to shoot down Soviet Communists. He made Mohammed a living character, not just selling arms but personally ordering weapons from his frontline troops to be sent to the holy warriors. This was the one morally unambiguous crusade of our time, he would say over and over again. Everyone was secretly a part of it—the British, French, Canadian, and German intelligence services; even Singapore was doing its part.

And then he would always bring up the ugly thing that always struck a responsive chord, even if no one else would say it publicly: "This is our chance to send the Soviet young men home in body bags like they sent our boys back in body bags. Let's make this a Vietnam for the Soviets." He always concluded that they—Congress, the House, the liberal Democrats, and his fellow subcommittee members—were the patriots funding this war. Not the great anti-Communist president, not the Pentagon or the CIA or State. It was their war. In conference he might say it was the entire Congress's war. With Tip, it was the Democrats. But in the subcommittee, where it all began, he would look at his eleven colleagues and say that this was their war.

These sophisticated, cautious politicians, even the liberals, were proud men who loved representing the most powerful nation in history, and each felt some primitive chord resonate in them when Wilson talked about this good cause and their right to pay the Evil Empire back. They liked it when he talked about the exotic rule breakers they were funding. They liked it when he personalized the war and made them feel that it was theirs, too.

But Wilson was anything but charming when he met opposition. One of the staffers remembers all too well: "He would cajole, threaten, rant, and

rave like a pit-bull dog. He was way ahead of the government on everything. At markups [where the committee lays down its first budget] if a
staffer called for cuts in one of his programs he would say, 'Now that we've
heard from the Communists, let's hear from the real Americans—the
people who were voted into office.'"

Jim Van Wagenen, one of the senior defense staffers who handled
the black accounts, recalled being in Wilson's office one day when a Pentagon official said, "We can't do that." Wilson responded, "Let me have
the staff tell you how you can do it." "He didn't give a tinker's damn how
he was going to get what he wanted," remembers the staffer. "He'd say, 'It
will hurt you, or you can make it easy on yourself.'"

On day five of this eleventh-hour campaign, Gust and Charlie thought
they were on the verge of pulling off the $300 million reprogramming when
one of Charlie's friends on the House Intelligence Committee told him there
was a seven-to-seven deadlock vote and that the chairman, Lee Hamilton,
intended to let the program die. Ordinarily Charlie moved the House through
humor, charm, and by doing things for his fellow representatives. But in this
case there was no time, so he sought out his secret benefactor, Tip O'Neill,
and told the Speaker that the Democrats would be embarrassed if Hamilton
didn't back down. He didn't need to say anything more. He knew that
O'Neill, in spite of his leadership of the opposition to Reagan's Contra war,
hated to have the party accused of being unpatriotic. "Tip, do you want
the Democrats to be responsible for pulling the rug out on the mujahideen?
There ain't no nuns over there, Tip, so you don't have to worry about that,"
Wilson added, referring to O'Neill's passionately antiwar sister who was
a Maryknoll nun.

When asked about Charlie's maneuvers to outflank Hamilton, the
former Speaker acknowledged that he had intervened to get the committee's approval. "We ironed things out behind the scenes, which was custom-
ary in those days," the Speaker explained. It also helped that Charlie had
delivered for Tip in the past.

The battle now shifted to the task force, which had only a couple of
days before the fiscal year ended, at midnight on September 30. It was again
a matter of "use it or lose it," but by now Gust had become a master at
playing this game. Hilly Billy, his finance guru, had taught him that the
money does not actually have to be spent in a given year so long as it has

been obligated to be spent. But that still meant that the task force only had a few days to get $300 million worth of contracts signed.

It was almost comical, this mad dash to spend the money. Gust, Vickers, and the logistics chief, Tim Burton, had prepositioned agents all over the world—Egypt, Switzerland, Pakistan, Singapore, and China—just waiting for an okay to commit the funds. Right up until midnight on the thirtieth, the wires were burning up as the cables confirming the contracts rolled in on deadline.

In the end, Gust not only committed the $300 million but a bit more, just to be safe. Soon after, he and Casey flew off to Saudi Arabia to hit the Saudis up for their matching share. Now Vickers had $600 million to add to the already immense budget.

It had all taken place without a vote on the floor of Congress and without any public acknowledgment, but it was another turning point in the war and the Kremlin had no idea that yet another enormous escalation was in the works. Because of the way the $300 million had to be committed ahead of time but not actually spent, Vickers realized that the CIA wouldn't have to spend it all by the next fiscal year as it normally would, with the rest of its congressionally appropriated budget. He convinced Gust they could ration this money so that their budget could be maintained at about three quarters of a billion dollars for the next two years. The Saudi matching funds, however, were not subject to the same congressional regulations.

The Wilson-Avrakotos partnership had now managed to elevate the Agency's Afghan program beyond the normal budgetary control of Congress. Inexplicably, no one on the Hill—much less in the press—seemed to know about or pay any attention to this dubious achievement, in spite of the hyperactive scrutiny that Wilson's liberal colleagues were subjecting the Agency to, with questions and accusations about every possible detail of the flagging Contra operation.

It was another first, and Gust decided it was time to make some meaningful gesture to the man who had made all of this possible. Almost as a reward, or perhaps as an acknowledgment of the dominant role Wilson had come to play in this unprecedented CIA operation, Gust invited Wilson to come out to headquarters to visit his Dirty Dozen in the war room. It was all a thrill for Charlie, and to Avrakotos's surprise, when Charlie walked through the door, the task force members spontaneously stood and broke into applause. "I don't know what it did for his health, but you could see the rays of sunshine and pleasure emanate from him," remembers Avrakotos. "And you know what, it was sincere. No matter what each individual might once have thought of him, you could tell they were genuinely honored that Charlie, the great benefactor who was giving them the wherewithal to beat the shit out of the Russians, was visiting them."

The additional $600 million, on top of the already huge budget for 1986, represented such a radical increase that Avrakotos and Vickers had no choice but to prepare a detailed report, known as a memorandum of notification (MON), to alert the president to the fundamental change in the nature of the Afghan operation. It's a requirement that anytime a CIA operation leaps out of the boundaries authorized by a finding an MON must be submitted to the White House to make sure the president is still prepared to go along with it.

Once again Vickers was tasked with drafting the report, which had to begin by addressing the concern that the Agency's escalation might be on the verge of provoking a Soviet invasion of Pakistan. For months now Avrakotos had figured that if he were in command in Kabul, he never would have allowed a CIA escalation without responding in kind deep inside Pakistan. By now he would already have burned down the port of Karachi, where the CIA weapons and ordnance ships were unloading tons of explosives each week. He would have sent saboteurs to seek out and bomb the munitions dumps spread out all around Peshawar. A hillside in Islamabad next to a mosque contained enough hidden explosives to blow up the capital. These were the obvious targets. There had been terrorist bombings and assassinations but mostly in the border areas and not on a scale large enough to shake Zia's resolve. And so when this didn't happen, Gust argued that the Kremlin had already blinked and the Agency was, in effect, free to escalate at will.

That was the line of reasoning that Vickers set forth in the draft of the MON that Gust sent on to the seventh floor for review. Bill Casey, Clair George, Bob Gates (later to become DCI), and even the cautious John McMahon endorsed this call for all-out secret war—the CIA was going for broke.

The fall of 1985 witnessed something new in the CIA's six-year-old Afghan war: the national security bureaucracy suddenly discovered its significance. Charlie Wilson had started the bandwagon moving, but as in all great endeavors, others were now sensing opportunities and scrambling to jump on. It was impossible not to recognize that the Contra war was all but dead, but the president was now personally committed to the Afghan freedom fighters, and Congress was pouring unprecedented amounts into the Agency's war chest. Afghanistan no longer looked like a sideshow. In the fall of 1985, the bureaucrats from State, the Pentagon, and the NSC who gathered in Room 208 of the Old Executive Office Building were demanding the right to get in on the action.

The CIA was simply not prepared for this new crowd of enthusiasts, who arrived on the scene armed with the deepest suspicions about the Agency itself. Included in the entourage were some of the Vlasov's army advocates, as well as others who were beginning to argue that the Pentagon might be better suited to run this war. It was hard for any of the participants to appreciate how large and bold and radical the CIA's weapons and training program had already become. On one key point, however, they shared a common concern with Wilson: finding a silver bullet to shoot down the invincible helicopter gunships.

The moving force in this group was an engaging, well-born conservative intellectual named Mike Pillsbury, then serving as the Pentagon's deputy undersecretary in charge of overseeing covert programs. Pillsbury, a former Senate staffer and China expert, had been an early believer in the Afghan campaign. He'd worked for Senator Gordon Humphrey at one point but had also served as a kind of foreign policy Machiavelli for a string of other conservative senators, including Jesse Helms, Orrin Hatch, Chip Hecht, and, to a certain extent, the chairman of the Senate Intelligence Committee, Malcolm Wallop.

Repeatedly during 1985 he had tried to persuade the National Security Council to authorize the introduction of the American-made Stinger surface-to-air missile, widely acknowledged as the most effective mobile anti-aircraft weapon available. But each time Pillsbury had attempted to win approval, he'd failed. According to Pillsbury, his boss, Assistant Undersecretary of Defense Fred Ikle, had told him to give up the fight. But, undaunted, he redoubled his efforts to forge a critical alliance with Ambassador Mort Abramowitz—Secretary of State George Shultz's intelligence chief—and had brought in his own collection of aggressive, conservative senators to support his effort.

Pillsbury's conviction (and hence that of his Senate group) was that the Afghans were not being given meaningful support, such as Stingers, because overly cautious and cowardly CIA officials were blocking it. His main source for these views was Vince Cannistraro, the veteran CIA officer whom the White House had put in charge of reviewing intelligence operations, despite a recent reprimand for his role in the infamous Contra assassination manual.

But among conservative intellectuals in the Reagan administration, like Pillsbury, Cannistraro was seen as a martyr to the cause of anti-Communism. Pillsbury says that he and other members of the 208 Committee were deeply swayed by Cannistraro's description of a CIA that had lost its way: "He told us that Clair George was the enemy and that George and McMahon were stopping the Stinger. He said the only way to turn Casey around to support the Stinger was to do in McMahon." Pillsbury now suspects that Cannistraro was, in effect, running a black propaganda operation out of the White House to bury John McMahon, the official responsible for derailing his career. At a bare minimum, he managed to unleash an unprecedented public attack on McMahon. From the moment Cannistraro took Andrew Eiva aside in the Old Executive Office Building and told him that McMahon was the enemy of the mujahideen as well as the one responsible for blocking the Stinger, the desperately earnest Eiva had known what he had to do.

With the exception of Philip Agee, American critics of the CIA have generally observed certain rules of engagement. The idea of identifying an Agency official by name, accusing him of treasonous practices that cannot be verified, and mounting a political campaign to get him fired was simply unthinkable. But with Cannistraro's words ringing in Eiva's ears, that was the course of action that he and Free the Eagle adopted when they launched a massive direct mailing to get the traitor. One hundred thousand letters were sent out to Free the Eagle's archconservative supporters, seeking money to mount the campaign.

"Why does the CIA persist in failing to supply effective weapons to the Afghan Freedom Fighters?" the letters asked. "Why does the CIA choose to send weapons that are old, defective, and in some cases useless? Who's behind this massive—and deadly—blunder? To be perfectly honest, my friend . . . it's because a certain public official—namely John McMahon—is failing to carry out American policy. . . . That's why I am asking you to sign the enclosed letter addressed to White House Chief of Staff Donald Regan and then mail it to him at the White House. . . . John McMahon must change his ways or he must go!"

Donald Regan had been targeted by Free the Eagle's founder, Neil Blair, because they moved in the same conservative circles. "I would buttonhole him in person at dinners or White House receptions and ask, 'Why are you keeping a son of a bitch like McMahon over at the CIA?'" Blair was brutally frank about his methods of persuasion. "If you want to know where our strengths came from, we raised and gave funds in the primary and general elections to key Republican senators, and when the Republicans took the Senate in 1982 they took over key committees and subcommittees and they were beholden to us. And when they came to power they opened doors for us; they kicked ass for us. They'd call George Shultz and chew him out. They'd call CIA people over and hold their feet to the fire on issues like Afghanistan. And that's how our influence began and everything spread from there." At its height, the campaign became so intense that every time Regan attended a fund-raiser, someone from Free the Eagle would leap out of the crowd demanding to know when the White House was going to deal with the saboteur.

The CIA higher-ups simply didn't know what to do. One of the problems was that it was supposed to be a secret operation. As a matter of policy, agents don't discuss covert operations. And even if they had decided to try to defend themselves, the Agency wouldn't have dared advertise what it was, in fact, doing in Afghanistan. How could it possibly explain that it was now riding the tiger of militant Islam—fully committed to the single biggest and most ruthless secret war in its history? In reality, the CIA had given its liberal Democratic critics just about every conceivable ground agreement to go on the attack and to question whether such a runaway operation, gargantuan in size and ruthlessness, made sense. But not a peep had been heard from the Left.

It should be acknowledged that McMahon was in fact a voice of caution in Bill Casey's CIA—alarmed at the Contra excesses, furious at some of the Iran dealings, and always worried that the Afghan war might precipitate a Russian invasion of Pakistan. But those concerns were hardly unreasonable. What must have seemed most unfair to the deputy director was that although he'd initially insisted on banning sniper rifles and had fought the introduction of American weapons like the Stinger, he had nevertheless been a key element in making the unprecedented escalation possible. And Avrakotos, the ultimate rule breaker, always saw him as a critical ally. In late 1985 and early 1986, it was preposterous to accuse McMahon or anyone at the CIA of lacking in courage or resolve when it came to providing meaningful support to the Afghans. But McMahon had no choice but to keep silent: "Technically we weren't supposed to be supporting the Afghans at all, so there was no way I could defend myself or the Agency," he says.

Ed Juchniewicz, then number two man in the Directorate of Operations, maintains that Free the Eagle's campaign, quickly picked up by congressional conservatives like Senator Malcolm Wallop of the Intelligence Committee, ultimately contributed to McMahon's resignation. "Most of us shrugged the attacks off, but they had a tremendous impact on John. He felt they were definitely out to get him. It was a hell of a thing to happen to the deputy director of the Agency, Casey's right-hand man."*

While Eiva and Free the Eagle were moving on the low road, Pillsbury says that Cannistraro, sounding much like a cultural anthropologist explaining the conduct of an insular and paranoid tribe, was doing a good job of portraying the Agency in an equally dark light. He would invariably begin by describing McMahon as a "very nice man" who, unfortunately, had been traumatized by the intelligence scandals of the 1970s. Cannistraro explained that ever since then, McMahon had done his best to keep the Agency out of covert operations that might get them in trouble. That's why he was blocking the things that needed to be done to give the Afghans a chance. Listening to Cannistraro, Pillsbury assumed that the only thing McMahon and the Agency really cared about was making sure they didn't get in trouble.

It was in this climate that the final bureaucratic battle over the Stinger was waged. Mike Pillsbury had become so obsessed with this mission that he arranged for the entire 208 Committee, accompanied by his conservative senators, to fly to Pakistan to lobby Zia to endorse the effort to de-

---

*Eiva had a particularly close relationship with one of the extreme right-wing aides of Senator Malcolm Wallop, then the chairman of the Senate Intelligence Committee, and his influence was definitely a factor in Wallop's later public denunciation of McMahon. It was a truly terrifying time for the CIA's number two man, now a senior executive at Lockheed. Although he makes a brave effort to claim that it did not bother him so much, that is not the way his colleagues on the seventh floor remember the experience.

ploy the Stinger. Zia had always insisted on personally approving each new weapon introduced into the jihad. Six months earlier, Zia had told Senator Sam Nunn, chairman of the Armed Services Committee, that he had no objection to the Stinger. Gust had accompanied Nunn on this trip, but by then the Agency had learned that Zia often played a double game with the Americans, saying one thing and then letting his intelligence chief take a different position. This time, with a delegation of Senators present, Zia's green light had a major impact on the debate in Washington.

Soon after that trip, Pillsbury's boss, Fred Ikle, persuaded the Joint Chiefs to drop their objections, and with that the CIA lifted its opposition. Now even Secretary of State George Shultz joined the bandwagon, calling for the deployment of the Stinger as a means of quickly increasing the costs of the war to the Soviets. U.S. policy, he argued, should seek to persuade the new Communist party boss, Mikhail Gorbachev, to cut his losses and get out before Afghanistan turned into Gorbachev's war. There was a green light from the National Security Council, a signature from President Reagan, and suddenly the ladies of Building 600 were assembling Stingers for the fundamentalist followers of Allah in Afghanistan.

At least a half dozen officials claim major credit for this breakthrough, among them Pillsbury and Cannistraro. Entire books are being written about this decision, based on the assumption that the fate of the Afghan war hinged on the decision to deploy the Stinger. Ironically, neither Avrakotos nor Wilson was directly involved in this decision and claims any credit. But in truth Wilson had already fought and won this battle two years before, when he'd forced the Agency to break the color line and buy the Swiss Oerlikon. It was Charlie's Oerlikon victory that opened the door to the British Blowpipe and the American Stinger.

More important, now that the Agency was running a covert war budgeted at over three quarters of a billion dollars annually, no one could realistically argue that America's handprint, indeed its flag, was not all over this war. What Wilson had forced the Agency and the White House to acknowledge was that if the Soviets hadn't already lashed out after the introduction into the war of more than a billion dollars' worth of weapons, it seemed safe to assume that they would not be shocked to discover that one of the weapons was made in the United States.

Wilson was thrilled to learn of the Stinger decision, but not because he thought it would be decisive. At that point no one had any idea just how devastatingly effective a weapon it would prove to be. "We figured the more shit we put in there, the better," remembers Wilson. "But we had already been disappointed by the SA-7s and the Blowpipes. And when the Paks first tried out the Stingers they didn't hit anything. We thought the Stinger was just adding another component to the lethal mix we were building." From Wilson's standpoint, the best thing about the Stinger decision was that, at last, no one was pretending anymore.

According to Wilson, there still remained the question of whether Zia would be willing to deploy the Stinger, risking Soviet fury by removing this last fig leaf from the American secret war. At dinner in Islamabad that February, Charlie had taken advantage of his private session with Zia to bring up the Stinger question. By then Wilson had come to think of Zia as almost a surrogate father, and Zia looked to Charlie as if he were one of his own trusted advisers. When Zia had confided that he was still uncertain about letting the Stingers into the jihad, Wilson had suggested that he should consider an important benefit beyond the weapon's battlefield value to the mujahideen. The Stinger, he'd said, would become a symbol of the special relationship that had been forged between the United States and Pakistan. It would serve to identify the two countries as partners in the great battle against Soviet tyranny. It would further cement the bond between Zia and the Reagan administration, and in turn, Charlie had said, it would make it far easier for him to continue to increase U.S. military and economic assistance to Pakistan.

Wilson had caught Zia's attention with this argument. The military dictator had already walked Pakistan way out on a limb by turning his country into the base camp for the Afghan jihad. There would have been no jihad without Zia, but without the massive U.S. military and economic assistance that had poured into Pakistan, the dictator would never have been able to justify the sacrifices he had forced upon his country. Pakistan had become the third largest recipient of U.S. foreign aid, and year after year Charlie Wilson had been solely responsible for increasing that U.S. foreign assistance by tens of millions of dollars.

Wilson's importance to Zia and Pakistan went beyond the extra money. Every year the Appropriations subcommittee members fought a battle royal over charges that Pakistan was actively pursuing an Islamic bomb. And every year Wilson, sometimes single-handedly, beat back those accusations. The fact is, Pakistan *was* working on the bomb, as Wilson, the

CIA, and almost everyone else knew. Furthermore, it was not about to stop. The one thing all serious Pakistani politicians agreed on was the need for a nuclear deterrent. It was the only way, they believed, they could survive against a militarily superior India, which had already overrun the country in three previous wars.

Zia knew that as long as Pakistan was backing the mujahideen, Charlie Wilson would be with them, whether they had the bomb or not. As usual, the kind of negotiation that Charlie had with Zia over dinner in February would have horrified the State Department. And, as usual, it worked. That night when Wilson left Zia's residence it was with a powerful sense of accomplishment. His idea had always been to bring America fully into the battle, and now that was going to happen.

So in the spring of 1986, the ladies of Rancho Cucamonga were unknowingly tasked by their country to become the armorers of a Muslim jihad. They were piecing together the delicate circuits and parts of an innocuous-looking weapon that would soon be revered by the holy warriors of Afghanistan as the most sacred of all the instruments that Allah had placed in their hands. On each of the weapons cases given to the Afghans was a mysterious name, inscribed in black letters: GENERAL DYNAMICS. Few of the mujahideen could read English, but all of them knew that Allah writes straight with crooked lines, and whatever the words might say, the silver bullet that had been given to them was a gift from God.

CHAPTER 29

The Stinger

THE OTHER
SILVER BULLET

I t does not remotely detract from Milt Bearden to call him the luckiest station chief in the CIA's history. By most accounts he was so devilishly effective during his three years running the Afghan program that he earned the good fortune with which he began his tour. Bearden was like a man who had inherited great wealth and, instead of screwing it up, managed to build an even greater fortune.

Avrakotos had personally recruited Bearden in early 1986 to take over the Islamabad station. Ever since Howard Hart had left, the station had been run by a competent but weak personality named Bill Piekney. Gust had taken advantage of his weakness. Using Charlie's money as leverage, he had trampled on the tradition of the chief of station as king and had managed to call the shots from Langley. But by February 1986 Vickers's redesign was over and Piekney was in trouble. He had been falsely accused, but the miniscandal confused the political scene and Avrakotos seized the opportunity to push for his early departure.* As Gust saw it, you either have strength in Washington or strength in the field, and with Vickers's work completed, he figured the program needed a classic field marshal.

Milt Bearden was not the kind of man that Avrakotos was going to be able to push around, and Gust wanted it that way. Bearden was a Texan,

---

*Vickers had thought highly of Piekney and praised him to Avrakotos. He felt the station chief had done a good job making sure the Pakistanis went along with the Agency's radical escalations.

a great storyteller, a natural salesman, and a very tough customer. At the time Avrakotos approached him, he wasn't yet a legend, but he was the veteran of twenty-five years of operations who had roamed the Third World managing dictators like the Sudan's Numiery. He had won Gust's admiration when Gust had been running the station in Boston, and the two had successfully teamed up to recruit a spy. Later Avrakotos had spent an evening drinking with him in Texas. They liked each other, and when Gust found out that Bearden was languishing as deputy division chief for the Far East—an impressive enough title but filled with bureaucracy and no way back into the field for at least two years—he hit him with an offer: "I've got a job that will knock your socks off."

"If it's so great, why aren't you taking it?"

"I would if I could, but Clair won't let me have it."

"Tell me more," Milt said.

Gust amazed him with the description of the size of the program and his conviction that it was working, no matter what the press and the analysts might be saying. And then he described the role of "the crazy congressman from Texas who is behind the program. I told him he would love Charlie and Charlie him. And in fact Charlie did fall in love with Milt. They're both from Texas."

Of the many wonders Bearden discovered about the program upon arriving in Islamabad, the one he found most appealing was that the American press corps was not really asking any questions.

It remains one of the great mysteries of this entire history that virtually no one in the press—or Congress, for that matter—seemed to care that the CIA was running the biggest operation in its history: that it was supporting efforts to kill thousands of Soviets, that it was fighting a very dirty war, that it was arming tens of thousands of fanatical Muslim fundamentalists. Bearden couldn't quite figure out why no one was concerned about these facts, but he loved it. The only thing the reporters seemed to want to do was get an Afghan to take them into the war zone for an adventure tale of being with the mujahideen in the Hindu Kush.*

---

*The other kinds of public criticisms dealt with Pakistani corruption, occasionally with charges that the mujahideen were selling drugs, and finally that the CIA was refusing to give the freedom fighters the kind of weapons they needed. This latter charge was, of course, almost welcome because it provided cover for what the Agency was, in fact, doing.

Bearden recognized another stroke of good fortune: the *New York Times* man in Pakistan, Arthur Bonner, announced just as Bearden arrived that the war was, in effect, over. The headline read, "Guerrillas Are Divided and at Risk of Being Conquered." Since the *Times* is a kind of American bible insofar as political judgments are concerned, Bearden realized that there was no place for his operation to go but up. Indeed, even the following year, Dan Rather would host a CBS special report concluding that all was lost, and henceforth no reporter would be able to go in.

In fact, as Gust had told him, the tide was already turning. No doubt one of the reasons why American reporters and politicians and, indeed, the public they represented didn't pay any attention to the occasional references to how much this war was costing was because they had all learned to disregard money as being helpful in solving problems. Government wasted money. The poverty program didn't solve poverty; it might have made it worse. The billions spent in Vietnam had backfired. *Washington Post* cartoonist Herb Block loved to draw Caspar Weinberger walking around with a thousand-dollar toilet seat around his neck. And everyone knew that the CIA screwed up everything it did.

Perhaps reporters felt some sympathy toward the poor Afghans. At that time the mujahideen cause was almost universally embraced throughout the world. Journalists seemed to find it difficult to undermine the CIA's effort, which appeared to be inadequate in the first place. Whatever the underlying reason, Bearden thought it totally charming that no one was hunting him down, eager to humiliate and expose him and the giant operation he had just taken over.[*]

All of this was just the beginning for the station chief, compared to the great good fortune that began to erupt that summer. On August 26, the skies of Kabul burst into flames, and Milt, the Afghans, and even the CIA bathed in the glory. The unmistakable conclusion was that the biggest Soviet arms depot in Afghanistan had just been blown up as a result of a very skilled CIA-backed guerrilla maneuver.

---

[*]Operatives like Bearden explain that their main reason for hating the press is that whenever a reporter says anything about them, whether good or bad, true or false, it inevitably triggers a query from headquarters to respond in writing. That eats up time and, depending on the situation, results in bad feelings about the officer or at best leaves him no better off than before the interruption of his work. So the idea of being left alone to simply "kill Russians" was considered too good to be true.

Bearden, who does not shy from taking credit for his triumphs, offers a disarmingly humble explanation of the Agency's role. "This was one that Allah really did do all by himself," he says. But to properly enjoy Bearden's explanation of how this killer blow against the 40th Army was delivered, you have to imagine yourself in the presence of a master storyteller using a Texas accent and knowing that his listener is likely to think that he was personally responsible for placing the C-4 explosives in just the right spot.

"Think of an old muj," he begins. "Lucky Mohammed, I call him. He's carrying a thirty-seven-pound rocket that costs ninety-two dollars. Now, Mohammed's mule has died and he's tired. He stops at a teahouse in the mountains on the outskirts of Kabul. And when he goes to lay the rocket down, it falls into a tandoori oven and it explodes. The rocket strikes a dove over the teahouse as it takes off. This changes its trajectory. As a result the rocket goes straight down the smokestack and blows up the whole dump."

At this point Bearden's audience understands that the much-ballyhooed incident in which a 107mm rocket knocked off fifty thousand tons of ammunition was not the product of the CIA's ingenious planners. "A free-flight rocket is a free-flight rocket," explains the station chief.

Bearden now reverts back to a straight briefing, explaining that news of this hit—complete with dramatic still photographs and video—was immediately picked up and shown all around the world. Meanwhile, the press corps' favorite Afghan commander, Abdul Haq, immediately claimed credit for the hit. He began to include pictures of the explosions in his party's brochures. Bearden thought this was just fine, since he wanted to give the impression to the Soviets that everything the mujahideen did was the result of precision planning. "So what if it happened by utter chance—you turn it into a precision operation and let Abdul Haq's story stick. And shit, everyone needs a hero, so let Abdul Haq be a hero and write ballads about being the man who knocked off the 40th Army."

Actually, it wasn't all quite the piece of abstract luck that Bearden describes. By the time Lucky Mohammed launched his mortar round, the mujahideen had taken to launching rocket attacks on Kabul almost daily. These attacks were not very accurate because the Soviets had built up a defensive ring perimeter eleven miles out. On top of that, the mujahideen didn't want to risk being caught by the gunships, so they tended to fire only at night, knowing they would have time to escape before first light, when the Hinds could lift off seeking revenge.

Even so, the fact was that the mujahideen were shelling Kabul virtually every day by the time Bearden arrived on the scene. If you fire enough rockets for long enough at the same general target, one day one of them is bound to strike. And this one didn't just explode a lot of enemy ammunition; it made everyone suddenly think that the mujahideen were finally learning how to really hurt the enemy.

That, in fact, was exactly what was happening in the sealed-off indoor-training area just outside the Pakistan capital the month Bearden arrived to take up his job. There a select group of mujahideen had been tapped to learn how to fire the Stinger.

Engineer Ghaffar was one of the Afghans' most successful gunners, a member of Gulbuddin Hekmatyar's archfundamentalist Hezb-i-Islami party. Like his leader, Ghaffar is not the kind of Muslim who smiles on America. So one might wonder how the good engineer felt when he was first handed the dull green seven-foot tube. And how he felt when the red-faced Texan, the American named Milt, went with him to the border to wish him well as he walked off with his band of men.

As Ghaffar crossed the Pakistan border, moved into the tribal zone, and then began traveling across the dry and wasted landscape of southern Afghanistan, he and his men looked little different from their great-grandfathers, who had twice shattered British invasions in the nineteenth century. The green tubes they carried with them hardly seemed menacing, and if the truth were known, no one at the CIA or the ISI knew whether they would be effective. The Stinger had never yet been deployed in actual combat.

The eyes of the CIA, in the form of satellites specially detailed for the operation, were very much upon the holy warriors as they continued on their way. Only the green tubes offered an evidentiary link to their American suppliers. They carried with them a map of the target area, drawn so artfully as to resemble a quick mujahid scroll but actually derived from the subtlest of American satellite photographs. The sketch depicted the best approach and escape routes from the airfield at the Soviet garrison in Jalalabad.

This was approximately the same spot where, 144 years earlier, Dr. Brydon had struggled alone along the Kabul road, bringing the appalling news

that he was the lone survivor of the British expeditionary force that had rid-
den into Afghanistan ten months earlier to take control of Kabul. The grisly
story of Dr. Brydon and the fate of the nineteenth-century British invaders
was told over and over again with great pleasure by U.S. ambassadors and
CIA men once the Afghans started to look as if they might actually defeat
the Soviets.

Brydon had been part of the proud British Indian army that had
marched into Kabul with their fine uniforms and lethal weapons to install
their own king. After more than a year of being hacked away by snipers
and attackers, the British realized they had no choice but to withdraw. They
thought they had negotiated an agreement of safe passage for their troops
and dependents. But from the first day of retreat, the mountain men began
to take their revenge, cutting off sections of the column, destroying the
infidels one by one, as often as possible in the most horrible manner. Dr.
Brydon's good fortune is assumed to be the consequence of an old tactic
of Muslim warfare: to leave behind one man to tell the tale. And so the
doctor carried the message that would echo down through the centuries—
of the fate that awaits any future enemy of the faith.

Ghaffar stood proudly in the tradition of his Afghan ancestors. It was
about 3 P.M. on September 26, 1986, when he and his men approached the
Jalalabad airfield. They moved in closer to the landing zone than their ISI
trainers, running off the CIA target studies, had specified.

Until this moment the three-man crews that flew the Hinds had never
really known fear. Never in the six years of the war. They could kill at
will, and no one could kill back. But now, preparing to pierce that invul-
nerability, Engineer Ghaffar sighted his shouldered weapon and he and
his fellow soldiers looked out near dusk at four Hinds flying into Jalalabad.

To explain the functioning of a Stinger is demanding—just as it takes
far more time to explain how a clock works than it does to teach a person
that the clock's purpose is to tell time. Engineer Ghaffar may not have
known what electrical forces cause the Stinger's warhead to launch out of
its tube or what makes it turn and twist in the air in pursuit of its target.
That sort of detail was between the weapons designer and Allah. But he
did know that the Stinger was what the Americans call a fire-and-forget
weapon. Somehow, with its infrared sensors it could chase through the skies
seeking heat from the exhaust of the Hind's engines. For Ghaffar the task
was to lock the beast in the Stinger's sights and then pull the trigger.

There was one thing more—something the instructors had not taught the Afghans but that none ever forgot. As the missile rocketed past Ghaffar's eyes at twelve hundred miles per hour, he uttered the cry of the faithful: *"Allahu Akbar,"* God is Great.

But now the engineer's faith was put to the test, because the Stinger had misfired and three of the Hinds were closing in.

At CIA headquarters that day, Mike Vickers was nowhere to be found. He had, by then, left the CIA. For Gust Avrakotos, returning from the front a few months earlier, the news that his irreplaceable strategist had decided to quit had been traumatic.

Avrakotos was not one to become dependent on anyone, but over the course of just a year and a half, Vickers had become Gust's right hand: his tutor, his troubleshooter, his counselor on all aspects of the war. Vickers had taught Avrakotos to look at the big picture and not get caught up in the details or panic at temporary setbacks. He had created an entirely new vision of how to arm and train this mass of primitive individualists. And already they were transforming themselves into a force that could torment and defy the invincible Red Army.

It was Vickers who had taught Avrakotos that his own instincts had been right: the Afghan war was winnable. But it was also Vickers who had given Avrakotos the shock of his life by showing him that the monetary price for getting into the winning game was far, far higher than he or anyone else at the CIA could have imagined.

Early on Avrakotos decided that Vickers was a military and tactical genius and that he would let him call the military shots. As he backed his strategist's brash plan to build the largest operation the CIA had ever run, Avrakotos came to rely on an almost unreal aspect of Vickers's performance: he didn't seem to make mistakes.

In early 1985, when the program had hit a half billion a year and a nervous John McMahon had called in the Pentagon to review the strategy, the Joint Chiefs could find nothing to criticize. When the White House had become alarmed about corruption charges and had ordered a full policy review, Vickers had managed to turn the exercise on its head. He'd not only put down the corruption concerns, he'd also successfully argued that the president should abandon the old "bleeding policy" and sign off on a new U.S. policy to drive the Red Army out "by all means available."

In February 1986, as Avrakotos sat contemplating life without his strategist, he realized that he had bet the store on Vickers and he had never once been disappointed. He now realized that he loved this young man—this bright, hardworking, patriotic ethnic kid who reminded him of what he had been like when he'd first joined the Agency in the early 1960s. Vickers wasn't burdened with quite the same rough edges that Gust had brought with him from Aliquippa, but still he was an ethnic and Gust had found it rewarding to see how the kid flourished when given the right kind of assignment by the right kind of boss. It was as if he had been proving what Gust might have been able to do for the Agency and for his country had he been given the same chance that Archie Roosevelt's prep school roommate would have had.

For Avrakotos, the idea of running the Afghan program without Vickers was like being told he had to have an arm amputated. He felt almost betrayed—or perhaps abandoned.* At a time when the press was still predicting defeat and ruin, and before Vickers's new mix of weapons and training and theories had been given a chance to kick in, their guide and all-important strategist was just walking out.

Bert Dunn got into the act, offering to make sure that after the Afghan program, Mike would get an assignment to whatever overseas post he wanted. But by then Vickers had analyzed his situation and reached several surprising conclusions simultaneously, all of which told him it was time to leave.

His first conclusion was typical of this wildly confident intellect. Vickers told Gust that his work was basically done. It would be another year or two before the full impact of what they had set in motion would surface on the battlefield, but the weapons decisions had all been taken, the contracts let, the training programs developed, the logistical system and delivery schedules established. He had put it all into the task force

*Gust figured he had made Mike Vickers. No other GS-12 in the Agency had ever had such a commission. One of the reasons Avrakotos had refused Bill Casey's request that he reorganize his group into an official task force was that he knew he would have then been compelled to fill Vickers's position with a military specialist several grades above Mike.

plans, and for all practical purposes the rest of the CIA's efforts could go on automatic pilot.

It was hard for Avrakotos to accept this until Vickers began to break it down for him. While Gust had been in Pakistan, Vickers explained, he had put into place the last major element of the weapons program—the Stinger training and deployment strategy.

He was confident that the Stinger would add a lethal new dimension to the anti-aircraft mix that was already beginning to pay off. He had gone to great lengths to make sure the Afghans would be properly trained. In the past, U.S. trainers had taught the Pakistanis how to use new weapons, and the Pakistanis had then instructed the mujahideen. This time Vickers proposed that the American specialists go into the camps dressed like mujahideen to personally supervise the training.

He was also hopeful about the hunter-killer strategy he and Nick Pratt, the marine colonel in charge of training, were implementing with the Stingers. Instead of using them just to counter planes or helicopters that might attack Afghan positions, the mujahideen would be trained to take them to where they knew or suspected Soviet aircraft would be taking off or landing. The idea was to turn the tables and let the mujahideen hunt the gunships for a change. It had worked with the SA-7s and Blowpipes, but the Stinger made the strategy all the more effective.

Now that the anti-aircraft strategy was in place, Vickers insisted that his master plan, spelling out precisely how the CIA should support the Afghans for the next three years was complete. Had it been anyone else making this claim, Avrakotos might have doubted that such a thing was possible. But he knew better than to question Vickers. At times Gust felt that his young military adviser was almost inhuman. "He could be frightening when he started talking numbers," Gust says.

Avrakotos remembered his amazement when he'd first watched the way Vickers had gone about making his decisions about the number of rounds the mujahideen would need to keep their AK-47s fed, factoring in not only combat engagements but also joy shots, hoarding, and black marketeering. Including such details had become an integral part of the effortless art of Mike Vickers, allowing for life as it is on the battlefield but applying science, discipline, and accountability whenever possible. Logistics, supply lines, medical care—such things are fundamental to war but are particularly challenging in covert warfare. Every aspect of trying to support the Afghan holy warriors had its own special logistical challenge. And so all of Vickers's calculations had to take into account maneuvers with Swiss bank accounts, shadowy purchasing agents, safe houses, phony corporations, contracts, lawyers, disguised boats, fleets of trucks, trains, camels, donkeys, mules, warehouses, disguised satellite-targeting studies, and secret payments to the families of the fighters.

Almost all of this work was done from a rather dull, colorless set of offices tucked away in the peaceful woods of Langley, Virginia. That wasn't at all the kind of work Mike Vickers had envisioned doing when he'd signed on with the CIA; he'd had visions then of becoming a modern T. E. Lawrence. But Vickers was, above all, a man of modern times and new technologies and he quickly came to feel that had Lawrence spent his time with the mujahideen, he might not have made much of a difference at all.

The Agency's paramilitary cowboys were always coming upstairs, urging him and Gust to let them mount special operations in Afghanistan. In his own daydream, Vickers would head off into the Panjshir Valley to advise Massoud, the Afghan he most admired. The two men were born the same year, and he would have loved nothing more than to disappear into the mountains with the Lion of the Panjshir to trap and hunt and harass the common foe. But Vickers knew it was of no value for a few Americans to run operations in Afghanistan. The mujahideen (and, when needed, the Pakistan ISI) were doing that kind of work for themselves. The creative thing in this war was for the CIA to transform these men into technoguerrillas.

It required a certain kind of imagination to visualize from paper the army Vickers was sculpting. Vickers had read long and deep into the history of unconventional warfare. He knew he had a historic commission. He was designing a new prototype, and to him it was a work of military art. Vickers is one of those rare men who basically mark their own report cards, and in February 1986 he was able to peer into the future, see the creature he had been bringing to life, and pronounce it a full-blown success.

Upon seeing those satellite photos of the carnage on the Gardez-to-Kabul Highway, Vickers had felt great satisfaction. From then on he had little doubt that the CIA's strategy would succeed, and he told Gust this when he said he had reached his decision to leave the Agency. But in all fairness, it's highly unlikely that Mike Vickers, after almost three years in the CIA, would have suddenly decided to leave simply because he believed that the important creative contribution he had to offer was largely complete.

What happened was that Vickers had focused his analytic powers not just on the strengths and weaknesses of the mujahideen and the Red Army but on the way things worked in his own spy agency, and he hadn't liked what he'd discovered.

By the beginning of 1986 Vickers realized he was calling the shots on 57 percent of the Directorate of Operations' total budget. He had by then grown accustomed to running the biggest CIA paramilitary campaign in history. But an experience the previous month had jolted him into the realization that on paper he was not running anything. Twenty thousand people worked at CIA. It was a bureaucracy. It had its rules and its routes to power and responsibility, and as far as the official record was concerned, he was one of the lowest case officers involved. Gust might be using him to do the equivalent work of an army field commander at war, but in the official records, he was the equivalent of a captain or major. And army captains and majors don't get to do the job of a General Schwarzkopf.

The previous fall Gust and Bert Dunn had sought a promotion for Vickers. The promotion board had gone along only after Dunn had threatened to have Clair George overrule them if they refused. But the officer in charge had given Vickers the sobering news that he would have been far better off doing what ordinary junior case officers do than performing a function that could not really be recognized since he wasn't supposed to be doing it. A senior CIA official had told him earlier that it would be another ten or fifteen years, if he was lucky, before he could count on getting such responsibility again. The official told Vickers that the Afghan operation was the highlight of his own twenty-year career.

Vickers was now coming to recognize just what a strange aberration this Afghan operation had been. Nothing he had been able to do would have been possible without Gust, but Avrakotos's license to operate came from Bert Dunn, who was about to leave to become Clair George's assistant deputy director of operations. That should have strengthened Gust's position, but there was a catch. The front-runner to inherit Dunn's job was Tom Twetten, and if that happened, Vickers's all-important patron, Gust Avrakotos, was going to be seriously out of luck.

Technically, Tom Twetten, as Near East Division deputy chief, had been Avrakotos's boss for over two years. But Gust had carved out a strange and independent role, dealing with Wilson at times, with Casey at other times, and always with a direct line to Dunn. And for his own perverse reasons, Gust had chosen simply to ignore Twetten whenever possible and sometimes to taunt him for no good reason at all.

Part of it was just a personality thing. Gust used to refer to Twetten as Mr. Rogers when talking with the Dirty Dozen, and the nickname had caught on. The one thing professional spies do well is build information networks, and Twetten was a pro who'd quickly learned his nickname.

One of the ways Avrakotos and Wilson had initially developed a rapport was by telling crude jokes at Tom Twetten's expense. And for some reason Gust used to refuse to answer Twetten's calls until he had kept him waiting for at least a minute. His secretary would find it excruciating to keep Twetten on hold while Gust would read his mail until he felt he had made his point, then pick up the phone and gruffly say hello as if he had far more important and pressing business to tend to than taking a call from Tom Twetten.

All that might have mattered little had it not been for the ugly incident the month before. Oliver North had stormed out to the Agency demanding access to a Swiss bank account to deposit the proceeds from one of the Iranian arms for hostages sales. He wanted it immediately, and Twetten wanted to satisfy this important White House emissary. Gust said no.

This time Avrakotos was not acting out of some adolescent need to tweak the deputy division chief. He thought the request was asinine and dangerous, and to him it was a matter of principle to resist. So far no one had bothered the Agency about its Afghan operation. No one was demanding the same kind of conformity to the rules as they were in Central America, and Gust knew the program couldn't stand examination. All they needed was to have one scandal break and the floodgates would open.

The deputy division chief was asking him to mingle Iranian arms-for-hostages funds with the Saudi account—an account that to Gust was sacred. The Saudis were giving a fortune to the CIA with no strings attached. And that money had an added value because it didn't have to be accounted for the way congressionally appropriated moneys did.

Gust had bent over backward to make sure nothing jeopardized this Saudi connection. When the king had sent his son to Langley for a month, Avrakotos had made sure the young prince was treated like a prince of old. He'd even consulted the Agency's great expert on Saudi Arabia and Iran, George Cave, who'd advised that because of Muslim prohibitions on usury, the Agency probably should not put the money in an interest-bearing account. Gust had put the choice to the Saudis, who thanked the Agency for its sensitivity to their religion and opted for the no-interest alternative.

As far as Gust was concerned, Twetten was so eager to please Oliver North and the White House that he was prepared to jeopardize this Saudi connection. Avrakotos wasn't going to let him do it. Twetten called on a secure line to ask for the account number.

"What for? You don't have a need to know," Avrakotos answered.

"I certainly do. Call Clair."

"Fuck you—have Clair call me."

Soon after that conversation, Hilly Billy, Gust's finance man, said he was being pressured to cough up the number. "Refer the calls to me," Gust said. When Twetten called back citing the orders of the National Security Council, Avrakotos ended the exchange by saying, "Have Casey order me." Gust says he also told Twetten, "You're going to go to jail."

Twetten finally managed to get the head of finance to give him the account number.*

Even more disquieting, however, were the other things going on with Iran-Contra. For starters, Clair George had sealed off the special Iran room and denied Avrakotos access. What was known was that at least part of the Iranian account had been taken from Avrakotos. Gust's political fortunes within the Directorate of Operations were once again coming under a cloud.

It didn't help Gust one little bit that John McMahon had already resigned that February. Andy Eiva and Free the Eagle tried to claim that

---

*When news of this commingling of funds surfaced several months later, during the Iran-Contra scandal, Wilson was so worried that the entire program might founder that he cut short his worldwide junket with Sweetums to find out what happened and then to hold a press conference to help the Agency put out the fire. The scandal never spread because the money was kept in the account only overnight, and according to congressional investigators the Afghan funds were not affected.

they were responsible and that they had saved the day for the Afghans by getting rid of their one true enemy inside the Agency. But McMahon had been one of Gust's most important patrons. His had always been a voice of caution in Bill Casey's CIA. He had insisted on old-fashioned efforts to conceal the American hand, but John McMahon had also been a key friend of the program who'd ultimately backed every major escalation. Every single person in the Directorate of Operations, including Avrakotos, had stood in line to shake hands and say good-bye to the thirty-year veteran.

Ed Juchniewicz, the ADDO who had appointed Gust to his job when Clair George was out of town and who had continued to serve as an ally, was also stepping down. Something even seemed to be wrong with Bill Casey. There were rumors about his health and about investigations under way.

Vickers had the option of staying on in his current job, certainly as long as Gust remained in charge. If that didn't appeal to him, Bert Dunn was offering to get him his choice of a foreign assignment anywhere he wanted to go if he stayed for another year. But it all seemed so incredibly small-time compared to what he had become used to.

A meeting with the CIA's career management staff confirmed Mike Vickers's fears. Avrakotos and Dunn might have pushed to get him promoted to GS-12 due to the nature of his work, but it would be at least five years before he could expect to make GS-13. According to the career management officer, Vickers would have to complete two overseas tours of two years each before he would be eligible for promotion to the next level.

He thought it through again and again, and every time he projected out the likely course of a CIA career without Gust and Bert and the Afghan program it always came out dull as dishwater. It might have been different if Vickers had felt that Gust really needed him. Had he honestly believed that there was that much more to do, he might have been persuaded to stay. But by now, his calculations and projections were complete. The program's next three years were set. Any competent officer could implement it. Even the Stinger deployment had been fully prepared.

Later Gust would have to acknowledge that his young friend was right. Because so much of the money they would need to sustain their effort was already obligated for future weapons delivery, no one would be able to change the plan that Vickers had set in motion. It didn't matter how powerful the chief of station in Islamabad might be or how differently he or someone at headquarters might want to do things. They had to go along with the weapons and ammunition deliveries or else give back the money to the Treasury. That was the nature of obligated money; it didn't have to be spent that year, but once obligated, the contracts were set in cement. Almost anyone could now run Vickers's program because his hand would be at the helm for the next three years, guiding each new shipment of goods to the front.

At the time, Avrakotos did not doubt Vickers's claim that the tide was already turning and that what he and the Agency and the mujahideen had set out to do was more or less accomplished. The unmistakable signs of the chinks in the Soviet armor had surfaced. The Afghans had tasted blood, and the best weapons were just about to arrive in their hands. As far as the redesign was concerned, the program could now go on automatic pilot.

There was no great farewell. Bert spent ten minutes telling Vickers what a remarkable contribution he had made. Gust took him to dinner and offered a toast to him. And then Mike left the Agency for the Wharton business school. He had very large visions for the future and assumed that one day he would return to the realm of national security work. But for now he thought he would begin by mastering the principals of business administration.

Mike Vickers left Langley with absolutely no fanfare or recognition, but when he drove out through the main security gate at the age of thirty-two he left quite a legacy. The great Muslim army in the greatest of all modern jihads had been reconstituted because of his vision. Right now, the invincible Red Army stood confused and harassed by this angry mass of undisciplined mujahideen, who somehow seemed to be operating with a new kind of intelligence and striking power. He had told Gust that it would probably not be until 1987 that they would see the full force of their efforts surface. But the die was cast. The battle was won. It was just a matter of time.

It was now just a matter of seconds before the contest between Engineer Ghaffar and the three Soviet helicopters closing in on him was resolved. The first Stinger had given away their precise location and the gunships were now turning to finish them off. But in the words of George Patton, "Wars are fought with weapons but won by men." Ghaffar rose to the occasion and, seizing a second grip stock, and issuing the same cry to his god, he fired the second Stinger and suddenly in the sky over Jalalabad the stake finally ripped through the heart of the beast.

The Hind was suddenly just a broken toy drifting down from the sky, and from beside Ghaffar had come a second and third cry to Allah and now it was not just one, but *three* Hinds, splintered to destruction before their eyes. God was indeed great.

It was a turning point. The Stinger worked, and the Afghans would soon demonstrate an uncanny ability to use this weapon. According to the CIA's estimates, seven out of every ten times a mujahid fired a Stinger, a helicopter or airplane came down. Each MiG cost an average of $20 million or more, contrasted with $60,000 or $70,000 for each Stinger. That was the kind of Cold War return on an American dollar that the CIA loved. But the Stinger's real impact went well beyond the simple number of planes and gunships it killed.

Now Soviet combat pilots had to begin worrying about when they might be coming within range of a Stinger. As a defensive measure they began constantly dropping flares from the Hinds; it was the only way to head off a heat-seeking missile that might be shooting up into the sky looking for the plumes of their exhaust. "What we wanted was to make them pucker up their asses," Wilson had said, and that was precisely what was happening as they visibly maneuvered to keep the American warhead from flying right up into the steaming, open orifice of their once invulnerable gunship.

The mujahideen considered it a triumph just to witness the aerial acrobatics the Soviets were now putting on over Bagram each day. The pilots came in for landings high and corkscrewed down in violent maneuvers to keep the mujahideen from being able to lock in on a target. But the biggest compliment they paid the Afghans and the most useful thing for the war effort was the way the Hind pilots began flying routine missions.

The Russian journalist Alexander Prokhanov, who was intimate with the Soviet General Staff and who covered the Afghan war from the very beginning, offered this derisive sketch of the Hind pilots before and after the introduction of the Stinger: "They used to be kings of Afghan and everyone saluted them. But after the Stinger they took to flying very high to keep out of range. They had little value up there, and the ground troops began referring to the pilots as 'cosmonauts.'"

By 1987, the mujahideen, with all of their weapons, were shooting down a Soviet or Afghan army aircraft a day. And now that the gunships were no longer sweeping in low to shoot up mule and camel caravans, much more ammunition and supplies started to make its way to the fighters.

None of this happened immediately. It took time to train operators, and even then there were only so many Stingers to cover a country the size of Texas. But the hunter-killer teams had begun moving out toward all of the major airfields, and the Soviets could never know when they might be waiting for them. Close to two hundred aircraft would be brought down by Stingers in the next year.

The main impact, as Bearden reported back to Langley, was in the morale and spunkiness of the mujahideen. They now had the psychological edge. Without the Hind, the Soviets were not ten feet tall. Mohammed with his thirty-five-pound General Dynamics Stinger was now ten feet tall. It created an entirely different balance of forces when a convoy was to be attacked. As long as they had a Stinger along, the mujahideen weren't running from the gunships. In fact, they were taunting the gunships to come out and fight. They would not only sneak up on airstrips but sometimes attack a garrison with the explicit objective of luring a gunship out for the kill.

"It became a force multiplier, a juju amulet, a Saint Christopher medallion—you name it," explains Bearden. "Before, all these guys were waiting around to be martyred. Now they were walking around, heading into Dodge City on purpose looking for trouble."

At Jalalabad on September 26, after he and his fellow mujahideen had fired their Stingers, Ghaffar made sure they carefully packed each of the spent tubes onto their mules before escaping into the mountains. They had reason to make haste, but the rules of accountability for this weapon were very strict: the only way they could get another of these magical missiles was by turning in a spent one. Beyond that, there were specific plans for the one that brought down the first Hind. It was to be given to a special friend.

In Islamabad that afternoon, after Ghaffar signaled word of his triumph, Bearden held fire until the following morning, when a CIA satellite sailed over the Hindu Kush at first light and took pictures of the tangled gunships at the end of the Jalalabad runway. Minutes later a call from the Afghan task force chief went into Charlie Wilson: three Hinds have been shot down at Jalalabad. The Stinger works.

For three years, Charlie Wilson had gone to bed each night knowing that he might be woken by the gunships. The nightmare had been his confusing companion, both terrifying and energizing him. But after this call from Langley, it never returned. Once the Hinds stopped hovering over the Afghan villages and their pilots started acting like cosmonauts, the grinning Slav would never wake Charlie again.

In the coming days and weeks, as confirmation of other Hind kills came in, Wilson knew the corner had finally been turned. He had been waiting three years to bring down a Hind, and after that first call he had told his secretary that his Agency friends were on their way over to celebrate.

CHAPTER 30

Gust

THE BROWN BOMBER

It was a bittersweet moment for Gust Avrakotos when he was informed of the Stinger hits. By September 1986 he had long since grown accustomed to immediately sharing such experiences with Charlie. But he was in deepest Africa when he read the cable, no longer a part of the Afghan program. As far as he was concerned, he had been banished to a hot Siberia and he wasn't even allowed to call Charlie on the phone.

Wilson had no idea what had actually happened; only that Gust had suddenly come to see him, saying that he was being reassigned. He had introduced him to his successor, a tall Irishman whom Wilson got on with just fine. But it was all quite odd. There was no longer any answer on his friend's old phone. All Charlie could get was the explanation from Norm Gardner, the CIA liaison man, that this was standard operating procedure and that Gust was off on an important new assignment.

The truth was that Avrakotos was now in purgatory, and from the moment the Stingers brought down their first kills, others at the CIA would ride to victory on the tiger he had unleashed. Others would receive the citations and the merit pay, the awards and the speeches and, especially, the promotions to the very top. He would only have his memories and his honor to console him.

No matter how many times Avrakotos went over the events that had led to his fall from grace, there was never any question in his mind that he'd done what Oscar Lascaris Avrakotos's son had had to do. Two things were more important than anything else, his father had taught him: there was never too much that he could do for his country, and he had to feel right about himself when he looked in the mirror. He hadn't gone into the CIA to make money, nor was he there to watch out for his career. He was just a simple second-generation ethnic patriot who had fallen in love during Camelot with the idea of doing something for his country that might make a difference. That's what had made his father proud when Gust had come back from a tour in Greece not willing to tell him what kind of things he had been doing for the CIA. "That's all right, Gust, I'm proud of you," he had said. And so, in spite of the risk to his career, Gust had not had a second thought about making his move to try to stop the Agency from becoming embroiled in what everyone would come to know as Iran-Contra.

Avrakotos never told Wilson about his growing troubles with Clair George and the system. They had begun in 1985 during the great Afghan buildup and had come to a head just before he had left for Pakistan. Gust was still in charge of Iran then, so he was one of the first to be told of the White House's idea that it was time to try to cut a deal with Khomeini's Iran. Part of what triggered his distress was that the proposal to sell arms to Iran was being pushed by the same kind of zealots, including Oliver North, who had dreamed up the Vlasov's army madness.

In the beginning the Agency was only indirectly involved. The Israelis were pushing the scheme. They had convinced Bud McFarlane and North that there were moderates in Iran who could be dealt with. At that point Iran was losing its war with Iraq, and the Israelis seemed to believe that if the president allowed them to sell some of their U.S.-supplied Hawk missiles, it would not only lead to the release of the hostages but to the beginning of a new strategic alliance that would prevent the Soviets from getting a foothold in Iran.

Operatives like Avrakotos always ask the question "Who profits?" when they consider such propositions. What Avrakotos instantly concluded was that Israel stood to profit the most from an arms sale to Iran, but it was very hard for him to see what possible good could come to the United States.

Avrakotos knew too much about Israel's complicated relationship with Iran—how the Mossad had "had half of the mullahs on its payroll" before the revolution. But mainly he factored in why Israel would want to be building up Khomeini. The answer was simple: Israel's most dangerous enemy was Saddam Hussein's Iraq, and right then Iraq looked as if it might be on the verge of winning its war with Iran. What better way for Israel to do in its enemy and rebuild its alliance with Iran than to get the United States to finance it? That was enough to call into question Israel's motives, but ultimately what enraged Avrakotos was the vision that Oliver North and the others had of a group of Iranian moderates just waiting to deal honorably with the Great Satan.

Of the many things that Avrakotos felt he brought to the Agency, one of the most valuable was an intuitive understanding of the way the Old World worked. He never permitted wishful thinking to cloud what he saw as the obvious way certain nationality groups think and act. Bosnia didn't come as a surprise to Avrakotos; he had seen it all in the drunken passions of the Serbs and Croats back in Aliquippa when he used to deliver beer to their political halls. And what he knew about the Iranians was that they had been consistently "fucking" the United States ever since the Ayatollah had overthrown the man the CIA had put in power.

Avrakotos's thinking was not terribly complicated. He could not figure out any reason why he or the CIA should be engaged in the efforts that Oliver North and the NSC staff were trying to push. The stated policy of the United States was not to bargain with terrorists. Specifically, it was not to arm Iran, which was responsible for backing the men holding the U.S. hostages in Beirut and which, indirectly at least, had to be held accountable for the capture and torture of the CIA station chief William Buckley.

Avrakotos hadn't liked Buckley, but he would have risked his life to save him, and he was repelled by the idea of dealing with Iran. It wasn't just because of the principle; there was no rational justification for believing that the scheme being pushed—bribing the Iranians with Hawk missiles to win the release of the hostages—would work.

He knew who North was relying on: the Israelis and a scumball named Manucher Ghorbanifar. Avrakotos was in charge of the Iran side of the Directorate of Operations at headquarters; the government's most knowledgeable experts on Iran reported to him. They insisted that there were no moderates in power in Tehran, that Ghorbanifar was lying, that he was simply a huckster out to make money, and that the Israelis had their own reasons for pushing this scheme, which had nothing to do with U.S. interests.

On one of the Agency's polygraph tests Ghorbanifar had managed to pass only two of his fourteen questions—his name and his nationality.

At Avrakotos's direction, the Agency had put out a burn notice in 1984 saying that he was a fabricator and no one should deal with him. But in 1985 Ghorbanifar came in through the CIA's back door via the Israelis, claiming that he could win the release of Buckley and the other hostages.

Gust knew these men. They didn't do favors for the Great Satan. They might be religious zealots, but they were smart and they knew how to bring down presidents. They knew the value of hostages to the country that was causing them such misery in their war with Saddam Hussein. The only way to deal with these people was to bomb their religious shrines, or, in the case of Ghorbanifar, stick a knife in his eyeball.

As far as Avrakotos was concerned, the people advocating this policy were part of the lunatic fringe. North had been part of the Vlasov's army madness, and this was every bit as crazy. This hopelessly naive arms-for-hostages scheme—which would soon grow into an arms-for-hostages scheme with the profits going to fund the Contras—was nothing short of recklessness, and Gust mobilized to put a stop to it.

Avrakotos had no problem stretching the rules to the breaking point and no doubt violating many of them. But he was not about to have his department—the Iran branch—drawn into this madness. Beyond that, he wanted to protect the Agency from the disaster he saw in the works. He had had his troubles with Clair George, but he wanted to protect his old friend as well.

Finally, he decided to take a preemptory strike to protect himself, his division, and the Agency from any further involvement in this operation. He gathered together his best experts and told them to prepare a document explaining why the Agency should not be involved. He agreed to sign it himself and not include their names. He knew that Clair George was being pulled into North's operation, and he didn't want his subordinates to catch George's wrath.

George may not have liked anything about North's operation, but the Agency, which was offering no solution to the hostage problem, was hard put to say no to the White House's plan. As Gust saw it, there was another reason why George might retaliate against the drafters of the memo. He was a contender for John McMahon's job, and it never helps to alienate the White House.

But that was not Avrakotos's concern. In fact, he deliberately drafted the memo with the explicit purpose of making it all but impossible for

George or Casey to go forward. Among other things, the memo said that
Ghorbanifar was a crook and that the operation was illegal, or at least some
of the things the Agency was being asked to do were illegal, immoral, and
unworkable. Then he added an explosive line predicting that if the Agency
went along, it would end up with the same kind of disastrous consequences
as Watergate. He sent it off just as the CIA was being asked to move into
the operation in a big way. And he sent it in such a way that it would enter
into the official records of the Directorate of Operations.

Clair George has a highly emotive and temperamental personality.
He is capable of enormous charm as well as terrifying temper tantrums,
and Avrakotos knew him better than anyone else at the Agency. He knew
that George was a ballroom dancer who could maneuver with his wife,
Mary, much like Fred Astaire. He was an elegant choreographer, and when
he got involved in blowups it might look spontaneous to everyone else but
not to Gust. In Athens he had learned to be able to predict when George
was about to have a tantrum in front of a case officer or visiting dignitary;
there were certain histrionics he would go through for effect. Once Clair
realized that Gust had broken his code, it infuriated him. He didn't like
someone who could see through him.

Up in the DDO's office, the CIA's top spy appeared to be going truly
nuts with anger, but Avrakotos was not intimidated. He watched his old
friend as if he were at the theater, noting, however, that behind the show
there was genuine fury. He knew why. The Agency had been created
mainly by military men. Its predecessor, the OSS, had been part of the military. General William J. Donovan, the founder, had worn a uniform. Military tradition survives very much in force in the Clandestine Services,
where people call one another by their first names and don't salute, but
they always follow orders.

What Gust had done with this unsolicited report was in effect insubordination. He had now made it part of the official record and had even
gotten Bert Dunn to sign off on it. In George's eyes there was little question that the intention of the memo was to make it damn difficult for the
Agency to go along with the White House's plans.

"Casey's never going to see this," Gust remembers him shouting. "Do
you know what I think of this?" he said, as he crumpled the report Gust
had given him. "This is what I think of it," he shouted, as he pantomimed
using the papers to wipe his ass and then threw them on the floor.

Avrakotos just stared at George for a beat. "You better pick those up and save them, because they're going to save your ass one day," he said before he walked out.

Shortly after this Avrakotos was taken out of the loop on the special Iran project. A new door was brought into Gust's empire, with a cipher lock and peephole. Behind it was the Agency's new component for North's arms-for-hostages operation. George ordered Avrakotos removed from all cable traffic and denied him access to the weird room. But the key operatives, like George Cave, were Avrakotos's friends and confidants. And the case officer Gust had running the Iran branch, Jack Devine, was nervous and continued to come to him for advice. Avrakotos watched with them in disbelief as North and Bud McFarlane, the recently retired national security adviser, flew off to Tehran carrying a key-shaped cake, symbolizing an opening for new relations, and a Bible—which someone in the entourage apparently thought would flatter the followers of the Ayatollah.

As far as Avrakotos was concerned, it was now only a matter of time before something blew. Gust's three-year tour happened to come up just at that moment. Under any other circumstances he believes he would easily have been able to extend it as long as he liked. "It was the most successful program *ever* against the Russians, and I had taken a losing program and turned it into a winner." Dunn knew that Gust wanted to stay, and so did Clair George, who sent his division chief to give Avrakotos the bad news.

"You're not going to like this, and neither do I, but Clair wants you to go to Africa." Gust had listened without comment as Dunn tried to make the assignment as the number three man in the African Division sound exciting. He spoke of the Savimbi war in Angola, but Avrakotos knew he was being banished and he also knew there was nothing he could do to change George's mind. "I could have gone to Clair and pleaded my case, but I knew it would have given him sadistic pleasure to turn me down. He would have thought, Even the great Gust had to kiss my ass and let me know I was boss." Gust had defied George, and now George was going to extract his revenge.

Avrakotos lived by his instincts. He fancied that he was a good judge of when he could bluff and when he could fight and win. And perhaps for the first time in his life he felt there was really not much of anything he could do. He knew Clair George through and through. They had been to war together—in Athens, when they'd both been hunted men. Gust had protected Clair and taught him how to navigate. They had shared confidences; Gust had given George his genuine friendship, and because he knew him so well he knew that his old friend was more than prepared to make life very miserable for him.

Later Avrakotos would have reasons other than insubordination to explain why Clair might have wanted him out of the Near East Division. The Agency was walking on the very edge of illegality in its Iran-Contra involvement. If and when the scandal hit, which now appeared likely, Avrakotos was on record as having passionately warned George and the Agency become further involved. One of Congress's biggest problem in investigating the Agency is that it never knows whom to question or what to ask for. In this case, however, the official supervising the Iran branch would certainly be one of the first questioned, and if Gust were in the Africa Division in another job, someone else could explain the Agency's position.

It was painful enough to have George take his beloved program away just when it was about to turn the corner, but the DDO now struck with a second blow designed to make sure the Aliquippan was fully neutered. He had Bert Dunn pass on his order for Gust to break off all contact with Charlie Wilson.

At this point Avrakotos understood that George was running an operation. He was tying Gust's hands, robbing him of his ability to reach out in any way. Through Charlie Wilson, Gust had the ability to strike almost anywhere in Washington and George knew it. But he also knew that Wilson had become a professional friend of the Agency. He was now close to Tom Twetten, and he had strong ties to Bert Dunn as well as McMahon. If Avrakotos could be taken out of the equation, it was almost a sure thing that Wilson would continue to see the Agency as a friend and ally to support.[*]

When Dunn relayed George's order, Gust didn't complain. He didn't say much. He was being punished—banished again, really. What was sur-

---

[*]Later, the House Democratic leadership, enraged by what they learned about Iran-Contra, tried to pass a law calling for instantaneous alerts whenever a covert operation was launched. Wilson, from his Intelligence Committee slot, killed it in spite of the fact that it probably would have passed.

prising was that this man who'd never backed down from a fight and who'd been taught by his mother to seek revenge at almost any cost seemed to accept his fate without protest. He didn't even accept Wilson's offer to intervene, even though Wilson was not only on the Defense Appropriations subcommittee that doles out the Agency's funds but was now also a member of the Intelligence Committee in charge of overseeing the CIA. Wilson had more than enough leverage to back George down.

But Avrakotos concluded that he had no choice but to take this punishment "like a man." It had nothing to do with him personally. He was about to marry a young case officer he had been living with for the last year, and by then his son Gregory had joined the Agency. As Avrakotos analyzed his predicament, he was forced to conclude that Clair now had hostages, and his fiancée and Gregory would be the ones to suffer if he caused trouble.

So there was no breast beating, no cursing, no heart-to-heart talks asking for sympathy from anyone. Instead he took his successor, Jack Devine, a six-foot–six-inch Irishman from Pennsylvania, to meet Wilson.* There he told Charlie, "I've got some good news and I've got some bad news. The bad news is I'm leaving the program . . . the good news is Jack is taking it over."

That was it. After all they had gone through, that was the way Gust broke the news to Wilson. And despite Charlie's efforts to find out what was going on—to see if he could be of help—Gust chose to say that this was just the way things worked in his secret world. The time had come for him to go, and the best thing Charlie could do for him and the Afghans was to make things work for Gust's successor. The strangest part of this sad drama is that Gust was actually still living in McLean, Virginia, just a few minutes from the main gates of the CIA, though he had been ordered to tell Charlie he was in Africa. When Charlie called Gust's old number one night, the recorded message said merely that the telephone had been

---

*Devine, a veteran of the Latin American Division, was most proud of his role in the intensely controversial coup against Salvador Allende in Chile. He felt that this was one of the great accomplishments of the CIA during the Cold War. Before getting Avrakotos's job he had served as Gust's head of the Iranian task force and had been deeply involved in all of the Agency's Iran-Contra efforts. Later, after the Afghan war ended in victory, he was promoted to chief of the Latin American Division.

taken out of service. As far as Charlie knew, Gust was somewhere in Africa, and because of the rules of his tribe they could no longer talk.

Avrakotos's next move required discipline. It's human nature not to want the person who takes over your position to flourish. It doesn't make you look good. Better to see the successor sink. But the Afghan program was his pride and joy, his crowning achievement, and he managed to overcome the impulse and, instead, throw himself into the transition. He set aside a month to take Jack Devine to Egypt, Pakistan, England, China, and Saudi Arabia to meet the players, and he himself announced the changing of the guard. One of the senior officers in the program later commented that it was the best transition he had ever witnessed.

It was a horrible time for Avrakotos. The Agency had been created to contain and ultimately help defeat the Soviet empire. Of all its anti-Communist crusades, Afghanistan had clearly extracted the greatest toll on the Soviets. In time, those who followed him on the Afghan program would reap the rewards for this effort, but when he left it in the summer of 1986 the Agency's leadership had never once recognized any of his outfit's contributions. Time after time Avrakotos had gone into the CIA auditorium and listened to the director call off the names of those who had performed brilliantly. Dewey Clarridge and Alan Fiers, two of the officers who would later be indicted for their part in the Iran-Contra scandal, were repeatedly honored with the greatest awards.

Gust always sat in what he called the "section with the secretaries and the couriers." He and Mike and Larry the consigliere, and Art Alper the demolitions man, and Tim the logs chief, and Hilly Billy the finance wizard—the whole Dirty Dozen would sit and listen as the director singled out the chiefs of the Contra program for their remarkable service. It was always hard for them to figure out why anyone would reward the Central American task force for its bloated staff, its micromanagement, and its complete failure to in any way threaten the Sandinista government. About the only thing it had been able to deliver was constant scandal, and yet here were Clarridge and Fiers being handed $25,000 checks in recognition of their great service.

At times it would eat away at Avrakotos. "It's hard to work without getting any sort of recognition on the outside," he says. You don't expect to get your name in the papers. You're the little gray men. But it's different with your peer group. It matters. When we had those big ceremonies in the auditorium, Mike never got any recognition and I never did. No one on the task force ever got any. We were the fucking losers. Black sheep are used to not being recognized. We were used to getting fucked, right. But that's what motivated us . . . because we were winning and they were losing."

There was a moment that fall when Gust thought perhaps he might be taken out of purgatory. Bert Dunn called him at home to see if he would take on a special operation. For the second time in recent memory, there had been a plane disaster, this one directly involving the Central American task force chief, Alan Fiers, the man Gust had outmaneuvered to get the Afghan job.

Dunn said that there had been an incident with a plane that had gone down and they needed Gust to find out what had happened. It could not have been pleasant for a man like Alan Fiers to have Gust Avrakotos with a prosecutor's writ moving into his secret world. For reasons that could not be explained, Fiers had dispatched a resupply plane to a destination so far away that the plane's supply of gas would not allow it to make the return trip. Given this simple fact, it was not surprising that the plane had crash-landed inside Nicaragua. It was just pure luck that, unlike the Contra supply plane shot down with ex–CIA agent Eugene Hasenfus aboard, no one found out about it.

Avrakotos was tasked with looking into that one royal screwup, but it was really a metaphor for a disastrous six-year operation. As he flew down to Central America his mind flashed back to his first sense of the disaster brewing for the Agency over this divisive covert operation. It had been the same time in January when he had tried to get George to cut off the Iran madness. There had been a terrible snowstorm, and Gust was at home when Joe Fernandez, one of Alan Fiers's station chiefs, called to ask if he could come over. The man said he needed to talk.

Avrakotos liked Fernandez. He was a former cop, a good Catholic with seven children—not one of your Ivy Leaguers—and he was in trouble. Oliver North had asked him to help the Contras build an airstrip in Costa Rica at a time when Congress had made it illegal for the CIA to do anything to help the Contra army.

Fernandez had been impressed when North had dropped the president's name and perhaps overly awed when the marine lieutenant colonel had taken him for a tour of the White House and actually introduced him to the president. North had made him think that everything he asked Fernandez to do came directly from the president. But now Fernandez was being accused of breaking the law, and he was terrified that he would be fired and lose his pension, which would kick in just a few months later. Fernandez knew that Avrakotos had been close to Clair George, and he thought Gust could put in a good word for him.

Avrakotos did his best to counsel this man he identified with and in the end told him the truth as he knew it. Fernandez should not expect any kindnesses from the director of operations. And Gust was not the man to bring up his case.

As he said good-bye to Fernandez that cold winter day, Gust could almost peer into the man's fate. It was the Halloween Day Massacre all over again. Fernandez wasn't a blue blood; therefore, he was expendable. Sure enough, two months before his fiftieth birthday, Joe Fernandez was fired. At fifty he would have qualified for his pension, but now the Agency took the position that it had no responsibility for this man with the seven kids and the twenty-five years of service. The Agency wasn't there for him when the grand jury handed up the criminal indictments. His boss Alan Fiers wasn't there for him either. Gust knew that Fernandez didn't understand what was happening to him. He didn't yet understand that his beloved CIA could betray him. Gust did.

Eleven months later Avrakotos was stunned at Alan Fiers's hopeless foul-up. It was a mind-bending performance from the man who had pompously declared in front of Avrakotos and Casey that the Agency's money was being wasted in Afghanistan—that the real victory over Communism would begin in Central America and that Gust's Afghan money should be turned over to him.

Now, with the Contra war engulfed in scandal and all but bankrupt, Avrakotos urged Bert Dunn to let him take it. He had credibility on the Hill, and even his past opposition to Iran-Contra could be put to the Agency's advantage. Clair George, however, chose once again to banish Avrakotos from the limelight.

Six years later, it wasn't easy for Gust to be charitable as he watched the news accounts and spoke to his old comrades about George's ordeal. The man the press was calling America's top spy was trapped in federal court in Washington. The CIA wasn't picking up the bills for his five-count felony prosecution. His lawyer portrayed him as a patriot who had served his country ably and stressed his brave service in Athens under the threat of assassination. But Gust was watching the bottom line: Clair George's own government was now trying to put him in jail. And who should come forward during the proceedings as star witness for the prosecution but Alan Fiers.

Never before had a case officer breached the code of *omertà* and snitched on another member of the Clandestine Services. What made the betrayal so vivid was that Fiers was not moved by principle but was simply attempting to trade the old spymaster for a lighter sentence.

Gust didn't bad-mouth George during those days. He didn't like what the government was doing, and he didn't like what Fiers had done. But he felt a grim satisfaction in seeing his prophecy come true. When one of the defense team called to ask if he would testify for Clair, Avrakotos agreed. "But I told them if the prosecutor asked me anything about Iran-Contra, Clair would go to jail."

It had been painful for Avrakotos when George had lost faith and turned on him. Clair's wife, Mary, had often told Avrakotos that he had saved her husband's life in Athens. And in truth, Gust had loved this man, at some point probably admiring him more than any other colleague. But in Gust's eyes, all this had been overridden in the bitter spring of 1986 when Clair George let the Agency be marched into the Iran-Contra swamp, putting career and the goodwill of Colonel North over Agency and country alike. George had chosen to treat Gust as a saboteur. He hadn't worried about what was best for the Afghan program, and he hadn't thought about what was best for the CIA or the United States. As far as George was concerned, Gust had put him in a compromised position and now the Aliquippan could go to Africa and rot.

Gust would never again have a job at the CIA that interested him. His career was basically over—he had been done in by his old friend. It certainly didn't have to have gone that way. He could have held on to his principles and still survived if he had been willing to take a lesson from Bert Dunn.

Dunn was the good guy in Avrakotos's book—the officer who had joined with him in making Afghanistan possible. He was also a pro who had backed Gust's efforts to halt the Iran disaster. But when it became perfectly clear to the veteran officer that the tide was running against him, Dunn always managed to be out of town.

There was a standing joke at the task force that everyone needed to be on guard whenever Bert was off on a hunting or fishing trip. Those were the days when compromising decisions would be made, and Dunn knew enough not to be there to have to fall on his sword or go on record in support of something absolutely mad. To men like Dunn, that was the way a professional had to act. Some would even say that by his refusal to accept the larger realities, Avrakotos was demonstrating that he just didn't have the makings of a truly first-class officer. If he couldn't smile and get out of the way in his own bureaucracy, how could he be trusted to con the enemy?

As Gust slipped into the obscurity of the Africa Division, sealed off from Charlie and from the growing successes of the Afghan program, he had little to carry with him by way of recognition for a job well done. Normally, in such situations, a party would be given to help cushion the blow of what was, after all, a dismissal under a cloud of sorts. Normally these affairs don't mean much. But the one Bert Dunn organized for Gust was just right. There were no official speeches, no gold watches, and certainly no Agency medals like the many Howard Hart had left with.

But close to five hundred CIA men and women came to say goodbye. The war room and the rest of Gust's domain had been sanitized for the occasion. Bert had unleashed the logs men to smuggle whiskey, gin, beer, and wine into the supposedly dry Agency offices. At the entrance, the big Russian solider in his frightening suit now held a Stolichnaya bottle in one hand and a Budweiser in the other. Red, white, and blue bunting was hung everywhere, framing the huge posters of the mujahideen and the large green banners with *Allahu Akbar* written in both Arabic and English.

There was much good cheer, even for Gust's people, who knew how complicated the moment was for their boss. The Dirty Dozen had commissioned a tribute of their own—a framed photograph showing a group of heroic mujahideen firing off mortars. The photo interpreters and the people who concoct fake pictures had then superimposed a picture of a Greek *efzone*, a World War II warrior, leaping into the air. In the old days Greek warriors wore dresses, body stockings, and funny shoes with tassels. And that's what this warrior, who had Gust's face superimposed onto his body, was wearing. Nothing could have delighted the departing chief of South Asia Operations more. "Here was this wild *efzone* jumping up in the air in joy as the mortars were going off," Gust says. "It was just great."

That was it from the traditional CIA. Nothing more. But one organization at the Agency had decided that Gust deserved their official recognition. Esther Dean, an effusive 325-pound black woman from Cleveland, was acting that day as if she were giving the party when Bill Casey came down from the eighth floor to pay his respects. He and Bert Dunn were moving about talking to members of the task force when Esther and Gust began laughing about some secret memory.

Esther had a special feeling about Gust. Two years before, she had been his secretary when everything had fallen apart for her. In exasperation one day Gust made a racist remark: "Esther, I know you're a fat nigger and can't talk well, but what's wrong with you?" She explained that she had gotten herself $34,000 in debt on credit card charges and that she was about to lose everything unless a senior-grade officer would sign off on a credit union loan. Would he?

"On one condition," Gust told her. With that he asked for her wallet, took out her ten credit cards, and sliced them all up. He then had her agree to a new cash regime, signed the loan, and nursed Esther back to financial health.

"Are you going to miss Mr. Avrakotos?" Casey asked Esther, not really expecting anything but a polite response.

"Oh, Mr. Casey, I never thought I'd say this, but I'm going to miss him. I'm going to miss him a whole bunch. I never thought I'd say this, because he used to call me 'you black nigger' four or five times a day, but he's good, he's a good boss." With that, big Esther Dean gave Gust Avrakotos a great hug and a kiss on the cheek.

Casey had no way of knowing what to make of this strange spectacle. The director, who was preoccupied with the unraveling Iran-Contra affair, and who was about to be diagnosed with a brain tumor, didn't mention the Afghan program. But Gust appreciated his stopping by. "See you around" was all Casey said as he left.

That was when Linda, another big, spirited black woman, tapped Gust on the shoulder and told him that she and some of the other blacks would like him to come downstairs. They wanted to recognize him.

Downstairs, the blacks of the CIA's Directorate of Operations were waiting for him in the records room. He knew most of them surprisingly well. In fact, he had become something of a legend with these people who manned the underbelly of the Agency. They were part of Gust's intelligence network, part of what had made it possible for him to wander the halls for almost seven months and face down Clair George in that first test of wills.

Gust also viewed them differently from all of his colleagues. Who knows what's going on in the director's office? The secretary knows. And what do you do if there is a message too sensitive to send over the wires? You give it to the couriers? They're the GS-1s and 2s and 3s and most of them were all staring at Gust right there in the records room.

"I had gone to bat for many of them," Gust recalls. The word among them was if you're having trouble and being picked on, go see Gust. He had given many of them practical counsel, just as he had with Esther Dean. When they were getting a raw deal, if he knew their supervisor he would put in a word for them. He ate lunch with them, he talked dirty to them, and mainly he gave them a fair shake.

Thea was the spokesperson for the gathering. The CIA's blacks had an award they gave each year to one of their own who had distinguished him- or herself. It was called the Brown Bomber Award, and it had never gone to a white guy.

A good-looking black woman with a beautiful smile, Thea was radiant as she offered Gust the highest possible praise: "We want to give this award to the blackest motherfucker of us all."

That is the only formal citation from the CIA that Gust Lascaris Avrakotos ever got. It sits by his desk with the picture of the mad Greek *efzone* leaping with joy into the air. There is also a picture of Charlie Wilson on a white horse. But for the professional underdog from Aliquippa, for the conqueror of the Evil Empire, the Brown Bomber Award has a special place of honor.

CHAPTER 31

"IT'S MY WAR, GODDAMN IT"

N othing illustrates the power that Charlie Wilson was able to wield on behalf of the Afghans better than the story of a humiliating incident he was subjected to on one of his trips to Pakistan with Sweetums.

The incident took place in 1986 at the end of a particularly satisfying tour in which he had been received as a conquering hero everywhere he went. As usual, he had flown into the Northwest Frontier Province to give blood at the IRC hospital in Peshawar and then meet with the mujahideen commanders who had gathered specially to see him. As usual, the Defense Intelligence Agency plane attached to the U.S. embassy in Islamabad, was assigned to fly him and his party to their various stops in Pakistan. At the end of the day the plane was scheduled to fly him and Sweetums to Lahore for an official dinner being held in his honor.

Moments before boarding the plane, everything collapsed. It turns out that the embassy's military attaché, an air force colonel, had taken it upon himself to scrutinize the rules, and discovered that civilians other than wives or relatives of congressmen were not cleared to fly on his military spy plane.

The colonel had done his duty as he saw fit and, without hesitation, ordered the pilots not to let Sweetums come aboard. It didn't matter to him that on previous trips Wilson's friends—Snowflake, Joanne, and even his belly dancer—had all flown on that very same plane. Nor did it concern the colonel that the congressman and his companion were scheduled to be the guests of honor in Lahore that evening, nor was it of interest to him that no commercial flights were available until the following day.

The colonel, it appears, had no idea that he might be picking a dangerous fight. He seemed to believe that Wilson was little more than a braggart without any leverage. The Texan was, after all, an elected official, and the colonel had caught him red-handed, trying to appropriate one of the nation's precious spy planes to ferry a beauty queen about the North-West Frontier province. It was, as the attaché saw it, a clear abuse of power and hardly an issue Wilson would like to risk surfacing in public.

One of Wilson's escorts had tried to warn the colonel that he was making a mistake. "If I were you, I'd interpret those regulations loosely or else you guys are going to lose your airplane." But now it was too late. The colonel had phrased his cable to Washington in such a way that the Pentagon had no choice but to deny permission for Sweetums.

It must be remembered that Charlie Wilson was a senior member of the subcommittee responsible for the Pentagon's annual budget. He had been around for over two decades and knew well how quickly the Pentagon was prepared to bend the rules to accommodate their congressional patrons. This colonel was trying to say that his precious $200,000 plane was too good for Sweetums and that she would have to wait a day in Peshawar until the next scheduled flight left. Wilson says that for the first time in twenty years, he lost his temper: "This was first time I actually swore and shouted. I just went bug-fuck."

At one point Wilson found himself screaming at the tough old U.S. ambassador, who was clearly trapped in a no-win situation. In exasperation, the congressman finally ordered the colonel to get the president of Pakistan on the phone.

Wilson had never asked Zia for a personal favor before, and the Muslim dictator immediately understood the gravity of the situation. Without hesitating, he told his friend Charlie that his personal plane was on its way to rescue Sweetums. That afternoon, as Wilson prepared to board Pakistan's equivalent of Air Force One, he told the offending officer: "This is not the end of this story, Colonel."

Just to make sure the colonel understood whom he had a picked a fight with, Wilson issued a humiliating order that the colonel was not in a position to refuse. The DIA plane was not to return to Islamabad, where the colonel and the pilots had been counting on attending an office picnic. Instead the plane was to fly parallel to Zia's plane, with Charlie's personal baggage and poor Colonel Rooney (Wilson's military aide) along as the official cargo. Stepping aboard the plane an awkward Rooney had told the furious pilots: "I'm just a little pissant on the crossroads of life. I had nothing to do with it." That didn't calm them down a bit. Enraged, they proceeded to warn Rooney that the Defense Department was going to get Wilson for this and that perhaps they wouldn't allow Sweetums's bag to be put on the plane. Rooney replied, "Don't even touch that one. It's absolutely foolish."

Zia had congratulated Charlie on his chivalry but Wilson was now hellbent on revenge. Back in Washington he addressed his Defense Appropriations colleagues in the room under the great dome: "Gentlemen, the honor of the coequal branch of government has been challenged. They have insulted the committee on Appropriations, they have insulted me, and they have insulted my true love, Sweetums. I want you to give me revenge."

Everyone on Appropriations understood that this was a petty, if not reckless, act of revenge that Wilson was calling for. But they also knew that it was something they had to do for their colleague. It was a professional courtesy, in effect. And lurking behind their vote to support their colleague was the recognition that it was not healthy to allow a lowly colonel to insult a member of Defense Appropriations.

For all these reasons the subcommittee moved to remind the Pentagon once and for all how to regard a member of Defense Appropriations: "Them that has the gold makes the rules." Ultimately, the whole sorry story surfaced in a front-page exposé in the *New York Times*. It turns out that by order of Congress, the offending DIA plane, along with one more for good measure, was permanently removed from the military spy agency's fleet. And, just to make sure the Pentagon got the message loud and clear, the two planes were reassigned to duty with the Texas Air National Guard.

Typically, Wilson seemed not in the least concerned about the resulting scandal and controversy. For a time, it seemed to overshadow all of the positive things Wilson had achieved in the region. In spite of that he wore the attention almost proudly. For over three years Wilson had been the real magic bullet of the Afghan War, all but invisibly hurtling through the entrails of the U.S. government. For the first time he had publicly demonstrated his willingness to bite, and he knew the story would only add to the legend that it was suicidal for any American bureaucrat to get in the way of Congressman Charlie Wilson and his Afghan obsession. For Pakistan's President Zia it had been a pleasure to be able to help his friend and the great patron of the jihad. But on Wilson's next trip to Pakistan, when once again he became troublesome to another military man, Zia found himself in a very different frame of mind, determined to do everything in his power to prevent his all-important ally from getting his way.

Brigadier Mohammad Yousaf went to bed on the night of November 15, 1986, with the certain belief that his work would earn him a place in Paradise. The big, barrel-chested, bug-eyed fundamentalist was then in his second year directing the ISI's supersecret Afghan cell. The excitement that swept over the CIA's Afghan task force once the tide began to turn that year was nothing compared to how this Muslim warrior felt. He was in operational command of the biggest and greatest of all modern jihads, and for the first time, he was convinced the mujahideen were going to win.

Brigadier Yousaf distributed the weapons, ruled on special operations, coordinated training, controlled the C-4 explosives and the Stingers, and passed on the satellite targeting studies. His officers were in radio contact with mujahideen commanders throughout the war zone. He even had teams of ISI soldiers, dressed as Afghans, operating alongside the mujahideen or conducting their own special operations.

Yousaf was at the very heart of everything, and more often than not he had been a royal pain in the ass for the Americans. The brigadier had not forgotten the insult of being taken blindfolded to the Agency sabotage school. He had responded with his own petty revenge: only occasionally allowing the CIA to visit the training camps. It was a great concession when he let in the Near East Division deputy chief, Tom Twetten— but only at night and in the clothes of the mujahideen. Yousaf even found it a badge of honor that after twenty-two requests he still had not given his home phone number to the two station chiefs who had asked for it. The CIA was a necessary evil, but he was quite determined to keep it at arm's length.

Yousaf was certain that the Americans had recruited spies in his own intelligence service. Many of his men trained in the United States, and he wondered what kind of bribes they'd been offered. His sense of the CIA's power was no doubt so exaggerated as to be detached from reality, but it was a perception shared by many of his countrymen. He was quite convinced that the Americans hated and feared his religion and that the Agency was helping Pakistan only because of its Cold War with the Communists. He was sure that the same CIA spies helping him with the mujahideen were at the same time trying to halt his country's efforts to build an Islamic bomb. He knew that they feared such Afghan fundamentalists as Gulbuddin Hekmatyar, his favorite commander, whom the ISI had had on its payroll for more than a decade. The fundamentalist mujahideen were the ones he and his intelligence chief had always favored, and he was offended when the U.S. embassy and the press corps called on the ISI to cut off these true warriors of Allah and turn the jihad over to the washed-out Muslims. This he refused to do.

It was an awesome responsibility that had been placed on his shoulders, and in the 1407th year of the Islamic calendar, Brigadier Yousaf considered it a unique privilege as a Pakistan army officer to stand astride this greatest of all modern jihads. So he went to sleep on November 15 filled with pride, a man who bowed only to Allah. In truth, his loyalties ran almost as deeply to his imperial ISI chief, General Akhtar Abdul Rahman, who woke him up in the middle of that night with an urgent directive from the president himself, General Zia ul-Haq.

An American official with a woman is trying to enter Afghanistan from Pakistan, Akhtar said. The brigadier must locate this man and stop him; it was of the utmost importance. Akhtar sternly added a proviso: Yousaf must not reveal that the ISI or the Pakistani government was involved.

The American official headed to Afghanistan, was of course, Charlie Wilson, but Zia had it wrong about the woman's destination. Sweetums had no intention of going into the war zone. It was not her idea of a good time. In fact, she was quite put out about having to sit around Peshawar while her man went off on his rite of passage. But Wilson had sweet-talked her into another one of those junkets that she would never forget, and Annelise had somehow allowed her hopes to rise again.

Though the incident with the DIA plane was still fresh in his mind, Wilson was truly pushing the envelope with this latest junket. He envisioned the trip as the ultimate romantic vacation: the Amalfi Coast; the baby elephant orphanage in Sri Lanka; the shopping wonders of Hong Kong; the exotic, teeming streets of Shanghai; and the Great Wall of China—all of this leading up to Sweetums's lifelong fantasy, a week in Tahiti. The monthlong trip began in Rome, where Bertie van Storer, the Oerlikon representative, would entertain them; there was a stopover in London; and then on to Pakistan for a closer look at the war. He had arranged for his favorite Pentagon traveling aide, Colonel Rooney, to come along to handle logistics, including him even in the nonbusiness-related legs of the trip that Wilson was paying for out of his own pocket. It was not only pleasant having the personable colonel along to share the sights; it was necessary in order to justify having the main portions of the junket picked up by Defense Appropriations. When they reached Pakistan, Sweetums was perplexed to learn that Charlie intended to leave her alone in the hotel while he disappeared into Afghanistan. He explained that he had developed a deep need to experience combat with the mujahideen.

Given Charlie's relationship to the program, you might think he would have tried to keep this CIA covert operation a secret. But he was now becoming just a bit flaky, and he had brought along a Texas reporter to chronicle his trip into the war zone.

He was offering the young man the experience of his life. But the morning before they were scheduled to go in, they went to the Khyber Pass, where the journalist looked down with horror at the sight of a Red Army tank brigade in ferocious action.

Wilson experienced some butterflies himself, but the reporter had a wife and two children at home; he didn't want to be a war correspondent. Ever the gentleman, Charlie gracefully let him bow out. Actually, it only made him feel all the more heroic when he embraced Sweetums in his Afghan robes and strode out onto the street to meet the mujahideen who had come to take him off to fight the Russians. She said she would be waiting for him at the American consulate when he returned.

In a four-wheel-drive, surrounded by bearded Afghans carrying AK-47s, with an extra one set aside for him, Charlie felt that he had now crossed the Rubicon. He had, however, made one major mistake. Over dinner the night before in Islamabad, he had told Zia of his plans. The Pakistani president, famous for his perpetual smile, had kept his poker face. He had even told Charlie that he envied him. *Inshallah,* God willing, they would meet soon to discuss Wilson's great adventure. But even as Wilson was passing through the gate of Zia's residence, the president, who ruled his country by martial law, had ordered his intelligence chief, General Akhtar, to stop Wilson. They couldn't afford to lose this man. He was too important to Pakistan.

This was not the kind of mission Brigadier Yousaf relished, but he set off for Peshawar at 4:30 in the morning, and by 6:30 he had mobilized all of the ISI assets throughout the frontier city. Yousaf had spies everywhere in Peshawar. The ISI had bugged Dean's Hotel, where Crandall had held his Cross Border meetings; they had waiters, hotel managers, and telephone operators throughout the city. Most important, the ISI had eyes and ears everywhere in the vast Afghan population—particularly in the headquarters and in compounds where the commanders and leaders of the different political parties lived with their armed followers.

It was only a matter of hours before Yousaf's men spotted a tall foreigner entering Abdul Haq's walled compound. Haq was the natural choice for Wilson's guide to the jihad. He was probably the U.S. reporters' favorite mujahideen commander, a brave, young fundamentalist with enormous charm.

Yousaf controlled Haq's right to be in Peshawar, not to mention his access to CIA weapons; nevertheless, Haq refused to consider his directive. The Afghan said he had no choice but to take the congressman in, no matter what Zia or the brigadier or anyone else said. Yousaf had just run head-on into the Pashtun's ancient code of honor, hospitality, and revenge. Haq explained that he had already given his word; Wilson was now under his protection, and by his code he must fulfill his commitment to take the American into the war zone and return him safely.

So in spite of Brigadier Yousaf and the iron control of the ISI, later that day the congressman was speeding through the tribal zone in Haq's four-wheel-drive, one of those vehicles that Larry Crandall's Cross Border program had given to the commander to spread goodwill. Dressed like a holy warrior, Wilson was preparing himself emotionally for whatever they might run into, when a jeep coming from the border signaled them to pull over. The driver reported heavy fighting between two tribes up ahead. Wilson's driver got a very worried look on his long Afghan face when a Pakistani tribal guard ran up to them with news that the entire road was caught up in the fighting.

With the sound of intense gunfire and explosions close by, the driver turned the vehicle around and headed back to Peshawar. Apologizing profusely, he explained that his orders had been to take Wilson into Afghanistan, to protect him there, and to bring him back safely. He would not be forgiven if he led Commander Haq's guest to his death before they had even crossed the border.

It didn't take Wilson long to figure out what had happened, and by the time he burst into the Peshawar house of Kurt Loebeck, the CBS stringer who had introduced him to Abdul Haq, Wilson was beside himself with rage. He knew he had been taken. Loebeck listened with amazement as the congressman got General Akhtar on the phone and lit into the intelligence chief: "It's my war, goddamn it. I'm paying for it, and I'm damn well going to see it."

Under normal circumstances, Akhtar did not take well to outsiders lecturing him. In his shadowy ISI empire, his word was law. But Akhtar had absolutely no interest in provoking Wilson's fury. Nor did Foreign Minister Yaqub Khan, who remembers this confrontation as a matter of the gravest national concern. "We had to ask, What if he were killed on such a trip. . . . For Charlie it was a romantic adventure. For us it was a horrible position without any possible benefit."

Ultimately it was Zia's dilemma, so the call was passed on to him. Zia had many reasons for not wanting Charlie to go into Afghanistan, not the least of which was that it violated his strict rule against any U.S. government officials entering the war from his country. He did not even acknowledge that Pakistan was helping the mujahideen, much less that it was working with the CIA, and here Wilson had been planning to take a reporter in with him. But the real reason went far deeper than that, and Zia could not spell it out.

Pakistan was then facing a historic threat to its own survival, and strange as it may seem, Zia saw Charlie Wilson as an indispensable part of the country's national defense. That year that India had mobilized again, and Zia and his staff had been forced to contemplate Pakistan's chances if war should break out. The picture was incredibly grim. For one thing, India had the bomb. It had exploded a nuclear device back in 1974, and no one doubted that it had the ability to wipe out Pakistan. Beyond that, India's huge army had already defeated Pakistan in three wars. To add to Zia's paranoia, he considered India a virtual client state of the Soviet Union. With Hinds now being shot out of the sky by ISI-delivered Stingers, and Black Tulips flying even more dead soldiers back to Russia, no one needed to point out to Zia that this was a moment when Moscow might well encourage India to go for broke.

The great unpredictable element in this entire mix, the unknown that threatened to unravel absolutely everything for Zia, was the matter of the bomb—or, rather, the intense national effort then being mounted in Pakistan to build an Islamic bomb. If the American Congress were confronted with evidence that Pakistan was on the verge of having a bomb, there was no question it would trigger an immediate move to cut off all foreign aid.

It was all quite unfair from Zia's point of view. No one in the Reagan administration had any illusions about Pakistan's bomb-building program. Even Zia's democratic predecessor, Zulfikar Ali Bhutto, had been working on the bomb. Nor would it have escaped any of the Reaganites that once Pakistan had a bomb, it would use American F-16s if it ever wanted to drop one on India.

The dirty little secret of the Afghan war was that Zia had extracted a concession early on from Reagan: Pakistan would work with the CIA against the Soviets in Afghanistan, and in return the United States would not only provide massive aid but would agree to look the other way on the question of the bomb.

Zia understood, however, that if he were ever caught red-handed, the White House could not protect him from the wrath of Congress. That was where Wilson, with his seat on the Appropriations subcommittee, came in. By now Zia knew how critical this committee was to Pakistan's fate. There had already been one close call in 1985, when a Pakistani agent had been caught in the United States trying to buy Kryton high-speed triggers, the switching devices used to fire nuclear weapons. Steve Solarz, the powerful chairman of the South Asia subcommittee, had immediately called for hearings and it looked as if he were going to lead a battle to cut off the dictator. The CIA's seventh floor was alarmed at what might happen to the Afghan program in the event of a cutoff. Ironically, the CIA had helped to bring on the crisis; part of its job was to expose Zia's bomb-building efforts,* and every station chief in Islamabad had given this a high priority.

At one point, Vernon Walters, a former CIA deputy director and Reagan's U.N. ambassador, flew to Pakistan to warn Zia of the dangers for everyone if he persisted in this effort. Zia had looked him straight in the eye and told him the reports were not accurate. Pakistan was not building the bomb. It was as clear and sincere a statement as any head of state could make. When later asked about another outright misrepresentation he had once made, Zia explained to two high-level State Department officials, "It is permissible to lie for Islam."

But in 1985 there was no way for Zia to explain away the Kryton triggers. Nor was it possible to imagine a more perfect issue for Steve Solarz to pursue than the bashing of Zia ul-Haq. What could be more popular for a leading Jewish congressman from New York than to kill an Islamic bomb?

The White House had done what it could to convince Congress not to cut off Pakistan. Wilson understood that this was a battle that could not be won with debating points; reportedly, he went to Solarz armed with certain classified intelligence about India's nuclear program. He is said to have suggested that India might be more exposed than Pakistan when it came to the issue of the bomb.

---

*Avrakotos says that Wilson had complained in 1985 when he'd discovered that the Agency had managed to penetrate Pakistan's nuclear program and was reporting on its progress toward completing the bomb. Gust explained that they had no choice; it was part of their mandate, and they could not pull their punches. However, Avrakotos also says that he pulled off one of his black-clothes performances at a private briefing for Solarz, the subcommittee chairman. "I came late, dressed in black, and told him I had been at a funeral for a member of my family," Gust said; he knew this would be disarming. He says that Solarz had been impressed to find that the Agency was so effective in its reporting and somewhat dismayed by Avrakotos's suggestion that Congress might find itself in a terrible position if it cut off aid and Zia changed the rules of the Afghan campaign. He might, for example, begin charging the United States for the services of the ISI and all of the logistical facilities or he might simply cut off the program. If he charged the CIA, the bill would be many billions of dollars a year. Avrakotos also suggests that Wilson may have communicated to Zia the need to back off because in the middle of this, the agents monitoring the Pakistani nuclear operation were able to report that they had been given a signal that Pakistan was halting a critical part of the program.

The crisis passed, but Pakistan didn't halt work on the nuclear program. Zia was no less committed to this objective than Roosevelt had been during World War II when he'd commissioned the Manhattan Project. The acquisition of essential devices like Kryton triggers, which could be acquired only in the United States, would have to be pursued. With the Indian threat looming, the Pakistanis were not about to stop taking risks, and Zia had every reason to believe that somewhere, sometime, another of his agents might well be caught. If that happened, he would need Charlie as his last line of defense on the nuclear issue.*

These were some of the thoughts that weighed heavily on the president of Pakistan when he found himself on the phone with an enraged Charlie Wilson. Zia had always gone the extra mile to be flexible with Charlie. The strict Muslim, so vilified for reimposing fundamentalist Islamic codes, had never complained about the congressman bringing his beauty queens and belly dancers to his strict Islamic state. But now Charlie was demanding the right to experience combat with the mujahideen. He wanted the dictator to help him risk his life in Afghanistan.

As a true believer, Zia was ultimately a fatalist. It was either written in the Great Book that Charlie Wilson should die at this time or it was not. On the phone he told his very difficult American friend that he would send his helicopter to Peshawar the next morning to pick him up. In Islamabad they would make plans for the trip inside. But Charlie would have to give Akhtar time to set it up properly. There would be no reporters, no loose talk to alert the Soviets to his intentions. The trip would be everything Charlie wanted, but he would have to do it on Zia's terms.

Once Zia had given his word, Charlie was mollified. And so with Colonel Rooney running interference, the congressman and his true love headed off for the exotic leg of their junket. In Hong Kong, Charlie bought clothes for Sweetums and several suits and shirts for himself. The Red Chinese were circumspect. There were no brass bands and no entry to their secret weapons factories. At Wilson's request they did arrange to

---

*Zia also knew that Wilson was responsible for putting Pakistan and Israel together. They now apparently had a back channel of communications and areas of mutual interest that they were pursuing. This was of enormous value to Pakistan, which otherwise would have had to worry more about Israel sending planes or saboteurs to blow up its nuclear facilities, as Israel had done against Saddam Hussein several years earlier.

have several survivors of the great Long March brief this important con-gressman on how Mao, Chou En-lai, and the Communists had made their way to victory in the 1948 revolution and how they had later trained and armed the North Vietnamese.

Sweetums endured all of this in anticipation of the last stop in Tahiti. But, as always happened with Charlie's grand junkets, nothing ever quite worked out for Annelise. And sure enough, she stayed out in the sun so long their first day in Tahiti that she had to be taken to the hospital with sun poisoning. By the time she returned, Charlie was preoccupied with a news story that made him think the entire Afghan program was in jeopardy. The article claimed that the CIA had commingled proceeds from the Iranian arms deal with Afghan funds in a secret Swiss bank account. Reporters were asking the obvious question: had the CIA diverted Afghan funds to the Contras? Charlie was beside himself.

As of that time, seven years into the war, no member of Congress had yet stood up on the floor to challenge the CIA's operation. It was one of the legislative miracles of all time. Everything had been worked out in the shadows, behind closed doors, and as a result it had the look of having total bipartisan support. But Wilson knew that backing for any CIA program was at best a mile long and about a millimeter deep.

Back in Washington, Wilson confronted Tom Twetten, demanding to know what was going on. He had no idea that Gust had tried to stop the Iran operation—or that Twetten had created the problem by overruling Avrakotos and forcing the finance chief to give him the Swiss bank account number. But Gust was gone, and Twetten was able to draw on his three years of dealings with Wilson. He assured him that no funds had been diverted. There had only been an overnight parking of the money. So Wilson moved quickly to control the damage. His press secretary, Elaine Lang, sent out word that the congressman would be holding a press conference to talk about the Iran-Contra diversion.

Not since the cocaine scandal had so many reporters crowded into Wilson's office. The networks, the wires, and the major papers were all expecting him to reveal a CIA crime or misdeed. Wilson prefaced his remarks by saying he knew more about the Afghan program than any other single person—that he had exhaustively investigated the matter. He had even grilled Director Casey. He was there to personally guarantee that no Afghan money had been diverted. Due to an accounting error, the Contra money had been in the wrong account for a day or two, but that was the end of it.

The reporters had come in search of red meat and weren't at all happy to be told there was no scandal, but Wilson had effectively put them off the trail. Short of calling him a liar, there was nothing left to report. Charlie had not hesitated to throw himself into the defense of the program. Still, for just a moment, he did find himself first perplexed, then furious at the idea that the CIA had been helping Khomeini. When Bill Casey came before him in a closed session of the Defense subcommittee, he asked for an explanation.

Casey mumbled and rambled. The effects of his brain tumor were showing, and Wilson couldn't figure out what he was trying to say— something to do with OSS days and how they should have assassinated Hitler. Wilson just shook his head. Without Gust he no longer had any way of knowing what was really going on inside the Agency. Anyway, he had already thrown in his lot with the CIA; he figured the Agency needed him more than ever now.

He also realized that once again there was a silver lining in the Iran-Contra disaster. Rarely can the government and the press handle more than one great scandal at a time. The Contra war had always been a heaven-sent distraction, and once again congressional staffers, reporters, and politicians were climbing all over the supposedly covert Nicaraguan operation. Meanwhile, in Afghanistan it was a completely free ride.*

Charlie Wilson felt that 1986 had been the magic year of his life. In November he had won reelection to a seventh term with 68 percent of the vote. His congressional office was virtually running itself in terms of constituent services, and he had finally secured a seat on the Intelligence Committee. He was now on the three committees that decided everything connected to the Afghans. No congressman had ever even dreamed of holding so much influence over any foreign policy, certainly never over a huge

---

*Andy Eiva and the occasional reporter continued to carp about Pakistani corruption. Some even began to question the CIA's backing of Afghan fundamentalists. But the stories never went anywhere. The energy and attention of the moment was focused on Oliver North and Iran-Contra. Once again, the mujahideen had been given a clean license to operate without the tut-tutting overview of the coequal branches of government.

and critically important covert foreign policy. By this time, even the officials at State had come to embrace him as a vital partner in anything they might need to accomplish. Robert Peck, the late deputy assistant secretary of state for the Near East offered a virtual eulogy in describing Wilson: "Charlie made himself in many ways the central figure in the Afghan war. He did it by being an honest broker. He could create problems, too, but that's not why you went and opened your heart to him. It's because he delivered. You could put that money in the bank and draw on it. Charlie always delivered."

When it came to Afghanistan, Wilson was operating throughout the governmental bureaucracies, but his most distinctive role came as an absolute equal, if not superior, to the Agency people working the program. Tom Twetten, the Near East division chief on his way to becoming the operations director, owed Charlie a big one for rescuing him on the diversion issue. Gust's successor, Jack Devine, considered it an important part of his job to keep Charlie both informed and happy. And the new station chief in Pakistan, Milt Bearden, had already become a brother in arms. Incredibly, these senior agency officials now began to attend Charlie's raucous fund-raising parties—not as contributors but simply to demonstrate their respect.

That Christmas, Charlie went to Texas to be with his sister Sharon's family. It was the first anniversary of his mother's death and almost eighteen months since he had gone on the wagon. Not only had he stopped drinking, but for the first time ever, he had stopped squandering his potential.

Everything might have been going right for a change, but Charlie was born to ride a roller coaster. Without a cause to lose himself in, he always reverted to Good-Time Charlie. The Afghans had unlocked something powerful in him, but now that the war had turned the corner, somehow the drug was wearing off. Perhaps that's why he'd felt the need to go inside the war zone for a fix. He had to drink deeply of the waters of the jihad. As he put it, "I felt that I didn't have total legitimacy unless I shared the risk in some way. I felt I needed to expose myself."

Zia had promised to give him this opportunity, but just now the magic was fading. That New Year's Eve, on the grounds that it was a special occasion and he had accomplished much, he decided to reward himself with one evening of champagne and cognac and romance with Sweetums. Just one.

Even the cardiologist who had finally given Charlie hope had told him that alcohol was the one thing that his heart could not cope with. Dr. Cashion had said it was the equivalent of a poison pill. But life is fleeting, and perhaps Charlie was preparing himself for that time when his moment of glory would pass. He did limit himself to that one binge, but the sober, focused man who had performed so brilliantly for the last eighteen months was once again battling the alcoholic within him.

And then he was rescued from temptation by a message from Zia. It was explicit: there would be no reporters; he didn't need a visa; he was not even to bring a passport. The ticket agents at Pakistan International Airways were expecting him.

CHAPTER 32

A JIHAD TO REMEMBER

No other Americans were in the first-class compartment when the two ISI men boarded the plane and escorted Charlie off before any of the other passengers. This time Zia meant it when he said over dinner that he dearly wished he too could go inside. They agreed that when victory came, the two of them would ride down the main street of Kabul on white horses. "You'll have this memory until the day you die," Zia told Charlie warmly as he said good-bye.

Brigadier Yousaf had brought two different Afghan outfits for Wilson to choose from. This time he'd been ordered to make sure that Wilson got into Afghanistan. It was an even more thankless assignment than the last, since the president expected the ISI to both insert Wilson into a hot combat zone and then to make sure he returned safely.

Charlie was amazed at how tense Yousaf and his men were when they hit the road from Bannh to Miram Shah. Hereditary kidnappers dominate the area. Pakistan has absolutely no control over these tribesmen, and about all the ISI men could do was drive fast and be ready to fight it out. It seemed terribly odd to Charlie that things could be so dangerous just trying to get to the war.

As they approached the border, the scenes Charlie saw gave him the sensation of moving backward in time. They passed through towns that reminded him of stagecoach stops—only there were no women on the streets. The butchers' freshly slaughtered sheep and goats hung on hooks. The tribesmen all carried weapons; most wore black or white cotton turbans; and their eyes blazed like car headlights. It wouldn't do to stare; these were not men to trifle with.

Charlie found himself thinking of life in the Old West as Yousaf told him about the Pashtuns' warrior tradition: How children are taught to withstand pain. How no boy cries after the age of six. Of the towering importance of revenge. How a Pashtun will wait generations, if necessary, to get even. He talked of their astonishing courage and orneriness, their total religious faith and their uncanny marksmanship. Of how little they needed to sustain themselves in the field and how they would bury their fallen comrades in the clothes and in the precise locations in which they'd died. For them there is no greater honor than to be *shaheed*, to die in the jihad.

Wilson had, of course, heard most of this before. But as he watched the spectacle of these people moving before his eyes, it was as if he were hearing it for the very first time—particularly when they came upon the mules and camels assembled for weapons runs inside. "Just acres and acres of camels and mules," Wilson remembers. He was never fully able to express the wonder of seeing this sight at the end of the twentieth century—to actually see and smell and feel the oddness of it, the sense of being in another time and the realization that *this* was the way these people fought their war: with camels and mules. He had known it and talked about it a hundred times, but it was different here, seeing it firsthand.

That was the beginning of Charlie's bright shining moment. He was only in Afghanistan for four days, but he did it all. He actually rode a white horse. He wore the armor of these Muslim knights—a Chitrali hat, *shalwar kameezes*. An elite guard of the Pakistan special forces, dressed as mujahideen, had been sent along to watch over him. Two Stinger teams kept him in sight at all times. Charlie figured that not even Genghis Khan had ever had such bodyguarding.

On the second day Charlie climbed the mountains overlooking Khost with Rahim Wardak, one of the two Afghan commanders chosen to guide him. They were moving from heat into the cold mountain air when it began to sleet, then snow. The Pakistanis told Wardak that Wilson had a terrible heart condition, that he shouldn't walk long distances. They tried to make him ride a horse, but he insisted on walking and he was thrilled when they let him fire a salvo of rockets at a Soviet garrison. This was real. Instead of fighting the Communists with words and legislation, Charlie was blasting a Soviet garrison with a CIA multiple-barrel rocket launcher. His money had bought the weapon and now it was his finger pulling the trigger.

This was not a free ride for the congressman, however, and before long the garrison's artillery was answering back, shells bursting close enough to fill the air with dirt and pebbles. This sent the combat-hardened Pakistani colonel into a panic. To Wardak's amazement, Colonel Mujahed leaped onto Charlie and pushed him to the ground. "I think someone told him he would be shot if anything happened to Charlie," Wardak says, adding that the entire Pakistan special forces contingent was in a state of constant tension those days, ready on a second's notice to hurl themselves into the defense of their charge. In marked contrast, the mujahideen, with their total faith in Allah's will, acted as if the shells were not bursting by their sides. They just kept walking.

For Wilson these real-life combat moments were at once terrifying and exhilarating. The adrenaline allowed him to keep up with these inexhaustible mountain men, and on the outside, at least, he maintained a soldier's calm. Ironically, the only time he almost lost it came when he and Wardak approached a mujahideen stronghold on a hillside over Khost.

The Afghans, acting as if they were being attacked, issued forth great cries of *"Allahu Akbar"* and went on the offensive. "They just opened up with all their small arms," remembers Wilson. "It just scared the shit out of me and I was already pretty anxious." Even Wardak acknowledges that it felt very much as if the mujahideen were shooting right at them. But it was all meant as a friendly gesture—thousands of joy shots fired as a salute in honor of the great patron's arrival.*

Only once did Wilson come close to embarrassing himself in front of the warriors. They had decided it would be an insult to their guest if they failed to bring down a Hind while he was there, so they initiated a noisy rocket barrage of the nearby garrison to draw the gunships to come out looking for them.

Wilson had lived with the nightmare of the Hind too long not to be spooked by the thought of one of them sweeping in to napalm or rocket or machine-gun him to death. Two were now overhead but high up. Charlie, helped along by his Pakistani protectors, scrambled for cover behind a rock.

---

*When Yousaf found out about it later he was furious, complaining about all the mule trips it would take just to replace the bullets wasted in that one gesture. But no one could do anything about it; it was the price the Afghans demanded for fighting.

The Stinger operators, however, stood tall on the high ground. They were furious at the congressman's companions, hurling insults at them and demanding that they get into the vehicles and drive up and down the road to kick up dust and lure the Hinds back in for the kill.

It was the only time Wilson drew rank. He had no conviction about there being a place in Paradise for him, so he sternly told the commander, "If you're doing this for me, please stop." By now the aircraft had passed, and the Afghans did not interpret Wilson's words as an act of cowardice. That was inconceivable. They assumed he was just trying to protect their pride for having failed to bring down a beast in front of his eyes.

Only later did Wilson fully appreciate the significance of what he had witnessed. The tables had been turned in this war. He was moving with an army of technoguerrillas swaggering about the Hindu Kush looking for the opportunity to take on the biggest and baddest the Soviets had to offer.

It's hard to fault Wilson for seeing only good in these men. Most American reporters were also dealing in two-dimensional portraiture when they sought to describe the Afghans. But in the dream Wilson was walking through, these were men without flaws. "Goodness personified" is the way he described Commander Haqqani, the fundamentalist mullah who guided him around Khost.

The curious thing about Wilson's romance with these warriors is that he never got to know any one individual mujahid. Deep down, he probably understood that he didn't dare; the magic might wear off. These were people whose language he did not speak, whose religion he did not share, and whose ordinary way of life, had it been imposed on Trinity, Texas, would have turned him into a revolutionary against them. But being with them in their mountains, as they defended their way of life, put Wilson in touch with a people who existed for Americans in the twentieth century only in the world of myths and legends.

There was a profound calmness to these men. They didn't move quickly, but they always moved deliberately. They turned together toward Mecca to pray to their god five times a day, but their faith was somehow an individual affair. Even young boys seemed transformed when they spoke of their religion. It was hard for Wilson not to admire and almost envy their faith. When they spoke, it was as if they were revealing divine truths. They were fighting Allah's battle against the atheists. They told him it was Allah who had caused Charlie Wilson to come to Paktia province to accept the hospitality of His most faithful mullah, Jalaluddin Haqani. It was the miracle of God that He had put kindness and mercy in the heart of the American congressman. "We had stood alone at first against the Soviet invader with bare hands. It is the bravery of the Afghan people that has attracted the foreigner to help."

Charlie Wilson moved about the hills of Afghanistan those four days in February as if under a spell. There were dinners in caves surrounded by men with beards and guns and centuries of heroism behind them. They ate lamb and yogurt and the flat Afghan bread. There was tea and talk of the different ways of killing Russians. Charlie was in the cave with the descendants of men who had stood their ground as Alexander's armies moved into the Khyber Pass. Who had chased the British invaders down and, according to legend, murdered every last one but the messenger. And best of all, he was now one with these men of destiny as they looked with contempt on the army of the Evil Empire, knowing that victory would be theirs.

On his last morning, hundreds of mujahideen came to Haqani's post to say good-bye to the congressman. Before leaving, Charlie posed on a white steed with three of these warriors next to him. The picture captured the last pure moment of the fairy tale: Charlie Wilson's war.

When Brigadier Yousaf came to take the congressman back to General Akhtar and President Zia, he noticed something different about the American. His men told him of Wilson's valor and endurance—of how he had impressed even the mujahideen. Yousaf, who was not wild about Americans, couldn't help but be taken by this one. "He was a brave man, full of energy, a man who dominated the scene," the general says. "I had a lot of respect for him. He wanted to take revenge for American blood spilled in Vietnam."

Yousaf, like the Afghans, admired this impulse of Wilson's. In the brigadier's culture, revenge is one of the highest categories of manly virtue. But what attracted him most about Wilson was the old cowboy business. "I had seen lots of cowboy movies when I was a young boy—too many of them," he says. "The cowboy was a tough guy who always stands for justice. Who is prepared to shoot left and right at any time. Who would go out to fight against the cow thieves or to get revenge of his father or go out against the Apaches. You know, superior somehow and always alone. He fights for the weak people. All the possible good qualities you find in a warrior, you find in a cowboy, with a little bit of the showoff included."

For Charlie Wilson the trip had been his rite of passage. "I felt I had entered the ranks of the initiated," he recalls. "I had dinner right afterward at Army House with Zia and Akhtar. Zia got all carried away about how he wanted to get in there and fight them himself. He was particularly jealous when I told him the muj had let me fire some of the volleys. I was most grateful to Zia and Akhtar for letting me do this. It had been far more than I had expected."

Milt Bearden's first words to Wilson were harsh. He told the congressman that what he had done was unconscionable. He had placed the entire program in jeopardy, and everyone was very upset. Having made his statement for the record, the exuberant station chief then laughed loudly and demanded that Wilson tell him everything. Charlie recounted his adventure to Bearden and then said he had tried to find one thing wrong with the program. He had asked every Afghan what they needed and what they were not getting, and he had not been able to find so much as a flaw. Never in his entire career in government had he encountered a program so perfect.

Bearden had a special treat for Wilson. The station chief believed in inspiring the troops, and so he had arranged to build what he called the Stinger Museum. Every spent gripstock that had shot down a Soviet aircraft had been brought back and mounted on a wall, with the famous lines from Kipling inscribed on a huge plaque: "When you're wounded and left on Afghanistan's plains . . ."

Charlie was the first to be taken to see this temple of Soviet doom. There Bearden had assembled a delegation of ISI officers and mujahideen. With great solemnity, the station chief, on behalf of the CIA, the ISI, and the Afghan freedom fighters, presented Charlie with the spent gripstock from the Stinger that Engineer Ghaffar had used to bring down the first Hind. It was mounted beautifully on a dark mahogany frame. Charlie had it sent back on a McCollum flight and hung it over the door to his office—a dull green tube that meant so many things to this very complicated man. It was the silver bullet of the Afghan war. Others could claim they were the ones responsible for the Stinger. But to Milt Bearden, to Akhtar, Zia, and the Afghans, the first Stinger belonged to the congressman from East Texas. It was to serve as an explanation for the uninitiated that behind those doors sat the real magical weapon of the Afghan jihad.

Wilson was somehow not the same man when he returned to Congress. He was bigger now. He was in a world of men and women who operate only with words and in committee—funding legislation or telling real men of action what they can't do. But now he was no longer just responsible for funding an exotic, important foreign policy. Now, in the minds of his colleagues, it really was becoming Charlie Wilson's war. Charlie was personally fighting the Russians. They were talking about him on his white horse.

The Democrats, meanwhile, had been reduced by Ronald Reagan to a party of whining naysayers. While Wilson had been off on his adventure, the Democrats had been on national television attacking the CIA and the Reagan administration for Iran-Contra. But no political party likes to be identified only as opposing policy. With Afghanistan, Charlie was giving them something they could claim credit for. This was the good war. It was also Congress's war. And, mainly, it belonged to the House.

Just at this time, Charlie's old adversary Steve Solarz saw the picture of Wilson on the white horse with a bandolier of machine-gun bullets strapped across his chest. Solarz, who is an avid reader of the Flashman historical novels, experienced one of those "aha!" moments: Charlie Wilson was a dead ringer for the books' hero.

"This is you," he told Charlie when he gave him a copy to read. It was actually not a very flattering tribute. The hero, Colonel Harry Flashman, is nothing short of a cad—an Englishman obsessed with chasing women, a coward at heart who owes his remarkable rise to fame and glory to astonishing coincidence, good luck, and the occasional surfacing of extraordinary talent and virtue.

Flashman can be found at the Charge of the Light Brigade, thinking that he is running away from the battle until he learns that he is in fact riding right into the ranks of the enemy. Then, as in every drama in the Flashman series, the charming, dissolute, skirt-chasing rogue, having gotten himself by mistake into the thick of a noble challenge, performs with astonishing courage and effectiveness.

Whether dealing with Otto von Bismarck, with the British army in China, or with the sorry expeditionary force that wanders into Afghanistan in 1848, Flashman is the ultimate antihero, a man forever doing the right thing for the wrong reason. No matter how dissolute or poorly intentioned he is most of the time, there always comes a moment when he rises to become a true hero. But the sad truth about Flashman is that if he had things his way, he would simply have frittered away his life in pursuits that would win him the disrespect and contempt of any organization that employed him.

Curiously, Charlie took immediately to the Solarz analogy and declared that he was indeed Flashman. It may be that he liked the cover; Flashman was, after all, a man caught up in great historical dramas. Even if he were a lout at heart, he did come through in the pinch, and Charlie found it easier to make this identification with his Afghan role than he did trying to define himself in a serious vein. He was just not able to dwell on himself as a hero without first loudly proclaiming that it was a lie. He actually began promoting the Flashman image. He created his own elite club of "Flashman's Raiders." Those he chose to initiate into this inner circle would get copies of the novels and a leather jacket with the club's name embroidered on the back. He even wrote to Gust at Langley describing the new organization and granting his old friend honorary membership.

Very much in the spirit of Flashman and to Sweetums's distress, Charlie began drinking again. It didn't seem to matter all that much. He was keeping it under control, and altogether things were at last going very, very well.

Even though no one was yet predicting victory, the CIA's battlefield reports were amazing. The mujahideen had even run an operation over the border, crossing into what Bill Casey had called "the soft underbelly of the Soviet Union," where tens of millions of Muslims lived. The Agency was terrified that this kind of provocation inside the Soviet Union might precipitate a fearsome response. Still, it showed how brazen the mujahideen had become.

In Geneva, the State Department had begun claiming that the Russians seemed genuinely interested in negotiating a way out. And then the law of the unexpected struck in the Achilles' heel of the whole program. In July, just after Congress had passed legislation authorizing a new aid package to Pakistan, a man widely believed to be Zia's agent, Arshad Pervez, was caught in Philadelphia trying to buy twenty-five tons of a specialty steel alloy vital to the building of a nuclear bomb.

It was dramatically worse than the Kryton-trigger affair of 1985. This time there was a Solarz amendment on the books that would force the White House to stop all aid. There was no realistic way to avoid it: Congress was going to cut Zia off, and Solarz was the first to alert Wilson to this likelihood when he informed him on the floor of the House about what his Pakistani friends had done now. "I believe Steve told me about Pervez with some glee," recalls Charlie.*

Wilson would later call his subsequent efforts to save Zia's military aid "my greatest achievement in Congress." Perhaps he remembers it this way because he is at heart a political artist and can assess the value of an accomplishment by the difficulty of the task. Everything else he had accomplished had been carried out in the shadows and behind closed doors. Here he had to operate publicly against a coalition of virtuous liberals. He had the thankless task to trying to defend the right of a Muslim dictator to break U.S. law in order to build an Islamic bomb while still qualifying for massive U.S. foreign aid. And he had to do it in the name of protecting a massive CIA killing-war.

On the face of it, this was a lost cause. U.S. policy was firmly committed to nuclear nonproliferation. A law had clearly been violated. The president had no choice but to trigger the Solarz amendment and cut off Zia's aid. Even if Reagan claimed a national security waiver, Congress was now committed to enforcing its own law.

But Wilson would end up forcing his colleagues to abandon their pretense of ethical deliberation. For this lone issue, he would strip Congress down to a body that operates solely on the basis of power and horse trading. Here, he would call in every chit and, to the horror of his liberal friends, win.

As Wilson and the CIA saw it, all might be lost if the United States publicly slapped Zia in the face and withdrew its aid. They knew that without Zia running Pakistan by martial law, there could be no Afghan war. Officially there was no Pakistani involvement with the mujahideen, but the population of Pakistan certainly knew about it and didn't like it. The Soviets were bombing their borders, sponsoring terrorist attacks. There were three million Afghan refugees and tens of thousands of armed warriors in Pakistan. And all of this at a time when Pakistan had to worry about a new war with India. The only reason Zia was able to maintain the loyalty of his army in the continuation this policy was because of the billions he was re-

---

*These two engaged in an annual face-off on this issue, with Wilson always attending Solarz's hearing with the explicit objective of spoiling his tea party. In February 1988 this is how he began his testimony: "Incidentally, Mr. Chairman, before we start, I would like to congratulate all of the friends of India on their acquisition of the peaceful nuclear submarine that has just arrived [from the Soviet Union]."

ceiving in U.S. military and economic aid. If that was taken away, all bets were off.

At the Pakistan embassy over dinner, former national security adviser Zbigniew Brzezinski confronted Steve Solarz with a question: "Steve, what are your objectives in cutting off aid to Pakistan? Because if you do, I foresee the following things happening: one, the Afghan resistance collapsing and the Soviets triumphing; two, the present government in Pakistan will disappear; and three, you'll have an anti-American government in Pakistan in possession of the bomb. Is that what you want?"

But for Solarz and fellow Democrats dedicated to nuclear nonproliferation, the issue had gone beyond debate. A law had been violated and a Muslim dictator was thumbing his nose at America. Solarz summoned the CIA to closed hearings and expressed outrage at what he saw as a pattern of gross violations by Pakistan. A brilliant young CIA analyst delivered devastating testimony at these hearings, which Wilson attended simply "to try to intimidate Steve a bit." Lurking behind Wilson's presence was always the threat of retaliation against India. But none of that mattered with the Pervez outrage.

Charlie had been worried about Pakistan's aid package well before the Pervez incident. That February in Islamabad he had told Zia that he couldn't hold the line alone anymore. "I told him that the antinuclear and disarmament forces were becoming increasingly strident, that he now had the third biggest AID program, and that I was having troubles with Obey. Solarz was holding hearings. Glenn and Pressler were getting adamant in the Senate. I said it was all going to come to a head that fall in the appropriations bill and I needed a pit bull to help me."

Zia responded by hiring a friend of Charlie's, the devilishly effective lobbyist Denis Neill. "There's no one in his class," Wilson explained. "He had made all the contributions to the Appropriations and Foreign Affairs members. He had courted the staff. That's where Denis wrote the book. Hill and Knowlton are great at social stuff, but that's not what wins these kinds of fights. In the Foreign Operations Committee in the middle of the night, you know who sends in pizza and beer. It's Denis. He's always in the wings. He can't go in but he's there."

The Pervez arrest had come at an awkward time. Thanksgiving was upon them. But the two old pros decided they had to win converts from different political persuasions who could argue their case. Zia agreed to receive a delegation, and Charlie began twisting arms, calling members' wives, promising the experience of a lifetime. Finally he put together a delegation of seven key members and their wives, who'd agreed to spend Thanksgiving in Pakistan. The fire-breathing conservative Bob Dornan, the much-respected California liberal George Brown, and the former all-American basketball player Tom McMillen were included in the group. Wilson had chosen members others would listen to.

Charlie knew exactly how his colleagues would react to the training camps. The idea was to make them fall in love with the mujahideen, to feel the patriotic drama under way and recognize that Pakistan's bomb issue was really about whether these freedom fighters were going to be abandoned. The congressmen were predictably impressed by the courage and ferocity and faith of the warriors. They might even have been somewhat transported by donning mujahideen outfits for the trip to the secret training camps and then watching Wilson give blood, shaming some of them into following suit.

By now Peshawar was filled with American volunteer doctors and nurses being funded by Crandall. The atmosphere was electric. But it was at the official state dinner that Wilson and Zia performed their magic for the delegation.

The ugly unspoken issue was the Islamic bomb, and when Wilson stood up he confronted the issue in his own uniquely outrageous manner. "Mr. President, in history I have three heroes. Winston Churchill, President Lincoln, and President Zia ul-Haq." He looked directly at his colleagues before he continued. "But for Zia's presence at the helm of Pakistan, the history of mankind and the free world would be different. After consolidating their gain in Afghanistan, the Russians would have fulfilled their centuries-old dream of reaching the Indian Ocean and dominating the world." And then he addressed the bottom line: "Mr. President, as far as I'm concerned you can make all the bombs you want because you are our friends and they, the Indians, are our enemies. But not all Americans feel the same way, and there are some questions, Mr. President, that you have to answer because this issue is getting hot."

A solemn Zia now approached the rostrum, his glasses and a prepared speech in hand. Charlie's intuition pulled him back to his feet: he didn't want a canned performance, so he complained that since he had not had the benefit of glasses or a speech, nor should the president of Pakistan.

"My friend Mr. Charles Wilson," Zia began, "has complained that I should not use my glasses or notes because he has neither on his person. So I cannot be unfair to my esteemed friend Charlie. And since he has taken away my official brief I will speak from my heart."

The dictator ordered the servants to leave the banquet hall and had his aide-de-camp bolt the doors from the inside. Zia was not above lying in the interest of Islam, particularly when it came to such things as the bomb. But his words this day had the ring of sincerity to them.

He spoke of the dilemma of a loyal husband making assurances to his wife. "Sometimes she must rely on his word. She can't always ask for proof." His country's nuclear program was exclusively for peaceful purposes. He asked that they accept his word: Pakistan had no intention of building a delivery system.

He then began a moving history of what he and Charlie and their two countries had done together. He spoke of the valor of the Afghans and the significance of the moment. "Now, if at this stage our American friends cut us off or threaten to cut off aid then it would be a betrayal of history, and the judgment of history would be very severe on those who take this decision. We did not accept the conditions of America"—he was referring to when he'd rejected Jimmy Carter's aid program as "peanuts"—"at the early stage, so how can Americans expect us to do so at this stage when we have bled the Russians nearly unconscious? Whether there is American aid or not we will continue to fight. We'll continue to fight, and I don't know how much more cost in human lives and limbs we will have to pay. So please go back and assure my American friends and all those who are now insisting that we should succumb to American pressure that Pakistan is not ready to accept any conditional elements. The task may be difficult, but with Mr. Charlie Wilson on Capitol Hill it is not impossible."

At the airport later, when the Pakistani press asked for comments, Wilson deferred to his liberal colleague George Brown. It was part of Charlie's political artistry to know when to yield and to let the issue become Brown's, not his.

Back in Washington, however, only one congressman stepped forward to lead the battle. With Denis Neill by his side, Charlie was now moving through the congressional directory calling every person he had ever done anything for. "This is payback time," he would say. It was that basic. He was calling in his debts.

Neill offers the best explanation of why Charlie (and he) finally pulled off their victory at 5 A.M. in the House-Senate conference. "Most of Congress is about words and debating, and you can never really resolve anything. But Appropriations is simply about money and it's very practical." The trade-offs were explicit: Charlie wanted money for Zia. He wanted his colleagues to give him the money. He had done it for them before; he would do it for them again. "Are you with me or are you with Solarz?" is the way he put it to each of his colleagues. Everyone knew that Charlie would remember forever which side they chose.

The morning of the showdown, Charlie Schnabel, who had come in to the office early, long before anyone else, picked up the phone, which would not stop ringing. It was Zia calling simply to pass on encouragement: "Tell Charlie to put on his wrestling togs and do battle."

At stake were hundreds of millions of dollars. Pakistan had become America's third biggest aid recipient after Israel and Egypt, and the battle to cut it off culminated at the House-Senate conference that night. As Denis Neill described it; "The Joint Conference is like a poker game. To be a real player you have to know what you're doing. You have to know how to read the other players, and you have to know when to make your move." When the game began, the master lobbyist could only sit outside the door and wait to see how his ace would fare.

Wilson's profound difficulty that night was that the anti-Pakistan coalition on the committees had the votes to defeat him. Understandably, they wanted and repeatedly asked for a straight up-and-down vote, but Charlie used his first maneuver to trump them. He was, in effect, able to set the agenda insofar as aid to Pakistan was concerned because he had a deal with subcommittee chairman Dave Obey. The first thing he had done was to make sure the divisive issue would not be brought up until the very end, when members would be tired and eager to get home. Secondly, he knew that Obey would find a way not to permit a direct vote.

David Obey didn't like Zia or his bomb one little bit, but he owed Wilson. Charlie was the chairman's secret instrument for maintaining discipline and control of the subcommittee. Charlie wasn't exactly a conservative. He was, in fact, a liberal when it came to domestic matters—civil rights, women's issues. But on gun control, anti-Communism, and defense, he was a hard-liner second to none. And that permitted him to position himself as an honest broker for Obey with the conservatives. With Charlie on board, Obey could always report out a full bill without having to worry about it being opened up on the floor. He thus avoided the risk of losing all of the horse trading and consensus building that had gathered those endless line items into a semblance of coherence. That's what Wilson gave to Obey, but it was a two-way street; on this occasion it meant the chairman had to hold his nose and champion Charlie's bomb-hungry Muslim despot.

"I'd never seen the chairman let another member dominate an issue like that," recalls staffer Steve Goose, who became increasingly distraught at what he saw as a mind-bending power play on Wilson's part. Goose had walked in certain that the liberal coalition, his boss Bob Mrazek, had helped organize was going to cut Zia's aid. "We had the votes, and we had the law on our side."

By 3 A.M., however, Charlie had already pulled off a legislative miracle, with a large portion of the administration's original funds restored to Pakistan. But Wilson still wasn't happy, and neither Obey nor Obey's Senate counterpart, Chairman Daniel Inouye, were willing to risk his anger. They both realized that Wilson was prepared to go to the floor if he didn't get what he wanted.

That was the second trump card Charlie held that night. He and Neill believed that if they took the issue to the floor, they had the votes to win. For Obey and Inouye, there could be no greater nightmare than to fail to report out a complete bill. Anarchy would break out if the two chambers began voting on each individual line item.

And so the late-night and now early-morning poker game of bets and bluffs continued, with Inouye repeatedly putting the question to Wilson: "Will you accept a compromise?"

"No, I can't live with that."

That was all he said—time after time, as the senator and Obey tried to force him to make some compromise: "No, I can't live with that."

It was an extraordinary effort, and as Inouye's frustration level began to rise, an element of unreasonableness came to mark Wilson's position. He was not bending an inch.

In Afghanistan earlier that year, Wilson had caused Brigadier Yousaf to see him as the lone cowboy standing up for the mujahideen. Now in the U.S. Capitol, this tall Texan in his bright striped shirt, with his trademark epaulets and suspenders, was once again standing alone—this time on the battlefield where he did his real fighting in the Afghan war. He was not acting as just another congressman seeking money for a campaign contributor; Charlie had a covenant to fulfill. For him this was a deeply moral issue. He could feel the responsibility of speaking for the million Afghan dead, for the six million who had been displaced, for the army of freedom fighters just then going into battle with America's true foe. He was not about to let anyone take this war from him, from Zia, from the Afghans. This night he stood his ground and won.

And so Zia remained the honored ally. The mujahideen continued to shoot down Soviet aircraft at a rate of one a day. The full force of the training and of the Vickers mix of weapons was surfacing, and it was clear that time was on the side of the holy warriors.

The all-night joint conference was not the sort of incident that would ever be recorded in a chronicle of a war. But it can be argued that the great event of the Afghan war in those critical last weeks of 1987 and the first few days of 1988 was what didn't happen in Washington because Charlie Wilson triumphed.

The decision may well have already been taken in Moscow to end the Red Army's unhappy occupation. No matter what the outcome at the joint conference, the Soviets might have moved to withdraw anyway in precisely the same time frame. But perhaps not. All one can say is that Washington's strongest suit so far was its demonstration that for once it was committed for the long haul. When Zia survived the aid cutoff battle, there were no hopeful signs left for the hard-liners in the Kremlin. In fact, they were now facing a movement that no one knew how to cope with.

It was at this time that Eduard Shevardnadze drew his unexpected intimate, George Shultz, aside at Geneva to tell him secretly that the Kremlin had reached a decision to withdraw. Barring the unforeseen, Charlie Wilson's war was about to end.

CHAPTER 33

Charlie and Zia ul-Haq

THE PRICE OF GLORY

It was an ordinary Sunday in Pakistan, the second workday of the week, as in all Muslim countries. The early-morning streets of Islamabad and nearby Rawalpindi had the usual mix of Third World and First World activities: vendors, colorful motor scooters, men going into mosques, boys carrying tea trays, schoolchildren sitting in disciplined rows, government buildings opening for business.

And then the world seemed to split wide open. Shrapnel tore into buildings, glass shattered, people were maimed indiscriminately. A half mile from what appeared to be the epicenter of the first explosion, strange apparitions were seen screaming through the air, tearing apart cars as they moved along highways. There was wave after wave of explosions as the thundering blasts seemed to feed on themselves, and a mushroom cloud of dark smoke and fire billowed thousands of feet into the sky. Confusion seized the population, who believed that the capital was under attack.

In the panic, rumors began to fly. Everyone knew that India had some kind of nuclear device. The more sophisticated presumed it was the Red Army taking its revenge. Many seemed sure that the Israelis had just bombed Pakistan's secret nuclear facilities. Still others insisted it was the CIA. Curiously, only this last speculation came close to the truth.

Milt Bearden's Islamabad station had not, of course, launched this attack. But every one of those exploding weapons killing Pakistanis that day had come directly from the CIA. The source of the disaster was a stockpile of some ten thousand tons of ordnance haphazardly stored at the Ojhiri military camp, just between the capital and Rawalpindi. The massive arms deliveries had been part of a huge, last-ditch operation to funnel enormous quantities of sophisticated weapons and ordnance in to the mujahideen before an agreement to end the war was signed in Geneva.

The Russians go to extraordinary lengths to honor their patriotic heroes. Every day of the entire Afghan War—in Moscow, Leningrad, or wherever Soviet veterans of World War II gathered—a commonplace drama occurred. Invariably, the old men would wear their medals on their chests when they went out in public, and as they entered a bus or subway, their fellow citizens would stand. Not just young children, but even old women would offer their seats, out of respect and gratitude for the sacrifice these veterans had made for them and as a thank-you for their valor in defeating the Nazis in "the Great Patriotic War." On May Day, Red Square would be filled with these veterans, most men covered with medals as adoring crowds clapped and cheered. Not a day would pass that their country did not bathe them in glory for their deeds, in thanks for their sacrifice.

In stark contrast, the Soviet veterans of the Afghan war did not exist. By official policy for more than five years, they were not fighting a war. Yes, there was a limited contingent of Soviet advisers helping to build socialism and advising the Afghan revolutionary government in its efforts to suppress the terror campaigns of the bands of Dushman or bandits, as they called the mujahideen. But there had been no invasion of Afghanistan, and there were not 120,000 combat troops there. Soviet airmen were not carpet bombing villages and laying waste to the countryside. There was no war, and no one was being killed or maimed there.

It was strange then when the tin coffins began coming home in the special airplanes known as Black Tulips. These couriers of death would deliver their harvest with very explicit instructions for the mothers: they were not to note on the gravestones the fact that their sons had died in Afghanistan. A mother would be told that her son had not died in combat in Afghanistan and that he couldn't be awarded a medal for valor because there was no war.

The Soviet people were told that the enemy was broadcasting lies on its Voice of America and through the BBC, claiming there was a Soviet war in Afghanistan. But then came the ugly whispers and the agonized drunken stories that the thousands of young men were bringing back with them year after year. By 1986 it started to achieve a critical mass—the accumulation of these tales of the dark and ugly things that the young boys had had done to them in the far-off, exotic land where Soviets were seen as infidels, where friend and foe looked the same, and where nothing seemed safe.

Traditionally in Russia, when a young man dies, his mother is given time to grieve and to prepare her child for the next world. It is a searing, sad experience, but there is dignity in it. It belongs to her. Family, friends, and neighbors participate as she honors her fallen hero. But during this war that was not being fought, the Communist officials were forced to rob the mothers of Russia of their dignity. The mother of a fallen soldier was not permitted to acknowledge her son's heroism, his sacrifice, his patriotic duty.

It didn't sit well. How could it when the numbers started to mount into the thousands? Sometime in late 1985 the mothers began to organize, quietly at first. A mother who has lost her son in such a way feels she has nothing left to lose. She cannot easily be intimidated any longer. The veterans also began to organize. Unlike their American counterparts, the Vietnam veterans, who had returned home as individuals, the Soviet Afghan veterans had all gone off to war together as a unit from the same town or city, and when their tour was up they returned as a unit.

Throughout the Soviet Union, across its twelve time zones, entire units from the Afghan war began to resurrect themselves inside the civilian life of the country. They met at night to drink, to take drugs, and to recite poetry and sing songs of their experience. The songs contained the entire secret history of the war—an explicit account of all that the government insisted had not happened and was not then continuing. They told of the invasion, of the storming of Amin's palace. They told of the devilish Dushman and of their comrades who had fallen in battle. There were songs about the Black Tulips and the tin coffins and the instructions to the mothers to lie for the state.

The system that Lenin and Stalin had built had discipline, remarkable discipline, and for five or six years it had held up to the growing strains of the whispering campaigns that were being unleashed throughout the country. Everywhere the mothers were talking and complaining and asking questions. Worst of all, these young veterans now walking the streets were missing legs and arms, limbs lost in a war that never happened. The phenomenon only grew faster and more powerful because it was not allowed; by early 1986 everyone, everywhere, knew something of the horror of Afghanistan. Charlie's money had kicked in and Vickers's program was coming on-line. The mujahideen were suddenly on the march—everywhere they were taking to the offensive, ambushing convoys, assassinating Russian soldiers, setting off bicycle bombs and camel bombs and car bombs, shelling the Soviet embassy, shooting down helicopters and planes. They were dying, too. Oh yes, the mujahideen were continuing to die in far, far greater numbers than the Soviets and their Afghan allies. But the mujahideen go straight to Paradise, where the pleasures are so sweet. There is no heaven for the unbelievers.

The unbelievers had only the Black Tulip. What sort of end was it for them, their bodies packaged in tin coffins with a small window, if the boy's face had not been altered beyond recognition? And what of the mother, not willing to bury the metal coffin without checking to make sure her son was inside, yet not quite able to risk the sight and smell of what she might find if she opened the casket to see for herself? One of the songs the veterans back home sang was of a mother opening the casket and finding another young man's body. And even if it had been her son, what could she say? All she could write on his tomb to explain the sacrifice was: "Born July 28, 1964. Died February 8, 1985, fulfilling his international duties."

By the winter of 1986, a poison was loose in the spirit of the Soviet Union, and Gorbachev and his inner circle knew it. Their problem was that every year since the invasion things had gotten worse. And now, after the Varennikov offensive, they were faced with the disturbing signs that the resistance, instead of being crushed, was showing new signs of vitality and lethal ability.

In Afghanistan, the Soviets were, ironically, beginning to do themselves in with their own propaganda about how evil the mujahideen were. The idea had not been to frighten their own troops, but that's what was happening with their warnings not to wander forth alone at night, not to walk into a store in Kabul without fellow soldiers as protection. There were frightening posters and official briefings from the moment the soldiers got off the transport planes at Bagram Air Base, whispers about what had happened to their colleagues. They all knew about the fanatic Gulbuddin

Hekmatyar's practice of leaving armless and legless Soviet soldiers on the road. He wanted fresh troops to fly into a rage at the sight of their countrymen, twisting in a bloody pool, and come looking for revenge—right into his trap. They came to fear the sting in the back as a friendly shopkeeper talked to them, smiling, while an Afghan stuck them with a long pin with poison on its end to foul their lungs.

Every Afghan now was the enemy. There was no such thing as a reliable Afghan ally. The Kipling poem about the fate of the British who had come here began to haunt the Red Army: "When you're wounded and left on Afghanistan's plains, / And the women come out to cut up what remains, / Jest roll to your rifle and blow out your brains / An' go to your Gawd like a soldier."

According to the Russian journalist Artyom Borovik, writing later of what he saw in those days, the average Red Army soldier was now finding religion—the atheists were seeking God. They all seemed to be carrying an extra bullet to shoot themselves if captured. They were filled with superstitions. Many were becoming drug addicts, and the Afghans were selling them the dope—strong dope. Borovik describes them sitting around camp stoned, listening to Pink Floyd, and being terrorized by stories of the enemy waiting around every bend.

If only they had an enemy they could fight in one all-out battle and have it be over with. But it was the endlessness and the shapelessness of it all. It was like being chased by some huge formless blob. Even when Afghan soldiers were captured and the Soviets resorted to torture, they were horrified to find that they couldn't get a reaction. The Afghans' eyes just stared out blankly.

Gorbachev was trapped. The United States was escalating, and for the first time America looked as if it were prepared to stay the course. It was no longer clear that the Soviets could afford to pay the price of this war. It might take a half million soldiers or more to deal with this worsening situation. But that would force Gorbachev to go before the nation to admit that there had been a war in the first place and that the Red Army was losing. That was impossible.

That February Gorbachev acknowledged that Afghanistan had become a running sore in the side of the Soviet Union. No one at the Kremlin knew that several months after that speech, a U.S. Air Force plane landed in the dead of night at the same military airfield in Rawalpindi that the McCollum flights used. The CIA station chief was on hand to watch over the first shipment of Stingers. Brigadier Raza of the ISI was there as well, to make sure the special cargo was safely transported to the nearby facility where a group of handpicked holy warriors was waiting to begin its eight-week training course.

Almost everything was starting to go in the wrong direction for the Soviets. In April, as the new fighting season reopened in Afghanistan, General Varennikov was suddenly pulled out of Kabul for an urgent mission of the highest national priority: the biggest nuclear accident in history had spread from the nuclear reactor at Chernobyl, poisoning thousands of square miles. After dispatching Varennikov, Gorbachev went underground and acted as if nothing had happened, until eleven days later—and then only after an international outcry. Some 200,000 wretched citizens were evacuated and conscript workers sent in to try to clean up the disaster.

Instead of deploying a division to the border of Pakistan, Varennikov was now ordering suicide teams into the reactor chambers to clear out the deadly wastes. The world stood by horrified. At the White House, Reagan told his advisers that if Chernobyl had happened in America it would have forced an end to his defense buildup. Gorbachev will feel it too, he said.

Gorbachev was already feeling terrible pressures from all sides. The Soviet economy was on the verge of collapse; it couldn't afford the expense of keeping up with Reagan's menacing nuclear and conventional arms race. The Star Wars challenge had spooked the military establishment. Chernobyl couldn't possibly have come at a worse time. Varennikov had been incensed that month to discover that Reagan had just sent a guided missile, a smart bomb, into Qaddafi's tent. It was a humiliating, taunting move. Varennikov, the great strategist of the empire, felt the Soviets couldn't ignore such challenges, but he was also convinced that his own colleagues on the General Staff, led by Defense Minister Yazov, had virtually bankrupted the country. As he saw it, they had fallen into a U.S. trap of building totally unnecessary weapons systems that the country couldn't afford just because the United States was building them.*

---

*Varennikov cited the Soviets' ambitious efforts to build a weapon to compete with the MX mobile underground missile, which the United States had announced its intention to build. He said that Yazov had a far bigger one designed at a cost that

But the issue of how this crisis had come about was irrelevant. The bottom line for Gorbachev was that the center could not hold much longer. And so that spring in the Kremlin, historic internal debates began. Afghanistan was very much on the agenda. It was emblematic of the problems the Soviet system faced.

A totalitarian state like the Soviet Union, a country with the greatest landmass in the world, must control its diverse population by force. But there's only so much an army or a police force can do. Ultimately, control relies on the perception that the government is all-powerful, instantly willing to crush any rebellion with cruel efficiency. In 1986 in Afghanistan, however, the Soviet might was ineffective. The Soviet leaders were forced to think the unthinkable—they had all but given up hope of breaking the resistance.

Zia had stalled the U.N. talks in Geneva to give the CIA an extra month to rush in supplies. Once the accord was signed, both superpowers would be prohibited from any further arms shipments. Zia wanted to make sure that his (and the CIA's) Afghans were in a position to do in the Russian Afghan surrogates. But that morning the mujahideen's secret stash at Ojhiri was wiped out—thirty thousand rockets, millions of rounds of ammunition, vast numbers of mines, Stingers, SA-7s, Blowpipes, Milan antitank missiles, multiple-barrel rocket launchers, mortars. And they were not just exploding, they were killing Pakistanis—over a hundred people died, and more than a thousand were wounded.

That morning, as the rockets were still flying, the Pakistan dictator called his Washington ambassador, Jamsheed Marker, with terse instructions: "Get Judge Webster [Casey's successor at the CIA] and Charlie and tell them, for God's sake, to replace everything." Marker was amazed at his president's iron nerves: "He didn't ask for help to put out the fires or to tend to the wounded. He just wanted one thing. He wanted more missiles."

Varennikov knew the country couldn't afford. He set out to sabotage it by having a mock-up model made that was so huge that when a man stood by one of the giant wheels he almost couldn't be seen. The large version was scrapped, although the Defense Ministry went ahead and built the wildly expensive system to keep pace with the American peacekeepers.

It was a stunning performance from a man who just a few months before had been on the edge of losing all U.S. assistance. Now, with his capital in flames, he was calling on the CIA director to rush another $100 million worth of the most sophisticated weaponry. He told Marker that it was essential for the Russians to know that the United States was doing this, so that the Kremlin would not dare break the Geneva accords.

This was to be the last time that Zia called on the CIA and Charlie for help, and by all accounts it was one of the Agency's all-time great logistics triumphs. Within twenty-four hours, huge U.S. cargo planes were unloading Stingers and other weapons taken directly from the frontline stores of NATO. Charlie had called Mohammed that same day to tell him the Agency desperately needed mortars. "Send the plane," replied Abu Ghazala, who then ordered the mortars to be taken from his frontline troops.

In Islamabad, where the explosions continued intermittently for two days, Milt Bearden assumed the role of field commander. Bearden was now in his true element. This war had become so much fun that for a man like Bearden there was a downside to it ending so fast. There were so many new weapons and gadgets to test out under real conditions. For example, they still hadn't tried out the Texas Chainsaw, the fiber-optic-wire-guided drone that a mujahid could fly right into the window of an Il-76 to blow up $100 million worth of Scuds. And everyone was dying to see how the latest version of the Israeli Charlie Horse, a far cry from the original anti-aircraft cannon, would perform. This later weapon was designed to hurl hundreds of antipersonnel devices over a huge area, some floating down by parachute, all exploding at different altitudes with frightening impact.

But Bearden had not been sent to Islamabad to enjoy himself. He was a pro, and the whole idea was to bring this war to a close. Bearden now decided that the best way to encourage the Soviet retreat was to take the covert war public. For Bearden, the game became not just replacing lost weapons but sticking the knife into the Soviets and twisting it. Make them feel that the Ojhiri arms-depot explosion hadn't hurt a whit. So when the embassy initially protested the dispatch of resupply planes, on the grounds that they would be identified, Bearden shouted them down: "Paint the planes in fluorescent paint. Put on the lights."

At an embassy reception just after the explosion, the station chief, dressed in a dark business suit, spotted his KGB counterpart and invited him into the garden. Overhead the sky was filled with American C-141s and C-5s in holding patterns waiting to land. "Do you know what that is?" Bearden asked, looking up at the Agency's air bridge. "It's a beautiful sight, isn't it?" His message was clear.

On April 14, 1988, the signing of the Geneva accords was announced on Moscow television with little fanfare. Unlike the silence and mystery that had surrounded the Red Army's invasion nine years earlier, this was the silence of humiliation. From Islamabad Zia called the negotiated withdrawal "a miracle of the twentieth century."

With hindsight, it now seems that the great resupply effort at Ojhiri probably didn't matter a bit in terms of the Soviet withdrawal. Bitter and traumatic battles had already been played out in the politburo and the high command of the Red Army. No great power fails to recognize the implications of a visible military defeat—particularly not one whose Red Army had been legendary for its claim that where it went, it never left. The traumatic decision to accept defeat had already been taken. The empire was collapsing, and nothing could stop it.

But for the Afghan insiders, Ojhiri had been a glorious last hurrah— for Charlie and Zia; Milt and the CIA; Mohammed in the wings with the ever reliable Saudis coughing up their matching share. They had delivered their own personal message to Gorbachev: "We can make this easy on you or we can make it hurt."

Ojhiri had been the last run for secrecy and improvisation. The time had come for the regulars to reclaim the government's foreign policy. In Geneva, Secretary of State Shultz was now at center stage cutting the deal with the Russians. Under Secretary Mike Armacost had assumed Charlie's ad hoc role coordinating the bureaucracies. Gordon Humphrey—who, after all, was a senator—was broadly recognized as the Afghans' true congressional champion. And the officials who had moved the Stinger decision along were crowing about how they alone had made all the difference.

Wilson could be forgiven if, at this moment, he was possessed by the rather conventional impulse to claim a slice of the credit due him. A producer from *60 Minutes* had approached him, asking for help on a report about the Cross Border program. The Pakistanis had refused to let the Americans in, and they were seeking help. A loose agreement was reached that Wilson would be interviewed if he happened to be in Pakistan at the same time as *60 Minutes*.

That was when Charlie went to the CIA to ask for his first personal favor. Bill Casey had recently died of a brain tumor. His successor, Judge William Webster, had inherited Wilson without any of the controversy that had accompanied the congressman's troubled entry into the secret agency. Wilson was now a full partner whose calls were not only answered immediately but whose counsel was sought on every matter pertaining to Afghanistan as well as on any troubles the Agency might be having with Congress.

For all practical purposes, he was the Agency's station chief on the Hill, so much so that when he later became head of the Oversight subcommittee, in charge of ferreting out intelligence abuses, he immediately called his Langley friends to celebrate. Over lunch the new watchdog declared solemnly, "Well, gentlemen, the fox is in the henhouse. Do whatever you like."

It was typical Wilson bravado, but underneath it all the seventh floor knew that they could always count on him. No one else, at that moment when the CIA was in such bad odor, would have dared take the aggressive position he did, and the Agency had felt deeply indebted. So when Charlie sat down with the judge and his deputy director, Bob Gates, the Agency chiefs were hard put to deny him the one favor he asked. He wanted their help to take *60 Minutes* into Afghanistan.

Neither Webster nor Gates nor anyone Wilson spoke to thought this was a good idea. State and AID were horrified, and Sweetums insisted that Charlie would be skewered. The Pakistanis, with their aversion to such publicity, had absolutely no interest. But Zia, like everyone at this stage, could not say no to the man who had made everything possible.

Peter Henning, a veteran cameraman for *60 Minutes,* had filmed all over the world, been everywhere, seen everything. But back in May 1988, midway into the first day of filming Charlie Wilson inside the war zone, he realized that he had never seen or heard of a politician receiving such an elaborate reception under such dangerous and unusual circumstances.

The exotic scenes had begun the moment they'd hit the Afghan border. Out of nowhere a mujahideen honor guard on galloping horses had appeared, looking very much as if they had charged right out of the days of Genghis Khan. The mounted warriors led Charlie and the camera crew down what was billed as the Ho Chi Minh Trail of the Afghan war. At the front and rear of the caravan, five Stinger crews swept the skies for Soviet helicopters. Two hundred mujahideen, bristling with weapons, accompanied them as they drove through territory that looked like a moonscape of bombed-out villages. When they finally arrived at Ali Khel, the first liberated Soviet garrison, a horde of freedom fighters stood on their vehicles and cheered as the congressman got out of his vehicle.

Henning scrambled behind, filming, as the commanders asked Wilson to go with them inside the fort, where the Russians had left an open bottle of vodka with half-filled glasses on the table. They wanted their patron to see how the Communist infidels had run for their lives. Wilson's laugh was infectious, deep, rumbling. The mujahideen had looked at the American dressed in their clothes and suddenly they were laughing too. It was all so new and delicious for these men who had sacrificed so much, this moment when they were finally taking back their country.

But the oddest feature of it all, for Henning, was the way the mujahideen treated the congressman—almost as if he were one of their field marshals. Outside, the warriors had assembled an amazing collection of the weapons the CIA had provided them. They were carefully laid out in a giant semicircle. Each time, as the congressman approached a new gun emplacement, they would fire the weapons—the 14.5s, the multiple-barrel rocket launchers, the Dashikas, the Oerlikons. They always hit their targets, and with each success the bearded warriors would shout to their god, *"Allahu Akbar."* Wilson, with his great deep voice and his clenched fist pumping triumphantly in the air, joined in filling the valley with smoke, the sound of guns, and the cry of the jihad: *"Allahu Akbar."*

A cameraman lives by what he sees through his lens, and there was not a moment on this trip when Henning did not feel he was mining gold. At one point the congressman was posing on a mountaintop all but denuded by Russian napalm when—by magic, it seemed—Afghans in turbans and woolen vests emerged out of a small patch woods left, bearing great trays of chicken and lamb, stacks of flat Afghan bread, mounds of rice and yogurt. A long colorful cloth, like an Oriental rug, was spread on the ground. Twenty mujahideen commanders, with bandoliers across their chests and Russian assault rifles by their sides, sat cross-legged before their guest of honor. The Stinger operators guarded the skies as Wilson and his table of Afghan warriors began thrusting their right hands into the overflowing trays of food. Henning did not dare stop filming to eat.

When Wilson fired a 14.5mm at a mountain target and the mujahideen started cheering, the cameraman was struck with a sense of déjà vu. When the congressman mounted a white horse, it finally came to him: Lawrence of Arabia. From that moment on, Henning couldn't shake the peculiar feeling that somehow he was filming on a Hollywood set.

Peter Henning had no way of knowing how accurate his intuition would turn out to be. There had, in fact, been a master hand at work secretly choreographing the scenes that *60 Minutes* was taping, and it was none other than Milt Bearden.

When the congressman had first arrived in Islamabad, Bearden had told him that he had prepared the entire shooting schedule. Ever the master storyteller, the station chief chortled as he laid it all out for his special friend. Two of Bearden's case officers, in spite of the ban on Americans in the war zone, had already checked the area where Charlie would be going to make sure the land mines had been cleared. Bearden had arranged for the great semicircle of weapons, which the mujahideen would fire for their patron; Russian tanks would be smoldering along the roads. The station chief spoke, Wilson later said with some amusement, as if he were Cecil B. DeMille: "Charlie, you're not going to believe how fierce the muj are going to look."

The night before they'd crossed into Afghanistan, the station chief had accompanied Wilson to a dinner at the private headquarters of General Akhtar. There, in front of a collection of Pakistani officials, the intelligence chief, in a formal ceremony, made Wilson an honorary field marshal in the Pakistani army. Akhtar then presented Charlie with a perfectly tailored uniform, complete with medals and ribbons. He commended him for the service he had performed not only for Pakistan but for the cause of freedom everywhere. There was only one condition: the congressman was not to wear his uniform anywhere in Pakistan. And good luck on his trip tomorrow.

At first light the next morning, a Toyota Land Cruiser filled with men who looked like mujahideen pulled up to the main security gate of the American diplomatic compound. The guards waved the car through; even in his Afghan outfit they'd recognized General Jenjua, the Pakistani brigadier who now ran the CIA-Afghan operation. Jenjua's Land Cruiser rolled past the bougainvillea to the ambassador's residence and waited patiently for the congressman.

At the military airport General Jenjua took the congressman into a secure area and offered him a selection of hats to choose from. Wilson passed over the turban, which made him look like a buffoon, and settled on a pure white Chitrali hat. It was thoughtful of Milt to have taken such pains over his wardrobe, he reflected, and it was particularly considerate of the station chief to have arranged for the twin satellites to take a look that night at what the Soviets were up to across the border. The report had come back: all clear at Ali Khel. Still, President Zia had put the Pakistani army's border units on full alert while Wilson and his American guests were in the war zone. A squadron of F-16 interceptors had been moved onto the runway, their engines running. Helicopter rescue teams stood at the ready. On one level it was a repeat performance, but this time it was also Bearden's show.

The CIA was nowhere to be seen when the mounted mujahideen suddenly appeared at the border. But lurking in the background, following the caravan just over the horizon, plugged in with walkie-talkies, and dressed in the clothes of the mujahideen, was Bearden. Next to the station chief was his boss, Frank Anderson, who had flown in from Washington to make sure nothing went wrong. Minutes before Charlie's caravan arrived at Ali Khel, the two CIA men had entered the fort themselves.

By the very strict standards of their trade, Bearden and Anderson had strayed far off the reservation that day. They were acting a bit like two male dogs claiming their conquered territory by peeing over every strategic bush. The big, bad Red Army was running away, and they just couldn't help themselves from doing a small jig inside the fort. Before slipping away the two men posed for snapshots, then tacked a tin sheet on the garrison door. It was a coded welcome greeting to their friend—an engraving of a Russian bear swatting desperately at a swarm of stinging bees.

There is no way to explain Bearden and Anderson's high-risk gesture that day other than to say that it was payback time. And they weren't the only ones tipping their hats to Charlie Wilson. The State Department, the embassy in Islamabad, the Pakistani army and intelligence services— all were breaking the rules and doing whatever was necessary to try to acknowledge their debt to this curious rogue congressman. The idea was, quite simply, to help Charlie take credit for the biggest and most successful CIA operation ever—for what might well be considered the last true campaign of the Cold War.

It was left to Zia ul-Haq to deliver the ultimate tribute. He had made the jihad possible, and for ten years he had ruled on every aspect of the CIA's war. Until now he had deliberately wrapped the many faces of the jihad in so many layers of mystery that almost no one except himself could fully appreciate what had gone into it. Now, before the *60 Minutes* camera, he chose his words carefully as he pronounced Charlie's rightful place: "If there is a single man who has played a part that shall be recorded in history in golden letters, it is that right honorable congressman, Charles Wilson."

"But how is it possible," the veteran correspondent Harry Reasoner asked, somewhat puzzled, "for one lone congressman to have accomplished so much?"

"I'm afraid, Mr. Reasoner, that it is too early to explain it all to you," declared the arbiter. "All I can say is that 'Charlie did it.'"

That would end up being the title of the *60 Minutes* segment. It would be the writing on the screen at CIA headquarters when Wilson was brought in to receive his Honored Colleague award years later. But in the spring of 1988, with the Red Army rattling back through the northern passes, Wilson went with the *60 Minutes* team to the Khyber Pass, where he delivered what became the concluding words of the broadcast.

Reasoner, who had lived through Vietnam as a reporter and a father and who felt the sadness of such adventures, referred to the thirteen thousand Soviets who had already died and asked if Wilson did not feel a "sneaking understanding for what the Russians are going through—particularly the field troops—an enemy they can't understand, being supplied in mysterious ways?"

Some long-brooding force grew inside Charlie Wilson at that moment as he sat in the sunshine—tan-faced, square-jawed, with Afghanistan in the background and the Khyber Pass and all that it represented surrounding him. He was now talking to all America, and as he saw it, the more relevant statistics were that a hundred thousand Soviet troops were still in Afghanistan; three million Afghans were still huddled in refugee camps in Pakistan; and no one would ever know how many had died of violence, misery, hunger, and cold. When he spoke, he sounded almost menacing.

"Nobody enjoys the anguish that a twenty-year-old kid from Leningrad goes through here. And nobody enjoys the fact of his death, because he didn't have anything to do with it. . . . But, Harry, there were a hundred and sixty-seven funerals in my district," he said, referring to constituents who had died in Vietnam. "One hundred and sixty-seven boys from East Texas died from my little congressional district. And they didn't have anything to do with it either! And I love sticking it to the Russians. And I think most Americans do. They *need* to get it back, and they're getting it back. They're getting it back as we speak. They're digging in for their last stand at Gardez. And they're gonna lose! *And I love it!*"

This last point was made with such somber, Old Testament ferocity that Charlie might have been a mujahid talking about destroying the infidels. No American politician of any stature had said anything like that in two decades. It was so old in its Cold War zeal that it was new. It had nothing to do with that postwar, eastern-elite doctrine of foreign policy that called for containing Communism—no defeats, no victories. Wilson had helped introduce a new idea. This was not Korea with thirty thousand Americans dead for a line that, in the end, didn't change. Nor was it Vietnam or the Bay of Pigs or the nuclear stalemate. It was, above all, not the posturing, ill-conceived Contra war, which had ended in scandal. This was victory, and Wilson was shamefully vindictive.

Many of the millions of viewers who later watched the "Charlie Did It" segment had no idea how deeply America had been involved in Afghanistan, nor had any but a few heard of Congressman Charlie Wilson. And for anyone who heard those words coming at the camera from the Khyber Pass, Wilson must have looked like some caricature from a John Wayne movie, thirsting for Communist blood.

But Charlie hadn't moved a nation with such two dimensional motivation. The forces driving him and, through him, his cause were far deeper. At the heart of his story lay an old-fashioned belief in his country's mission: the spirit that Kennedy had summoned "to pay any price, bear any burden," which had fallen dormant; the "live free or die" code of the Afghans that made Charlie think of Bowie and Travis; those special voices the boy had heard in Trinity on the radio—Churchill during the Battle of Britain, Roosevelt rallying the nation. It was the sight of refugees shivering in tents; the appeal of those brave, desperate fighters for help against the demon in the sky; his mother teaching him always to stand up for the underdog.

That was why Charlie Wilson had set off with his rage and all of his cunning to bring down the Red Army. But Gust was equally right about his old friend: Charlie had also done it because it was plain and simple fun, because it was so exotic, and because in the end he had been able to turn it into his war and even pretend for *60 Minutes* at the Khyber Pass that he was an uncomplicated American patriot like John Wayne.

In truth, there was a very large element of uncertainty in the minds of the *60 Minutes* team as they closed down their shoot. Who was this man and what should a reasonable person think about him? At one point after the taping inside Afghanistan, Peter Henning was riding with the producer in the back of a truck filled with machine guns and mujahideen. "You know, George," he said, "you've got a big problem here. I've never seen anything like this before. You could turn Charlie Wilson into the biggest hero you've ever heard of . . . or a complete clown. It just depends which way you want to cut it."

That was the best one-sentence summary of the whole fifty-five years to date of Charlie Wilson's life. That had always been the way people looked at Wilson, and something disturbing did begin to happen to him back in Washington as the Russians continued their withdrawal and he waited to see how things would turn out.

It was the old story of the soldier coming back from the campaign and no one bothering to ask what had happened. Some colleagues offered congratulations after the Geneva accords, when the Soviets agreed to a timetable for a final withdrawal. Wilson was still included in all the serious decisions involving Afghanistan, but with the Red Army leaving, it was no longer clear that he had an essential role to play. He was not by any means going completely to seed at this point, but by now he had begun drinking again, which made life with Sweetums even more tense than before. For her it was like watching a man playing Russian roulette night after night. He was fifty-five; she only twenty-eight. Even for a strong-willed Miss World contestant, a tough Ukrainian beauty from Cleveland, it wasn't easy getting the conqueror of the Red Army to stop drinking whiskey.

The two Charlie Wilsons now were wrestling for center stage. Wilson needed someone like Gust to retool and reenergize him. Instead, thinking that Gust was somewhere in Africa, he sent a letter to the Agency notifying his old friend that he had been drafted into Flashman's Raiders. Already the bridge-crashing, hot-tub-soaking, Good-Time Charlie was beginning to elbow the secret statesman off to the side. More than ever, the endangered Charlie Wilson craved the hard-won right to continue thinking of himself as a genuine world figure.

One man alone held the key to this haunting need: Zia ul-Haq. Zia knew exactly who Charlie was, and that became Wilson's purchase on reality. Zia had become his anchor in a troubled sea: just knowing that there existed somewhere in the world a truly great man who knew that he was great too.

The smiling dictator had been Charlie's only real equal in the Afghan struggle, and in spite of every difference of religion, style, culture, and politics, they had bonded. Uncannily, Rudyard Kipling had foreshadowed this most unlikely brotherhood in a parable set in the very frontier mountains where, a century and a half before, the Afghans had turned back a British imperial army:

Oh, East is East, and West is West, and never the twain shall meet,
Till Earth and Sky stand presently at God's great Judgment Seat;
But there is neither East nor West, border, nor breed, nor birth,
When two strong men stand face-to-face, though they come from the
    ends of the earth!

Somehow Zia and Wilson had connected in spite of the clashing differences of their lives. And each had consistently astounded the other for six amazing years, until at last each had come to treat the other as a true friend and partner.

As the jihad approached its climactic hour, the two men faced one piece of unfinished business. They shared a sense that they had been great actors upon the fulcrum of history. When they met now, they talked about the need for a defining moment—like MacArthur on the deck of the U.S.S. *Missouri* accepting the unconditional surrender of imperial Japan. And from the start, they had always agreed on what form that moment should take: tens of thousands of freedom fighters in the central street of Kabul shouting *"Allahu Akbar"* and blasting off joy shots from their CIA-issued Kalashnikovs, as the two strong men from opposite ends of the earth rode side by side to savor victory for all the world to see.

"HERE'S TO YOU,
YOU MOTHERFUCKER"

It was out of character for Charlie to be in his office at 9 A.M. Usually he didn't roll in until it was time to go out for lunch. But on August 17, 1988, he was at his desk when Richard Armitage, the under secretary of defense, called with painful news: "President Zia's plane has gone down with Akhtar and the general, and we're acting on the premise that it's true." The U.S. ambassador, Arnie Raphel, had also been aboard, along with the American military attaché and nine of Zia's military high command. All were presumed dead.

Wilson knew immediately that the report had to be valid. "In my whole life," he said revealingly, "I've never received any bad news that didn't turn out to be true." Charlie got up, locked the door to his office, and didn't come out until well into the afternoon. Something inside him emptied in those long hours as, alone, he began to calculate the loss, or to try.

He'd miss Akhtar, the insular, almost debonair general with the British manners who, in spite of their similar ages, had always treated Charlie like a mischievous boy but who had become fond enough of him to get Zia to make him a secret honorary field marshal, even though the Pakistani army had no others.

And he'd only just begun to get to know Arnie Raphel, the brilliant young ambassador destined, everyone said, to be secretary of state one day. Charlie and Sweetums had recently spent a magical weekend with him in the Hunza Valley, the inspiration for Shangri-La, where everyone is said to be happy and to live to at least one hundred. They had stayed with the mir of Hunza, who lived on the roof of the world and wore little fairy-tale slippers that curled up at the toes. Raphel had just married a lovely State Department colleague, and it had been an idyll of springtime love, with all of them sharing the thrill of this historic moment.

"I loved all three almost equally," he would say, but it was losing Zia that crushed Charlie. At the state funeral in Islamabad, with a million Pakistanis and mujahideen crowding up to him, Charlie made his way to Akhtar's successor, Hamid Gul, and broke into tears. "I have lost my father on this day," he said.

Charlie had no children, and his parents were gone. His entire emotional life had become intertwined with the war. When he returned to Washington, the enormity of the catastrophe overcame him. He told Charlie Schnabel that he couldn't deal with the Afghans or even the Pakistanis anymore. Schnabel must take over the account.

For a long time Wilson's absence was not noted, because Schnabel had been moving in his name for so many years now that he could cover almost perfectly, but Schnabel was alarmed for his boss. "I couldn't even get him to come to the Sewing Circle," he said, as if describing a child too miserable to go to the ice-cream parlor.

With each Soviet battalion that crawled out of Afghanistan, it was as if the mujahideen reverted further and further to type. They could no longer be called freedom fighters, because their enemy had ceased to fight. Now they could be seen for what they were: Afghans pure and simple, with all the astonishing failings that accompany their amazing qualities.

In Pashtun, the word for *cousin* also means *enemy,* and the clans started to tear each other up even before the Russians had gone. A foreboding crept into the minds of the more observant American officials as they thought of the hundreds of millions of dollars' worth of weapons stored in mountain caves throughout Afghanistan.

Equally distressing were the questions being raised by State, as well as by some reporters, about those mujahideen factions that had received the bulk of America's support and that continued to get favored treatment. Many were Islamic radicals, not terribly different in attitude from the kind of Muslims elsewhere who were beginning to frighten the American government. Even Charlie Schnabel, who had become so enraptured with the guerrillas that he had converted to Islam one emotional night, had warned Wilson years before that the warriors of God, whom he had grown to admire and trust, themselves feared such true fanatics as Gulbuddin Hekmatyar, the special favorite of the ISI and the CIA.

Wilson, however, had been drawing his inspiration from the idea of the movement as a whole. He had purposefully never gotten to know the Afghans as individuals. It was their cause that he embraced and their cause that had been his elixir. He didn't dare differentiate.

Now the magic was all but gone; there would be no parade shoulder to shoulder with Zia. Still, as the deadline approached for the final Soviet withdrawal, he could not help but feel a pride of creation.

Again he wrote to Gust: "We miss you. Wish you were here. Hope you're having a good time in Africa. Watch out for the spears."

"Thanks for the kind words," replied Gust, "Caught two spears last month." The letter appeared to have originated in Africa, but Gust was still in McLean, Virginia.

For one glorious week Charlie basked in the glow of the *60 Minutes* profile, which included Zia's tribute and gave Wilson the lion's share of credit for what was fairly enough billed as the "largest and most successful CIA operation in history." And then what Zia had said would be "the miracle of the century" came about. On February 15, 1989, Boris Gromov, commander of the once-proud 40th Army, strode across Friendship Bridge in front of a worldwide television audience, the last Russian to leave Afghanistan.

From the station in Islamabad Bearden sent a simple cable: "We won." Charlie dashed off his own note to Gust: "We did it."

That afternoon Judge Webster threw a party at headquarters—"the most raucous and overt celebration they'd ever had there," says Wilson. The walls were covered with dozens and dozens of huge blowups of mujahideen with Stingers and their prey: wrecked helicopters and tanks. A band played as great supplies of food were consumed and whiskey drunk.

"There were so many happy people there, maybe a couple hundred," Wilson remembers. "They kept coming up to me: 'You did it, you did it.' 'This gives us our pride back.' 'This vindicates us.' 'You were the only one who thought it would work except us. You believed in us.' 'I just wanted to shake your hand.' There was a lot of hugging going on. I was hugging people I didn't know. Judge Webster was laughing and carrying on."

After the director spoke of his great pride in this astonishing accomplishment, he turned the podium over to Wilson, who began by expressing his wonderment at discovering "all the strange and brilliant anthropologists, psychiatrists, culturalists, linguists whom the Agency could just reach down and surface any time it wants. No institution in the world is so filled with such genius and talent and élan." He then singled out Gust and Frank Anderson and Jack Devine and Milt before speaking "for all of us." "No one thought we could do it when we started," he said in that booming voice of his. "And there were lots of times when we all had doubts. But as long as we live, no one will ever be able to take away from us the fact that we delivered a decisive blow to the Evil Empire from which they will never completely recover."

"It was almost like a pep rally," Charlie remembers. "I paid tribute to Casey and, of course, the muj, and there was thunderous sustained applause for the judge and me—lots of talk, like we've got to find us another war like this one. They were rowdy, extremely rowdy. All kinds of people kept coming up to me: 'I worked on overhead,' or 'I met you in Pakistan,' or 'I was involved in logistics.' I believe the judge finally walked me out. 'Thanks again,' he said. I thanked him."

"I don't remember what I did next," Charlie says, "but I'm sure I got very drunk, which is probably what I would have felt like doing because, you know, Gust wasn't there. My inclination is that I went back to the apartment and sat by myself in front of the fire and got drunk in honor of Zia and Akhtar and Arnie."

Gust was in Rome that day when Charlie was drinking himself to sleep and Boris Gromov was marching home. Avrakotos was now retired. When Tom Twetten had become the operations director he'd figured he didn't stand a chance of ever getting another good assignment. As he saw the Russians trying to paint a bright face on their withdrawal, he thought that they had gotten off easily. He figured that the mujahideen and the Agency were responsible for at least 25,000 dead, even if the Kremlin owned up to only half that.

He received just one call of congratulations that day—from a fellow Greek and his closest case officer friend, Peter Koromilas, who had given him his first shot at real responsibility when he was a new agent in Greece. Thanks to Koromilas, Gust, though only a GS-14, had operated through the colonels to virtually run the country and, as he saw it, had "kept it from going Communist." That day Peter gave him the perfect tribute: "*O Tolmon Nika*," an old Spartan war saying meaning "He who dares, wins."

Koromilas's call touched Gust and made him think of the young man he had bet on during the Afghan program. "No one will ever give you credit," he wrote to Vickers, "and in fact history will never record how big your contribution was to getting that fucking general to walk across Afghanistan into Russia."

Gust also, of course, thought of Charlie and longed to give him a call. But he figured that Wilson would be out celebrating with all of Avrakotos's old Agency crowd. He couldn't stand pity, and he didn't want to feel like an outsider. So he kept to himself in Rome.

It would have broken Gust's heart to see Charlie that night and to know how lonely his Texas friend was for him. So much had happened since Joanne Herring had first breathed fire into a rather aimless politician. She had seen the potential in him. She had urged him to link up with her hero, Zia ul-Haq, and to stand up for those marvelous freedom fighters who had only "courage as their weapon."

The political landscape of the world was tilting. Everything was changing so fast. The next morning when the sun woke him, Charlie turned on the television and stepped out onto the terrace. He looked down at the statue of the marines at Iwo Jima, which never failed to move him. Washington itself never ceased to move this bighearted kid of a man from Texas. He was admiring the gleaming white marble of the Capitol and the monuments when he realized that the TV was filled with images of Russians in fur hats, moving in their APCs and tanks. It was a tape rerun, and Gromov was about to walk over Friendship Bridge again. Charlie moved quickly to the refrigerator, where he always kept a bottle of Dom Pérignon for special occasions.

Positioning himself on the terrace before the TV image of the retreating Red Army and the city he loved, the tall man raised his glass to Boris Gromov: "Here's to you, you motherfucker."

EPILOGUE: UNINTENDED CONSEQUENCES

The morning of September 11, 2001, broke bright and shining in the nation's capital. As was his custom before leaving for work, Charlie Wilson walked out onto his terrace to take in the spectacular view. Never in history had a nation accumulated such dominance over the rest of the world as the United States had in the decade following the Soviet collapse. Wilson's name was all but unknown to most Americans, but as he looked out over the monuments and the historic houses of government, he had every reason to believe that he had played a part in the startling disappearance of America's greatest enemy.

A call from a friend interrupted his morning ritual: "Do you have your television on?"

The sight of the World Trade Center in flames stunned him, but like most Americans, he assumed it had to have been a horrendous accident. Some ten minutes later he was watching when the second plane appeared on-screen and flew straight into the second tower. A sickening realization gripped him: it had to be the work of terrorists, and, if so, he had little doubt that the killers were Muslims.

"I didn't know what to think, but figured if I got downtown I could learn more." By then Wilson had retired from Congress and was working as a lobbyist, with Pakistan as one of his main accounts. At 9:43 A.M., half an hour after the first attack, he was driving across the Fourteenth Street Bridge with the windows up and news radio blasting so loud that he didn't hear the explosion that rocked the Pentagon less than a mile away. A woman was in Wilson's condo and, as a measure of how different things were, she was his wife; he had been happily married for two years now. The shockwaves from the Pentagon were so intense that the floor under Barbara Wilson's feet shook.

That night, Charlie found himself back on the same terrace, where twelve years earlier he had toasted General Gromov on the day the Soviets marched out of Afghanistan. This time he was looking down the Potomac at the sight of the Pentagon burning. For five straight nights he watched, until the fires were finally put down and the smoke cleared. He didn't know what to make of it all at first. When the photographs of the nineteen hijackers appeared in newspapers across the country, he took some comfort in pointing out that they were all Arabs, not Afghans. "It didn't register with me for a week or two that this thing was all based in my mountains."

For most Americans, the events of 9/11 were quickly tied to Afghanistan when it was learned that the hijackers had all spent time there. Much was made of this by the Bush administration, which assailed the Taliban for harboring Osama bin Laden and for allowing Afghanistan to become a breeding ground for international terrorists. The American public rallied behind the president when he launched his "war on terror." But almost everyone seemed confused about who the terrorists were, and all but clueless to explain why they hated the United States so much.

For anyone trying to make sense of this new enemy, it would seem relevant that for over a decade in the 1980s and early 1990s, the U.S. government sponsored the largest and most successful jihad in modern history; that the CIA secretly armed and trained several hundred thousand fundamentalist warriors to fight against our common Soviet enemy; and that many of those who now targeted America were veterans of that earlier CIA-sponsored jihad.

While news reports explored every possible avenue that might explain America's new enemy, there was curiously little commentary on the role the United States had played in Afghanistan's recent past. The fact that the CIA had supported the Afghans in their guerrilla war against the Soviet Union was mentioned. But the impression left was of a nuisance campaign, like the one the Agency ran with the Nicaraguan Contras. And it was perhaps to be expected that no one from the administration chose to spell out the scope and nature of the CIA's role in the Afghan jihad. It would have been embarrassing at best. And there is no doubt that it would have complicated the president's effort to build a consensus for war. But that left the American people very much in the dark about their own immediate history.

Afghanistan was the largest and most successful covert operation ever mounted by the CIA. But the scope and nature of this campaign has still not registered in the consciousness of most Americans. Nor is it understood that such secret undertakings inevitably have unforeseen and unintended consequences, which in this case remained largely ignored. None of the sponsors of the campaign, least of all Charlie Wilson, has ever felt responsible for the path the CIA-sponsored jihad has taken; perhaps that's because their intentions were so pure and because the specific objectives they sought were initially so overwhelmingly successful.

The origins of this book go back to a time when the Afghans were viewed by most everyone in the U.S. government as freedom fighters, allies against a common foe. It was January of 1989, just as the Red Army was preparing to withdraw its last soldiers from Afghanistan, when Charlie Wilson called to invite me to join him on a fact-finding tour of the Middle East. I had produced a *60 Minutes* profile of Wilson several months earlier and had no intention of digging further into his role in the Afghan war. But I quickly accepted the invitation. The trip began in Kuwait, moved on to Saddam Hussein's Iraq, and then to Saudi Arabia—a grand tour that took us to all three of the countries that would soon take center stage in the Gulf War. For me, the trip was just the beginning of a decade-long odyssey.

There were two surprises on that trip, revelations that opened my eyes to a bigger story: the first was the princely reception given to Wilson wherever he went in the Arab world. The second was my introduction to Gust Avrakotos, recently retired from the CIA and reunited with his co-conspirator for the first time in several years. As we moved from Kuwait down to the battlefield of Basra, where hundreds of thousands had died in the closing battles of the Iran-Iraq War, I began talking to Avrakotos, and in short order I realized that the Afghan campaign had been anything but a typical CIA program.

When our commercial flight back to Baghdad was canceled, Avrakotos managed to get us onto a lavish Boeing 707 owned by a Saudi religious leader by telling him about Wilson's role in the Afghan war. We shared the flight with a delegation of holy men from the strict Wahhabi sect, some of whom were still sending money and Arab volunteers to the jihad in Afghanistan. The plane was, in effect, a flying mosque: luxuriously outfitted with solid-gold bathroom fixtures, soft leather seats, and numerous monitors that tracked the direction of Mecca for the plane's passengers. It was in this setting that Avrakotos began to tell me about the Afghan program and about a side of Charlie Wilson I had never seen. In marked contrast to the congressman's image as a good-natured, even-tempered fellow, Avrakotos described him as a man who struck terror in the bureaucrats at the CIA and the other agencies involved in the Afghan war. Soon it dawned on me that these two men had been engaged in an extra-governmental conspiracy, and that Avrakotos held the key to understanding the CIA side of it.

In Riyadh, a royal receiving party met us at the airport. A caravan of brand-new white Mercedes-Benzes, complete with police escort, swept us off to the palace for a meeting with the king's brother, Saudi defense minister Prince Sultan. After tea, Wilson delivered his message: he had come to thank the Saudi royal family for its extraordinary generosity in matching the Americans dollar for dollar in Afghanistan. It became clear that the gratitude went both ways when Wilson was shown to his quarters several hours later—a preposterously lavish suite with a living room that seemed to be the size of a football field.

"We want you to know, Mr. Congressman," the prince's aide said, "that these are larger quarters than we provided for George Bush. Mr. Bush is only the vice president. You won the Afghan war."

While Charlie Wilson greatly appreciated this princely salute, he still had unfinished business to attend to. Wilson knew that all great campaigns needed closure—that moment when victory is acknowledged and a grateful nation honors its heroes—and he was hell-bent on creating such an event to honor the mujahideen victory. More than just a yearning for his own personal glory, Wilson felt he owed it to the Afghans.

Throughout the Muslim world, the victory of the Afghans over the army of a modern superpower was seen as a transformational event. But back home, no one seemed to be aware that something important had taken place and that the United States had been the moving force behind it. Any chance of an American appreciation for the Afghan miracle was fast disappearing, as one incredible event after another began to unravel the Soviet eastern bloc. That August, Lech Walesa and his movement pushed aside the Communists and took power in Poland. Then in November, the ultimate symbol of Communist oppression, the Berlin Wall, came down. It was just nine months after the Red Army's humiliating retreat from Afghanistan, and the dominoes were now falling in central and Eastern Europe. As Charlie Wilson saw it, his Afghans had played a decisive role in helping to trigger and hasten the collapse of the

Communist eastern bloc. Some 28,000 Soviet soldiers were killed in the war, but more than a million Afghans had died, and no one had ever thanked them for their sacrifice.

That was precisely the message that Wilson and Zia had intended to deliver with the victory parade they had so carefully planned. These two patrons of the jihad, mounted on great white horses, were to ride side by side down the main avenue of Kabul. Freedom fighters would line the street as far as the eye could see, filling the air with thundering cries of *"Allahu Akbar,"* along with volley upon volley of CIA-dispensed joy shots. This celebration of freedom would be seen and remembered around the world, and the partnership of America and its Muslim friends would be seared into everyone's consciousness. That particular vision died with Zia, but Charlie had not given up.

In 1989, the year of the Afghan victory, Charlie brought his kid sister Sharon, Sweetums, Gust, and a collection of friends with him to Pakistan, where he was scheduled to receive the country's highest decoration. It should have been a moment of triumph, but Charlie found himself preoccupied by the unpaid debt to the mujahideen and by his need to make America discover and recognize the great victory it shared with the Afghans. That's when he came up with an idea so spectacular that even Cecil B. DeMille might have been impressed.

There are few stage sets in the world as dramatic and as filled with a sense of history as the parade grounds high up in the mountains of the Khyber Rifles, the regiment that guards the fabled pass leading into Afghanistan. Wilson took his entourage there to show them the site of the extravaganza he was planning. Ostensibly he was only organizing his wedding to Sweetums. When he had asked her to marry him that spring, he promised a ceremony no one would ever forget. What he didn't say was that he had now decided to have the wedding serve a dual purpose.

It's hard to surprise Gust Avrakotos. But watching Wilson that day, he was struck once again by the magic in this man. Somehow Charlie had managed to enlist the diplomatic and intelligence services of both Pakistan and the United States to assume responsibility for the logistics and planning of the wedding. Milt Bearden, along with the Pakistani intelligence chief, Hamid Gul, had accepted Wilson's commission to see to it that the streets and parade deck would overflow with bearded Afghan warriors. Without the mujahideen, Charlie explained, the event would have no meaning. The seven Afghan tribal leaders were to be enthroned at one end of the gathering; and thousands of mujahideen would fire off joy shots at every important interval in the service. Milt, as usual, had added a dramatic flourish with his offer to provide tracer rounds at a ratio of five to one in order to enhance the celebratory nature of the Afghans.

The ceremony itself was to be performed by Wilson's great friend from the Appropriations Committee, Bill Gray—the black congressman and former Baptist minister who was the number three man in the House Democratic leadership. That struck Avrakotos as quite typical of Charlie— bringing his own Baptist minister to the Khyber Pass. But it got better. Gray would be part of an official congressional delegation that Speaker Jim Wright had agreed to lead to Pakistan to attend the event, as if it were a state function. The delegation was to include the members of the Defense Appropriations subcommittee, where so many of the key battles of the war had been fought.

For best man, Charlie had tapped his old drinking buddy, field marshal Abu Ghazala, the defense minister of Egypt. Wilson's great friend, the high-placed Israeli Zvi Rafiah, would maintain a low profile somewhere in the crowd. There was no telling how many mandarins of the CIA and the Pakistan intelligence service would be in attendance, but there would be many. And all of Charlie's Angels would be on hand, along with Baron Ricky di Portanova, the baroness, Charles Fawcett, and Joanne Herring, the Christian godmother of the Muslim victory.

Listening to Wilson describe the guest list, it suddenly dawned on Gust what Charlie was doing. Here, on this magnificent stage on the roof of the world, he was planning to unveil all of the secret cast of characters who had played leading roles in the great drama he had just produced— the players who had changed history. And to make sure the world got the message, he invited me to come along with a *60 Minutes* camera crew.

It all might have happened if Charlie hadn't gotten careless a couple of weeks later. He had flown to California to serve as the grand marshal in the annual Mule Day parade, an honor recognizing all that the congressman had done to enlist Tennessee mules in the great anti-Communist jihad. But early that morning, when Sweetums called Charlie's hotel room, Snowflake answered the phone.

*   *   *

It was the end of the affair; there would be no wedding at the Khyber Pass, no parade. It was also the last time that Wilson, or anyone else, would even think about publicly glorifying the Afghans. Charlie had planned a victory parade, but in truth, the Afghan war hadn't ended. The Soviets were gone but their puppet government was very much in place, as was the CIA's Afghan war budget. This was the beginning of the dark side of the Afghan adventure.

Throughout the war, Wilson had always told his colleagues that Afghanistan was the one morally unambiguous cause that the United States had supported since World War II—and never once had any member of Congress stood up to protest or question the vast expenditures. But with the departure of the Soviets, the war was anything but morally unambiguous. By 1990 the Afghan freedom fighters had suddenly and frighteningly gone back to form, reemerging as nothing more than feuding warlords obsessed with settling generations-old scores. The difference was that they were now armed with hundreds of millions of dollars' worth of weapons and explosives of every conceivable type. The justification for the huge CIA operation had been to halt Soviet aggression, not to take sides in a tribal war—certainly not to transform the killing capacity of these warriors.

It was a turning point that demanded a reevaluation; someone in the U.S. government needed to take the lead in charting a new course. For a brief time, Wilson looked as if he might assume the role of a statesman. His model for enlightened leadership had always been the men who led America during and after World War II, when the United States defeated and then rebuilt Europe and Japan with the Marshall Plan. He proposed a billion-dollar U.S. aid package to begin rebuilding Afghanistan and did his best to rally support. At the end of that first year, he set off for Moscow to see what could be done to end the surrogate war that continued to rage. The Russians were pumping an estimated $3 billion a year into Afghanistan to prop up the puppet government led by Najibullah, while the CIA, with Saudi matching funds, maintained the enormous flow of weapons to the feuding warlords.

At his meeting with Andre Koserov, the future Russian foreign minister argued that the United States and Russia now had a common interest in stabilizing Afghanistan and particularly in preventing radical Islamic elements from taking power. The Soviets' preoccupation, Koserov explained, was Gulbuddin Hekmatyar, the mujahideen leader who had so impressed Joanne Herring and whose close ties to Pakistan's ISI made him the leading recipient of CIA weaponry. Koserov insisted that Gulbuddin's brand of militant Islam was just as dangerous to America as it was to the Soviet Union—a point Charlie had heard frequently that year from his own side.

What struck Wilson most on his visit was not Koserov's reasoned appeal, but the discovery that, whatever the sins of the Communist regime, the people of Russia had been liberated. He witnessed the explosion of religious faith after years of repression, and he attended a daring production of the musical *Hair* in the union hall of a cigarette factory. But everywhere, the scarcity of consumer goods shocked and saddened him. This, he realized, was a defeated nation.

When Charlie returned to Washington, the men running the CIA's Afghan program were alarmed to read an interview in the *New York Times* that presented him in a dovish light. Wilson says they immediately descended on his office to "whip me into shape. They complained about the interview and said it looked as if I had traded in my hound dog for a poodle and my pickup truck for a BMW." Beyond the jibing, Wilson says that the Saudis, who had just honored Charlie, expected the United States to hold firm in its support of the mujahideen.

It was sad to see how quickly Wilson's effort at statesmanship collapsed. He found that it wasn't easy to stop what he had started. He was a politician and a dealmaker, and as he put it, "I had asked the Saudis and the CIA to run with me. When they told me what they expected in return, I decided to go along with it. I didn't have the old fire and zeal, but I knew I had to pay back."

In the second year after the Soviet withdrawal, Wilson delivered another $250 million for the CIA to keep its Afghan program intact. With Saudi matching funds, the mujahideen would receive another half billion dollars to wage war. The expectation was that they would join forces for a final push to throw out the Soviet-backed Najibullah regime, restore order, and begin the process of rebuilding. The Agency even sent word to Wilson that as an act of gratitude for the renewed budget, the mujahideen planned to take Jalalabad by June 1, Charlie's birthday. It didn't happen. Instead the Najibullah forces held, as the Afghans bickered and disgraced themselves by massacring prisoners.

That year, Saddam Hussein invaded Kuwait; adding insult to injury, Gulbuddin and Sayaf—the mujahideen leader closest to the Saudis, whose men had guided Wilson into Afghanistan for the *60 Minutes* shoot—both publicly sided with Hussein against the United States. Their subsidies, however, continued.

With the news from Afghanistan growing darker, Charlie escaped so deep into drink that he began attending sessions of the congressional chapter of Alcoholics Anonymous. No member of Congress had ever acquired a position of such towering influence over the CIA as had Charlie Wilson at that particular time. He was consulted on every aspect of the Agency's dealings with Congress, and incredibly, at the same time, he chaired the committee that served as the congressional watchdog over the CIA. At best, though, Wilson was operating on automatic pilot, rarely attending the special briefings the Agency put on for him and refusing to meet with the mujahideen when they came to Washington. It was almost as if he didn't want to see or hear what was happening to his old freedom fighters.

Finally, on April Fools' Day, 1991, there was good news from the front —very good news. Wilson learned that his favorite commander, Jalaluddin Haqani, had "liberated" Khost. The first major Afghan city was now in the hands of the freedom fighters, and it was in no small measure due to the introduction of a series of lethal new weaponry that had come out of Wilson's Weapons Upgrade Program.

Soon after, I accompanied Wilson's administrative assistant, Charlie Schnabel, to meet up with Haqani and take stock of how the mujahideen were conducting themselves as they began to reclaim their country. The stories we heard once we reached Pakistan were alarming. The mujahideen were hijacking the AID trucks, making regular runs impossible. At Friday prayers, the mullahs were inflaming their followers with accounts of Western NGO volunteers teaching Afghan women to wash with soap. An enraged mob had marched on the facility that provided free health care to women, now convinced that the clinic was promoting free sex. They burned the facility to the ground and trashed seventeen cars—$1.8 million in damage in just one day. Afghan women working in refugee camps as teachers and nurses were threatened; one had just been kidnapped and murdered. In Peshawar, the American consul relayed a particularly horrific account of one of Gulbuddin's many outrages. A few months earlier he had sought to "liberate" Khost by shelling the civilian population of the city. Thousands fled their homes, and the embassy, sensing a massive humanitarian crisis, dispatched medics from the Cross Border program to care for the wounded and the refugees. As diplomat Janet Bogue told us, "The U.S. government now finds itself giving guns to a friend who shells civilian populations, and then we turn around and send in a humanitarian mission to deal with the refugees created by our own investment."

Khost was hardly the triumph that Schnabel and Wilson had envisioned. It was like a ghost town when we arrived. The bazaar, which had been full just days before, was empty. Everyone had fled the liberators. Nothing moved except armed mujahideen soldiers. Many of the warriors were said to be radical Arabs who had come to get in on the jihad. There was little sign of life and few prospects of people returning anytime soon.

The most chilling story we heard was of the sound trucks that Crandall's Cross Border program had dispatched to Khost as the mujahideen moved in to take the city. Instead of devoting its energies to rebuilding Afghanistan, as they had hoped, the Cross Border program found itself following the liberators in a desperate attempt to persuade them not to murder and pillage.

None of this attracted any real attention in the world press, which had either forgotten about or lost interest in Afghanistan—in spite of the fact that the CIA and KGB were continuing to mount the largest covert Cold War battle in history. For all practical purposes, the Cold War was over, and it seemed as if the United States and Russia had come to share roughly the same long-term goals in Afghanistan. The only logical explanation for why the two superpowers were now funding this mysterious war of the tribes was the force of inertia. Simply put, neither side wanted to be the first to pull back.

In Islamabad, however, someone with enough stature to call the entire program into question suddenly clocked in. Ambassador Robert Oakley was a hard-liner, a champion of the program. His wife, Phyllis, had been the Afghan desk officer when Wilson first took up the cause, and Oakley had been the NSC staff man for Afghanistan. He had taken over his current post when his predecessor, Arnie Raphel, died in the plane crash with President Zia.

Oakley was, in short, an activist, an ambassador who made sure that Bearden and the ISI chief, Hamid Gul, understood that when it came to intelligence matters, the three of them were a triumvirate. He was there when Gulbuddin and Massoud resumed their blood feud, when the mujahideen began stealing health funds, when two of the CIA's oldest Afghan allies came out for Saddam. He had been sufficiently concerned about the rise of anti-American sentiment in Pakistan during the Gulf War to evacuate the embassy and urge all Americans to leave the country. And now, watching the rise of radical Islam, he questioned whether the freedom fighters even existed any longer.

It was almost unthinkable, but he now wondered if our Afghans, no longer menaced by the Red Army, were any different from the Afghans whom the Russians were backing. In fact, it was the leaders of the Afghan puppet government who were saying all the right things, even paying lip service to democratic change. The mujahideen, on the other hand, were committing unspeakable atrocities and couldn't even put aside their bickering and murderous thoughts long enough to capture Kabul. Even if the mujahideen finally took the country, Oakley asked himself, "Would they be sympathetic to us and would we want anything to do with them?"

Oakley had looked down every alley for a rationalization for continuing the CIA program, and he always came upon the same signpost: "What's a nice group of kids like us doing in a place like this?" Without the Russians around, did we really want to be giving long-range Stingers, satellite-guided mortars, burst transmitters, and hundreds of millions of dollars' worth of ordnance to these men?"

Crandall's Cross Border program was all but powerless to stop the carnage. The image of the caravans following our warriors wherever they triumphed, blaring out messages of restraint—admirable though it may have been—seemed misguided. It was like a scene out of *Apocalypse Now*: lunatic, crazed shooting of everything that moved, followed by a heroic, humanitarian gesture to save a small dog or child.

This was not what had led Bob Oakley to become an American ambassador. He had been a hard-liner when the Russians were the Evil Empire. But as he assessed the U.S. presence in Afghanistan and Pakistan, he drew the conclusion that America's national interests were not being served. His recommendation was to cut off the mujahideen, and he began moving about in key political circles in Pakistan, telling the ISI and the mujahideen leaders that the United States was getting out: "We've given it the old college try. We've stayed with the mujahideen for two and a half years. It's actually been three and a half since Gorbachev told Reagan that the Russians were pulling out. It's up to them now."

Oakley's opinions counted: he was Jim Baker's former college roommate and a friend of President Bush. And he was prepared to suggest that American policy should have changed when the 40th Army withdrew. The mujahideen had helped end the Cold War; the Saudis had helped bankroll the effort; and both would consider it disloyal if the United States cut and ran. But the United States had done its part and each year it seemed that Najibullah only grew stronger and the mujahideen only more divided, less attractive, maybe even dangerous. Oakley's fear was that they might win and we'd have to cope with the spectacle of our freedom fighters running riot—all in the name of a CIA freedom campaign.

Wilson was surprised that spring to hear that the administration was not putting in a request for more money. There had been meetings in Wilson's office and talks with Judge William Webster, the new director of Central Intelligence, about the coming year's budget, but the Agency was no longer of a single mind. The Bush administration, however, wanted out of this game—so the CIA's seventh floor had no choice but to reflect the opinion of their masters in the White House.

But no one could just turn off Charlie Wilson's war like that. Not when the new men running the CIA's Afghan program had long since learned Gust's trick of appearing unannounced and without authorization to suggest that, in spite of official CIA policy, there were those in the Agency who felt that it would be a shame not to see this battle through to its proper conclusion.

With no request for funds, the Senate Select Committee met and reported out a bill with nothing in it for Afghanistan. On September 30, 1991, the end of the fiscal year, the flow of weapons, ammunition, and supplies that the mujahideen had so dearly loved would stop. But for Charlie Wilson, there was something fundamentally wrong with his war ending then and there. He didn't like the idea of the United States going out with a whimper. The president might want to end the war, but it wasn't his war to end. It had always been Congress's war, and just because there was disarray at the CIA didn't mean Congress should step back. That was the essence of the appeal Wilson made to his highly reluctant colleagues on the House Intelligence Committee when they met to consider the annual budget. Incredibly, he carried the day. No one knew how to say no to Charlie.

"Where will we get the money?" the chairman of the Intelligence Committee asked.

"It doesn't matter," Wilson said in his most selfless tone. "Take it from a Texas defense contract. Whatever. The main thing is: this body should not be cutting off the mujahideen."

"Well, shit. How about $25 million?" McCurdy asked, meaning $25 million per quarter, $100 million for the year.

"How about $50 million?" Wilson responded. And $50 million a quarter is what they ultimately agreed on. With the Saudi contribution, that meant another $400 million for the mujahideen.

It was only the beginning of the extraordinary maneuvers Wilson had to make to push this bill through a highly reluctant Congress. By then even his most reliable ally, John Murtha, the chairman of the Defense Appropriations subcommittee, wanted to end the CIA program. Murtha was appalled at reports of the mujahideen's drug trafficking, but in the end he stood with Charlie, and his support guaranteed the bill's passage in the House. It was passed in the Senate that fall. The secret appropriation was hidden in the $298 billion Defense bill for fiscal year 1992. When it was presented for a vote, no one but the interested few noticed the $200 million earmarked for the Afghans.

And so, as the mujahideen were poised for their thirteenth year of war, instead of being cut off, it turned out to be a banner year. They found themselves with not only a $400 million budget but also with a cornucopia of new weaponry sources that opened up when the United States decided to send the Iraqi weapons captured during the Gulf War to the mujahideen.

However disgraceful the mujahideen's conduct was in the following months, in April 1992 they managed to stop fighting one another long enough to take Kabul. Once again Charlie felt vindicated. He had stayed the course and allowed the victory that belonged to the Afghans to occur. But then everything became ugly. By August, the interim foreign minister, Gulbuddin Hekmatyar, was outside of the capital, with his artillery shelling the positions of his former comrade in arms, the interim defense minister Ahmad Shah Massoud. Kabul, which had survived the entire Afghan war relatively intact, was suddenly subjected to intense urban warfare. Before it was over, close to 40 percent of the housing was destroyed; the art museum was leveled; the palace ravaged.

Under normal circumstances, such misuse of American resources should have led to a scandal or at least entered the American consciousness as an issue of concern. But the anarchy in Kabul was completely overshadowed by the historic events sweeping the world. In December 1991, the Soviet Union ceased to exist. Everywhere across the twelve time zones of the former Soviet Union, statues of Lenin were coming down and freedom was breaking out in a Russia reborn. People everywhere were now referring to the United States as the world's lone superpower.

For the men who ruled the CIA, Afghanistan was acknowledged as the main catalyst that helped trigger these historic changes. Flush with the glory of tumbling dominoes and convinced that the Afghan campaign had been the key to it all, the Directorate of Operations moved to recognize the man who had made it possible. Without Charlie Wilson, Director Woolsey said in his comments, "History might have been hugely different and sadly different." It wasn't the parade that Charlie had sought, but then no other member of Congress, indeed no outsider, had ever been singled out by the CIA for such an accomplishment. If that's where it all had ended for Charlie Wilson—standing tall at Langley that day with the fear of nuclear war fast receding and America now the world's only superpower—then it truly would have been a Cold War fairy tale come true.

But that's not the way history works. Inevitably, great events have unintended consequences. What no one involved anticipated was that it might be dangerous to awaken the dormant dreams and visions of Islam. Which is, of course, exactly what happened.

There were many early warnings well before Charlie's award at Langley. In January of that year, a young Pakistani, Mir Aimal Kasi, walked down the line of cars at the gates of the CIA and calmly murdered two officers before escaping to Pakistan where he was embraced as a folk hero. The month after Kasi's shooting spree at the CIA in February 1993, the World Trade Center was bombed. What emerged from the smoke was a clear indication that some of the veterans of the Afghan campaign now identified America as their enemy.

As early as a year before at Khost, a haunting portrait of the future was already in place: battle-hardened Afghan mujahideen, armed to the

teeth and broken down into rival factions—one of the largest being a collection of Arab and Muslim volunteers from around the world. Pakistan's
former intelligence chief, Hamid Gul, maintains that over the course of
the jihad, up to thirty thousand volunteers from other countries had come
into Pakistan to take part in the holy war. What now seems clear is that,
under the umbrella of the CIA's program, Afghanistan had become a gathering place for militant Muslims from around the world, a virtual Mecca
for radical Islamists.

The man Charlie described as "goodness personified," Jalaluddin
Haqani, had long been a gateway for Saudi volunteers, and for years the
CIA had no problem with such associations. Osama bin Laden was one of
those volunteers who could frequently be found in the same area where
Charlie had been Haqani's honored guest. As the CIA's favorite commander, Haqani had received bags of money each month from the station
in Islamabad. In the aftermath of 9/11, he would emerge as the number
three target of the U.S. forces in Afghanistan.

As early as the Gulf War, Gulbuddin Hekmatyar, long the main recipient
of CIA weaponry, had articulated his belief that the United States was seeking world domination and control of Muslim oil. After the events of 9/11,
he too became a target of his old patron when the CIA attempted to assassinate him with a Hellfire missile launched from an Agency-controlled
Predator drone. Like the attempts on Haqani and bin Laden, the lack of
success only enhanced the aura of invincibility surrounding those seen as
enjoying Allah's protection.

The presumption at Langley had been that when the United States
packed its bags and cut off the Afghans, the jihad would simply burn itself
out. If the Afghans insisted on killing one another, it would be a shame but
not America's problem. Perhaps that policy would have worked out had it
been only weapons that we left behind. But the more dangerous legacy of
the Afghan war is found in the minds and convictions of Muslims around
the world. To them the miracle victory over the Soviets was all the work
of Allah—not the billions of dollars that America and Saudi Arabia poured
into the battle, not the ten-year commitment of the CIA that turned an
army of primitive tribesmen into techno–holy warriors. The consequence

for America of having waged a secret war and never acknowledging or advertising its role was that we set in motion the *spirit* of jihad and the belief in our surrogate soldiers that, having brought down one superpower, they could just as easily take on another.

The question that has puzzled so many Americans, "Why do they hate us?" is not so difficult to understand if you put yourself in the shoes of the Afghan veterans in the aftermath of the Soviet departure. Within months, the U.S. government "discovered" what it had known for the past eight years—that Pakistan was hard at work on the Islamic bomb. But with the Russians gone, sanctions were imposed and all military and economic assistance was cut off. The fleet of F-16s that Pakistan had already purchased was withheld. Within a year, the Clinton Administration would move to place Pakistan on the list of state sponsors of terrorism for its support of Kashmiri freedom fighters. The Pakistan military had long been the surrogates for the CIA, and every Afghan and Arab mujahid came to believe that America had betrayed the Pakistanis. And when the United States kept its troops (including large numbers of women) in Saudi Arabia, not just bin Laden but most Islamists believed that America wanted to seize the Islamic oil fields and was seeking world domination.

By the end of 1993, the six-year-old Cross Border Humanitarian Aid Program—the one sustained U.S. effort to create an infrastructure and blueprint for the rebuilding of Afghanistan—was cut off. The University of Nebraska educators who ran part of the program had appealed to the Clinton Administration for funds to at least warehouse the large store of textbooks that had already been printed, but even this was denied. There were no roads, no schools, just a destroyed country—and the United States was washing its hands of any responsibility. It was in this vacuum that the Taliban and Osama bin Laden would emerge as the dominant players. It is ironic that a man who had had almost nothing to do with the victory over the Red Army, Osama bin Laden, would come to personify the power of the jihad. In 1998, when bin Laden survived $100 million worth of cruise missiles targeted at him, it reinforced the belief that Allah had chosen to protect him against the infidels. Ironically, one of those cruise missiles struck the very spot where Charlie had slept in Haqani's camp.

It's not what Charlie Wilson had in mind when he took up the cause of the Afghans. Nevertheless, in spite of 9/11 and all the horrors that have flowed from it, he steadfastly maintains that it was all worth it and that nothing can diminish what the Afghans accomplished for America and the world with their defeat of the Red Army: "I truly believe that this caused the Berlin Wall to come down a good five, maybe ten, years before it would have otherwise. Over a million Russian Jews got their freedom and left for Israel; God knows how many were freed from the gulags. At least a hundred million Eastern Europeans are breathing free today, to say nothing of the Russian people. It's the truth, and all those people who are enjoying those freedoms have no idea of the part played by a million Afghan ghosts. To this day no one has ever thanked them.

"They removed the threat we all went to sleep with every night, of World War III breaking out. The countries that used to be in the Warsaw Pact are now in NATO. These were truly changes of biblical proportion, and the effect the jihad had in accelerating these events is nothing short of miraculous.

"These things happened. They were glorious and they changed the world. And the people who deserved the credit are the ones who made the sacrifice. And then we fucked up the endgame."

The story of Charlie Wilson and the CIA's secret war in Afghanistan is an important, missing chapter of our recent past. Ironically, neither the United States government nor the forces of Islam will want this history to be known. But the full story of America's central role in the Afghan jihad needs to be told and understood for any number of reasons. Clearly it's not helpful for the world of militant Islam to believe that its power is so great that nothing can stop it. But the danger exists for us as well. It may not be welcomed by a government that prefers to see the rising tide of Islamic militancy as having no connection to our policies or our actions. But the terrible truth is that the group of sleeping lions that the United States roused may well have inspired an entire generation of militant young Muslims to believe that the moment is theirs.

To call these final pages an epilogue is probably a misnomer. Epilogues indicate that the story has been wrapped up, the chapter finished. This one, sadly, is far from over.

SOURCE NOTES

The reporting for this book spans fifteen years. It included repeated trips to Afghanistan, Pakistan, the former Soviet Union, Russia, Saudi Arabia, and numerous locations in the United States where people who had figured prominently in the Afghan war could be found. Nearly all of the key figures responsible for running this secret enterprise were interviewed and were generous in their cooperation. However, this book tells the story of activities so concealed from the central authorities of the government itself that no complete account exists in any archive.

The extensive recollections of Charlie Wilson and Gust Avrakotos form the backbone of the greater part of this narrative. Equally important are the scores of other interviews with central figures involved in this operation who sometimes had conflicting opinions but were able to confirm crucial aspects of this most unlikely story.

It was my good fortune to accompany Wilson on a number of his trips—inside Afghanistan itself; into the new Russia; with the royal family in Saudi Arabia; at presidential headquarters in Pakistan; and, memorably, at Charlie's awards ceremony at Langley. The prickly Avrakotos was also generous with access on his travels, and much time was spent with him in Rome, Aliquippa, the Middle East, and McLean, Virginia.

In any story of this nature, the issue of motives needs to be addressed. The first point to make is that the core interviews were conducted in the enchanted light of a Cold War fairy tale come true during the early 1990s. At the time, inside the CIA, the Afghan campaign was seen as an authentic miracle. The participants were deeply proud of their roles and felt that this was a story that should be told.

In the time I spent with Gust Avrakotos over these many years, I was always haunted by Bernal Díaz's sad commentary in the preface to his classic book about the experiences he had shared with Cortes, as a conquistador, when they set off for the New World for God, for country, and for gold: "I am now an old man, over eighty-four years of age, and have lost both sight and hearing; and unfortunately I have gained no wealth to leave my children and descendants, except this true story, which is a most remarkable one, as my readers will presently see."

The following is an extensive, but by no means complete, list of those whose cooperation has made this history possible. As might be expected, some sources cannot be divulged. Certain people whose names it would be repetitious to list in every instance where their recollections were drawn on have been omitted.

Charlie in Texas, from boyhood to Congress: this account draws heavily on Wilson's own recollections. But also I drew on interviews with the late congresswoman Barbara Jordan; Charlie's sister Sharon Allison; Charles Schnabel; Charles Simpson, Charlie's close friend; Joe Murray of Cox Newspapers; Larry L. King of *Texas Monthly* and *Harper's* magazine; Molly Ivins of *Texas Monthly* and much else; and Paul Begala.

The general accounts of what Wilson himself describes as "the longest midlife crisis in history" come primarily from his own recollections. Many others supplied memorable details and flavor: Stuart Pierson, Wilson's lawyer; former governor Ann Richards; Charles Simpson; Charles Schnabel; Carol Shannon; Diane Sawyer; Lori White; Molly Hamilton; Agnes Bundy; Elaine Lang; and indeed many others.

With regard to Charlie as a visible and invisible power on the Hill, I drew upon the insights of former speakers Tip O'Neill, Jim Wright, and Tom Foley; former majority leader Tony Coelho; former whip Bill Gray; David Obey, lately chairman of Appropriations; and many others from the Appropriations world, notably Representative John Murtha, the late Clarence "Doc" Long, and Silvio Conte, the ranking Republican on Appropriations; Representatives Joe McDade, Louis Stokes, and Bob Livingston. I also drew on interviews with the Washington lobbyist Denis Neill; former representative Steve Solarz; Esther Kurtz of the American Israel Public Affairs Committee (AIPAC); Maurice Rosenblatt; Zvi Rafiah; Ed Koch; and Representatives Henry Hyde, Bob Mrazek, Tom Downey, Bob Dornan, Dave McCurdy, Lee Hamilton, Edward Boland, and Pat Schroeder.

Wilson's misadventures in Nicaragua are described again by Wilson himself but also by the late Tacho Somoza; Ed Wilson, formerly with the CIA but now serving a life sentence; Pat Derian, Jimmy Carter's assistant secretary of state for human rights; former Representative Jack Murphy; and Tina Simons, formerly of both Ed and Charlie Wilson's staffs, who is now in the federal witness protection program.

Wilson's entry into the Afghan arena in response to Dan Rather's report (as well as others') was described by Jim Van Wagenen of the Defense Appropriations subcommittee staff and was supplemented with Wilson's own account. Dan Rather was also interviewed.

Charlie himself described his trip to Sabra and Shatilla and his extreme disappointment and sadness at discovering that the Israelis had permitted a massacre of innocents. Wilson himself described the poisoning of his dog and the revenge that he took. He also described his first meeting with Zia ul-Haq, which occurred on this trip; Joanne and Zia discussed this first encounter, too.

The overall account of Wilson's struggles with the Agency to escalate the war, as well as afterward when he became their "station chief on the Hill," started from Wilson's own descriptions. In every instance, however, his version is accompanied by accounts of the same events from a broad range of CIA officers Wilson encountered, including Bob Gates, Tom Twetten, Clair George, Frank Anderson, Jack Devine, Milt Bearden, Howard Hart, Norm Gardner, Art Alper, Larry Penn, Mike Vickers, Charles (Chuck) Cogan, Ed Juchniewicz, John McMahon, and Gust Avrakotos.

Joanne Herring is the primary source for the account of her life in Texas, her global anti-Communist network, and her efforts to convince Charlie Wilson and President Zia to champion the Afghan cause. The account of Charles Fawcett's life and his involvement with the Afghans comes from Fawcett himself, who was very generous with his time. Arnaud de Borchgrave, the Baron and Baroness di Portanova, and Hasan Nouri also contributed.

The seduction of Doc Long and Wilson's legislative maneuvers to push through the Oerlikon draw on lengthy interviews with Jeff Nelson, Norm Gardner, and Jim Van Wagenen, as well as on accounts from Wilson, Joanne Herring, and Zia.

Primary night, 1984, was resurrected by Charlie's sister Sharon, Joanne Herring, Charles Fawcett, and Joe Murray.

Wilson's own descriptions of his travels were richly supplemented by those of the various women who accompanied him, most notably Trish Wilson, Carol Shannon, Cynthia Gale Watson (Snowflake), and Annelise Ilschenko (Sweetums), as well as by Joe Christie and Colonel Jim Rooney.

Gust Avrakotos himself evoked his steel-town childhood and his recruitment into the CIA's elite Clandestine Services. Readers will understand that several people who filled me in on Gust's early career there can be thanked but not identified. The story of Avrakotos's sessions with Nitsa, "the witch," and his hidden days at the CIA "underground in the underground" come from Avrakotos himself and others who asked that they not be named (a notable exception being the recollections of Art Alper, the demolitions expert).

This entire history hinges on the first unauthorized encounter between Wilson and Avrakotos in the Rayburn building. Both men gave memorable versions of that incident and of the consequences flowing from it.

How Gust tried and failed to deflect the Agency from the Iran-Contra scandal comes directly from Avrakotos himself and was further amplified by a number of people so well-placed they preferred not to be identified. George Cave, although he did not address the issue of Avrakotos's memo, provided useful context for understanding the concern of the profession.

The shadowy but indispensable Saudi connection was clarified by Gust Avrakotos, as well as by Prince Bandar (ambassador to the United States and chief of Saudi military), and Adel el Jabar.

The visit to Mohammed's arms bazaar was reconstructed from the recollections of many participants: Field Marshal Mohammed Abu Ghazala, General Yahia, Denis Neill, Trish Wilson, Gust Avrakotos, Charlie Wilson, and Art Alper.

For the inner history of the new weapons mix and the transformation of America's Afghan strategy, Wilson and Avrakotos were necessarily the prime sources, along with Mike Vickers and other more concealed participants. General Mohammad Yousaf provided an account from the Pakistani point of view.

The account of the birth and implementation of the McCollum flights and the Weapons Upgrade Program is drawn from interviews with Vaughn Forest, Charles Schnabel, Chuck Barnard, Edward Luttwak, General Richard Stillwell, Wilson, Avrakotos, and General Rahim Wardak.

Larry Crandall provided the most telling account of how the Cross Border Humanitarian Aid Program came into being and how it unexpectedly influenced the war; he made it impressively clear how much of the credit for massively increasing the program's funding goes to Wilson. Senator Gordon Humphrey, the program's principal patron in the upper house, also gave further valuable insight, as did Ambassador Dean Hinton and the late Ambassador Arnie Raphel, Professor Tom Gouttierre, Dr. Bob Simon, Ambassador Gerald Hellman, Hasan Nouri, Tajwar Kakar, and upwards of fifteen or twenty NGO and U.S. AID officials who worked in the program.

The intense conservative campaign to demonize the CIA as betraying the Afghans was richly evoked by Neil Blair, Andrew Eiva, Eli Krakowski, Michael Pillsbury, Vince Cannistraro, Karen McKay, Ludmilla Thorne, Senator Gordon Humphrey, Ed Juchniewicz, John McMahon, Gust Avrakotos, and Charles Schnabel.

Wilson's near-death experience was described by the "Angels," his sister Sharon, Charles Schnabel, Avrakotos, and numerous others.

For Charlie's overall relationship to Pakistan and Afghanistan, the interviews with the following officials were of great value: Bob Oakley, Phyllis

Oakley, Nick Pratt, Richard Hoagland, Craig Carp, General Akhtar, Hamid Gul, Khalid Khawaja, General Raza, General Jenjua, General Mohammad Yousaf, Colonel Mujahed, General Aslan Beg, Ambassador Jamsheed Marker, and Hamid Karzai (now president of Afghanistan).

How the hotly contested Stinger initiative came about in the first place and the extent to which its weapons transformed the war was pieced together from many sources, including President Zia, Mike Pillsbury, Andrew Eiva, Milt Bearden, Gust Avrakotos, and Wilson.

This book is indebted to Milt Bearden for his insightful descriptions of his experiences at the front line, especially his supervision of the initial deployment of Stingers. The account of the firing of the first Stinger came from an interview with Engineer Ghaffar, the mujahid who pulled the trigger.

For Charlie's trip into the war zone, I am indebted to the late Abdul Haq, Rahim Wardak, Ibrahim Jaqani, General Mohammad Yousaf, Kurt Loebeck, President Zia, and Ambassador Arnie Raphel. The showdown over the DIA plane was fleshed out by Colonel Rooney, Gust Avrakotos, Annelise Ilschenko, and once more, by Wilson himself.

With the collapse of the Soviet regime, Russia opened up, and interviews with Generals Varennikov and Gromov were immensely helpful in presenting events from the Red Army perspective. I'm particularly indebted to the late Artyom Borovik, through whom scores of veterans from the Soviets' Afghan campaign were interviewed.

The events that darkened the imminent victory—the arms depot catastrophe in Rawalpindi and the mysterious death of President Zia—were most tellingly portrayed by Milt Bearden, Richard Armitage, Ambassador Jamsheed Marker, Sahabzada Yaqub Khan, and Wilson.

For the first phase of the Afghan war, I interviewed Zbigniew Brzezinski, Vice President Walter Mondale, General William Odom, David Aaron, Gordon Stewart, and former CIA director Stansfield Turner.

Among the many mujahideen leaders whose cooperation is particularly appreciated: Gulbuddin Hekmatyar, Abdul Haq, Jalaluddin Haqani, Professor Mojadeddi, Massoud Khalili, Pir Gilani, General Safi, and Hamid Karzai.

I have not included all of the names of the Afghan mujahideen, the Pakistani soldiers and officials, as well as the many Russian officials and veterans of the Afghan war who were interviewed. There are simply too many to list. The same is true of the numerous U.S. congressional staffers, politicians, and others who were interviewed but whose interviews were not essential to my reporting.

Finally, I have not included the extensive list of interviews conducted in the months before and after 9/11. This research was essential to the thoughts conveyed in the epilogue, but a detailed accounting is perhaps best left for another day. However, I would like to thank the following for their cooperation: President Pervez Musharraf, Malik Shahid Ahmed Khan, and Khalid Khawaja, for serving as my guides into the world of Osama bin Laden and militant Islam.

ACKNOWLEDGMENTS

The inspiration for this book springs from the experience of covering the Afghans in an earlier time when we shared a common foe. Back in the 1980s, it was hard to find anyone who traveled among the mujahideen on the border or inside the war zone who was not permanently moved by their courage and sacrifice and by the hospitality, amidst so little, that the mujahideen always insisted on lavishing upon their guests.

It can be argued that the universal religion or spirit of the American people is the motto of the state of New Hampshire written on its license plates: "Live Free or Die." The Afghans—and not just a few but almost an entire nation—seemed to embody the very essence of that American idea. Granted, the way the Afghans deal with invaders or, for that matter, with one another inside their own borders is terrifying. But never once during their jihad against the Soviet Union did they resort to what we identify as terrorism outside of their own country—no embassies were bombed, planes hijacked, diplomats taken hostage, or civilians put at risk. And so far, they have not directly joined the terror campaign that their Muslim and Arab friends from other countries have launched.

One can only hope that this continues to be true and that this time, at the end of America's latest Afghan campaign, the United States will recognize its obligation to help in the rebuilding of this ravaged land. It is hoped that this book will revive the memory of the Afghans as we knew them back then, when—outmanned and outgunned—they faced our Cold War foe, the Red Army, and fearlessly took back their country.

Beyond the Afghans, an unlikely network of people made the telling of this story possible. I am indebted to the late president of Pakistan, Zia ul-Haq, who opened a window on the hidden war so that we could begin to tell the story. For all these years, the two extraordinary central figures in this history, Charlie Wilson and Gust Avrakotos, have occupied my imagination. There was never any question of what motivated these two men: a fierce love of country and the conviction that they had engineered a historic victory for America. They were so convinced of the virtue of their efforts that neither man placed any conditions on their coop-eration, in spite of knowing that I would be listening to others, many with rival viewpoints. Over the course of many years, my respect and affection for these two men has only grown.

This long venture began with one of those wonderful commissions from Don Hewitt and *60 Minutes* that allowed me to explore a world that grew bigger and more fascinating at each stop. Special thanks to Jeff Fager, Patti Hassler, Maureen Cashen, and *60 Minutes II* as a whole for their patience, encouragement, and generosity.

Speaking of which, Morgan Entrekin has gone above and beyond an editor's call of duty, first in his energizing belief in this story and then in his skillful editing of the text. Thanks to everyone at Grove/Atlantic for their ability to calmly cope with the unusual challenges posed by this project—particularly to Michael Hornburg and Muriel Jorgensen who repeatedly went above and beyond the call of duty.

Every author should have an agent as loyal and fiercely persistent as Andrew Wylie. He never wavered in his conviction and I appreciate his friendship as well as the efforts of Jeff Posternak and everyone at the Wylie Agency.

A book could be made out of the writing of this book. It is no ordi-nary experience navigating through the intelligence agencies of the United States, Pakistan, and all the other secretive worlds that came together for this campaign. It has taken a long time and more than a village—more like an international coalition—to finally nail it down.

Among those to whom I am indebted are Joe Spohn, Nicolas Beim, Tyler Clemens, Zeb Esselstyn, Reg Laing, James Morrow, Sam Osborne, Tasha Zemke, and the wise, late-night counsel of Otis Walters. Thanks to Roy Abrams for his dedicated efforts and Britta Fulla, the brilliant graphic designer who did the first-draft design for this book. Particular thanks go to two close friends who were essential to the project, one at the begin-ning and the other at the end: Neeraj Khemlani and Justin Oppmann.

Finally, there are three more people without whom this book would simply not exist. Timothy Dickenson has served as a kind of Oxford don to this project, a role he has often played for me since our days together at *Harper's* magazine. Every twist and turn of this chronicle has benefited from the endless store of historical wisdom and insight that Timothy has self-lessly provided.

The best of marriages involve a sharing of the good times and bad. I am forever indebted to my wife, Susan, for her steady support and love but mostly for her unusually wise full-time assignment of her sister, Barbara Lyne, to serve as my in-house editor. No wife has ever given a husband a more valuable gift.

Barbara was by my side from the beginning. Equally as transfixed as I by the almost surreal wonder of the story that emerged from our labors, there was not a day's work that was anything but sheer pleasure. And finally, it was only her quick and ruthless capacity to make judgments that made it possible for this book to come out in such a timely manner.

INDEX